Industrial Policy and Developme...

THE INITIATIVE FOR POLICY DIALOGUE SERIES

The Initiative for Policy Dialogue (IPD) brings together the top voices in development to address some of the most pressing and controversial debates in economic policy today. The IPD book series approaches topics such as capital market liberalization, macroeconomics, environmental economics, and trade policy from a balanced perspective, presenting alternatives, and analyzing their consequences on the basis of the best available research. Written in a language accessible to policymakers and civil society, this series will rekindle the debate on economic policy and facilitate a more democratic discussion of development around the world.

Industrial Policy and Development

The Political Economy of Capabilities Accumulation

Edited by

Mario Cimoli, Giovanni Dosi, and Joseph E. Stiglitz

OXFORD
UNIVERSITY PRESS

OXFORD

UNIVERSITY PRESS

Great Clarendon Street, Oxford OX2 6DP

Oxford University Press is a department of the University of Oxford.
It furthers the University's objective of excellence in research, scholarship,
and education by publishing worldwide in

Oxford New York

Auckland Cape Town Dar es Salaam Hong Kong Karachi
Kuala Lumpur Madrid Melbourne Mexico City Nairobi
New Delhi Shanghai Taipei Toronto

With offices in

Argentina Austria Brazil Chile Czech Republic France Greece
Guatemala Hungary Italy Japan South Korea Poland Portugal
Singapore Switzerland Thailand Turkey Ukraine Vietnam

Oxford is a registered trade mark of Oxford University Press
in the UK and in certain other countries

Published in the United States
by Oxford University Press Inc., New York

British Library Cataloguing in Publication Data

Data available

Library of Congress Cataloging in Publication Data

Data available

Typeset by SPI Publisher Services, Pondicherry, India
Printed in Great Britain
on acid-free paper by
Clays Ltd, St Ives plc

ISBN 978–0–19–923527–8 (Pbk.)

ISBN 978–0–19–923526–1 (Hbk.)

10 9 8 7 6 5 4 3 2 1

Acknowledgements

The book is the outcome of the research of a task force on Industrial Policy and Development of the Initiative for Policy Dialogue (IPD) at Columbia University, directed by Joseph E. Stiglitz and José Antonio Ocampo. IPD is a global network of over 250 economists, researchers, and practitioners committed to furthering understanding of the development process. We would like to thank all task force members, whose participation in provocative dialogues and debates on industrial policy informed the content of this book.

In addition to the contributing authors, we gratefully acknowledge the comments of a long list of friends who participated in various capacities to the gestation of this enterprise (without, of course, committing them to our analysis or conclusions) and in particular to Joao Ferraz, Yevgeny Kuznetzov, Akbar Noman, Stan Metcalfe, Carlota Perez, Luc Soete, Mauro Sylos Labini, Marianna Vintiadis (who contributed invaluably to putting together the team of authors), and Sid Winter. This work would not have been possible without the constant and professional dedication of Shana Hofstetter and Ariel Schwartz, and the assistance of Laura Ferrari. IPD also expresses its gratitude to Dora Beszterczey, Jill Blackford, Vitaly Bord, Dan Choate, James Giganti, Sarah Green, Anne Feldman, Farah Siddique, Wamiq Umaira, Sylvia Wu, and former Executive Director Shari Spiegel.

Finally, we are most grateful to The Ford Foundation, The John T. and Catherine D. MacArthur Foundation, The United Nations Development Programme, and the Commonwealth Secretariat for funding the work of the IPD Task Force on Industrial Policy and supporting IPD activities.

Contents

Contents

Part IV. Conclusion

List of Figures

List of Figures

List of Tables

List of Tables

List of Abbreviations

APLs	arranjos produtivos locais
BIT	bilateral investment treaty
BNDES	Banco Nacional de Desenvolvimento Econômico e Social
CGE	computable general equilibrium
CLADS	Centro Latinoamericano para la Competitividad y el Desarrollo Sostenible (Latin American Center for Competitiveness and Sustainable Development)
CORFO	Corporacion de Fomento de la Produccion
DCs	developing countries
EA	East Asia
ECLAC	Economic Commission for Latin America and the Caribbean
EPZ	export processing zone
FDI	foreign direct investment
FTA	free trade agreement
IFI	international financial institution
INCAE	Instituto Centroamericano de Administración de Empresas (Central American Business School)
IPN	international production network
IPD	Initiative for Policy Dialogue
IPR	Intellectual Property Rights
ISI	import substitution industrialization
LDC	least developed country
MNC	multinational corporation
MNE	multinational enterprise
NAFIN	Nacional Financiera
NIC	newly industrialized country
PPP	purchasing power parity

SDT	special and differential treatment
SEBRAE	Servicio Brasileno de Apoyo a las Micro y Pequenas Empresas (Brazilian Service of Support for Micro and Small Enterprises)
SEI	Statute for Encouragement of Investments
SMEs	small and medium-sized enterprises
SOE	state-owned enterprise
TRIMS	Trade-Related Investment Measures
TRIPS	Trade-Related Aspects of Intellectual Property Rights
USPTO	United States Patent and Trademark Office
USTR	United States Trade Representative
WTO	World Trade Organization

List of Contributors

Yılmaz Akyüz Special Economic Advisor, South Centre, and Former Director, Division on Globalization and Development Strategies, UNCTAD.

Alice H. Amsden Barton L. Weller Professor of Political Economy, Massachusetts Institute of Technology, Urban Planning.

Antonio Barros de Castro Emeritus Professor, Federal University of Rio de Janeiro, and Consultant of the President, Banco Nacional de Desenvolvimento Econômico e Social (BNDES)

Stephanie Blankenburg SOAS, University of London

Heloisa Borges PhD student and researcher, Institute of Economics, Federal University of Rio de Janeiro

Carolina Castaldi Department of Innovation Studies, Utrecht University

Mario Cimoli Economic Commission for Latin America and the Caribbean (ECLAC), United Nations, and Department of Economics, University of Venice (Ca Foscari)

Benjamin Coriat Professor of Economics, University Paris 13

Nelson Correa Economic Commission for Latin America and the Caribbean (ECLAC), United Nations

Carl J. Dahlman Henry R. Luce Professor of International Relations and Information Technology, Edmund A. Walsh School of Foreign Service, Georgetown University

Michele Di Maio Assistant Professor of Economics, University of Naples 'Parthenope', Italy

Giovanni Dosi Professor of Economics, Sant'Anna School of Advanced Studies, Pisa, and Visiting Professor, University of Manchester

Mike Hobday Professor of Innovation Management, CENTRIM, University of Brighton, United Kingdom

Mushtaq H. Khan Professor of Economics, SOAS, University of London

Bernardo Kosacoff Director, Economic Commission for Latin America and the Caribbean (ECLAC), Buenos Aires Bureau

Colin Mayer Peter Moores Dean, Saïd Business School, University of Oxford

Roberto Mazzoleni Hofstra University, New York

Richard R. Nelson George Blumenthal Professor Emeritus and Professor Emeritus of Business and Law, and Earth Institute, Columbia University, New York

José Gabriel Palma University of Cambridge

Wilson Peres Economic Commission for Latin America and the Caribbean (ECLAC), United Nations

Fernando Perini Programme Officer, International Development Research Centre (IDRC), and Visiting Fellow, Science and Technology Policy Research (SPRU), Freeman Centre, University of Sussex

Mario L. Possas Institute of Economics, Federal University of Rio de Janeiro

Annalisa Primi Economist/Policy Analyst, Science and Technology Policy Division, DSTI, OECD

Adrián H. Ramos Economic Commission for Latin America and the Caribbean (ECLAC), United Nations

Erik S. Reinert The Other Canon Foundation, Norway & Tallinn University of Technology, Estonia

Ajit Singh Emeritus Professor of Economics and Senior Research Fellow, Judge Business School, University of Cambridge and Chair in Economics, University of Birmingham Business School.

Joseph E. Stiglitz University Professor Columbia University, Co-President Initiative for Policy Dialogue, and Visiting Professor University of Manchester

1

The Political Economy of Capabilities Accumulation: The Past and Future of Policies for Industrial Development

Mario Cimoli, Giovanni Dosi, and Joseph E. Stiglitz

There was a time when 'industrial policies', for both developed and developing countries, were bad words not to be spoken either in public or in private by respectable people. It was the time of the (in)famous 'Washington Consensus' on development—dominant among international policy makers in the last part of the twentieth century—with its market fundamentalism, made of an invariant recipe good for all macro diseases (less government, fiscal sweat and tears, privatizations, etc.) in turn grounded in a very naïve and blackboxed microeconomics ('the market will take care of itself...hence do not mess around with micro behaviors'). At last, the realization of the impressive failures of the recipe (see, revealingly, World Bank, 2005 and 2008a) has finally sobered up a significant share of both economists and policy makers (although with significant exceptions in both camps). Indeed, at the time this book is sent to the publisher, the tsunami hitting the world financial markets is forcing even the most stubborn believers in the miraculous properties of 'markets' to accept markets as they exist and not as they are portrayed in economic textbooks.

This book, however, is not about beating a dead horse—notwithstanding the many horses still running around—and concerns only tangentially the so-called 'augmented Washington Consensus', that is the revisitation of the former one with a much greater emphasis on ancillary institutions. Rather, this book is about industrial policies seen as intrinsic fundamental ingredients of all development processes. Witness to that, every experience of successful industrialization, ranging from Germany and the USA, almost two centuries ago, all the way to Korea, Taiwan, Brazil, China, and India nowadays.

The notion of 'industrial policy' is understood here in a quite expansive manner. It comprises policies affecting 'infant industry' support of various kinds, but also trade policies, science and technology policies, public procurement, policies affecting foreign direct investments, intellectual property rights, and the allocation of financial resources. Industrial policies, in this broad sense, come together with processes of 'institutional engineering' shaping the very nature of the economic actors, the market mechanisms and rules under which they operate, and the boundaries between what is governed by market interactions, and what is not.

The accumulation of capabilities in the great industrial transformation

The contributions to this book analyze from different angles the role played by industrial policies, in the foregoing broad sense, and by institution building within that *great transformation*—borrowing Karl Polanyi's (1944) expression—leading from traditional, mostly rural, economies to economies driven by industrial activities (and nowadays also advanced services), able systematically to learn how to implement and eventually how to generate new ways of producing and new products under conditions of dynamic increasing returns.

Such a 'great transformation' entails a major process of *accumulation of knowledge and capabilities*, at the levels of both *individuals* and *organizations*. Certainly, part of such capabilities builds on education and formally acquired skills (what in the economists' jargon often goes under the heading of 'human capital'). However, at least equally importantly, capabilities have to do with the problem-solving knowledge embodied in organizations—concerning, for example, production technologies, marketing, labor relations, as well as 'dynamic capabilities' of search and learning.

Many contributions to this volume can be read in this perspective, which links with a growing literature on technology, innovation, and development (see, among others, Amsden, 2001; Bell and Pavitt, 1993; Chang, 2002; Chang and Cheema, 2002; Cimoli and Dosi, 1995; Dosi, Pavitt, and Soete, 1990; Mytelka, 2007; Nelson, 1982 and 2004; Reinert, 2007). More precisely, many of the chapters which follow tackle the impact of various forms of policy intervention upon the rates and directions of knowledge accumulation during the catch-up process and the ensuing effects upon the patterns of production and trade.

The inter-technological and intersectoral diversity of opportunities

That sectors and products matter in terms of learning opportunities is increasingly recognized well beyond the 'structuralists', Kaldorian and evolutionary camps where the conjecture was originally put forward (that is, from Prebisch, 1950; Kaldor, 1981; Dosi, Pavitt, and Soete, 1990; Freeman, 1994; Reinert, 1998; to Hausmann and Klinger, 2006; and Hausmann and Rodrick, 2006). The basic intuition is that specific technologies and specific sectors and products matter because they entail different learning opportunities and also different income elasticities of demand. Thus, today's specializations influence tomorrow's productivity growth, chances to innovate, and demand potential: we elaborate a bit on the point in Chapter 2, by Cimoli, Dosi, Nelson, and Stiglitz, and dwell on it in Dosi, Pavitt, and Soete (1990). If this is the case, however, 'industrial policies are a predicament'—as Hausmann and Rodrick (2006) put it—because countries inevitably have the choice of steering their future paths of capability accumulation, and together their patterns of production and trade. Even the choice of not having any (implicit or explicit) industrial policy is a choice in itself, that is, the acceptance of the current international division of intellectual and physical labor, and with that the current distribution of learning opportunities.

Ricardo versus List

On the issue—as we are reminded in Chapter 4 by Reinert (see also Reinert, 2007)—there is a divide, which can be traced back to the very origin of modern political economy, between a view *prescribing* on normative grounds the acquiescence in the 'revealed comparative advantages' one country inherits from its past, and an alternative view traceable back even beyond Hamilton and List, arguing that the 'productive forces' of a nation can and must be purposefully constructed, and that current comparative advantages are a luxury that only technological and market leaders can afford (indeed a major asset that they can exploit).

It happens that quite a few of the contributors to this volume bear to varying degrees sympathy with this latter view and show—we believe quite convincingly—how a wide array of policies and institutions have been behind the earlier catch-up successes of, for example, Korea and Taiwan and more recently of China and India.

Knowledge and business organizations

We have already mentioned that the accumulation of knowledge and capabilities does entail, but is not exhausted by, the upgrading of the skills of workers and technicians. Needless to say, such educational efforts are of paramount importance. And so is the construction of broader social capabilities in the sense of Sen (1985). However, there is a fundamental *organizational dimension* in such a process, as the whole body of literature from business economics inspired by *capability-based theories of the firm* has begun to reveal (for an overview, see Dosi, Marengo, and Faillo, 2008). It is not only or not *even primarily* an issue of entrepreneurship, which the lack thereof, contrary to common wisdom, might not be a peculiarity of underdevelopment. The presence of imaginative entrepreneurial efforts of economic survival under hardship, and even the level of entrepreneurial sophistication of Sicilian Mafia or the Medellin Cartel, bear witness that 'entrepreneurship' as such might not be a widespread bottleneck for development. Rather, the bottleneck is likely to concern much more some persistent 'inability to seize opportunities', paraphrasing Albert Hirschman (1958), regarding the productive manipulation of knowledge, especially when such manipulation has a complex collective dimension, involving also the intra-organizational coordination of several actors carrying diverse pieces of knowledge and most often diverse interests (on seemingly 'entrepreneurship' vs. 'intrapreneurship' within incumbent firms, see Chapter 18, by Hobday and Perini).

Indeed, *organization building* is one of the most difficult tasks facing developmental industrial policies. The idea that a Toyota, a Samsung, a Tata, an Embraer can just naturally spring up out of a multitude of peasants, just due, again, to the 'magic of the market', is a fairy tale that few ought to be ready to believe. In fact, the characteristics of the producers in the catching-up process, their organizational sophistication, and also their nationality (whether domestic or foreign) matters a lot in terms of learning patterns (see Amsden's Chapter 15).

Technological learning: a *primus inter pares*, not a magic bullet

We have been arguing that the changes in the patterns of accumulation and processing of information and knowledge are at the core of development patterns: the 'unbound Prometheus' systematically improving technological and organizational knowledge has been a crucial *deus ex machina* of early industrialization almost three centuries ago, and also of subsequent episodes of development (Landes, 1969; and Cipolla, 1965; cf. also Landes, 1999; Freeman, 1982; Reinert, 2007; Rosenberg, 1976; Mokyr, 1990; and Nelson, 2005). However this is far from being the identification of some 'magic bullet'. In fact, economic historians investigating the 'European exceptionalism' (Landes, 1999) leading to the Industrial Revolution do point at the advances of technical knowledge as a crucial factor in the industrial take-off. However, the European industrialization precisely illustrates that not even technological advances are such a magic bullet. Many of the technological advances upon which the Industrial Revolution drew were originally developed, or at least equally known, in other regions, China being a prime example. 'European exceptionalism' was made possible by a conjunction of complementary conditions ranging from the 'scientific attitude' of inquiry about nature which fostered knowledge accumulation and its codification and diffusion, all the way to the characteristics of the political structure and the relations between rulers and subjects. In this vein, C. Freeman (2008, which puts together an ensemble of his classic contributions) suggests that *national systems of innovation and production* develop and advance (or do not) on the grounds of the co-evolutionary dynamics among five sub-domains, and related institutions, governing (i) the generation of *scientific knowledge* (he is talking primarily of 'frontier' countries); (ii) the development, improvement, and adoption of new artifacts and new techniques of production (that is the domain of *technology*); (iii) the *economic machine* which organizes the production and distribution of goods, services, and incomes, and *together, information flows and patterns of incentives* amongst economic agents; (iv) the *political and legal structure*; and, finally, (v) the *cultural domain*, shaping values, norms, and customs.

Co-evolutionary dynamics

Several scholars are indeed adding substance (implicitly or explicitly) to this 'grand political economy' program: we have already mentioned a few contributors to the technology-focused literature, but the 'grand view' takes on board the complementary importance of the political economy of labor relations, income claims, property rights, and indeed, of culture (working our way backward, from Mokyr, 2009; North, 2005; Greif, 2006; and Boyer,1988; all the way to Karl Marx and Adam Smith).

This is not the place to discuss in any detail the long history of industrialization in general. Suffice it to say that if there is some truth in this co-evolutionary story, such truth does not apply only to the Low Countries four centuries ago or England three centuries back. It does apply equally well to all the later episodes of industrialization and subsequent self-sustained growth. The co-evolutionary point is indirectly revealed by the overall shaky results stemming from the quest for overarching invariant *institutional preconditions* for growth or invariant policy recipes for it.[1]

On the contrary, the co-evolutionary account rests on the sorts of *congruence conditions* between *ingredients* (including state variables which influence the subsequent dynamics) and *processes* wherein feature prominently the matchings or mismatchings between capabilities accumulation and the institutions governing the distribution of information and the incentive structures of any one economy. (Incidentally, note that if this view is correct, and successful episodes have been the outcomes of different *combinatorics* among institutional set-ups and learning dynamics, their essence is not likely to be statistically captured by heroic 'reduced form' estimations in a quest for some preconditions, or driving factors of differential growth—supposedly shielded from endogeneity—invariant in their effects across countries.)

By way of an illustration, consider the diagnostics of the underlying drivers of the different performances of East Asia and Latin America in the 1980s and 1990s, itemized in Table 1.1 (drawing upon Dosi, Freeman, and Fabiani, 1994, and Freeman, 2008, where one can find more detailed discussions). Notably such diagnostics of the significantly different economic outcomes highlight primarily *diverging processes* at both the microeconomic level (e.g. the different modes and intensity of technological search) and at a more aggregate one (e.g. the patterns of investments in ICT). Together, they also emphasize the *diverging institutional set-ups* (affecting education, income distribution, corporate learning, etc.). As we argue in the chapter that follows by Cimoli, Dosi, Nelson, and Stiglitz, policies and various measures of 'institutional engineering' have deeply shaped the patterns of growth throughout contemporary industrial history dynamics. In fact, many of the subsequent chapters add to our understanding

Table 1.1. At the roots of different East Asian and Latin American performances: divergences in national systems of innovation and production in the 1980s and 1990s

East Asia	Latin America
Expanding education system with high proportion of engineering studies	Deteriorating education system with proportionally lower output of engineers
Rapid growth of scientific and technical activities at enterprise level, especially R&D	Slow growth, stagnation, or decline of enterprise level R&D and other learning activities
Progressive integration of production design, marketing, and research activities within the firm	Weakening of R&D and absence or decline of enterprise marketing (especially on foreign markets)
Development of strong science–technology infrastructure	Weakening of science–technology infrastructure
Strong influence of Japanese models of management and networking organization	Continuing influence of outdated management models
High levels of investment	Generally lower level of investment
Heavy investment in advanced telecommunications	Slow development of modern telecommunication
Strong and fast-growing electronic industries with high exports	Weak electronic industries with low exports
More generally, patterns of specialization favoring goods with high income elasticities	Specialization in low income elasticity goods
Growing participation in international technology networks and agreements	Low level of international networking in technology
Rather sophisticated policy efforts aimed at fostering technological learning and generalizing rent-seeking even under regimes of protection of domestic markets (until the 1980s)	From generalized protection with little anti-rent seeking safeguards to 'wild market regimes' with little learning incentives
Relative egalitarian income distribution	Very unequal income distribution—and increasingly so

Source: Elaborations on Dosi, Freeman, and Fabiani (1994) and C. Freeman (2008).

of how policies and institution-building have shaped both the accumulation of technological and organizational capabilities and the political economy in which it is embedded.

Taking a centennial perspective, Reinert identifies a kind of invariance in the inspiring principle for successful catching-up policies, namely a philosophy of *emulation* vis-à-vis world technological leaders, irrespective of revealed comparative advantages. (More on that in the conclusions to this book.) This applies to pre-Industrial Revolution England; nineteenth-century Germany from the *Zollverein* onward; the United States since its constitution; Japan, starting from the Meiji restoration well into the second half of the twentieth century; post-WWII Korea; and also the policy antecedents of current successes of China and India. On the latter, see the (deliberately controversial) chapters below by Singh and Dahlman (Chapters 11 and 12 respectively).

A historical topography of policy experiences is in Di Maio's contribution (Chapter 5), while Peres (in Chapter 7) traces the somewhat shy comeback of industrial policies—ridden of implementation hurdles—in Latin America after the apotheosis of the 'Washington Consensus' (and the experience of its failed promises).

Some chapters reconstruct the role of both macroeconomic and industrial policies along the history of a country's development: see Castro on Brazil, Kosacoff and Ramos on Argentina, and Singh on India.

Other contributions explicitly compare different countries or groups of them in their performances and try to identify the role of policies underlying the different patterns of specialization and growth: see Palma on the comparison of East Asia versus Latin America, and Dahlman on a comparative assessment of both policies and outcomes of India and China.

Another group of contributions addresses, so to speak horizontally, specific policy domains. So, Akyuz revisits the importance of trade policies for local industrial development and assesses the consequences of the newly introduced constraints in their use stemming from the WTO regime of international exchanges. But even granted 'infant industry protection' (something that indeed is not granted any longer), what are the organizational loci where learning occurs and how does their nature affect knowledge accumulation?

Entrepreneurship, incumbent organizations, and development

Hobday and Perini analyze the role of entrepreneurship in the development process, dispelling also the myth of a diffused entrepreneurial potential for *industrial development* hidden in marginality and compressed by bureaucracy and red tape. As we already mentioned, developed capitalist economies have no monopoly of entrepreneurial effort. A distinguished feature of industrial economies, however, is that a significant share of such effort is devoted to the manipulation and improvement of products and production technologies, and the development and maintenance of organizations able to implement them. These are the types of entrepreneurial and managerial abilities required by the *great transformation*. And indeed, as Amsden's chapter argues, most often the accumulation of technological and managerial capabilities has historically occurred within *domestic* firms rather than within subsidiaries of foreign-owned firms. One of the reasons for this phenomenon (which is not going to disappear: see also the remarks in Chapter 3 by Castaldi, Cimoli, Correa, and Dosi) is that even when MNCs are an important source of capital investment, they often carry a relatively limited technology transfer, with the most tacit forms of knowledge and a good deal of R&D activities being kept in developed countries (indeed, often near the corporate headquarters). One could say that MNCs tend to bring in higher 'static capabilities' but also often entail greater obstacles to local 'dynamic' learning capabilities.[2]

Institutions supporting the great transformation

We have repeatedly emphasized knowledge accumulation as a central process within any industrialization strategy, occurring to a good extent *but not exclusively* within business firms. As Chapter 14 by Mazzoleni and Nelson shows, the process—when it occurs effectively—is supported and nurtured by the activities of applied research, training, consultancy, and adaptation of technologies to local conditions undertaken by universities and public laboratories.

Technological learning, of course, does not happen in thin air, but rather goes hand in hand with investment in physical equipment and intangibles. And, in turn, that requires the mobilization of financial resources and their transfer to industry. By now the economics profession is well aware of the implications of the fundamental informational asymmetries underlying industry financing, be it via credit or via equity (cf. Stiglitz and Weiss, 1981). This applies in general, and even more so to industrializing countries. How did earlier industrializers cope with such endemic and massive 'informational imperfections', and what may that experience teach current catching-up countries? The question is addressed in Chapter 16 by Colin Mayer drawing upon the early history of industrialization of England and Germany. The literature often emphasizes the difference between a supposedly market-based (and equity-based) English system and a credit-based German one. The chapter argues that the differences were less pronounced than it appears at a first glance, even if the two systems differed in the ways equities were intermediated. In fact, the crucial point—entailing also a major normative lesson for 'institutional engineering' in developing countries—concerns the development of institutional arrangements fostering relations of trust in equity intermediation (incidentally, note also that, notwithstanding 'globalization', these relations are bound to have an intrinsically 'local', possibly national, or even regional, dimension).

The appropriability of knowledge and the opportunities for imitation

Technological learning throughout the catching-up process, and especially in its early phase, involves a lot of imitation, reverse engineering, marginal modifications of products and processes, and straightforward copying (the point has finally come through even the official discourse of some international organizations: see World Bank, 2008; and ECLAC, 2008). It has been so in the past in England vis-à-vis the Netherlands, in the US vis-à-vis England, in Japan vis-à-vis the developed West, and it is so nowadays in the case of China.

However, the possibility of successfully undertaking such activities of imitation in the broadest sense depends, first, on the *absorptive capabilities* of the various countries (cf. Cohen and Levinthal, 1989, who write about firms, but the notion can be easily extended to countries composing interrelated ensembles of firms and complementary organizations). Absorptive capabilities fundamentally concern the ways in which past achievements in knowledge accumulation influence future learning potential (and, as such they impinge also on the degrees of path-dependency that the process of capability-building displays).

Second, given whatever absorptive capabilities, the easiness of imitation is modulated by the degrees of *appropriability* of the various technologies—by which we mean a measure of the ability of the originators/owners of the process and product technologies to keep to themselves the relevant underlying knowledge and/or the ensuing claims to the economic benefits coming from the exploitation of such knowledge. It happens that quite often appropriability conditions depend to a large extent on the nature of technological and production knowledge itself (cf. Dosi, Marengo, and Pasquali, 2006, and the literature cited therein). Imitating a Boeing or an Airbus is likely to be hard in itself irrespective of the legal conditions of knowledge appropriation, while these conditions might greatly affect the possibility of reproducing a new chemical entity. However, appropriability conditions are also affected by the regimes of *Intellectual Property Rights* (IPR). Clearly, other things being equal, tighter IPR regimes imply harder conditions for imitation. The issue is discussed in Chapter 19 by Cimoli, Coriat, and Primi. Historically, imitative activities by catching-up countries have occurred under quite lax conditions regarding the international enforcement of IPR, especially with regard to then developing countries. So, for example, until the mid-nineteenth century the United States was not recognizing patents to non-nationals and the pro-domestic bias continued long after. Germany and Japan originally allowed 'utility patents', covering also minor improvements over state-of-the-art technologies most often protecting local 'creative imitators'. In fields like pharmaceuticals—indeed the technological area where IPR count most—countries like Italy and Switzerland (the headquarters of some major drugs multinationals!) recognized IPR altogether only around three decades ago. Things have dramatically changed since, with the current scene featuring both TRIPS agreements and an unexpected novel aggressiveness of US and European companies in their IPR protection even against seemingly marginal infringements and even at the cost of world moral outrage, as in the case of anti-retroviral drugs. Does all this change the imitation opportunities of catching-up countries? If so, generally, or only in some technologies? While this book is not focused primarily on this issue,[3] the evidence discussed in Cimoli, Coriat, and Primi's chapter seems to suggest that a tighter IPR enforcement regime has effects on the imitation/catching-up process that range between the irrelevant and the quite harmful: certainly, the positive sign is hardly to be seen on the screen.

Incentives and rents in the political economy of learning

The reader will have already noticed that the thread of our argument rests more on notions such as knowledge, information, capabilities, and learning rather than incentives. This is also what distinguishes this line of interpretation of development processes from another one inspired by the principle of 'getting the incentives right and everything will follow'. The thrust of our argument is that, given whatever incentives, 'learning how to seize technological and organizational opportunities' is a fundamental driver of industrialization. Granted that, however, the two dimensions are far from orthogonal.

As discussed in detail in Chapter 13 by Khan and Blankenburg, the *political economy of (successful) industrialization* entails the compatibility of technological and organizational strategies with the political constraints arising from the distribution of power among social groups (and often also from external influences, including, of course, foreign economic and political entities). In this respect, the sad paradox of the political economy of development is that those supposedly in charge of leading the development strategies are the very groups which have huge vested interests in and derive huge rents from, the status quo. Hence the need to engineer what the authors call *systems of institutional compulsion* lending momentum to imitation, productivity growth, production expansion, and eventually innovation. In turn, this involves the political ability directly or indirectly to allocate *developmental rents* to the actors of the 'great transformation' (and also withdraw them according to performance). This is in fact what has happened in many Far Eastern countries, but not in most Latin American ones. And the comparison also vividly illustrates the circumstances under which unleashing the rent-seeking genie of capitalism has unleashed also the 'Unbound Prometheus' of technological progress as distinguished from those other circumstances whereby it just triggered the search for rents *full stop*.

Stick-and-carrot and rent governance issues emerge also at the more circumscribed domain of market regulation and competition policies, addressed in Chapter 17 by Possas and Borges. The framework is broadly speaking 'Schumpeterian', in that the virtue of competition policies is judged against the yardstick of the performance dynamism that a particular market structure fosters, rather than in terms of the standard textbook triangles of static allocation and welfare measures. At early stages of industrial development, infant industry considerations militate against the viability of competition policies either as a rent-curbing stick or an innovation-enhancing carrot. Thus, other institutional devices should be in place in order to govern 'developmental rents' and spur the 'developmental compulsion' discussed by Khan and Blankenburg, including performance-related allocation of finance, foreign currency, subsidies, and diverse taxation regimes. The first three decades of Korean industrialization are a good case in point. And older historical experiences reinforce it: competition policies have typically been introduced in all catching-up countries well after the initial industrialization drive—in the US as well as in Germany, Italy, and Japan. However, Possas and Borges argue that above a certain threshold of development competition policies become (or at least ought to become) an important ingredient of industrial policies, often under negligible trade-offs between rent-curbing and incentives to innovate, if any.

The consistency conditions among macro policies and industrial policies

Industrial policies, in the broad definition adopted here, are a constant presence in all historically observed successes in industrialization. However, they require *compatible macro policies*, including exchange rates, taxation, fiscal policies, public investment, governance of the labor market, and income distribution. This is another crucial facet of the political economy of industrialization. It is also a theme recurrent in several chapters, especially those analyzing the experience of single countries or comparing them (see in particular Chapters 8–10, by Palma; Kosacoff and Ramos; and Castro respectively). There is a more dramatic way to make the same point: there are combinations of macro policies which are bound to suffocate industrial development and sterilize most opportunities of success of more technology- and industry-oriented policies, even when tried. The point is well illustrated by the application of the 'Washington Consensus' policy package in Latin America (with the partial exception of Brazil), with its devastating effects on industrial production capacity and technological capabilities—which often disappeared together with the firms that were carrying them (for some evidence cf. also the chapter by Castaldi et al.).

This is even more striking when the effects of the Latin American macro shocks are compared with the outcomes at industrial level of much less orthodox responses to financial and exchange rate crises such as in Korea and other Far Eastern economies. We discuss these examples in Stiglitz (2002 and 2006).

Certainly, the sudden liberalization process together with orthodox macro policies in Latin America had a massive 'weeding out' effect. However, there is no guarantee—either in biology or even less so in economics—that a major *selection shock* allows any one species to survive. And in fact what happened in South America (outside Brazil) was that in the aftermath of the shock one found piles of rubble where before one had a variegated, even if often inefficient, industrial structure, with few survivors—except in some natural-resource based activities (these activities have experienced a boom in the recent past driven by the spectacular increase in demand for energy and raw materials especially by China, but a big question mark remains concerning their ability to lead the industrialization of whole countries: we shall come back to the issue in the conclusion).

How much are the lessons from the past helpful for the future?

In our view there is little doubt that the historical lessons point out the crucial importance of various ensembles of industrial policies and institution-building efforts in nurturing capabilities accumulation and industrial development. Indeed, the chapters which follow add several original insights to such evidence. However, even granted that, the last resort of the skeptic rests in the view that even what applied to the past will not apply to the future: the magic that was not performed by the Washington Consensus policy medicines is going to come around nonetheless as a natural by-product of 'globalization'. In order to address this conjecture, in the chapter by Castaldi et al. we set the current trends against secular background evidence on the international distribution of innovative activities, the patterns of technological diffusion, the structure of international trade flows and income growth. One major message of the analysis is that *divergence and heterogeneity* have been and continue to be the dominant tendencies in the world economy. Second, and relatedly, notwithstanding the hype, there appears to be a lot of globalization of (short-term) finance, but relatively little, if any, in terms of technological capabilities. In fact it could well be that under conditions of dynamic increasing returns, more international openness of capital and trade flows might well 'naturally' induce *divergence* across regions and countries. Hence, in our view, also the continuing importance of measures of discretionary policy intervention able to trigger and fuel what we have called the 'great industrial transformation'.

Clearly, the international conditions have changed compared to when, say, the United States was taking its first steps toward catching-up, and even compared to when Korea or Taiwan were entering the international scene. The WTO and the TRIPS agreements are putting some novel constraints on what policies can and cannot do with respect to both their domestic industry and to trade flows. First-world companies are as aggressive as ever before in the defense of their proprietary technologies. The very emergence of China as a major industrial player has profoundly changed the patterns of opportunities and constraints facing other actual or would-be industrializers. Despite all of the above being true, the processes of knowledge accumulation and industrial development continue to require relatively massive doses of public policies and institution-building to mold a national political economy friendly to technological and organizational learning.

Some of the basic building blocks of such policies will be spelled out in the conclusion.

Notes

1. Sachs and Warner (1997) is a known short example of the genre; more specifically on the role of institutions and policies within the 'new political economy' style of interpretation, cf. the somewhat diverging views of Acemoglu, Johnson, and Robinson (2001), Easterly and Levin (2003), Rodrik (2008). For a sharp critique of mono-causal explanations of underdevelopment, see Adelman (2001), together with a few other contributions to Meier and Stiglitz (2001).
2. Are these patterns going to persist also under the current 'globalized regime' of production? In fact the evidence suggests a significant increase in the internationalization of R&D activities (cf. the evidence critically reviewed in Narula and Zanfei, 2005). However such patterns involve primarily intra-OECD investments. While the question is certainly open, we tend to believe that the weakness of the incentives, if any, to purposefully transfer major 'dynamic capabilities' of innovative search to newly industrializing countries—including China—is likely to persist also in the future.
3. In fact, another task force of the IPD is currently preparing a report on the subject.

References

Acemoglu, D., Johnson, S., and Robinson, J. (2001). 'The Colonial Origins of Economic Development: An Empirical Investigation'. *American Economic Review*, 91: 1369–401.

Adelman, I. (2001). 'Fallacies in Development Theory and their Implications for Policies', in Meier and Stiglitz (2001).

Amsden, A. H. (2001). *The Rise of 'The Rest': Challenges to the West from Late Industrializing Economies*. Oxford/New York: Oxford University Press.

Bairoch, P., and Kozul-Wright, R. (1996). *Globalization Myths: Some Historical Reflections on Integration, Industrialization and Growth in the World Economy*. Geneva: UNCTAD Discussion Papers No. 113.

Bell, M., and Pavitt, K. (1993). 'Technological Accumulation and Industrial Growth: Contrasts between Developed and Developing Countries'. *Industrial and Corporate Change*, 2: 157–210.

Boyer, R. (1988). 'Technical Change and the Theory of "Regulation" ' in Dosi et al. (1988).

Chang, H.J. (2002). *Kicking away the Ladder: Development Strategy in Historical Perspective*. London: Anthem Press.

—— and Cheema, A. (2002). 'Conditions for Successful Technology Policy in Developing Countries'. *Economics of Innovation and New Technology*, 11: 369–98.

Cimoli, M., and Dosi, G. (1995). 'Technological Paradigms, Patterns of Learning and Development. An Introductory Roadmap'. *Journal of Evolutionary Economics*, 5: 243–68.

—— and Katz, J. (2003). 'Structural Reforms, Technological Gaps and Economic Development: A Latin American Perspective'. *Industrial and Corporate Change*, 12: 387–411.

Cipolla, C.M. (1965). *Guns, Sails, & Empires: Technological Innovation and the Early Phases of European Expansion, 1400–1700*. New York: Pantheon Books.

Cohen, W.M., and Levinthal, D.A. (1989). 'Innovation and Learning: The Two Faces of R&D'. *The Economic Journal*, 99: 569–96.

Dosi, G., Freeman, C., Nelson, R., Silverberg, G., and Soete L. (eds.) (1988). *Technical Change and Economic Theory: The Global Process of Development*, London: Pinter Publishers, and New York: Columbia University Press.

—— Marengo, L., and Faillo, M. (2008). 'Organizational Capabilities, Patterns of Knowledge Accumulation and Governance Structures in Business Firms. An Introduction'. *Organization Studies*, 28(8): 1165–85.

—— —— and Pasquali, C. (2006). 'How Much Should Society Fuel the Greed of Innovators? On the Relations between Appropriability, Opportunities and Rates of Innovation'. *Research Policy*, 35(8): 1110–21.

—— Pavitt, K., and Soete, L. (1990). *The Economics of Technological Change and International Trade*. Brighton: Wheatsheaf, and New York: New York University Press.

Easterly, W., and Levine, R. (2003). 'Tropics, Germs, and Crops: How Endowments Influence Economic Development'. *Journal of Monetary Economics*, 50: 3–39.

ECLAC (Economic Commission for Latin America and the Caribbean) (2008). *Structural Change and Productivity Growth, 20 Years Later: Old Problems, New Opportunities*, LC/G.2367(SES.32/3), May 2008.

Freeman, C. (1982). *The Economics of Industrial Innovation* (2nd edn.). London: Pinter.

—— (1994). 'Technological Infrastructure and International Competitiveness'. *Industrial and Corporate Change*, 13: 541–69.

—— (2008). *Systems of Innovation: Selected Essays in Evolutionary Economics*. Cheltenham, UK/Northampton, MA: Edward Elgar.

—— and Fabiani, S. (1994). 'The Process of Economic Development. Introducing some Stylized Facts and Theories on Technologies, Firms and Institutions', *Industrial and Corporate Change*, 3(1): 1–45.

Greenwald, B., and Stiglitz, J.E. (1986). 'Externalities in Economics with Imperfect Information and Incomplete Markets'. *Quarterly Journal of Economics*, 101: 229–64.

—— —— (2006). 'Helping Infant Economies Grow: Foundations of Trade Policies for Developing Countries'. *The American Economic Review*, 96(2): 141–6.

Greif, A. (2006). *Institutions and the Path to the Modern Economy: Lessons from Medieval Trade*. New York: Cambridge University Press.

Hausmann, R., and Klinger, B. (2006). 'Structural Transformation and Patterns of Comparative Advantage in the Product Space'. Cambridge, MA: Harvard University, Center for International Development, Working paper.

—— and Rodrik, D. (2006). 'Doomed to Choose: Industrial Policy as a Predicament'. Cambridge, MA: Harvard University. J. F. Kennedy School of Government, Working paper.

Hirschman, A.O. (1958). *The Strategy of Economic Development*. New Haven/London: Yale University Press.

Kaldor, N. (1981). 'The Role of Increasing Returns, Technical Progress and Cumulative Causation in the Theory of International Trade and Economic Growth', *Economie Appliquée*, reprinted in F. Targetti and A.P. Thirlwall (eds.). *The Essential Kaldor*. New York: Holmes & Meier, 1989.

Landes, D. (1969). *The Unbound Prometheus*. Cambridge: Cambridge University Press.

—— (1999). *The Wealth and Poverty of Nations*. New York: Norton.

Lundvall, B.A. (ed.) (1992). *National Systems of Innovation: Towards a Theory of Innovation and Interactive Learning*. London: Pinter Publishers.

Meier, G.M., and Stiglitz, J.E. (eds.) (2001). *Frontiers of Development Economics*. New York/Oxford: Oxford University Press.

Mokyr, J. (1990). *The Lever of Riches*. Oxford/New York: Oxford University Press.

—— (2009). *Enlightened Capitalism*. Forthcoming.

Mytelka, L.K. (ed.) (2007). *Innovation and Economic Development*. Cheltenham, UK/Northampton, MA: Edward Elgar.

Narula, R., and Zanfei, A. (2005). 'Globalization of Innovation: The Role of Multinational Enterprises', in Fagerberg, J., Mowery, D.C., and Nelson, R.R. (eds.) *The Oxford Handbook of Innovation*, Oxford: Oxford University Press, pp. 318–45.

Nelson, R.R. (1982). *Governments and Technical Progress*. New York: Pergamon Press.

—— (2004). 'Economic Development from the Perspective of Evolutionary Theory'. New York: Columbia University, mimeo.

—— (2005). *Technology, Institutions and Economic Growth*. Cambridge, MA: Harvard University Press.

North, D.C. (2005). *Understanding the Process of Economic Change*. Princeton: Princeton University Press.

Polanyi, K. (1944). *The Great Transformation: The Political and Economic Origins of Our Time*. Boston: Beacon Press.

Prebisch, R. (1950). *The Economic Development of Latin America and its Principal Problems*. New York: United Nations, ECLA.

Reinert, E. S. (1998). 'Raw Materials in the History of Economic Policy; or, Why List (the Protectionist) and Cobden (the Free Trader) Both Agreed on Free Trade in Corn?' in G. Cook (ed.) *Freedom and Trade: 1846–1996*. London: Routledge.

Reinert, E. S. (2007). *How Rich Countries Got Rich...and Why Poor Countries Stay Poor.* London: Constable.

Rodrik, D. (2004). 'Industrial Policies for the Twenty-First Century'. Cambridge, MA: Harvard University. J. F. Kennedy School of Government, Working paper.

—— (2008), 'Goodbye Washington Consensus, Hello Washington Confusion?'. *Journal of Economic Literature*, forthcoming.

Rosenberg, N. (1976). *Perspectives on Technology.* Cambridge: Cambridge University Press.

Sachs, J.D., and Warner, A.M. (1997). 'Fundamental Sources of Long-Term Growth'. *American Economic Review,* Papers and Proceedings, 87: 184–8.

Sen, A. K. (1985). *Commodities and Capabilities.* Amsterdam: North-Holland.

Stiglitz, J.E. (2002). *Globalization and its Discontents.* New York/London: W.W. Norton & Company.

—— (2006). *Making Globalization Work.* New York/London: W.W. Norton & Company.

—— and Weiss, A. (1981). 'Credit Rationing in Markets with Imperfect Information'. *American Economic Review,* 71(3): 393–410.

World Bank (2005). *Economic Growth in the 1990s: Learning from a Decade of Reform.* Washington, DC: The World Bank.

—— (2008). *Global Economic Prospects 2008.* Washington DC: The World Bank.

—— (2008a). *The Growth Report: Strategies for Sustained Growth and Inclusive Development.* Washington, DC: The World Bank.

Part I

General Introduction

2

Institutions and Policies Shaping Industrial Development: An Introductory Note

Mario Cimoli, Giovanni Dosi, Richard Nelson, and Joseph E. Stiglitz

There are two complementary ways to introduce the analysis of the institutions and policies shaping industrial development.

First, one may just build on the simple empirical observation that no example can be found in history of a process of development nested in an environment even vaguely resembling the institution-free tale of economic interactions that one finds in a good deal of contemporary economic theory. On the contrary, all historical experiences of sustained economic growth—starting at least from the English Industrial Revolution—find their enabling conditions in a rich set of complementary institutions, shared behavioral norms, and public policies. Indeed, the paramount importance of institutions and social norms appears to be a rather universal property of every form of collective organization we are aware of. Moreover, much more narrowly, discretionary public policies have been major ingredients of national development strategies, especially in catching-up countries, throughout the history of modern capitalism: see the contributions by Mazzoleni and Nelson, Perez, and Di Maio to this book, together with the historical experiences analyzed in the different country chapters.

Conversely, from a symmetric perspective, there are extremely sound theoretical reasons supporting the notion that institutions and policies always matter in all processes of technological learning and economic coordination and change.

Here we focus on the latter issue and outline some theoretical foundations for institution-building and policies.

A misleading point of departure: *market failures*

Conventionally, one would start from the very general question, when are public policies required from the point of view of the theory? And, as known, the standard answer would be, when there are market failures of some kind. However, albeit quite common, the 'market failure' language tends to be quite misleading in that, in order to evaluate the necessity and efficacy of any policy, it takes as a yardstick those conditions under which standard normative ('welfare') theorems hold. The problem with such a framework is not that market failures are not relevant. Quite the contrary: the problem is that hardly any empirical set-up bears a significant resemblance with the 'yardstick'—in terms of, for example, market completeness, perfectness of competition, knowledge possessed by economic agents, stationarity of technologies and preferences, rationality in decision-making, and so on (the list is indeed very long!). In a profound sense, when judged with standard canons, the whole world can be seen as a huge market failure!

Indeed, this is implicitly recognized in any serious policy discussion, where the argument about policy almost never is about whether the situation at hand is actually optimal, but rather about whether the problems with the incumbent institutional set-up are sufficiently severe to warrant active policy measures. In all that, most often the demand for 'proofs of failures' mainly plays as a device to put the burden of the evidence away from the believers in the dogma that in general 'more market is always better than less'.

Much nearer the empirical realities of markets and non-market institutions which govern production, exchanges, and economic coordination in modern economies, in the following we shall discuss issues of both (i) the boundaries between market and non-market forms of economic organization, and (ii) the embeddedness of markets themselves into complementary non-market institutions.

A rather universal role of institutions: the determination of the boundaries between non-market and market interactions

Which types of social activities are subject to (i) decentralized production and (ii) money-mediated exchanges, and which ones are not? There is an impressive range from the economically banal to the morally outrageous. Strategic goods? Pharmaceuticals? Natural monopolies? Public utilities? Education? Childcare? Retirement benefits? Health care? Human organs? Blood? Husbands and wives? Political votes? Children? Court rulings?

In another work one of the authors (Nelson, 2005) discusses precisely the *governance structure* of a few goods and services wherein their provision has often relied, in part or entirely, on non-market mechanisms.

Clearly the question of the determination of market boundaries applies to both developed and developing countries but is particularly crucial in emerging and ex-centrally planned economies where the boundaries between market and non-market institutions still have to be clearly defined. Far from the fury of market fundamentalism, our basic view there is that non-market institutions (ranging from public agencies to professional associations, from trade unions to community structures) are at the core of the very constitution of the whole socio-economic fabric. Their role goes well beyond the enforcement of property rights. Rather, they offer the main governance structure in many activities where market exchanges are socially inappropriate or simply ineffective. At the same time, they shape and constrain the behavior of economic agents toward competitors, customers, suppliers, employees, government officials, and so on. In that, they are also instrumental in curbing the 'self-destruction perils' for market economies flagged long ago by Polanyi (1957) and Hirschman (1982).

Moreover, notice that even when one encounters a prevailing 'market form' of governance, the latter is embedded in a rich thread of non-market institutions.

Pharmaceuticals is a very good case in point. Here in all countries with an effective, for-profit pharmaceutical industry, one finds government programs that support biomedical research, generally at universities and public labs. Together, the university parts of these programs are associated also with scientific training for people who, after finishing their education, go on to work in pharmaceutical companies. Moreover, in virtually all countries, public funds and programs play a major role in the procurement of pharmaceuticals. And, finally, in virtually all countries there are various forms of regulation of pharmaceuticals which go well beyond textbook guarantees of property rights and integrity of exchanges.

Or consider aircraft and airline services. In all countries that have major aircraft production, government funds play a significant role in R&D. And in most countries both the airports and the traffic control system are not only funded but run by government agencies. Even in the simple case of trucking and the use of automobiles, the public sector plays a major role: it builds and maintains roads, regulates safety and inspects vehicles, while a large part of the police is traffic police....

Indeed, even when the conditions which allow markets to work reasonably well are fulfilled—in terms of distribution of information, norms of interaction, etc.—we propose that their role should be evaluated not only in terms of allocative efficiency (whatever that means in ever-changing economies) but also as environments which continuously allow the experimentation of new products, new techniques of production, new organizational forms. In this perspective, markets, when they work, operate as (imperfect) mechanisms of selection. Also at this level, the ways the institutional architecture organizes the interactions amongst economic agents, and the ways policies regulate behaviors and forms of competition are of paramount importance.

The case of the generation, adoption, and economic exploitation of new scientific and technological knowledge

While the importance of institutions and policies is ubiquitous in all processes of economic coordination and change, this is particularly so with respect to the generation and use of information and knowledge. As we have known since the early works of Nelson (1959) and Arrow (1962), they are in many respects similar to a 'public good' in that the use of information is (i) non-rival (the fact that one uses it does not prevent others from using it too); and (ii) non-excludable (were it not for institutional provisions such as patent-based monopoly rights of exploitation). Moreover, the generation of information is subject to: (i) sunk, upfront costs of production, and basically zero cost of reproduction; and (ii) if anything, there are increasing returns to its use, in the sense that the more we use it the easier it is, and, dynamically, the higher is the likelihood of learning and producing ourselves better, novel, in some sense innovative further pieces of information.

One should note that these very properties of information intrinsically entail phenomena of market failures, to use the jargon just criticized above (also in that marginal prices are of no guidance to efficient market allocation, and equilibria might even fail to exist).

Further insights may be gained by distinguishing between sheer information and knowledge. Knowledge includes (i) the pre-existing cognitive categories which allow information to be interpreted and put to use; (ii) search and problem-solving heuristics irreducible to well-defined algorithms.

All forms of knowledge have a significant tacit aspect, highly complementary to codified information, which makes them person- or organization-embodied and rather sticky in their transmission. Indeed, this is one of the fundamental reasons why technological catching-up by developing countries remains a challenging task even in an era of globalization and free-information flows.

It happens that all processes of generation of new scientific and technological knowledge, as well as of technological imitation and adaptation, involve a rich variety of complementary actors, often including business firms, together with public training and research institutions, communities of practice, technical societies, and trade unions, among others.

In a fundamental sense, institutions and policies addressing technological learning have to do with the construction of *national systems of production and innovation*.

In fact, the process of catch-up involves innovation in an essential way. The innovating activities that drive the process of course differ from the innovating that is the focus of a good deal of research and technological learning in advanced economies. The new technologies, and new practices more generally, that are being taken on board, while new to the country catching up, generally are well established in countries at the frontier. And much of the innovation that is required is organizational and institutional. But what is going on in catch-up most certainly is innovation in the sense that there is a break from past familiar practices, considerable uncertainty about how to make the new practice work effectively, a need for sophisticated learning by doing and by using, and a high risk of failure, as well as a major potential payoff from success.

Together, the dynamics of industrialization rest upon major structural transformations which entail a changing importance of different branches of economic activity as generators of both technological and organizational innovations. The recent literature on innovation highlights the diversity in the sources of learning opportunities and the complementarities between them (Dosi, 1988a; Cimoli and Dosi, 1995; Mowery and Nelson, 1999). In fact in each epoch there appear to be technologies whose domains of application are so wide and their role so crucial that the pattern of technical change of each country depends to a large extent on the national capabilities in mastering production/imitation/innovation in such crucial knowledge areas (e.g. in the past, mechanical engineering, electricity and electrical devices, and nowadays also information technologies). Moreover, the linkages among production activities often embody structured hierarchies whereby the most dynamic technological paradigms play a fundamental role as sources of technological skills, problem-solving opportunities, and productivity improvements. Thus, these core technologies shape the overall absolute advantages/disadvantages of each country. The patterns of technical change of each country in these technologies do not average out with the technological capabilities in other activities but are complementary to them. These core technologies often also imply the construction of basic infrastructures and networks common to a wide range of activities (such as, for example, the electricity grid, the road system, telecommunication information networks). Historical evidence strongly supports the view that self-sustained technological dynamism in catching-up countries is hardly possible without a progressive construction of a widening manufacturing sector involving also indigenous skills in a set of 'core' technologies.

Complementarities, incentives, and coordination hurdles

So far, we have addressed some basic motivations underlying the policies and the institutions affecting primarily the mechanism of knowledge accumulation. But what about coordination problems, stemming in the first instance from the very interrelatedness among multiple heterogeneous agents?

Of course, the distinction is not as clear as that: 'coordination' involves also demand (Keynesian) feedbacks, and requires reasonable degrees of incentive compatibility among agents as well as coordination in learning processes. The fundamental coordination issues here are that of matching between decentralized behaviors and between distributed diverse pieces of knowledge: the radically different outcomes that such processes might entail depending crucially on the institutions in which they are nested.

Interestingly, the basics are quite clear to some founding figures of development economics as a discipline (including Nurske, Gerschenkron, Rosenstein-Rodan, Hirschman, and Prebisch).

Consider the following remarks by Nurske (1953):

in our present context it seems to me that the main point is to recognize how a frontal attack of this sort—a wave of capital investments in a number of different industries—can economically succeed while any particular industry may be blocked or discouraged by the limitation of the pre existing market. Where any single enterprise might appear quite inauspicious and impracticable, a wide range of projects in different industries may succeed because they will all support each other, in the sense that the people engaged in each project, now working with more real capital per head and with greater efficiency in terms of output per man-hour, will provide an enlarged market for the products of the new enterprises in other industries. In this way the market difficulty, and the drag it imposes on individual incentives to invest, is removed or at any rate alleviated by means of a dynamic expansion of the market thorough investment carried out in a number of different industries.

And by Gerschenkron (1962):

industrialization process begins only if the industrialization movement can proceed, as it were, along a broad front, starting simultaneously along many lines of economic activities. This is partly the result of existence of complementarity and indivisibilities in economic process. Railroads cannot be built unless coal mines are opened up at the same time; building half a railroad will not do if an inland center is to be connected with a port city. Fruits of industrial progress in certain lines are received as external economies by other branches of industry whose progress in turn accords benefit to the former. In viewing the economic history of Europe in the nineteenth century, the impression is very strong that only when industrial development could commence on a large scale did the tension between the preindustrialization conditions and the benefits expected from industrialization become sufficiently strong to overcome the existing obstacles and to liberate the forces that made for industrial policies.

Similar insights are behind Rosenstein-Rodan's *big push* theory (Rosenstein-Rodan, 1943; cf. also the contemporary revisitation in Murphy, Shleifer, and Vishny, 1989): as discussed in Hoff and Stiglitz (2001), a crucial feature on which the relevance of big push models rest is diffused externalities, where the interaction effects occur through system wide variables such as aggregate demand, industrial demand for inputs, or search costs.

These are all domains where appropriate mixes of policies may and do help—as historical experiences have shown—to 'delock' from the past and foster novel developmental trajectories. It has been so in the past, and, as we shall argue next, there is little reason to believe that it will be radically different in the future, notwithstanding so-called globalization.

Indeed, institutions can be seen as the social technologies (Nelson and Sampat, 2001) mastering externalities and matching/mismatching patterns between innovative activities, underlying incentives structures, investment, saving propensities, labor training, and socially distributed skills. In turn, the institutions governing such externalities and complementarities do so also governing interaction rules among agents, shaping their beliefs and the information they may access, their ethos and behavioral rules (for a more detailed discussion, see Hoff and Stiglitz, 2001).

The institutional development of technological capabilities, organizations, and incentive structures: a co-evolutionary dynamic

A fundamental element in countries that successfully caught up with the leaders during the nineteenth and twentieth centuries was active government support of the catch-up process, involving various forms of protection and direct and indirect subsidy. The guiding policy argument has been the need of domestic industry, in the industries of the day judged critical in the development process, for some protection from advanced firms in the leading nations. Alexander Hamilton's argument (1791) for infant industry protection in the new United States was virtually identical to that put forth decades later by Friederich List (1841) regarding Germany's needs. Gershenkron's (1962) famous essay documents the policies and new institutions used in Continental Europe to enable catch-up with Britain. The same story also fits well with the case of Japan, and of Korea and Taiwan somewhat later. In many countries these policies engendered not successful catch-up but a protected inefficient home industry. However, they also were the hallmark during the twentieth century of all the countries that have achieved their goals of catching up. We need to learn more about the circumstances under which infant industry protection leads to a strong indigenous industry, and the conditions under which it is self defeating, and indeed several contributions to this book shed new light on the issue.

These policies obviously angered companies in the leading countries, and their governments, particularly if the supported industry not only supplied its home market but began to invade the world market. While the case made after World War II for free trade was mostly concerned with eliminating protection and subsidy among the rich countries, and at that time there was sympathy for the argument that some infant industry protection was often useful in developing countries, the more recent international treaties that have been made increasingly have been used against import protection and subsidy in countries seeking to catch up from far behind.

Our belief is that Hamilton and List were and continue to be right that successful catch-up in industries where international trade is considerable requires some kind of infant industry protection or other means of support.

Moreover, during the nineteenth and early twentieth centuries, many developing countries operated with intellectual property rights regimes which did not restrict seriously the ability of their companies in effect to copy technologies used in the advanced countries. There are many examples where licensing agreements were involved, but we believe that for the most part these were vehicles through which technology transfer was effected for a fee or other considerations, rather than instances of aggressive protection of intellectual property by the company in the advanced country.

As with infant industry protection and subsidy, conflicts tended to emerge largely when the catching-up company began to encroach onto world markets, or even to export to the home market of the company with the patent rights. Increasing instances of this clearly were a major factor in inducing the treaty on Trade-Related Aspects of Intellectual Property Rights. But this treaty makes vulnerable to prosecution not just companies in developing countries that are exporting, but also companies that stay in their home markets.

More generally, what are the different domains of policy intervention and how do they map into different policy measures and related institutions?

Table 2.1 summarizes an exploratory taxonomy.

In the last resort, policies and other activities of institutional engineering affect together (i) the technological capabilities of individual and corporate organizations, and the rate at which they actually learn; (ii) the economic signals that they face (including of course profitability signals and perceived opportunity costs); (iii) the ways they interact with each other and with non-market institutions (e.g. public agencies, development banks, training and research entities, etc.).

It happens that all major developed countries present indeed relatively high degrees of intervention—whether consciously conceived as industrial policies or not—that affect all the above variables. And this applies, even more so, to the period when today's developed countries were catching up with the international leader. What primarily differentiate the various countries are the instruments, the institutional arrangements, and the philosophy of intervention.

In another work, one of the authors considers the case of Japanese policies, especially in relation to electronic technologies, after WWII, as a paradigmatic example of catching-up policies (Dosi, 1984).

Interestingly, Japan appears to have acted comprehensively upon all the variables categorized in our taxonomy. A heavy discretionary intervention upon the structure of signals (also involving formal and informal protection against imports and foreign investments) recreated the 'vacuum environment' that is generally enjoyed only by the technological leader(s). However, this was matched by a pattern of fierce oligopolistic rivalry between Japanese companies and a heavy export orientation which fostered technological dynamism and prevented any exploitation of protection simply in terms of collusive monopolistic pricing.

Table 2.1. Some classification of the variables and processes which institutions and policies act upon (in general and with particular reference to technological learning)

Domains of policy intervention	Policy measures	Related institutions
(i) Opportunities of scientific and technological innovation	Science policies, graduate education, "frontier" technological projects	Research universities, public research centers, medical institutes, space and military agencies, etc.
(ii) Socially distributed learning and technological capabilities	Broader education and training policies	From primary education to polytechnics, to US-type "land-grant colleges", etc.
(iii) Targeted Industrial Support Measures, affecting e.g. types of firms, etc.—*in primis* the structure, ownership, modes of governance of business firms (e.g. domestic vs. foreign, family vs. publicly owned companies, etc.)	From the formation of state-owned firms to their privatization, from "national champions" policies to policies affecting MNCs' investments; all the way to the legislation affecting corporate governance	State-owned holdings, public merchant banks, public "venture capitalist", public utilities
(iv) The capabilities of economic agents (in the first instance business firms) in terms of the technological knowledge they embody, the effectiveness and speed with which they search for new technological and organizational advances, etc.	cf. especially points (ii), (iii) and also R&D policies; policies affecting the adoption of new equipment, etc.	
(v) The economic signals and incentives profit-motivated agents face (including actual and expected prices and profit rates, appropriability conditions for innovations, entry barriers, etc.)	Price regulations; tariffs and quotas in international trade; Intellectual Property Rights regimes, etc.	Related regulatory agencies, agencies governing research and production subsidies, trade controlling entities, agencies granting and controlling IPRs
(vi) Selection mechanisms (overlapping with the above)	Policies and legislation affecting anti-trust and competition; entry and bankruptcy; allocation of finance; markets for corporate ownership; etc.	Anti-trust authorities, institutions governing bankruptcy procedures, etc.
(vii) Patterns of distribution of information and of interaction amongst different types of agents (e.g. customers, suppliers, banks, shareholders, managers, workers, etc.)	Governance of labor markets, product markets, bank–industry relationships, etc. all the way to collectively shared arrangements for within-firms information-sharing mobility and control; forms of cooperation and competition amongst rival firms, etc. (cf. for example the historical differences between Japanese vs. Anglo-Saxon forms of Industrial governance)	Basically, all of the above

It is tempting to compare the Japanese experience—notwithstanding, recent, mostly macroeconomic difficulties—with others, on average less successful, such as the European ones, which heavily relied upon a single instrument, financial transfers (especially R&D subsidies and transfers on capital account), leaving to the endogenous working of the international market both the determination of the patterns of signals and the response capabilities of individual firms. Certainly, there are country-specific features of the Japanese example which are hardly transferable. However, that case, in its striking outcome, points at a general possibility of reshaping the patterns of comparative advantages as they emerge from the endogenous evolution of the international markets.

The comparison between the experience of Far Eastern countries and Latin American ones is equally revealing (cf. Amsden, 1989 and 2001; Wade, 1990; Kim and Nelson, 2000; Dosi, Freeman, and Fabiani, 1994; among others).

In a nutshell, Korea—as well as other Far Eastern economies—has been able to 'twist around' absolute and relative prices and channel the resources stemming from 'static' comparative advantages toward the development of activities characterized by higher learning opportunities and demand elasticities (Amsden, 1989).[1] And they did that in ways which penalized rent-seeking behaviors by private firms. In fact, the major actors in technological learning have been large business groups—the chaebols—which were able at a very early stage of development to internalize skills for the selection of technologies acquired from abroad, their efficient use and their adaptation and, not much later, were able to grow impressive engineering capabilities (cf. Nelson, 1993).

This process has been further supported by a set of institutions and networks for improving human resources (Amsden, 1989). All this sharply contrasts with the Latin American experience, where the arrangement between the State and the private sector has often been more indulgent over inefficiencies and rent-accumulation, and less attentive to the accumulation of socially diffused technological capabilities and skills.

Ultimately, success or failure appears to depend on the combinations of different institutional arrangements and policies, in so far as they affect learning processes by individuals and organizations, on the one hand, and selection processes (including of course market competition), on the other.

Certainly, the historical experience shows a great variety of country- and sector-specific combinations between the types of policies illustrated above. Some subtle regularities nonetheless emerge.

First, a regularity, holding from nineteen-century Europe and the US all the way to contemporary times, is the centrality of public agencies, such as universities, and public policies in the generation and establishment of new technological paradigms.

Second, and relatedly, incentives are often not enough. A crucial role of policies is to affect the capabilities of the actors, especially in the case of new technological paradigms, but also in all cases of catching-up whereby no reasonable incentive structure might be sufficient to motivate private actors to surmount big technological lags.

Third, market discipline is helpful in so far as it weeds out the low performers and rewards the high performers within particular populations of firms. However, nothing guarantees that too high selective shocks will not wipe out those entire populations, thus also eliminating any future learning possibility.

Fourth, policies—especially those aimed at catching-up—generally face the need to balance measures aimed at capability building (and also at protecting the 'infant learner') with mechanisms curbing inertia and rent-seeking. For example, the latter are indeed one of the major elements missing in the old Latin American experience of import substitution while the former are what is lacking under many more recent liberalization policies.

Fifth, historically, a successful catching-up effort in terms of per capita income and wages has always been accompanied by catching-up in the new and most dynamic technological paradigms, irrespective of the initial patterns of comparative advantages, specialization, and market-generated signals. Our conjecture is that, *ceteris paribus*, the structural need for policies affecting *also* the patterns of economic signals (including relative prices and relative profitabilities) as they emerge from the international market will be greater, the higher the distance of any one country from the technological frontier. This is what Amsden (1989) has provocatively called policies of deliberately 'getting the prices wrong'. Conversely, endogenous market mechanisms tend to behave in a virtuous manner for those countries that happen to be on the frontier, especially in the newest/most promising technologies. This is broadly confirmed by historical experience: unconditional free trade often happened to be advocated and fully exploited only by the technologically and politically leading countries.

On some fundamental trade-offs facing institutions and policies in learning economies

In a world characterized by technical change (both continuous change along defined technological trajectories and discontinuous, related to the emergence of new technological paradigms), technological lags and leads shape the patterns of intersectoral and interproduct profitability signals and, thus, also the patterns of microeconomic allocation of resources. The latter, however, may affect the long-term macroeconomic dynamism of each country, in terms of both rates of growth of income consistent with the foreign balance constraint and of technological innovativeness. In the last resort, this happens because the effects of a multiplicity of signals (related to profitability, long-term demand growth, and technological opportunities) upon microeconomic processes of adjustments are likely to be *asymmetric*. In another work one of the authors elaborates on this point distinguishing between the notion of (i) allocative efficiency; (ii) innovative (Schumpeterian) efficiency; and (iii) growth efficiency of particular patterns of production (Dosi, Pavitt, and Soete, 1990). There we argue that, especially in countries far from the technological frontier, patterns of allocation of resources which are 'efficient' on the grounds of the incumbent distribution of technological capabilities and relative prices might well entail negative long-term effects in terms of demand elasticities of the goods one country will be able to produce (the 'growth efficiency') and of the innovative potential associated with that (the criterion of 'innovative efficiency'). Whenever trade-offs between different notions of efficiency arise, sub-optimal or perverse macroeconomic outcomes may emerge. Since the *future* pattern of technological advantages/disadvantages is also related to the *present* allocative patterns, we can see at work here dynamic processes which Kaldor termed as *circular causation*: economic signals related to intersectoral profitabilities—which lead in a straightforward manner to comparative advantages and relative specializations—certainly control and check the allocative efficiency of the various productive employments, but may also play a more ambiguous or even perverse role in relation to long-term macroeconomic trends.

Note that these possible trade-offs have little to do with the informational efficiency of market processes (even if, of course, various forms of informational asymmetries are likely to make things worse). Rather it is the general condition of an economic system that technological opportunities vary across products and across sectors. Moreover, within each technology and each sector the technological capabilities of each firm and each country are associated with the actual process of production and innovation in the area. Thus, the mechanisms regarding resource allocation *today* affect also where technical skills will be accumulated, (possibly) innovation undertaken, economies of scale reaped, and so on. However, the potential for these effects differs widely between technologies and sectors. This is another aspect of the irreversibility of economic processes: present allocative choices influence the direction and rate of the future evolution of technological coefficients. Whenever we abandon the idea of technology as a set of blueprints and conceive technical progress as a joint product with manufacturing, it is possible to imagine an economic system which is dynamically better off than otherwise (in terms of productivity, innovativeness, etc.), if it evolves in disequilibrium vis-à-vis conditions of allocative efficiency.

It is rather easy to see how such trade-offs between allocative efficiency and innovative efficiency can emerge. The patterns of specialization (with their properties of allocative efficiency) are determined, for each country, by the relative size of the sector-specific technology gaps (or leads) (more in Dosi, Pavitt, and Soete, 1990). Whenever the gap is highest in the most dynamic technologies (i.e. those characterized by the highest technological opportunities), allocative efficiency will conflict directly with innovative efficiency. We would suggest that the likelihood of such trade-offs between the two notions of efficiency is proportional to the distance of each country from the technological frontier in the newest, most dynamic, and most pervasive technologies.[2]

A similar argument applies to the trade-offs between allocative and growth efficiency: ultimately countries may well end up by 'efficiently' specializing in the production of commodities which a relatively small or even decreasing number of world consumers wants to buy thus tightening their ability to grow consistently with some foreign balance constraint.[3]

Under conditions of non-decreasing (often increasing) returns, there is no straightforward way in which markets can relate the varying growth and innovative efficiencies of the various commodities to relative profitability signals for the microeconomic agents.[4]

This defines also a fundamental domain for policies.

A detailed understanding of, and intervention on, patterns of signals, rules of allocative responses, and forms of institutional organization of the 'economic machine' are particularly important in those phases of transition from a technological regime (based on old technological paradigms) to a new one. These historical periods define a new set of opportunities and threats for each country: the patterns of international generation and diffusion of technologies become more fluid as do, consequently, the international trade flows and the relative levels of per capita income.

The contemporary economy—we believe—is undergoing such a change. In the process, comparative advantages become the self-fulfilling prophecy of a successful set of institutional actions and private strategies: *ex post*, technological and economic success makes 'optimal' from the point of view of the economist what *ex ante* is a political dream.

Some tricky operational questions

That having been acknowledged, interesting lessons are likely to come from the detailed comparison of the outcomes of different combinations of institutional arrangements and policy measures as historically observed.

For example, (i) what lessons can be drawn from the comparison between 'import substitution' versus 'export promotion' philosophies? (ii) how does capital accumulation complement technological learning? (iii) what is precisely the importance of the financial sector and its relationship with industrial activities? (iv) how do strategies of technological acquisition based on MNCs' investment compare with others relying on the growth of domestic firms? (v) what are the most effective policy devices aimed at curbing rent-seeking behaviors which often emerge as a by-product of the efforts to foster learning by domestic firms? (vi) what is the role of public research institutions in the process of catching-up? (vii) how is the latter affected by different IPR regimes?

and (viii) how do macroeconomic policies influence microeconomic behaviors and adjustment processes especially with regard to technological and organizational learning?

Indeed several of these questions—crucial to the understanding of the effectiveness of different policy combinations—are addressed by various contributions to this book.

However, possibly the trickiest question of all concerns the extent to which the lessons from the past can be useful under the current regime of international economic relations.

Policies in a globalized world: the new challenges

Our argument so far, we believe, applies to the generality of the processes of catching-up and industrialization, notwithstanding their obvious historical variety. But what are the specific lessons which can be drawn from the most recent phase of international development?

In fact, the last couple of decades of globalization have gone hand-in-hand with powerful efforts to impose a policy regime grounded in rather extreme forms of economic orthodoxy, which in the case of developing countries has gone under the name of 'Washington Consensus'. Of that, Latin America has been an exemplar victim.

Trade liberalization, leading eventually to free trade, was a key part of such a 'consensus'—sometimes imposed indeed at gunpoint. The emphasis on trade liberalization was natural: the Latin American countries, it was claimed, had stagnated behind protectionist barriers. Import substitution according to the same view had proved a highly ineffective strategy for development. In many countries industries were producing products with negative value added, and innovation was stifled. The usual argument—that protectionism itself stifled innovation—was indeed somewhat confused. Governments could have created competition among domestic firms, which would have provided incentives to import new technologies. It was the failure to create competition internally, more than protection from abroad, that was the cause of the stagnation. Of course, competition from abroad would have provided an important challenge for domestic firms. But it is possible that in the one-sided race, domestic firms would have dropped out of the competition rather than enter the fray. Consumers might have benefited, but the effects on growth may have been more ambiguous. In fact, the subsequent experience materialized all the worries in these respects. Trade liberalization may create competition, but it does not do so automatically. If trade liberalization occurs in an economy with a monopoly importer, the rents may simply be transferred from the government to the monopolist, with little decrease in prices. Trade liberalization is thus neither necessary nor sufficient for creating a competitive and innovative economy.

At least as important as creating competition in the previously sheltered import-competing sector of the economy is promoting competition on the export side. The success of the East Asian economies is a powerful example of this point. By allowing each country to take advantage of its competitive strength, trade increases wages and expands consumption opportunities. For the last few decades in the case of Far Eastern countries trade has been doing just that.

Moreover, as the comparison between different experiences in Latin America and in the Far East shows, a free-trade shock does not automatically trigger any increase in the accumulation of knowledge and innovative capabilities. On the contrary, in a world characterized by multiple forms of localized increasing returns (both localized in terms of technologies and in spatial terms), greater integration may well lead to phenomena of increasing differentiation with self-reinforcement and lock-in of particular production activities, specialization patterns, technological capabilities (or lack of them): compare the discussion above. Putting it another way, it is easy to show that a world which becomes, at some level, increasingly integrated—but not (even roughly) identical in initial conditions, institutions, technological capabilities, mechanisms of economic interaction, etc.—might be subject to various forms of 'local' virtuous or vicious circles, *even more so than in the past.*

Finally, the impact of greater integration is likely to depend on the modes through which it is implemented. The experience of many Latin American countries is a good case in point. When macro (globalizing) shocks suddenly induced higher selection upon domestic firms, massive mortality of firms did often entail an apparent reduction of the productivity gap vis-à-vis the international frontier. But this happens to come together—at least in Latin America—with striking increases in both unemployment rates (i.e. transitions of parts of the labor force from low productivity to zero productivity states) and with tightening foreign-balance constraints to growth, in turn the joint outcome of relatively low elasticities of exports to world growth and high elasticities of imports to domestic growth (cf. Cimoli and Correa, 2005).

Certainly both the recent changes in international—political and economic—relations and the ongoing 'ICT revolution' are reshaping the opportunities and constraints facing policy making and institutional engineering, but by no means have decreased their importance. On the contrary, they demand new forms of governance which one is only beginning to explore.

So, for example, on the technological side, the characteristics of productive knowledge have nowadays changed as compared to, say, the electromechanical paradigms within which countries like Germany and the USA caught up and overtook England nearly one century ago, and they might be also partly different from the type of knowledge—a good deal centered on 'first generation' ICT—through which, more recently, Korea and Taiwan approached the technological frontier. In turn, with changes in the type of knowledge countries need to accumulate and improve upon, often come also changes in the most appropriate policy packages concerning, for example, the type of education offered; the support to national incumbent firms versus MNCs versus new entrants; the role of public training and research centers. Indeed, many of the contributions to this book tackle these issues.

Major changes have come also in the regime of international trade and property right protection, associated with WTO, TRIPS, and several bilateral agreements. The new regime, first, has implied a reduction in the degrees of freedom developing countries can enjoy in their trade policies, while, to repeat, all catching-up countries in the preceding waves of industrialization could exploit a large menu of quotas, tariffs, and other forms of non-tariff barriers. Second, it involves a much more aggressive international policing of intellectual property rights and, thus, other things being equal, more difficulties in imitating and 'inventing around' existing products and production processes—again, activities which have been at the core of the first phases of industrialization, from the US to Switzerland, to Japan, to Korea....

Hence, a fundamental policy question concerns the degrees of freedom left for discretionary public interventions supporting in different ways specific technologies, sectors, and firms. How stringent are the new international constraints? Note that the answer here is likely to vary from sector to sector and from technology to technology. And it is likely to depend also on the distance of any country from the international technological frontier. For example, many African and some Latin American countries might not be directly affected by a tightening in the IPR regimes, having little capabilities to imitate to begin with (although they might still be badly affected by being forced to buy e.g. drugs or software at ridiculous prices from first-world MNCs rather than from more advanced but still 'imitating' countries). Conversely, tighter IPR regimes may well represent a major hindrance to more advanced catching-up countries.

Given that, how easy is it to play around with existing rules? That is, putting it the other way round, how urgent is it to reform the incumbent international trade and IPR regimes from a pro-development perspective?

On all these issues, it is time to build a 'new consensus' prominently featuring the exploration of forms of institutional governance which in developing countries also foster knowledge accumulation and render its efficient economic exploitation consistent with the multiple interests of profit-motivated agents. Such a consensus, we shall repeatedly argue, is going to be based on a pragmatic view of markets whereby the latter sometimes work in a developmental sense, sometimes do not, and even when they do work, their effectiveness cannot be separated from the contribution of supporting institutions and policies. And, last but not least, it must be a consensus sensitive to issues of equity and of access to the sharing of the benefits from growth stemming from technological and organizational learning.

The contributions to this book, from different angles, indeed move us in this direction.

Notes

1. On the 'perverse' importance of rent-seeking in the development process, cf. Khan (2000a, 2000b).
2. Somewhat similar conclusions on the crucial importance of the distance from the international technological frontier in terms of required mix of policy measures can be drawn also on the grounds of 'neo-Schumpeterian' models of growth: cf. Aghion and Howitt (2005).
3. In Dosi, Pavitt, and Soete (1990) and Cimoli (1988) one argues this proposition on the ground of a model nesting a Kaldor–Thirlwall growth dynamic onto diverse technology gaps at the commodity level. A similar proposition however can be shown to hold under more conventional assumptions: see Rodrik (2005).
4. If the same argument is put in a language more familiar to the economist, the widespread possibility of trade-offs between allocative, Schumpeterian, and growth efficiencies arises from the fact that the general case is one of non-convexity of production and consumption possibility sets and dynamic increasing returns and path-dependencies of technological advances. On the point, within a growing literature, see the complementary arguments of Atkinson and Stigliltz (1969), David (1988), Arthur (1994), Dosi, Pavitt, and Soete (1990), Krugman (1996), Antonelli (1995), Cimoli (1988), Castaldi and Dosi (2006).

References

Aghion P. and S. Durlauf (eds.) (2005), *Handbook of Economic Growth*, Elsevier, Amsterdam.
—— and P. Howitt (2005), 'Appropriate Growth Policy: A Unifying Framework,' The 2005 Joseph Schumpeter Lecture, Presented to the European Economic Association Congress, Amsterdam (August 25).
Amsden A. (1989), *Asia's Next Giant: South Korea and Late Industrialization*, Oxford University Press, New York.
—— (2001), *The Rise of 'the Rest': Challenges to the West from Late-Industrializing Economies*, Oxford University Press, Oxford.
Antonelli C. (1995), *The Economics of Localized Technological Change and Industrial Dynamics*, Kluwer Publishers, Boston.
Arrow K. (1962), 'Economic Welfare and the Allocation of Resources for Invention' in R. Nelson (ed.) *The Rate and Direction of Inventive Activity*, Princeton University Press, Princeton.
Arthur W.B. (1994), *Increasing Returns and Path Dependence in the Economy*, University of Michigan Press, Ann Arbor.
Atkinson A., and J. Stiglitz (1969), 'A New View of Technological Change,' *Economic Journal*, 79: 573–8.
Castaldi C., M. Cimoli, N. Correa, and G. Dosi (2004), 'Technological Learning, Policy Regimes and Growth in a "Globalized" Economy: General Patterns and the Latin American Experience,' LEM Working Paper 2004/01, Sant'Anna School of Advanced Studies, Pisa.
—— and G. Dosi (2006), 'The Grip of History and the Scope for Novelty: Some Results and Open Questions on Path Dependence in Economic Processes' in A. Wimmer and R. Kössler (eds.) *Understanding Change*, Palgrave Macmillan, 99–128.

Cimoli M. (1988), 'Technological Gaps and Institutional Asymmetries in a North–South Model with a Continuum of Goods,' *Metroeconomica*, 39: 245–74.

—— and G. Dosi (1995), 'Technological Paradigms, Patterns of Learning and Development. An Introductory Roadmap,' *Journal of Evolutionary Economics*, 5: 243–68.

—— and N. Correa (2005), 'Trade Openness and Technological Gaps in Latin America: A "Low Growth" Trap' in J. A. Ocampo (ed.) *Beyond Reforms, Structural Dynamics and Macroeconomic Vulnerability*, Stanford Economics and Finance, Palo Alto.

David P.A. (1988), 'Path Dependence: Putting the Past into the Future of Economics,' Technical Report 533, Stanford University, Institute for Mathematical Studies in the Social Science.

Dosi G. (1984), *Technical Change and Industrial Transformation*, Macmillan, London and St. Martin Press, New York.

—— (1988), 'Institutions and Markets in a Dynamic World,' *The Manchester School of Economic and Social Studies*, 56: 119–46.

—— (1988a), 'Sources, Procedures and Microeconomic Effects of Innovation,' *Journal of Economic Literature*, 26(3): 1120–71.

—— K. Pavitt, and L. Soete (1990), *The Economics of Technical Change and International Trade*, Harvester Wheatsheaf, London, New York University Press, New York.

—— C. Freeman, and S. Fabiani (1994), 'The Process of Economic Development: Introducing Some Stylized Facts and Theories on Technologies, Firms and Institutions,' *Industrial and Corporate Change*, 3: 1–45.

Freeman C. (1982), *The Economics of Industrial Innovation*, 2nd edn., Francis Pinter, London.

—— (2004), 'Technological Infrastructures and International Competitiveness,' *Industrial and Corporate Change*, 541–69.

Gerschenkron A. (1962), *Economic Backwardness in Historical Perspective*, Harvard University Press, Cambridge, MA.

Greenwald B. and J. Stiglitz (1986), 'Externalities in Economics with Imperfect Information and Incomplete Markets,' *Quarterly Journal of Economics*, 101: 229–64.

Hamilton A., (1791), 'Report on the Subject of Manufactures' in H.C. Syrett et al. (1966) *The Papers of Alexander Hamilton: Vol. X.* Columbia University Press, New York.

Hausmann R., J. Hwang, and D. Rodrick (2005), 'What You Export Matters,' CID Working Paper No. 123, Center for International Development, Harvard University, Cambridge, MA.

Hirschman A.O. (1958), *The Strategy of Economic Development*, Yale University Press, New Haven.

—— (1982), 'Rival Interpretations of Market Society: Civilizing, Destructive, or Feeble?' *Journal of Economic Literature*, 20: 1463–84.

Hoff K. (1996), 'Market Failures and the Distribution of Wealth: A Perspective from the Economics of Information,' *Politics and Society*, 24: 411–32.

—— and J. Stiglitz (2001), 'Modern Economic Theory and Development' in Meier and Stiglitz (2001).

Khan, M. (ed.) (2000a), 'Rents, Efficiency and Growth' in *Rents, Rent-Seeking and Economic Development: Theory and Evidence in Asia*, Cambridge University Press, Cambridge.

—— (ed.) (2000b), 'Rent-Seeking as Process' in *Rents, Rent-Seeking and Economic Development: Theory and Evidence in Asia*, Cambridge University Press, Cambridge.

Krugman, P.R. (1996), *The Self-Organizing Economy*, Blackwell Publishers, Cambridge, MA/Oxford.

Lall S. (2000), 'Selective Industrial and Trade Policies in Developing Countries: Theoretical and Empirical Issues,' QEH Working Paper Series 48, University of Oxford, Oxford.

Landes D. (1969), *The Unbound Prometheus*, Cambridge University Press, Cambridge.

List F. (1841), *The National System of Political Economy*, trans. S.S. Lloyd. Longmans, Green and Co., London.

Meier G. and J. Stiglitz (eds.) (2001), *Frontiers of Development Economics*, Oxford University Press, Oxford/New York.

Mowery D. and R.R. Nelson (1999), *Sources of Industrial Leadership: Studies of Seven Industries*, Cambridge University Press, Cambridge.

Murphy K., A. Shleifer, and R.W. Vishny (1989), 'Industrialization and the Big Push,' *Journal of Political Economy*, 97: 1003–26.

Nelson R.R. (1959), 'The Simple Economics of Basic Scientific Research,' *Journal of Political Economy*, 67: 297–306.

—— (1982), *Government and Technical Progress*, Pergamon Press, New York.

Nelson R.R. (1993) *National Innovation Systems: A Comparative Analysis*. Oxford University Press, New York.

—— (1994), 'The Co-Evolution of Technology, Industrial Structure and Supporting Institutions,' *Industrial and Corporate Change*, 3: 47–64.

—— and B. Sampat (2001), 'Making Sense of Institutions as a Factor Shaping Economic Performance,' *Journal of Economic Behavior & Organization*, 44: 31–54.

—— (2004), 'Economic Development from the Perspective of the Evolutionary Theory,' Columbia University, New York, mimeo.

—— (ed.) (2005), *The Limits of Market Organization*, Russell Sage Foundation, New York.

Nurske R. (1953), *Problems of Capital Formation in Underdeveloped Countries,* Oxford University Press, New York.

Ocampo J.A. (ed.) (2005), *Beyond Reforms, Structural Dynamics and Macroeconomic Vulnerability*, Stanford University Press, Palo Alto.

—— (2005), 'The Quest for Dynamic Efficiency: Structural Dynamics and Economic growth in Developing Countries' in Ocampo (2005).

Polanyi K. (1957), *The Great Transformation*, Beacon Press, Boston.

Rodrik D. (1995), 'Trade and Industrial Policy Reform' in J. Behrman and T.N. Srinivasan (eds.) *Handbook of Development Economics, Vol. III*. North Holland, Amsterdam.

—— (ed.) (2003), *In Search of Prosperity: Analytic Narratives on Economic Growth*, Princeton University Press, Princeton.

—— (2005), 'Growth Strategies' in P. Aghion and S. Durlauf (2005).

Rosenberg N. (1976), *Perspective on Technology*, Cambridge University Press, Cambridge.

—— (1982), *Inside the Blackbox*, Cambridge University Press, Cambridge.

Rosenstein-Rodan P. (1943), 'Problems of Industrialization of Eastern and Southeastern Europe,' *Economic Journal*, 53: 210–11.

Stiglitz J.E. (1994), *Whither Socialism?* MIT Press, Cambridge, MA.

—— (1996), 'Some Lesson from the East Asian Miracle,' *World Bank Research Observer*, 11: 151–77.

Stiglitz J. E. (2001), 'More Instruments and Broader Goals Moving toward the Post-Washington Consensus' in H. Chang (ed.) *The Rebel Within*, Wimbledon Publishing Company, London. (Originally presented as the 1998 WIDER Annual Lecture, Helsinki, January).

Veblen T. (1915), *Imperial Germany and Industrial Revolution*, Macmillan, London.

Wade R. (1990), *Governing the Market: Economic Theory and the Role of Government in East Asian Industrialization*, Princeton University Press, Princeton.

3

Technological Learning, Policy Regimes, and Growth: The Long-Term Patterns and Some Specificities of a 'Globalized' Economy

Carolina Castaldi, Mario Cimoli, Nelson Correa, and Giovanni Dosi

Introduction

The purpose of this chapter is to offer a frame of interpretation for the international patterns of technological innovation and diffusion, and their relations with income growth, in general, but with a particular emphasis on the possible role played by the so-called 'globalization' processes of the last couple of decades. As such, it is meant also to offer a background for the discussions of the role of policies and of various measures of institutional engineering in different countries and different historical periods presented in the other chapters of this book. The field to cover is huge, and our only ambition here can be to provide a rather telegraphic set of propositions and some suggestive evidence (much more may be found in the literature we shall draw upon.)[1]

It is useful to start from the broad picture and recall some basic long-term features of technological accumulation and income growth, in particular in their international dimension (see the next section). Given those secular trends, which—as we shall see—tend to display divergence as the dominant characteristics, to what extent and in which directions are they influenced by the contemporary processes coming under the fashionable and rather fuzzy heading of 'globalization'? In order to address the question one requires a clarifying detour, spelling out which phenomena—real or imagined—underlies globalization itself (see the third section). We shall also focus on trends related to the ICT revolution, highlighting the still rather limited impact of the New

Economy and offering an interpretation in terms of 'retardation factors' which affect the establishment of new 'techno-economic paradigms' (see the fourth section). Together, we investigate the impact, especially on developing countries, of those dimensions of 'globalization' having to do with the 'diffusion' or imposition of that particular policy regime of management of macro variables and market governance which goes under the heading of 'Washington Consensus' (cf. J. Williamson, 1990). Notwithstanding relevant international differences in the implementation procedures, the general philosophy grounding such a policy archetype has ultimately involved the commitment to: (i) blood-and-tears macro-stabilization policies, (ii) 'private-is-better-than-public-no-matter-what' market governance policies, and (iii) quite unconditional, *most often asymmetric*, international liberalization of trade and financial flows. In this respect, an 'experiment'—striking both from an interpretative point of view and for its dramatic social outcomes—is offered by many Latin American countries over the past quarter of a century. The evidence provides a powerful example of how laissez-faire policies may produce a 'vicious' growth path leading to 'low growth traps' whenever a country is not able to decrease its technology gap with respect to the international frontier and improve its trade balance at the same time.

As we argue in the final section, neither the contemporary evidence nor the theory supports the view that globalization naturally goes hand-in-hand with international convergence: in quite a few cases, the opposite holds. This supports the view that policy variables continue to be fundamental to the engineering of development processes.

Technological and income divergence as secular patterns

The basic phenomenon to start from is indeed the highly skewed international distribution of innovative activities which have emerged since the Industrial Revolution (Dosi, Pavitt, and Soete, 1990) starting from previously rather homogenous conditions at least between Europe, China, and the Arab World (Cipolla, 1965). It is certainly true that technological 'innovativeness' is hard to measure, but irrespectively of the chosen proxy, the picture which emerges is one with innovation highly concentrated in a small group of countries. An illustration using patents registered in the US is presented in Table 3.1.

Indeed, the club of major innovators has been quite small over the whole period of around two centuries and half since British industrialization, with both restricted entry (with Japan as the only major entrant in the twentieth century, and Korea and Taiwan as recent additions) and a slow pace of change in relative rankings.

At the same time, since the Industrial Revolution, one observes the explosion of diverging income patterns, starting from quite similar pre-industrial per

Table 3.1. US patents granted, by country of applicant and year (% of non-US recipients)

	1883	1900	1929	1958	1973	1986	1995	2007
OECD								
Australia	1.11	2.33	1.96	0.60	0.89	1.14	1.00	1.63
Austria	2.62	3.36	2.47	1.12	1.05	1.09	0.74	0.59
Belgium	1.59	1.35	1.30	1.14	1.25	0.74	0.87	0.67
Canada	19.94	10.54	10.25	7.99	5.95	4.01	4.61	4.27
Denmark	0.56	0.46	0.71	0.74	0.68	0.56	0.44	0.50
France	14.22	9.79	9.76	10.36	9.47	7.24	6.18	4.03
Germany	18.67	30.72	32.36	25.60	24.68	20.94	14.45	11.64
Italy	0.24	0.92	1.19	3.02	3.35	3.04	2.36	1.67
Japan	0.16	0.03	1.40	1.93	21.82	40.35	47.64	42.90
Netherlands	0.24	0.75	1.57	5.71	3.03	2.21	1.75	1.61
Norway	0.32	0.49	0.71	0.61	0.37	0.25	0.28	0.32
Sweden	0.95	1.32	3.19	4.64	3.37	2.70	1.76	1.36
Switzerland	1.75	2.27	4.46	8.80	5.86	3.70	2.31	1.33
UK	34.55	30.52	22.23	23.45	12.61	7.35	5.43	4.23
NICs								
Israel					0.37	0.58	0.84	1.42
Singapore					0.03	0.01	0.12	0.51
Taiwan					0.00	0.64	3.55	7.88
South Korea					0.02	0.14	2.54	8.10
Hong Kong					0.07	0.09	0.19	0.43
India					0.09	0.05	0.08	0.70
China					0.04	0.03	0.14	0.99
Latin America								
Argentina					0.12	0.05	0.07	0.05
Brazil					0.08	0.08	0.14	0.12
Mexico					0.19	0.11	0.09	0.07
Venezuela					0.03	0.06	0.06	0.02

Source: Elaborations on US Patent and Trademark Office (USPTO) data.

Table 3.2. Estimates of trends in world income: per capita GDP of regions relative to the US and Western offshoots

Regions	1700	1820	1870	1913	1950	1973	2001
Western Europe	210	100	81	66	49	71	71
Eastern Europe	127	57	39	32	23	31	22
Former USSR	128	57	39	28	31	37	17
US and Western offshoots	*100*	*100*	*100*	*100*	*100*	*100*	*100*
Latin America	111	58	28	28	27	28	22
Japan	120	56	30	27	21	71	77
Asia (excluding Japan)	120	48	23	13	7	8	12
Africa	88	35	21	12	10	9	6
World	129	55	36	29	23	25	22

Western Offshoots: Australia, Canada, New Zealand and the United States.

Source: Own elaborations on per capita GDP, 1990 million international dollars, 1700–2001 from Maddison (2001).

capita levels. Table 3.2 presents estimates showing that before the Industrial Revolution the income gap between the poorest and the richest region was probably of the order of only 1 to 2. Conversely, the dominant tendency after the Industrial Revolution is one with fast increasing differences among countries and overall divergence. Bairoch and Kozul-Wright (1996) have discussed how the period between 1870 and 1914, taken as an era of early globalization, was already characterized by increasing divergence and concentration of high growth in a few countries only. Even in the post World War II period, commonly regarded as an era of growing uniformity, the hypothesis of global convergence, that is convergence of the whole population of countries toward increasingly similar income levels, does not find support from the evidence (De Long, 1988; Easterly et al. 1992; Verspagen, 1991; Soete and Verspagen, 1993; Durlauf and Johnson, 1992; Quah, 1996; and Castaldi and Dosi, 2008 and 2009, among others). Moreover, the process of divergence in incomes has speeded up over time. Clark and Feenstra (2003) claim that: 'Per capita incomes across the world seemingly diverged by much more in 1910 than in 1800, and more in 1990 than 1910—this despite the voluminous literature on exogenous growth that has stressed the convergence of economies, or, to be more precise, "conditional" convergence'(op. cit. p. 277).

Indeed, one finds some, although not overwhelming, evidence of *local* convergence, that is, convergence within subsets of countries grouped according to some initial characteristics such as income levels (Durlauf and Johnson, 1992) or geographical locations. The typical patterns are impressionistically illustrated in Figure 3.1 from Durlauf and Quah (1998), showing the appearance

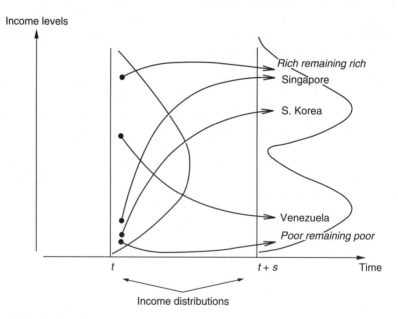

Source: Durlauf and Quah (1998).
Figure 3.1. Evolving cross-country income distributions

of a two-humped distribution of countries with low (albeit positive) transition probabilities between the 'poor' and 'rich' clubs (and vice versa, too).

Bimodality hints at a separating tendency between poor and rich countries, characterized by markedly different income levels. At the same time, the other part of the story, as discussed at length in Quah (1997), is that the same shape of a given distribution may conceal very different intra-distribution dynamics. Is it the case that poor countries have been converging to a common income level and rich countries to their own high level of income or that the two modes are also the result of shifting in ranking between poor and rich countries? The issue at stake is the respective weight of persistence and mobility of countries inside the distribution. Quah (1997) finds evidence that the period 1960–1988 has been characterized by high persistence of relative rankings, notwithstanding some important exceptions. The main events contributing to mobility have been the 'growth miracles' of countries like Hong Kong, Singapore, Japan, Korea, and Taiwan and 'growth disasters' including some sub-Saharan African countries, but also Venezuela which was among the first richest countries in 1960 and has dramatically fallen in the 'poor' countries club.

Recent evidence on the world income distribution has shown that population-weighted measures of inequality have decreased in the last two decades, mainly due to China and India (see the discussion in Bourguignon et al. 2004). While the finding provides evidence indeed for the convergence hypothesis, it does not shed light on the increasingly frequent episodes of 'marginalization' (cf. Melchior and Telle, 2001). Authors such as Dowrick and DeLong (2003) agree on the convergence of OECD economies and also within a broader group including the East Asian economies, and with China and India too after 1980. 'However, these episodes of successful economic growth and convergence have been counterbalanced by many economies' loss of their membership in the world's convergence club' (op. cit. p. 193).

At the same time, across-group differences in growth performances appear to be rather persistent. Likewise, one observes persistently wide and in some cases widening (such as in a few Latin American cases) productivity gaps vis-à-vis the international frontier (cf. Table 3.3 for estimates of labor productivity relative to the US). As discussed also in van Ark and McGuckin (1999) all available evidence witnesses a persistent dispersion in productivity measures. More specifically, while countries in the OECD area appeared to have moved on average closer to the US benchmark, the same cannot be said for the rest of the world.

A delicate but crucial issue concerns the relation between patterns of technical change and patterns of economic growth. Of course, technological learning involves many more elements than simply inventive discovery and patenting. Equally important activities are imitation, reverse engineering, and adoption of capital-embodied innovations, learning by doing and learning by using (Freeman, 1982; Dosi, 1988; Patel and Pavitt, 1994). Moreover, technological

Table 3.3. Labor productivity relative to US (real GDP in 1990 international dollars per person employed)

	1870	1913	1950	1973	1990	1998	2007
OECD							
Austria	*60.6*	*56.4*	31.4	61.4	76.7	81.7	77.1
Australia	*153.2*	*106.4*	74.2	71.7	76.3	76.6	77.3
Belgium	*96.1*	*71.9*	58.2	75.5	93.1	90.5	86.9
Canada	*75.7*	*86.9*	85.1	85.8	83.2	81.0	77.2
Denmark	*69.0*	*68.6*	59.6	66.5	74.9	76.8	75.0
Finland	*38.1*	*36.2*	34.1	53.5	70.8	77.5	79.7
France	*60.6*	*56.0*	46.3	76.4	93.7	90.8	86.0
Germany	*66.0*	*58.7*	42.9	72.2	72.5	70.9	66.8
Ireland			35.0	47.9	74.8	82.8	88.8
Italy	*45.4*	*40.6*	40.8	69.5	85.5	83.7	72.7
Japan	*20.3*	*20.9*	18.7	56.9	77.5	71.3	71.1
Netherlands	*107.8*	*80.4*	67.1	82.4	80.5	75.9	72.6
Norway	*52.7*	*46.7*	51.8	63.9	79.4	84.9	83.3
Spain		*45.0*	22.2	50.0	75.1	73.5	60.5
Sweden	*53.9*	*50.2*	57.4	68.2	69.1	74.3	76.9
Switzerland	*68.3*	*65.0*	75.5	82.4	76.6	70.2	65.2
UK	*113.9*	*84.8*	65.2	65.6	73.2	76.8	78.5
US	*100.0*	*100.0*	100.0	100.0	100.0	100.0	100.0
Latin America							
Argentina			52.4	52.9	36.1	47.4	40.7*
Brazil			23.0	27.9	21.9	22.6	19.4*
Chile			48.2	40.3	39.6	52.1	46.7*
Colombia			28.5	29.3	30.0	28.9	25.9*
Mexico			34.1	45.9	36.7	32.5	30.7
Peru			27.5	31.2	16.8	20.5	21.0*
Venezuela			97.7	92.4	54.4	46.8	46.4*
NICs							
Israel				61.2	74.1	70.5	65.7*
Hong Kong			87.0	43.3	76.8	78.9	94.7*
Singapore				39.5	58.8	64.8	74.2*
Korea			*10.7*	21.3	43.1	51.6	61.7
Taiwan			*10.9*	28.7	50.5	65.8	71.6*
India			*5.8*	6.1	6.9	9.6	18.9
China			*5.5*	4.8	7.4	8.4	10.9

Source: Total Economy Database, GGDC (2006), historical values (in italics) are from Maddison (2001). Values with the star (*) correspond to the year 2006.

change often goes together with organizational innovation. Still, it is important to notice the existence of significant links between innovative activities (measured in a rather narrow sense, i.e. in terms of patenting and R&D activities) and GDP per capita (for the time being, we shall avoid any detailed argument on the direction of causality), which however tend to change over different historical periods.

As discussed in Dosi, Freeman, and Fabiani (1994), evidence concerning OECD countries appears to suggest that the relationship between innovative activities and levels of GDP has become closer over time and is highly significant after World War II (Table 3.4). Moreover, innovative dynamism, measured

Table 3.4. Correlation coefficients between levels of innovative activity and GDP per capita, OECD countries

Year	Correlation of GPD per capita with	
	US patents per capita	R&D per capita
1890	0.20	
1913	0.38	
1929	0.56*	
1950	0.63**	
1963	0.73**	0.79**
1967	0.72**	0.69**
1971	0.74**	0.71**
1977	0.88**	0.61**
1981	0.65**	0.62**
1985	0.61**	0.49*
1991	0.63**	0.68**
1996	0.50*	0.62**
2006	0.55*	0.76**

* Significance at 5% level.
**Significance at 1% level.
Source: Pavitt and Soete (1981) until 1977 and own elaborations for later years.

by the growth of patenting by different countries in the US, always appears positively correlated with per capita GDP growth, even if the relation is quite noisy and period-specific (see results from Tables 3.5 and 3.6).[2]

The link is particularly robust between 1913 and 1970. Conversely, a sign that the regime of international growth might have changed in the 1970s is that in this period the relation gets weaker and loses statistical significance. The link becomes strong again in the 1980s, loses significance again in the 1990s, and regains it in the most recent period: in our view, this is circumstantial evidence of turbulent and uncertain dynamics in the 'political economies' of different countries governing the combined dynamics between technological learning, demand generation, and growth.

In general, at least since World War II, the rates of growth of GDP appear to be closely correlated with: (i) domestic innovative activities, (ii) the rates of investment in capital equipment, and (iii) international technological diffusion (De Long, 1988; Soete and Verspagen, 1993; Meliciani, 2001; Laursen, 2000; among others). In particular Fagerberg (1988) finds a close correlation between the level of 'economic development', in terms of per capita GDP, and the level of 'technological development', measured with the R&D investment level or with patenting activity.[3]

There is no strong evidence of convergence of innovative capabilities (PT and pt indicators in Tables 3.5 and 3.6), but there is some continuing sign of convergence in income. In turn, capability of innovating and quickly adopting new technologies is strongly correlated with successful trade performance (Dosi, Pavitt, and Soete, 1990).

Carolina Castaldi, Mario Cimoli, Nelson Correa, and Giovanni Dosi

Table 3.5. Correlation coefficient between innovative activity and output, 1890–1977, 14 OECD countries

	GDP Growth (g)	GDP per capita growth (y)	US patents per capita at t = 1 (PT)	US patents per capita growth (pt)	GDP per capita at t = 1 (Y)
1890–1913					
g	1.00	0.60*	0.60*	−0.22	−0.18
y		1.00	0.20	0.05	−0.66**
PT			1.00	−0.61*	0.22
pt				1.00	−0.67**
Y					1.00
1913–1929					
g	1.00	0.76**	−0.12	0.66**	−0.41
y		1.00	−1.21	0.67**	−0.62*
PT			1.00	−0.55*	0.38
pt				1.00	−0.43
Y					1.00
1929–1950					
g	1.00	0.82**	0.31	0.66**	0.37
y		1.00	0.41	0.58*	0.40
PT			1.00	0.22	0.56*
pt				1.00	0.67**
Y					1.00
1950–1970					
g	1.00	0.75**	0.38	0.89**	−0.76**
y		1.00	0.40	0.71*	−0.76*
PT			1.00	−0.48	0.63*
pt				1.00	−0.84*
Y					1.00
1970–1977					
g	1.00	0.91**	−0.67**	0.29	−0.47
y		1.00	−0.60*	0.16	−0.48
PT			1.00	−0.28	0.66**
pt				1.00	−0.16
Y					1.00

* Significance at 5% level.
** Significance at 1% level.
Source: Pavitt and Soete (1981).

Moreover, despite technological diffusion taking place at rather high rates, at least among OECD countries, important specificities in national innovation systems persist, related to the characteristics of the scientific and technical infrastructure, local user–producer relationships, and other institutional and policy features of each country (Lundvall, 1992; Nelson, 1993; Archibugi, Howells, and Michie, 2001). In a historical perspective, Freeman (2002) convincingly argues how catch-up of countries has critically relied on the ability to build successful national innovation systems. This has been, in turn, the case for England, US, Japan, and, most recently, the Asian Tigers.

To repeat, the dominant tendency throughout the foregoing secular picture hints at long-term divergence in relative technological capabilities,

Table 3.6. Correlation coefficient between innovative activity and output, 1970–2006, 21 OECD countries

	GDP growth (g)	GDP per capita growth (y)	US patents per capita at t = 1 (PT)	US patents per capita growth (pt)	GDP per capita at t = 1 (Y)
	1	2	3	4	5
1970–1977					
g	1.00	0.88**	−0.60**	0.37	−0.87**
y		1.00	−0.49	0.18	−0.70**
PT			1.00	−0.21	0.73**
pt				1.00	−0.14
Y					1.00
1977–1984					
g	1.00	0.88**	−0.36	0.78**	−0.76**
y		1.00	−0.25	0.82**	−0.54*
PT			1.00	−0.26	0.64**
pt				1.00	−0.63**
Y					1.00
1984–1991					
g	1.00	0.96**	−0.15	0.94**	0.94**
y		1.00	−0.13	0.89**	−0.49*
PT			1.00	−0.24	0.61**
pt				1.00	−0.58**
Y					1.00
1991–1998					
g	1.00	0.96**	−0.48*	0.37	−0.34
y		1.00	−0.46*	0.30	−0.25
PT			1.00	−0.27	0.63**
pt				1.00	−0.39
Y					1.00
1998–2006					
g	1.00	0.92**	−0.44*	0.67**	−0.33
y		1.00	−0.36	0.64**	−0.39
PT			1.00	−0.23	0.60**
pt				1.00	−0.12
Y					1.00

*Significance at 5% level.
**Significance at 1% level.
Source: Own elaborations on data from OECD and USPTO for a sample of 21 OECD countries.

production efficiencies, and incomes. Together however, they present two more hopeful messages.

First, notwithstanding prominently divergent patterns, one has also witnessed secularly increasing average levels of technological knowledge within most countries, and together also in the levels of per capita income. Second, while it holds true that the 'innovators' club' has been remarkably small and sticky in its membership, one ought to notice both the possibility of entry by a few successful latecomers (in different periods, the US, Germany, and Japan being the most striking examples) and also the possibility of falling behind by very promising candidates to the club (cf. the vicissitudes of Argentina over the last century).

Given all that, how is such a long-term scenario affected by those recent changes of the economic and political relations in the international arena collectively coming under the banner of globalization? In order to offer some tentative answer, one ought to start by specifying what precisely 'globalization' stands for.

A necessary detour: globalization of what?

Let us briefly go through a few domains in which an often anecdotal literature identifies the forces of globalization. For much more detailed analyses that we largely share, compare Eatwell (1996); Stiglitz (2002); Meier, Stiglitz, and Stern (2000); Kleinknecht and ter Wengel (1998); Bairoch and Kozul-Wright (1996); see also Bowles (2002) and the discussion in Berger and Dore (1996) and Hollingsworth and Boyer (1997). Globalization is often defined as a process of integration. This generic definition stresses the multidimensional nature of this phenomenon.

There are at least six relevant dimensions or forces that drive this integration process. The primary force is seen in the development of international trade, that is, the integration process of the commodity markets. Globalization is not only related to the trade of final goods, but also affects the markets for inputs. Thus, the integration of labor markets and financial markets are two other fundamental dimensions. Relatedly, an increased mobility of inputs also results in new productive structures, changes in technology specializations and in institutional arrangements that are required for a country to achieve successful development. Hence, we present here some of the recent evidence on the above dimensions.

International trade

A globalizing process of international trade has indeed taken place since World War II at quite rapid rates. However, in order to put things into perspective, remember that the ratio of international trade (exports and imports) over GNP of many countries overtook that of 1913 only around the late 1970s/early 1980s (see Table 3.7 for the evidence on some major developed countries).

These results are consistent with the argument of Findlay and O'Rourke (2003): tariff barriers were low at the beginning of the century, increased during the interwar period, and followed a declining path after 1950. Currently, even if tariff barriers are lower than in 1913, there are important exceptions such as in Britain, China, and India. The authors also stress that there is a consensus on the fact that non-tariff barriers have increased. Moreover, note that the institutional and tariff impediments to globalization have remained the highest in product areas in which developing countries are often more competitive such as

Table 3.7. Exports and imports of goods as a percentage of GNP (current prices)

	1913	1950	1973	1995	2007
France	30.9	21.4	29.2	44.3	54.8
Germany	36.1	20.1	35.3	47.8	85.9
UK	47.2	37.1	37.6	57.1	55.3
Netherlands	60.0	70.9	74.8	111.4	140.2
US	11.2	6.9	10.8	23.2	28.9
Japan	30.1	16.4	18.2	16.9	33.6

Source: Kleinknecht and ter Wengel (1998). Own elaborations for the last two years using data from IMF (International Financial Statistics, June 2008).

agricultural products, textiles, and so on (see also the evidence in Rodrik, 2002c).

Finally, one observes the persistence of striking international price differentials even in tradable commodities that are subject to low trade barriers (cf. the discussions in Rodrik, 2002a, and Bradford, 2003). Notice that if we observe an increase in the levels of imports and exports, we cannot use it as evidence for a process of globalization, simply because the increase could be the result of some other process. But if globalization was indeed the force behind this increase we would necessarily also observe a reduction in the price gap among different countries. Instead we still observe significant international price differentials.

Production by multinational companies

There is some evidence that multinational companies have somewhat increased production activities outside their home countries. A strong trend over the last ten years has been the increasing outsourcing of activities by manufacturing firms in developed economies. The very properties of ICT technologies have enabled the dislocation of non-core activities and services to other regions of the world (cf. Miozzo and Soete, 2001). Within this trend, a number of countries have been able to reap the benefits of attracting foreign firms to their sites or simply directly exporting services. In fact, developing economies are playing an increasingly large role in ICT-enabled services, with success stories including Singapore for financial services and India for software. As discussed by Cantwell and Janne (1999), the recent emergence of more global chains of production has made it more important for firms to take strategic decisions not only on which activities to outsource abroad but also on which countries to select as host countries. In this respect the availability of cheap labor is attractive for foreign firms only if it is accompanied by good local infrastructures, high quality labor, and, also, tax advantages.

However note that: (i) multi-nationalization of production has mainly been an intra-OECD phenomenon, with limited impact, if any, on developing and ex-communist countries (cf. Kleinknecht and ter Wengel, 1998; Archibugi and Iammarino, 2002); (ii) at least with respect to OECD countries, country-specific patterns of specialization continue to be rather persistent and path-dependent (cf. Meliciani, 2001; and Scarpetta, Bassanini, Pilat, and Schreyer, 2000); and (iii) when one observes significant ruptures in such patterns of specialization, such as in a few developing countries, they seem to be mostly the outcome of major macroeconomic and institutional shocks (cf. many Latin American countries) with a highly controversial impact upon production and technological capabilities (see also the section headed 'Different modes of insertion in the global economy').

Labor markets

Not by any far cry, have labor markets globalized, with the partial exception of the top tail of the skills distribution (i.e. engineers, scientists, managers, etc.) together with 'new economy gurus' of various sorts, actors, and football players...[4] The high-tech labor force deserves however a special mention. Lazonick (2007) discusses the 'off-shoring' phenomenon: in the first half of the 2000s US-based companies started to transfer large amounts of the ICT labor force to locations abroad, primarily India, China, and East Asian countries including Korea and Malaysia. Off-shoring is not a new phenomenon, as it already happened in a similar way for the semiconductor industry in the 1960s, with Mexico being the prime location then.

The claim of Lazonick is that off-shoring should be understood as complementary to the movements of large numbers of highly educated individuals from East Asia to the US. For successful Asian countries, some of the brain drain is in fact mitigated as soon as living standards in the home countries rise and indigenous companies emerge. For instance, while Korea can count on successful home-based companies, Malaysia is still strongly dependent on the investment decisions of multinationals. Ultimately the results of the globalization of the high-tech labor force depend on 'a triad of investment strategies of multinational companies engaged in foreign direct investment, national governments that construct indigenous science and technology infrastructures, and indigenous companies that build on the investment strategies of foreign companies and domestic governments to become world-class competitors in their own right' (op. cit. p. 63).

While the ICT and high-tech labor force is an importance case, one should not forget that for all other jobs national labor markets remain persistently national. At the same time, high and persistent asymmetries in the skills of the population remain the rule: compare Table 3.8 for evidence of cross-country differences in educational attainments.

Table 3.8. Mean years of schooling

	1970	1980	1990	2000
OECD				
Australia	10.2	10.3	10.4	10.9
Austria	7.4	7.3	7.8	8.4
Belgium	8.8	8.2	8.9	9.3
Canada	9.1	10.3	11.0	11.6
Denmark	8.8	9.0	9.6	9.7
Finland	6.1	7.2	9.4	10.0
France	5.7	6.7	7.0	7.9
Germany			9.9	10.2
Ireland	6.8	7.5	8.8	9.4
Italy	5.5	5.9	6.5	7.2
Japan	7.5	8.5	9.0	9.5
Netherlands	7.8	8.2	8.8	9.4
New Zealand	9.7	11.5	11.3	11.7
Norway	7.2	8.2	11.6	11.9
Portugal	2.6	3.8	4.9	5.9
Spain	4.8	6.0	6.4	7.3
Sweden	8.0	9.7	9.5	11.4
Switzerland	8.5	10.4	10.1	10.5
UK	7.7	8.3	8.8	9.4
US	9.5	11.9	11.7	12.0
NICs				
Israel	8.1	9.4	9.4	9.6
Singapore	5.1	5.5	6.0	7.1
South Korea	4.9	7.9	9.9	10.8
Hong Kong	6.3	8.0	9.2	9.4
Latin America				
Argentina	6.2	7.0	8.1	8.8
Brazil	3.3	3.1	4.0	4.9
Chile	5.7	6.4	7.0	7.6
Mexico	3.7	4.8	6.7	7.2
Venezuela	3.2	5.5	5.0	6.6
India	2.3	3.3	4.1	5.1
China		4.8	5.9	6.4
World				
Mean	4.2	4.9	5.8	6.4
Coeff. of variation	1.6	1.8	2.0	2.3

Source: Own elaborations on data from UN (2001).

Patterns of generation and diffusion of innovations

One has already mentioned the continuing concentration of innovative activities—notwithstanding remarkable new entrants such as Finland, Korea, Taiwan, and to a lesser extent Brazil, China, and India.

Not surprisingly, such patterns in innovative outputs are matched by persistent international differences in the share of resources devoted to formal technological learning (also revealed by privately financed R&D). So, while Korea overtook developed countries like Italy quite a while ago, most LDCs continue to display negligible levels of private investment in R&D (Figure 3.2).

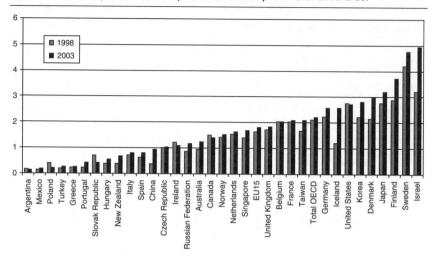

Source: Own elaborations on data from Main Science and Technology Indicators, OECD (2005b).
Figure 3.2. Intensity of firm level R&D

Table 3.9. Number of researchers (per thousand labor force)

	1991	1994	1997	2000	2003	2004
EU15	4.4	4.7	5	5.5	5.9	
Finland	5.5	6.4	10.6	13.4	15.9	
France	5.2	5.9	6	6.5	7.1	
Germany	6.1	5.9	5.9	6.5	6.8	
Ireland	3.8	3.7	4.6	4.9	5.4	
Italy	3.1	3.3	2.8	2.8	3	
Sweden	5.8	7.2	8.4	9.7	10.6	
UK	4.4	4.8	5.2			
US	7.6	7.7	8.4	9	9.1	
Japan	7.5	8.1	9.2	9.6	10.1	
Argentina			1.8	1.8	1.8	1.9
Brazil		0.8		0.8	0.9	0.9
Chile	0.9	1.0	1.0	1.1	1.9	2.0
Mexico		0.5	0.6	0.6	0.8	0.9
Venezuela				0.5	0.5	0.6
Singapore		3.9	5.2	7.6	9.3	
Taiwan			5	5.7	6.7	
South Korea			4.7	4.9	6.6	
China	0.7	0.8	0.8	1	1.1	

Source: Own elaborations on Main Science and Technology Indicators, OECD (2005b).
Data for Latin America are from Ricyt (2000).

Evidence on the number of researchers (Table 3.9) also points to large gaps across countries worldwide, and even within the EU.

Certainly, ICT technologies have determined easier diffusion of information. However, there is hardly any evidence of a generalized acceleration in the rates of adoption of both new (e.g. ICT-related) and old technologies (from tele-phones to tractors). Let us begin with the latter. Even in this case there is hardly any evidence of *generalized* patterns of convergence in their use at world level: see Figure 3.3.

As for new technologies, diffusion of the new ICT technologies is occurring in highly asymmetric fashions across countries. This applies to OECD countries and, even more so, to the universe of countries in the world economy. Most of the data available refer to developed countries. But, if gaps are found for those economies, even larger gaps are to be expected for developing ones.

It is useful to start by distinguishing the relative impact on production and consumption.

As for production, there has been an increasing investment in ICT capital for the last 30 years and rising factory automation, all the way from mechanical engineering to continuous cycle processes. At the same time, the evidence reinforces the view—discussed above—that we are still in an initial phase of the diffusion of ICT technologies, certainly with a consistent unexpressed potential. And, again, this applies even more so to developing countries. So, even in the United States ICT investment represents less than 30 percent of total investment and the share reduces considerably for European countries (see Daveri, 2002). Relatedly, the degree of automation in production has greatly increased, but one is still very far from saturating levels (see the evidence reported in Castaldi et al. 2004).

A complementary but different picture comes out from data on expenditure for Information Technology which can be taken as a proxy for the overall automation of the economy. The percentages remain quite small (Table 3.10). The evidence indicates that Japan and Europe lag behind the US in terms of total automation (as proxied by the level of ICT investment), while on the contrary the US lags behind in terms of factory automation (the same circumstantial evidence was already pointed out long ago in Arcangeli, Dosi, and Moggi, 1991, see also Freeman, 2001, for a discussion of the US national innovation system).

As for consumption, the evidence again points to a diffusion of new technolo-gies that is highly uneven across countries, even within the OECD. Table 3.11 reports on the strength of the IT infrastructure in a sample of countries. The ranking of countries now changes. The US is far ahead in the 'informatization' of its society and the other developed countries follow at considerable distance (the only relevant exception comes from mobile phones). Note the impressive inter-national differences in the diffusion of ICT technologies: compare for example Finland with Poland or East Asia with Latin America. Interestingly, there is also evidence of a 'digital divide' within the United States (Greenstein and Prince, 2007), with non-urban areas lagging behind in terms of high-speed Internet connection as the better alternative to low-speed/dial-up connection.

At the same time communication costs still remain a barrier to ICT use in a number of OECD countries (OECD, 2003).

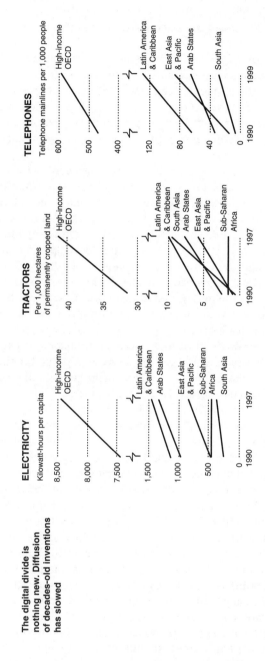

Figure 3.3. Diffusion of 'old' technologies

Source: United Nations, Human Development Report (2001).

Table 3.10. IT expenditure (Information Technology, excluding Communication), as a percentage of GDP

Country	1992	1996	2001	2006
US	4.45	4.93	5.30	3.3
Japan	3.83	3.60	4.00	3.4
EU15	3.03	3.17	4.17	2.7
Sweden	4.37	4.73	6.77	3.8
UK	4.43	4.90	5.62	3.5
Netherlands	3.96	3.84	5.19	3.3
Denmark	3.94	4.10	4.99	3.2
France	3.59	3.74	4.75	3.1
Belgium	3.38	3.34	4.48	2.8
Finland	2.93	3.36	4.38	3.2
Germany	2.94	2.96	4.22	2.9
Austria	2.73	2.80	3.78	2.8
Norway	3.24	3.26	3.66	2.4
Italy	1.8	1.78	2.48	1.7
Ireland	2.35	2.18	2.25	1.5
Spain	1.62	1.56	1.94	1.4
Portugal	1.24	1.48	1.93	1.8
Greece	0.71	0.90	1.20	1.2

Source: Elaborations of Eurostat data.

The most recent evidence about the participation of developing countries in the ICT-based regime shows that East Asian countries such as Korea, Malaysia, and Philippines have the highest share of employment and value added of the ICT sector (both manufacturing and services). Korea and Taiwan have in fact for a couple of decades ceased to be developing countries and have joined the quite exclusive club of innovators. Conversely, most Latin American countries and a few Eastern European ones remain at the bottom of the list (UN, 2006, chart 1.15).

The OECD Information Technology Outlook 2006 reports the geographical distribution of the top 250 ICT firms. While 116 of these are US firms, followed by 39 Japanese firms, the newcomers are also represented (11 for Taiwan, 6 for Korea, 3 each for Hong Kong and India). Mexico is the only Latin American country included (with 2 top ICT firms).

At the same time, the internationalization of innovative activities by MNCs beyond the home countries has somewhat increased, but one is still talking about rather low proportions. Most studies indicate that patenting by MNCs originating in countries different from that of their own origin is of the order of 10–15 percent of their total patenting, roughly comparable to their share in the total patenting of the host countries. Moreover, most of these research activities abroad occur within OECD countries (for discussion of the evidence cf. Patel and Pavitt, 1997; Pavitt, 1999; Cantwell, 1992; and Archibugi and Pietrobelli, 2003).

Table 3.11. Indexes of ICT diffusion, per 100 population

	Telephone lines and cellular subscribers			Internet users			Personal computers		
	1990	1998	2004	1990	1998	2004	1990	1998	2004
OECD									
Austria	42.9	78.9	143.6	0.1	15.4	47.5	6.5	23.8	57.6
Australia	46.7	77.2	141.3	0.6	22.4	65.3	15.0	36.8	68.9
Belgium	39.7	66.7	133.4	0.0	7.8	40.2	8.8	21.5	34.7
Canada	58.7	84.2	111.0	0.4	25.6	62.3	10.7	32.1	69.8
Denmark	59.6	102.4	160.0	0.1	22.6	50.4	11.5	37.7	65.5
Finland	58.6	110.2	141.0	0.2	25.4	51.4	10.0	34.9	48.2
France	50.0	77.6	129.8	0.1	6.3	39.3	7.1	23.2	48.7
Germany	44.5	73.7	152.6	0.1	9.9	42.7	9.0	27.9	48.5
Ireland	28.8	69.6	143.3	0.0	8.1	29.6	8.6	27.3	49.7
Italy	39.2	81.0	152.9	0.0	4.5	46.8	3.6	13.3	31.3
Japan	44.8	86.8	118.2	0.0	13.4	62.2	6.0	23.7	54.2
Netherlands	47.0	80.5	139.7	0.3	22.2	61.6	9.4	32.4	68.5
Norway	54.8	113.4	150.9	0.7	36.0	39.0	12.1	40.5	57.8
Spain	31.7	57.7	131.0	0.0	4.4	35.1	2.8	10.9	25.4
Sweden	73.5	118.6	180.0	0.6	33.4	75.5	10.5	39.5	76.1
UK	46.0	80.5	158.5	0.1	13.5	47.0	10.8	26.8	60.0
US	56.9	90.7	122.7	0.8	30.8	63.0	21.8	45.2	76.2
Russian Fed.	13.99	20.36	79.1	0.0	0.81	12.9	0.34	3.46	13.2
Hungary	9.62	44.09	121.9	0.0	3.92	26.7	0.96	6.48	14.6
Poland	8.64	27.74	*76.96*	0.0	4.08	23.4	0.79	4.91	19.1
Latin America									
Argentina	9.3	28.1	58.1	0.0	0.9	16.1	0.7	5.5	*8.2*
Brazil	6.5	16.5	59.8	0.0	1.5	12.0	0.3	3.0	10.7
Chile	6.7	27.1	83.6	0.0	1.7	27.9	0.9	6.3	13.9
Colombia	6.9	20.0	40.1	0.0	1.1	8.5		3.2	5.5
Mexico	6.6	13.9	53.9	0.0	1.3	13.4	0.8	3.7	10.7
Peru	2.6	9.3	22.1	0.0	1.2	11.6		3.0	9.7
Venezuela	7.7	19.8	45.0	0.0	1.4	8.4	1.0	3.9	8.2
NICs									
Israel	34.6	82.8	149.0	0.1	10.0	21.8	6.3	20.1	73.4
Hong Kong	47.5	105.5	173.2	0.0	14.5	50.3	4.7	26.0	60.5
Singapore	36.3	73.2	132.7	0.0	19.1	57.9	6.6	37.0	*62.2*
Korea	30.8	75.1	131.4	0.0	6.8	65.7	3.7	18.2	54.5
India	0.6	2.3	8.4	0.0	0.1	3.2	0.0	0.3	1.2
China	0.6	8.9	49.7	0.0	0.2	7.2	0.0	0.9	4.1
World									
Average	14.9	28.2	*46.7*	0.0	3.7	*13.1*	3.4	8.0	*12.8*
Coeff Variation	1.2	1.1	*1.0*	4.6	1.9	*1.3*	1.4	1.4	*1.3*

Source: Elaborations on United Nations Millennium indicators. Values in italics refer to 2003.

In terms of outsourcing of R&D activities, multinational companies have been much more reluctant to transfer key research labs to developing countries. One of the reasons for firms to decentralize R&D activities is to relocate in the neighborhood of technological centers of excellence in order to enjoy agglomeration economies and spillovers of new knowledge concentrating in that area (Dunning, 1993). But most key geographical technological clusters are still

Table 3.12. Geographical distribution of R&D foreign affiliates, 2004

Region/economy		Number
Total world		**2584**
Developed countries		**2185**
of which	Western Europe	1387
	United States	552
	Japan	29
Developing countries		**264**
of which	Africa	4
	Latin America and the Caribbean	40
	Asia	216
	South, East and South East Asia	207

Source: UNCTAD, based on the Who Owns Whom database of Dun and Bradstreet.
The data are based on a sample of 2284 majority-owned foreign affiliates identified in the db as engaged in either:
  (i) commercial, physical and educational research (SIC code 8731)
  (ii) commercial economics and biological research (SIC code 8732)
  (iii) non-commercial research (SIC code 8733)
  (iv) testing laboratories (SIC code 8734)

found in the developed world. As shown in Table 3.12, the great majority of R&D foreign affiliates are still located in developed countries and only about 10 percent in developing countries, of which 8 percent are in Asian countries. Note that, also in this case, the growth figures may be impressive but the levels are not.

There is also evidence that until recently R&D facilities located abroad were mostly responsible for adapting existing products to local needs and tastes, while most fundamental and strategic R&D efforts were maintained in-house in the home countries (Pearce, 1989). 'Support laboratories' (in the definition of Pearce, 1999) are simply responsible for short-term technology transfer and facilitate the assimilation of the technologies for local affiliates. Long-term goals may only be achieved if multinationals move from 'support laboratories' to 'locally integrated laboratories' and even 'international independent laboratories'.

Financial markets

The liberalization of financial markets has been indeed the most striking phenomenon which has forcefully taken off over the last quarter of a century (cf. Blundell-Wignall and Browne, 1991). Just to provide an order of magnitude, in the 1990s one day of foreign exchange trade was typically more than a hundred times bigger than world yearly trade (see Eatwell, 1996). Together, barriers to capital movements have hurriedly come down and with that has grown the volatility of financial flows. The increased volatility of financial flows has also played a major role in a series of financial crises of the last decade including the ones in Mexico in 1994–1995, in East Asia and Russia in 1997–1998, and in Argentina in 2001–2002. These crises have taught us that even if financial integration can bring benefits to the world economy as a whole, these benefits are distributed unevenly among the participants and developing countries usually bear the highest risks.

Remarkably, even in this case, globalization has gone much faster with respect to 'hot', short-term, speculative finance, with much lower impact—if any—upon long-term activities of investment and production (see the discussion for the Latin American case in Ocampo, 2002). A plausible conjecture is indeed that in a few countries the latter activities have been made more marginal and more 'national'. Kose et al. (2006) argue that financial globalization has brought some benefits, but only after certain threshold conditions were met. Such conditions include the quality of institutions, the development of financial markets, and the integration of macroeconomic policies. In their review of the current evidence, Rodrik and Subramaniam (2008) show how countries growing the most are in fact the ones who have resorted the least to capital inflows stemming from financial globalization.

At the same time, savings and investments have remained stubbornly national. In this respect, one of the major puzzles in international economics is the persistence of the so-called *Feldstein–Horioka Puzzle*. Feldstein and Horioka (1980) found a high correlation between national saving rates and domestic investment rates for OECD countries in the period 1960–1975. Recent cross-country estimates (Obstfeld and Rogoff, 2000) confirm a high correlation coefficient. Note that the higher the correlation, the lower the capital mobility.[5] These results feed the puzzle because under a full integration of capital markets one would expect capital to flow to countries with higher expected returns. In principle savings should be directed to the most productive investments, hence one would predict that capital from rich developed countries would contribute to investments in poor, but growing, developing countries.[6] As discussed in Eatwell (1996), there are at least three elements that strongly point to an effective lack of integration across national capital markets. First, real rates of return persistently diverge and they diverge in ways which hardly seem to reflect just 'country risks'. Second, net capital flows tend to be directed to developed countries, the US in particular, and not to developing countries. Third, the capital flows directed to developing countries are more volatile and investments are usually in the most liquid financial assets. While foreign direct investment has recently increased for many developing countries, a huge amount of capital flows has instead been of a short-run, speculative nature. For the Latin American case, Stallings and Peres (2000) argue that the boom in FDI flows to Latin America in the 1990s is for the most part explained by the investment undertaken, which represented around 47 percent of the accumulated stock of FDI. This process of takeover has resulted in an increase of transnational corporation subsidiaries in the region. Moreover, the overall financial capital in Latin America has become more volatile: short-term claims (up to one year) increased from 37 percent in 1991 to 52 percent in 1999.

Institutional arrangements

Certainly, the current globalized regime of international and political relations is linked with the diffusion, or in many circumstances the imposition at gun point, of specific institutional set-ups, drawn from a particular form of Western capitalism—the laissez-faire Anglo-Saxon one—ranging from Stock Exchanges to Intellectual Property Right regimes. However, the piecemeal diffusion of elements of the 'Anglo-Saxon model' is far from producing an international convergence to a unique institutional archetype, notwithstanding the violence through which it is often forced upon the international community by the organizations enforcing the so-called 'Washington Consensus' (for thorough discussions see Berger and Dore, 1996; Stiglitz, 2002; Krugman, 1999; Rodrik, 2002b).

Another—equally important and deeply related—level of analysis regards the impact of broad *policy regimes* upon both processes of knowledge accumulation and ultimately growth patterns. It happens that at the level of policy and institutional design Latin America represents a striking albeit socially sad experiment.

Different modes of insertion in the global economy

The last couple of decades of globalization have gone hand-in-hand with powerful efforts to impose a policy regime grounded in rather extreme forms of economic orthodoxy, which in the case of developing countries has gone under the name of 'Washington Consensus'. Of that Latin America has been an exemplar victim. Indeed, for the past quarter of a century most Latin American countries have been undergoing a process of structural adjustment which has included, among other policy measures, the elimination of the trade barriers adopted during the import substitution industrialization phase, the privatization of large domestic firms, and the deregulation of the labor and financial markets.

Let us consider in particular the tangled relationships between technology, trade, and growth, against the background of the orthodox prescription according to which openness was crucial for industrialization and would have enhanced growth opportunities in developing countries (Krueger, 1980, 1997; Srinivasan and Bhagwati, 1999).

Several years into this process, one is in a position to assess the link between trade liberalization and growth and indeed it does not turn out the way it had been expected to. The poor results of liberalization as a strategy for supporting a prosperous growth path are increasingly emerging. Moreover, the weakness of such a purported link does not merely appear to be a pathology specific to certain countries and/or historical accidents. Rather, it is a widespread pattern demonstrated by most of the Latin American countries, who have been unable to achieve the growth rates that prevailed in the 'import substitution' period (Rodriguez and Rodrik, 1999; ECLAC, 2002; Ocampo, 2003).

The current debate on the effectiveness of liberalization policies is stressing faulty expectations and the mistakes made by proponents of the Washington Consensus. In fact, as Rodrik (2007) points out, 'the countries that did best ... were hardly poster children for open markets and laissez-faire economics' (p.2). Countries like China, India, and Vietnam, indicated by the World Bank as 'star globalizers' were instead among the most protected countries in the 1990s, while Latin American countries followed all prescriptions and performed disappointingly. A simple causal relation between openness and growth does not hold, as standard liberalization policies cannot exert the same effect on all countries. Instead, different countries might benefit or not from globalization depending on individual circumstances largely influenced by specific national institutional arrangements.

Laissez-faire regimes, trade openness, and technology gaps in Latin America: a 'low growth trap'

One way to determine how policies aimed at trade liberalization and the adoption of an 'outward' orientation have influenced growth is to investigate the main tendencies and constraints that characterized the Latin American economies following economic reform (Ocampo, 2003).

Let us start by comparing a few relevant macro-variables referring to different key periods before and after the implementation of reforms. For our purpose here, it is useful to distinguish between: (i) the 'Import Substitution Golden Age' (IS Golden Age), which includes the years 1950–1973 for all countries in our sample; (ii) a 'Pre-Trade Reforms' period of shocks and adjustments (Pre-Reforms); and (iii) a 'Post-Trade Reforms' regime (Post-Reforms).

Most analyses investigate only the last two periods and basically refer to the timing of the 'Before reforms' and 'After reforms' periods used in Stallings and Peres (2000) and Ramos (1997). The 'Before reforms' period is defined as quite a long set of years which in fact covers a rather uncertain phase including also the 'lost decade' of the 1980s. For some countries this period does *not* entail trade liberalization, but most often does present rather wildly restrictive macro-policy shocks. We choose to include in our analysis also the IS Golden Age. Hence, we are able to detect even more dramatically the impact of liberalization reforms on Latin American countries.

As the region opened up, it did witness a large increase in both exports and imports (Table 3.13). Exports rose after economic reforms were implemented, but import requirements increased even more, thus *tightening further* the trade balance constraint on GDP growth. Overall, empirical evidence shows that the average growth rate of GDP decreased dramatically after the liberalization

Table 3.13. Indicators of growth and trade balance performance for three different periods

Country	Period	Years	Growth rate	Import elasticity	Export elasticity	Change in productivity gap
Argentina	IS Golden Age	1950–1973	3.49	0.42	0.71	
	Pre-Reform	1974–1990	0.34	−3.10	14.29	0.84
	Post-Reform	1991–2003	1.81	2.66	3.81	0.91
Brazil	IS Golden Age	1950–1973	7.20	0.80	0.78	
	Pre-Reform	1974–1989	4.07	−0.27	1.98	0.55
	Post-Reform	1990–2003	1.83	3.74	3.64	0.76
Chile	IS Golden Age	1950–1973	3.64	1.45	0.60	
	Pre-Reform	1974–1984	1.63	−0.38	3.81	1.60
	Post-Reform	1985–2003	5.34	2.07	1.70	0.65
Colombia	IS Golden Age	1950–1973	5.20	0.57	0.88	
	Pre-Reform	1974–1989	4.12	0.82	1.28	0.58
	Post-Reform	1990–2003	2.71	2.35	1.64	1.03
Mexico	IS Golden Age	1950–1973	6.56	0.66	0.69	
	Pre-Reform	1974–1985	4.58	0.58	2.37	0.67
	Post-Reform	1986–2003	2.88	4.42	3.23	0.68
Peru	IS Golden Age	1950–1973	5.12	1.19	0.99	
	Pre-Reform	1974–1989	0.75	−5.46	2.85	−0.92
	Post-Reform	1990–2003	3.74	1.87	2.19	0.78
Uruguay	IS Golden Age	1950–1973	1.55	−0.12	−0.25	
	Pre-Reform	1974–1977	3.67	−0.14	4.23	1.33
	Post-Reform	1978–2003	1.03	3.44	3.02	0.77
Latin America	IS Golden Age	1950–1973	3.04	0.58	0.74	
Weighted Average	Pre-Reform	1974–1989	3.12	0.58	2.42	0.43
	Post-Reform	1990–2003	2.45	3.64	3.31	0.74

The table reports average growth rates of income, elasticities of imports and exports. The change in productivity gap is the percentage change in productivity for the country relative to the same change in the international technological frontier (the US). Thus a value higher than 1 stands for catching-up.

Source: Own elaborations on ECLAC statistics and Bureau of Economic Analysis (US Department of Commerce).

reforms. Together the trade deficit widened. Indeed, both import and export elasticities appear significantly higher in the last period, but the elasticity of imports remains generally greater than the elasticity of exports. In that, the role played by the balance of payments as a determinant of domestic economic performance emerged clearly in the post-reform period (see also Moreno-Brid, 1999; Perez and Moreno-Brid, 1999; Frenkel and Gonzalez, 1999; Holland et al. 2001).

Remember that, in order to balance its foreign accounts, the growth of any one country is constrained, at least in the long-term, by the dynamics of its current-account balances, which in turn are basically determined by the dynamics of exports and imports plus the net remittances from labor and capital employed abroad by the country and tourism. As a qualification, it is possible to think of a country which grows *less* than the constraint because of a systematic outflow of financial resources on the *capital* account. It is harder to think of a country which grows more than the constraint despite a *negative current and capital account*. The only exception *so far* is obviously the United

States, as long as the rest of the world is prepared to finance American growth in exchange for green IOUs of increasingly dubious value.

Back to our central point. The export-led orientation in many Latin American countries came together with a sharp increase in import elasticities which was less than compensated by some acceleration in the catch-up in relative productivity.[7] A vicious growth pattern came out to be reinforced: for a discussion of how one can formally model vicious and virtuous growth patterns, we refer the reader to the analysis in Castaldi et al. (2004).

Moreover, if economic and trade performance of most countries in the region appear to deteriorate after liberalization reforms as compared to the uncertain phase of the 'Pre-Reforms' period, the evidence is a fortiori stronger when the comparison is carried out with respect to the Golden Age.

All this contrasts sharply with the experience of some Asian economies, such as Korea. In this case, it is interesting to note that the productivity gap shrank and, at the same time, the elasticity of demand for imports decreased (Table 3.14). Thus, a virtuous growth pattern was established.

In addition to aggregate growth performance and trade balance changes it is useful to look at the specialization patterns of Latin American countries and at how these have changed after the liberalization reforms. Table 3.15 provides a synthetic appreciation of the 'dynamic quality' of export specialization of various economic regions. Japan and the Asian Tigers appear to have been the most successful in reaping the benefits from fast-growing markets, while Latin American countries' exports have been mainly in commodities characterized by low income elasticity with respect to international demand.

Geographically, two separate patterns appear to have emerged for Mexico and the Central American countries, on the one hand, and South America, on the other. The South American countries have intensified their specialization

Table 3.14. Indicators of growth and trade balance performance for three Asian Tigers before and after the Asian financial crisis, different periods

		Growth rate	Import elasticity	Export elasticity	Change in productivity
Hong Kong					
Early Industrialization	1960–75	8.7	0.88	0.99	0.89
Pre-crisis	1976–97	6.8	1.95	1.81	3.04
Post-crisis	1999–06	5.5	1.70	1.87	2.39
Korea					
Early Industrialization	1960–75	8.0	2.10	3.42	2.49
Pre-crisis	1976–97	7.7	1.56	1.62	3.94
Post-crisis	1999–06	5.2	1.98	2.33	1.78
Taiwan					
Pre-crisis	1977–97	10.6	1.43	1.41	6.45
Post-crisis	1999–06	4.0	1.81	2.11	1.62

Source: Own elaborations on data from World Development Indicators, Taiwan Statistical Office and GGDC.

Table 3.15. Dynamic efficiency of the regional patterns of specializations: ratio of market shares in OECD imports in 'dynamic' vs. 'declining' commodities, 1961–2002

	Period							
	1963–1971		1971–1989		1979–1989		1989–2004	
USA	1.22	1.22	1.63	1.39	1.72	1.60	1.01	0.88
Japan	2.45	3.52	1.64	3.15	3.40	3.34	2.43	1.87
EU (12 first members)	1.52	1.23	1.55	1.21	1.98	1.40	0.92	0.91
Central and Latin America	0.38	0.22	0.21	0.39	0.28	0.36	0.70	0.80
Asian Tigers	1.48	2.29	2.38	2.58	3.40	3.08	1.27	1.90

Note: 'Dynamic' commodities are those which have undergone above average growth of OECD trade (imports) over the considered period.
Source: Elaborations by O. Mandeng on the CAN databank, ECLAC, Santiago de Chile, and by the authors.

in natural resources and standardized commodities. These are now highly capital-intensive industries with low domestic value added. Firms producing for local markets—which are labor-intensive and engineering-intensive—have suffered most from trade liberalization and market deregulation initiatives. Conversely, countries such as Mexico and the Central American nations have greatly globalized their manufacturing and assembly activities based on cheap labor. The structural features of the specialization pattern have affected the capacity to achieve equilibrium on the current account (Katz and Stumpo, 2001).

The Chilean experience is an interesting one, which at a first look is in conflict with the thrust of our argument. Indeed, between the mid-1980s and the end of the 1990s, Chile experienced an impressive rate of growth for a country whose export bundle consisted almost exclusively of natural resource-based products and standardized commodities characterized by low income elasticity of demand. However, emerging difficulties in diversifying manufacturing output and in developing local technological and productive linkages (Moguillansky, 1999) suggest that even Chile might find it hard to keep average growth rates comparable with those of the 'import substitution golden age' (Ocampo, 2002).

Some microeconomic roots of persistent technology gaps: low knowledge content of specialization patterns and forms of new dualism

Let us begin to explore the micro-dynamics of production and technological learning underlying Latin American Countries (for empirical evidence and an analytical formalization, see Cimoli and Katz, 2001; and ECLAC, 2000, 2002). So far, we have mostly discussed aggregate patterns concerning, for example, productivity, exports, and income growth. However, the transition to laissez-faire, free-trade, regimes has also implied profound changes in the sectoral composition of output, in the patterns of technology accumulation and diffusion, and in the 'demography' of firms. It is in the underlying microeconomics that one has ultimately to nest the interpretation of the worsening trade balance in Latin America.

In the first place, the weak link between exports and growth may be understood as the result of a new dualism in the production system and in the pattern of technology accumulation which has emerged as an effect of the liberalization shocks.

There is little doubt that such shocks have increased competitive selection and induced strong modernization pressures. However, the final outcomes in terms of knowledge accumulation are much more blurred. Many production activities have been seriously disrupted by trade liberalization and by the massive inflow of imports, particularly in technology-intensive fields. These industries have rapidly begun to de-verticalize their production organization technologies, replacing domestically produced intermediate inputs with cheaper (and sometimes better) imported ones and reorganizing their production activities more as assembly-type operations based on a much higher unit import content.

At the same time, the disappearance of many activities along the 'value chain' of production has often broken down local networks of user–producer links and the related processes of knowledge diffusion. The heterogeneity of responses has been quite striking, not only across production sectors, but also across individual firms within narrowly defined industries. Thus, failure and success tend to occur side by side even within the same production activity. The share of large firms—either local subsidiaries of transnational corporations or domestically owned conglomerates—in GDP increased significantly during the adjustment process, while countless SMEs were forced to exit the market altogether. Only a very small group of modernized domestic-owned and export-oriented firms are becoming global in terms of their production orientation and their capacity to acquire and creatively build upon foreign technology in international networks. Note also that even these modernized firms are, in fact, characterized by fewer linkages with domestic institutions of higher education and with local research centers and laboratories than in the past.

In terms of specialization patterns, following the trade reforms, many Latin American economies increased their share of production in (i) natural resources and natural resource processing industries (such as pulp and paper, iron and steel, vegetable oil, etc.) and (ii) maquila industries (that is largely assembly activities in sectors like electronics, television sets and video equipment, etc.).[8] Conversely, other industries, such as footwear, garments and furniture, and industries that produce engineering- and knowledge-intensive products (capital goods, agricultural machinery, machine tools, pharmaceuticals), have seen their share decline throughout the continent.

In fact a fundamental paradox stands out. After trade liberalization Latin America as a whole did *not* witness any adjustment in the specialization profiles toward more labor-intensive sectors, but it did—if anything—toward more resource-intensive *and capital-intensive* production structures.

At the same time the share of the *informal sector* in total employment appears to have dramatically increased (up to 46%, according to Cimoli et al. 2006).[9] In this respect, even the 'Import Substitution (IS) Golden Age' did not fare particularly well: even in the presence of a sustained GDP growth, one is hardly able to absorb within the 'formal' sector a constant share of the labor force attracted to urban areas (Cimoli et al. 2006). However, the last couple of decades have been particularly disappointing. The end result is a widening *dualism* whereby an increasing share of the whole economy is composed of activities typically characterized by a low knowledge content and low opportunities for technological and organizational learning.

Another relevant issue is the role played by large domestic firms and subsidiaries of multinational enterprises (MNEs). Subsidiaries of MNEs, in, for example, motor vehicles, other consumer durables, etc., have adopted the technologies developed by their parent companies in industrialized countries. Conversely, a few—too few perhaps—domestic Latin American firms during the 'IS Golden Age' tried to pursue economies of scale and learning procedures which happened to enable them to compete in the international market after the economy was opened up. This involved the adaptation of production and product designs for the domestic market, to begin with, as well as efforts to improve organization and increase production capacity. Examples of such firms include large groups in the chemicals, brewing, and glass container sectors, which did not only increase their production capacity to internationally visible levels, but revealingly also carried out earlier R&D activities during the IS phase.

Under brutal policy shocks it happened that the long-term accumulation of local technological capacity has been hampered by the replacement of engineers with machines in the process of reorganizing production. Similarly, entire R&D and project engineering departments have been eliminated as firms have become part of worldwide integrated production systems and R&D and engineering efforts have been transferred to headquarters. The same is observed in the case of public firms providing telecommunications, electricity, and transport services, which, after privatization, discontinued their domestic R&D and engineering departments and relied instead on their respective central offices for technology and engineering services. These changes in the organization of production forcefully entail the destruction of human capital and domestic technological capabilities and their replacement with 'capital embodied' technologies and with foreign-supplied R&D and engineering services. Some of the skills and technological capabilities made redundant by the new production organization arrangements can and have been successfully transferred to other areas of the economy, for example, to a newly emerging and rapidly expanding software industry. Others, however, have remained idle.

In the last resort, the emerging patterns of production specialization turn out to be strongly biased against domestic knowledge generation (cf. also the discussion in Cimoli and Katz, 2001; and ECLAC, 2002). This process means that, while Latin America does actively participate in the globalization of production, its participation in the globalized scientific and technological activities is very limited, as multinational companies transfer only a limited amount of their R&D activities to the region.

To sum up, Latin America's poor growth performance in the wake of liberalization strategies encapsulates a complex set of issues related to the interaction between trade balances, specialization patterns, and the process of technological learning. Certainly, the trade liberalization shock has acted upon both exports and imports, inducing a significant increase in both. However, the 'bad' patterns of specialization, biased in favor of commodities characterized by low income elasticities, has meant a relatively tighter foreign balance constraint to growth, less than compensated by some catching-up in relative productivity vis-à-vis the international frontier. The end result appears to be a vicious pattern of export-led growth. At the same time, the modern part of the economy has shrunk, yielding a dual production structure with relatively small dynamic enclaves floating within a sea of relatively stagnant and marginal activities.

Finally, knowledge-intensive industries appear to be losing ground as a proportion of GDP while non-tradable activities, natural resource processing industries, and maquila-type assembly operations (catering mostly to United States markets) increase their share. The sources of technological change and productivity growth have also shifted significantly, with a rapidly increasing share of external (foreign) sources emerging at the expense of domestic ones.

Note that all these considerations apply strictly to the last quarter of a century and continue to apply also to the most recent years when a few countries— those rich in natural resources—have experienced remarkably higher rates of growth due to the rising prices of minerals, fuels, and several agricultural commodities. Certainly, with everything said concerning technological learning, industrial structures, and patterns of specialization continues to hold. The only question mark regards whether a country can sustain a durable growth in per capita income just driven by the export of natural resources notwithstanding persistent gaps in domestic capabilities (even assuming that the terms of trade continue to improve). The historical experience of Arab oil-producing countries suggests a strikingly negative answer. However, one will come back to the point in the conclusion.

Beyond the 'globalization hype': some concluding remarks

In a nutshell, if our interpretation is correct, so-called 'globalization' has mainly to do with: (i) the international liberalization of capital movements and

(ii) (a rather asymmetric) liberalization of trade flows, while bearing rather controversial effects upon the international patterns of technological learning and the related distribution of growth possibilities among countries. The evidence that we have presented in this chapter points to persistent diversity in levels of incomes, growth rates, and technological capabilities, also under (or even partly because of) a globalized international economy. These ought to be the fundamental 'stylized facts'. Relatedly, let us conclude by proposing three key considerations.

First, a myth to dispel is that globalization—in the sense of higher international integration—comes naturally together with convergence or higher uniformity in technological capabilities. As argued at greater length in Pavitt (1999) and (2002), and Dosi, Orsenigo, and Sylos Labini (2003), knowledge as distinct from sheer information, tends to be rather sticky in its transmission, embodied, as it often is, in specific people, organizations, and local networks.

Second, in a world characterized by multiple forms of localized increasing returns, greater integration may well lead to phenomena of increasing differentiation with self-reinforcement and lock-in of particular production activities, specialization patterns, technological capabilities (or lack of them).[10] Putting it another way, it is easy to show that a world which becomes, at some level, increasingly integrated—but not (roughly) identical in initial conditions, institutions, technological capabilities, mechanisms of economic interaction, and so on—might be subject to various forms of local virtuous or vicious circles.

Third, the impact of greater integration is likely to depend on the modes through which it is implemented. The experience of many Latin American countries is a good case in point. When macro ('globalizing') shocks suddenly induce higher selection upon domestic firms (especially in Latin America), massive mortality of firms does often entail an apparent reduction of the productivity gap vis-à-vis the international frontier. But this seems to come together—at least in Latin America—with striking increases in both unemployment rates (i.e. transitions of parts of the labor force from low productivity to zero productivity states), and with tightening foreign-balance constraints to growth, in turn the joint outcome of relatively low elasticities of exports to world growth and high elasticities of imports to domestic growth (cf. Cimoli and Correa, 2005).

The continuing divergent tendencies across countries and across social groups within them reiterate the secular historical lesson today, like two centuries ago, that there is no 'natural drift' toward the international frontier in technologies and income. Quite the contrary. However, a few experiences of successful catch-up also tell a story of 'windows of opportunities', which appropriate mixtures of policies and institution-building might help to seize. Indeed a good number of the chapters which follow are precisely about the nature of the processes by which such opportunities are seized.

Notes

1. More detailed discussions by two of the authors are in Dosi, Pavitt, and Soete (1990), Cimoli and Dosi (1995), Dosi, Freeman, and Fabiani (1994), and Dosi, Orsenigo, and Sylos Labini (2003).
2. Tables 3.4 and 3.5 are based on Pavitt and Soete (1981) for the years until 1977. Their original sample included 14 OECD countries. Results for most recent years in Tables 3.4 and 3.6 are obtained for an updated sample of 21 OECD countries (Australia, Austria, Belgium, Canada, Denmark, Finland, France, Germany, Hungary, Ireland, Italy, Japan, Korea, Mexico, Netherlands, New Zealand, Norway, Spain, Sweden, Switzerland and United Kingdom). Our elaborations are based on data from OECD (real GDP, population and R&D spending in the business sector) and USPTO (historical series of granted patents).
3. His sample includes most world economies and covers the years 1960–1982.
4. For a discussion of the lack of globalization of labor markets and its implications cf. Rodrik (2002a).
5. It should also be noted that this high correlation between saving and investment is not found at the regional level, *within countries* (cf. Obstfeld and Rogoff, 1996), which hints at the specificity of the patterns of capital mobility across different institutional systems.
6. This argument is also presented in Lucas (1990), which again discusses why capital flows more from rich to rich countries than from rich to poor.
7. The case of Chile is exceptional, with a significant shrink in the productivity gap in the period 1974–1984 and import elasticities falling. This is at least partly due to cyclical factors since imports shrink in the end years due to the crisis which peaked in 1982.
8. Another sector which grew, in *some countries*, is the automotive one, but in this case, first, liberalization was no shock on local producers because there were none but mostly subsidiaries of world multinationals, and, second, the latter have been able, when needed, to bargain tariff and trade exceptions.
9. The distinction between 'formal' and 'informal' sector follows the rather expansive definition provided by ECLAC, trying to capture the traditional activities as opposed to the non-traditional ones (thus, in addition to personal services it includes all commercial and manufacturing activities undertaken in entities with fewer than five workers).
10. On this point, within a growing literature, see the complementary arguments of Arthur (1994), Dosi, Pavitt, and Soete (1990), Krugman (1996), Antonelli (1995), Cimoli (1988).

References

Amsden, A.H. (1989), *Asia's Next Giant: South Korea and Late Industrialization*, Oxford: Oxford University Press.

—— (2001), *The Rise of 'The Rest', 1850–2000: Late Industrialization Outside the North Atlantic Economies*, Oxford: Oxford University Press.

Antonelli, C. (1995), *The Economics of Localized Technological Change and Industrial Dynamics*, Boston: Kluwer Publishers.

Arcangeli, F., Dosi, G., and Moggi, M. (1991), Patterns of Diffusion of Electronics Technologies: An International Comparison with Special Reference to the Italian Case, *Research Policy*, 20, 515–29.

Archibugi, D., Howells, J., and Michie, J. (2001), *Innovation Policy in a Global Economy*, Cambridge: Cambridge University Press.

—— and Iammarino, S. (2002), The Globalization of Technological Innovation: Definition and Evidence, *Review of International Political Economy*, 9, 98–122.

—— and Pietrobelli (2003), The Globalisation of Technology and its Implications for Developing Countries: Windows of Opportunity or Further Burden?, *Technological Forecasting and Social Change*, 70, 861–83.

Arthur, W.B. (1994), *Increasing Returns and Path-Dependence in the Economy*, Ann Arbor: University of Michigan Press.

Bacha, E.L. (1978), An Interpretation of Unequal Exchange from Prebisch–Singer to Emanuel, *Journal of Development Economics*, 5.

Bairoch, P. and Kozul-Wright, R. (1996), *Globalization Myths: Some Historical Reflections on Integration, Industrialization and Growth in the World Economy*, UNCTAD Discussion Paper.

Bassanini, A. and Scarpetta, S. (2002), Growth, Technological Change, and ICT Diffusion: Recent Evidence from OECD Countries, *Oxford Review of Economic Policy*, 18, 324–44.

Berger, S. and Dore, R. (1996), *National Diversity and Global Capitalism*, Ithaca and London: Cornell University Press.

Blundell-Wignall, A. and Browne, F. (1991), *Macroeconomic Consequences of Financial Liberalisation: A Summary Report*, Working paper 98, OECD Department of Economics and Statistics.

Bordo, M.D., Taylor, A.M., and Williamson, J.G., (eds.), (2003), *Globalization in Historical Perspective*, Chicago and London: University of Chicago Press.

Bourguignon, F., Levin, V., and Rosenblatt, D. (2004), Declining International Inequality and Economic Divergence: Reviewing the Evidence through Different Lenses, *Economie Internationale*, 100, 13–15.

Bowles, S. (2002), Globalization and Redistribution: Feasible Egalitarianism in a Competitive World in R. Freeman, (ed.), *Inequality Around the World*, Oxford: Macmillan.

Bradford, S. (2003), Paying the Price: Final Goods Protection in OECD Countries, *Review of Economics and Statistics*, 85, 24–37.

Cantwell, J. (1992), The Internationalization of Technological Activity and its Implications for Competitiveness, in D. Granstrand, L. Hakanson, and S. Sjolander (eds.), *Technology, Management and International Business*, Chichester and New York:Wiley.

—— and Janne, O. (1999), Technological Globalization and Innovative Centres: The Role of Corporate Technological Leadership and Locational Hierarchy, *Research Policy*, 28, 119–44.

Castaldi, C., Cimoli, M., Correa, N., and Dosi, G. (2004), *Technological Learning, Policy Regimes and Growth in a 'Globalized Economy': General Patterns and the Latin American Experience*, LEM Working Paper 2004/01, Sant'Anna School of Advanced Studies, Pisa, Italy.

Castaldi, C. and Dosi. G. (2008), *Technical Change and Economic Growth: Some Lessons from Secular Patterns and Some Conjectures on the Current Impact of ICT Technologies*, presented at the seminar 'Growth, Productivity and ICT', ECLAC, Santiago de Chile, March 2007, LEM Working paper 2008–1, Sant' Anna School of advanced studies, Pisa, Italy.

—— —— (2009), The Patterns of Output Growth of Firms and Countries: New Evidence on Scale Invariances and Specificities, LEM Working Paper 2004-18, Sant'Anna School of Advanced Studies, Pisa, Italy. Forthcoming, *Empirical Economics*.

Cimoli, M. (1988), Technological Gaps and Institutional Asymmetries in a North–South Model with a Continuum of Goods, *Metroeconomica*, 39, 245–74.

—— and Correa, N. (2005), Trade Openness and Technological Gaps in Latin America: A 'Low Growth' Trap, in Ocampo, J.A. (ed.), *Beyond Reforms: Structural Dynamics and Macroeconomic Vulnerability*, World Bank, Washington D.C.: Stanford University Press.

—— and Dosi, G. (1995), Technological Paradigms, Patterns of Learning and Development: An Introductory Roadmap, *Journal of Evolutionary Economics*, 5, 243–68.

—— —— Nelson, R.R., and Stiglitz, J.E. (2008), *Institutions and Policies Shaping Industrial Development: An Introductory Note*, this volume.

—— and Katz, J. (2001), *Structural Reforms, Technological Gaps and Economic Development: A Latin American Perspective*, document presented at the DRUID–Nelson and Winter Conference (Aalborg, 12–15 June), <http://www.business.auc.dk/druid/conferences/nw/>.

—— Primi, A., and Pugno, M. (2006), Un modelo de bajo crecimiento: la informalidad como restriccion estructural, *Revista de la CEPAL, 88, Abril*.

—— and Soete, L. (1992), A Generalized Technology Gap Model, *Economie Appliquée*, 3.

Cipolla, C. M. (1965), *Guns and Sails in the Early Phase of European Expansion, 1400–1700*, London: Collins.

Clark, G. and Feenstra, R. (2003), Technology in the Great Divergence, in Bordo et al. (2003).

Colecchia, A. and Schreyer, P. (2002), ICT Investment and Economic Growth in the 1990s: Is the United States a Unique Case? A Comparative Study of Nine OECD Countries, *Review of Economic Dynamics*, 5, 408–42.

Coriat, B. (2002), The New Global Intellectual Property Rights Regime and its Imperial Dimension. Implications for 'North/South' Relations, presented at the Seminar 'New Paths of Development' organized by *BNDES*, Rio de Janeiro, September, 12–13, 2002.

Daveri, F. (2002), The New Economy in Europe, 1992–2001, *Oxford Review of Economic Policy*, October 2002, pp. 345–62.

David, P.A. (1990), The Dynamo and the Computer: An Historical Perspective of the Modern Productivity Paradox, *American Economic Review Papers and Proceedings*, 80, 355–61.

—— (2001), Understanding Digital Technology's Evolution and the Path of Measured Productivity Growth: Present and Future in the Mirror of the Past, in E. Brynolfsson and B. Kahin (eds.), *Understanding the Digital Economy*, Cambridge, MA: MIT Press.

De Long, B. J. (1988), Productivity Growth, Convergence and Welfare, *American Economic Review*, 78, 1138–54.

Dosi, G. (1988), Sources, Procedures and Microeconomic Effects of Innovation, *Journal of Economic Literature*, 26, 1120–71.

—— and Castaldi, C. (2002), *Local and Divergent Patterns of Technological Learning within (Partly) Globalized Markets. Is There Anything New? And What Can Policies Do about It?: A Concise Guide*, LEM working paper 2002-22, Sant'Anna School of Advanced Studies, Pisa.

—— Freeman, C., and Fabiani, S. (1994), The Process of Economic Development: Introducing some Stylized Facts and Theories on Technologies, Firms and Institutions, *Industrial and Corporate Change*, 3, 1–45.

—— Orsenigo, L., and Sylos Labini, M. (2003), *Technology and the Economy*, in N.J. Smelser and R. Swedberg (eds.), *Handbook of Economic Sociology*, 2nd edn.

—— Pavitt, K. and Soete, L. (1990), *The Economics of Technical Change and International Trade*, London: Harvester Wheatsheaf.

Dowrick, S. and DeLong, B. (2003), Globalization and Convergence, in Bordo et al. (2003).

Dunning, J.H. (1993), *Multinational Enterprises and the Global Economy*, Reading, Mass., and Wokingham, England: Addison Wesley.

Durlauf, S.N. and Johnson, P.A. (1992), *Local Versus Global Convergence across National Economies*, NBER Working paper 3996.

—— and Quah, D. (1998), *The New Empirics of Economic Growth*, London School of Economics, Center for Economic Performance, Discussion paper 384.

Dutt, A. (2001), *Income Elasticities of Imports, North–South Trade and Uneven Development*, Notre Dame, Indiana, University of Notre Dame, mimeo.

Easterly, W., King, R., Levine, R., and Rebelo, S. (1992), *How Do National Policies Affect Long-Run Growth? A Research Agenda*, World Bank, Discussion paper.

Eatwell, J. (1996), *International Financial Liberalisation: The Impact on World Development*, ODS UNDP, Discussion paper 12.

ECLAC (2000), *Equity, Development and Citizenship* (LC/G.2071/Rev.1-P), Santiago, Chile. United Nations publication, Sales No. E.00.II.G.81.

—— (2002), *Globalization and Development* (LC/G.2157(SES.29/3)), document prepared for the Twenty-ninth session of ECLAC (Brasilia, Brazil, 6–10 May), Santiago, Chile.

Fagerberg, J. (1988), Why Growth Rates Differ, in G. Dosi, C. Freeman, R. Nelson, G. Silverberg, and L. Soete, *Technical Change and Economic Theory*, London: Pinter Publisher.

Feldstein, M. and Horioka, C. (1980), Domestic Saving and International Capital Flows, *Economic Journal*, 90, 314–29.

Findlay, R. and O'Rourke, K.H. (2003), Commodity Market Integration, 1500–2000, in Bordo et al. (2003).

Freeman, C. (1982), *The Economics of Industrial Innovation*, London: Francis Pinter.

—— (2001), A Hard Landing for the 'New Economy'? Information Technology and the United States National System of Innovation, *Structural Change and Economic Dynamics*, 12, 115–39.

—— (2002), Continental, National and Sub-National Innovation Systems: Complementarity and Economic Growth, *Research Policy*, 31, 191–211.

—— and Perez, C. (1988), Structural Crises of Adjustment: Business Cycles and Investment Behavior, in G. Dosi, C. Freeman, R. Nelson, G. Silverberg, and L. Soete (eds.), *Technical Change and Economic Theory*, London: Pinter.

Frenkel, R. and Gonzalez, M. (1999), Apertura comercial, productividad y empleo en Argentina, in V. Tokman and D. Martinez (eds.), *Productividad y empleo en la apertura econ'omica*, Lima, ILO Regional Office for Latin America and the Caribbean, International Labour Organization.

GGDC (2006), Total Economy Database, <http://www.ggdc.net>, Groningen Growth and Development Centre, University of Groningen.

Greenstein, S. and Prince, J. (2007), Internet Diffusion and the Geography of the Digital Divide in the United States, in R. Mansell, C. Avgerou, D. Quah, and R. Silverstone (eds.), *The Oxford Handbook of Information and Communication Technologies*, Oxford: Oxford University Press.

Holland, M., Vieira, F.V., and Canuto, O. (2001), *Economic Growth and the Balance of Payments Constraint in Latin America*, mimeo.

Hollingsworth, R. and Boyer, R. (eds.), (1997), *Contemporary Capitalism: The Embeddedness of Institutions*, Cambridge: Cambridge University Press.

Hufbauer, G. C. (1966), *Synthetic Materials and the Theory of International Trade*, London: Buckworth.

ITU (2003), *Telecommunication Indicators*, International Telecommunication Union.

Katz, J. and Stumpo, G. (2001), *Regmenes sectoriales, productividad y competitividad internacional*, CEPAL Review, No. 75 (LC/G.2150-P), Santiago, Chile, December.

Kennedy, C. and Thirlwall, A.P. (1979), Import Penetration, Export Performance and Harrod's Trade Multiplier, *Oxford Economic Papers*, 31, 303–23.

Kim, L. (1993), National System of Industrial Innovation: Dynamics of Capability Building in Korea, in R. Nelson (ed.), *National Innovation Systems,* Oxford: Oxford University Press.

—— and Nelson, R.R. (2000), *Technology, Learning and Innovation: Experiences of Newly Industrialising Economies*, Cambridge: Cambridge University Press.

Kose, M.A., Prasad, E.S., Rogoff, K.S., and Wei, S.J. (2006), *Financial Globalization: A Reappraisal* (August 2006). IMF Working Paper No. 06/189.

Kleinknecht, A. and ter Wengel, J. (1998), The Myth of Economic Globalisation, *Cambridge Journal of Economics*, 22, 637–47.

Krueger, A.O. (1980), Trade Policies as an Input for Development, *American Economic Review*, 70, 288–92.

—— (1997), Trade Policy and Economic Development: How we Learn, *American Economic Review*, 87, 1–22.

Krugman, P.R. (1996), *The Self-Organizing Economy*, Cambridge, MA, and Oxford: Blackwell Publishers.

—— (1999), *The Return of Depression Economics*, New York: W.W. Norton.

Kuznets, S. (1980), Recent Population Trends in Less Developed Countries, and Implications for International Income Inequality, in R. A. Easterlin (ed.), *Population and Economic Change in Developing Countries*, Chicago, Illinois: University of Chicago Press.

Laursen, K. (2000), *Trade Specialisation, Technology and Economic Growth: Theory and Evidence from Advanced Countries*, Cheltenham, UK: Edward Elgar.

Lazonick, W. (2007), Globalization of the ICT Labour Force, in R. Mansell, C. Avgerou, D. Quah, and R. Silverstone (eds.), *The Oxford Handbook of Information and Communication Technologies*, Oxford: Oxford University Press.

Lucas, R. (1990), Why Doesn't Capital Flow from Rich to Poor Countries?, *American Economic Review*, 80, 92–6.

Lundvall, B.A. (1992), *National Systems of Innovation: Towards a Theory of Innovation and Interactive Learning*, London: Pinter Publisher.

Maddison, A. (2001), *The World Economy: A Millennial Perspective*, Paris: OECD.

Meier, G.M., Stiglitz, J.E., and Stern, N. (2000), *Frontiers of Development Economics: The Future in Perspective?*, Oxford: Oxford University Press.

Melchior, A. and Telle, K. (2001), Convergence and Marginalisation, *Forum for Development Studies*, 28, 75–98.

Meliciani, V. (2001), *Technology, Trade and Growth in OECD Countries*, London, New York: Routledge.

Miozzo, M. and Soete, L. (2001), Internationalization of Services: A Technological Perspective, *Technological Forecasting and Social Change*, 67 (2&3), 159–85.

Moguillansky, G. (1999), *La inversion en Chile: el fin de un ciclo de expansion?*, Santiago, Chile, Economic Commission for Latin America and the Caribbean (ECLAC)/Fondo de Cultura.

Moreno-Brid, J.C. (1998), On Capital Inflows and the Balance-Of-Payments Constrained Growth Model, *Journal of Post-Keynesian Economics*, 21, 2, Winter.

—— (1999), Mexico's Economic Growth and the Balance Of Payments Constraint: A Cointegration Analysis, *International Review of Applied Economics*, 13, 2, May.

Nelson, R.R. (1993), *National Innovation Systems*, Oxford: Oxford University Press.

Obstfeld, M. and Rogoff, K. (1996), *Foundations of International Macroeconomics*, Cambridge, MA: MIT Press.

—— —— (2000), *The Six Major Puzzles in International Macroeconomics: Is There a Common Cause?*, NBER, working paper 7777, Cambridge, MA.

—— and Taylor, A.M. (2003), Globalization and Capital Markets, in Bordo et al. (2003).

Ocampo, J.A. (2002), *Globalization and Development*, presented at the Seminar 'New Paths of Development' organized by *BNDES*, Rio de Janeiro, September, 12–13, 2002.

—— (2003), *Lights and Shadows in Latin American Structural Reforms*, Informes y estudios especiales series, No. 14, Santiago, Chile, Economic Commission for Latin America and the Caribbean (ECLAC).

—— and Taylor, L. (1998), Trade Liberalization in Developing Economies: Modest Benefits but Problems with Productivity Growth, Macro Prices, and Income Distribution, *The Economic Journal*, 108, 1523–46.

OECD (2000), *A New Economy? The Changing Role of Innovation and Information Technology in Growth*, Paris: OECD.

—— (2002), *Measuring the Information Economy*, Paris: OECD.

—— (2003), *International Trade and Competitiveness Indicators, edn. 2*, Paris: OECD.

—— (2005a), *Economic Outlook edn. 2*, Paris: OECD.

—— (2005b), *Main Science and Technology Indicators 2005-2*, Paris: OECD.

Patel, P. and Pavitt, K. (1994), Uneven (and Divergent) Technological Accumulation among Advanced Countries: Evidence and a Framework of Explanation, *Industrial and Corporate Change*, 3, 759–87, reprinted in K. Pavitt (1999).

—— (1997), The Technological Competencies of World's Largest Firms: Complex and Path-Dependent, but Not Much Variety, *Research Policy*, 26, 141–56.

Pavitt, K. (1999), *Technology Management and Systems of Innovation*, Cheltenham, UK: Edward Elgar.

Pavitt, K. (2002), *Knowledge about Knowledge since Nelson and Winter: A Mixed Record*, SPRU Electronic Working papers 83.

—— and Soete, L. (1981), International Differences in Economic Growth and the International Location of Innovation, in H. Giersch (ed.), *Emerging Technologies: Consequences for Economic Growth, Structural Change and Unemployment*. Tubingen: JCB Mohr.

Pearce, R.D. (1989), *The Internationalisation of Research and Development by Multinational Enterprises*, London: Macmillan.

—— (1999), Decentralised R&D and Strategic Competitiveness: Globalised Approaches to Generation and Use of Technology in Multinational Enterprises (MNEs), *Research Policy*, 28, 157–78.

Perez, E and Moreno-Brid, J.C. (1999), Terms of Trade, Exports and Economic Growth in Central America: A Long-Term View, *Banca Nazionale del Lavoro Quarterly Review*, 211, December.

Prebisch, R. (1950), *The Economic Development of Latin America and its Principal Problems*, New York: United Nations.

Quah, D. (1996), Twin Peaks: Growth and Convergence in Models of Distribution Dynamics, *Economic Journal*, 106, 1045–55.

—— (1997), Empirics for Growth and Distribution: Stratification, Polarization and Convergence Clubs, *Journal of Economic Growth*, 2, 27–59.

Ramos, J. (1997), *Neo-Liberal Structural Reforms in Latin America: The Current Situation*, CEPAL Review, No. 62 (LC/G.1969-P), Santiago, Chile, August.

Ricyt (2000), *El Estado de la Ciencia: Principales Indicadores de Ciencia y Tecnologia Iberoamericanos/Interamericanos 2000*, Buenos Aires: Ricyt.

Rodriguez, F. and Rodrik, D. (1999), *Trade Policy and Economic Growth: A Skeptic's Guide to Cross-National Evidence*, NBER Working Paper, No. W70801, Washington, D.C.

Rodrik, D. (2002a), *Feasible Globalisations*, Harvard University, mimeo.

—— (2002b), After Neoliberalism, What?, presented at the Seminar 'New Paths of Development' organized by *BNDES*, Rio de Janeiro, September, 12–13, 2002.

—— (2002c), *Globalization for Whom?*, Harvard Magazine, July 2002.

—— (2004), *How to Make Trade Regimes Work for Development. A Few Thoughts on the Doha and Post-Doha Trade Agenda*, Kennedy School of Government.

—— (2007), *How to Save Globalization from its Cheerleaders*, Harvard University, September 2007.

—— (2008), Goodbye Washington Consensus, Hello Washington Confusion?, *Journal of Economic Literature*, forthcoming.

—— and Subramaniam, A. (2008), *Why Did Financial Globalization Disappoint?*, Harvard University, March 2008.

Rosenberg, N. and Birdzell, L.E. Jr. (1987), *How the West Grew Rich*, New York: Basic Books.

Scarpetta, S., Bassanini, A., Pilat, D., and Schreyer, P. (2000), *Economic Growth in the OECD Area: Recent Trends at the Aggregate and Sectoral Level*, OECD Economics Department working papers 248.

Soete, L. and Verspagen, B. (1993), Technology and Growth: The Complex Dynamics of Catching Up, Falling Behind and Taking Over, in A. Szirmai, B. van Ark, and D. Pilat, (eds.), *Explaining Economic Growth*, Amsterdam: Elsevier Science Publishers.

Srinivasan, T.N. and Bhagwati, J. (1999), *Outward Orientation and Development: Are Revisionists Right?*, Working Paper, No. 806, New Haven, Connecticut, Economic Growth Center, Yale University.

Stallings, B. and Peres, W. (2000), *Growth, Employment, and Equity: The Impact of the Economic Reforms in Latin America and the Caribbean*, New York, Brookings/ECLAC.

Stiglitz, J.E. (1994), *Whither Socialism?*, Cambridge, MA: MIT Press.

—— (2002), *Globalization and its Discontents*, New York: W.W. Norton.

UN (2001), *Human Development Report*, United Nations.

—— (2006), *Information Economy Report 2006: The Development Perspective*, United Nations.

—— (2008), *Development and Globalization: Facts and Figures*, United Nations.

van Ark, B., Inklaar, R., and McGuckin, R. (2002), 'Changing Gear' Productivity, ICT and Services: Europe and the United States, Groningen Growth and Development Center, working paper GD-60.

—— and McGuckin, R.H. (1999), International Comparisons of Labor Productivity and Per Capita Income, *Monthly Labor Review*, July, 33–41.

Vernon, R. (1966), International Investment and International Trade in the Product Cycle, *Quarterly Journal of Economics*, 80, 190–207.

Verspagen, B. (1991), A New Empirical Approach to Catching Up or Falling Behind, *Structural Change and Economic Dynamics*, 2, 359–80.

—— (1993), *Uneven Growth between Interdependent Economies: An Evolutionary View on Technology Gaps, Trade, and Growth*, Avebury, Aldershot, UK: Ashgate Pub.

Wade, R. (1990), *Governing the Market: Economic Theory and the Role of Government in East Asian Industrialisation*, Princeton: Princeton University Press.

Williamson, J. (1990), What Washington Means by Policy Reform, in Williamson, J. (ed.), *The Progress of Policy Reform in Latin America*, Institute for International Economics.

Part II

Industrial Policies in a Historical Perspective

4

Emulation versus Comparative Advantage: Competing and Complementary Principles in the History of Economic Policy

Erik S. Reinert

The objective of this chapter is to show how economic policies based on completely different principles—one described as 'emulation' and the other as 'comparative advantage'—have been strategically employed in order to achieve economic development when nations have made the transition from poor to wealthy. It also briefly describes key aspects of the process by which Europe, through emulation, developed from a collection of fiefdoms ruled by warlords into city-states and later to nation-states. It is argued that the timing of the strategic shift from emulation to comparative advantage is of utmost importance to a nation. Making this policy shift too early will hamper development much as a late shift will do. It is argued that these principles, although sometimes under different names, were well known and employed by European nations from the seventeenth century onwards—in the United States all the way to the end of the nineteenth century—and that the Marshall Plan implemented more than 60 years ago owed its success to putting the principle of emulation chronologically *ahead of comparative advantage*.

The *Oxford English Dictionary* defines emulation as 'the endeavor to equal or surpass others in any achievement or quality'; also 'the desire or ambition to equal or to excel.' In eighteenth-century political and economic discourse, emulation was essentially a positive and active effort, to be contrasted with envy or jealousy (Hont, 2005). In modern terms emulation finds its approximate counterparts in the terminology of US economist Moses Abramowitz, whose ideas of 'catching-up,' 'forging ahead,' and 'falling behind' resonate with the same understanding of dynamic competition. In his 1693 work

English economist Joshua Child made the emulative nature of English catching-up very clear: 'If we intend to have the Trade of the World, we must imitate the Dutch, who make the worst as well as the best of all manufactures, that we may be in a capacity of serving all Markets, and all Humors.'

By focusing on barter alone, leaving out the dynamics of innovation and competition, Ricardian trade theory neglects a core element inherent to capitalism. There is no forging ahead, nor is there any falling behind, in Ricardian economics, nor in any other type of economics based on metaphors of equilibrium. In a Schumpeterian framework, the rents created by innovation, and later eroded by competitors emulating that innovation, represents the core of what capitalism is all about: relentless innovation in order to create innovation rents, followed by relentless emulation that dilutes and reduces the same rents. The precondition for Thorstein Veblen's 'pecuniary emulation' is a Schumpeterian 'technological emulation.' This chapter aims to establish a skeleton for a Schumpeterian theory of international trade as it relates to uneven economic growth.

A frequent nineteenth-century continental European and US criticism of Ricardian economics is that it operated with 'units void of any qualitative characteristics' (*qualitätslose Grössen*). This chapter argues that Ricardian trade theory—by visualizing the world economy as the bartering of labor hours void of any qualitative factors (importantly also knowledge)—abstracts from and leaves out the qualitative changes, or development, that take place in human society over time. The qualitative difference between one labor hour in Silicon Valley and one in African subsistence agriculture may in fact account for the failure of free trade to even out factor prices of labor in the two areas.

Finally the chapter discusses the important timing aspect of the transition from emulation to free trade. Clearly both free trade and industrialization will have their special interest groups, and promoters of both can revert to cronyism and corruption to get their favorite policies accepted. The US Civil War represents a classic case of infighting between a 'comparative advantage' South insisting on immediate free trade and an 'emulative' North insisting on following England's path to industrialization. It is argued that the negative effects from an overdose of emulation are considerably less than from an overdose of premature free trade; a nation will be better off in the long run if the North rather than the South wins its civil war.

Emulation and 'management by gut feeling'

A key argument in this chapter is that in many situations emulation is the intuitive gut reaction to a problem. Therefore emulation—especially when it blatantly contradicts ruling trade theory—will tend to be used intuitively in situations close to home, whereas comparative advantage tends to be imposed scientifically on nations far away. The oxymoronic concept of 'managed free trade' is the result of this tension between home turf intuition (e.g. Europe's conviction today that they also need a manufacturer of large commercial airplanes to compete with Boeing) and a simultaneous scientific conviction in Europe that African countries are better off sticking to their comparative advantage in agriculture. I further argue that the principle of 'first emulation, then comparative advantage' has been the strategy followed by all presently wealthy nations, with the *possible* exception of naturally wealthy nations that were void of raw materials and happened to be the first to industrialize. The Dutch Republic and Venice would be the prime examples of such states, wealthy as compared to the laggard countries at the time (Reinert, 2007a and 2009).

This chapter explains the main building blocks of the anti-Ricardian intuition underlying technological change and progress that create the tacit and intuitive logic of emulation.

Emulation generally requires initial tariffs, what John Stuart Mill and many scholars thereafter called infant industry protection. No businessperson expects an industrial company to make money from day one; he or she is willing to sustain losses for several years until the company starts making money. The similar logic was used for centuries as regards industrial systems. A new industry could not be expected to be profitable immediately. Indeed England protected her manufacturing industry heavily for more than 350 years, the United States only for about 100 years, and Korea for only 40 years. However, the *timing* of this protection was crucial: the same institution that in one context would cause *increased* welfare would, in another context, *decrease* welfare. Once a certain domestic industrial capacity has been reached, however, competitiveness can only be maintained through access to larger markets. If industrial dynamics are to decide, as they did in the United States towards the end of the nineteenth century, beyond a certain point the not-so-infant industry will be interested in freer trade in order to stay competitive a) because new technology tends to come with larger capacity and b) because of domestic competitive pressure. If industrialization is then successful, and protection keeps companies on their toes, the same type of industrial vested interests that once favored protection will now favor freer trade in order to conquer foreign markets. The vested interests behind new and expanding technologies and a large scale of production will tend to crowd out the less dynamic ones favoring continued protection, all leading to a 'natural' transition from protection to free trade. However, when 'bad protection' (as defined later) dominates, a nation may get stuck with a sub-scale and technologically mature manufacturing sector. The general rule is, as was observed by an anonymous Italian political economist traveling in Holland in the eighteenth century, 'Tariffs are as useful for introducing the arts in a country, as they are damaging once these are established.' (Anonymous, 1786) This observer in fact constructed a core principle of a

Schumpeterian trade theory based on an underlying assumption of industrial dynamics.

Comparing two sets of countries over a period of 50 years, Figure 4.1 illustrates the activity-specific nature of economic growth. Korea was for a long time poorer than Somalia, but was allowed to shift its comparative advantage away from a natural comparative advantage in diminishing returns activities to a man-made comparative advantage in increasing returns activities. Singapore was for a long time poorer than Peru, but took off in the 1970s. The curve also shows how an inefficient and overly protected manufacturing sector in Peru produced a higher standard of living than a de-industrialized Peru. Both cases illustrate the problem of creating middle-income countries: countries seem to cluster in a successful group and a race-to-the-bottom group. This chapter suggests approaches to creating such middle-income countries.

Renaissance: the birth of the politics and economics of emulation and economic growth

It's commonly said that capitalism arrived in the United States when the first boats landed on North American shores. We can say even more confidently that industrial policy arrived in Europe with the same boats as did the Renaissance. Philosophers from the Byzantine Empire were instrumental in creating the Renaissance—literally re-birth—in Italy. In addition to bringing new texts of classical Greek philosophy, particularly by adding Plato to Aristotle, who had been known earlier, they also brought to Italy a new religious interpretation of Man as a creative being. Creation became Man's pleasurable duty (Reinert and Daastøl, 1997). The most influential of these philosophers from Byzantium was Georgios Gemistos Plethon (c.1360–1452) whose lectures in Florence inspired Cosimo Medici to establish a Renaissance milestone: the Platonic Academy. Plethon, the contemporary living individual who more than anyone else influenced Renaissance philosophy, also brought with him a view on economic policy: 'Plethon praised protectionist policy as a means to stimulate a Byzantine economy suffering from the competition of Italian industry and trade.'[1]

In a somewhat macabre way, Plethon's economic policy and the plight of his dead body together illustrate the most important principle of Europe's successful economic policy during the last 500 years: the policy of emulation (Hont, 2005; and Reinert, 2007a). 'The propensity for emulation...is of ancient growth and is a pervading trait of human nature' said Thorstein Veblen in his *Theory of the Leisure Class* (Veblen, 1899). In twentieth-century economics, emulation tended to be limited to Veblen's pecuniary emulation on an individual level by 'keeping up with the Joneses' in terms of consumption. Starting in the Renaissance, and even more self-consciously during the Enlightenment,

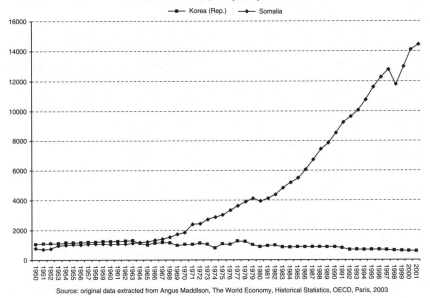

Source: original data extracted from Angus Maddison, The World Economy, Historical Statistics, OECD, Paris, 2003

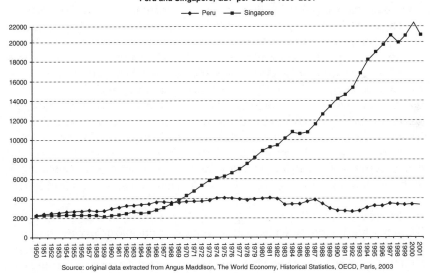

Source: original data extracted from Angus Maddison, The World Economy, Historical Statistics, OECD, Paris, 2003

Source: Reinert, Amaïzo, and Kattel (2009).

Figure 4.1. Emulation vs. 'wrong' comparative advantage

83

from the point of view of a city-state or nation-state, emulation on the production side was a perquisite for emulation of consumption.

In his works *Luxury and Capitalism* (1913a) and *War and Capitalism* (1913b), Werner Sombart outlines the role of emulation both through luxury, where art was an important element, and by the way of warfare for the development of capitalism.[2] Just as trade later was seen as 'war by other means,' also emulation in luxury and in war were intertwined. There is no reason to believe that Leonardo da Vinci (1452–1519)—who was born near Florence the year Plethon died—was less proud of his ingenious war machines than of his wonderful art. In fact the rulers' patronage of art was part of a competition between states not unlike war. Artists were patronized by rulers for similar reasons as were mercenaries, as tools for catching-up and forging ahead to use the language of Moses Abramowitz.

Sigismondo Malatesta (1417–1468), the ruler of Rimini, was one of the worst and most violent tyrants of the Renaissance. At the same time, he shared and promoted the Renaissance cult of art and letters (Hutton, 1926). Sheltering many humanists and poets at his court, Malatesta epitomizes the Renaissance when it can be argued that economic emulation and capitalism consciously were promoted in order to channel human passions and activities away from violence into more constructive activities. This point is made brilliantly by Albert Hirschman in his book *The Passions and the Interests* (1977).

In 1438, the same year Plethon lectured in Florence, Sigismondo Malatesta was engaged in a serious game of emulation with Florence. That year Malatesta brought Filippo Brunelleschi, the father of Renaissance architecture, to Rimini. Two years earlier Brunelleschi had finished the Florence cathedral. Subsequently, the greatest architectural theorist of the age, Leon Battista Alberti, led a team of distinguished designers in remodelling an ancient Franciscan basilica into a church-monument to Sigismondo and his ancestors, transforming it into an edifice without parallel in the peninsula. In this temple, now known as the Tempio Malatestiano, the famous artist Piero della Francesca adorned the interior with a fresco and a painting of Sigismondo (now in the Louvre), and Florence's most admired sculptor Agostino di Duccio embellished the building with the most important work of his career. Sigismondo Malatesta simultaneously epitomizes the most barbaric violence and the most refined art of the Renaissance.

Later in life, after most Italian states—including the Papal State—had turned violently against him, Sigismondo Malatesta sought new fortune as general for Venice in its war against the Ottoman Empire, as a field commander in Peloponnesus (1464–1466). On his way home, Malatesta engaged in what was by then a traditional European act of emulation: adding to the prestige of a city through the acquisition of saints' body parts. The most spectacular, and at the same time most successful, act of emulation through dead bodies took place in the year 828 when Venetian sailors stole the body of St. Mark from Alexandria.

St. Mark was later made the patron saint of the city, where the cathedral built above his crypt still dominates the city today.

It was typical of Sigismondo Malatesta and his time that when he returned from Peloponnesus in 1465, he brought as a souvenir back to Rimini not the traditional hallowed remains of some Eastern Christian Saint but—sensitive to the shift towards veneration for knowledge rather than for sainthood—he brought back to Europe the bones of Georgios Gemistos Plethon, the man who with Plato also brought industrial policy to Europe. The last 'primitive' warlord in Europe had the remains of Plethon buried in the Tempio Malatestiano in Rimini. The actions of Sigismondo Malatesta—'The Mastiff of Rimini'—testify to the role of emulation in three key areas in the creation and shaping of modern capitalism: the emulation in war, in luxury (as shown by Sombart), and in learning (in what Veblen called 'idle curiosity'). And, we might add, as a Veblenian example of the conspicuous consumption that came to characterize capitalism, Malatesta exhibited Plethon's stone coffin outside the main church in Rimini. There it can still be found today.

Novelty, Diversity, Scale, Synergy: bringing non-Ricardian elements back in

With Adam Smith's influence on economics, several factors which had been prominent until then became peripheral. These were the most important insights of Renaissance and Enlightenment economics: novelty (innovation), diversity (heterogeneity), scale (increasing returns), and synergy. Although the labor theory of value can be traced back all the way to Arab historian and economist Ibn Khaldoun (1331–1406), compared to those of his predecessors Adam Smith's greatest innovation was reducing production and trade into a single unit of measurement: labor. A higher theoretical level of extraction was achieved by abstracting from the complications and vicissitudes inherent to production. On the basis of this, a generation later David Ricardo constructed his theory of international trade and comparative advantage with the bartering of goods embodying labor hours of identical quality as the key feature of the world economy.

In order to appreciate the history of economic policy, it is necessary to recreate a theoretical structure by adding back in the key elements left out by Ricardo, or perhaps more accurately stated, by his followers. Pre-Smithian economics would not have accepted that the international economy could possibly be represented as a system ultimately centered around the barter of labor hours. Pre-Ricardian logic had an underlying understanding that what a country produced would determine how wealthy it was: if all stockbrokers are wealthier than all the personnel cleaning their offices, a nation of stockbrokers will be considerably wealthier than a nation of cleaning personnel. Any static Ricardian gain from specialization will in this case be totally dwarfed by the qualitative and activity-specific differences between the profession of being a stockbroker and that of cleaning floors.

I suggest the elements that Ricardian economics left out of the profession can be captured under the headings of Novelty, Diversity, Scale, and Synergy and the interaction between these factors. *Novelty*, or innovation, is at any point in time focused in few activities, in the stone industry in the Stone Age and in cotton spinning during the first Industrial Revolution. This creates *diversity* or *heterogeneity* as a key feature of economic life (Audretsch, 2004). As we shall discuss below, technological change and increasing returns—*novelty* and *scale*—though very different phenomena often come packaged as Siamese twins. In a world with oligopolistic competition some economic activities may catapult the real wages of a nation relative to others (Ireland is a recent example. See Reinert, 2007a; see also the examples of Korea and Singapore in Figure 4.1), while other nations specialize in activities bereft of innovation and novelty, seriously limiting the possibilities for growth (classical *maquila* industries). When judged with the standard canon perfect-competition model, successful development projects are indeed gigantic 'market failures' (compare Cimoli, Dosi, Nelson, and Stiglitz in Chapter 2). The models of the standard canon, assuming non-increasing returns and perfect competition, in fact describe the situation in raw material producing poor countries much more accurately than they describe the situation in the rich world (Singer, 1950, presents an argument based on the same asymmetry).

Pre-Smithian economics saw economic growth and welfare as a synergy-based phenomenon, and that the existence and strength of such synergy is determined by the presence or absence of novelty and diversity. This perspective is still exceedingly relevant in order to understand the world distribution of wealth and poverty. We shall return to this when discussing Johann Heinrich von Thünen's economic theories.

Facing diversity and heterogeneity forces choices upon the researcher. Between a position where all human beings are alike as economic agents ('perfect information') and dealing with 6 billion unique individuals, finding an appropriate level of abstraction for analysis is difficult. This presents the economics profession with a trade-off between relevancy and accuracy. As Schumpeter says, 'The general reader will have to make up his mind, whether he wants *simple* answers to his questions or *useful* ones—in this as in other economic matters he cannot have both' (Schumpeter in Zeuthen, 1930). In the spirit of Schumpeter's first book (Schumpeter, 1908) one should first pose a question and then enter into theory at a level of abstraction where one is likely to find an answer to the question. If the question we want answered is one of diversity in development experience between countries, a theory that—like Ricardian trade theory—a priori *excludes* all diversity, hierarchies, and learning processes is unlikely to be of much help. In fact it may be argued that the conclusion of standard trade theory, economic harmony and factor price equalization, is indeed already built into the assumptions on which this theory rests. A theory that starts out with no diversity is not likely to have diversity as an outcome.

Another problem related to this emerges from what Abramowitz calls the 'factor-bias' of economic development. Different economic activities also have different factor-biases. Oil refining has a much stronger bias towards the use of capital and knowledge than does the production of slippers. Likewise, the indivisibility and scale-bias of an oil refinery also pulls in the same direction: barriers to entry (see Bain, 1956, among many others) in petroleum refining are likely to establish much higher wages there than in the slipper factory, regardless of skill level. As a Ugandan politician once told me, the barriers to entry and monopolistic competition in the production of beer in Uganda produce wage levels among brewery cleaning personnel approaching that of high government officials. And nepotism flourishes.

Diversity: economies as hierarchies

Adding a dynamic dimension to this we can use Nathan Rosenberg's observation that technological change at any point in time tends to be focused in certain areas (Perez, 2002 and 2004). Figure 4.2 attempts to establish a Quality Index of Economic Activities that brings together the qualitative elements, static and dynamic, from which Ricardian trade theory abstracts (Reinert, 1994). The Quality Index pulls together the factors that explain why the world's most efficient producers of such a low-tech product as baseballs—in Haiti or Honduras—have a real wage that is only a fraction of the wage of the world's largest producer of golf balls. A tiny static gain from trade through specialization may indeed be completely overshadowed by the loss one nation suffers from specializing at the bottom of the hierarchy of skills. This is an attempt to codify the Myrdalian notion that increased specialization and trade may indeed *increase* rather than *decrease* international wage differentials.

This hierarchy argument comes in two parts, one which is essentially static and one that is dynamic and developmental.

First the static argument. By failing to differentiate qualitatively between disparate units of labor hours, standard Ricardian theory fails to account for the qualitative differences between economic activities and, paired together, the possible ensuing benefits that comparative advantages might carry with them. We fail to grasp the fact that the real world consists of hierarchies of different sorts, within companies and institutions and between them.

Take into account the way that most of the Ricardian assumptions underlying the advantages of specialization neglect all differential learning economies. I shall discuss, focusing on the following example involving a vertically integrated activity which includes a 'high-skill' and a 'low-skill' part.

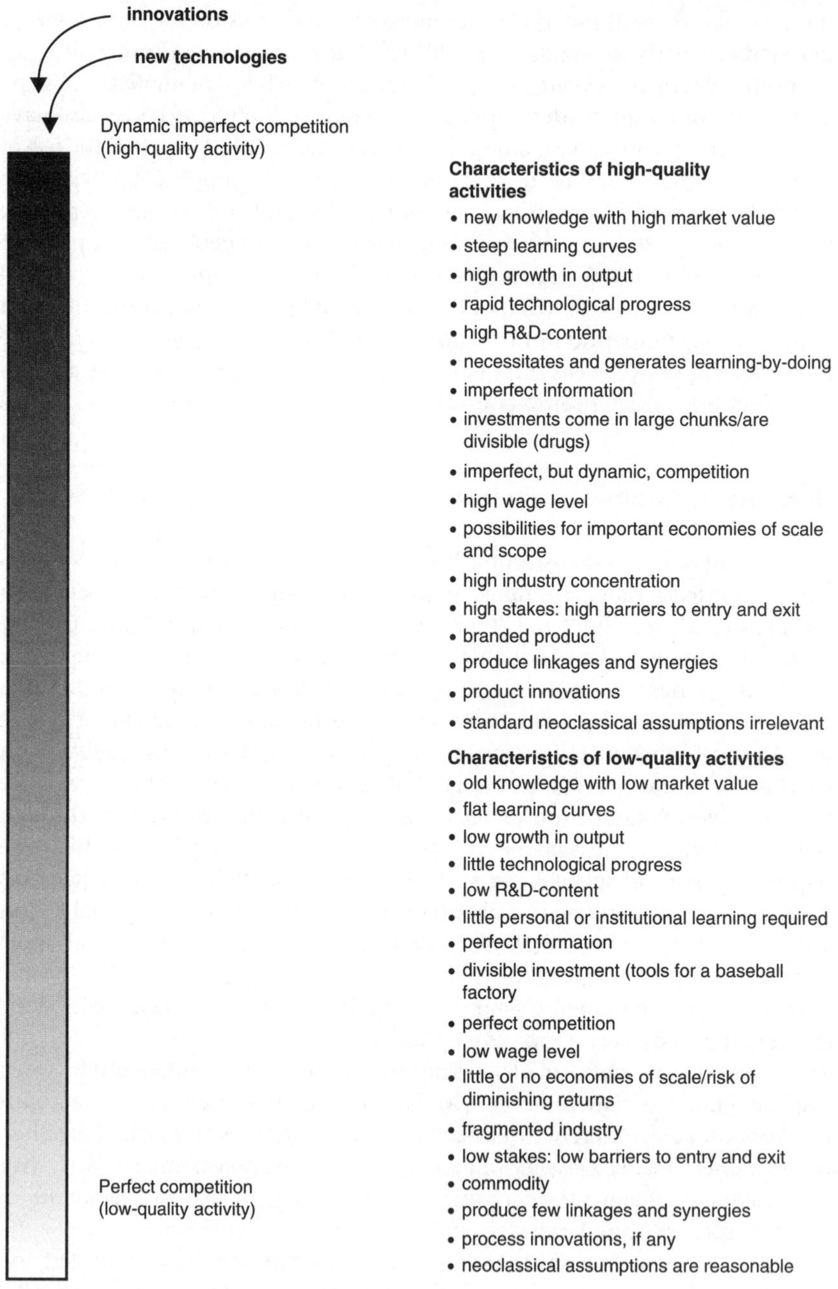

innovations

new technologies

Dynamic imperfect competition
(high-quality activity)

**Characteristics of high-quality
activities**
• new knowledge with high market value
• steep learning curves
• high growth in output
• rapid technological progress
• high R&D-content
• necessitates and generates learning-by-doing
• imperfect information
• investments come in large chunks/are
  divisible (drugs)
• imperfect, but dynamic, competition
• high wage level
• possibilities for important economies of scale
  and scope
• high industry concentration
• high stakes: high barriers to entry and exit
• branded product
• produce linkages and synergies
• product innovations
• standard neoclassical assumptions irrelevant

Characteristics of low-quality activities
• old knowledge with low market value
• flat learning curves
• low growth in output
• little technological progress
• low R&D-content
• little personal or institutional learning required
• perfect information
• divisible investment (tools for a baseball
  factory
• perfect competition
• low wage level
• little or no economies of scale/risk of
  diminishing returns
• fragmented industry
• low stakes: low barriers to entry and exit
• commodity
• produce few linkages and synergies
• process innovations, if any
• neoclassical assumptions are reasonable

Perfect competition
(low-quality activity)

Figure 4.2. The quality index of economic activities

Let us illustrate the relationship between hierarchies and standard of living. If we abstract from geography and assume a world economy consisting only of hospital services, we could create a world economy where all the specialized medical staff lived in one country, and all the nurses lived in another. Suppose also that both in the 'autarchic' world and in the integrated one, the cost of each input is determined by the technology of its training (i.e. its labor content). Assume it is equal to 1 in both countries for nurses, while for doctors it is 2 in country A and 3 in country B. In the system of autarchy a unit of hospital services (one doctor plus one nurse) costs 3 in country A and 4 in country B. Now let them integrate, while continuing to assume that incomes are proportional to the (direct and indirect) content of labor. After integration, B will fully specialize in nurses and A in doctors. Overall 'world average costs of production' will be 3. (i.e. 1 for the nurse and 2 for the doctor) but country B will see its share of world income fall to one half of that of country A (i.e. the relative price of nurses to doctors). Putting the children of the nursing personnel in the same schools as those of the medical doctors would foster social mobility and income growth under autarchy. However, if they are placed in different countries, the socially mobile children of cleaning personnel who manage to get an education as a doctor will migrate to the rich countries in order to increase their income. As Gunnar Myrdal predicted, in this way the market frequently tends to enlarge already existing differences in income rather than to narrow them.

The logic that a nation could upgrade its hierarchy of skills in the same way that a person could is found in the work of US economist Daniel Raymond, whose 1820 book heavily influenced the establishment of the protectionist American System of Manufactures. Through the early decades of the nineteenth century, England was the only country with a comparative advantage in manufacturing, and it was fairly obvious that it used Ricardo's logic in an attempt to prevent other countries from industrializing. The frequent response from other countries that followed its path to industrialization was a biblical quote, Joshua 9:23, pointing precisely to the fact that the world economy corresponded to a hierarchical structure: 'and now, cursed are ye, and none of you is cut off from being a servant, even hewers of wood and drawers of water, for the house of my God.' Today's wealthy nations followed England into industrialization, against the recommendations of Ricardo's trade theory, because they did not wish to be at the bottom of the world's economic hierarchy as hewers of wood and drawers of water.

It is now time to introduce dynamics into the hierarchy (Figure 4.2). From both sides of the political spectrum, Karl Marx and Joseph Schumpeter agree on the sterility of capital alone as a source of wealth. Innovations, rather than savings and capital per se, drive welfare forward. The world economy functions similarly to the world of *Alice in Wonderland*, where one of the strange figures tells Alice 'this is how fast you have to run here in order to stand still'; only constant innovations sustain welfare. Once the builders of sailing ships topped the world hierarchy of ship builders, but they were pushed down after the steam engine and the diesel engine were invented. The world's best producer of kerosene lamps soon became poor with the advent of electricity. Status quo leads to poverty as technical change pushes old technologies, and those who stick to them, further down in the economic hierarchy. This is, of course, precisely what makes the capitalist system so dynamic, but this mechanism also contributes to creating such large differences between rich and poor countries. By introducing emulation as an alternative to comparative advantage, it is possible to introduce these dynamics into trade theory.

Schumpeter used a metaphor to describe society as a *dynamic* hierarchy, saying 'the upper strata of society are like hotels which are...always full of people, but people who are forever changing' (Schumpeter, 1934). The dynamics of radical technological change give rise to great fortunes and a new circulation of elites. Henry Ford brought in new technologies and new management principles and also created a financial fortune through them. A new set of people joined the upper strata through both production and finance-related gain on the new principles. More than half a century later new techno-economic paradigms fostered a new wave of 'creative destruction,' a new wave of entry and new dominant positions both within countries and across countries (Freeman and Perez, 1988; Perez and Soete, 1988; Perez, 2002). In Perez's scheme, economic development consists of what in my terminology are 'productivity explosions', technological breakthroughs that produce explosive increases in labor productivity. Figure 4.3 shows, as an illustration, the productivity explosion of the first Industrial Revolution, that of cotton spinning.

For the purposes of this chapter, what is important to notice is that novel techno-economic paradigms also entail new windows of opportunities (Perez and Soete, 1988) and novel threats for the possibilities for poorer countries to catch up—with quite different outcomes (see also Castaldi et al. in Chapter 3).

Novelty and scale: accounting for qualitative change

During the most dramatic qualitative changes in contemporary economic history—during both the first and the second Industrial Revolutions—the economics profession developed ways of describing the change that was taking place by ways of theories of *stages* of qualitatively different historical periods. Such stage theories have been used in most of the social sciences (Ely, 1903; Reinert, 2000). In my view, if they do not become mechanical exercises they are useful tools for understanding technological and institutional change.

The two types of stage theories discussed above—David Ricardo vs. the early German and US theories—produce vastly different economic policies. As it is intuitively obvious that a hunting and gathering tribe will not be

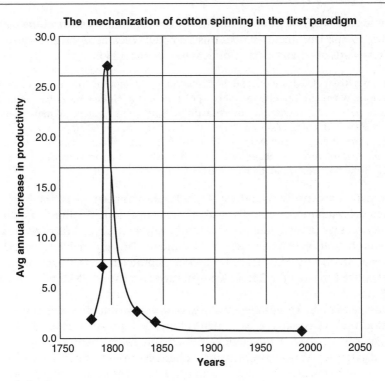

The mechanization of cotton spinning in the first paradigm

Source: Carlota Perez.

Figure 4.3. A quantum jump in productivity

able to compete successfully with an industrial society, similarly emulation into the same technological age as the world's leading nation is a prerequisite before free trade's comparative advantage may take over as a guiding principle.

The logic accompanying such theories of qualitative economic change is that free trade is always beneficial between nations at the same level (stage) of development. Bringing back an old UNCTAD term, we could say that exchanging industrial goods for other industrial goods both produced under increasing returns represents 'symmetrical trade' which is beneficial to both parties, while exchanging commodities produced under non-increasing returns for goods produced under increasing returns conditions represents 'asymmetrical trade' and is only beneficial to the industrialized partner. We have argued elsewhere that the theories of 'good' and 'bad' trade that represented the mainstream of Enlightenment economics were based precisely on this same principle (Reinert and Reinert, 2005; for a formal argument along similar lines, see Dosi, Pavitt, and Soete, 1990).

In his four-volume work on the history of economic thought in the United States, Joseph Dorfman describes this very well when accounting for the attitude towards free trade in the Unites States around 1830:

Of course, free trade is the ideal, and the United States will proclaim the true cosmopolitan principles when the time is ripe. This will be when the United States has a hundred million people and the seas are covered with her ships; when American industry attains the greatest perfection, and New York is the greatest commercial emporium and Philadelphia the greatest manufacturing city in the world; and when 'no earthly power can longer resist the American Stars.' Then 'our children's children will proclaim freedom of trade throughout the world, by land and sea.' (Dorfman, Vol. II)[3]

Dorfman here explains the principle that I argue has been the path taken by all industrialized nations: an initial state of protective emulation has been a mandatory passage point for all presently in industrial nations. With the possible exception of the very first leaders (Venice and the Dutch Republic) all presently rich nations have been through a period of protection. The sequencing has always been 'emulation' before 'comparative advantage' (Reinert, 2007a and 2009).

Integrating nations at different stages of development creates forms of integration that we could call 'asymmetrical' (see Reinert and Kattel, 2004, for a taxonomy of types of integration). When this form of integration is done rapidly through shocks, an important phenomenon can be observed. When two nations at widely different technological levels integrate, the first casualty is *the most advanced* economic activity in *the least advanced* nation. I have referred to this as the Vanek-Reinert effect and argue that it represents one of the mechanisms of primitivization that accompany premature globalization. This Vanek-Reinert effect in turn contributes to falling employment for skilled people, to factor price *polarization*, and migration of skilled labor. For example, the effect can be observed with the unification of Italy during the late nineteenth century.

The mechanisms behind this effect are relatively straightforward. Abruptly freeing imports creates a shock in terms of reduced demand for national production. The companies with the highest relative fixed costs compared to variable costs are the hardest hit on their profit and loss statement. The companies that still have a high amount of machinery and equipment to be amortized are hit long before mature industries with depreciated machinery. Young industries that are cash-starved are hit long before mature cash-cows. All of this contributes to the opposite effect of what one might have meant: a too rapid economic integration leads to the loss of precisely those industries one would wish to promote, modern industries employing new technologies. The last economic activity to be hit from a free trade shock is subsistence agriculture where people simply withdraw from market activities back into self-sufficiency.

Diversity and synergy: Heinrich von Thünen's stages simultaneously spread across geography

While economists presently attempt to reintroduce geography (a process which has seen Paul Krugman as a major contributor), German economist Heinrich von Thünen is an early protagonist. Thünen (1783–1850) drew a map of civilized society with four concentric circles around a core of increasing returns activities—the city.[4] Moving outwards from the city core, the use of capital gradually decreased and the use of nature gradually increased. Near the city the most perishable products are produced, such as dairy products, vegetables, and fruit; grain for bread is produced further out; and in the periphery there is hunting in the wilderness. Economists today have rediscovered Thünen's approach to economic geography, but many totally miss the crucial point he stresses, that the increasing returns on city activities needed tariff protection in order to get the entire system to function. Thünen understood that the development machine at the core of the concentric circles—the urban increasing returns industries (manufacturing)—needed, for a time, targeting, nurturing, and protecting. In other words, the presence of an emulating city would also determine the standard of living in the rest of the country, in these outer circles.

Thünen drew the stage theory onto a map where the most 'modern' sector, manufacturing, formed the city core, and the most 'backward' sector, hunting and gathering, formed the periphery furthest from the city. Moving outward away from the city, the use of nature increases and the use of capital decreases. Only the city has authentic increasing returns, free from nature's flimsy supply of resources of different qualities.

As one moves outwards from the city, man-made comparative advantage (subject to increasing returns) gradually diminishes and nature-made comparative advantage (subject to diminishing returns) increases. As we move outwards in the circles, the carrying capacity of the land in terms of population also diminishes.

The importance of the linkages and synergies for agricultural development, seeing the benefits accruing to agriculture from the proximity of manufacturing, was perhaps the most important new insight in economics during the early 1700s. 'Husbandry...is never more effectually encouraged than by the increase of manufactures,' says David Hume in his *History of England* (1767, Vol. III).

Thünen's model pictures all the stages of development inside one nation-state, one labor market, one school and university system, and one social security system. The synergies that David Hume points to are partly the result of an equal access to basic institutions and government services accruing to the 'hunters' in the outermost circle as well as to the city dweller. The local city market does to national agriculture what an international market can never do. Proximity to a city in the same labor market, rather than abroad, assures employment for the second and third son on the farm. The wage pressure from the city activities makes labor more expensive in the countryside, allowing for technological change that would never be profitable with low wage rates. The proximity to the city gives access to advanced technology and expertise that a rural-only nation would never achieve. All in all von Thünen's model provides a useful picture for development as a synergy between town and countryside.

Novelty and scale: understanding capitalism and the absence of economic development

In the post-Cold War setting we are increasingly made aware of nation-states with radically different political structures from those of Western democracies: 'fragile,' 'failed,' or 'failing' states ruled by warlords, such as Somalia or Afghanistan. Going back to pre-Cold War German and American theories of capitalism, it was generally considered that such political structures were products of particular modes of production (a term in no way exclusive to Marxism). As we shall see below, such states were defined as not being part of 'capitalism.' During the twentieth century Fordist mass production was the dominant mode of production in the US, Europe, and what the League of Nations called 'areas of recent settlement' (Canada, Australia, New Zealand), but not in the colonies.

This development implied use of technologies where economies of scale (and, relatedly, fixed costs) increased heavily over time. The transition from town economies to national economies was made possible by a larger division of labor—potentially favorable both to producer and consumer—because of the lower costs originating in technical change and increasing returns. A greater degree of impersonality—no longer knowing the person who produced your shoes—was the price society and the individual had to pay for getting cheaper shoes. On the production side, capitalism was a system driven by technological change and increasing returns. While perfectly distinguishable in theory, as they tend to develop over time, *increasing returns* and *technical change* are in fact so intertwined that they are often inseparable. The technology Ford used to produce cars was never available for a car producer who wanted to produce profitably at a household or village level. Schumpeter therefore coined a term which is extremely useful for the study or economic history: 'historical increasing returns' (a combination of both).

This combined technology-scale phenomenon hit different economic activities at different points in time, but when it hits it hits in an explosive way. In the industries that had been hit by this combined scale-technological change phenomenon, no return to perfect competition would be possible. The minimum efficient size of operations would create a pattern of competition where scale of operations created barriers to entry and consequently a type of competition that was by definition oligopolistic. The successful result of taming the imperfect competition between these huge players would, as John Kenneth Galbraith always pointed out, be a societal balance of countervailing powers between 'big business,' 'big labor,' and 'big government.'

The transition from handicraft (implying production made to order) to industrial production (implying production for an unknown group of consumers) also implied a transition from production 'in order to make a living' to production 'for profit.' Competition became a relentless game of oligopolistic innovation and emulation, seeking the rents that could be harvested from successfully getting a share of the oligopoly. As long as the rents are Schumpeterian rents which slowly erode rather than static rents, this rent-seeking is in fact a core mechanism explaining capitalist dynamics.

Werner Sombart's definition of colonies not being part of capitalism

During the Cold War two different definitions of capitalism crystallized. First: in the 'free world,' capitalism gradually came to be defined as a system of private ownership of the means of production, where all coordination outside firms is left to the market. This developed into a definition that excludes any reference to production: as long as they bartered without central planning one would almost assume that a Stone Age tribe could be considered 'capitalist.' Second: in Marxism capitalism was mainly defined as a system defined by a relationship between two classes in society, the owners of the means of production and the workers.

However, a third definition of capitalism exists, a definition that dominated until the Cold War, a definition that was crowded out because it could not be neatly placed along the right-left-axis. If we follow German economist Werner Sombart's definition of capitalism, we get an understanding of why capitalism—as it is defined today—is a system where it is possible to specialize in being rich, or in being poor.

Werner Sombart considers capitalism as a kind of historic coincidence, brought together by a whole range of circumstances which hold even if economic wealth is a result of a range of necessary although not sufficiently conscious policies. The driving forces of capitalism, which create both the foundation and the conditions for the system, are according to Sombart (1928): (i) *The entrepreneur,* who represents what Nietzsche calls the 'capital of human wit and will': the human agent who takes the initiative to have something produced or traded. (ii) *The modern state,* which creates the institutions enabling improvements in production and distribution, that creates the incentives that make the vested interest of the entrepreneur coincide with the vested interests of society at large. Institutions encompass everything from legislation to infrastructure, patents to protect new ideas, schools, universities, and standardization, for example, of units of measurements. (iii) *The machine process*, that is, what was long called *industrialism*: mechanization of production creating higher productivity and technological change with innovations under economies of scale and synergies, embodied within 'national innovation systems' (in contemporary literature the notion is associated with Christopher Freeman, 1988 and 1994; Bengt-Åke Lundvall, 1992; and Richard Nelson, 1993).

In Sombart's definition of capitalism, the rich countries were those who emulated the leaders into the industrial age. With capitalism defined in this way, it is actually correct to say that the rich countries are the ones that joined the *mode of production* called capitalism.

Still according to Sombart, when these elements are in place capitalism demands the following ancillary elements in order to function and to be able to develop fully: (i) capital, (ii) labor, and (iii) markets.

These three elements—the very core of standard economic theory—are in Sombart's mind *not* the driving forces of capitalism, but simply auxiliary factors to the main driving forces. Without the driving forces, these ancillary factors, as important as they are, turn out to be sterile. Both Marx and Schumpeter agree that capital in itself, without innovations and without entrepreneurship, is sterile.

The most interesting aspect of this pre-Cold War definition of capitalism is that with this approach capitalism had not reached the colonies. At its core, colonialism was a technology policy: a key aspect of colonial policy was to prohibit manufacturing there. The following quote from English economist Joshua Gee, from his 1729 work, *Trade and Navigation of Great Britain Considered*, is typical of colonial economic policy:

That all Negroes shall be prohibited from weaving either Linnen or Woollen, or spinning or combing of Wooll, or working at any Manufacture of Iron, further than making it into Pig or Bar iron: That they be also prohibited from manufacturing of Hats, Stockings, or Leather of any Kind...Indeed, if they set up Manufactures, and the Government afterwards shall be under a Necessity of stopping their Progress, we must not expect that it will be done with the same Ease that now it may.

The rebellion against these anti-emulation policies—which are less racist than they sound because they were also applied against the predominantly white settlements in North America at the time—has in all cases been accompanied by a strategy of emulation into manufacturing industries. Decolonization meant embarking on a program of industrialization. Not all of these attempts were equally successful, but if human welfare—rather than free trade per se—is our goal, we have to face the fact that in a majority of countries' real wages were considerably higher when an 'inefficient' manufacturing sector was present than when it was not.

Not all protectionism is equally efficient. In another work *How Rich Countries got Rich...and Why Poor Countries Stay Poor* (Reinert, 2007a) we try to identify two ideal types of protectionism, 'good' (East Asian) protectionism and 'bad' (Latin American) protectionism.[5] In many poor countries protectionist policies were clearly of the bad kind, but this bad protectionism produced real wages about twice as high as the wage level after structural adjustments and deindustrialization. Data reproduced in Reinert (2007a) make it evident that maximizing world trade clearly is not the same as maximizing world real wages. The Washington Consensus system of 'conditionalities' created an anti-emulation effect.

Anti-emulation policies were also very frequent within Europe. Venice prohibited the migration of her skilled glass workers from finding work abroad with the penalty of death, while England for many years prohibited the export of machinery. If we see the debate on when to stop protection—when to switch from emulation to comparative advantage—as perhaps the most important economic debate in the times to come, the English machine case provides an interesting insight. England only stopped the export prohibition of machinery when the English machine producers themselves successfully argued that if they were restricted from competing in world markets they would lose ground to foreign machine producers. In other words, if the kind of protection employed is what we define as good protection policies, market forces can to some extent be relied on for fostering the transition to free trade and comparative advantage. Successful emulation provides the seeds of its own destruction, and the key underlying mechanism is Schumpeter's 'historical increasing returns' (the combination of technological change and increasing returns).

I have argued (Reinert, 2007a) that the only time Adam Smith uses the term 'invisible hand' in the *Wealth of Nations* is precisely when describing such a transition from emulation to comparative advantage. Smith praised the Navigation Acts protecting English manufacturing and shipping against Holland, arguing 'they are as wise . . . as if they had all been dictated by the most deliberate wisdom' and holding them to be 'perhaps, the wisest of all the commercial regulations of England.' The term invisible hand is used only when it supports the key import substitution goal of mercantilist policies, when—after successful emulation—the English consumer preferred domestic industry to foreign industry. This could only happen when the market had taken over the role previously played by protective measures, and national manufacturing no longer needed such protection. While Adam Smith tends to be used more these days to provide ideology than to provide theoretical solutions to contemporary problems, let us suggest that he can also be legitimately seen as an enlightened mercantilist who truly understood the transition from emulation to comparative advantage. Successful emulation through protection has been a mandatory passage point in all capitalist countries, but it must at one point yield to free trade.

The economist who more than anyone else had the transition from protectionism and free trade at the very core of his theoretical edifice was Friedrich List

(1841). He was the visionary of a united Europe, when emulation through protection had successfully reached all nations of Europe. The 1846 Repeal of the Corn Laws was at the time understood as an attempt by the English to convince the rest of the world that their free trade in agricultural products meant that the rest of the world should adopt immediate free trade in manufacturing. In fact List had always argued for free trade in corn (Reinert, 1998).[6]

The Marshall Plan (1947) as the last successful project of emulation

In June 1947, in a speech delivered at Harvard University, US Secretary of State George Marshall announced a re-industrialization plan for a war-torn Europe— later called the Marshall Plan (formally the European Recovery Program). This plan represents the logic of emulation at its most creative: compared to the United States, Europe (it was believed, even if somewhat off mark) did not have a comparative advantage in industrial production. In spite of this—and totally contrary to Ricardian principles—a generous infusion of capital as well as tolerance of needed developmental policies ensured the rebirth of modern Europe as industrial states.

Over the next couple of decades, as the same type of economic development policy spread in Asia following the Korean War, the Marshall Plan developed into what is probably the most successful economic development assistance project in human history. Politically, it created a *cordon sanitaire* of wealthy countries from Western Europe to Northeast Asia, successfully containing the spread of Soviet influence, while ensuring rapid growth throughout the world during what has been termed the post-war 'Golden Age.'

Apart from its historical importance, it is worth taking a fresh look at the Marshall Plan because it delivers valuable insights to the logic of emulation that have relevance today. First, it is important to recall that the Marshall Plan represented a complete reversal of the preceding Morgenthau Plan, named after US Secretary of the Treasury Henry Morgenthau, Jr. Germany had started two world wars, and in his 1945 book, *Germany is Our Problem*, Morgenthau announced a de-industrialization plan 'converting Germany into a country principally agricultural and pastoral' to make sure it could never again go to war.

By late 1946, however, economic hardship and unemployment in Germany were worrying the Allies, and former President Herbert Hoover was sent there on a fact-finding mission. Hoover's third report of March 18, 1947 noted: 'There is the illusion that the New Germany left after the annexations can be reduced to a "pastoral state." It cannot be done unless we exterminate or move 25,000,000 people out of it.' He well understood that a purely agricultural country would only be able to sustain a much smaller population than a mixed agrarian and industrial nation.

Faced with the real possibility of an excess of people in need of work that a loss of industry would bring, the only option was to re-industrialize, which is what the Marshall Plan facilitated. Less than three months later, Marshall's early June speech reversed policy. Germany and the rest of Europe were to be re-industrialized with policies that, in practice, included heavy-handed economic interventions such as high duties, quotas, and import prohibitions. Free trade was there, but it was envisaged as viable only after reconstruction and international competitiveness had been achieved. The 1948 Havana Charter may still serve as a blueprint for this approach, putting employment, welfare, and social goals as priorities to be achieved before free trade is introduced.

George Marshall's short speech[7] made four other important points. In describing how Germany's economy had ground to a halt, Marshall noted the breakdown of trade between city and countryside: 'The farmer has always produced the foodstuffs to exchange with the city dweller for the other necessities of life,' stressing that 'this division of labor is the basis of modern civilization.' With this, Marshall recalled centuries-old European economic insight: the only wealthy nations were those with cities that held a manufacturing sector. 'The remedy lies in breaking the vicious circle and restoring the confidence of the European people.' Marshall's use of the expression 'vicious circle' was to become the vogue in development economics in the 1950s and 1960s.

'Our policy is directed not against any country or doctrine but against hunger, poverty, desperation, and chaos. Its purpose should be the revival of a working economy in the world so as to permit the emergence of political and social conditions in which free institutions can exist,' said Marshall. Contrary to today's conventional wisdom, Marshall argued that free institutions emanate from certain productive arrangements, not the other way around (Reinert, 2007b).

Marshall was also very insightful about how to ensure that aid would be truly developmental. 'Such assistance, I am convinced, must not be on a piecemeal basis as various crises develop. Any assistance that this Government may render in the future should provide a cure rather than a mere palliative.' Unfortunately, much of today's ostensible development initiatives are palliative, ignoring Marshall's caveat.

During recent decades, structural adjustment and forced trade liberalization have created effects similar to that of the Morgenthau Plan in many countries. While some large nations—like China and India—that had protected their industries for half a century and had given high-level education to significant portions of their populations have benefited from globalization, many of the other developing countries saw their real wages virtually halved by de-industrialization and unfettered global competition. Incipient industrialization in many parts of Africa regressed. During the last twenty years, premature and sudden exposure to world markets has brought about a steady loss of industry, decline in agriculture, and de-population in many regions now subject to vicious circles of immiseration.

We must rediscover the ancient art of emulation that died out sometime in the 1970s. More attention must be paid to rebuilding the productive structure of poor nations. This process requires a simultaneous build-up of the supply and demand sides—of productive capacity and purchasing power—just as the European economies did during the crucial decades following Marshall's speech in June 1947. This seemingly roundabout development road is, in fact, the only one that can create a lasting peace.

The very last traces of Marshall Plan logic were seen in the integration of Spain into the European Union during the 1980s, gradually lowering tariffs and making sure that the Spanish automotive industry, with its layers of suppliers, survived. When the former centrally planned economies were integrated into Europe some two decades later, the medicine was shock therapy which left large parts of Eastern Europe virtually de-industrialized. The economies of the European periphery, in countries like Moldova, have many similarities to Third World peripheries (Reinert and Kattel, 2004).

Conclusion: industrial policy and poverty

On the basis of an analysis of the last 500 years of the history of economic policy, this chapter argues that all countries that have moved from being poor to wealthy have done so by going through a period of emulation—of infant industry protection—in order to work their way into the areas where techno-logical progress is concentrated at the time. This has been a mandatory pas-sage point in human history. This emulative stage reduces the asymmetry in knowledge and technologies between rich and poor countries. The lack of skills and the lack of markets combine (vicious circles) to make any technology transfer simply not profitable without these added incentives. Only after this step has been achieved will it be in the interest of the catching-up country to specialize symmetrically according to its comparative advantage *within* the leading paradigms.

I have compared attempts to achieve this transition without artificial incen-tives to a businessperson expecting a new industrial company to make money from day one of operations. This is something that only happens in theory. Amazon.com's many years in red ink may be compared to a nation weaning itself from industrial start-up costs.

Starting with the economic theory of Antonio Serra in 1613 economic devel-opment has been associated with economic activities subject to increasing returns and a large division of labor (Reinert and Reinert, 2005). I have labeled these Schumpeterian activities, contrasting them with what I have summarized under a 'Malthusian' archetype that only produces poverty (Table 4.1).

Table 4.1. Characteristics of Schumpeterian and Malthusian activities

Characteristics of Schumpeterian activities (= 'good' export activities)	Characteristics of Malthusian activities (= 'bad' export activities if no Schumpeterian sector present)
Increasing returns	Diminishing returns
Dynamic imperfect competition	'Perfect competition' (commodity competition)
Stable prices	Extreme price fluctuations
Generally skilled labor	Generally unskilled labor
Creates a middle class	Creates 'feudalist' class structure
Irreversible wages ('stickiness' of wages)	Reversible wages
Technical change leads to higher wages for the producer (e.g. 'Fordist wage regime')	Technical change tends to lower price to consumer
Creates large synergies (linkages, clusters)	Creates few synergies

This chapter argues that both neoclassical economics and Ricardian trade theory fundamentally misrepresent the very nature of capitalism in that they fail to identify the very core of the process of relentless rent-seeking through innovation and emulation that *is* economic development.

Perfect competition ceased to be a feasible proposition already during the First Industrial Revolution. A combination of technical change and increasing returns (Schumpeter's 'historical increasing returns') increased the minimum efficient size of operations and consequently barriers to entry and exit, making oligopolistic competition the name of the game in manufacturing industries.

Rent-seeking in a sea of oligopolistic competition is therefore what capitalism is all about. As labor also became oligopolistic through unionization, the stage was set for a system of big business, big labor, and big government (Galbraith, 1956 and 1983). Regulations aiming at a just degree of imperfect competition turned this system into one of triple rent-seeking: capital, labor, and government colluded to share the oligopolistic rents. Minimum wages is an important tool for insuring such a 'collusive' distribution of the rents from innovations.

The presently wealthy nations have all been through a stage where they employed a strategy of emulation into the paradigm-carrying activities of the day. The Marshall Plan—the giant plan for reindustrializing Europe after World War II—was the last big emulation plan that opened up for successful free trade later. Presently the United States and European economies are emulating each other in creating gigantic rent-seeking machines based on very oligopolistic competition—like Boeing and Airbus. As a rapidly increasing part of world trade takes place in patented goods—i.e. legalized rent-seeking—it is almost indecent of First World economists to suggest that Third World countries should not be allowed to engage in industrial policies that produce rent-seeking. This is a blatant example of double standards: the strategy 'perfect competition for you and imperfect competition for us' was the core of an industrial policy called colonialism. The Third World will increasingly see the present stance as neo-colonialism.

Both vested industrial interests and plain institutional inertia will easily lead to keeping the strategy of emulation in place longer than warranted before comparative advantage takes over. India and China are probably both examples of that. However, if we compare the situation of India and China on the one hand and that of Somalia and Tanzania—both nations richer than Korea and Singapore 50 years ago—on the other, the cost of keeping the strategy of emulation in place too long is infinitely smaller than that of never embarking on it. Capitalism *is* rent-seeking. Choosing between the option of keeping a system of industrial rent-seeking that is relatively too static, thus creating an economic system that only partly exploits its dynamic potential, is infinitely better than failing on the opposite side with no emulation, which results in unemployment, hunger, and disease—as is the case of fragile, failing, and failed states in Africa and elsewhere. Failing on the side of keeping the protective barriers too long leads us to live pleasantly in a country like Argentina in 1970. Failing to embark on emulation at all leads us to live in a country like Somalia in 1995. The choice is not really difficult.

I have argued that by establishing free trade uncompromisingly as the linchpin of the World Economic Order we have closed our eyes to many of the trade-offs that actually face us when we make economic decisions. As the absoluteness of the Gold Standard blocked Keynesian reforms for many years in the 1930s, the absoluteness of Free Trade plays a similar role today. I have argued that while 'emulation' is the logical intuitive choice in many situations, the counterintuitive choice of 'comparative advantage' is more than often imposed on countries far away. To use the term coined by US economist Thorstein Veblen, Ricardian (and much more so, Washington Consensus/neo-classical) economics may 'contaminate our instincts.' Not only that, in my view Ricardian trade theory is also about to contaminate our ethics. By seeing rent-seeking through import restrictions as something close to the cardinal economic sin, we may actually indirectly favor other forms of rent-seeking that may be even less palatable. During the US Civil War the South would be our ethical choice because they were in favor of free trade. Rent-seeking in the South was based on something else, on slavery. The North on the other hand based their economic policy on rent-seeking through import substitution. Which would we favor today, rent-seeking through import substitution or through low-wage slavery?

As did the United States after the defeat of the South in the Civil War, after World War II many countries raised their standards of living through an active industrial policy of the Schumpeterian kind described in this chapter. When protection was abruptly radically reduced or removed with the structural adjustment programs of the Washington Consensus, beginning in the 1970s, real wages fell precipitously in a large number of countries from Peru to sub-Saharan Africa, Moldova, and Mongolia (Reinert, 2007a). Clearly in many countries industrial policies were inefficient, but historically the only reasonable reaction to having an inefficient manufacturing sector is to make it more efficient, through the promotion of more competition internally or from countries at similar levels of development. And, centuries of experience (Steuart, 1776; List, 1841) insist that whatever changes are made to industrial policy should be made slowly—not through shock therapy—in order to allow companies to adjust their productive structures.

Notes

1. *The Oxford Dictionary of Byzantium*, Vol. 1.
2. Sombart (1928) gives the complete story. See Mitchell (1929) for an English résumé.
3. We should note that 'cosmopolitan principles' was the term used to refer to Ricardian economics, against which Friedrich List coined the term 'National Economics' (which still is the term for economics in Sweden). The other protest term against the cosmopolitan principles was 'Social Economics' (as economics was referred to in Norwegian until very recently) because the cosmopolitan principles, just as today, tended to disregard serious social consequences.
4. The inventor of the concentric circles to explain the role of cities was Johann Heinrich Gottlob von Justi, in his *Gesammelte Politische und Finanzschriften über wichtige Gegenstände der Staatskunst, der Kriegswissenschaften und des Cameral und Finanzwesens, 1761–4*, Vol. 3.
5. See also Dosi, Freeman, and Fabiani (1994) for a similar concept.
6. Modern agricultural protectionism originates from only towards the very end of the nineteenth century, and is not an emulation project. At the early stages of industrialization it was generally argued that the farmers were much better off than the industrial workers because they had enough food. When workers' rights and the embryonic welfare state had been established, it was discovered that then the city was exploiting the poor farmers who had to be protected from the even poorer farmers abroad. It is extremely important to understand the very different motivations behind the two types of protectionism. I have previously referred to emulative manufacturing protection as 'aggressive protectionism' and to agricultural protectionism as 'protective protectionism.'
7. <http://www.oecd.org/document/10/0,2340,en_2649_201185_1876938_1_1_1_1,00.html>.

References

Anonymous (1786), *Relazione di una scorsa per varie provincie d'Europa del M. M . . . a Madama G. in Parigi*. Pavia, Nella Stamperia del Monastero di S. Salvatore.

Audretsch D. (2004), 'Diversity: Implications for Income Distribution' in E. Reinert (ed.) *Globalization, Economic Development and Inequality: An Alternative Perspective*. Edward Elgar, Cheltenham.

Bain J. (1956), *Barriers to New Competition*, Harvard University Press, Cambridge, Mass.

Castaldi C. et al. (2009), 'Technological Learning, Policy Regimes and Growth in a "Globalized" Economy: Some General Patterns,' this volume.

Cimoli M., G. Dosi, R. Nelson, and J. Stiglitz (2009), 'Institutions and Policies Shaping Industrial Development: An Introductory Note,' this volume.

Dorfman, J. (1947–1959), *The Economic Mind in American Civilization*, Harrap, London (vols. 1–2) & Viking, New York (vols. 3–4).

Dosi G. et al. (ed.) (1988), *Technical Change and Economic Theory*, Pinter, London.

—— K. Pavitt, and L. Soete (1990), *The Economics of Technical Change and Industrial Trade*, Harvester Wheatsheaf, New York.

—— C. Freeman, and S. Fabiani (1994), 'The Process of Economic Development. Introducing some Stylized Facts and Theories on Technologies, Firms and Institutions' in *Industrial and Corporate Change*, Vol. 3.

Ely R. (1903), *Evolution of Industrial Society*, Chautauqua Press, New York.

Freeman C. and C. Perez (1988), 'Structural Crises of Adjustment, Business Cycles and Investment Behaviour' in G. Dosi et al. (eds.) *Technical Change and Economic Theory*, Pinter, London.

—— (1994), 'Technological Infrastructure and International Competitiveness'. *Industrial and Corporate Change*, 13: 541–69.

Galbraith J. K. (1956), *American Capitalism: The Concept of Countervailing Power*, Houghton Mifflin, Boston.

—— (1983), *The Anatomy of Power*, Houghton Mifflin, Boston.

Gee J. (1729), *Trade and Navigation of Great Britain Considered*, Bettesworth & Hitch, London.

Hirschman A. (1977), *The Passions and the Interests: Political Arguments for Capitalism before Its Triumph*, Princeton University Press, Princeton.

Hont I. (2005), *Jealousy of Trade: International Competition and the Nation-State in Historical Perspective*, Harvard University Press, Cambridge, Mass.

Hutton E. (1926), *The Mastiff of Rimini: Chronicles of the House of Malatesta*, Methuen, London.

Hume D. (1767), *The History of England from the Invasion of Julius Caesar to the Revolution in 1688 (6 vols.)*, A. Millar, London.

Jomo K. S. and E. Reinert (2005), *The Origins of Development Economics, How Schools of Economic Thought Have Addressed Development*, Zed Publications, London/Tulika Books, New Delhi.

Justi J.H.G. von (1761–4), *Gesammelte Politische und Finanzschriften über wichtige Gegenstände der Staatskunst, der Kriegswissenschaften und des Cameral- und Finanzwesens (3 vol.)*, Rothenschen Buchhandlung, Copenhagen and Leipzig.

Krugman P. (1991), *Geography and Trade*, MIT Press, Cambridge, Mass.

—— (1995), *Development, Geography, and Economic Theory*, MIT Press, Cambridge, Mass.

List F. (1841), *Das Nationale System der Politischen Ökonomie*, Cotta, Stuttgart.

Lundvall B.-Å. (ed.) (1992), *National Systems of Innovation: Towards a Theory of Innovation and Interactive Learning*, Pinter, London.

Mitchell W. (1929), 'Sombart's Hochkapitalismus,' *The Quarterly Journal of Economics*, 43(2): 303–23.

Morgenthau H. (1945), *Germany is Our Problem: A Plan for Germany*, Harper, New York.

Nelson R. (1993), *National Innovation Systems. A Comparative Analysis*, Oxford University Press, New York.

—— (2006), 'Economic Development from the Perspective of Evolutionary Economic Theory,' The Other Canon Foundation and Tallinn University of Technology Working

Papers in Technology Governance and Economic Dynamics No. 2. Available at: <http://hum.ttu.ee/tg/>.

The Oxford Dictionary of Byzantium (1991), Oxford University Press, New York.

Perez C. (2002), *Technological Revolutions and Financial Capital: The Dynamics of Bubbles and Golden Ages*, Edward Elgar, Cheltenham.

—— (2004), 'Technological Revolutions, Paradigm Shifts and Socio-Institutional Change', in E. Reinert (ed.) *Globalization, Economic Development and Inequality: An Alternative Perspective*, Edward Elgar, Cheltenham.

—— and L. Soete (1988), 'Catching Up in Technology: Entry Barriers and Windows of Opportunity' in G. Dosi et al. (eds.) *Technical Change and Economic Theory*, Pinter, London.

Raymond D. (1820), *Thoughts on Political Economy*, Fielding Lucas, Baltimore.

Reinert E. (1994), 'Catching-up from Way Behind: A Third World Perspective on First World History', in J. Fagerberg, B. Verspagen, and N. Tunzelmann (eds.) *The Dynamics of Technology, Trade and Growth*, Edward Elgar, Aldershot.

—— (1998), 'Raw Materials in the History of Economic Policy; or, Why List (the Protectionist) and Cobden (the Free Trader) Both Agreed on Free Trade in Corn?' in G. Cook (ed.) *Freedom and Trade: 1846–1996*, Routledge, London.

—— (2000), 'Karl Bücher and the Geographical Dimensions of Techno-Economic Change' in Jürgen Backhaus (ed.) *Karl Bücher: Theory—History—Anthropology—Non-Market Economies*, Metropolis Verlag, Marburg.

—— (2007a), *How Rich Countries Got Rich and Why Poor Countries Stay Poor*, Constable, London/Carroll & Graf, New York.

—— (2007b), 'Institutionalism Ancient, Old and New: A Historical Perspective on Institutions and Uneven Development' in H-J. Chang (ed.) *Institutional Change and Economic Development*. United Nations University Press, New York/Anthem, London.

—— (2009), 'Emulating Success: Contemporary Views of the Dutch Economy before 1800' in O. Gelderblom (ed.), *The Political Economy of the Dutch Republic*, Ashgate, Aldershot.

—— and A. Daastøl (1997), 'Exploring the Genesis of Economic Innovations: The Religious Gestalt-Switch and the Duty to Invent as Preconditions for Economic Growth,' *European Journal of Law and Economics*, 4(2/3).

—— and R. Kattel (2004), 'The Qualitative Shift in European Integration: Towards Permanent Wage Pressures and a "Latin-Americanization" of Europe?' Praxis Foundation Working Paper No. 17, Estonia. Available at: <http://www.praxis.ee/data/WP_17_2004.pdf>.

—— Y. Ekoué Amaïzo, and R. Kattel (2009), 'The Economics of Failed, Failing and Fragile States: Productive Structure as the Missing Link,' The Other Canon/Tallinn University of Technology Working Paper Series No. 18.

—— and S. Reinert (2005), 'Mercantilism and Economic Development: Schumpeterian Dynamics, Institution Building and International Benchmarking' in K.S. Jomo and E. Reinert (eds.) *Origins of Economic Development*, Zed Publications, London/Tulika Books, New Delhi.

Ricardo D. (1974), *The Principles of Political Economy and Taxation*, Dutton, London, Dent [1817].

Schumpeter J. (1908), *Das Wesen und der Hauptinhalt der theoretischen Nationalökonomie*, Duncker & Humblot, Munich and Leipzig.

Schumpeter J. (1934), *Theory of Economic Development*, Harvard University Press, Cambridge, Mass.

Singer H. (1950), 'The Distribution of Gains between Investing and Borrowing Countries,' *American Economic Review*, 40.

Sombart W. (1913a), *Luxus und Kapitalismus*, Duncker & Humblot, Munich and Leipzig.

—— (1913b), *Krieg und Kapitalismus*, Duncker & Humblot, Munich and Leipzig.

—— (1928), *Der moderne Kapitalismus (6 vol.)*, Duncker & Humblot, Munich and Leipzig. [Partial French trans. (1932), *L'Apogée du Capitalisme (2 vol.)*, Payot, Paris. Partial Spanish trans. (1946), *El Apogeo del Capitalismo (2 vol.)*, Fondo de Cultura Economica, Mexico. Partial Italian trans. (1967), *Il Capitalismo Moderno*, Unione Tipografico-editrice Torinese, Torino.

Steuart J. (1776), *An Inquiry into the Principles of Political Economy: Being an Essay on the Science of Domestic Policy in Free Nations. In which are particularly considered population, agriculture, trade, industry, money, coin, interest, circulation, banks, exchange, public credit, and taxes (2 vol.)*, A. Millar & T.Cadell, London.

Thünen J.H. von (1826), *Der isolierte Staat in Beziehung auf Landwirtschaft und Nationalökonomie, oder Untersuchungen über den Einfluss, den die Getreidepreise, der Reichtum des Bodens und die Abgaben auf den Ackerbau ausüben*, Penthes, Hamburg.

Veblen T. (1899), *The Theory of the Leisure Class*, Macmillan, New York.

Zeuthen F. (1930), *Problems of Monopoly and Economic Welfare. With a Preface by Professor Joseph A. Schumpeter*, Routledge, London.

5

Industrial Policies in Developing Countries: History and Perspectives

Michele Di Maio

Introduction

This chapter presents a historical and empirical account of the role played by government intervention in the form of industrial policies in spurring development and growth in developing countries in the last 50 years.

Here, in line with Chapter 2, we adopt a broad definition of industrial policies meant to include i) innovation and technology policies; ii) education and skill formation policies; iii) trade policies; iv) targeted industrial support measures; v) sectoral competitiveness policies; vi) competition-regulation policies.

The starting point of this chapter is the acknowledgment that industrial policies have always accompanied the growth process of rich countries and that, for this reason, they should be considered as a permanent feature of the 'constitution of markets' and an essential part of their functioning (Dosi, 1988). Government intervention has indeed a long history.[1] In fact, there is abundant historical evidence showing that all the current developed countries have widely adopted targeted government interventions in trade and industry during their catching-up process (Landes, 1970). Starting from the Renaissance period, several European kingdoms created, supported, and protected activities characterized by increasing returns and high technology intensity. According to Reinert (1994), historical evidence clearly shows that a state forcing entrepreneurs into specific activities has indeed been a *necessary* step in the development process of most countries. Moreover, in a number of cases, when this was not possible, it became itself an *entrepreneur of last resort* (Reinert, 1999). The state also played a very important role in pushing the technological frontier by being a source of high-quality demand for national production. Infrastructure projects and warfare have been particularly important in this respect.

Two historical examples are particularly instructive in showing the role of government intervention through industrial polices in the development process of existing developed countries: Germany and Japan. The catching-up process of Germany in the second part of the nineteenth century is a clear example of successful use of industrial policies for inducing growth. The German development model was based on the Listian idea that acquiring new technologies, learning how to use them, and improving upon them were the three necessary steps for catching-up (List, 1845). To this end, the government designed an education and training system with the objective to transform the process of creation and diffusion of innovation in a continuous activity at the national level. For instance, German universities were the first to institutionalize a system of science laboratories and post-graduate training. In fact, far beyond protectionism, the key to the German (and US) catching-up process was precisely the leadership in the new technologies (namely chemistry and electrical engineering) and their widespread application to the economic system. This has been achieved through the development of an excellent education system and the government provision of incentives for innovators (Freeman, 2004).

A Listian philosophy also shaped the Japanese development model involving the modification of the country's economic structure through innovation and the *creation* of comparative advantages in dynamic sectors. As in the case of Germany (and the US), the Japanese model also entailed a strong emphasis on education and the creation of a domestic innovation system. The government played a fundamental role in this. Moreover, a high quality education system was complemented by what Freeman (2004) identifies as the second ingredient of the Japanese success: a long-term approach to investment in which consideration of the dynamics of world demand had a pre-eminent role in identifying strategic priorities in R&D investments, and in which government, again, played a central role, directing investment through the provision of a wide set of incentives (and directives).

Government intervention has also played a fundamental role in the development processes of Latin America and Far Eastern countries other than Japan.

The objective of this chapter is to describe the attempt made by latecomers after WWII to use industrial policies in order to speed up the rate of industrialization and economic growth rates. We will see that their results have been mixed, with similar policies producing very different outcomes. A thorough comparative exercise is a necessary precondition to the understanding of their varied degree of success. This chapter is meant to contribute to this task.

The work is structured as follows. The next section describes, adopting the taxonomy proposed in Cimoli et al. (this volume), the set of industrial policies implemented since the end of WWII in a number of developing countries. In particular, the focus is on the experiences of Latin American countries and the so-called East Asian Tigers (South Korea, Taiwan, Singapore, Hong Kong). The objective is to identify the main lines of intervention asking a number of important questions, namely, which are the characteristics of successful industrial policies? Are there industrial policies, among the ones that have worked in the past, which can also be useful in the present context? Is there a one-size-fits-all recipe, or does the high degree of country heterogeneity make it impossible to identify any 'general' effective industrial policy? The third section analyzes how the acceleration of the globalization of production and the introduction of the new World Trade Organization (WTO) rules have modified the available set of instruments, practices, and institutions to support industrial development and how the governments of developing countries have reacted to it. Together, the section describes the set of industrial policies that have been implemented by latecomers in the last 15 years, emphasizing the similarities and diversities among the experiences of different countries.

Industrial policies: historical experiences and empirical evidence

Industrial policies in developing countries after WWII

In the 1950s, if not earlier, many governments of developing countries started extensively to intervene in the economy with the objective to spur the industrialization process. Government intervention took different forms, from complete economy-wide plans to different packages of industrial policies. Let us follow the taxonomy put forward by Cimoli et al. in this volume and distinguish between policies affecting i) opportunities of scientific and technological innovation; ii) socially distributed learning and technological capabilities; iii) the set of economic signals and incentives profit-motivated agents face; and iv) modes of governance of private firms.

We begin discussing the least controversial areas of government intervention, namely technological and innovation policies on the one hand and education and skill formation policies on the other.

OPPORTUNITIES OF SCIENTIFIC AND TECHNOLOGICAL INNOVATION: INNOVATION POLICIES AND TECHNOLOGICAL PROJECTS

While at the beginning of the development process all countries bought rather than made technology (Amsden, 2001), later on a few governments made an effort to stimulate the domestic production of technological knowledge. These attempts showed mixed results.

Beginning in the 1940s, a large number of public firms and public research institutions were created in almost all Latin American countries. At the time, public laboratories and publicly owned firms were the most important source of domestic research and development (R&D) activity. Indeed, it was inside the publicly owned firms that the first engineering departments of the region were created to modify imported technologies and products in order to make them fit for the local environment. In the 1950s, specific public institutions started to be established to promote science and technological advances and to coordinate scientific research with firms' production activities.[2] National Research Councils were established in most of the countries. They had a number of missions: (i) funding technological development; (ii) coordinating R&D programs; and (iii) diffusing technological information.

During the 1960s and 1970s, a rich institutional infrastructure to support innovation and technological change was already active in several Latin American countries. At the time *National Development Plans* usually also incorporated a *Science and Technology Program*. Generally, their declared objectives were to coordinate public research, to establish priorities in R&D activities, and to increase the cooperation between public research institutes and the private sector. Governments have also used the national legislation to facilitate and foster domestic knowledge accumulation. For instance, in several countries,[3] national laws meant to force (with limited success) foreign investors to disinvest in favor of local ones after some years were instituted, and profit repatriation was legally limited (Alcorta and Peres, 1998). The preeminent role of the state in the knowledge accumulation process is testified by the fact that, during the import substitution industrialization (ISI) period, more than 80 percent of Science and Technology (S&T) total expenditure was publicly funded (Katz, 2000). Business-performed research and development activities were mainly carried out by large public firms operating in sectors such as telecommunications and transport, together with research institutes working in the areas of agriculture, energy, mining, forestry, and aeronautics (ECLAC, 2004). Specific public research institutes were created to support this technology accumulation strategy. In Argentina in 1954, the National Atomic Energy Commission (CNEA) was set up, followed by the National Institute of Industrial Technology (INTI) (Yoguel, 2003) while Brazil created, in the early 1950s, the Aerospace Technology Centre (CTA). Similarly, the National Institute for Nuclear Research (ININ), the Electrical Research Institute (IIE), the Mexican Institute of Water Technology (IMTA), and the Mexican Petroleum Institute (IMP) were set up in Mexico to promote technological innovation and development in their respective industries (Casalet, 2003).

Interestingly, governments' efforts to develop R&D capabilities were not confined to the manufacturing sector. For instance, in 1957 the Argentinean government established the National Institute of Agricultural Technology

(INTA) while at the beginning of the 1970s, the Brazilian government created the Agricultural Research Enterprise (EMBRAPA) with the objective to coordinate the R&D activities in the agricultural sector (Pacheco, 2003).

Development banks also had an important role in financing programs for technological development during the 1970s. For instance, in Brazil, the National Development Bank (Banco Nacional de Desenvolvimiento Economico e Social, BNDES) had two special funds to finance the training of specialized technical personnel and the development of a local capital goods industry (Dahlman and Frischtak, 1993). In Mexico, the industrial technology development program (Fondo de Equipamiento Industrial, FONEI) had a risksharing program in collaboration with the CONACYT, and another one funded by the World Bank, to subsidize technological adaptation and innovation (Alcorta and Peres, 1998).

An important and widely used instrument to induce domestic technological accumulation was local content rules, sometimes in the form of a condition for receiving development banks' loans. While this type of condition may have severe drawbacks (Pack, 2000), there is anecdotal evidence showing that in some cases such arrangements have been very successful. A very interesting case in this sense is the automotive sector in Brazil. Brazil started an automotive plan in 1956 as part of its ISI strategy (Shapiro, 1989). The automotive sector was targeted because it was thought to be able to attract foreign capital and technology and thus, through the creation of backward linkages, to act as a leading sector for the whole economy. In particular, the plan restricted imports and forced multinational companies to accept local content rules in exchange for permission to access the (potentially large) domestic market.[4] This early experiment in sectoral planning proved to be successful. Internal prices started to decrease in the mid-1960s, and foreign exchange savings were significant. By the beginning of the 1970s, the industry was relatively cost-efficient by international standards. What made this success possible was that the Brazilian market was large enough to make a domestic industry viable and to induce foreign investors to accept local content rules. Moreover, the automobile was still a luxury good, which made it easier for the producer to pass the burden of the cost of local content rules on to the consumers. This success story[5] shows that there are conditions under which industrial policies and MNC strategies can be made to be complementary.

Governments' commitment to technological development has been even stronger in the case of the East Asian Tigers. From the early 1960s, the South Korean government supported domestic technological upgrading in several ways. The import of technology was strongly subsidized: transfer costs of patent rights and technology import fees were tax deductible, income from technological consulting was tax-exempt, and foreign engineers were exempt from income tax. Private R&D was directly promoted with the creation of public funds to finance domestic technological innovation. In addition, the process of technological upgrading of domestic production has been accompanied and facilitated by the simultaneous increase of the government's activity in financing domestic technological innovation. As early as the 1960s, the South Korean government already started to promote a rich set of public policies whose primary goal was to foster the development of indigenous technological capabilities, and thus to reduce the dependence of domestic companies on foreign technology (Amsden, 1989).[6]

Even more so than in Latin America, the East Asian Tigers' governments acted as venture capitalists and as pioneers, especially in high-technology sectors such as informatics, semiconductors, and telecommunications. Taiwan is the clearest example of this. Given an industrial structure characterized by small and medium-sized enterprises (SMEs), the creation of high-tech firms needed an initial period of acquisition of foreign technologies. To this aim the import, adaptation, diffusion, and development of new technologies was heavily stimulated. The Taiwan Industrial Technology Research Institute (ITRI), founded in 1973, was established precisely to import and rapidly to diffuse advanced technologies among Taiwan's firms. In addition to policies to attract foreign direct investments (FDI), a favorite instrument of technology development has been the creation of *science parks* and *technology clusters*. Even when cooperation between the public and the private sector is a characteristic feature of the technological upgrading strategy of the country (Lall, 2003), the public sector has also developed new technologies on its own. Public enterprises entered several 'heavy' and high-technology industries when the private sector was unable to develop the necessary capabilities. In addition, the government elaborated a number of venture capital projects and comprehensive *Technology Plans* to guide the allocation of resources.

In most of the East Asian Tigers, accumulation of technological capabilities was also stimulated by high quality government demand. Two interesting examples of this are the (now well-known) story of the shipping industry in South Korea (Amsden, 1989) and the development of the ICT industry in India which took its start from government demand for defense industry equipment (Singh, Chapter 11).

An important aspect in which latecomers differ from each other is the way they manage FDI. While access to foreign technology is an obvious prerequisite in order to take off, the *form* in which this happens (i.e. FDI, the purchase of capital equipment, licensing, venture capital agreements, etc.) matters a lot. Indeed, it determines the possibilities and modes of developing *domestic* technological capabilities and thus has a great impact on the characteristics of the growth process (Amsden, Chapter 15). Historically, FDI inflows have been (and still are) the most important of these forms of access, but developing countries have used this channel to very different extents (Table 5.1).

Table 5.1. Net foreign direct investment as percentage of gross domestic capital formation

	1960–64	1965–69	1970–74	1975–79	1980–84	1985–89
Argentina	1.0	0.5	0.2	1.2	2.0	4.4
Brazil	–	7.6	5.7	4.2	3.8	2.0
Chile	−1.3	3.0	−7.0	3.9	7.8	4.6
Mexico	3.5	4.4	4.1	3.4	3.2	7.1
South Korea	0.2	0.6	2.7	0.8	0.2	1.5
Taiwan	4.4	−4.9	1.5	1.0	0.8	1.7
Malaysia	–	10.2	12.3	12.5	11.9	8.7

Source: Amsden (2001) based on IMF data.

Concerning the attitude towards FDI, Amsden (2001) identifies two groups of countries. The characteristics of the first group, called *independents*,[7] are i) minimal reliance on FDI and MNCs; ii) the technology development of a country relies on strengthening domestic firms and a heavy emphasis on domestic skill building and R&D; iii) a pervasive use of industrial policies in order to create *national champions*. In some cases the state acts as a venture capitalist or as a pioneer. The second group, called *integrationists*,[8] itself comprises two groups. The a*ctive integrationists* rely on the *spillovers* from MNCs to access new technology and make a significant use of selective policies to move into high value added activities. The *passive integrationists*, instead, do not select MNCs but attract them through the use of a large number of welcoming policies, offering a stable macro environment, low wages, disciplined and semi-skilled labor, and good location.

South Korea clearly belongs to the *independents* group. In the 1960s and 1970s, FDIs were permitted only if they were the only way of obtaining some technologies or gaining access to world markets. But, even in those cases, they were subject to tight state control. Somewhere in between, FDI has been an important engine of the Brazilian development process (Castro, Chapter 10). During the industrialization process, the Taiwanese government also made a substantial effort to attract FDI in technologically advanced sectors in which domestic firms were still very weak. The government sought to maximize benefits from FDI for domestic firms by (i) promoting local sourcing and subcontracting; (ii) imposing local content rules and (iii) introducing the obligation for foreign firms to transfer skills and technology to subcontractors, with the objective to raise the technological capabilities of domestic firms. At the other extreme, Singapore's technological upgrading process has been dominated by MNCs, which provided state-of-the-art technologies and access to their global networks (Lall, 2000). Singapore's government attracted MNCs by using a wide set of welcoming policies, selective investments in skills, technology, and infrastructure. Interestingly, all these policies were directed at meeting the specific needs of selectively *targeted* FDI (Lall, 1996).

SOCIALLY DISTRIBUTED LEARNING AND TECHNOLOGICAL CAPABILITIES: EDUCATION AND SKILL FORMATION POLICIES

A natural complement to innovation policies and indeed a prerequisite are education and skill formation policies. While there is no doubt that firms from late-coming countries, need to access and acquire technologies developed in advanced countries the necessary condition is a training and education system that gives a multitude of firms access to a labor supply with the needed skills.

We have already mentioned how important education policies have been in the historical experiences of Germany and Japan.[9] Similarly, they have been a fundamental part of the development strategy of *latecomers* after WWII. But the experiences of the East Asian Tigers and Latin America have differed considerably in this respect, as well.

The progress developing countries have made in all dimensions of education in the last century is evident, but highly uneven. Even concerning the level of illiteracy (Table 5.2), differences across regions are large. Indeed, the reduction of illiteracy that took place in Latin America during the twentieth century was impressive considering the levels of illiteracy at the beginning of the century, but less so if compared with the dynamics in other countries. The Philippines

Table 5.2. Illiteracy rate, total (population with age >15)

	1900	1950	1960	1970	1980	1985	1990
Argentina	53	14	9	7	6	5	5
Brazil	65	51	29	34	26	22	19
Chile	50	20	16	15	19	8	7
Mexico	77	35	25	26	17	15	13
South Korea	na	78	na	11	7	5	4
Philippines	51	na	40	17	17	10	5
Thailand	na	48	na	21	12	7	na

Source: UNESCO Statistical Database.

Table 5.3. Gross enrollment ratios in tertiary education

	1950	1960	1970	1975	1980	1985	1990
Argentina	5	11	13	27	22	36	38
Brazil	1	2	5	10	11	na	11
Chile	2	4	9	15	12	16	21
Mexico	2	3	5	10	14	16	15
South Korea	–	–	7	9	15	34	39
Philippines	–	–	17	16	24	25	28
Singapore	–	–	6	8	8	14	19
Thailand	–	–	3	3	15	19	na

Source: UNESCO Statistical Database.

Table 5.4. Share of engineers in total tertiary students (%)

	Share in	
	1960	1990
Argentina	13.0	12.0
Brazil	12.0	9.6
Mexico	20.0	16.9
South Korea	19.0	21.7
Taiwan	19.8	30.2

Source: Amsden (2001).

and Thailand, for example, which in 1950 had illiteracy rates as high as that of Mexico and slightly lower than that of Brazil, achieved reductions in illiteracy much larger than did those countries.

A similar picture emerges from the data on tertiary education (Table 5.3). Access to tertiary education in all developing countries expanded most during the 1960s and 1970s, albeit from extremely small levels. But by 1990 the access to higher education was much lower in Latin America than in the East Asian Tigers. While one third of young Argentineans were attending colleges and universities, the rest of the Latin American countries were well below this level.

There are few doubts that the available supply of highly skilled workers is one of the conditions that allowed the Asian Tigers to take off. Indeed, by the 1960s their educational indicators were much higher than those of other countries of comparable income. In particular, there was near-universal primary-school enrollment, and the literacy rate was nearly double that of other developing countries (Rodrik, 1995a). In Asian Tiger countries, the education systems were strongly biased in favor of technical degrees and were (and still are) characterized by an extremely high number of engineers (Table 5.4).

In this respect, it is interesting to note that Singapore, which with Hong Kong has been the least 'interventionist' among the East Asian Tigers, has also widely invested in education and technical training, obtaining very high levels of scientific education indicators. Indeed, by mid-1980, it ranked second in the world in the number of engineers and students enrolled in a scientific discipline as a percentage of total population (Kim, 1993). There is little doubt that the high-skilled labor force has been key to the rapid acquisition of imported technology and to its efficient exploitation and subsequent improvement.

The positive achievements of the education systems in the East Asian Tigers have been the result of active public policies.[10] This is particularly evident for South Korea and Taiwan. Starting from very low education indicators, South Korea has constantly and heavily invested in education and high skill formation: the number of researchers went from nearly zero at the beginning of the 1950s to about 6,000 in 1970, most of whom were employed in government research institutes and universities (Kim, 1993). At the beginning of the 1970s, South Korea was able quickly to match a fast increase in the demand for technical skills. As soon as South Korean industrial policy moved towards targeting high-tech sectors, the government started investing in the creation of general and technical skills too. As a result, the average number of years of schooling and the number of engineers increased at an impressive rate: in fact they are now among the highest in the world (see also Castaldi et al. Chapter 3).

Similarly, the Taiwanese government has been very committed to increasing the country's supply of educated workers. Compulsory education was extended to nine years in 1968, and vocational education and manpower training was strongly promoted from the early 1970s.

The importance of educational policies for catching-up is also confirmed by the Indian case. As shown by Singh (Chapter 11), Indian government intervention in supplying high quality education (especially engineering) has been a fundamental ingredient of its industrial policy. The considerable effort by the government in establishing engineering colleges laid the basis for the export boom of the 1990s in ICT, and also for the establishment of the biotechnology and pharmaceutical industries (see also below).

Similarly, Latin American governments have also tried to support high-skill formation as part of their ISI strategy. Among them the most active was again Brazil. Already in the late 1950s, the Coordenação de Aperfeiçoamento de Pessoal do Ministério da Educação (CAPES) and the la Financiadora de Estudos e Projetos (FINEP) were established to provide scholarships for advanced studies. Yet in most of the countries of the region, research in public universities and laboratories has worked in isolation with respect to the needs and priorities of the private sector (Katz, 2000; Cimoli and Primi, 2004).

From this brief historical overview it is clear that a high-level education system has been a fundamental ingredient for catching-up. Accumulation of physical and human capital turns out to be a necessary if not sufficient condition for growth. It is important to note that successful latecomers have also implemented, in addition to policies directed to increase the general level of education, focused education policies with the objective of building engineering skills. This strategy has been essential for both the *independent* and the *integrationist* models. Indeed, the building-up of domestic technological capabilities obviously calls for heavy investments in higher education. But this is also true for the integrationist model because the acquisition of technology is far from being an easy process: without infrastructural investment in education, training, and domestic R&D, very little can be accomplished through technology imports alone.

The economic signals and incentives profit-motivated agents face: import substitution, trade policies, and openness

Trade policy, affecting the degree of international competition to which firms are exposed, contributes to determining the profitability of different production activities and thus plays an important role in influencing firms' investment decisions. For this reason, such policies have been a key part of the import substitution industrialization (ISI) strategy that has characterized developing countries at least since WWII. In fact, in using trade policy to support industrialization, they did not do anything different from what developed countries did before them. Indeed, Britain was protectionist when it was trying to catch up with Holland. Germany was protectionist when trying to catch up with Britain. The United States was protectionist when trying to catch up with Britain and Germany, and Japan was protectionist for most of the twentieth century up to the 1970s (Wade, 2003).[11] Yet, while there is historical evidence that all now-developed countries were protectionist during their catching-up process, the motivation for using trade policies and their effects are still highly controversial.

At the beginning of the 1950s, protectionism and import substitution were common practices in all developing (and some developed) countries. The idea was to protect the domestic market in order to make it easier for domestic firms to learn, innovate, and grow. Later on countries started differentiating their strategies, with some of them transforming 'protected' sectors into exporting ones. Two elements characterize all the successful examples of sustained export growth. The first is the level of commitment of the government (and of the bureaucracy) to export success. An interesting example of this is South Korea where, under the Park Chung Hee military regime, there were monthly meetings between top government officials (chaired by the President) and leading exporters. Export targets were set at the industry, product, and firm levels by bureaucrats who were also held responsible for the achievement of these export targets in the industries assigned to them, and who obviously had to keep in close touch with exporting enterprises (Rhee et al. 1984). A second fundamental element is the existence of a set of policies and institutions created to mobilize exports. Starting in the 1960s, in all the East Asian Tigers, import substitution policies were usually *coupled* with export promotion policies. Firms were given subsidies and the right to sell in the protected domestic market under the commitment to export. The super-profits earned through selling in the domestic market were then invested in order to create the learning and scale economies necessary to export and thus to acquire new licenses. In South Korea, import protection was high, prolonged, and selective but, at the same time, export performance was used as the disciplinary device for both firms and bureaucrats (Amsden, 1991). In Taiwan, exporters were given preferential tax treatment and access to credit on favorable terms. The government extensively used tariffs and quantitative restrictions in order to direct the sectoral evolution of the economy (Wade, 2003).[12] Export growth was also favored by the provision of long-term investment capital to those import-substituting industries that were expected to become exporters. The commitment of the governments to increase exports is also demonstrated by the creation, during the ISI period, of highly skilled and professional trade promotion centers in all the East Asian Tigers.[13] These institutions played a fundamental role in increasing exports by facilitating SMEs in establishing contacts with foreign buyers and to enter new markets (Lall, 2003).

Also Latin American governments largely used trade policy to promote domestic industrialization during the ISI period. But, differently to what happened in East Asian countries, protectionist policies were not coupled with incentive schemes to promote production efficiency and domestic competition. In particular, in Latin America, the implementation of active export policies has been much more limited. The only partial exception has been Brazil. In fact, starting in the 1960s, the Brazilian government designed a set of export incentives in the form of tax rebates and duty drawbacks and a special program authorized duty-free imports or a firm-specific incentive package in exchange for the commitment to export.

An interesting example of the contrasting effects of trade policies implemented in Latin America is given by the case of the machine tool industry. During the 1960s and 1970s, several Latin American countries attempted to develop a domestic machine tool industry as part of their ISI strategy. Machine tools was considered a strategic industry in that it embodied innovative knowledge with widespread applications. Indeed, after an initial period in which companies were acquiring licenses for foreign technology and designs, own design and engineering have quickly became common among several Latin American producers. But the protectionist polices that were part of the ISI strategy created a number of problems for the users. First, the prices of domestically produced machine tools were higher than world prices. The reason for this was mainly the lack of scale economies and of production specialization. A second (and related) problem was the high costs of components. While domestically produced components were expensive due to a too small scale of production, the imports of foreign ones was made expensive by the high trade barriers (tariffs and quotas) and transport costs. Third, imports were strictly controlled to reduce foreign competition. Even if imported machine tools were locally available, they were normally subjected to an import license. Although licensing requirements varied across countries and over time, they were quite restrictive and normally involved: (i) justification of the purchase; (ii) proof of lack of local production; (iii) a certificate of availability of foreign exchange. The process was extremely complicated, subject to delays and (sometimes) to the approval of local manufacturers, who were afraid of foreign competition. As a result small firms' access to advanced machine tools was extremely limited and only public or multinational firms could acquire foreign equipment (even if not always at the required moment) (Alcorta, 2000).

The historical experiences of East Asian Tigers clearly show that the use of trade protection policies is not per se harmful to growth. On the contrary, one of the keys to the success of those countries has been indeed the selectivity of the country's selection (e.g. opening some markets to international competition while keeping others closed) (Amsden, 1989). In fact, import substitution policies only performed poorly when: (i) they were not complemented by export promoting policies; and (ii) there was no external or internal competition. In particular, protection has resulted in failure when there were no check mechanisms (i.e. competition either at home or abroad, benefits transfers based on some predefined standards, etc.) (Amsden, 2001). Indeed, in some cases, the negative effect of trade policies was simply the result of badly designed measures. There are a number of examples of this in the way Latin American countries implemented the ISI strategy. We have already mentioned that several governments in the region imposed licenses to import capital goods to favor domestic capital goods firms. However, since licenses were granted on the basis of installed capacity, the final effect was an extremely low level of capital utilization. The mismanagement of the exchange rate has been equally harmful. In contrast to the East Asian Tigers, Latin American countries have often adopted a largely over-valued exchange rate. This, by making the import of capital goods cheaper, was a way indirectly to subsidize capital formation and, at the same time, to control inflation. But this strategy had important shortcomings too. First, it greatly penalized export. Second, by favoring imports, it hindered the creation of those (domestic) production linkages that Hirschman (1958) argued were the key to development and that were precisely at the core of the restrictions on imports of capital goods discussed above.

As a matter of fact, it is rather difficult to identify instances of export successes in Latin America and in East Asia (outside raw materials) which did not involve government support at some earlier stage. Among these, the most notable are the establishment of Posco in South Korea, Embraer in Brazil, and the salmon industry in Chile, with the first two being clear examples of import substitution under public ownership and the last one a case of the success of a quasi-public agency acting as a venture fund (Rodrik, 2007). Similarly the now prevailing view that India's growth at the beginning of the 1990s has been induced by the reduction of high import duties and non tariff barriers is very controversial. As argued by Singh (Chapter 11), the growth of the Indian economy started well before the trade and liberalization episode in the 1990s. Instead, industrial polices implemented in the decades before played a fundamental role in creating conditions for the take-off. As the empirical evidence shows, protectionist trade policies alone are (obviously) not sufficient to induce growth, and if they are badly designed can even depress the economy. But combined with other policies, they can be extremely effective. In particular, their positive impact is higher when they are coupled with export policies and targeted technological policies. In any case their main importance rests in the creation of the temporary 'vacuum environment' that is so crucial for infant industries to grow and that is normally enjoyed only by the technological leaders (Dosi, 1988).

Modes of governance and targeted industrial support measures: development banking, credit rationing, and fiscal incentives

Targeted industrial support measures are among the most controversial industrial policies. Criticisms are obviously related to the rent-seeking argument (Krueger, 1985) and to the purported lack of effectiveness of any 'picking winner' strategy (Noland and Pack, 2002). As a matter of fact, during the take-off phase, governments of both developed and developing countries have made large use of targeted measures.

Historically, an important domain of targeted intervention has been discretionary credit lending to specific sectors or firms by development banks (Amsden, 2001).

At different times after WWII, in many developing countries, governments created national development banks with the objective to facilitate the creation and growth of the domestic manufacturing industry through preferential credit. This was nothing new in economic history. Indeed, state-supported development banks had a fundamental role in spurring industrialization for late industrializers in Europe during the nineteenth century (Gerschenkron, 1962).

The development bank was the state's agent for financing private and public investment and a crucial source of long-term lending to industry (Table 5.5). Development banks raised capital at home and abroad using it to lend to domestic firms at below-market interest rates and sometimes to buy equities in private and public firms. Interestingly, their activity showed similar sequence and target criteria in most of the countries. Although targeting

Table 5.5. Share of development banks in total manufacturing investments, 1970–1990

	1970	1980	1990
Brazil (BNDES)	11.0	18.7	18.1
India (AIFIs)	7.6	16.8	26.0
South Korea (Korea Development Bank)	44.7	10.1	15.3
Mexico (NAFINSA)	35.5	11.4	10.3

Source: Amsden (2001) based on National Development Banks data.

criteria varied across countries, the most common ones were: (i) the presence of a large backward and forward linkage effect; (ii) high market potential; (iii) high technology intensity; (iv) high-value added.[14]

In the case of the East Asian Tigers, development bank loans were usually conditioned on the fulfillment of some requirements that were firm-specific and included in the client's contract. One of the most used conditions for loans was the local content rule for the inputs used (Shapiro, 1989). This condition aimed at: (i) inducing domestic firms to develop their own technology and to source local engineers and machinery; (ii) facilitating the establishment and growth of national firms; (iii) enriching the technological content of domestic production; (iv) saving foreign exchange. Development banks also played a crucial role in supporting the process of technological accumulation (reserving special funds to finance programs for technological development) and the country's effort to increase exports (giving exporting firms access to *long-term subsidized capital*).

Governments largely used development banks to condition the firms' behavior. This attitude was particularly clear and also effective in South Korea. In the 1960s, the South Korean military regime nationalized all banks, giving the state control of all financial flows and thus of all investment decisions in the economy. In addition, the regime started tightly to control foreign exchange, foreign loans, and foreign direct investments. Investment subsidies were mainly given under two forms: (i) loans at negative real interest rates; and (ii) direct subsidies. The government subsidized investments also through the socialization of risk: entrepreneurs were induced to enter new strategic sectors by the guarantee that the state would bail them out in case the business was not profitable (Rodrik, 1995a).[15] Finally, the government also introduced extensive tax incentives for the selected industries.

The Taiwanese government too made widespread use of subsidized and direct credit (Amsden, 2001). But, unlike in the South Korean case, the government did not promote giant conglomerates or the entry of domestic firms into heavy industries. On the contrary, since the Taiwanese economy was characterized by a large number of medium-sized and small firms, the development bank's intervention took the form of credit for technology adoption and innovation (Lall, 2003). Taiwan also had a very effective fiscal incentive program (Statute for Encouragement of Investments, SEI), under which participating firms could choose either tax exemption or accelerated depreciation on capital equipment. The SEI ran from 1961 to 1990, available to both domestic and foreign firms, with the targeted industries changing during the decades: all exporting sectors (1960s), capital-intensive sectors (1970s), technology intensive sectors (1980s).

The role and effectiveness of development banks' activities in Latin America have been much more heterogeneous than in the case of the East Asian Tigers. At the two extremes one finds Brazil and Argentina, with the Chilean experience in the middle. The Brazilian national development bank (Banco Nacional de Desenvolvimiento Economico e Social, BNDES) played a central role in the country's development process. As in the case of the East Asian Tigers, the government's main objective was to create a domestic industry, but an additional constraint was present. The BNDES had to achieve this result while preventing, at best, economic concentration from increasing, in a country where income distribution was already highly unequal, the consequence being the unwillingness to create national manufacturing champions (Amsden, 2001). BNDES activity has been important for financing Brazilian firms entering strategic heavy industries (e.g. the aircraft and space industry, communications). In Chile, a similar role has been played by CORFO (Corporacion de Fomento de la Produccion); during the 1950s and 1960s it financed both public and private investments in different sectors (in particular machinery and equipment). The CORFO programs allowed the creation of the industrial production structure and facilitated the investment in human capital formation and innovation. Even though these programs were clearly effective, the neo-liberal structural reforms by the military regime after the *coup d'état* in 1973 drastically reduced CORFO's role and the number of sectoral interventions (Cimoli and Di Maio, 2004). Argentina, on the other hand, represents the example of a total failure. Created in the 1940s and active until 1977 when financial reform was introduced, the national development bank (often) granted loans at negative interest rates following the directives of government economic policy (see also Kosacoff and Ramos, Chapter 9). Yet the development bank has never really contributed to the development process because of a lack of any coherent industrial strategy and also because of mismanagement and corruption (Lewis, 1990).

Governments used development banks to direct the evolution of economic activity. However, in many cases, government intervention has been even more pervasive. The cases of Korea and India are the most noteworthy in this sense. In South Korea, the government tightly controlled economic activity through price ceilings and controls on capital movements. The government also used a large set of tax exemptions and government subsidies to direct investment activity in selected 'strategic' sectors (Amsden, 1991). As in South Korea (and China), so also in the case of India the government played a central role in guiding the industrialization process. Since the end of World War II, the government has tried to guide industrial development through centralized planning, meant to facilitate coordination of decisions in both the public and the private sectors,[16] and a large number of industrial policy measures, such as protecting and/or subsidizing some industries and investment (Possas and Borges, Chapter 17).

The concession of credit at favorable conditions to targeted sectors and firms has been an essential piece of the developmental state's toolbox, but development banks' activities have been characterized by a very different level of effectiveness. International historical comparisons show that bank performance depended on: (i) the presence, or lack thereof, of some form of conditionality on the loans; (ii) the ability of the bureaucracy to control and direct firms' behavior; (iii) the lack of corruption of the bureaucracy itself. With few exceptions, in Latin America control mechanisms or conditionality rules were in most cases lacking, while in East Asia they were always present. This is one important difference explaining the diversity in the contribution of development banks to the growth process of the countries in the two regions. In the next section we describe other complementary explanations to the differing impacts of similar industrial policies in Latin America and East Asia.

Evaluating industrial polices under the Developmental State

Though still dominant in the profession, the market-fundamentalist view arguing against any industrial policy is now challenged by an increasing number of contributions showing that government intervention has been much more effective than the orthodox account suggests. It is interesting in this regard to consider the way in which the discipline has analyzed the impressive economic performances of the East Asian Tigers. For a long time their economic success has been described as the 'natural' effect of correctly implemented export-led growth strategies (Krueger, 1985; World Bank, 1993). The orthodox account focused, in particular, on the change in policies that took place between the mid-1950s and the 1960s in South Korea and Taiwan. In effect, at the end of the 1950s, when the first stage of import substitution strategy was already exhausted, governments in both countries started to implement polices aiming at inducing export growth (e.g. unification of exchange rates, a partial liberalization of the import regime, etc.). Thus the export boom that took place in the mid-1960s has been interpreted as the consequence of such policy change and of the fact that the countries had specialized according to their (static) comparative advantages. It is evident that in this account the role of the state in the development process is very marginal. The government supposedly only set the new rules favoring export and allowed the markets to work freely: then, automatically, the economy took off (Krueger, 1990). In fact the causal relationship between export and investments (and growth) has been the other way around, with the government playing the leading role. Rodrik (1995a) presents convincing evidence that in both the South Korean and the Taiwanese cases, exports followed investment growth. Export growth was a *consequence*, a forced response, to the increase of the demand for imported capital goods triggered by the investment boom, in turn induced by governments which implemented a wide range of industrial policies aimed to overcome the (investment) coordination failures and to induce entrepreneurs to invest in new strategic industries.

The orthodox view is also contradicted by the historical evidence that in the period following WWII, if not earlier, governments all around the world have largely used trade policies, subsidies, public enterprises, direct credit allocation as instruments to *shape* comparative advantages and to guide investments and industrialization, obtaining, in quite a few cases, remarkable results (Amsden, 1989, 2001; Wade, 2003). In particular, even if the orthodox view argues that *good* selectivity is impossible (see e.g. Noland and Pack, 2002), there are a number of cases showing that the *picking winners strategy* may work. For example, in the 1960s the Taiwanese government hired the Stanford Research Institute to identify promising industries in order to promote them using trade and industrial policies. In most of them, Taiwan is now a world leader. To explain why this strategy has been successful, Amsden (2001) correctly points out that, contrary to the orthodox view, the picking winners strategy is indeed simple because, in the case of latecomers, the information requirement for implementing it is relatively small. To select the *right* sector thus it would be sufficient to see what developed countries have already done and (creatively) imitate them. Moreover, as we have seen, in most cases governments have also *created* winners using mainly two instruments. First, they allowed the possibility of borrowing (and copying) more advanced technologies from abroad, eliminating the high sunk costs related to discovery and innovation. Second, government intervention (i.e. in the form of subsidies) offered the *additional* incentives that firms in developing countries needed in order to adopt new technologies. The final result has often been that, because of lower labor costs (and sometimes higher availability of raw materials), developing countries' firms have ended up producing at lower costs than their competitors in developed countries. Actually, as Rodrik (2007) points out, the performance of countries that in their recent economic history have made large use of industrial policies is much less disappointing than usually argued by the conventional wisdom.

Still, why did (apparently) similar industrial policies produce such different results in the East Asian Tigers and in Latin America? It is by now a shared view that the recipe for the success of the East Asian Tigers has been the effective combination of incentives with discipline (Amsden, 2001; Hausmann and Rodrik, 2003). Incentives were provided through subsidies and protection, while discipline was obtained through direct government control and the use of export performance as a selection and monitoring device for both the entrepreneurs and the bureaucrats. The failure of the Latin American experience lies precisely in the lack of the joint presence of these two elements. Indeed, during the ISI period Latin American firms received considerable incentives, but faced very little discipline. The mistake has been to ignore efficiency considerations and to assume away capability problems. The assumption was that the necessary capabilities were already available within the country, or, in case of necessity, they would be created automatically and without extra cost (Cimoli et al. 2004). This is certainly an important difference between the two models but it is not the only one.

According to Lall (2003), the East Asian Tigers' model was also based on: (i) strict selectivity and time limitation of government intervention; (ii) the use of public enterprises to enter risky sectors (for limited periods); (iii) massive investment in skill creation and technological and physical infrastructure building; (iv) the centralization of strategic industrial decisions in competent authorities; and (v) a highly selective use of FDI.

There are two further features about the East Asian Tigers' model that are important in order to understand its success. First, governments have provided stable and predictable incentive frameworks that have favored investments. Second, governments have kept a close and continuous dialogue with the private sector, and, most importantly, they were 'strong' (Chang, 1994). Indeed, as in all the other developing countries where they have been implemented, industrial policies in the East Asian Tigers did create inefficient firms too. But, unlike what happened elsewhere (e.g. in many Latin American countries), the state was able to withdraw support whenever firms' performance was not satisfactory and imposed exporting performance and fierce competition in domestic markets as selecting devices for firms to be targeted (Westphal, 1990).

The Latin American model, on the other hand, was characterized by: (i) an 'anti-export' biased version of the ISI strategy; (ii) the lack of clear performance criteria to evaluate the policies implemented; (iii) the inexperience and inability of civil servants to implement the different policies; (iv) a lower (with respect to the East Asian Tigers) expenditure in education and S&T as a share of GDP. Brazil is an exception on many grounds but not with regards to its educational policies.

A particularly important element that differentiates the Latin American countries with respect to the East Asian Tigers concerns science and technology policies implemented after WWII. In fact, the evaluation of the effects of government intervention on innovation during the ISI period in Latin America shows mixed results. While there are a number of case and country studies showing a positive effect of industrial policies on the accumulation process of technological capabilities in the region (Katz and Kosacoff, 1998), the innovative apparatus built around public intervention that started to take form during the ISI period has never become, contrary to expectations, the engine of growth. There are three main reasons for that. First, governments in the region have always considered increasing foreign investment the most effective innovation policy. Second, Latin American national innovation systems (that have been predominantly built around public firms and public research institutes) have never been able to create strong cooperative links with the private sector. On the one hand, the public centers have been increasingly characterized by a bureaucratic production of knowledge: in particular knowledge transfer to local firms was not a priority at all (Katz, 2000). On the other hand, technology policies have never been effective because of the lack of any control mechanism. Since micro economic conduct was not regulated, Latin American firms did not respond to government incentives designed to induce the adoption of technology produced by public research institutes. Third, as we have seen, the Latin American version of the ISI strategy was characterized by high trade protection. This protectionist environment, coupled with ill-conceived technology policies, favored the emergence of a multitude of small and medium-sized firms producing products well below the international standard. In these firms, in many cases, capital goods were second hand, most of the instruments were homemade, and the organization of production was rudimentary (Katz, 1987). The East Asian experiences show, on the contrary, the positive effects of a direct and extensive government intervention in the technological domain. In particular, the effectiveness of the implemented policies is witnessed by the high technological dynamism that has characterized the East Asian Tigers starting from the 1960s and by the continuous increase in the number of firms producing technologically complex products and competing in the world market (Kim and Nelson, 2000).

All this said, a question remains: *Why was it possible* to implement growth-friendly industrial policies in the East Asian Tigers and not elsewhere? There are three crucial differences between the East Asian Tigers and Latin American countries that have made (and still make) the former more industrialization-oriented. First, in the East Asian Tigers there was no opposition to social change coming from the traditional land-owning class, which, on the contrary, was extremely powerful in Latin American countries. Second, East Asian Tigers were characterized by a more equal distribution of income that allowed the rapid expansion of domestic markets without reducing the savings rate. Finally, the *direct* economic power of the state in the East Asian Tigers was substantial, with the government controlling strategic inputs, banks, and industries (e.g. through state-owned enterprises) while keeping a grip on firms' behavior. The situation was completely different in Latin America where financial interests (and the landed class) *controlled* the state and not vice versa. The final outcome of this was the establishment of a rentier attitude of the capitalist class.[17]

'New' industrial policies in a neo-liberal world

The 'old' policies and the 'new' world

The industrial policy toolbox of the developmental state was severely attacked starting from the mid-1970s. On one hand, on the 'rhetorical' side, an increasing number of theoretical arguments showing the negative effects of industrial (and in particular trade) policies in developing countries made the case for policy reform increasingly louder (Rodrik, 1995b). On the other, two 'real world' events forced governments deeply to modify their use. The first one was the explosion of foreign debt and the consequent 1982 debt crisis. The second was the proliferation of multilateral, regional, and bilateral trade agreements that, to a large extent, limited the scope for government intervention. In particular, the multilateral agreements progressively obliged countries to reduce tariff and non-tariff barriers to trade. In addition, the new WTO rules have also restricted the use of both selective subsidies and safeguards. I shall briefly consider these in turn.[18]

The use of selective subsidies has been severely limited by the new WTO agreements. Export subsidies (also in the form of the creation of export processing zones, EPZs) and subsidies for the use of domestic (rather than imported) inputs is now prohibited.[19] Local content requirements and quantitative restrictions on imports are now banned. As we have seen, export promotion policies have been a fundamental instrument of industrial policy during the developmental state era, even if their effects in terms of induced technological spillovers are somewhat controversial (Rodrik, 2004). In any case, the WTO rules still allow the use of trade policy interventions in the form of selective subsidies to promote (i) domestic R&D; (ii) regional development; (iii) environment friendly activities.

The WTO, like the GATT, enables members to use safeguard measures to protect themselves only in two cases: (i) when imports can destabilize their balance of payments (*Article XVIII*); and (ii) when foreign competition threatens a specific industry, due to an import surge (*Article XIX* on temporary safeguards) or an unfair trade practice (*Article VI* on anti-dumping and countervailing duties). The novelty is that WTO rules strictly limit the duration of safeguards to a maximum of eight years. The imposition of a time limit to the use of safeguards is coherent with the attempt to make trade policies as transparent as possible. For the same reason the WTO rules have forbidden the use of voluntary export restraints. The new WTO rules still give countries chances to promote and select strategic sectors: a good deal of discretionary power is left to governments in promoting science and technology activities, in particular by subsidizing private and public R&D and giving firms incentives to locate in 'science parks'. In effect, Rodrik (2004) argues that in fact the most serious obstacle to implementing industrial policies comes from bilateral agreements with the US in which developing countries 'voluntarily' relinquish a relevant part of their policy autonomy. The US is also responsible for the extension of the Uruguay Round to trade in services, which includes foreign investment. In the interest of developed countries, the TRIPS agreement has been designed to protect rather than liberalize the access to proprietary know-how. The effect is greater difficulty in employing the strategies of reverse engineering and copying that have been so important during the developmental state period (see e.g. the South Korean case) (Amsden, 2000). This hinders possibilities to catch up for developing countries at least in some sectors (Nelson, 2004; Cimoli, Coriat, and Primi, Chapter 19). Yet, some good news may come from new regional and multi-regional trade agreements if they become opportunities to implement larger industrial policy plans (see e.g. the Mercosur experience in the automotive sector, Rodrik, 2004).

New policies: a regional overview

A closer look at the current behavior of developing countries' governments shows that industrial policy and direct state intervention have far from disappeared. They have changed names and sometimes content, but they are still there. Let us briefly discuss the characteristics of the most important industrial policies as they have been implemented in Latin America and in the East Asian NICs in the last two decades.

LATIN AMERICA

Three common elements are found in most of the official documents describing governments' plans for industrial development in the region produced in the last 15 years. First, they are clearly designed to take into explicit consideration the characteristics of the new international scenario and the new WTO rules, especially concerning direct subsidies and trade protection. Second, they are characterized by a certain degree of national experimentation, with governments trying to find original ways to stimulate innovation in the region. Third, one of the governments' objectives is (still) to modify the current international division of labor, attempting to increase manufacturing exports and decrease countries' dependence on primary-sector related exports (Peres, 2002).

In general, it is possible to point out a (partial) abandonment of the ISI philosophy of discretionary industrialization policies in favor of horizontal policies. Among these, an important novelty is the introduction of competition policies to create a more competitive and efficient market context (see Possas and Borges, Chapter 17). These policies were generally part of the reform package Latin American countries introduced in the 1980s, after the debt crisis, as part of the requirements of the international institutions, that is, the World Bank and the IMF. Yet, most of these competition regulations have not been fully implemented.

As a matter of fact, despite the official declarations, in the last decade there has been a revival of industrial policy by Latin American governments (more on this in Peres, Chapter 7). This is clearly witnessed by the proliferation of new programs to increase exports, productivity, and outputs but also innovation capabilities and diversification of production.

There are two main characteristics of the set of industrial policies that are currently employed by Latin American countries. First, tax incentives are used only marginally. The reason for this is that they are seen as both sources of distortion in resource allocation (whatever this means) and contributing factors to recurrent fiscal imbalances, with their sequel of macroeconomic destabilization (Melo, 2001). Second, in the last two decades, industrial policies have (primarily) been *competitiveness policies*: the aim has been to increase production efficiency and thus the shares in the world market of existing sectors rather than the entry into new activities.

In the last two decades governments in the region have dedicated a lot of effort to designing effective export promotion policies. This aim has been mainly pursued through international trade negotiations to obtain access to *new markets* and the design of a number of policies directed to attract FDI (ECLAC, 2004). In order to attract MNCs with the objective of increasing exports three sets of instruments have been used (Mortimore and Peres, 1998). First, a number of governments have created export processing zones (EPZs) and *maquiladoras* and have also provided tax breaks and incentives for foreign investors. In some cases, these measures are also coupled with special trade agreements. In Ecuador, for example the *maquila* sector operates under a special tax regime and benefits from trade preferences granted by the US.[20] Second, there has been an attempt to build a more efficient market environment (better law enforcement, amelioration of the physical infrastructure to reduce the country's distance from world markets, etc.) in order to induce MNCs to invest in the country. Third, in the same vein, governments have tried to increase the supply of skilled workers. In fact, MNCs have been attracted mostly by offering them the possibility to exploit the host country's natural resources (Peres, 1998).

Governments have also provided export promotion policies for domestic producers. These can be classified into three categories: (i) policies that affect the availability and/or cost of credit; (ii) fiscal incentives; and (iii) provision of non-financial services to exporters. As Tables 5.6 and 5.7 show, there is by now no shortage of incentives to increase exports, and each country has its own package. What are the results of this large effort? In fact, results are highly disappointing as these activities did not generate the positive externalities and the spillovers they were supposed to produce.[21] Thus, according to Rodrik (2004), given the available evidence, it would be fair to say that subsidizing foreign investors with the objective of increasing exports is, in most cases, a 'silly policy' because it results in transfers from poor country taxpayers to rich country shareholders.

Besides exports, governments have tried also to increase their country's aggregate output. Table 5.8 reports the set of policies used by governments to increase the production capacity of each economy (i.e. policies intended not to change the composition of output but 'just' to increase it). Both horizontal

Table 5.6. Financial incentives to export

	Tax refund scheme	Drawback schemes	Temporary admission schemes	EPZ
Argentina	X	X	X	X
Bolivia	X	X	X	X
Brazil	X	X	X	X
Chile	X	X		
Colombia	X	X	X	X
Costa Rica		X	X	X
Ecuador		X	X	X
Mexico	X	X	X	X
Peru	X	X		
Uruguay	X	X	X	X
Venezuela	X	X	X	X

Source: adapted from Melo (2001).

Table 5.7. Fiscal incentives to export

	Credit export agency	Export credit line in the Development Bank	Export credit insurance	Loan working capital	Finance for entire investment	Finance for Marketing	Buyer's credit
Argentina	X		X	X	X	X	X
Bolivia							
Brazil		X	X	X			X
Chile		X		X		X	X
Colombia	X		X	X		X	X
Costa Rica				X			
Ecuador			X	X			
Mexico	X	X	X	X	X	X	X
Peru		X		X			
Uruguay		X	X	X			
Venezuela	X		X	X			X

Source: adapted from Melo (2001).

and sectorally targeted policies are present. For instance, in addition to horizontal credit policies, several countries have special credit lines favoring particular sectors and/or regions within the country. In general, it is interesting to note that, while during the ISI period, the favorite target of any policy was the manufacturing sector, interventions are now mainly directed to the primary sector and to tourism.[22] Moreover, while horizontal tax incentives are not very diffused, tax incentives for particular regions or sectors are widely used (Rodrik, 2007).[23]

In most countries, policies to support small and medium-sized enterprises (SMEs) have been the main component of the competitiveness policies pursued by governments in the last decade. This is so because SMEs have been

Table 5.8. Industrial policies in support of production and investment—Latin America

	Loans to specific sectors	Credit program particular regions	Tax incentives specific sectors	Tax incentives particular regions
Argentina	X	X	X	
Brazil	X	X		X
Bolivia			X	
Chile		X	X	X
Colombia	X	X		X
Costa Rica			X	
Ecuador			X	
Mexico	X		X	X
Peru			X	X
Uruguay			X	
Venezuela			X	

Source: adapted from Melo (2001).

deemed to become the engine of growth. For this reason, several national development banks have created specific credit lines for smaller firms. For instance, the Mexican industrial development bank Nacional Financiera (NAFIN) has played a fundamental role in supporting and financing SMEs in Mexico after its entry into the NAFTA. While all countries in the region have introduced in one form or the other some policy to support SMEs, differences are found both concerning the total amount of resources devoted to them and the design and coordination capabilities of the institutions devoted to their implementation. During the 1990s, a number of new programs[24] were initiated, with some of them obtaining significant results. The primary novelty of these programs was the attempt to create and strengthen the linkages between SMEs and larger firms and to induce cooperation among SMEs in order to reduce some of the sunk costs that characterize access to export activity. One important limitation concerns the still low organizational and institutional capabilities of the agencies, with the notable exceptions of SEBRAE[25] in Brazil and CORFO in Chile. Indeed, in less advanced countries, programs are mostly one-shot and in many cases totally dependent on the availability of foreign aid for implementation.[26]

The design and implementation of policies to promote technological modernization have been one of the primary concerns of the governments in the region during the last two decades. National Science and Technology Councils, Agencies, and Technology Programs to foster science and technology activities by domestic firms are now present in all countries. However, there are considerable differences among countries in terms of magnitude of administered budgets, objectives, and mix of horizontal and selective policies employed (Cimoli et al. 2004). There are also notable differences concerning the financial instruments used. Resources to finance S&T activities are usually channeled through 'technology funds'. In some cases, technology funds are meant to create and strengthen a technological service market while in other cases they aim to coordinate innovation activity at the sectoral level. An example of the first approach is the Argentinean Fondo Tecnologico (FONTAR) that has, for example, a dedicated fund to support the technology development of SMEs through technology import and technology consultancy.[27] The Brazilian case represents the main example of the second type of funds. In fact, the Brazilian program is currently the best articulated and most ambitious technology program of the region. It groups sectors into two classes: the first group includes those sectors in which the country has already developed some technological capability, that is, information technology and automation; aerospace technology; nuclear technology; and agriculture; and the second group consists of sectors where Brazil's technological knowledge is still very low, that is, optical electronics and biotechnology. While the policies for the first group are intended to induce firms to make private investments, for the second one the main policy is the creation of publicly funded 'research centers of excellence' devoted to basic and applied research (Cimoli and Primi, 2004).

Governments in the region still also used (traditional) fiscal incentives as policy instruments to support innovation. In the 1990s, fiscal incentive schemes essentially took the form of: (i) tax credits and deductions for different types of R&D activities according to the categories of actors involved, or (ii) public development bank loans. While there are some programs providing risk capital, this instrument is still marginal in the technology development strategy of the governments in the region.

In most countries, technology policies are now usually complemented by programs for human-resource development. Important examples in this sense are the Mexican program to financially support firms retraining their workers and managers, and the Brazilian government program offering training to highly qualified professionals.[28] In the same vein, regional S&T policies are increasingly directed to facilitate interaction and coordination between the public sector (mainly universities and research laboratories) and the private one in the R&D activity and technological upgrading. In Uruguay, for instance, a public–private partnership in seed development through the Instituto Nacional de Investigacion Agropecuaria turned out to be extremely successful (Rodrik, 2007). Still, these efforts did not seem to have significantly increased the technological accumulation capabilities of domestic firms in most of the countries. This is most probably due to the mismatch between demand and supply of technological knowledge which hampers the impact of technology policies in the region (Cimoli and Primi, 2004).

While there are few doubts that policies' design has improved in the last decades, there are still substantial problems concerning the implementation process and also its evaluation (see Peres, Chapter 7). As the past experience of East Asian NICs suggests, a fundamental element for successful industrial policies is indeed the possibility to evaluate *both* (i) (how good has been) the process of implementation of a specific policy and (ii) the results obtained. From both points of view, many Latin American programs are (still) highly disappointing. In addition, since the economic signals these policies send to the private sector are much 'weaker' than the protectionist policies of the ISI period, there is much more uncertainty about their functioning. The final result is that the enterprisers do not 'believe' the incentive system of the new policies and do not exploit their possibilities for development (Peres, 2002).

Even if rigorous evaluation is still missing, some good news comes from anecdotal evidence about encouraging experiments of cooperation between the government and the entrepreneurs concerning the design and sometimes also the implementation of industrial policies. This is the case of Uruguay, where the public sector has played an identifiable and important role in providing key inputs and support for inducing private investment in a number of new economic activities (Rodrik, 2007). In some cases the entrepreneurial association has also taken the lead in making policy proposals (i.e. Colombia and Mexico). Peres (2002) considers this trend to be positive because it goes in the direction of a co-responsible attitude of government and private agents. On the contrary, apart from very few exceptions, workers unions and the academic community still do not take part in the policy design or implementation processes.

EAST ASIAN NEWLY INDUSTRIALIZED COUNTRIES (NICs)

During the last two decades, governments' interventions in NICs in East Asia have focused on the achievement of two main objectives. First, to induce domestic firms to enlarge their scale of production. Second, to foster innovation and knowledge accumulation. Both objectives have been pursued implementing a combination of old and new industrial policies.

In recent years, governments in the region have constantly induced, by using a number of different incentives and laws, domestic firms to become bigger, with the idea that size matters for competing at world level. With this objective in the 1990s, the South Korean government forced some of the biggest business firms to merge and to acquire each other's subsidiaries. In exchange, *chaebols* received extensive tax benefits and financial support. Partially to counterbalance this concentration process, the government has also started promoting high-technology small firms through the creation of dedicated credit lines by local and regional banks and the establishment of a venture capital industry. The small scale problem is more acute in the Taiwanese economy, which is still characterized by the preponderance of small and medium-sized enterprises. To cope, the Taiwanese government guided the restructuring of the domestic economy providing direct subsidies and incentives for the creation of cooperation agreements between firms. Starting from the second half of the 1990s, the Chinese government, like the South Korean one, also adopted policies to increase national firms' size inducing domestic mergers and acquisitions and the reorganization of different industries, in particular petrochemicals, steel, automobiles, and the consumer goods industries (Amsden, 2001). In fact, the government's attempt to favor the growth of domestic firms is pursued also in countries where antitrust law has been formally introduced. For instance, in India the new antitrust law gives the Competition Commission a strong discretionary power in deciding whether to act against anti-competitive behavior by domestic firms and concerning the criteria for determining whether mergers and acquisitions have adverse effects on competition.[29]

During the last two decades, governments have also made a strong effort to increase countries' knowledge assets. The results have been impressive. In most of the countries in the region both the GDP share of science and technology investments and the share of R&D spending in the manufacturing sector have substantially increased. In addition, differently from what happened in Latin America, the private sector share in R&D has also significantly increased, reaching in the cases of South Korean and Taiwanese levels comparable with those in the US and Japan. These results have been the effect of the combination of a number of policies. First, starting from the 1980s, governments in the region have gradually liberalized their technology transfer policies. This has increased the number of collaborations between domestic and foreign firms. Second, during the 1990s, governments' promotion of high-tech sectors changed also in response to the strengthening of the IPR regime that has reduced the possibility of imitative reverse engineering. In the last two decades, the South Korean government has strongly funded the R&D activity of both large and small domestic firms.[30] The government has also launched an ambitious Highly Advanced R&D Project to support 11 selected R&D research projects by domestic firms. In addition the government, through the Korean Development Bank, has provided loans with low interest rates and guarantees for technology loans to SMEs (Lall, 2000). At the same time the South Korean government has reorganized its numerous programs to foster innovation creating a unique national innovation master plan. The focus of the industrial policies has shifted from the promotion of strategic industries to the support and development of strategic activities within sectors, in particular innovation-related ones. In general the private sector has taken up a larger role. With broadly the same objectives, the Taiwanese government increased the number of science parks but restricted the admission criteria.[31] In addition, in order to overcome the scale problem concerning R&D and technology investments for SMEs, the government has supported the creation of *R&D consortia* (Mathews, 2002). These have proved to be one of the most successful and distinctive tools of industrial policy used recently in Taiwan. Most of these consortia are in the information technology sectors but they have also emerged in automotive engines, motor cycles, electric vehicles, and now in the services and financial sector as well.

Together educational and skill formation policies have been strengthened. The South Korean government, in order to support knowledge accumulation and the process of technological upgrading, has strongly invested in higher education transforming a number of universities into research-oriented schools and establishing the Science and Research Centers and Engineering Research Centers (Kim, 1999). In Singapore, the government has largely financed tertiary education and the creation of links between the academy and industry. In particular, the government finances a number of industrial training courses, some run by MNCs, some jointly with foreign governments. A Skill Development Fund to fund the full cost of training by SMEs was introduced beside a scheme of subsidies to large firms for providing training to low-skilled workers. Finally, the government complements these policies with a free entry policy towards skilled expatriates (Lall, 2003). Starting from the 1990s, the Indian government has financed the creation of 'centers of excellence' in order to make available well-prepared professional technicians for national firms in strategic sectors. In addition, the legislation concerning technology production was modified in order to make it more profitable for private firms to engage in R&D. In particular, the software and services industries have received support from the government (Singh, Chapter 11) both in the form of tax incentives and of specific incentive measures. That has proved to be quite effective in favoring the development of these industries and their export growth. There is now no doubt that these industrial policies, albeit of a new form, have been necessary to allow these industries to be competitive at the world level in the new scenario of globalization and liberalization of markets.

Similarly, the Chinese government has heavily invested in domestic human capital accumulation. In the mid-1990s, the Chinese State Planning Commission announced the creation of approximately 100 national laboratories in selected fields of basic science in which Chinese capabilities already excelled (Amsden, 2000). In the last two decades, the government has made a large effort to design and implement policies and programs to support innovation. The instruments used spanned from tax breaks and subsidized credit to the creation of science parks and national R&D projects. Targeted industries were given tax breaks and loans at favorable conditions from state banks. But the biggest innovation has been the creation of the Science and Technology (S&T) enterprises (Lu, 1997). Although these enterprises were nominally independent, the government forced them to meet a number of requirements including the percentage of technology personnel, the percentage of sales brought in by new products, and the percentage of products exported. This, admittedly, sounds quite 'old-fashioned' and not very orthodox. But, till now, it has shown to be quite successful: isn't there a lesson to be learned from this?

While the rules of the game have changed, governments in the region have clearly not abandoned industrial policies within the broader objective of guiding economic development (Table 5.9). Even the Singapore government,

Table 5.9. Industrial policies in support of production and investment—East Asian NICs

	Loans to specific sectors	Credit program particular regions	Tax incentives specific sectors	Tax incentives particular regions
India	X	X	X	X
China	X	X	X	X
Malaysia	X	X	X	X
South Korea	X	X	X	X
Taiwan	X	X	X	X

Source: adapted from Rodrik (2004) and Lall (2003).

one of the most market friendly of the region, has centralized the management of industrial policy and FDI targeting in the efficient Economic Development Board (EDB), part of the Ministry of Trade and Industry (MTI) that gives overall strategic direction. The government undertakes periodic competitiveness studies to chart the industrial evolution and upgrading of the economy, and adjusts the design strategy to improve the country's competitiveness. Since its 1991 Strategic Economic Plan, the government has focused its strategy around *industrial clusters*. The public sector, among other roles, still plays a catalytic one by setting up R&D laboratories. The public sector strictly cooperates with the private sector and the MNCs, which, unlike in most other countries are actively involved in the strategy formulation process. Also the survival of the Planning Commission in India demonstrated continuity in the process of defining a national industrial development program. While less intervention-ist with respect to the Developmental State period, the Indian government still plays a fundamental role in coordinating investment activities and promoting some specific sectors.

Conclusion

All the currently rich countries have in their past made large use of a variety of industrial policies in order to induce structural change and growth. The same has been done by more recent *latecomers* during their development process in the last 50 years. This chapter has described these policies and their effects with a particular focus on the Latin American countries and East Asian Tigers' experiences since the end of WWII. By way of a conclusion, the main findings of the chapter could be summarized as follows. First, the historical and empirical evidence here reviewed clearly shows that industrial policies are necessary for take-off and long-run growth. Second, the degree of effectiveness of industrial policies varies a lot.

In the search for effective industrial policies, there are important lessons to be learned from the historical experience of *latecomers*. In particular, even acknowledging that each country has specific initial structural and socio-economic conditions and that the rules of the game have changed a lot in the last decades, it is still possible to identify some stylized facts that should be taken into consideration when designing industrial policies. First, as recent empirical evidence convincingly demonstrates, trade liberalization, contrary to the orthodox view, is not a *panacea*. Instead, the most effective policies in spurring growth seem to be the ones directed to support investments in education and innovation. Second, selective-targeted policies need to be accompanied by *some* form of control mechanism. Third, there are no ready-to-wear policies. On the contrary, experimentation and innovation are essential ingredients in the process of figuring out how to make government interventions and industrial policies growth enhancing. Four, 'initial' conditions and comparative advantages can be (and historically have been) created. If this is the objective, then, there are few doubts that a leading role in this process must be played by a strong educational system and by public research centers (Mazzoleni and Nelson, Chapter 14). Thus, the main challenge for developing countries is to identify which characteristics their public research system should have in order to contribute to the increase of firms' learning and innovation performance. This is not an easy task and it is not a short process but this is not surprising. As emphasized by Freeman (2004), only adopting a very *long-term* view in designing and applying industrial policies, well beyond current market signals, is it possible to create a sustained growth process.

Notes

1. For a long-term historical account of different modes of government interventions see Reinert (Chapter 4).
2. The Brazilian National Council for Scientific and Technical Development (CNPq) was established in 1951, the Argentinean National Council for Scientific and Technical Research (CONICET) in 1958, and the Mexican National Council for Science and Technology (CONACYT) in 1970 (Cimoli and Primi, 2004).
3. These countries were Bolivia, Colombia, Ecuador, Peru, and Venezuela.
4. The required average local content share varied from 90% to 95% of the value (Shapiro, 1989).
5. In 1987, the first Volkswagen model totally constructed in Brazil entered the US market.
6. As noted by Mazzoleni and Nelson (Chapter 14) this was also a way to mitigate the brain drain problem. See below.
7. South Korea, Taiwan, China, India.
8. Indonesia, Malaysia, Thailand, Argentina, Brazil, Chile, Mexico, Turkey.
9. On the evolution of the education system in Japan since the nineteenth century see Mazzoleni and Nelson, Chapter 14.

10. For a thorough discussion on the role of education polices in the development process in East Asian countries see, Ashton et al. (1999).

11. As List put it: 'In order to allow freedom of trade to operate naturally, the less advanced nation [read, Germany] must first be raised by artificial measures to that stage of cultivation to which the English nation has been artificially elevated' [cited by Wade, 2003].

12. Note that the conclusions of Wade (2003) are in open contrast with Little's (1979) classical study where Taiwan's exceptional growth performance was primarily attributed to a low level of trade protection, the availability to exporters of inputs at international prices, and a conservative macroeconomic policy.

13. The Hong Kong Trade Development Council (HKTDC), the Korean Trade Promotion Council (KOTRA), Taiwan's China External Trade Development Council (CETDC), and the Singapore Trade Development Board (SRDB) were all established at the beginning of the 1970s.

14. In this respect India was an exception: the criteria were much more political. Indeed, the government favoured small firms, regardless of the sector of activity.

15. A classical example of this type of government intervention is the entry of Hyundai in the shipbuilding industry, see Amsden (1989).

16. For instance, the 1951 Industrial Development and Regulation Act (still in force) empowers the state to control the direction and pattern of public and private investments, as well as to bring strategic industries and firms under public ownership Chakravarthy (2004).

17. This interpretation of the different results of industrial policy in South Asia and Latin America largely overlaps with an explanation, based on the political economy of growth, pursued by Khan and Blankenburg (Chapter 13).

18. For a thorough discussion of the implications of the new WTO rules see Akyüz (Chapter 6).

19. Export subsidies are still allowed for countries with per-capita income $\leq$ $1,000.

20. As noted by Rodrik (2007) this is clearly an industrial policy in all but name.

21. For a thoughtful discussion of the characteristics and results of one such program, namely the Industrial Specialization Regimen (ISR) in Argentina, see Sirlin (1999).

22. Agriculture is still largely supported in Argentina, Brazil, Mexico, Costa Rica, and the Dominican Republic.

23. Horizontal tax incentives are, on the contrary, largely used in Caribbean countries.

24. These are the Servicio Brasileno de Apoyo a las Micro y Pequenas Empresas (SEBRAE), the Programas de Fomento of CORFO in Chile, Program de Calidad Integral y Modernizaccion (CIMO) and the Centre Regionales de Competitividad Empresarial in Mexico, the Centros de Desarrollo Empresarial (CDE) in Argentina, and the Centros de Desarrollo Tecnologico (CDT) in Colombia (Peres and Stumpo, 2002).

25. During the 1990s, the SEBRAE activities supported more than 3.5 million SMEs belonging to all sectors of the Brazilian economy.

26. For a thorough assessment of policies supporting SMEs see Hobday and Perini (Chapter 18).

27. Representatives of academies and research centers, members of the Ministry for Science and Technology, of the business sector, and of regulatory bodies constitute a mixed management committee that runs each of the 12 sectoral technological

funds which are in place according to a coordinated and consensual strategy. For a detailed description of technology funds in Argentina, Brazil, Chile, and Mexico see Cimoli et al. (2004).

28. The Argentinean National Plan for Technology and Production Innovation, the Bolivian National Secretary for Science Technology and Innovation, the Colombian National Program for Industrial and Technological Development, the Mexican National Council for Science and Technology (CONACYT), and the Uruguayan National Service for Science and Technology (SENACYT), all support postgraduate studies through credit and grants systems. The Brazilian government has an articulated system of grants and loans for financing university postgraduate studies which alone sponsors around 7,000 PhDs per year (Cimoli et al. 2004).

29. The Competition Bill argues that the contribution to economic development by a domestic firm may be a justification for allowing anti-competitive actions (see Possas and Borges, Chapter 17).

30. The government designated R&D programs have funded 50% of R&D of large firms and 80% of SMEs' investments in new technologies (Lall, 2003).

31. The admission to science parks depends on the evaluation of a committee that consisted of representatives from government, industry, and academia. The government's objective is to attract firms developing the most advanced technologies (microelectronics, precision machinery, semi-conductor, biotechnology). Benefits include tax exemptions, low interest loans, as well as special educational facilities. In exchange, companies have to meet criteria related to operating objectives, pollution prevention, and management (Amsden, 2000).

References

Akyüz, Y. (This Volume). Industrial Tariffs, International Trade, and Development.

Alcorta, L. (2000). New Economic Policies and the Diffusion of Machine Tools in Latin America. *World Development*, vol. 28 (2), 1657–72.

—— and Peres, W. (1998). Innovation Systems and Technological Specialization in Latin America and the Caribbean. *Research Policy*, vol. 26, 857–81.

Amsden, A. (1989). *Asia's Next Giant: South Korea and Late Industrialization*. New York and Oxford: Oxford University Press.

—— (1991). Diffusion of Development: The Late-Industrializing Model and Greater East Asia. *American Economic Review* Papers and Proceedings, vol. 81, 284–6.

—— (2000). Industrializing under the New WTO Law. Mimeo, UNCTAD.

—— (2001). *The Rise of the Rest: Challenges to the West from Late-Industrializing Economies*. Oxford: Oxford University Press.

—— (This Volume). Nationality of Firm Ownership in Developing Countries: Who Should 'Crowd Out' Whom in Imperfect Markets?

Ashton, D., Green, F., James, D., and Sung, J. (eds.) (1999). *Education and Training for Development in East Asia*. London: Routledge.

Casalet, M. (2003). Políticas científicas y tecnológicas en México: evaluación e impacto, FLACSO.

Castaldi, C., Cimoli, M., Correa, N., and Dosi, G. (This Volume). Technological Learning, Policy Regimes, and Growth in a 'Globalized' Economy: Some General Patterns.

Castro, A. (This Volume). The Impact of Public Policies in Brazil along the Path from Semi-Stagnation to Growth in a Sino-Centric Market.

Chakravarthy, S. (2004). India's New Competition Act 2002: A Work Still in Progress. *Business Law International*, vol. 5 (2), 204–93.

Chang, H.J. (1994). *The Political Economy of Industrial Policy*, Macmillan.

Cimoli, M. and Di Maio, M. (2004). Has the Chilean Neo-Liberal Experiment Run out of Fuel? A View on Technological Gaps, De-Industrialisation and Catching-Up. *Quaderni del Dipartimento di Economia Politica*, Università degli Studi di Siena, n. 426.

—— Ferraz, J.C., and Primi, A. (2004). Science and Technology Policies in Open Economies: The Case of Latin America and the Caribbean. Mimeo, ECLAC.

—— and Primi, A. (2004). Las polìticas para la creaciòn y difusiòn del conocimiento. Mimeo, CEPAL.

—— Coriat, B., and Primi, A. (This Volume). Intellectual Property and Industrial Development: A Critical Assessment.

—— M., Dosi, G., Nelson, R., and Stiglitz, J. E. (This Volume). Institutions and Policies Shaping Industrial Development: An Introductory Note.

Dahlman, C. J. and Frischtak, C. R. (1993). National Systems Supporting Technical Advance in Industry: The Brazilian Experience, in Nelson, R. (ed.), *National Innovation System*. Oxford University Press, 414–50.

Dosi, G., (1988). Institutions and Markets in a Dynamic World. *Manchester School*, vol. 56 (2), 119–46.

ECLAC (2004). *Productive Development in Open Economies*. Santiago de Chile, ECLAC.

Freeman, C. (2004). Technological Infrastructure and International Competitiveness. *Industrial and Corporate Change*, vol. 13 (3), 541–69.

Gerschenkron, A. (1962). *Economic Backwardness in Historical Perspective*. Cambridge: Harvard University Press.

Ground, R. L. (1988). The Genesis of Import Substitution in Latin America. *CEPAL Review*, n. 36, 180–203.

Hausmann, R. and Rodrik, D. (2003). Economic Development as Self-Discovery. *Journal of Development Economics*, vol. 72, 414–50.

Hirschman, A. O. (1958). *The Strategy of Economic Development*. New Haven: Yale University Press.

Hobday, M. and Perini, F. (This Volume). Latecomer Entrepreneurship: A Policy Perspective.

Katz, J. M. (ed.), (1987). *Technology Generation in Latin American Manufacturing Industries*. London: Macmillan.

—— (2000). Pasado y presente del comportamento tecnològico de Amèrica Latina. *Serie Desarollo Productivo*, no. 75, CEPAL.

—— and Kosacoff, B. (1998). Aprendizaje tecnologico, desarrollo instituional y la microeconomia de la sustitucion de importaciones. *Desarrollo Economico*, vol. 37, 483–503.

Khan, M. and Blankenburg, S. (This Volume).The Political Economy of Industrial Policy in Asia and Latin America.

Kim, L. (1993). National System of Industrial Innovation: Dynamics of Capability Building in Korea, in Nelson, R. (ed.), *National Systems of Innovation: A Comparative Analysis*, 357–83. Oxford University Press.

—— (1999). Building Technological Capabilities for Industrialization: Analytical Framework and Korea's Experience. Industrial and Corporate Change, vol. 8 (1), 111–36.

—— and Nelson, R. (2000). *Technology, Learning and Innovation: The Experience of Newly Industrializing Countries*. Cambridge University Press.

Kosacoff, B. and Ramos, A. H. (This Volume). Microeconomic Evolution in High Uncertainty Contexts: The Manufacturing Sector in Argentina.

Krueger, A. O. (1985). The Experiences and Lesson of Asia's Super Exporters, in V. Corbo et al. (eds.), *Export Oriented Development Strategies: The Success of Five Newly Industrializing Countries*. London: Westview Press.

—— (1990). Government Failures in Economic Development. *Journal of Economic Perspectives*, vol. 4 (3), 9–23.

Lall, S. (1996). *Learning from the Asian Tigers: Studies in Technology and Industrial Policy*. London: Macmillan.

—— (2000). Selective Industrial and Trade Policies in Developing Countries: Theoretical and Empirical Issues. *QEH Working Paper Series*, 48.

—— (2003). Reinventing Industrial Strategy: The Role of Government Policy in Building Industrial Competitiveness. Mimeo.

Landes, D. S. (1970). *The Unbound Prometheus: Technological Change and Industrial Development in Western Europe from 1750 to the Present*. Cambridge: Cambridge University Press.

Lewis, C. M. (1990). *The Crisis of Argentinian Capitalism*. Chapel Hill: University of North Carolina Press.

List, F. (1845). *The National System of Political Economy* [English translation by S.S. Lloyd (1904), Longmans].

Little, I. (1979). An Economic Reconnaissance, in W. Galenson (ed.), *Economic Growth and Structural Change in Taiwan: The Postwar Experience of the Republic of China*, Ithaca: Cornell University Press.

Lu, Q. (1997). *Innovation and Organization: The Rise of New Science and Technology Enterprises in China*. Cambridge MA, Harvard University Press.

Mathews, J. A. (2002). The Origins and Dynamics of Taiwan's R&D Consortia. *Research Policy*, vol. 31 (4), 633–51.

Mazzoleni, R. and Nelson, R. (This Volume).The Roles of Research at Universities and Public Labs in Economic Catch-up.

Melo, A., (2001). Industrial Policy in Latin America and the Caribbean at the Turn of the Century, IADB, Departamento de investigaciòn, Working Paper 459.

Ministèrio do Desenvolvimento, Indùstria e Comèrcio Exterior (Brasil) (2003). Diretrizes de Polìtica Industrial, Tecnològica e de Comèrcio Exterior. November.

Mortimore, M. and Peres, W. (1998). Policy Competition for Foreign Direct Investment in the Caribbean Basin: Costa Rica, Jamaica and the Dominican Republic. *Serie Desarrollo Productivo*, no. 49, CEPAL.

Nelson, R. (2004). The Changing Institutional Requirements for Technological and Economic Catch-Up. Mimeo, Columbia University, June.

Noland, M. and Pack, H. (2002). Industrial Policies and Growth: Lessons from the International Experience, in Loayaza, N. and Soto, R. (eds.) *Economic Growth: Sources, Trends and Cycles*. Santiago de Chile: Central Bank of Chile, 251–307.

Pacheco, C. (2003). As reformas da Politica Nacional de Ciencia Tecnologica e Inovacao no Brazil, Mimeo CEPAL.

Pack, H. (2000). Industrial Policy: Elixir or Poison. *World Bank Research Observer*, vol. 15 (1), 47–68.

Palma, J. G. (This Volume). Flying Geese and Waddling Ducks: The Different Capabilities of East Asia and Latin America to 'Demand-Adapt' and 'Supply-Upgrade' their Export Productive Capacity.

Peres, W. (ed.) (1997). *Polìticas de Competitividad Industrial en Amèrica Latina y el Caribe.* Mèxico, D.F.: Siglo XXI Editores.

—— (ed.) (1998). *Grandes Empresas y Grupos Industriales Latinoamericanos.* Mèxico, D.F.: Siglo XXI Editores.

—— (2002). Industrial Competitiveness Policies in Latin America and the Caribbean in the 1990s, in Huber, E. (ed.), *Models of Capitalism. Lessons for Latin America.* Pennsylvania State University Press, ch. 3.

—— (This Volume), The (Slow) Return of Industrial Policies in Latin America and the Caribbean.

—— and Stumpo, G. (ed.) (2002). Las pequenas y medianas empresas industrials en Amerca Latina y el Caribe. Mèxico D.F.: CEPAL–Siglo XXI Editores.

Possas, M.L. and Borges, H. (This Volume) Competition Policy and Industrial Development.

Reinert, E. S. (1994). Catching-Up from Way Behind: A Third World Perspective on First World History, in Fagerberg, Jan et. al. (eds.) *The Dynamics of Technology, Trade, and Growth,* Aldershot: Edward Elgar.

—— (1999). The Role of the State in Economic Growth. *Journal of Economic Studies,* vol. 26 (4/5), 268–326.

—— (This Volume) Emulation versus Comparative Advantage: Competing and Complementary Principles in the History of Economic Policy

Rhee, Y., Ross-Larson, B., and Pursell, G. (1984). *Korea's Competitive Edge,* Baltimore: Johns Hopkins.

Rodrik, D. (1995a). Getting Interventions Right: How Korea and Taiwan Grew Rich. *Economic Policy,* vol. 20, 55–107.

—— (1995b). Trade and Industrial Policy Reform, in Behrman, J.R. and T.N. Srinivasan (eds.) *Handbook of Development Economics,* Vol. III. Amsterdam: North Holland, 2925–82.

—— (2004). Industrial Policy for the Twenty-First Century. Mimeo, UNIDO.

—— (2007). Normalizing Industrial Policy. Mimeo, Harvard University.

Shapiro, H. (1989). State Intervention and Industrialisation: The Origins of the Brazilian Automotive Industry. *Journal of Economic History,* vol. 49 (2), 448–50.

Singh, A. (This Volume). The Past, Present, and Future of Industrial Policy in India: Adapting to the Changing Domestic and International Environment.

Sirlin, P. (1999). Argentina's Industrial Specialization Regime: New-Generation Industrial Policy or Merely a Transfer of Resources? *CEPAL Review,* 68, 101–14.

Wade, R. (2003). *Governing the Market: Economic Theory and the Role of Government in East Asian Industrialization.* Princeton University Press.

Westphal, L. E. (1990). Industrial Policy in an Export-Propelled Economy; Lessons from South Korea's Experience. *Journal of Economic Perspectives,* vol. 4, 41–59.

World Bank (1993). *The East Asian Miracle*. Public Policy and Economic Development, Washington, DC.

Yoguel, G. (2003). La política científica y tecnológica argentina en las últimas décadas: algunas consideraciones desde la perspectiva del desarrollo de procesos de aprendizaje. Mimeo, CEPAL.

6

Industrial Tariffs, International Trade, and Development

Yılmaz Akyüz

Introduction

The past two decades have witnessed rapid liberalization of trade in industrial products in developing countries. Much of this has taken place unilaterally or as a result of bilateral and regional trade agreements or conditionalities attached to multilateral lending by the Bretton Woods Institutions. The Uruguay Round also resulted in the elimination of non-tariff barriers and reduction of industrial tariffs, but until now developing countries have enjoyed considerable freedom in the WTO in choosing which tariff lines to bind and where to bind them. As a result, in most of them tariffs have remained either unbound or bound at relatively high levels compared to applied rates.

This situation is set to change. A main objective pursued by developed countries in the current (Doha) round of negotiations on industrial products is to bind and reduce all tariffs so as to harmonize them across both countries and products. This would in effect translate unilateral liberalization by developing countries into WTO commitments, bring tariffs much closer to levels in developed countries, reduce tariff dispersion among different product categories, and result in further cuts in applied rates.

In the debate on the implications of these proposals for developing countries attention has focused on two issues: their immediate impact on trade,

* This is a revised and abridged version of an earlier paper, 'The WTO Negotiations on Industrial Tariffs: What is at Stake for Developing Countries?', prepared for and published by the Third World Network. I am grateful to Ha-Joon Chang, Bhagirath Das, Martin Khor, Richard Kozul-Wright, Kamal Malhotra, Jorg Mayer, Chakravarthi Raghavan, and Irfan U1 Haque for helpful comments and suggestions. They are not responsible for remaining errors.

production, and employment in the sectors affected by tariff cuts and increased market access; and their impact on government revenues from trade taxes, particularly where such taxes account for an important part of the budget. Less attention has been paid to the implication of tariff cuts for industrialization in developing countries and their participation in the international division of labor. While it is generally agreed that there may be temporary costs, there is also a widespread belief, in accordance with the prevailing orthodoxy, that proposed tariff reductions would be beneficial to developing countries when adjustment to a more liberal trade regime is completed and existing resources are fully redeployed and utilized according to new incentives.

For developing countries what matters is not one-off gains or losses resulting from reallocation of existing resources, but the longer-term implications of proposed binding and cuts in industrial tariffs for capital accumulation, technical progress and productivity growth since these hold the key to narrowing income gaps and catching up with richer countries. Even if there could be an instantaneous, costless adjustment to a new set of incentives allowing developing countries to fully mobilize their existing endowments and capabilities, an irreversible commitment to low tariffs across a whole range of sectors would carry the risk of locking them into the prevailing international division of labor.

It is true that tariff protection is not always the only or the best way to promote technologically advanced and dynamic industries. However, many of the more effective and first-best policy options successfully used in the past for industrial upgrading by today's mature and newly industrialized countries are no longer available to developing countries because of their commitments in the WTO, notably in agreements on subsidies, TRIMS, and TRIPS. The loss of freedom to use policy tools in these areas increases the risks entailed by narrowing policy autonomy further through irreversible commitments for deep cuts in industrial tariffs.

This chapter focuses on the implications of the proposed multilateral regime for industrial tariffs for the industrialization of developing countries. The next section gives an overview of its key elements without going into technical details of various proposals. This is followed by a brief review of the historical experience of today's advanced countries regarding the use of tariffs in the course of their industrialization in comparison with the actual situation prevailing in developing countries today and the proposals put forward by industrial countries. The fourth section discusses the sectoral pattern and evolution of tariffs that may be needed in the course of industrial development in comparison with the constraints that would result from these proposals, and advances a simple alternative that can help reconcile policy flexibility with multilateral discipline. This is followed by a critical evaluation of benefits claimed from tariff cuts to developing countries. The chapter will conclude with a summary of the features that a multilateral regime for industrial tariffs needs to have in order to accommodate longer-term development trajectories of developing countries.

The multilateral regime for industrial tariffs as advocated by developed countries

The multilateral regime for industrial tariffs advocated by developed countries would have four distinct features:[1]

First, all tariffs would ultimately be bound. While most developed countries have almost full binding coverage, this is not the case for the majority of developing countries, particularly outside Latin America. This would lead to a considerable reduction in the scope to use trade policy for industrialization, particularly since WTO commitments are not time-bound, to be renegotiated after a pre-specified period. Various rules that permit countries to resort to anti-dumping or safeguards measures are exceptional and temporary provisions. They are not designed to allow developing countries to pursue effective trade and industrial policies in order to promote competitive firms in more dynamic, high value-added sectors.

Second, whatever their initial positions, countries are expected to lower their tariffs over time in successive rounds. Indeed, an overarching objective pursued by some of the most advanced countries such as the United States is a rapid convergence to free trade in industrial products. Furthermore, with some minor exceptions, liberalization is to be pursued on a line-by-line basis; that is, tariff cuts would be applied to all product categories.

The third feature advocated is to narrow tariff dispersion across countries. Currently the difference between average weighted bound tariffs of developed and developing countries is over 11 percent. This would be reduced to some 4 percentage points in some proposals or disappear altogether in others (Laird et al. 2003). Again, there would be considerable compression of tariff dispersion among developing countries, with the standard deviation of average bound tariffs falling from more than 20 percentage points to less than 3 percentage points.[2]

Finally, the proposals seek a significant compression of tariff dispersion across industrial products. On some proposals dispersion, as measured by standard deviation of bound tariffs, could fall by more than two-thirds.[3] The EU has proposed to compress tariffs into a range with an overall cap of 15 percent. The consequences of such a move for developing countries could be much more serious than is commonly appreciated since it could severely reduce their ability to differentiate among industrial sectors in the provision of infant industry support and protection.

A brief history of industrial protectionism: good for the goose, but not for the gander

The goose

These principles espoused by developed countries do not conform to their historical experience regarding the use of tariffs for industrialization. As documented in the literature on the economic history of Western Europe and its offshoots, protectionism was the rule, free trade the exception during the industrialization of today's mature economies (Bairoch, 1993). While industrial leaders often favored free trade, followers used all kinds of policy tools to support and protect their infant industries in order to catch up with the more advanced economies (Wade, 2003).

In the Western European core, following the widespread mercantilism that pervaded the earlier centuries, there was a brief period of free trade beginning in the 1840s.[4] This coincided with the emergence of Britain as the industrial hegemon, achieved under high barriers to imports, and started with the repeal of the Corn Laws. Tariffs on manufactured imports were brought down to zero by the 1860s from levels as high as 50 percent in the 1820s. Liberal trade policy spread to Europe after the Anglo-French trade agreement of 1860. However, this episode of liberal trade policy was followed by a protectionist backlash in the late 1870s and early 1880s, leading to increases in industrial tariffs in several follower countries including Germany and France. In the period until the First World War, tariffs remained at relatively high levels outside Britain, the Netherlands, and a few smaller European countries. In the interwar period, there was a proliferation of tariffs and non-tariff barriers, including in Britain which started to feel the competitive pressures from the newly emerging industrializers, notably Germany and the United States, and eventually resorted to high tariff barriers on the eve of the Second World War. The postwar era witnessed another wave of liberalization with gradual declines in industrial tariffs in the developed world, this time driven by the new industrial hegemon, the United States. However, 'one of the elements which permitted this trend towards tariff liberalization was an incipient tendency to apply measures of a flexible nature (non-tariff measures) on an increasing scale, a tendency to manage trade in certain sensitive sectors, and a tendency to apply such restrictive measures on a discriminatory basis.'[5]

It is also notable that throughout its industrial development the United States was more protectionist than other early industrializers. It was indeed described as 'the mother country and bastion of modern protectionism' (Bairoch, 1993). From the beginning of the nineteenth century until the 1840s its average tariffs varied between 20 percent and 50 percent while its industrial tariffs were as high as 40 percent in 1820, a level which was generally maintained until the 1840s (Irwin, 2003). The United States also entered a period of more liberal trade policy in the late 1840s, but its tariffs were still kept at much higher levels than in the Western European core. Moreover, this liberal episode lasted even shorter, with average tariffs returning to 40–50 percent levels in the 1870s when custom duties accounted for more than 50 percent of the United States government revenue (Irwin, 2002a). Until the First World War, tariffs were also higher in all other European offshoots including Australia, Canada, New Zealand, and Argentina than in the core countries (Irwin, 2002b). In the United States there was a brief easing of tariffs around the First World War, before they were raised again to exceed 35 percent in the mid-1920s, and 48 percent with the onset of the Great Depression. It was only after the Second World War that the United States started to move to sustained trade liberalization, having successfully established its industrial dominance behind protectionist barriers. Even then, as noted by Chang (2002), 'the USA never practiced free trade to the same degree as Britain did during its free-trade period (1860–1932).'

The historical evolution of industrial tariffs in the United States is described in Figure 6.1. Its average industrial tariffs were relatively low at its early stages of industrial development, rising rapidly in intermediate stages, and falling with maturity. Figure 6.1 excludes two periods where tariffs temporarily diverged from their long-term path; that is, the liberal episode of 1846–1861, and the Smoot–Hawley increase during the Great Depression. However, not only were these extreme episodes temporary but, as noted above, declines in the former period and increases in the latter were quite moderate compared to levels prevailing previously.

Evidence shows that there was a strong correlation between protectionism and economic growth in the United States throughout the nineteenth century

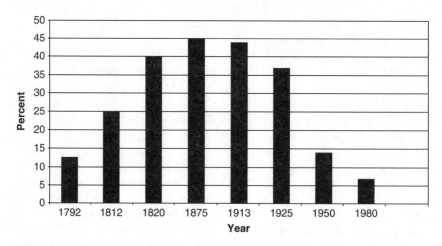

Figure 6.1. United States industrial tariffs (average applied tariffs)

and until the Second World War (Bairoch, 1993; O'Rourke, 2000; Clemens and Williamson, 2001). Indeed during that period, not only did the United States have the highest tariffs, but also it was the fastest growing economy. Although it is true that the correlation between high tariffs and economic growth does not imply causality and there are many other factors than infant industry protection that contribute to rapid growth (e.g. Irwin, 2000 and 2002b), it is notable that not only was the correlation valid for several Western European countries, but also it was robust after taking into account other factors affecting growth in cross-country regressions (O'Rourke, 2000).

While the United States was protectionist across a wide range of industries, Japan (like Germany and Sweden) was more selective (Chang, 2002), providing high levels of protection to capital-intensive and high value-added sectors, including those producing machinery and equipment (World Bank, 1993). Korea followed in the footsteps of Japan, except that it was less willing to move to free trade: 'even by 1983, when Korea's success had become an established fact, most sectors were still protected by some combination of tariffs and non-tariff barriers. While Korea utilized a variety of instruments, especially export targets and rebates, to ensure that exporters faced international prices for their tradable inputs, there was considerable protection of goods sold on the domestic market' (World Bank, 1993).

And the gander

Compared with the historical experience of mature and newly industrialized countries, trade policy in developing countries today appears to be unduly liberal. Table 6.1 makes a comparison of the historical experience of the three core Western European economies and the United States with the current situation in developing countries and least developed countries (LDCs), and three large developing economies: (i) At the end of the nineteenth century when per capita income (measured in purchasing power parity) in the United States was at a similar level to that in developing countries today (that is, some $3,000 in 1990 dollars), its weighted average applied tariffs on manufactured imports was close to 50 percent, compared to 8.1 percent in developing countries and 13.6 percent in LDCs today. (ii) In 1950 when the United States was already an undisputed industrial hegemon with a per capita income of almost three times the per capita income of developing countries today, its average applied industrial tariff rate was higher not only than the average rate applied by developing countries but also by LDCs today. This is also true, to varying degrees, for Germany, France, and the United Kingdom. (iii) When the United States had the same levels of per capita income as Brazil or China today, its applied tariff rates were four times higher. When its per capita income was similar to that of India today (that is, around the mid-nineteenth century), its average tariff was twice as high. Again, all Western European core economies had higher industrial protection than Brazil, China, and India today when they had similar per capita income levels.

The figures in Table 6.1, however, do not fully reflect the extent of protectionism in industrial countries in the past in comparison with developing countries today. High tariffs in the earlier period came on top of much higher transportation and information costs than today, which provided natural protection from imports, particularly for the European offshoots (Clemens and Williamson, 2001). Moreover, the productivity gap between industrial leaders and followers is much greater now than in earlier times (Chang, 2002). For instance, even though the United States in 1913 had the same per capita income as Brazil today, it was already one of the most developed economies in the world with effectively no productivity gap with the industrial leader of the time, the United Kingdom. Since Brazil now faces a larger income gap with industrial leaders, the same level of tariffs would provide much less protection to its industry today than it did for the United States in the earlier period.

Although major industrial countries have had continuous tariff liberalization in the postwar era, the tariff levels reached by 1980 are not very much different from the average rate of applied tariffs in developing countries today.

Table 6.1. Industrial tariffs: historical comparison between developed and developing countries

Country/Year		Per capita income (at 1990$)	Average applied tariffs (%)
US	1820	1257	35–45
	1875	2445	40–50
	1913	5301	44.0
	1950	9561	14.0
	1980	18577	7.0
Germany	1913	3648	13.0
	1950	3881	26.0
	1980	14113	8.3
France	1913	3485	20.0
	1950	5270	18.0
	1980	15103	8.3
UK	1913	5150	0
	1950	6907	23.0
	1980	12928	8.3
Developing Countries	2001	3260	8.1 (2.1)*
LDCs	2001	898	13.6 (13.6)*
Brazil	2001	5508	10.4 (4.0)*
China	2001	3728	12.3 (1.2)*
India	2001	1945	24.3 (9.0)*

*Average tariffs that would result from the application of a Swiss formula according to what Fernandez de Cordoba et al. (2004b) call 'hard scenario'.

Source: Per capita income from Maddison (2001) at 1990 dollars based on multilateral PPP. The latest available figures (1998/99) are adjusted for subsequent growth to arrive at estimates for 2001. Tariffs for developed countries from Bairoch (1993, table 3.3, p. 40) and for developing countries Fernandez de Cordoba et al. (2004b, Appendix).

Furthermore, there was widespread resort to non-tariff measures which were 'applied to approximately one-quarter of Switzerland's total imports and more than one-tenth of the imports of Japan, Norway and the European Economic Community', even without the inclusion of voluntary export restraints in the inventory of non-tariff measures (UNCTAD TDR, 1984). Some of the formulas currently proposed by developed countries imply that tariff cuts in developing countries would be much deeper cuts than those made by most major developed countries in the 30 years after the Second World War (Table 6.1).

The current push for greater harmonization of industrial tariffs across countries also stands in sharp contrast with the historical experience of today's industrial countries. Even though the leading industrial nations used their political, military, and economic leverage throughout the nineteenth and much of the twentieth century to promote liberalization-cum-harmonization in weaker countries, cross-country dispersion of tariffs was much greater than is the case today.

Lack of trade policy autonomy in colonies was a factor favoring greater harmonization of tariffs. There was indeed a high degree of correlation among the tariff levels of imperial powers and colonies throughout the nineteenth and twentieth centuries. This was particularly true for British and Dutch colonies in Asia which operated under imperial tariff policies. This imperial dominance goes a long way in explaining why colonies in Asia kept much lower tariffs than independent Latin American countries through the nineteenth century and until the Second World War. Tariffs in the former region were aligned to relatively liberal regimes in Britain and the Netherlands, while Latin American countries kept high tariffs in view of excessive protectionism in their main trading partner, the United States (Clemens and Williamson, 2002b; and Williamson, 2003).

Powerful countries also exerted a strong influence over tariff policies of independent but weak states through the so-called unequal treaties. This includes the gunboat diplomacy in Asia forcing Japan and China to open up their markets to the United States and Britain respectively, as well as the 1860 trade agreement imposed on the Ottoman Empire by Britain when the country defaulted on its external debt, and public finances were effectively taken over by the creditors.[6] Since the main objective in such instances was to make the weaker states open their markets, such treaties did not always promote harmonization, particularly when the imposing countries were protectionist. This was certainly the case when the United States forced Japan to open its markets while protecting vigorously its own.

An important factor that favors greater harmonization is that once countries establish industrial dominance behind protectionist walls, they tend to advocate free trade in order to *kick away the ladder* from the followers and consolidate their dominance, as argued by Chang (2002) reviving the term originally introduced by the German economist Friedrich List. As noted above this was certainly the case for Britain in the mid-nineteenth century which led the liberalization drive in Europe. The United States followed a similar path a hundred years later.

Despite these tendencies making for greater liberalization-cum-harmonization, there was still considerable diversity among the contemporaneous industrializers in the core during both the nineteenth century and the first half of the twentieth century. For instance, in the interwar period the cross-country dispersion of industrial tariffs was quite wide; tariffs ranged from zero in the United Kingdom to 6–10 percent in the Netherlands, 20 percent in Germany, 30 percent in France, 46–50 percent in Italy and the United States. As shown in Table 6.2, the dispersion of tariffs among developed countries, as measured by standard deviation, was close to 11 percentage points even in 1875 when trade was relatively free. This figure almost doubled by 1913 after the globalization backlash, before coming down to 7 percentage points in 1950. Thus, cross-country dispersion of industrial tariffs was quite high during the industrialization of today's developed countries, not only in absolute terms but also relative to average tariffs (as demonstrated by the coefficient of variation in the last column of Table 6.2), coming down only after followers narrowed the development gap with the leaders.

For a broader range of countries, both in the core and the periphery, the dispersion was even larger. It was also in the wrong direction as tariffs in many poor countries in the periphery were lower than those in more advanced economies. For instance, a study contrasting the behavior of tariffs over 1865 and 1938 in six regions found 'enormous variance in levels of protection between the regional averages' (Williamson, 2003). It is even more striking that, as shown in Table 6.2, the dispersion of average tariffs applied by developed

Table 6.2. Average applied tariffs and their dispersion

	Year	Average applied tariff	Dispersion (percentage)	Coefficient of variation
Developed countries[1]	1875	12.1	10.8	0.9
Developed countries[1]	1913	23.1	21.8	0.9
Developed countries[1]	1950	15.8	7.1	0.5
Developed and developing countries[2]	1870	13.8	10.7	0.8
Developed and developing countries[2]	1890	15.2	12.6	0.8
Developed and developing countries[3]	2001	9.3	5.7	0.6
Developed and developing countries[3]	After harmonization	4.1	2.9	0.7

[1] Industrial tariffs for 14 developed countries for 1875 and 1913, and 10 developed countries for 1950, calculated from Bairoch (1993: 40, table 3.3.).

[2] All tariffs for 27 countries, calculated from Irwin (2002b: 27, Appendix table 1).

[3] Industrial tariffs for 84 countries (excluding LDCs), calculated from Fernandez de Cordoba et al. (2004b: Appendix table A1). Harmonization refers to tariffs that would result from what the authors call 'hard scenario.'

and developing countries was much higher, both in absolute and relative terms, during the nineteenth century than at present, despite harmonizing influences associated with imperial rule and gunboat diplomacy in the earlier period. This is true whether one takes the figures during the liberalization episode (1870) or during the tariff backlash (1890). Table 6.2 also shows that the application of the non-linear Swiss formula could take harmonization between developed and developing countries much further than was ever achieved under imperial rule or gunboat diplomacy.

Industrial development and tariffs

Stages of industrial development

The key question raised by multilateral negotiations on industrial tariffs is the extent to which the proposals put forward by developed countries would affect industrialization prospects of developing countries. In examining this issue, it is important to bear in mind that successful industrialization is a cumulative process involving movements from one stage to another through the establishment of new industries with higher value-added and technology contents. In the earliest stages of economic development, production and exports consist largely of primary commodities while imports comprise mainly manufactures, both capital and labor-intensive products. Exporting at such a stage provides a vent for surplus; that is, it allows production to increase by making use of formerly unemployed resources because of lack of domestic demand. As these sectors enjoy natural resource-based comparative advantages of the kind emphasized by the Ricardian theory of trade, their mobilization does not call for specific support and protection.[7] It does, however, raise other policy issues linked to distribution of rents, particularly when foreign firms are involved (Prebisch, 1950; Singer, 1950).

How long a country can rely on the exploitation of natural resources before moving to industry depends, inter alia, on the relative size of its resource endowments. However, evidence strongly suggests that rich natural resources, even when combined with a well-developed human resource base, do not automatically lead to processing and diversification. Without active policies designed to promote and support such activities, being rich in natural resources can be detrimental to diversification away from unprocessed commodities. On the other hand, even though commodity processing provides early industrialization opportunities, the possibilities of maintaining rapid development through deepening and diversification in the primary sector are limited. Manufactures offer better growth prospects not only because they allow for a more rapid productivity growth and expansion of production, but also because they avoid the declining terms of trade that have frustrated the growth prospects of many commodity-dependent economies. Countries rich in natural resources can delay industrialization, but in general they cannot reach high income levels without a strong industrial base.[8]

The early stages of industrialization are characterized by sectoral specialization in exploiting endowments of natural resources and unskilled labor. This is followed by diversification into a wide spectrum of more technologically advanced activities, accompanied by increased internal integration through a dense set of linkages among sectors.[9] With industrial maturity there is again a move towards sectoral specialization, this time at the top end of the technology ladder. This pattern is also confirmed by empirical evidence on the evolution of sectoral allocation of labor in the course of industrial development. A study using data from a variety of sources covering a wide cross-section of countries found

robust evidence that economies grow through two stages of diversification. At first, labor is allocated increasingly equally between sectors, but there exists a level of *per capita* income beyond which the sectoral distribution of labor inputs starts concentrating again. In other words, the sectoral concentration of labor follows a U-shaped pattern in relation to *per capita* income . . . The non-linearity holds above and beyond the well-known shifts of factors of production from agriculture to manufacturing and on to services. (Imbs and Wacziarg, 2000)

The turnaround from sectoral diversification to specialization occurs quite late in the development process around a per capita income of $9,000.

During the initial expansion in resource-based and labor-intensive manufactures, the support and protection provided to industry will likely be phased out after a relatively short period of learning and expansion in world markets, since such sectors tend to be technologically less demanding. As traditional industries mature and become competitive, a new generation of infant industries would need to emerge and establish themselves. Indeed, an effective industrialization strategy should recognize that currently successful industries may, over time, confront difficulties in competing in international markets as domestic wages rise, low-cost competitors emerge, and the limits of learning and productivity growth are reached. Hence, more dynamic and skill- and technology-intensive industries would need to be promoted simultaneously as resource-based and labor-intensive manufacturing successfully carries the economy forward. Such an approach underpinned successful modern industrializers such as Korea which started to build up from an early date scale- and technology-intensive industries, including shipbuilding, steel, and automotive industries. Rather than seeking to maintain competitiveness by keeping down wage costs or protecting traditional industries with high tariffs, they chose to upgrade rapidly as a way of raising productivity, exports, and incomes.

Eventually these scale- and technology-intensive industries will have to compete with firms in more mature economies which enjoy the advantage of having begun sooner and progressed further on the technology ladder. But, as argued by Gomory and Baumol (2000) 'entry into one of these industries, against an entrenched competitor, is slow, expensive, and very much an uphill battle if left entirely to free market forces.' They would thus need to be supported, including with industrial tariffs and various forms of subsidies, of the kind widely used in both mature and newly industrialized countries in the past. Such support would likely be higher and maintained for longer periods compared to less demanding, resource-based and labor-intensive manufacturing.

In this process, as new and more dynamic industries emerge, the traditional ones are phased out and may even be left entirely to countries at earlier stages of development. This pattern of modern industrialization, dubbed 'the flying geese paradigm', was originally formulated in Japan in the 1930s when it was still a comparatively poor economy (UNCTAD TDR, 1996). It provides a description of the life cycles of various industries in the course of economic development and their relocation from one country to another through trade and foreign direct investment (FDI) in response to shifts in competitiveness. In this process, imports from more advanced economies allow new goods and technology to be introduced in less advanced economies. The next stage is to promote indigenous industries to replace imports in meeting domestic demand, to be followed by exports. When a country loses competitiveness in a particular product, its domestic production is phased out and replaced by imports from the followers.[10]

While the flying geese paradigm assumes an outward-oriented strategy, it is not a market-driven process. Success in industrial upgrading would require policy intervention in the form of infant industry support and export promotion, in order to even the playing field with firms from more advanced economies. Initially there would be no need for tariffs on products for which the economy relies entirely on imports. Subsequently, as indigenous industry is established, tariffs are introduced for infant industry protection. And eventually protection and support would be removed as the industry matured. In this process, the economy goes through a series of overlapping industries according to their life cycles, constantly raising productivity as it moves up the technology ladder.

Similarly, building on the work of Young (1928), Kaldor (1966) described industrialization as a cumulative process going through four stages, based on a distinction between consumer and capital goods. In the first stage a local consumer goods industry emerges, substituting imported manufactured consumer goods. As competitiveness is established, the economy moves to the second stage, exporting consumables but still dependent on imported capital goods. The third stage is characterized by mass production and export of consumables combined with the emergence of a local industry to replace imported capital goods, to be followed by capital goods and technology exports. In this process, scale economies and learning play a crucial role. While industrialization follows a clear trajectory of progress, it does not converge to a predefined point. Rather, selection is involved across a whole range of industries and products in each stage of development, influenced by policy including import restrictions.[11]

Pattern and evolution of optimum industrial tariffs

These considerations suggest a pattern of optimal tariffs in the course of industrial development as described in Figure 6.2. Four different categories of products (industries) are selected according to a broad classification developed in UNCTAD TDR (1996 and 2002): resource-based and labor-intensive manufactures (RL), and low (LT), medium (MT) and high (HT) technology- and skill-intensive products.[12] Tariffs are introduced once a particular line of industry is entered, and kept at their initial (maximum) levels for a certain period before being brought down at a constant rate as the industry matures.[13] For the reasons already noted, technology-intensive industries have higher initial levels of protection and support than resource-based and labor-intensive manufacturing.[14] As technological capacities are built successfully, subsequent shifts to more advanced sectors become relatively easier than the earlier move from labor-intensive to technology-intensive activities. Accordingly, in Figure 6.2, peak tariff rates are assumed to follow a non-linear path, rising initially during the shift from RL towards LT and MT industries, and falling afterwards. In the early stages of development, there would be no need for infant industry protection against imports of MT and HT products since industries producing these goods are not yet in existence. By the time the economy moves to MT products, protection for RL products is assumed to have been fully phased out.

In this process the economy moves through a technological trajectory which determines its position in the international division of labor. In other words, what a country produces, imports, and exports, and how much support and protection its emerging industries need depends very much on its stage of technological development vis-à-vis the rest of the world.[15] Clearly the process of sequencing industries can differ from country to country depending on factors such as geography, size, and endowments. In accordance with the evidence noted above, industrial specialization in Figure 6.2 follows a non-linear path, with greater sectoral concentration at the early and late stages of industrial development, and diversification in between. In each stage there is a diverse set of industries while different stages are characterized by different levels of selection. Selection made in different countries in each stage of industrial development can show considerable variations depending on a host of factors including institutional arrangements and endowments.

Figure 6.2 describes the pattern and evolution of optimum tariffs that would be needed for infant industry protection in late industrializers in order to overcome their technology and skill gaps with the more advanced economies at each stage of industrial development. For industrial leaders where technological advance depends on innovation rather than adaptation of foreign technology, industrialization would not call for the kind of infant industry protection described in Figure 6.2, but a host of other policies that help promote innovation and internalize its benefits.

In reality tariffs tend to be set and evolve in quite different ways from the pattern depicted in Figure 6.2 since they are imposed, inter alia, for balance-of-payments and government revenue reasons. Furthermore, pressures by interest groups or distributional considerations could push tariffs from the levels that would maximize their economic benefits.[16] Even though it would not generally be efficient to have all four types of industry operating simultaneously, labor-intensive sectors are often maintained behind barriers in economies which have attained technological maturity. Indeed, in many developed countries textiles, clothing, and footwear and leather goods receive far greater protection than technology-intensive sectors against competition from low-cost developing country producers, in large part because of the country's failure to upgrade the skill profile of labor and to deal effectively with rising unemployment.

Much like the major industrial countries, many middle-income countries have been unable to maintain competitiveness in traditional labor-intensive products against cheaper new producers and persisted in such sectors behind barriers, in part because their producers have found it difficult to upgrade and

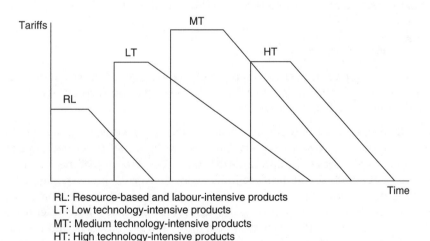

RL: Resource-based and labour-intensive products
LT: Low technology-intensive products
MT: Medium technology-intensive products
HT: High technology-intensive products

Figure 6.2. Tariff profile of sequenced industries for infant industry protection

diversify.[17] Again, in some developing countries there have been attempts to establish MT or even HT industries under strong protection at relatively early stages of development, before achieving efficiency in labor-intensive manufacturing. More generally, under import-substitution regimes tariffs were often levied on an ad hoc basis with the consequence that 'a great hodgepodge of rates appeared, with virtually no evidence of any consideration of costs or efficiency' (Bruton, 1998). More recently the tendency has been towards indiscriminate liberalization without much regard to its consequences for industrial development.

The use of tariffs in the course of technological upgrading along the lines described in Figure 6.2 implies that countries at the intermediate stages of development would have relatively low tariffs for products both at the top and bottom ends of the technology spectrum, and higher tariffs on middle-range products. By contrast, industrially advanced countries would have higher tariffs at the top end. Available evidence from a recent study distinguishing tariffs on low, intermediate, and high value-added products suggests that in reality this happens only to a limited extent (Fernandez de Cordoba and Vanzetti, 2005). Both developed and developing countries have lower applied tariffs on low value-added industrial products. Developing countries have higher average applied tariffs for intermediate products than for high value-added products, while in developed countries average tariffs are higher on high value-added products. Nevertheless, in developed countries tariffs on intermediate products are only marginally lower than those on high value-added products, reflecting in large part tariff peaks on products of export interest to developing countries. On the other hand, both developing countries and LDCs keep relatively high tariffs for high value-added products even though most of them have not yet advanced beyond labor-intensive and resource-based industries (Akyüz, Kozul-Wright, and Mayer, 2004).

Implications for trade negotiations

The pattern of tariffs needed to support overlapping generations of industries in developing countries conflicts with the objectives pursued by developed countries in the WTO in several respects:

(i) At any point in time effective use of tariffs for industrialization would require coexistence of very low and very high tariffs. In Figure 6.2 at initial stages of industrialization, tariffs are zero for MT and HT products, high for LT products, and moderate for RL products. Similarly during industrial maturity, tariffs are zero for RL and LT products, moderate for MT products, and high for HT products. In the intermediate stages tariffs are concentrated on LT and MT products, and there is no need for tariff protection for the RL industries because they are competitive, nor for the HT industries because they are not yet in existence. Briefly, since at any point in time different industries would require different degrees of infant industry protection, dispersion across tariff lines can be very wide.

(ii) Over time tariff dispersion may be rising or falling according to the stage of industrial development reached. In Figure 6.2 it is initially increasing as the economy moves towards more demanding industries, but subsequently decreasing with industrial maturity.

(iii) In the course of industrialization tariffs are raised on some products but lowered for others; that is, there is no continuous liberalization on a line-by-line basis.

(iv) The behavior of average tariffs in Figure 6.2 in the course of industrial development is quite similar to the evolution of industrial tariffs in the United States shown in Figure 6.1; they rise in the intermediate stages of industrialization as the economy diversifies away from resource-based and labor-intensive manufactures and then start falling with industrial maturity.

(v) Since countries at different stages of industrial development can coexist, there would be little harmonization across countries. Mature industrial countries would have relatively low average applied tariffs compared to those at the intermediate stages of industrialization, but not necessarily lower than those at the early stages of industrialization. In other words, countries at the intermediate stages of development need higher average applied tariffs than both mature industrial countries and LDCs. However, while mature industrial countries are expected to dismantle tariffs over time, LDCs would need to move towards higher tariffs as they enter technology-intensive industries.

Although Figure 6.2 is a highly simplified picture of the possible evolution of optimum infant industry support and protection that may be needed at different stages of industrial development, the results above do not depend on a particular description of this process. A key conclusion is that in a process of sequential build-up of competitive industries under temporary infant industry protection, the optimal level and structure of tariffs would change over time. Consequently, focusing on the needs of existing industries or taking current levels of tariffs as the basis for commitments in the WTO could subsequently present serious setbacks to technological upgrading. A country at an earlier stage of industrialization might be inclined to have low bound tariffs for high-tech products because it has not yet entered into such sectors, aiming, instead, at retaining high bound tariffs for labor-intensive and low-technology manufactures in order to protect its existing industries. But emphasizing short-term benefits to the neglect of longer-term industrialization could lock it into the current pattern of industrial specialization, making it difficult to move up on the technology ladder. Similarly, whether or not bound tariffs allow sufficient policy space for industrialization should be assessed in terms not of currently applied rates, but of the rates that may be needed when the time comes to enter higher value-added, more dynamic industries.

The key issue here is how to reconcile multilateral discipline with policy flexibility needed for industrial development. As shown earlier, developing countries do not need high tariffs for all sectors and all the time. But they should have the option of using tariffs on a selective basis as and when needed for progress in industrialization. They should not be expected to keep moving tariffs downward from one trade round to another, but be able to move them in both directions in different sectors in the course of industrial development.

The analysis above suggests that this kind of flexibility is best accommodated by binding the average tariff without any line-by-line commitment; that is, to leave tariffs for individual products unbound, subject to an overall constraint that the average applied tariffs should not exceed the bound average tariff. Clearly, the average bound tariff should be high enough to accommodate the needs of different sectors at different stages of industrial maturity. This would not necessarily lead to high bound average tariffs. On the contrary, it could result in lower average tariffs than would be the case under a line-by-line commitment.

This is illustrated by the example given in Table 6.3 which draws on the pattern in Figure 6.2 wherein countries go through various phases of industrial development, moving through a sequence of overlapping industries in LR, LT, MT, and HT products. The bold numbers are the maximum tariffs that would be needed for each product for infant industry protection. Numbers in the last column give the average applied tariffs in each phase of industrialization. As in Figure 6.2, over time tariffs are lowered in some sectors but increased in others. In this example, on a line-by-line commitment, a country at the first phase of industrial development would want to bind its sectoral tariffs at the maximum

Table 6.3. Tariffs at different phases of industrialization (percent)

Phase	RL	LT	MT	HT	Average
I	20	0	0	0	5.0
II	10	40	0	0	12.5
III	0	30	50	0	20.0
IV	0	20	40	40	25.0
V	0	10	30	40	20.0
VI	0	0	15	25	10.0
VII	0	0	5	15	5.0
VIII	0	0	0	0	0.0

RL: Resource-based and labour-intensive products; LT: Low technology-intensive products; MT: Medium technology-intensive products; HT: High technology-intensive products.

Notes: Bold numbers are the maximum tariffs initially needed for infant industry protection for each product.

rates needed, ending up with an average bound tariff of 37.5 percent. For an economy in phase II, the resulting average bound rate would be 35 percent, and in phase III 30 percent. But for these economies an average maximum bound tariff of 25 percent would be sufficient to provide infant industry support to all sectors in all phases of industrial development provided that they are free to set applied tariffs for different sectors as needed.

Average applied tariffs would remain below 25 percent in early stages of industrialization, rising gradually in the intermediate stages and eventually falling with industrial maturity. A country with an average bound rate of more than 25 percent would be willing to cut it provided that it retains the freedom to set sectoral rates as needed. Furthermore, once phase IV is reached, it would be possible to reduce the average bound tariff gradually while maintaining higher applied tariffs for more advanced sectors.

As countries are free to choose their applied tariffs for individual industries/products subject to the overall constraint of an average bound tariff, such an approach would balance multilateral discipline with policy flexibility. It would also have the additional advantage of encouraging countries to view tariffs as temporary instruments and to make an effort to ensure that infant industry protection succeeds in establishing competitive industries. This is because in order to stay within the overall limit of the bound average tariff, they would need to cut tariffs in industries at the lower end before moving up towards the higher end. For instance, a country cannot effectively move into phase III and establish MT industries under tariff protection without first lowering its tariffs on RL and LT industries from their initial levels, since this would result in an average tariff of higher than 25 percent. Finally, it would encourage developing country trade negotiators to take a long view in making multilateral commitments, rather than focusing on the immediate needs of their industries.

Assessing costs and benefits: are the gains worth the pains?

Doubling the effort

Fanaticism, according to the Spanish philosopher George Santayana, means redoubling your effort when you have forgotten your aim. Economics is no exception to such thinking. Thus, developing countries are once again facing intense pressure to liberalize trade in industrial products even though the extravagant benefits claimed from the Uruguay Round have been belied by subsequent experience.[18] According to one estimate, the Uruguay Round's combined liberalization increased global economic welfare by $75 billion, of which almost $70 billion went to developed countries, $5 billion to newly industrialized countries (NICs; Korea, Singapore, and Taiwan), and none to developing countries taken together.[19] Despite this, recent years have seen a proliferation of similar exercises, claiming large benefits from further trade liberalization for the world economy in general and for developing countries in particular. The gains estimated by various studies from full liberalization of goods and services trade, or trade in goods alone, range from a couple of hundred billion dollars to more than $2,000 billion.[20] On some accounts, the incidence of gains to developing countries reaches as much as 65 percent of the total.

It has also been argued that while a successful outcome of the Doha Round would greatly improve the growth prospects of developing countries, these benefits would come primarily from liberalization in these countries themselves. According to a scenario designed by the World Bank (2004) universal liberalization of agricultural and manufacturing trade would generate some $290 billion, of which $160 billion would go to developing countries and $132 billion to developed countries. Manufacturing liberalization in developed countries would carry a small loss to themselves while benefiting developing countries. Developing countries would gain significantly more from their own reforms than from increased access to markets in developed countries.

Other estimates are less sanguine about the potential benefits to developing countries from liberalization of trade in industrial products. According to one study, the global gain from the Uruguay Round was in the order of $90 billion, of which $65 billion went to mature industrial countries, $6 billion to NICs, and less than $20 billion to developing countries (Brown et al. 2001). The same study estimates that a one-third reduction in post-Uruguay Round manufacturing tariffs would benefit industrial countries by $160 billion, NICs by $16 billion, and developing countries by $30 billion.

Only a few attempts have been made to estimate the costs and benefits of the various formulas proposed for reducing industrial tariffs in the current negotiations on industrial tariffs. Simulations of various scenarios including universal free trade, ambitious liberalization, and a simple formula designed to reduce tariff peaks and escalation predicts modest welfare gains for the world economy as a whole, between $28 billion and $42 billion (Fernandez de Cordoba et al. 2004a). Under free trade, winners are concentrated in Asia. Developing countries would obtain less than a third of the total gains from cuts in tariff peaks and escalation. Their exports increase as much as in developed countries, partly due to increase in exports to other developing countries, while their imports increase faster.

Modeling the benefits, assuming away the costs

The estimates above are one-off static gains expected to result from reallocation of resources after trade liberalization.[21] They are derived from computable general equilibrium (CGE) models based on the neoclassical paradigm of competitive equilibrium where markets always clear and resources are fully employed.[22] These estimates do not provide a reliable guide to what might happen in reality because of two interrelated shortcomings of the CGE models.

First, the structure of a particular model determines the range of results that can be obtained, and it is often the underlying theory and assumptions that determine what the numbers would show. A CGE model founded on conventional trade theory will generally behave and yield results in the manner determined by its underlying assumptions, but shed no light on the validity of the theory itself (Stanford, 1993). For this reason it is almost impossible to find any CGE model fashioned on the traditional trade theory which does not predict gains from trade liberalization (Anderson, 2004).

As one commentator remarked, the 'best definition of a CGE model is: "theory with numbers" ' (O'Rourke, 1995), rather than an empirical test of a theory. But it is a theory that assumes away various imperfections and rigidities that pervade developing economies and lead to market failures, including externalities, incomplete markets, imperfect and asymmetric information, monopolies or imperfect competition. The incorporation of any of these could lead to problems for the stability and even the existence of equilibrium. They could also yield multiple equilibria, leading to uncertainty about the outcome of trade liberalization.

The second problem is that although these are comparative statics exercises, the *difference* between two equilibrium states is often presented as a *change* from one to another. This tendency has long been noted:

Following Joan Robinson's strictures that it is most important not to apply theorems obtained from the analysis of differences to situations of change (or, at least, to be aware of the act of faith involved in doing this), modern writers usually have been most careful to stress that their analysis is essentially the comparison of different equilibrium situations one with another and that they are not analysing the actual processes. Nevertheless, in their asides, they sometimes speak as if their results were applicable to a world of change and as if 'back-of-an-envelope' excursions into the statistics can provide 'realistic' orders of magnitude to try out their theorems.   (Harcourt, 1972)

The CGE models compare two equilibrium states of an economy differing in trade policy but similar in all structural aspects. From the way the economies are assumed to work follows the prediction that the equilibrium state with lower tariffs will have higher income and welfare. But even then, this does not mean that a reduction in tariffs would necessarily lead to another equilibrium state with a higher level of income. This depends on how the economy will react to disequilibria generated by liberalization. The kinds of problems involved were explained by John Hicks some 40 years ago:

Even if the equilibrium exists, it has still to be shown that there is a tendency towards it . . . Even in the single market, under perfect competition, and such that the existence of equilibrium is indubitable, there may be no *tendency* to equilibrium, if speeds of reaction to price change are perverse. Something has to be specified about reactions to disequilibrium before the existence of a tendency to equilibrium can be asserted. (Hicks, 1965)

The CGE economists do not specify reactions to disequilibrium brought about by policy shocks, but assume that a new equilibrium is always reached. Nevertheless, they also hedge by taking refuge in the concept of adjustment costs, acknowledging that in the transition from one equilibrium state to another, resources may be temporarily unemployed, skills may be eroded, equipment may become obsolete, government revenues may fall, trade imbalances may emerge, or there may be all kinds of costs in learning to live with the new set of incentives. Thus the World Bank (2004) argues that the 'positive impact on overall growth, accompanied by a sharp boost in trade and a poverty outlook improvement leaving all regions better off in aggregate, does not signify that the reforms are without adjustment costs, even over the long term.'

However, these 'adjustment costs' are almost never quantified and incorporated in the estimated benefits from trade liberalization simply because the CGE economists are engaged in comparative statics, making comparisons between two equilibrium states (i.e. two solutions, for different tariff rates, to a set of simultaneous equations) without specifying how the economy moves from one state to another. There are attempts to incorporate some of the deviations from neoclassical assumptions into these models, such as labor market inflexibility, as causes of adjustment costs. While this would alter the comparative statics effects of liberalization, as measured by welfare *differences* between two equilibrium states, it would not account for what happens in between, which is what the adjustment cost is about. More importantly, the very same deviations from the conventional assumptions of the CGE models that lead to adjustment costs could also prevent the economy from moving towards a new equilibrium with an improved allocation of resources, or could actually lead to an equilibrium with lower income and employment levels, making temporary adjustment costs permanent. But this question is rarely asked, let alone answered.

When adjustment costs out-of-equilibrium are relatively large, there may be no net benefits from liberalization even if comparative statics show positive results, 'since in discounting streams of costs and benefits for welfare calculations, the near-present counts more heavily than "the long run" ' (Baldwin et al. 1980). But there is hardly any work on developing countries in the CGE tradition specifying the time path of adjustment to a new equilibrium, assessing the adjustment costs and measuring them against comparative static benefits. Despite lack of rigorous work and evidence, there is a tendency to downplay such costs. A good example is a recent paper from the WTO. After arguing that 'although the economy may be worse off in the short-run, the gains from trade will outweigh short-run adjustment costs in the medium to long-term', the authors go on to recognize that 'measures of adjustment costs in existing empirical work are crude and imprecise' and 'the empirical evidence... is restricted to industrialized countries', and 'may not be representative for the case of other countries' since 'the institutional settings and the functioning of domestic markets will affect the size of adjustment costs.'[23]

Until adjustment paths are properly defined and out-of-equilibrium reactions and costs are properly specified, the assumed one-off benefits of trade liberalization in developing countries would remain an act of faith, and estimates based on CGE models would provide little guidance to commercial policy. But there are reasons to doubt whether a sound analysis of trade liberalization could really be undertaken in models premised on the neoclassical tradition. As long argued by Keynesian economists, 'comparisons of equilibrium positions one with another are *not* the appropriate tools for the analysis of out-of-equilibrium processes or changes, and that the neoclassical procedure is singularly ill-equipped to cope with the problem of time' (Harcourt, 1972). This is also reflected by a sloppy use of the concepts of short-term and long-term in the CGE literature. In economic analysis, short-term typically refers to a situation where, inter alia, resources are fixed while long-term implies capital accumulation, technical progress, and economic growth, none of which really happen in the CGE models.

Beyond adjustment costs: industrialization

The key question for developing countries is not what they can gain or lose from trade liberalization as a result of one-off reallocation of existing resources, or even the temporary adjustment costs generated when passing from one resource allocation to another. Rather, it is the implications of leaving industrial progress, technological upgrading, and economic growth to global market forces dominated by large and mature firms from advanced industrial countries. Even if developing countries could avoid adjustment costs and instantly benefit from improved allocation of resources and increased access to markets in industrial countries, these one-off benefits may be quite insignificant compared to longer-term losses that may be incurred as a result of losing policy space for rapid industrialization. Thus, as explained by Dosi, Pavitt, and Soete (1990): 'From such a perspective, it is the relationship between technology, trade and growth which is at the centre of the analysis, rather than the question about the short-term gains from trade stemming from the open-economy allocation of resources, so crucial in the conventional view.'

According to conventional trade theory, under free trade developing countries with abundant unskilled and semi-skilled labor should specialize in labor-intensive activities while industrial countries concentrate on skill- and technology-intensive sectors. Thus, with a significant move towards free trade in industrial products, developing countries would be expected to exit partly or wholly from skill- and technology-intensive and *potentially* high value-added sectors maintained behind tariff and non-tariff barriers. The same goes for industrial countries for labor-intensive products.

Detailed studies of the sectoral impact of trade liberalization on employment and production are hard to come by. Nevertheless, as expected, available evidence from a series of CGE model simulations is quite consistent with the traditional trade theory. One study estimates that in both Japan and the United States trade liberalization in agriculture, industry, and services would lower output and employment in low value-added, labor-intensive sectors including textiles, wearing apparel, and leather products, but raise them in almost all other manufacturing sectors including transportation equipment, metal products, and machinery and equipment (Brown et al. 2001). In the same study a simulation of a free trade agreement among ASEAN plus 3 (China, Japan, and Korea) shows employment losses for Japan in textiles, wearing apparel, leather products, and gains in all other manufacturing sectors. For China, there are sizeable losses in chemical industry, metal products, transportation equipment, machinery and equipment, but gains in almost all the sectors in which Japan experiences losses. These are also broadly confirmed by the results obtained from a CGE model simulating the sectoral impact of various formulas for cuts in industrial tariffs (Fernandez de Cordoba et al. 2004a).

Thus, the mainstream theory and the CGE models tell us that at the current levels of technological capability, firms in developing countries cannot compete with those in advanced industrial countries in skill- and technology-intensive products so that any rapid move towards free trade implies that developing countries would withdraw from these sectors and move to low value-added, resource-based and labor-intensive industries. In other words, it would have the consequence of establishing an international division of labor based entirely on competitiveness as determined by existing endowments and capabilities. Still, the pace of industrialization and growth in developing countries would depend on how fast they move away from such a division of labor by improving their technical and skill endowments and establishing more dynamic and challenging industries that promise higher productivity and per capita income. In other words, the return on industries that developing countries would be exiting is potentially greater than industries in which they are expanding. Therefore, the key question is: can developing countries re-enter and successfully establish such high value-added, technologically dynamic activities over time without being able to provide them infant industry protection and support because of their commitments in the WTO?

In answering these questions the conventional trade theory and the CGE models are even less useful since 'they can't unlock the secrets of economic growth' (O'Rourke, 1995). This issue is addressed by another class of ad hoc models linking trade to growth. However, there is no generally accepted theory that economies that are more open grow faster. Furthermore, several cross-country studies which show a positive relation between growth and some measure of openness have come under strong criticism because of their methodological and conceptual weaknesses, as well as their failure to account for causality—that is, whether greater openness causes faster growth or faster growth allows greater openness. The more recent experience also shows not only that import liberalization does not guarantee a strong export performance, but also that improved export performance is not always mirrored by acceleration of industrialization and growth (Akyüz, 2005).

While evidence on the link between growth and tariffs appears to be mixed for advanced industrial countries, the relation between the two is generally found to be positive in developing countries. As already noted, O'Rourke (2000) finds a positive correlation between tariffs and growth among Western European countries and their offshoots during 1875–1914 while Clemens and Williamson (2001) contend that this was reversed after 1950.[24] Edwards (1992) finds a negative relation between growth and tariffs for a sample of 20 developing countries, but the relationship is statistically insignificant. By contrast Yenikkaya (2003) provides cross-country evidence for 100 countries that initial tariffs were positively correlated with subsequent growth during 1970–1997, particularly in developing countries. According to a more recent study, the relationship between tariffs and growth is negative and significant among developed countries but positive among developing countries (DeJong and Ripoll, 2005).

These studies all focus on average tariffs while one of the conclusions of the analysis here is that success in the use of tariffs for industrial development depends not so much on their average level as their pattern and evolution over time. Consequently, two countries at the same level of development and with the same average level of tariffs may obtain different results in industrial development and economic growth depending, inter alia, on the sectoral profile of their tariffs. This is all the more important since, as noted, in reality tariffs often diverge from the pattern maximizing their dynamic economic benefits. In general success comes where they are designed to protect learning in dynamic sectors rather than deep-seated inefficiencies or vested interests in sunset industries.[25] Indeed, a rational tariff structure based on selective and temporary protection appears to be one of the factors distinguishing East Asian economies such as Taiwan and Korea from less successful countries which had similar or even lower average tariff protection and price distortions.[26] Given the evidence against the orthodox idea of technological leapfrogging through big-bang liberalization, 'some form of protection for learning is necessary... The major policy issue then is to design protection measures that induce learning rather than the easy life' (Bruton, 1998).[27]

To sum up, while infant industry protection is no guarantee for successful industrialization and growth, there is no example of modern industrialization

167

based on laissez-faire. Consequently, there is little economic rationale for developing countries to narrow their options to use tariffs for industrialization by agreeing to bind and lower them significantly in the WTO. First, the one-off comparative static benefits that may be brought by the reallocation of their existing resources are likely to be small, and there may even be net losses. Second, they can face high adjustment costs resulting from dislocation and disequilibria generated by trade liberalization, and these costs can in fact wipe out static benefits. Finally, over the longer term such a commitment can create serious difficulties in industrial progress and development. Even when net benefits in the short-term are positive, they are unlikely to be large enough to justify losing policy space and jeopardizing development prospects.

Conclusions: the way forward

According to the traditional theory, while opening up to trade is mutually beneficial, the distribution of its benefits among trading partners is indeterminate, susceptible to being influenced, inter alia, by power, intra- or extra-market. Certainly there is considerable power play in negotiations on industrial tariffs in the WTO. But if current negotiations are to live up to their characterization as a Development Round, industrial tariff cuts should be so designed as to provide maximum benefits to developing countries. This is not the case with the proposals put forward by major industrial countries and a different approach would be needed.

First of all, developed countries should not use tariffs on products of export interest to developing countries, notably labor-intensive manufactures, as bargaining chips. Even though these sectors have long lost their viability in the face of the emergence of low-cost producers in the developing world, they have been maintained behind barriers for the reasons already explained.[28] Such protection is not temporary since these sectors have no chance of regaining competitiveness vis-à-vis cheaper producers in the South. Developed countries are in effect offering to cut such tariffs in return for across-the-board cuts in tariffs by developing countries, including those protecting learning in skill- and technology-intensive industries that should eventually be removed with maturity. These should be cut as part of unfinished business as rapidly as possible irrespective of the commitments to be undertaken by developing countries.

As for the import regime for industrial products in developing countries, the crucial issue is how to reconcile policy flexibility with multilateral discipline. The proposals on the table leave little room not only because they stipulate deep cuts in industrial tariffs in developing countries, but also because they require tariff binding and reduction on a line-by-line basis. Such an approach could pose a number of problems not only for developing countries but also for the trading system as a whole.

There are more than 5,000 tariff lines in the Harmonized System for customs tariff classification. Even if commitments were to be made for broad categories of products rather than for individual tariff lines, an attempt to shape national commercial policy through multilateral commitments at the lowest layers of public intervention could pose problems of practicality and potential conflicts that may surpass even those caused by the proliferation of conditionalities attached to lending by the Bretton Woods Institutions. If countries are forced to make commitments which they cannot fulfill without suffering from serious disruptions, they might be inclined to resort to other, less transparent means of import restrictions, thereby creating trade frictions and weakening multilateral discipline. Recent history of international development policy is replete with examples showing an inverse correlation between proliferation of rules and conditions on the one hand, and the degree of compliance, on the other, particularly when rules are set without a full understanding of their consequences.

One way of addressing these difficulties would be to have a fixed lifespan for the agreements so that they can be automatically renegotiated after a certain period. This was the case with almost all free trade agreements of the nineteenth century, including the Anglo-French agreement which had a lifetime of 20 years, and was not renewed after its expiration. It would represent an important advance over current procedures for the renegotiation of tariffs. Such an option should be worth considering on its own merits regardless of how tariffs are bound.

Setting maximum (bound) line-by-line tariffs at sufficiently high levels so as to accommodate all contingencies would provide considerable flexibility to developing countries, but it would also render multilateral commitments superfluous. The proposal developed in this chapter, binding the average industrial tariff without line-by-line commitments, does not only have the advantage of simplicity compared to a complex system of tariff commitments. It would also reconcile multilateral discipline with policy flexibility since countries would be subject to an overall average ceiling in setting tariffs for individual products. Furthermore, for most countries in the early and intermediate stages of industrial development, it could result in lower average tariffs than would be the case under line-by-line commitments. In practice it would have the effect of balancing tariff increases with reductions; a country would need to lower its applied tariffs on certain products in order to be able to raise them elsewhere. This would encourage governments to view tariffs as temporary instruments, and to make an effort to ensure that they effectively serve the purpose they are designed for; that is, to provide a breathing space for infant industries before they mature and catch up with those in more advanced economies.

Notes

1. For a detailed discussion of these proposals see Khor and Goh Chien Yen (2004).
2. For bound tariffs before and after the application of various formulas see Fernandez de Cordoba et al. (2004b).
3. These estimates are based on Fernandez de Cordoba et al. (2004b).
4. For the historical evolution of industrial tariffs in the developed world the classic reference is Bairoch (1993). See also O'Rourke and Williamson (2000); and Chang (2002). For the evolution of tariffs in general see Williamson (2003).
5. UNCTAD TDR (1984). There was also a general upward drift in the use of subsidies after the early 1950s (Hufbauer, 1983). Shutt (1985) argues that liberalization was an illusion as tariff cuts were offset by a greater resort to market-distorting state interventions.
6. On the gunboat diplomacy see Clemens and Williamson (2002b), and the Ottoman predicament Kiray (1990).
7. For the distinction between natural and nurtured comparative advantages see Gomory and Baumol (2000).
8. Countries such as Finland and Sweden diversified on the basis of their natural resources, but their success in industrialization depended on moving to technology-intensive manufacturing. For a discussion of processing and diversification in timber and iron-related industries see UNCTAD TDR (1996).
9. For a discussion of the importance of internal integration in economic development and the trade-offs and complementarities involved between internal and external integration see Wade (2003).
10. Vernon's (1966) product-cycle theory also gives a similar description of shift of production across countries. However, it focuses on the behavior of TNCs and sees trade and FDI as successive stages in production for foreign markets.
11. See Argyrous (1996) who distinguishes between low-end and high-end capital goods with the former referring to standard, off-the-shelf equipment, the latter to custom-made machinery built for special purposes.
12. This classification based on products does not capture all aspects of manufacturing production. Many technology-intensive products involve labor-intensive processes, such as the assembly of imported electronic parts and components in developing countries participating in international production networks (IPNs). These should appear in the RL category; see Akyüz (2003 and 2005).
13. It is also possible to have non-linear paths for tariffs, falling at an accelerated or decelerated rate.
14. Since subsidies are substitutes for tariffs in maintaining domestic production above the level that would be possible under free trade, the vertical axis may be conceived as including also the tariff equivalent of subsidies. The horizontal axis could be defined in terms of per capita income rather than time, but the latter is preferred here in order to emphasize the sequence of industries.
15. For technology-driven trade, as opposed to endowment-driven trade, see Dosi, Pavitt, and Soete (1990).
16. Several ad hoc theoretical and empirical models have been developed to account for political-economy influences on tariff policy. For a survey see Gawande and Krishna (2003).

17. These countries thus run the risk of being squeezed between the bottom and top ends of the markets for manufactured exports, and contribute to a global glut in labor-intensive manufactures and the deterioration of manufacturing terms of trade of developing countries: see Akyüz (2003).

18. For predictions of potential benefits of the Uruguay Round see Martin and Winters (1996).

19. Brown et al. (2001). These estimates do not take into account the kind of adjustment costs discussed in the following section. They thus overestimate the benefits of liberalization. See Dorman (2001) for a critical assessment.

20. For a survey of these studies see Anderson (2004).

21. Some of the exercises noted above attempt to incorporate dynamic effects. For instance in the World Bank (2004) scenario, trade is assumed to induce productivity growth so that 'dynamic' gains would be a multiple of static gains.

22. Not all CGE models generate full employment equilibrium. This depends on the assumption about what is called 'macro-closure'; that is, how the equilibrium in the product market is attained. While the neoclassical closure gives full employment, under Keynesian closure aggregate demand and supply (or savings and investment) can be brought into equilibrium at less than full employment. For a classification of empirical CGE modeling see Thissen (1998). The estimates surveyed here generally use the GTAP (Global Trade Analysis Project) model developed at Purdue University, assuming neoclassical competitive equilibrium; see Anderson (2004).

23. Bacchetta and Jansen (2003). According to one of the few models, again designed for developed countries, that specifies the adjustment path between steady states and accounts for training costs of unemployed labor, aggregate adjustment costs could reach 90 percent of the comparative statics gains from freer trade even under modest assumptions regarding training costs and the discount factor; see Davidson and Matusz (2001).

24. However, as noted above, while tariffs lost their relative importance, other forms of intervention including subsidies, non-tariff barriers, and voluntary export restraints have proliferated in the postwar era. For an attempt to test possible explanations for this reversal, including widespread use of non-tariff barriers, see Clemens and Williamson (2002a).

25. According to a study of 63 countries including LDCs and advanced industrial countries, the average tariff is uncorrelated with growth, but countries that focus protection on skilled manufacturing exhibit faster growth than those with higher protection for unskilled manufacturing (which includes several industries classified as RL and LT here) (Nunn and Trefler, 2004). Higher protection for unskilled industries is associated with rent-seeking behavior. While this is highly plausible for advanced and even middle-income countries, higher tariffs on RL and LT products in LDCs dependent on primary commodities cannot always be said to reflect the inability of governments to prevent rent-seeking behavior, rather than a rational choice. For the same reason it is doubtful if higher protection for skilled industries in Bolivia, Ghana, and Haiti are more beneficial (or less harmful) to growth.

26. For tariffs and price distortions in East Asia compared to other 'interventionist' developing countries see Bruton (1998), and Wade (2003).

27. It is sometimes argued that because of increased participation of developing countries in IPNs organized by TNCs, tariffs are no longer needed for industrial progress. However, working with TNCs promises no more leapfrogging than liberalizing trade or even faster learning (Bruton, 1998; and Akyüz, 2005). For instance tariffs on imported skill- and technology-intensive parts and components can help encourage TNCs to contribute to indigenous learning of national firms by making greater use of local products. This may indeed be an effective way of increasing the domestic content of production in sectors dominated by TNCs in view of restrictions placed on domestic content requirements through TRIMS. For a discussion of the impact of the rise of TNCs on the ability of developing countries to conduct strategic industrial policy see Chang (2003).

28. On the concentration of high tariffs (tariff peaks) in developed countries on such products see Fernandez de Cordoba et al. (2004b).

References

Akyüz Y. (ed.) (2003), *Developing Countries and World Trade: Performance and Prospects*, Zed Books, London.

—— (2005), 'Trade, Growth and Industrialization: Issues, Experience and Policy Challenges,' TWN Trade and Development Series 24, Third World Network, Penang.

—— R. Kozul-Wright, and J. Mayer (2004), 'Trade and Industrial Upgrading: Catching Up and Falling Behind' in Will Milberg (ed.) *Labour and the Globalization of Production: Causes and Consequences of Industrial Upgrading*, Palgrave Macmillan, New York.

Anderson K. (2004), 'Subsidies and Trade Barriers,' Copenhagen Consensus Challenge Paper, Centre for International Economic Studies, University of Adelaide.

Argyrous G. (1996), 'Cumulative Causation and Industrial Evolution: Kaldor's Four Stages of Industrialization as an Evolutionary Model,' *Journal of Economic Issues*, 30 (1): 97–119.

Bacchetta M. and M. Jansen (2003), 'Adjusting to Trade Liberalization: The Role of Policy Institutions and WTO Disciplines,' *Special Study* 7, WTO, Geneva.

Bairoch P. (1993), *Economics & World History: Myths and Paradoxes*, University of Chicago Press, Chicago.

Baldwin R., J. Mutti, and J. Richardson (1980), 'Welfare Effects on the United States of a Significant Tariff Reduction,' *Journal of International Economics*, 10: 405–23.

Brown D., A. Deardorff, and R. Stern (2001), 'CGE Modelling and Analysis of Multilateral and Regional Negotiating Options,' University of Michigan School of Public Policy Research Seminar in International Economics, Discussion Paper 468.

Bruton H. (1998), 'A Reconsideration of Import Substitution,' *Journal of Economic Literature*, 36: 903–36.

Chang H-J. (2002), *Kicking Away the Ladder: Development Strategy in Historical Perspective*, Anthem Press, London.

—— (2003), *Globalization, Economic Development and the Role of the State*, Anthem Press, London.

Clemens M. and J. Williamson (2001), 'A Tariff–Growth Paradox? Protection's Impact the World Around 1875–1997,' NBER Working Paper 8459.

—— —— (2002a), 'Why Did the Tariff–Growth Correlation Reverse after 1950?' NBER Working Paper 9181.

—— —— (2002b), 'Closed Jaguar, Open Dragon: Comparing Tariffs in Latin America and Asia Before World War II,' NBER Working Paper 9401.

Davidson C. and S. Matusz (2001), 'On Adjustment Costs,' GEP Research Paper 24, University of Nottingham.

DeJong D. and M. Ripoll (2005), 'Tariffs and Growth: An Empirical Exploration of Contingent Relationships,' University of Pittsburgh.

Dorman P. (2001), 'The Free Trade Magic,' Briefing Paper, Economy Policy Institute.

Dosi G., K. Pavitt, and L. Soete (1990), *The Economics of Technical Change and International Trade*, Harvester Wheatsheaf, New York.

Edwards S. (1992), 'Trade Orientation, Distortions, and Growth in Developing Countries,' *Journal of Development Economics*, 39: 31–57.

Fernandez de Cordoba S. and D. Vanzetti (2005), 'Now What? Searching for a Solution to the WTO Industrial Tariff Negotiations,' UNCTAD, Geneva.

—— S. Laird, and D. Vanzetti (2004a), 'Trick or Threat? Development Opportunities and Challenges in the WTO Negotiations on Industrial Tariffs,' UNCTAD, Geneva.

—— —— —— (2004b), 'Blend it like Beckham: Trying to Read the Ball in the WTO Negotiations on Industrial Tariffs,' UNCTAD, Geneva.

Gawande K. and P. Krishna (2003), 'The Political Economy of Trade Policy: Empirical Approaches' in J. Harrigan and E. Choi (eds.) *Handbook of International Trade*, Basil Blackwell, Oxford.

Gomory R. and W. Baumol (2000), *Global Trade and Conflicting National Interests*, MIT Press, Cambridge, MA.

Harcourt G. (1972), *Some Cambridge Controversies in the Theory of Capital*, Cambridge University Press, Cambridge.

Hicks J. (1965), *Capital and Growth*, Clarendon Press, Oxford.

Hufbauer G. (1983), 'Subsidy Issues after the Tokyo Round' in W. Cline (ed.) *Trade Policy in the 1980s*, Institute for International Economics, Washington, DC.

Imbs J. and R. Wacziarg (2000), 'Stages of Diversification,' CEPR Discussion Paper 2642.

Irwin D. (2000), 'Tariffs and Growth in Late Nineteenth Century America,' NBER Working Paper 7639.

—— (2002a), 'Interpreting the Tariff–Growth Correlation of the Late Nineteenth Century,' NBER Working Paper 8739.

—— (2002b), 'Did Import Substitution Policies Promote Growth in the Late Nineteenth Century?' NBER Working Paper 8751.

—— (2003), 'New Estimates of the Average Tariff of the United States, 1790–1820,' NBER Working Paper 9616.

Kaldor N. (1966), *Causes of the Slow Rate of Economic Growth of the United Kingdom*, Cambridge University Press, Cambridge.

Khor M. and G. Yen (2004), 'The WTO Negotiations on Non-Agricultural Market Access: A Development Perspective,' TWN, Geneva.

Kiray E. (1990), 'Turkish Debt and Conditionality in Historical Perspective: A Comparison of the 1980s with the 1860s' in T. Aricanli and D. Rodrik (eds.) *The Political Economy of Turkey: Debt, Adjustment and Sustainability*. Macmillan, Hong Kong.

Laird S., S. Fernandez de Cordoba, and D. Vanzetti (2003), 'Market Access Proposals for Non-Agricultural Products,' UNCTAD, Geneva.

Maddison A. (2001), *The World Economy: A Millennial Perspective,* OECD, Paris.

Martin W. and A. Winters (eds.) (1996), *The Uruguay Round and the Developing Countries,* Cambridge University Press, Cambridge.

Nunn N. and D. Trefler (2004), 'The Political Economy of Tariffs and Growth,' University of Toronto.

O'Rourke K. (1995), 'Computable General Equilibrium Models and Economic History,' University College, Dublin <http://www.gams.com/solvers/mspge>.

—— (2000), 'Tariffs and Growth in the Late 19th Century,' *Economic Journal,* 10(4): 456–83.

—— and J. Williamson (2000), *Globalization and Economic History: The Evolution of Nineteenth Century Atlantic Economy,* MIT Press, Cambridge, MA.

Prebisch R. (1950), 'The Economic Development of Latin America and Its Principal Problems,' *Economic Bulletin for Latin America,* 7, United Nations, New York.

Shutt H. (1985), *The Myth of Free Trade,* Basil Blackwell, Oxford.

Singer H. (1950), 'The Distribution of Gains between Investing and Borrowing Countries,' *American Economic Review,* 15: 473–85.

Stanford J. (1993), 'Continental Economic Integration: Modeling the Impact on Labor,' *Annals of the Academy of Political and Social Science,* 526: 92–110.

Thissen M. (1998), 'A Classification of Empirical CGE Modelling,' SOM Research Report 99C01, University of Groningen.

United Nations Conference on Trade and Development (UNCTAD) (Various issues), *Trade and Development Report,* United Nations, Geneva.

Vernon R. (1966), 'International Investment and International Trade in the Product Cycle,' *The Quarterly Journal of Economics,* 80: 190–207.

Wade R. (2003), *Governing the Market,* 2nd edn, Princeton University Press.

Williamson J. (2003), 'Was It Stolper–Samuelson, Infant Industry or Something Else? World Tariffs 1789–1938,' NBER Working Paper 9656.

World Bank (1993), *The East Asian Miracle: Economic Growth and Public Policy,* Oxford University Press.

—— (2004), *Global Economic Prospects,* Washington, D.C.

Yenikkaya H. (2003), 'Trade Openness and Economic Growth: A Cross-Country Empirical Investigation,' *Journal of Development Economics,* 72: 57–89.

Young A. (1928), 'Increasing Returns and Economic Progress,' *Economic Journal,* 38(152): 527–42.

7

The (Slow) Return of Industrial Policies in Latin America and the Caribbean

Wilson Peres

Introduction

This chapter is based on the hypothesis that, to empower their development processes, the countries of Latin America and the Caribbean need to implement policies aimed at creating new sectors or modernizing mature ones, within the constraints imposed by the size, development level, and economic structure of the individual national economies. Diversification of the production structure, thereby improving the product mix and the vector of international specialization, is decisive for closing the productivity gap in relation to the international technology frontier, and, hence, for quickening the pace of aggregate productivity growth in open economies. Such diversification allows for better domestic linkages, thereby reinforcing the positive impact of economic growth on aggregate productivity (Cimoli, Correa, and Primi, 2003).

The experience of public–private consensus-building efforts in Latin America in the 1990s suggests that opportunities for bringing about change in the structure and dynamics of industry through marginal policies may have been exhausted. These efforts—for example, the National Competitiveness Council in Colombia or the Production Development Forum in Chile—focused on identifying specific competitiveness problems in production chains or sectors, and then proposing particular actions to address them. This approach was

* This chapter has benefited from comments by the participants at the second meeting of the Task Force on Industrial Policy of the Initiative for Policy Dialogue (IPD), held in Rio de Janeiro in March 2005. In particular, the author is grateful for comments made by Antonio Barros de Castro (who was the main discussant), Alice Amsden, Giovanni Dosi, Bernardo Kosacoff, Yevgeny Kuznetsov, Richard Nelson, Gabriel Palma, and Annalisa Primi. Parts of this chapter have already been published in ECLAC (2004a), ch. 8.

akin to identifying market failures and designing policies to correct them. A competitiveness benchmark was identified for a sector or chain, and actions were designed to correct the problems that caused the gap between the actual conditions and the benchmark—by building some infrastructure, for example, or simplifying an administrative procedure, or changing a rule. While these decisions were not always put into practice, they were an improvement compared to the laissez-faire approach that characterized the first half of the 1990s. The evidence, however, shows that the results achieved were less than outstanding, except with regard to exports that possessed comparative natural or labor advantages. And, we all agree that backwardness and inaction are especially harmful where technology and innovation are concerned.

Time has also passed. The gap between the region and the developed and newly industrialized economies has grown in terms of productivity and competitiveness, while the pace of the technological revolution has accelerated. Continued reliance on marginal measures may fall short of what is required to attain objectives such as 'competitive insertion in the world marketplace', 'joining the knowledge society', or, to be less presumptuous, 'adding value to exports'.

Naturally, it may be argued that big problems do not always require big solutions, and that a few well-chosen actions may serve as catalysts. There is, however, no evidence that any real progress has been made in determining whether such catalysts exist, and, if they do, what they are. The usual discourse is that an action can serve as a catalyst when its importance is acknowledged, but no significant resources are allocated to it. Another approach advocates a large number of marginal actions leading toward change. This view may be correct; however, hundreds of measures have been identified using consensus-building mechanisms, and only a few have been implemented. Today, it does not appear to be significantly easier to implement hundreds of actions than it was a decade ago, given the scarce progress made in the development and strengthening of policy institutions. Consequently, changing the structure of industry does not appear to be a costlier alternative, especially since there is little time left to enter the technology and innovation race, if the goal is truly to achieve 'competitive insertion in the world', 'join the knowledge society', or 'add value to exports'.

In this context, deliberate sectoral strengthening policies can increase the density and complexity of a country's production structure; and those variables are positively correlated with the stability of its growth rates, and the speed and flexibility of its response to external shocks (Castaldi, 2003). A dense and complex production structure creates domestic counterweights to the transmission of shocks, thereby generating automatic stabilizers. Specialization, in conjunction with increased knowledge content and diversification, makes it possible more fully to exploit the increasing returns to scale implicit in technical progress, which leads directly to virtuous cumulative causation processes (Young, 1928; Stigler, 1951; Kaldor, 1966).

In short, the core of a policy to speed up long-run productivity growth involves a combination of knowledge accumulation and diversification of the production structure. The first generates the possibilities, while the second materializes them. Both of these dimensions are present in this essay, which is organized in five sections. Following this introduction, which also reviews the broad currents of industrial-policy experience during the import-substitution (ISI) period, the second section describes current policy practices in the region and develops a typology of the strategies that underlie them. The third section describes the main lines of action and policy instruments, while the fourth analyzes issues relating to the evaluation of their implementation and impact; the fifth section concludes.

Policies to create new sectors were at the heart of industrial policy in the ISI model.[1] Even now, industrial policy is frequently defined as one that seeks to alter the production vector of goods and services (Chang, 1994; Melo, 2001), which necessarily implies the creation of new activities. The aim of that policy was to complete a country's industrial fabric, endogenizing the effects of domestic demand growth, particularly investment, which would otherwise fuel imports and put pressure on the external constraint. In the 1970s there was a growing perception that the effects of investment were being split in two: on the one hand, an expansion of production capacity, thereby boosting aggregate supply; but, on the other, a derived demand for capital goods which, owing to insufficient domestic supply, fuelled import demand and thus dissipated the potential spillover effects of the investment on the rest of the domestic economy. At that time, industrial policy, sectoral policy, and policy to develop the production of capital goods were understood as closely related concepts.

The main tools of industrial policy combined trade protection with promotion of direct investments (frequently state or foreign) and financing by national development banks. The clearest examples in the 1970s, prior to the break triggered by the debt crisis, were the Second National Development Plan in Brazil, and the National Industrial Development Program 1979–1982 in Mexico, which coincided with the boom in oil exports.

Industrial policies organized the expansion of domestic supply and were at the heart of plans and programs aimed at diversifying the production structure. Three interrelated factors strengthened this role: (i) the public-sector development institutions were organized into sectoral and even subsectoral structures;[2] (ii) private enterprise was also organized in sectoral chambers, which were the principal defenders of the pattern of trade protection; and (iii) international trade negotiations, such as the framework of Latin American Integration Association (LAIA), the Central American Common Market (CACM), the Caribbean Community (CARICOM) or the Andean Pact, were based on negative or positive sectoral preference lists. Although policies tended to focus on the agricultural and manufacturing sectors, the weight of the latter was such that the term 'sectoral policy' tended to be confused with industrial policy.

From that central position, industrial policies steadily fell from favor during the 1980s, and were practically excluded from the new economic model that was established along with the structural reforms, at least in its more strict formulation. There were several reasons for this: (i) the public enterprises that had traditionally invested directly in new sectors were either privatized or closed, reflecting the new view that the state should only play a subsidiary role in economic growth; (ii) the need to balance public finances meant eliminating subsidies, particularly fiscal ones, and the subsidy components of credit operations; and (iii) there was a (sometimes controversial) perception that many investments suffered from bad planning, poor project management, and corruption, and in some cases were actually useless—the so-called 'white elephants.' This loss of legitimacy did not occur in all parts of the world. For example, in several countries of East and Southeast Asia, active sectoral policies, sometimes with targeting at the firm level, remained in force until well into the 1990s; but they subsequently faded as those countries gradually, and at different rates, joined the free-market wave and the new international trade regime.[3]

Apart from the economic arguments against industrial policy, political opposition to the new economic model came from agents who supported the previous paradigm, thereby consolidating the 'developmental versus neo-liberal' stereotype. Agents in favor of structural reforms countered that opposition by promoting a discourse that portrayed sectoral industrial policies as a distortion in resource allocation and the cause of fiscal imbalances that fuelled inflationary processes. Although this critical attitude towards industrial policy was shared by a growing number of governments in the region,[4] such an extreme view did not always coincide with the facts. Even strongly reformist governments, such as those of Menem in Argentina, Collor de Melo in Brazil, and Salinas de Gortari in Mexico, maintained certain sectoral policies, in particular for the automotive industry.

Practice and strategy of industrial policies

The region's experience

Much of the region's current experience in industrial policy is encapsulated in the term 'competitiveness policies' (Peres, 1997).[5] Ongoing policies in the region can be organized in four broad groups. First, there are policies following the line developed under the ISI model which aim to expand a given sector and deepen it by integrating new segments, through a combination of trade protection, and tax and financial incentives. The regimes covering the automotive industries of the Mercosur countries and Mexico, which aimed to organize and expand the investments of auto makers and auto-part producers, provide a clear example of this type of initiative (ECLAC, 2004b). Many of the region's countries have provided sporadic support for sensitive sectors (of weak competitiveness) such as textiles, clothing, footwear, electronic products, and toys. Numerous examples can also be found of policies to stimulate agricultural and mining production. Although these vary from country to country, they have generally been much more stable than the incentives given to manufacturing activities. Even in sectors with clear comparative advantages, such as large segments of the agriculture sector, it has frequently been necessary to design support schemes in response to short-term crises[6] or to meet longer-term challenges arising from a relative loss of competitiveness.[7]

In the agriculture sector, several countries (including Central America, Brazil, and Colombia) intervene directly in basic grain markets (wheat, maize, rice). Nonetheless, direct market intervention (through guaranteed prices, for example) and the granting of subsidized loans through programs targeting small-scale producers (who tend to be the hardest hit by trade liberalization) are progressively being replaced by horizontal instruments (such as expenditure on animal and plant health, irrigation, or land titling programs) (FAO, 2001; ECLAC, 2003). Measures with a geographic or local scope are also gaining ground (e.g. tax incentives in poor regions, or comprehensive rural development programs that combine investment in infrastructure with training and technical assistance).

Secondly, a number of measures originally targeted on specific sectors have developed into policies that impact the economic system as a whole. This is the case of policies for the electronics and computer industry, which began as import-substitution policies for hardware and later shifted to supporting the development of an intangible product (software), before being subsumed under policies for the development of information and communication technologies (ICTs), and to promote the information society in the region.[8] The widespread prevalence of scope and networking economies, and complementarities between activities, means that these should be viewed as cross-cutting policies, reaching beyond sectoral or institutional boundaries which, themselves, tend to be increasingly ill-defined and vague.

A third group of policies focuses on activities that are highly concentrated as a result of scale and network economies (electric power, telecommunications, oil and natural gas). Policies for these sectors, nearly all of which were decided upon following privatization processes, have aimed to develop efficient regulatory frameworks, including creation and strengthening of regulatory bodies, adaptation of the legal framework, and efforts to link the expansion of sectoral investments to greater coordination with suppliers located in the country, the intensity of which varies from case to case.[9] In Brazil, technology funds were created to support scientific and technological development programs in each of the sectors in question, using funds obtained from royalties paid by the firms.[10]

A fourth group consists of policies to support clusters, particularly of small and medium-sized enterprises, or activities in which there are many enterprises of that size under the leadership of larger firms. This approach has become increasingly accepted in Andean and Central American countries; and, like other industrial policies, it has been aimed more at increasing the competitiveness of existing sectors than at creating new activities. At the subnational level, significant measures to develop clusters have been implemented in countries such as Mexico and Brazil, such as support for the footwear sector in Guanajuato or the electronics industry in Jalisco, Mexico (Unger, 2003; Dussel, 1999), or the measures implemented by the Brazilian Service of Support for Micro and Small Enterprises (SEBRAE) throughout that country, in the framework of the project to develop local clusters known as APLs (*arranjos produtivos locais*).[11] The legitimacy enjoyed by such policies, even among international financial organizations, has facilitated their acceptance by governments and resulted in actions being included in this category that have neither a production-chain nor a geographic-conglomerate scope.[12]

A typology of national strategies

The revival of interest in active microeconomic and sectoral policies in the mid-1990s generated three ways of looking at competitiveness policies. In some countries, basically Brazil, Mexico, and the English-speaking Caribbean, policy documents were designed that specifically targeted the industrial sector and its linkages with technological development and participation in the international economy.[13] The fact that, strictly speaking, these documents constituted work agendas between the government and the private sector rather than industrial plans or programs led their critics to accuse them of being 'programs without targets' and even 'without resources.'

In the Andean and Central American countries, the predominant approach aimed to enhance the competitiveness of the economy as a whole, without giving preference to the industrial sector; and national competitiveness strategies were based on the cluster methodology, albeit under a variety of names: industrial agglomerations, production arrangements, or conglomerates.[14] From the policy-implementation standpoint, that approach resulted in the negotiation and implementation of sectoral agreements encompassing complete value chains, between private agents and the government, with the latter playing the role of catalyst or facilitator.

Lastly, Argentina, Chile, and Uruguay eschewed industrial policies or national competitiveness strategies, preferring horizontal policies[15] that sought to avoid discrimination between sectors, and were implemented by providing demand incentives for firms, in contrast to the supply subsidies typical of the previous model. Nonetheless, when problems arose that had a clearly sectoral dimension, horizontal policy instruments would be brought to bear, ignoring the fact that this would negate their essentially neutral character. Chile was where this type of intervention was conceptualized and implemented most forcefully, although direct subsidies for the forestry and mining sectors and for export activities were maintained in that country for a long time (Moguillansky, 2000).

Unlike in other areas of development policy, there is no convergence on sectoral policy among the countries of the region in the early 2000s. Whereas some countries promote a discourse that rejects such policies outright, despite providing ad hoc sectoral support in practice, elsewhere they are recognized as valid for increasing the competitiveness of activities that have potential to break into external markets or are facing strong competition from imports. There is also a double standard in the treatment of such policies: countries that deny their usefulness, especially when they support the manufacturing sector, use them openly in numerous agricultural and service sectors (e.g. tourism) without making any attempt to legitimize them.

On the basis of this historical analysis of policy design, the region's countries can be classified or ranked according to three categories: the aim of the intervention, its frequency or intensity, and the degree to which the actions that implement it are coordinated through a broader-scope strategy.

In terms of the *intervention target*, as mentioned above there are three types of countries: (i) those that have maintained or even revived sectoral policies; (ii) those in which sectoral policies are basically seen in terms of cluster development; and (iii) countries that have adopted neither of these two perspectives and use only horizontal policies, which, nonetheless, sometimes target a specific sector.

While horizontal policies are broadly accepted everywhere, what distinguishes countries in the first two categories is their use of policies that go further. Available information reveals the existence of loans from development banks and fiscal incentives targeting specific sectors.[16] In seven of the region's countries (Argentina, Brazil, Colombia, Costa Rica, and Mexico, among others) public development banks extend credits with a sectoral focus, while 18 countries have designed tax incentives to benefit specific sectors. One form of incentive that is even more widespread consists of special regulations for establishing free trade zones for export or maquila plants.

The overall analysis of the information highlights an initial departure from the practices of the previous model. Whereas, in the latter, manufacturing industry was privileged, now it is one of the sectors of least weight. The most favored activities have been tourism; primary sectors such as oil, mining, and forestry; and various services (ranging from infrastructure to cinema). The importance of policies targeting the agriculture sector varies widely between the different countries of the region, if measured in terms of the public expenditure that implements them (including production development programs, investments in rural infrastructure, and social spending in rural areas).[17] Public development banks, meanwhile, make a major contribution to financing that sector in countries such as Argentina, Brazil, Costa Rica, the

Dominican Republic, or Mexico (Acevedo, 2002). Credit is generally extended under near-market conditions, with interest-rate subsidies being provided in programs to strengthen small-scale agriculture.

The foregoing point needs to be nuanced by analyzing the credit portfolios of six development banks in five of the region's countries. Industrial activity continues to absorb roughly half of all credit extended by Banco Nacional de Desenvolvimento Econômico e Social (BNDES) of Brazil, Banco Nacional de Comercio Exterior (BANCOMEXT) of Mexico, and Banco de Comercio Exterior of Colombia (BANCOLDEX); and it accounts for roughly 25 percent of the entire portfolio of Corporación Financiera de Desarrollo (COFIDE) of Peru, and under 15 percent of the Banco Nacional de Costa Rica (BNCR), and Nacional Financiera (NAFIN) of Mexico. Given that BANCOLDEX and BANCOMEXT make loans to finance foreign trade, of the six institutions, only BNDES would seem to play a major role in financing the domestic manufacturing sector.[18]

Secondly, countries differ in the *frequency* or *intensity* with which they implement sectoral policies: countries that implement a wide range of measures at the sector level (e.g. Argentina, Brazil, Colombia, Guyana, Mexico, Uruguay, and Venezuela); those that support only a few activities (Bolivia, Chile, the Dominican Republic, and Peru, among others); and countries where such policies are virtually non-existent (Haiti, Paraguay, and Suriname). The intensity of sectoral policies can be detected through measures that do not involve fiscal and financial subsidies, such as in Colombia, which has a very active policy of sectoral agreements that are not based on this type of incentive, or in El Salvador, which has an active policy in support of clusters (Alonso, 2003).

In Mexico, the 2002 Economic Policy for Competitiveness specifies a total of 12 priority sectors as the targets of sectoral programs, of which four are currently in operation (fibers–textiles–clothing; leather–footwear; electronics and high-technology industries; and software). Progress has also been made in relation to the automotive industry, maquila exports, and the chemical industry.[19]

In 2003, the Brazilian Government announced Guidelines on Industrial, Technology, and Foreign-Trade Policy, which set out its strategic sectoral alternatives in four knowledge-intensive activities (semiconductors, software, pharmaceuticals and medicines, and capital goods), and the creation of an institution to coordinate the implementation of that policy, the Brazilian Industrial Development Agency.[20] The PITCE marked the return of industrial policies to the country's development agenda.

In May 2008, Brazil launched a new industrial policy which has an even stronger sectoral focus. Beyond horizontal, basically fiscal, measures and six strategic technological programs (health, ICT, defense, nuclear energy, bio and nanotechnologies), this policy includes seven programs targeted to leading sectors (aeronautics; oil, natural gas, and petrochemicals; bioethanol; mining;

steel; pulp and paper; meat) and 12 industrial competitiveness programs. Resources for policy implementation would consist of financing to industry and services, financing to R&D, and tax incentives (Government of Brazil, 2008). This program represents the most advanced industrial policy in Latin America, both in terms of policy design and institutional coordination.

After 2003, Argentina has selected nine production chains to be supported by the Programa Foros Nacionales de Competitividad Industrial de las Cadenas Productivas (wood and furniture, leather and leather products, textiles and apparel, agricultural machinery, building materials, software, biotechnology, natural gas for automobiles, and cultural industries).[21] Other countries, such as Costa Rica, Peru, and Uruguay, target development actions in even greater detail, supporting individual projects in certain firms. Examples include investment incentives in megaprojects in the Peruvian mining sector,[22] measures taken by the government of Costa Rica to encourage Intel to establish operations in the country,[23] or tax exemptions in support of projects declared to be in the national interest in Uruguay.[24]

The third category—the degree to which measures are coordinated—entails considering an additional dimension within the rationale of those policies, namely their integration or lack of integration in a more general national strategy. Here again countries fall into three categories: countries with frequent measures contained in explicit public-intervention strategies, generally expressed through official plans or programs (e.g. Brazil, Colombia, El Salvador, and Mexico); those with frequent measures but no explicit strategy (Costa Rica and Uruguay); and countries that implement measures sporadically (the vast majority).

The three categories considered have remained very stable in each country over time, reflecting their capacity and experience in industrial policy design and implementation. Changes of government, even when that entailed a sudden break with the country's past policy, such as in Mexico in 2000 or Uruguay in 2005, have not produced major changes in attitudes towards industrial policies. Two examples, albeit in different directions, are the continued minor importance of sectoral policies in Chile, and the continuity of sectoral agreements (export competitiveness) in Colombia during the governments of Presidents Samper, Pastrana, and Uribe. Such agreements encompassed 41 production chains and sectors accounting for 86 percent of all non-traditional exports.[25]

Although definitely positive, this display of institutional maturity should not be overstated, because regional experience also abounds in examples of programs that were developed to alleviate efficiency problems but came to nothing.[26] Even Brazil's policy for the automotive industry in the 1990s contained elements that suggest the rescue of a sector in crisis that is unable to face external competition—that is, industrial restructuring, as it used to be called in the 1980s (Bonelli and Motta Veiga, 2003).

Lines of action and instruments

As has been stated repeatedly in the literature,[27] the region's competitiveness policies, including those with a basically sectoral scope, have focused much more on enhancing the efficiency of existing sectors than on creating new ones—an emphasis that is consistent with the search for greater penetration in international markets, founded essentially on static comparative advantages (unskilled labor and natural resources). This has been the case both in countries with a diversified production structure, such as Brazil and Mexico, and in those that are more specialized. In the more diversified countries, it could be argued that there are few non-existent sectors, so a sectoral policy would only be detected at the level of specific products. Although that is true, the evidence, especially for Brazil until the 2008 industrial policy and to a lesser extent for Mexico,[28] suggests that sectoral measures have focused on strengthening and expanding pre-existing sectors. The clearest example is the automotive industry, as mentioned above.

The creation of new activities appears sporadically as a policy objective, and two basic lines of action have been pursued for this purpose: international trade negotiations to ensure market access, based on bilateral or multilateral free-trade agreements, and the attraction of foreign direct investment (FDI) to develop export platforms, including activities in duty-free zones and maquila plants.

In most countries of the region, policies to attract FDI have been the key mechanism used to develop new sectors. Policy initiatives include a deepening of Mexico's export platform in the framework of NAFTA (automobiles and auto parts, electronics, and clothing); promotion of the most elementary activities of first-generation maquila industries in a number of Central American and Caribbean countries (clothing); and investments in privatizations in the services and primary sectors in South American countries (Mortimore, 2000; Peres and Reinhardt, 2000). The different combinations between sector-level public policy and the strategies of the transnational enterprises providing FDI have been the main determinants of activities resulting in more diversified production structures. Nonetheless, this has clearly had limitations, such as low levels of value-added resulting from a focus on assembly activities with weak linkages to the rest of the domestic economy.

The instruments used to attract foreign enterprises can be classified into three broad groups (Mortimore and Peres, 1998): (i) attraction on the basis of incentives, essentially of the free-zone and fiscal type; (ii) attraction based on rules, that is, creating efficient business conditions (rule of law, transparency, assured access to international markets, efficient infrastructure, and so on); and (iii) attraction based on the creation of specialized factors of production, particularly skilled labor. Although the region's countries have applied these three types of instrument with varying degrees of intensity, with few exceptions the first two have predominated.

In addition to specific instruments for attracting FDI, two others have targeted investment of any type (i.e. domestic or foreign). Besides financial and fiscal incentives, they include a broad set of measures whereby governments seek to establish competitive environments for enterprises to operate in (defense of competition and regulation of monopolies), lower transaction costs (e.g. reduction of administrative controls), or to promote the exploitation of scale economies based on collective action by firms (sectoral agreements across production chains, support for partnerships between firms, etc.).

The remaining lines of policy designed in the region can be organized in three groups: winning policies, losing policies, and emerging policies (Peres, 1997). Winning policies include those that are generally accepted by governments, that is, they enjoy strong legitimacy. In addition to the policies for export development and FDI attraction mentioned above, this group also includes policies to promote technological development, human resource training, and small firms and microenterprises—generally by supporting the establishment or consolidation of business networks or clusters—and production development at the local or subnational level, the latter two being closely linked. Recently, policies to foster innovation are increasingly accepted throughout the region, as is shown by the number of science and technology plans released in the last years, even in some of the smallest countries.[29] Acceptance of these policies stems from their assumed neutrality since they act on factor markets (technology and human resources development), or because of their (also supposed) positive impact on job creation, basically at the subnational or local level.

Losing policies, in contrast, are most clearly contrary to the existing development model based on trade openness and the reduction of the public-sector deficit. They include direct fiscal subsidies, directed credit with subsidized interest rates, foreign trade tariffs, and use of the power of state procurement. In terms of the latter, the situation varies from one country to another: while some use it nationally or subnationally, as in the program for the support of software production in Mexico, mentioned above, in other countries it is off the policy agenda because its use is deemed contrary to the goals of expenditure efficiency and transparency. Given that financial and fiscal subsidies are instruments for the implementation of the winning policies, a sharp contradiction arises. Policy implementation suffers from the fact that governments that want to support industrial development through the winning policies are seldom able to implement them because of the lack of effective action in the fiscal and financial fields.

Lastly, emerging policies—which, among other things, encompass defense of competition, improvement of corporate governance regimes, regulation of infrastructure sectors where markets do not operate efficiently—while enjoying great legitimacy, have yet to reach maturity, and their development varies widely across countries. Some countries have modern legislation and relatively strong institutions to implement them; whereas in others, they are still at the discussion and decision stages, and in some cases such policies are not yet a significant item on the policy agenda.

Aside from national differences, the region displays strong convergence in terms of the content of policy documents over the last decade, centered around four basic elements: (i) emphasis on increasing international competitiveness; (ii) generalization of the legitimacy of horizontal or neutral instruments, which, as mentioned above, are actually far from horizontal or neutral *ex post*; (iii) support for small businesses and microenterprises, basically for reasons linked to their job-creation capacity; and (iv) the focus of attention on subnational or local economic areas. Programs to support clusters provide the clearest examples of at least three of these elements, and the SEBRAE program to support APLs in Brazil is possibly the most important in the region.

Evaluation of implementation and impact

Evaluation of the implementation and impact of the policies that have been applied is hampered not only by a lack of available information, but also because the design of the instruments deployed seldom explicitly establishes the criteria and mechanisms to be used to evaluate them. This is compounded by the technical complexity of evaluating policies that contain numerous objectives and lines of action. Data on the financial resources channeled into programs or projects are scarce,[30] so it is hard to conduct an overall assessment. Nonetheless, with few exceptions, it appears that many of the policies announced in the region have not actually been implemented—as shown in Peres (1997), and in particular the analyses of Alonso (2003) on the situation of the five Central American countries, and by Fairbanks and Lindsay (1997) on the Andean countries that designed competitiveness strategies based on a cluster approach.

Various factors can be blamed for widespread implementation failures (government failures) and the consequent shortfall between what was decided and what was actually executed in the studies mentioned:

The inclusion of *non-operational or unachievable goals* in policy design, which shifts the real decision on their effective implementation to the budgetary appropriation stage. In such cases, the problem consists of shortcomings of design, the contents of which often are more declarative statements than instruments of resource allocation. An evaluation of success factors in the 41 Colombian sectoral agreements shows that: (i) those with well-structured, quantifiable commitments and specific time horizons are easier to monitor and fulfill; (ii) agreements with few and simple commitments tend to be more successful; (iii) the leadership and decision-making power of the individuals who negotiate the agreements play a fundamental role; and (iv) chains in which work is carried out prior to the agreements achieved better results.[31] As practice in the region often makes no attempt to take these success factors into account, policy documents tend to be shopping lists of needs and objectives. Although the multiplicity of goals may reflect the involvement of many stakeholders in complex societies, it also indicates an inability to choose priorities and build consensus around a small number of implementable goals.

Lack of human and financial resources to implement policies. This is particularly serious in the smaller and poorer countries which often depend on external funding (loans or grants) to design and implement their programs. In addition to a lack of resources, policies are usually announced without considering their cost and the corresponding financing, assuming once again that 'first we decide and then we see what can be done and with what resources.'

Nearly all of the region's countries display *weak institutional capacity* for policy implementation, even in policies that are not complex. This shortcoming is greater when policies aim to approach best international practice, rather than respond to the needs of the countries interested in applying them. This results in designs that are disconnected from reality, often promoted by state mechanisms of little weight in the power structure of governments, or business associations that are unrepresentative and have little economic and political weight, which makes the situation even more difficult. The problem is further aggravated by the regional tendency to separate the design of policy instruments from their implementation. Although countries can increase their institutional capacity over time, and some have done so in the region, institution building and innovation require stability of objectives for longer periods than those typical of a government in the region (between four and six years), together with financial resources that confer action capacity. In that regard, the wide range of tax burdens in the region's countries, from less than 10 percent to over 30 percent of GDP, introduce structural differences in terms of what can be achieved in this domain.

Government agreements to implement policies with the private sector are weak, as can clearly be seen when executing public expenditure or investment commitments in conjunction with the private sector. There is also a proliferation of plans and programs designed merely to respond to political pressures from economic stakeholders, obtain international funding, or comply with legal or constitutional provisions. The strength with which the business sector defended protectionism until the late 1970s has not been seen in its promotion of policies to diversify and enhance productive specialization in the countries of the region.[32]

In the case of industrial policies, implementation problems are compounded by the *weak economic signals* emitted by programs that seek to create or expand new activities. Compared to the strength and clarity of the signal associated with trade protection, which made it possible to fix domestic prices and thus maximize profitability (typical of the ISI model), now, at best, the entrepreneur is offered a package that is complex to conceptualize and operate, and whose impact on profitability is uncertain and far from clear. It is hardly surprising that there is such a perception that policies do not work.

Implementation failures and the perception that 'policies do not work' undermine their legitimacy and the interest they arouse, especially among their main targets, namely entrepreneurs. This gives rise to the paradox that entrepreneurs bemoan the lack of resources available for policies, while at the same time failing to make full use of what is available. Overcoming these implementation failures and making sure that instruments designed actually function is one of the key challenges facing productive development policies.

Despite the problems outlined above, progress has been made on relations between public authorities and business chambers for policy design and, in some cases, implementation. Although stand-off situations still persist, significant progress has been made in developing public–private dialogue. The process has gone beyond strengthening of dialogue and has now reached a stage in which the leadership of policy proposals has often been exercised by business entities. Examples include the Asociación Nacional de Industriales (ANDI) of Colombia, the Confederación de Cámaras de la Industria de Transformación (CANACINTRA) in Mexico, the Asociación de Industriales in the Dominican Republic, the Cámara de Industrias in Costa Rica, or the Federación de Cámaras Industriales de Centroamérica (FECAICA), which promoted the industrial modernization agenda in Central America. In these countries and elsewhere, it is even possible to speak of public–private co-responsibility in policy formulation, rather than mere policy consensus (Peres, 1997).

Business chambers have also participated actively in negotiating forums to design measures in support of competitiveness, such as the National Competitiveness Council in Colombia, the Production Development Forum in Chile, or the sectoral forums in Brazil.[33] In some cases, long-term proposals have even been made to stabilize policy design beyond government terms of office, as happened for example with 'Visión 2020' promoted by the Mexican Confederation of Industrial Chambers (CONCAMIN).

Policy coordination with other civil-society organizations has been much weaker. Although labor unions have participated in discussion forums, in general their presence has not been decisive for the dynamic of such mechanisms. An exception, however, is the role played by unions in the sectoral chamber of the automotive industry in Brazil. Other bodies have played an even smaller role, an exception being participation by the academic sector in the efforts made by the National Competitiveness Council in Colombia.

The situation in terms of impact evaluation is equally unsatisfactory. Although there are evaluations of a number of specific programs, such as those supporting small businesses in Chile,[34] together with general assessments of what happened after policy implementation, these do not make it possible to specify the causes of the events they describe. Examples include the expansion of non-traditional exports in chains with sectoral agreements in Colombia (Velasco, 2003); growth of mining exports in Peru (Fairlie, 2003); income growth among rural producers, and even increased productivity of their land plots, based on large-scale Mexican agricultural programs (Villagómez, 2003); and discussion on whether or not self-employment incomes have risen among producers supported by the National Institute for Agricultural Development (INDAP) in Chile (Kjöllerström, 2004).

The shortfall, between what is decided and announced and what is actually done and evaluated, naturally raises the issue of what can be done to rectify the situation. Lines of action in three mutually non-exclusive groups seem promising and call for more in-depth analysis.

First, policy design should be accompanied, not followed, by explicit consideration of the institutions that will have to implement the policies. This means industrial policy stakeholders becoming involved in issues relating to reform of the state. The structure of the latter continues to respond to realities organized on the basis of productive sectors and subsectors, while seeking to implement systemic or cross-cutting policies, which, by definition, encompass more than one sector or implementing entity. This is particularly important for policies that evolved from the strictly sectoral towards a more general scope, such as strategies to support the dissemination and use of information and communication technologies, whose cross-cutting nature has been referred to before. Although reform of the state and the consequent institutional development are not issues that are close to the industrial organization specialist, they need to be addressed to reduce implementation failures.

Given the lack of human resources skilled in areas of the state relating to policy implementation, a second type of measure would involve reassigning highly qualified personnel from design areas to implementation. This would not undermine capacity-building measures, because their time horizons are different; while the latter necessarily operate in the long term, human resources could be reallocated in the short run. It should be assumed that this reallocation will entail high costs, in terms of both efficiency and personal careers; but it is an alternative if the foregoing diagnosis is accepted.

A third line of action is to develop and strengthen the operators of policy, that is, the institutions and individuals that have to combine design and implementation. Three courses of action are available for that purpose: strengthen public institutions; search for leaders in the private sector; and strengthen intermediate agents such as business associations and NGOs.

Long-term institutional development in the state is a reality both in ministries responsible for macroeconomic policy and in the region's central banks; such experience could and should be replicated in areas linked to industrial development. Private leadership of policies has been efficient in some cases (e.g. in the development of a number of local clusters), and should be used whenever possible; but experience in the region shows that it is hard to systemize and is not distributed according to implementation needs. Thus, economically weak areas that need major efforts from policy operators tend also to have weak leaderships. The strengthening of intermediate implementation bodies has been a successful strategy in countries such as Chile, where it has been used to implement productive coordination promotion programs (PROFO), although the predictable problems of adverse selection and moral hazard still arise.

None of these measures is a panacea, or easy to implement; but they do open up alternatives and deserve to be explored from perspectives that combine the economic, institutional, and management dimensions.

Conclusions

The review undertaken in this chapter shows that Latin American and Caribbean countries have alternatives to develop policies to improve their productive specialization, and they have used them to formulate three types or modes of policy, reflecting the objectives, experience, and economic and institutional capacities of each country. Actions that range from direct sector-based interventions to horizontal policies focused on specific sectors (including cluster promotion based on a value-chain approach) have been designed, but seldom implemented.

Industrial policies are the core of specialization or diversification strategies. Four points need to be considered when proposing such a strategy: criteria for selecting the sector to be promoted; the policy instruments that are available; constraints imposed by the size of domestic markets and the accumulated capacities of the various countries in the region; and the political will that exists to deploy this type of measure.

The choice of sectors should recognize that, while there are no universally used criteria for deciding which activities to promote, extensive international experience shows that countries have in fact chosen and continue to choose sectors; and they do so on the basis of a few more or less precise criteria. These include the knowledge-intensity of the activities in question; their dynamism in the international market as a result of high elasticity with respect to world income, particularly that of developed countries; and the potential for productivity growth.

These criteria are supported by others related to the strategic nature of certain activities, which basically reflect their importance in output, exports, or employment, usually at the national level, but also with a local or subnational dimension. The policy review undertaken in the previous sections amply demonstrates how those criteria have been used, albeit not always explicitly, in the countries of the region.

As from the 1980s, the technological dimension has increasingly been used to define the scope of industrial policies. Although a group of activities have traditionally been thought of as a sector when all of them produce goods or services with high price cross-elasticity, it is also possible to define as a 'sector' activities that share a technological path (Robinson, 1953). One can therefore speak of the aerospace, biotechnology, or information and communications technology sectors. To promote activities encompassed by a given technology, there are as many experiences centered on horizontal policies as others involving direct intervention at the level of firms, market segments, or knowledge networks. As in the case of productive coordination, where industrial policies tended to be expressed through policies to promote clusters, in this field such policies are confused in practice with innovation or technological development policies.

As policies acquire systemic scope, their impact on competitiveness in the economy at large requires special attention. The higher costs associated with the initial stages of learning curves should not be so high that they endanger the competitiveness of firms that use new goods or services that are being incorporated into the basket, particularly when those firms have a strong foreign-trade orientation. The balance between supporting the diversification of the domestic productive structure and taking advantage of opportunities to import cheaper capital goods or better technology is not easy to strike; it can only be found through processes of experimentation, and trial and error—that is, pragmatic rather than doctrinaire policies. As pragmatic policies are frequently of a reactive type, a major challenge for the region is to combine pragmatism with much more proactive policies.

The tools available to implement this type of policy are well known and present in the policy discourse in Latin American and Caribbean countries. The big difference with respect to past experience in the region and elsewhere stems from the current open-economy scenario, in which it is impossible to use instruments involving widespread and permanent trade protection. This constraint weakens the economic signal (expected profitability) sent to potential investors in new activities, and causes a significant portion of the cost of development activities to fall on the fiscal area. This leads to problems, both in setting priorities for the allocation of budgetary resources, and for the stability of those resources at times of fiscal constraint. The sustaining of long-term development instruments, possibly spanning more than one government term, remains a challenge that the countries of the region have so far been unable to tackle successfully. Another powerful tool of sectoral policy, direct investment by the state, is off the policy agenda in most countries; but the degrees of freedom in this subject are large, as shown by various experiences, particularly at the local or subnational level. Experience in the region seems to suggest that the policy packages applied thus far have not had the inductive force of protection, although the cumulative effects remain to be evaluated.

Apart from these constraints, it has been argued that small countries with less institutional capacity not only should not develop policies of sectoral scope, but in fact cannot do so. Without denying the importance of using the domestic market to achieve economies of scale and learning, it should be remembered that the issue is less important in open economies, as shown by the experience of numerous small countries that operate as highly competitive export platforms. Although institutional capacity can also be a major constraint, especially in the short run, this does not mean it is impossible to implement productive development policies, rather that their scope should be in accordance with those capacities. In other words, the alternative is to focus efforts down rather than shooting wildly into the air. In this regard, the region's experience of cluster policies shows that even small countries have been able to formulate policies to improve their pattern of specialization.

Despite these considerations, from the standpoint of political will, sectoral measures face ambivalence in the region—enjoying high levels of legitimacy in some countries, although always less than during the ISI period, but very low levels in others. Nonetheless, even in countries that do not consider them legitimate, actual practice is far more ad hoc, and often specific measures are implemented to support sectors in crisis. Given the need for these policies to move development forward in the region, it is worth asking what needs to be done to increase their legitimacy.

There are two priority areas of action. First, implementation capacity needs to be improved, to narrow the gap between policy design and institutional capacity for effective implementation, the persistence of which undermines the credibility of policy makers and hence the policies themselves. Secondly, significant progress also needs to be made in evaluating the impact of the initiatives implemented in terms of their ultimate objectives: economic growth, technological progress, increased productivity. When public resources are scarce, only robust evaluations can create space to divert resources from other policy areas to these ones.

Although these points are not new, they are crucial.[35] Some progress has been made on this issue, two examples being the Business Development Program of Mexico 2001–2006 and the 2008 Brazilian industrial policy, which explicitly mention quantitative targets,[36] thereby demonstrating clear progress with respect to previous programs. Nonetheless, progress at the regional level is clearly insufficient. This is very serious for policies that have to justify their own *raison d'être* and compete for fiscal resources with others that enjoy greater legitimacy, such as basic education, public health, or citizen safety. As these policies are crucial for diversifying the productive structure and quickening the pace of productivity growth, industrial policies need to regain their legitimacy by demonstrating their impact.

From a broader perspective, some crucial questions remain unanswered. If, in the late 1990s, an analyst who advocated industrial policies had been asked to design an ideal political scenario for their acceptance and implementation in the region, he or she hardly could have hoped for a better environment than that which exists today. At present, at the end of the decade of 2000, parties or coalitions of parties that based much of their long-term adversarial platform, in almost every instance, on the rejection of 'economic laissez-faire' are in power in Argentina, Brazil, Bolivia, Chile, Ecuador, Nicaragua, Paraguay, Uruguay, and Venezuela. Production development policies—including industrial policy— were frequently mentioned by these parties as a substantive part of their strategic guidelines for achieving sustainable development with greater social justice.

Reality appears not to have fulfilled those expectations. The dominant perception today is that, where policy development is concerned, the most significant developments have taken place in Brazil, where industrial policy guidelines were approved in 2003, a strong industrial policy was formulated in 2008, and an industrial development agency with a coordinating role was created in 2005. The 2006 development plan adopted in Bolivia includes a chapter on the subject, and interest has been expressed in Argentina in the implementation of programs to strengthen production chains. In Chile, Uruguay, and Venezuela, there is no evidence that any significant decisions have been made in this field, despite partial information on strategy and policy debates within the governments of those countries. Even in the most advanced example of policy development and actions (Brazil), the long-run perception is that not enough has been done in terms of what is needed to change the productive structure of the country, and that the most significant actions are still those of BNDES and, more recently, those of sectoral technology funds. In short, there has been no significant effort in any of the countries mentioned above to change the current model, in terms of its pattern of productive specialization, through the application of industrial policies.

Two explanations may be attempted. The first would be that the discourse of the opposition was rapidly constrained, upon its rise to power, by the pressure of global markets and the existing consensus as to what constitutes a responsible macroeconomic policy, and that, as part of the same move toward international acceptance, the discourse of structural change was relegated to second or third place. The fact that structural-change measures were correctly assumed to be expensive, and to produce doubtful results that could only be achieved in the long term, could not but speed their decline, even within the official discourse.

Another explanation might be that, without denying the significance of the factors mentioned above, the structural-change or industrialist discourse lacked the strength to show that it could be translated into specific operational proposals, capable of yielding at least a few results that were attainable within the space of a single administration (four to five years). If the second explanation is correct, one might conclude that the chief concern of structural policy analysis should be to pay attention to governments that wish to carry out such policies, do not know how to do so, and, if they did, would scarcely have the time needed for those policies to yield results that strengthen the government and allow it to remain in office.

Even if policies to diversify the productive structure can technically demonstrate their capacity to generate positive impacts, it is by no means clear which social stakeholders would be interested in generalizing them in the region's countries. In other words, which stakeholders are likely to put their economic and political resources behind initiatives that go beyond support for cluster development, when the vast majority of them do not have an abundance of resources? Industrial policies have been making a (slow) return in Latin America and have been able to operate, albeit on a small scale, in open economies and with orthodox macroeconomic policies—contrary to the previous conventional wisdom that they were incompatible. Enhancing their, if not minimal, then at least marginal, status requires social stakeholders, including the state, to take ownership of them and commit their power and resources behind them. And therein lays the rub: who are the stakeholders interested, or likely to be interested, in supporting proactive industrial policies with the power and resources to change the current pattern of productive specialization?

Notes

1. In this chapter, the term 'industry' is used in a broad sense to include, not only manufacturing industry, but also non-manufacturing sectors such as agriculture and mining.
2. For example, Ministries of Industry, Agriculture, Mining, and others, and the corresponding general directorates for food, metal manufactures and machinery, chemicals, capital goods, and so forth.
3. Although the debate on the effect of industrial policies in Asia is very wide-ranging and has not yet concluded, the 1997 crisis significantly diverted attention away from the 'Asian Miracle.' For arguments in favor of such policies, see Amsden (1989), Rodrik (1995), and Wade (1990); for the opposite view, see World Bank (1993), Krugman (1994), and, more recently, Noland and Pack (2002). On the other hand, the agricultural policies implemented in industrialized countries show that sectoral policies are by no means peculiar to a number of underdeveloped countries in the past.
4. In the early 1990s, it was frequent to hear high-ranking macroeconomic policy officials propounding the view that 'the best industrial policy is no industrial policy.' Although simplistic, that phrase aptly reflected their position on the subject.
5. Issues relating to the impact of economic reforms and of macroeconomic policy on the industrial dynamics are outside the scope of this chapter. Nonetheless, it has to be stressed that reforms such as trade openness or privatization, and monetary and exchange-rate policy measures, have often had a major impact on that dynamics,

thereby making it possible to classify them as genuine 'implicit industrial policies'.

These implicit policies were often decided upon without adequate knowledge of the microeconomics of the region, i.e. the specific behavior of its enterprises and markets. See Stallings and Peres (2000).

6. For example, tax exemptions extended to sheep meat producers during the foot-and-mouth crisis in Uruguay, mentioned by Scarone (2003). Data for Brazil show significant support for sectors such as electric power, information technology, automobiles, and electrical appliances, see Balbi (2003).

7. Some examples are 'sun-and-sand' tourism in much of the English-speaking Caribbean (Hendrickson, 2003) and the promotion of crops of higher value-added and market opportunities, as a goal of the Alianza para el Campo in Mexico (Villagómez, 2003).

8. For a general discussion of this subject, see ECLAC (2005); for national analyses, see Bonelli and Motta Veiga (2003), for Brazil; Scarone (2003), for Uruguay; and Henry (2003), for the Caribbean.

9. See Sergeant et al. (2003), for Trinidad and Tobago.

10. Similarly, Chile's rents from copper mining will be channeled to support innovation through R&D as an instrument of the National Innovation Strategy for Competitiveness released in February 2007.

11. In an APL, a large number of firms operate around a productive activity that is predominant in a given location, with shared forms of cooperation and governance mechanisms. Measures to support APLs are implemented locally, reflecting the Brazilian experience that state-level policies tend to have a substantial sectoral component. Examples of this are programs to support the automotive industry (subsidies and even capital contributions from a number of state governments), electronics and information technology, textiles, clothing and footwear. See Bonelli and Motta Veiga (2003).

12. See Velasco (2003) on sectoral agreements in Colombia.

13. Pérez (2003) highlights the intensity of sectoral incentives in the Caribbean economies, particularly in member countries of the Association of Eastern Caribbean States, and in Barbados and Guyana, the latter having the broadest package of incentives in the region. Those incentives basically target the manufacturing and service sectors, particularly hotels and tourism (Hendrickson, 2003).

14. This approach was developed on the basis of Porter (1990), and was materialized in papers by *Monitor Company* in the Andean countries in the early 1990s, and in the project entitled 'Central America in the Twenty-First Century: An Agenda for Competitiveness and Sustainable Development,' coordinated by INCAE/CLADS in the middle of that decade.

15. The term 'neutral' or 'horizontal' policy, which is widely used in the region, conceals the fact that any policy is bound to favor some sectors more than others *ex post*. This is because such policies aim to enhance the operating efficiency of markets for factors of production which are used with varying intensity according to the sector or product in question. In some cases, policies are presented as neutral to gain greater legitimacy, despite being aimed at specific sectors from the outset. This frequently happens with technological development policies.

16. The available data does not make it possible to quantify the implicit subsidies in credit operations and fiscal incentives. For a detailed analysis, see Melo (2001).

17. Annual expenditure per producer amounted to US$900 in Chile and Mexico in 2000, but was less than US$50 in Bolivia. In that same year, agriculture expenditure as a percentage of sectoral GDP was 35% in Mexico, 21% in Chile, and slightly over 5% in Bolivia (Kerrigan, 2001).

18. In the NAFIN portfolio the 'Other' category, which represents 97% of the total, probably includes operations targeting domestic production. See ECLAC (2004a), table 8.2.

19. The remaining five sectors are aeronautics, agriculture, tourism, commerce, and construction. *Economic Policy for Competitiveness* (website of the Ministry of Economic Affairs, October 2005, <http://www.economia-cgm.gob.mx/?P=1131>).

20. The document in question states that those sectors were selected because (i) they display sustained and increasing dynamism; (ii) they account for significant proportions of international investments in research and development; (iii) they open up new business opportunities; (iv) they are directly related to innovations in processes, products, and modes of use; (v) they increase the density of the production structure; and (vi) they are important for the future of the country and have potential for the development of dynamic comparative advantages (Ministry of Development, Industry and Foreign Trade, 2003, p. 16). These guidelines were strengthened by the Growth Acceleration Program, enacted in February 2007, which relies mainly on fiscal incentives.

21. See Subsecretaría de Industria, <http://www.industria.gov.ar/foros/institucional.htm>.

22. In Peru, the main policies implemented in support of the mining sector in the 1990s were as follows: promotion and guarantees for foreign direct investment; privatization of state-owned enterprises; approval of a framework law guaranteeing free enterprise and private investments; tax, exchange-rate, and administrative stability; modernization of the mining concessions process; tax benefits (reinvested profits are exempt from income tax); tax incentives for investment in megaprojects (income-tax exemptions and advance drawback of the general sales tax). See Fairlie (2003).

23. See Alonso (2003).

24. The 1998 Investments Act allows the government to promote specific investments by declaring a project to be in the national interest. Benefits can be general or specific to a given project; general benefits can be automatic or discretionary. See Scarone (2003).

25. Of these, 31 are national and 10 regional; 29 correspond to goods and 12 to services. Not all of them are programs for production chains strictly defined; some target specific sectors (potatoes, farmed shrimp, tuna, trawled shrimp, flowers, coffee, and bananas). The relatively loose application of the production-chain concept reflects the fact that most of the agreements were signed for pragmatic reasons aimed at mobilizing entrepreneurs (Velasco, 2003).

26. See Scarone (2003) on most policies in Uruguay; Villagómez (2003) on the 2002–2010 electronics industry program in Mexico.

27. IDB (2001), Melo (2001), Peres (1997).

28. See Bonelli and Motta Veiga (2003) for Brazil; Unger (2003) and Villagómez (2003) for Mexico.

29. Some examples are the *2006–2010 National Science, Technology and Innovation Plan* in Panama issued in 2006, the 15-year Chilean *National Innovation Strategy for*

Competitiveness and the Colombian *National Science, Technological Development and Innovation Plan*, both released by early 2007.

30. The best-documented cases relate to funds allocated to agriculture policies, in particular in the framework of large-scale programs such as PROCAMPO, Alianza para el Campo, and the marketing support program in Mexico; see Kjöllerström (2004); Villagómez (2003), for Mexico; Scarone (2003), for Uruguay.
31. Velasco (2003).
32. Moreover, differences between the government and the private sector, although less than before, are far from having disappeared, as shown by Alonso (2003) for Guatemala, and Scarone (2003) for Uruguay.
33. In Brazil, the expression 'cámara sectorial' [sectoral forum] does not refer to a business association, but to a tripartite government–entrepreneurs–workers negotiation space.
34. For that country, see the evaluations of development programs in Silva and Sandoval (2003).
35. This idea has already been highlighted in Peres (1997), Stallings and Peres (2000), and Peres and Stumpo (2002).
36. The program proposes to create a public evaluation system including strategic indicators, oversight mechanisms, coordination and participatory evaluation mechanisms, periodic accountability, and a monitoring unit for micro, small, and medium-sized enterprises, as an information source. Secretaría de Economía (2001), p. 56.

References

Acevedo R. (2002), 'ALIDE y el financiamiento de la agricultura y el medio rural,' document presented at the conference Development of Rural Economies in Latin America and the Caribbean: Sustainable Management of Natural Resources, Access to Land, and Rural Finance, Fortaleza, Ceará, March.

Alonso E. (2003), 'Centroamérica: políticas para el fomento de los sectores productivos,' Desarrollo Productivo Series No. 140, United Nations Economic Commission for Latin America and the Caribbean (ECLAC), Santiago, Chile.

Amsden A. (1989), *Asia's Next Giant: South Korea and Late Industrialization*, Oxford University Press, New York.

Balbi S. (2003), 'Crise e divergência travam política industrial,' *Folha dinheiro*, November 2, p. B1.

Bonelli R. and P. Motta Veiga (2003), 'A dinâmica das políticas setoriais no Brasil na década de 1990: continuidade e mudança,' *Revista brasileira de comércio exterior*, 75.

Castaldi C. (2003), *Essays on the Process of Economic Growth*, Scuola Superiore Sant'Anna, Pisa.

Chang H-J. (1994), *The Political Economy of Industrial Policy*, Macmillan and Saint Martin's Press.

Cimoli M., N. Correa, and A. Primi (2003), 'Crecimiento y estructura productiva en economías abiertas: lecciones de la experiencia de a América Latina,' Santiago, Chile, unpublished.

Dussel Peters E. (1999), 'La subcontratación como proceso de aprendizaje: el caso de la electrónica en Jalisco (México) en la década de los noventa,' Desarrollo Productivo Series No. 55, United Nations Economic Commission for Latin America and the Caribbean (ECLAC), Santiago, Chile.

Economic Commission for Latin America and the Caribbean (ECLAC) (2003), 'Istmo centroamericano: los retos de la sustentabilidad en granos básicos,' ECLAC Subregional Headquarters in Mexico, Mexico City.

—— (2004a), *Productive Development in Open Economies*, United Nations, Santiago, Chile.

—— (2004b), *Foreign Investment in Latin America and the Caribbean: 2003 Report*, United Nations, Santiago, Chile.

—— (2005), 'Políticas públicas para el desarrollo de sociedades dela información en América Latina y el Caribe,' United Nations, Santiago, Chile.

Fairbanks M. and S. Lindsay (1997), *Plowing the Sea: Nurturing the Hidden Resources of Growth in the Developing World*, Harvard Business School Publishing.

Fairlie A. (2003), 'Políticas sectoriales y cadenas productivas en el Perú reciente,' United Nations Economic Commission for Latin America and the Caribbean (ECLAC), Santiago, Chile, unpublished.

Food and Agriculture Organization (FAO) (2001), *Review of Basic Food Policies*, United Nations, Commodities and Trade Division, Rome.

Government of Brazil (2008), 'Inovar e Investir para Sustentar o Crescimento', Agencia Brasileira de Desenvolvimento Industrial, Banco Nacional de Desenvolvimento Econômico e Social, Ministério da Fazenda and Ministério do Desenvolvimento, Indústria e Comercio Exterior, Rio de Janeiro.

Hendrickson M. (2003), *Caribbean Tourism: Trends, Policies and Impact, 1985–2002*, ECLAC Subregional Headquarters for the Caribbean, Port of Spain.

Henry L. (2003), 'Sectoral Policies: Information and Communications Technology in the Caribbean. Trends, Policies and Impact: 1985–2002,' United Nations Economic Commission for Latin America and the Caribbean (ECLAC), Santiago, Chile.

Inter-American Development Bank (IDB) (2001), *Competitividad. El motor del crecimiento*, Washington, DC.

Kaldor N. (1966), *Causes of the Slow Rate of Growth of the United Kingdom*, Cambridge University Press, Cambridge.

Kerrigan G. (2001), 'Gasto público hacia el sector agrícola y desarrollo de las áreas rurales: tablas por países,' document presented at the Seminar on Public Spending for Agricultural and Rural Development in Latin America and the Caribbean for the Food and Agriculture Organization of the United Nations (FAO), Santiago, Chile, August 28–31.

Kjöllerström M. (2004), 'Competitividad del sector agrícola y pobreza rural: el papel de los gastos públicos en América Latina,' United Nations Economic Commission for Latin America and the Caribbean (ECLAC), Santiago, Chile.

Krugman P. (1994), 'The Myth of Asia's Miracle,' *Foreign Affairs*, 73(6).

Melo A. (2001), 'Industrial Policy in Latin America and the Caribbean at the Turn of the Century,' Research Department Working Paper No. 459, Inter-American Development Bank (IDB), Washington, DC.

Ministério do Desenvolvimento, Indústria e Comércio Exterior (2003), *Diretrizes de política industrial, tecnológica e de comércio exterior*, Brasilia, Brazil.

Moguillansky G. (2000), *La inversión en Chile. El final de un ciclo de expansión?* Fondo de Cultura Económica, Santiago, Chile.

Mortimore M. (2000), 'Corporate Strategies for FDI in the Context of Latin America's New Economic Model,' *World Development*, 28(9).

—— and W. Peres (1998), 'Policy Competition for Foreign Direct Investment in the Caribbean Basin: Costa Rica, Jamaica and the Dominican Republic,' Desarrollo Productivo Series No. 49, United Nations Economic Commission for Latin America and the Caribbean (ECLAC), Santiago, Chile.

Noland M. and H. Pack (2002), 'Industrial Policies and Growth: Lessons from the International Experience,' Working Paper No. 169, Banco Central de Chile, Santiago, Chile.

Peres W. (ed.) (1997), *Políticas de competitividad industrial en América Latina y el Caribe*, Siglo XXI Editores, Mexico City.

—— and N. Reinhardt (2000), 'Latin America's New Economic Model: Micro Responses and Economic Restructuring,' *World Development*, 28(9).

—— and G. Stumpo (2002), *Pequeñas y medianas empresas industriales en América Latina y el Caribe*, Siglo XXI Editores, Mexico City.

Pérez Caltendey E. (2003), 'Policies for Productive Development in Caribbean Economies,' ECLAC Subregional Headquarters for the Caribbean, Port of Spain.

Porter M. (1990), *The Competitive Advantage of Nations*, The Free Press, New York.

Robinson J. (1953), 'Imperfect Competition Revisited,' *The Economic Journal*, 63: 251.

Rodrik D. (1995), 'Getting Interventions Right: How Korea and Taiwan Grew Rich,' *Economic Policy*, 20.

Scarone C. (2003), 'Las políticas sectoriales de Uruguay 1998–2002,' United Nations Economic Commission for Latin America and the Caribbean (ECLAC), Santiago, Chile.

Secretaría de Economía (2001), *Programa de Desarrollo Empresarial 2001–2006*, Mexico City.

—— (2003), 'Política económica para la competitividad,' Mexico City.

Sergeant K., S. Racha, and M. James (2003), 'The Petroleum Sector: The Case of Trinidad and Tobago. Trends, Policies, and Impact. 1985–2002,' United Nations Economic Commission for Latin America and the Caribbean (ECLAC), Santiago, Chile.

Silva I. and C. Sandoval (2003), 'Políticas de desarrollo productivo en Chile, con especial énfasis en el nivel regional y local,' Santiago, Chile, unpublished.

Stallings B. and W. Peres (2000), *Growth, Employment and Equity: The Impact of Economic Reforms in Latin America and the Caribbean*, The Brookings Institution, Washington, DC.

Stigler G. (1951), 'The Division of Labor is Limited by the Extent of the Market,' *Journal of Political Economy*, 59(3).

Unger K. (2003), *Clusters industriales en México: especializaciones regionales y la política industrial*, United Nations Economic Commission for Latin America and the Caribbean (ECLAC), Santiago, Chile.

United Nations Industrial Development Organization (UNIDO) (2003), *Competir mediante la innovación y el aprendizaje. Informe sobre el desarrollo industrial correspondiente a 2002/2003*, Vienna.

Velasco M. (2003), 'Una evaluación de las políticas de competitividad en Colombia,' United Nations Economic Commission for Latin America and the Caribbean (ECLAC), Santiago, Chile, unpublished.

Villagómez A. (2003), 'Una revisión de la política sectorial en México 1995–2003,' unpublished.

Wade R. (1990), *Governing the Market: Economic Theory and the Role of Government in East Asian Industrialization*, Princeton University Press, Princeton.

World Bank (1993), *The East Asian Miracle: Economic Growth and Public Policy*, Washington, DC.

Young A. (1928), 'Increasing Returns and Economic Progress,' *Economic Journal*, 38(4).

Part III

National and Regional Experiences

8

Flying Geese and Waddling Ducks: The Different Capabilities of East Asia and Latin America to 'Demand-Adapt' and 'Supply-Upgrade' their Export Productive Capacity

José Gabriel Palma

The world of foreign trade is one of change. It makes a great difference to the trade of different countries, and to the impact of trade on them, whether they are capable of changing with the world... Capacity to transform is capacity to react to change, originating at home or abroad, by adapting the structure of foreign trade to the new situation in an economic fashion.

C. Kindleberger

The obsession with competitiveness is not only wrong but dangerous, skewing domestic policies and threatening the international economic system.

P. Krugman

Introduction

During the 1992 US presidential campaign President Bush's head economic adviser was questioned about the decline in the technological content of US

* I would like to thank Alice Amsden, Stephanie Blankenburg, Mario Cimoli, Mushtaq Khan, José Luis Fiori, Daniel Hahn, Michael Hobday, Richard Kozul-Wright, Carlos Lopes, Ousmene Mandeng, Carlota Perez, Annalisa Primi, Bob Sutcliffe, Fiona Tregenna, and especially Giovanni Dosi and Julie McKay for helpful observations. Also, participants at seminars in Bangkok, Bilbao, New Delhi, Kuala Lumpur, Rio de Janeiro, Santiago, and Sydney made constructive comments on this chapter and on two previous drafts (Palma, 1998 and 2006). The usual caveats apply.

exports; he replied that he saw no problem in it as there was no difference between exporting micro-chips or potato-chips. This chapter investigates whether this is really the case, especially for developing countries (DCs). Are there major economic consequences for the growth path of DCs (especially for its pace, nature, and sustainability) from an export orientation based on one or the other type of product? In particular, what are the consequences in terms of the long-term productivity growth potential of the export sector itself, for the capacity of exports to induce productivity growth in the rest of the economy, for institution building, and for the welfare gains from specialization (e.g. issues related to the terms of trade)? Do DCs have a choice in this matter? And are regional dynamics, particularly the role of the regional power, an important component of the likelihood of DCs exporting one or the other type of product?

The general issue of 'potato-chips versus micro-chips' will be analyzed through the examination of the diverse export and growth performances of Latin America (LA) and East Asia (EA) since 1960. In this chapter I argue that their experiences support at least four hypotheses. First, that growth is a 'product specific' phenomenon. Second, that the role played in it by exports relates at least as much to *what* a country exports as to how much it exports— that is, that the capacity of exports to generate and sustain (trade-induced) GDP growth is related not only to the volume but also to the composition of exports. Third, that the capacity of an economy continuously to shift resources towards more growth-enhancing export activities is related to the effectiveness of the state to implement appropriate trade and industrial pol-icies; and that this effectiveness is associated not just with the ability of the state to create rents, but (much more importantly) to its capacity to compel the corporate sector to invest them in productive capacity diversification—that is, continuously to shift resources towards products that would help to *supply-upgrade* along the so-called 'learning curve', and *demand-adapt* a country's export productive capacity to an ever-changing international demand. And fourth, that regional dynamics have played a significant role in growth, export diversification, and gains from specialization, especially due to the specific type of leadership that Japan has exerted in East Asia (as opposed to that shown by the US in the Americas).

Economic growth: regional diversities

One of the main stylized facts of the world economy since the beginning of 'globalization' and economic reforms is the different economic performances of LA and Asia. Figure 8.1 highlights this remarkable phenomenon.

If between 1960 and 1980 Brazil practically doubled the gap between its GDP per capita and that of India (see left-hand panel), between 1980 and 2006 it

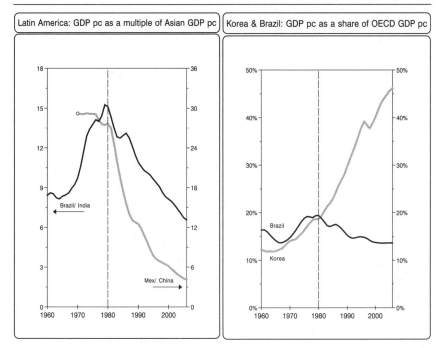

GDP pc = gross domestic product per capita. **Mex/China** = GDP per capita of Mexico as a multiple of that of China. 3-year moving averages.

Figure 8.1. GDP per capita growth: Latin America vs. Asia

was India's turn to more than halve this gap. At the same time, while before 1980 Brazil was closing its income per capita gap vis-à-vis the countries of the OECD in a similar fashion to Korea (see right-hand panel), after 1980 only Korea was able to continue to do this. And comparing Mexico and China, the GDP per capita of the former as a multiple of the latter collapsed between 1980 and 2006 from a factor of 28, to one of just 4.[1]

The primary objective of this chapter is to discuss some trade issues related to these remarkable asymmetries and their regional dimensions.

East Asian versus Latin American development strategies

Differences between LA's and EA's trade and industrial policies have been well documented. The primary benefit of these policies for EA (and now for China, India and Vietnam) was that EA was able to increase simultaneously its shares of exports and of manufactures in GDP. By contrast, LA, which throughout the first half of the twentieth century had been the region with the largest share of exports in GDP, between 1950 and the first oil crisis of the 1970s experienced a near-halving of this share. This decline followed both a weakened demand for primary commodities in OECD markets since the Korean War and trade and industrial policies characterized by strong anti-export bias. As a result, and despite a strong growth performance in some countries until 1980, particularly in Brazil and Mexico, the rapid increase in the share of manufactures in GDP resulting from import-substituting industrialization (ISI) came at the expense of exports.[2]

Although LA's growth strategy during ISI had left the region vulnerable to external shocks, especially due to continuous current account deficits and growing foreign debt, nothing had prepared the region for the one artificially created by Paul Volker following his appointment to the Fed in 1979. In fact, the consequences for LA of Volker's 'macho-monetarism' were of a magnitude not felt in the region since 1929.[3] And as had happened in the 1930s, a massive and long-lasting external shock (that found LA in an extremely vulnerable position) not only brought about the need for a sudden and very painful internal and external macroeconomic adjustment, but also laid the foundations for a radical and widespread change in the economic paradigm of the region. In this case, it was characterized by an extreme move towards trade and financial liberalization, wholesale privatization, and market deregulation, along the lines experimented with in Chile since 1973. Therefore, the key element to understanding these reforms, particularly the purely ideological and remarkably rigid and unimaginative way in which they were implemented throughout the region, is that they were mostly carried out as a result of perceived economic *weaknesses*—that is, an attitude of 'throwing in the towel' vis-à-vis the previous growth strategy of state-led ISI. In fact, the economic discourse ended up resembling a compass whose 'magnetic north' was simply the mechanical reversal of as many aspects as possible of the previous development strategy.[4] The mere idea that alternatives could exist met with a mixture of amusement and contempt.[5] This helps to explain the remarkable differences with which the reforms were implemented in LA, as distinct from EA.

As I have argued elsewhere (Palma, 2004), it is not that EA did not implement its economic reforms partly out of necessity (and also because of mounting external political pressure from the US to do so); but its economic weaknesses were very different in nature and intensity. Since the 1960s, EA integrated into the world economy in a different way to LA. Instead of accepting their traditional, path-dependent comparative advantages (i.e. based on traditional resource endowment, subject to decreasing returns), East Asian countries acquired a more flexible and growth-enhancing set of comparative advantages mainly by following a 'flying-geese' pattern of production and upgrading.[6] This was achieved through increased export penetration of OECD markets for manufactured goods, within a process of the regionalization of production led by Japan (see especially Figure 8.6 below). Their extraordinary success was based on several factors. On the external front, the fast rate of expansion of international trade in these goods, and OECD (especially US) market openness were key.[7] Internally, it was due to several factors such as the ability to build a structure of property rights and incentives, an institutional capability, and a political settlement that allowed them to produce globally competitive manufactures; an ability to upgrade exports continuously through the 'flying geese' path;[8] to their ability to generate the high levels of investment and saving required for this upgrading; and their achieving an effective coordination of this investment through different forms of industrial and trade policies, which succeeded in *simultaneously* insulating domestic markets and outwardly orienting tradable production.

However, in the late 1980s and early 1990s, problems emerged for many East Asian economies. First, in part due to the increased standardization of inputs to the electronics industry, some of their most important exports faced rapidly falling prices. In response, the corporate sectors massively expanded their productive capacity, attempting to turn falling prices to their advantage via increased market shares.[9] An obvious casualty was profitability; consequently, the composition of the finance for investment had to move away from profits towards (domestic and foreign) debt.[10] The increasing need for access to finance was one of the key domestic pressures behind the drive towards financial liberalization.

Another problem was that in the same period, China became a formidable competitor in many markets crucial to the second-tier East Asian NICs (Newly-industrialising countries), affecting profitability and contributing to an increased need for external finance. At the same time, the second-tier NICs reached a point where further upgrading of exports to higher value-added products was becoming increasingly difficult. In particular, it became more and more complicated to break away from a 'sub-contracting' type of industrialization. So (as China, India and Vietnam would do later), in a far more pragmatic way than in LA, East Asian countries increasingly looked towards trade and financial liberalization, and economic deregulation in general, not (as in LA) as a way of changing but of *strengthening* their existing ambitious growth strategy.

The capacity to 'demand-adapt' a country's export profile to a rapidly changing OECD import-demand structure

The rapidly evolving structure of demand in world markets is a well-known characteristic of international trade, especially since the Second World War. This phenomenon raises the issue of the need for a more flexible approach to the concept of comparative advantages within an export-led growth strategy; that is, from the point of view of gains from specialization the key issue becomes how to develop the capability continuously to adapt one's export productive capacity to the ever-changing patterns of international demand.

Since the introduction of the Prebisch–Singer hypothesis in the 1950s,[11] and the related research at ECLAC in the 1960s,[12] DCs have fretted over the changing nature of international demand, and in particular about the declining purchasing power of unprocessed primary commodities exports resulting from their low income and price elasticities of demand. Figure 8.2 shows the remarkable changes in the structure of OECD demand for imports until 2000 (i.e. before the short cyclical upturn for commodities following 9/11) and its anti-unprocessed-primary-commodity bias (except for the erratically changing fortunes of oil).

Figure 8.2 shows the most important characteristic of the structure of OECD imports between 1963 and 2000: the collapse of the share of non-oil primary commodities (SITC groups 0, 1, 2, and 4). In fact, even including unprocessed oil commodities lost about *three-quarters* of their share in OECD imports during this 37-year period, falling from 41 percent of the total in 1963 to just

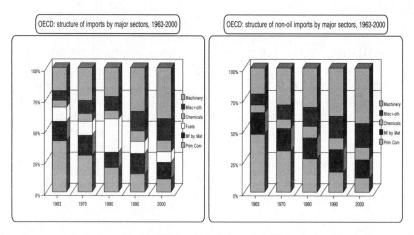

Prim Com = primary commodities (SITC groups 0, 1, 2, and 4); **Mf by Mat** = Manufactures goods classified chiefly by materials (SITC group 6); **fuels** = Mineral fules, lubricants and related materials (SITC group 3); **Chemicals** = Chemicals and related products (SITC group 5); **Misc + oth** = Miscellaneous manufactured articles and commodities and transactions not classified elsewhere (SITC groups 8 and 9); and **Machinery** = machinery and transport equipment (SITC group 7).

Note: The Trade-CAN program was originally developed by Ousmene Mandeng at ECLAC in the 1980s; it has been updated periodically by ECLAC and the World Bank. The data source is the UN Com-trade on-line database (which starts in 1963). Unless otherwise stated, the program is the source of all trade statistics quoted in this paper, and all export-groups quoted will correspond to the SITC classfication, Version 2, at a 4-digit level.

Source: Trade-CAN (2005).

Figure 8.2. OECD: structure of overall imports and non-oil imports by major sectors, 1963–2000

10.6 percent in 2000 (left-hand panel); and excluding oil from both the numerator and denominator, they fell from 46 percent to 11.5 percent, respectively (right-hand panel).[13] However, primary products with a higher level of manufacturing value added (e.g. SITC group 6) maintained their share in OECD imports at a relatively stable level (about 15% of the total). By contrast, imports of machinery and transport equipment (SITC group 7) more than doubled their OECD import-share during this period (from 18.4% to 41%).

Quite apart from supply-side issues discussed below (such as the different long-term productivity growth potentials that exports of manufactures and unprocessed commodities may have), to insert oneself into the international division of labor through exporting products characterized by slow-growing (or even declining) markets does not augur well for long-term welfare gains from international specialization. In fact, during the second half of the twentieth century, the terms of trade of non-oil exporting LA fell (cyclically) by half from its Korean War peak, reaching before the 9/11 crisis a level even below that of the post-1929 crash. What Latin American policy makers and their economic advisors seem to forget these days is that, from the point of view of demand, exports are just an indirect way of producing imports; and by their exporting low-income and low-price elasticity of demand products, declining terms of trade makes the (indirect) production of those imports ever more expensive. In fact, in a Ricardian sense, the region's increased export efficiency may sometimes even act as an 'own-goal' because although increased competitiveness may help GDP growth, if it is done too much at the expense of the terms of trade, it may seriously harm the purchasing power of that GDP growth—that is, in extreme cases output growth may be outweighed by deteriorating terms of trade.[14]

As if the problem of the (cyclical) long-term declining level of LA's non-fuel terms of trade was not serious enough, the instability of these terms of trade adds a further uncertainty to the region's economic life. In fact, the average (absolute) percentage variation of LA's non-oil terms of trade reached 6.7 percent per annum during the 86-year period between 1920 and 2006. To give an indication of the magnitude of this instability problem (and assuming an average share of exports in national income of one-third, with everything else constant), a country facing this amount of instability in its export markets will have its national income changing randomly by an average of 2.2 percent per annum for this reason alone!

However, demand dynamics in international markets is a more complex issue than just a generic one between unprocessed commodities or manufactures. There is also a significant diversity within manufactures in this respect.

Figure 8.3 illustrates that the rapid growth of OECD demand for manufactures is concentrated in just two types of product: one requiring intense R&D and one of moderately intense R&D (road vehicles, including their engines and non-electrical parts). These two groups had a sector-share increase

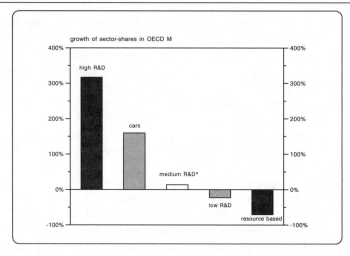

Industries are grouped on the basis of their R&D intensity. **Cars** = road vehicles, engines, and their non-electrical parts; **medium R&D*** = medium R&D, excluding vehicles and engines.

Source: Trade-CAN (2005), using the OECD classification for product content of R&D.

Figure 8.3. OECD imports: demand dynamics and sector content of R&D, 1963–2000

between 1963 and 2000 of 317 percent and 160 percent, respectively. Sector shares of other manufactured products with a medium content of R&D increased by only 14 percent during this 37-year period, while that of manufactured products with a low content of R&D actually declined by 23 percent (in part due to falling prices due to China's export success). In turn, the market share of resource-based products collapsed by 71 percent! Figure 8.3 also reveals the remarkable correlation between demand dynamism and technology content of OECD imports. Therefore, the degree of dynamism of OECD demand for imports of a product could also be understood as a proxy for the technology content of that product (see Figure 8.10 below).

Given the fact that OECD demand for imports is a rapidly moving target, one of the key differences between LA and EA during this period was that while EA was able to develop its skills at keeping an eye on this moving target (and kept shifting resources accordingly), LA continued aiming as though at a fixed target (increased competitiveness in non-demand-dynamic products; see Figures 8.4, 8.9, and 8.10). In fact, one could argue that the real comparative advantage acquired by EA during this period was not on a set of products, but on learning how to develop a flexible export productive capacity.[15]

Writing at the beginning of the period studied in this chapter, Kindleberger (1962, p. 10; see introductory quotation) predicted this rapidly changing structure of world trade, and prescribed developing 'the capacity of changing with the world' as a necessary skill for maximizing gains from trade. Figure 8.4

presents a statistical indicator for a country's capacity to react to changes in world demand via a 'demand-adaptability index'. This index is constructed using the ratio of a country's or region's market share in 'demand-dynamic' sectors (adjusted by the weight of demand-dynamic sectors in all sectors of OECD imports), to that of its market share in demand-sluggish sectors (adjusted by these sectors' share in OECD imports).[16] A value of 1 for this index at the end year of a period indicates that during the preceding years a country was able to 'track' changes in demand in OECD markets—that is, it was able to 'demand-adapt' its export structure to reflect the changing structure of OECD imports.[17]

Figure 8.4 shows LA's tendency to underinvest in productive capacity diversification in its export sector; this could hardly be blamed merely on the fact that the region happens to be rich in natural resources. Abundance of natural resources could hardly be considered a sufficient condition for lack

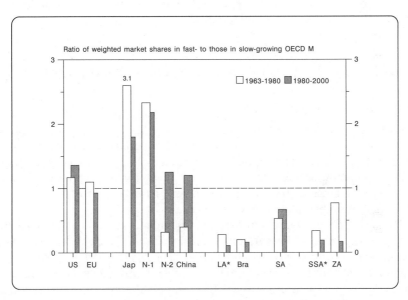

Excludes oil, **M** = imports; **Jap** = Japan; **N-1** = first-tier NICs (Korea, Singapore and Taiwan; Hong Kong has been excluded due to its transformation into a financial centre); **N-2** = second-tier NICs (Malaysia and Thailand); **LA*** = LA (excluding Mexico and Brazil); **Bra** = Brazil; **SA** = South Asia (India and Pakistan); **SSA*** = Sub-Saharan Africa (excluding South Africa); **ZA** = South Africa. See Appendix 1.

Note: The index for Mexico is not included in the graph due to the distorting effect of its 'maquila' exports, which in trade statistics are measured in terms of gross value of production (i.e., including imported inputs); 'maquila' exports accounted for about half its manufacturing exports, but almost 80% of the value of output was made from imported inputs (see Palma, 2005a). The share of imported inputs is also very high in the rest of manufacturing exports (see Capdevielle, 2005; and Moreno-Brid et al., 2005).

Figure 8.4. 'Demand adaptability' to the changing structure of OECD imports: 1963–1980 and 1980–2000

of investment efforts in product diversification and upgrading. That is, a rich resource endowment could not be blamed in itself (as the resource-curse hypothesis seeks to do) for a country ending up being a waddling-duck rather than a dynamic goose.[18]

One obvious way for primary commodity rich countries to improve their 'demand-adaptability' is to increase the degree of processing of these commodities, as the Scandinavian and some East Asian countries (especially Malaysia) have shown. Another is the upgrading of their domestic productive capacity in terms of acquiring comparative advantages and export capabilities in the production of the inputs needed for their commodity production.[19] Both paths (up- and down-stream) would lead to export products that are more 'demand dynamic' in world markets. Yet another path is the targeting of high-value low-volume commodity niches, taking advantage of the hyper-segmentation of markets that characterizes the current process of globalization.[20] The process of export upgrading (both up- and downstream) is the subject of the next section of this chapter.

The capacity to 'supply-upgrade' a country's export profile

Upgrading resource-based exports

Increasing the degree of manufacturing value added of resource-based exports allows resource-rich countries to attain an export structure characterized not just by stronger demand in international markets, but also by products with higher long-term productivity growth potentials. Figure 8.5 shows the contrast between Finland and Malaysia on the one hand, and Brazil and Chile on the other, in timber-based export products.

The differences in long-term productivity growth potentials characteristic of processed and unprocessed timber are well known. There are also substantial differences in their demand-dynamics in OECD import markets: while the sector share in total OECD imports of wood-chips fell by 54 percent and that of pulp by 71 percent between 1963 and 2000, those of wood manufactures increased by 74 percent and of furniture by 400 percent during this period.

As Figure 8.5 shows, Finland's high market shares in OECD imports of the more technologically advanced timber-based products were acquired gradually as they moved along the value-added learning curve of the industry. A large part of Finland's timber-based exports in the 1960s consisted simply (as in Brazil and Chile) of wood-chips and pulp. However, by the 1970s Finland had all but stopped exporting wood-chips, had substantially cut its exports of pulp, and was using these raw materials as inputs for increased production and export of paper and paperboards, wood manufactures, and furniture. Also, by

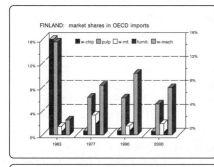
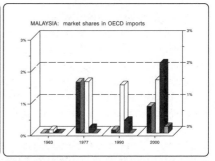
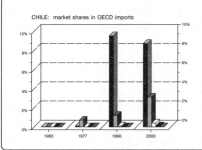
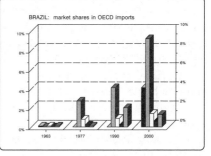

W-chip = wood-chips; **pulp** = pulp and waste paper; **w-maf** = wood manufactures; **furnit** = furniture; **W-mach** = paper mill and pulp mill machinery. Finland also managed a substantial share in OECD imports of paper and paperboards (not included in the graph), reaching in 2000 a market share in OECD markets of 14% (in that year, the respective market shares for Brazil and Chile were just 0.6% and 0.1%).

Figure 8.5. Finland, Malaysia, Chile and Brazil: vertical integration in the processed-timber industry

then Finland's market shares in OECD markets for machinery for the paper mill and pulp mill industries had exceeded 8 percent—a substantial achievement for such a small country.[21]

Figure 8.5 also reveals large disparities in export upgrading in the processed-timber industry between LA and EA. In the 1960s, neither had a processed-timber export industry. In the 1970s, while Chile and Brazil continued to export basic timber products, Malaysia had already added some wood manufactures, aided by the successful implementation of an industrial policy that included restricting exports of unprocessed timber. By 2000, Brazil's and Chile's exports still consisted entirely of products at the lower end of processing, while Malaysia's exports of processed-timber products consisted almost entirely of wood manufactures and furniture.[22]

The upgrading in the timber-based industry is, of course, a complex phenomenon, full of investment indivisibilities, high-entry costs, huge economies of scale, intricate financial engineering, specific skills, technological complexities, and environmental issues. For example, even the relatively simple operation of upgrading from wood-chip to 'MDF' requires considerable investments and skilful institutional arrangements.[23] Basically, one could easily end up in the business of transforming high quality timber into worthless furniture. As a result, many advise DCs not to tackle these market failures in the export-upgrading business (those that tend to keep them trapped in their traditional comparative advantages), and to try to make the best of their sub-optimal growth path. It would be wiser to be risk averse in this matter of 'acquiring' more growth-enhancing comparative advantages. For example, some may remember the World Bank reports and academic publications of the late 1950s and early 1960s that were intrigued by Japanese corporations transforming world-class steel and other high-quality inputs into sub-standard cars, which could be sold only to captive domestic customers or exported at highly subsidized prices.[24] Korean corporations followed suit in the 1970s, and the 'usual suspects' again wondered about what could be the rationale for building low or negative value-added production lines that used profits from captive markets to subsidize unprofitable exports? Who would voluntarily choose to buy a 1970s' Korean car, unless it was a home-customer with no choice, or an international one only able to afford a (massively subsidized) cheap product? But in fact, it did not take all that long for the Japanese and Korean car industry to turn the tables completely on their competitors.[25]

Asymmetries in the dynamics of international demand for iron, steel, and metal-working machinery are similar to those of the timber industry: while the sector shares in total OECD imports of iron ores and concentrates fell in value by 82 percent between 1977 and 2000, those of metal-working machinery significantly improved their relative position in OECD imports. However, in 2000 Chile exported practically only iron ores and Brazil's market share in OECD imports of iron ores was 15 times larger than its share in processed iron and steel. As mentioned above, this can hardly be justified simply by LA's natural resource abundance or US protectionist policies. Korea, by contrast, soon transformed the initial exports of iron ores into steel; then developed further into exporting metal-working machinery. Taiwan, in turn, had by the 1980s also already developed a significant export industry of metal-working machinery.

Although it is well known that as many countries which have tried this type of product-upgrading and demand adaptation have failed as have succeeded, the fact is that EA has developed the habit of succeeding while post-reform LA has even stopped trying. Not surprisingly, when FDI decides to get involved in this type of value-chain it tends to invest in resource-extraction in LA and resource-processing in EA.[26]

In fact, post-reform LA has not only invested very little in productive capacity diversification in order to move up the 'technology ladder' in terms of the processing of exports, but in several cases the movement has actually been in the opposite direction. Post-1973 Chile, for example, not only abandoned its previous 'pro-industrialization' agenda, but even ended up severely *reducing* the share of domestic value added in its copper exports, with the proportion of refined copper in total exports being drastically reduced in favor of the far more primitive copper 'concentrates' (see below).

Supply-upgrading in resource-poor countries: the flying-geese phenomenon

The Japanese economist Akamatsu coined the phrase 'flying geese' to characterize the East Asian supply-upgrading industrialization model (Akamatsu, 1962). The analysis that follows will characterize two very distinct components of this flying-geese phenomenon, not distinguished properly by Akamatsu and often confused in the literature: what I have called here the 'sequential movements' and the 'parallel movements' along the learning curve. Although each process is characterized by a very different dynamic, both have a crucial common element in that nearly all products involved are demand-dynamic from the point of view of world trade. What is characteristic of the first (and better-known) component of this 'flying-geese' process of industrialization, that which 'moves *sequentially* along the learning curve', is the involvement of products that Japan can no longer competitively produce and export and, therefore, allows its productive capacity to be transferred to the geese that are following them. For Japan, these products are either too labor-intensive to be produced competitively at Japanese wages, or they have already exhausted their productivity growth potentials (Figure 8.6, left panel).

In this 'sequential-movement' export productive capacity of products that tend not to be very high up the 'learning curve' is successfully transferred from Japan to the first-tier NICs, and then from these countries to the second-tier NICs, then to China, Vietnam, and so on. The crucial issue here is that when productive capacity is transferred to the geese that are following them, these *substitute* the exports of the more advanced goose in world markets, creating a sequence of 'inverted U-paths'—a phenomenon widely acknowledged in the traditional flying-geese literature.

The second (and usually ignored) component of the flying-geese phenomenon, that of 'moving in *parallel*' along the learning curve (Figure 8.6, right panel), reflects a different regional dynamic. This relates to products in which Japan does not relinquish its productive capacity easily, and often vigorously fights back against the challenge of other Asian countries. Japan's reluctance to 'concede' is due either to the fact that these products still have substantial productivity growth potential left in them and/or because they are among the products with the highest demand-dynamics in world trade.[27]

As Figure 8.6 indicates, Japan's share of exports in these 20 sectors eventually began to decline under the competitive pressure of the other East Asian geese;

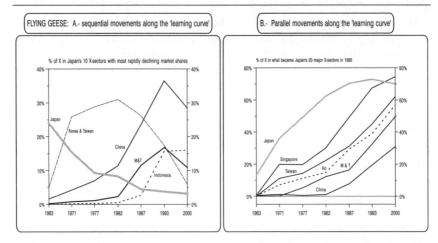

Panel A = percentage of exports in the respective countries in products that made up Japan's 10 export sectors with most rapidly declining market shares between 1963 and 2000 (SITC groups 843, 851, 037, 034, 894, 899, 666, 842, 761, and 762; for a detailed analysis of these products, see Palma, 1998). **Panel B** = the same but for Japan's 20 major export sectors in 1995 (SITC groups 781, 752, 764, 784, 776, 759, 778, 713, 763, 894, 782, 785, 751, 772, 749, 898, 874, 882, 728, and 736). **M&T** = Malaysia and Thailand; and **Ko** = Korea.

Figure 8.6. Flying geese: sequential and parallel movements along the learning curve

even in these extremely demand-dynamic markets, there is limited space for market entry. So, here we find not 'inverted U-paths', but parallel trajectories; the crucial issue here is that this process involves products that are much higher up in the 'learning curve'. These are products which Japan is reluctant to give up, and East Asian countries (with lags in time associated to their relative level of development) attempt to compete with Japan (rather than substitute its exports, as in the 'inverted-U' case).

One of the first casualties of EA's moving 'parallel' along the learning curve was the US; this was due to the fact that this pattern of imitation-with-a-lag leads to an *incremental* East Asian market share (right-hand panel of Figure 8.7). This is not the case with the other component of flying-geese industrialization, the 'sequential' movement in less attractive export products, as EA's aggregate market share hardly increased as productive capacity was systematically moved from one country to the other.

The contrast between EA and the Americas in both components of the East Asian 'flying-geese' pattern of industrialization is remarkable. On the one hand, in terms of Japan's *declining* sectors, the US and non-Mexico-LA maintain remarkably low and stable market shares for most of the period (left-hand panel in Figure 8.7). Yet, on the other, during this period the US lost *half* its market share in OECD imports in the second (more growth-enhancing) group of products (right-hand panel in Figure 8.7). In turn, LA (excluding 'maquila'

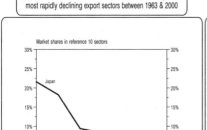

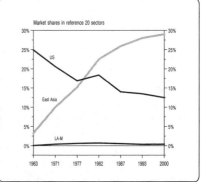

LA-M = Latin America, excluding Mexico; **East Asia** = Combined market shares of Japan, the NICs-1, NICs-2, and China in Japan's 20 major export sectors in 1995. (For a list of these export sectors see Figure 6; NICs-1 stands for first-tier NICs, and NICs-2 for second-tier NICs.)

Figure 8.7. Not the flying geese: market shares of the Americas in what became Japan's 10 most rapidly declining export sectors between 1963 and 2000; and market shares of the Americas in what became Japan's 20 major export sectors in 1995

Mexico) is on a completely different productive-capacity planet as far as these products are concerned.

However, to test whether or not there is a 'flying-geese' phenomenon in the Americas one should compare LA's exports with those of the US rather than with those of Japan. Figure 8.8 does that vis-à-vis the US's 20 major and most 'dynamic' export sectors.[28]

Within LA, Brazil was the only country that had a slow but steady increase of the share of its exports in the US's 'top-20' sectors (left-hand panel in Figure 8.8), reaching 22 percent of its exports in 2000; however, more than one-fifth of this increased share is made up by a single product, and a primary commodity at that: soybeans! The rest of 'non-maquila' LA had no significant amount of export-shares in these products (though Argentina was also rapidly increasing its soybean exports towards the end of this period).

One could hardly characterize this as a regional flying-geese pattern of industrialization and upgrading, one in which exports follow either a sequential or a parallel path between the US and LA. Of the US's 20 most dynamic export sectors (right-hand panel in Figure 8.8), 16 are primary commodities and fuels. Not surprisingly, the combined sector-share of these 20 sectors in all OECD imports fell steadily from 10.4 percent in 1963 to just 4.4 percent in 2000. Contrast this with Japan's 20 most dynamic export sectors, which doubled their sector-share over the same period. Moreover, as the right-hand

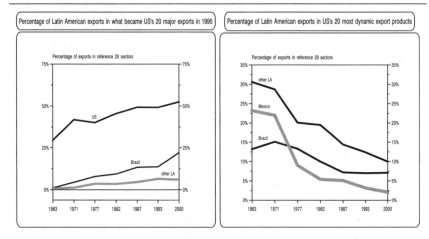

US's 20 major export sectors in 1995 were: SITC groups 792, 752, 784, 759, 781, 776, 874, 714, 764, 713, 931, 541, 778, 898, 772, 598, 749, 222, 322, and 892. US's 20 most 'dynamic' export sectors (i.e. those which had the fastest increase in market shares) between 1963 and 2000 were: SITC groups 246, 785, 034, 289, 112, 035, 061, 323, 014, 634, 036, 659, 248, 001, 871, 072, 223, 247, 287, and 291 (to avoid spurious growth rates in the calculation of US's 20 most 'dynamic' export sectors, a 'filter' was used to include only those export sectors that had an export-share of at least 0.3% of the total in 1963).

Figure 8.8. Not the flying geese: percent of Latin American exports in what became USA's 20 major exports in 1995; and percent of Latin American exports in USA's 20 most dynamic export products

panel of Figure 8.8 shows, in the US's 20 most *dynamic* export sectors the 'goose leader', the US, flies *in reverse*: that is, trying to penetrate markets that are being relinquished (partly as a result of competitive preasurs from US producers) by supposed geese-following Latin American countries! That is, it is in the 20 sectors in which the US had the highest *increase* in OECD market shares that one of the most bizarre aspects of the US's regional influence emerges. The US was increasing its export-share in (rather unattractive, mostly primary) products in which LA was *reducing* its export-share. Rather than an East Asian flying-geese pattern of succession, the (more magical realist) Americas present a scenario in which the leader follows the followers...[29]

Figure 8.9, which compares the changes in the overall levels of competitiveness and the capacity to move into 'high-tech' products in the regions studied here, illustrates several related issues.[30]

First, Figure 8.9 shows that in 1963 neither LA nor the first- and second-tier NICs and China exported 'high-tech' products. However, secondly, it also indicates that East and South East Asian countries were already 'competitive' in the (non-high-tech) products that they exported at the time (products that were rather similar in nature to those exported by LA). Thirdly, it shows that among Latin American countries during the 1960s, only Brazil and Mexico

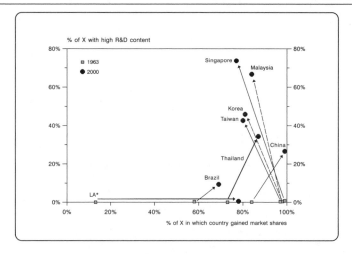

'High-tech' products = products with high content of R&D. **X** = exports; LA* = Latin America, excluding Brazil and 'maquila' Mexico and Central America. Excludes oil.
Vertical axis: percentage of exports with high content of R&D in 1963 (first observation) and in 2000 (second observation). **Horizontal axis**: percentage of *all* exports (with or without high content of R&D) in which the respective country or region gained market shares in OECD imports between 1963 and 1971 (first observation), and between 1990 and 2000 (second observation).

Figure 8.9. Latin America and East Asia: different export-trajectories in high-technology exports, 1963 and 2000

(not included in the graph) were relatively competitive in their exports and were gaining market shares in a significant proportion of them (58% of exports in both countries); that is, LA's ISI-anti-export-bias affected more intensively the export competitiveness of the small and medium-sized countries (including Argentina). Fourthly, it shows that during the 1990s (after trade liberalization) LA was able massively to increase its competitiveness in OECD markets (i.e., the proportion of exports in which it was gaining market shares)—in several cases, from less than 20 percent to about 80 percent of their exports. Fifthly, even though during the 1990s LA reached East Asian levels of export competitiveness, it did so only in its traditional-type exports.[31] If international demand had not discriminated in such an extreme form against unprocessed commodities, and if these products had had the same long-term productivity growth potential and growth-enhancing 'pulling' effect as those higher up in the 'value-chain', this remarkable increase in competitiveness would have been an unqualified regional success. Unfortunately, this was clearly not the case. Finally, Figure 8.9 also illustrates East Asian countries' remarkable capacity to 'reinvent' themselves, by diversifying their export productive capacity towards 'high-tech' products; further, they did so while retaining most of their former extremely high levels of export competitiveness.

219

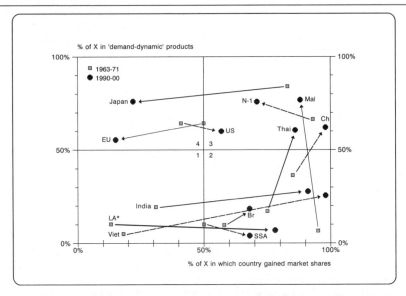

Excludes oil. **X** = exports; **Br** = Brazil; **Ch** = China; **EU** = European Union; **LA*** = LA (excluding Brazil; maquila Mexico and Central America); **Mal** = Malaysia; **N-1** = Korea, Singapore and Taiwan; **SSA** = Sub-Saharan Africa (excluding South Africa); **Thai** = Thailand; **Viet** = Vietnam.

First observation: export profile of country or region between 1963 and 2000. **Second observation**: that between 1990 and 2000. **Vertical axis**: percentage of exports of a country or region of products that became 'demand-dynamic' in OECD imports (i.e. products that increased their share in OECD imports during respective periods due, for example, to their higher income elasticity). **Horizontal axis**: percentage of exports in which the respective country or region gained market shares in OECD imports during the relevant period. Therefore, if an observation is in **quadrant 1** this indicates an 'uncompetitive' country (i.e. less than half its exports have gained market shares) exporting 'non-demand-dynamic' products (i.e. less than half its exports are 'demand-dynamic' products); if it is in **quadrant 2**, it shows a 'competitive' country exporting 'non-demand-dynamic' products; if in **quadrant 3**, a 'competitive' country exporting 'demand-dynamic' products; and in **quadrant 4**, an 'uncompetitive' country exporting 'demand-dynamic' products.

Notes: i) Data for Taiwan correspond to those reported in the second edition of the Trade-CAN software; this edition includes data only until 1995. The third edition (used for all other countries) does not provide data for Taiwan; ii) The first observation for Vietnam corresponds to the period 1973–1984 (i.e. from the date when US combat troops left Vietnam until the beginning of economic reform; Trãn Văn Thọ, et al. 2000); the seond observation is for the 1990s; and iii) See Appendix 2 for a more formal definition of the four quadrants.

Figure 8.10. 'Anti-clockwise' export-trajectories between the 1960s and the 1990s

Overall export-trajectories between the 1960s and 1990s

Finally, one could compare export profiles between the 1960s and the 1990s not just by looking at the capacity to move into 'high-tech' products (Figure 8.9), but also into 'demand-dynamic' products in general, whether 'high-tech' or not (Figure 8.10).

Figure 8.10 illustrates that the remarkable increase in export competitiveness in LA between the 1960s and the 1990s (i.e. the rapid movement from quadrants 1 to 2), was not accompanied by an improvement in the 'quality' of its exports. Figure 8.9 has shown that LA's improved export competitiveness did not include many high-tech products; Figure 8.10 indicates that it did not include many other demand-dynamic products either. In EA, in contrast, it indicates an intriguing aspect of the flying-geese pattern of industrialization and exports: the different trajectories of young-industrializers (second-tier NICs and China), to those of middle-aged ones (first-tier NICs) and of more 'mature' ones (Japan). Basically, the rapid movement into demand-dynamic products of the second-tier NICs and China—their sharp movement from quadrants 2 to 3—eats away some degree of export competitiveness in the first-tier NICs. This process is more acute with Japan (and the EU) because the aggregate competitive pressure of all NICs and China (in addition to other domestic economic problems) has driven these countries from quadrants 3 to 4. With the exception of the US (mostly due to the export dynamism of the Clinton years), the overall pattern that emerges in Figure 8.10 is one of a clear anti-clockwise trajectory.

For LA and other countries moving into quadrant 2, the crucial trade- and industrial-policy issue is whether there are endogenous market forces that would lead them eventually in an upwards movement from quadrants 2 to 3. Or whether there are market failures that would lead them to get trapped in being ever more competitive in products that tend to be ever more marginalized (in value terms) from world markets (except for temporary cyclical periods such as those that benefited many commodities, such as oil, between 9/11 and the 2007 financial crisis). In fact, especially in commodity markets, excessive competitive struggle for market shares by DCs often leads to self-defeating fallacy of composition problems.[32]

So far, there is little (if any) evidence of 'upward endogenous forces' at work that would help bring a country from 2 to 3. Countries in quadrant 2 seem to need an exogenous push such as the trade and industrial policies that characterized the movement from 2 to 3 in most East Asian countries. However, for these policies to be implemented effectively, what is needed is the type of institutional arrangements that allowed them to be effective in EA. These include a strong state, capable not only of devising trade and industrial policies to generate rents that would create incentives to the transfer of resources towards demand-dynamic export products, but also capable of making sure that these rents are used effectively. That is, a state not only capable of generating rents, but also one capable of imposing performance-related conditionalities in order to 'discipline' the capitalist elite to use them productively. Furthermore, for these policies to succeed it is also necessary to have a state capable of withstanding clientelist pressures from 'intermediate classes'.[33]

If these policies and the institutional arrangements necessary for their success are not implemented, the potential GDP-growth-enhancing effect of further increases in export competitiveness in LA would continue to be restricted by the generally low productivity growth potential of unprocessed commodity exports (sometimes after an initial one-off boost), and by their modest positive externalities and spillover effects and low capacity to induce productivity growth in the rest of the economy in general. Furthermore, lack of an upward movement from 2 to 3 could also seriously affect the welfare gains from trade specialization in terms of the purchasing power of exports.[34]

Existing evidence for LA indicates that the (not so) invisible hand of globalized markets is only creating incentives leading towards further penetration into quadrant 2. There is little evidence that existing market incentives, the current domestic structure of property rights and institutional arrangements, or the present domestic political settlements are helping the region to move upwards in the direction of quadrant 3. One example is Chile, the most successful country in post-reform LA (at least for the period between the 1982 debt crisis and the 1997 East Asian financial crisis), whose export trajectory is a horizontal (in fact, slightly downward) movement from quadrant 1 to 2, which resulted from increasing the share of competitive exports from 12 percent to 79 percent, while actually *decreasing* the share of exports of demand-dynamic products from 12 percent to 6 percent. The performance of its copper export industry is a good example of this peculiar combination of increased competitiveness with no 'upward push'; in fact, while rapidly gaining market share, Chile was actually *reducing* the average share of manufacturing value added in its copper exports. As a result, the proportion of refined copper (i.e. with more than 99% metal content) has fallen from 97 percent of total copper exports in 1973 to just about half, in favor of the far less processed form of copper 'concentrates' (with less than one-third metal content).[35] There is ample evidence that the sharp slowdown in Chile's growth since the end of the 1990s is partly due to this underinvestment in upward productive diversification.[36]

Finally, the analysis of the past 40 years of international trade (and Figures 8.7 and 8.8 above) clearly shows that LA's long-delayed transition towards quadrant 3 can expect little (if any) pulling help from the US (as East Asian countries had from their 'leading-goose').[37]

A simple test for the different capabilities of EA and LA to use exports effectively as an engine of growth

LA's economic performance since the beginning of trade and financial liberalization, and the switching back of the engine of growth to the export sector, has been characterized by dynamic exports and sluggish growth in the rest of the economy. Figure 8.11 shows the average growth of GDP and exports since 1980 for a group of countries, as well as the conditional expectation for this relationship.

In most of LA, as in many other DCs, economic reform has certainly succeeded in shifting the 'engine of growth' towards the export sector. However, for any engine to be effective, the power it generates must be properly harnessed. Asian countries seem to have mastered this process rather well, while those in LA

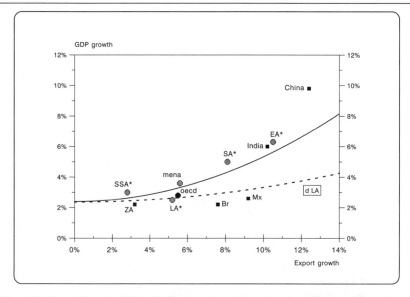

EA* = NICs-1 and NICs-2 (excluding China); **LA*** = Latin America (excluding Brazil, Mexico and Vene-zuela); **d LA** = interactive dummy for Latin American countries; **mena** = North Africa and the Middle East; **oecd** = average of 15 high-income OECD countries; **SA*** = South Asia (excluding India); **SSA*** = Sub-Saharan Africa (excluding South Africa). **Br** = Brazil; **Mx** = Mexico; and **ZA** = South Africa.

Notes: The regression line is obtained form a cross-country regression in which GDP growth is the dependent variable and export growth squared is the explanatory one; the sample consists of all countries for which the WDI reports data for both variables during this period (94). It is important to emphasize here that the aim of this regression is simply to represent a cross-sectional description of cross-country GDP-growth differences, categorized by export-growth performance. Therefore, this regression should not be interpreted as 'predictive', because as is well-known there are a number of difficulties with a regression of this type estimated from a single cross-section, especially regarding the homogeneity restrictions that are required to hold. This regression passes all the relevant diagnostic tests. The R^2 is 54% and the 't' static of the explanatory variable is 10.8, and the 't' of the dummy is 3. The 't' statistics are based on 'White's heteroscedasticity adjusted standard errors'. For a discussion of the econometrics of cross-section regressions, see Pesaran, et al. (2000).

Source: Constructed by the author using data from WDI (2007).

Figure 8.11. Regional averages: exports and GDP growth, 1980–2006

(especially Brazil and Mexico, formerly the most dynamic economies of the region) and in sub-Saharan Africa (including South Africa) remain far from doing so. Figure 8.12, in turn, shows the degree to which the performance of the export engine seems to be region-specific, and the remarkable underper-formance of LA.

As is clear from the graph, the Latin American export engine tends to perform badly compared to those of EA and South Asia in terms of its capacity to be associated with GDP growth in the rest of the economy. In fact, it performs poorly in relative terms even when compared with that of other commodity-exporting countries. Basically, during this period sub-Saharan countries achieved disappointing growth rates on both exports and GDP, while Asian

223

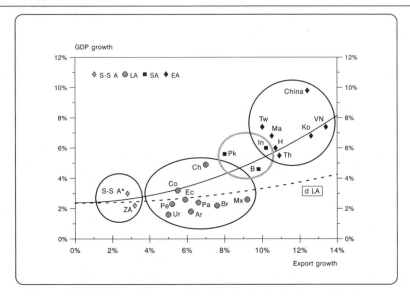

EA = East and South-East Asia; **LA** = Latin America; **d LA** = interactive dummy for Latin American countries; **SA** = South Asia; **S-S A** = Sub-Saharan Africa; and **S-S A*** = Sub-Saharan Africa (excluding South Africa). **Ar** = Argentina; **B** = Bangladesh; **Br** = Brazil; **Ch** = Chile; **Co** = Colombia; **Ec** = Ecuador; **H** = Hong-Kong; **In** = India; **Ko** = Korea; **Ma** = Malaysia; **Mx** = Mexico; **Pa** = Paraguay; **Pe** = Peru; **Pk** = Pakistan; **Th** = Thailand; **Tw** = Taiwan; **Ur** = Uruguay; **VN** = Vietnam; and **ZA** = South Africa. Vietnam's export growth is 14.7%.

Note: The WDI database does not provide information for Taiwan. Data for this country has been obtained form The Republic of China Yearbook of Statistics.

Figure 8.12. Export and GDP growth in four developing regions, 1980–2006

countries managed dynamic growth on both fronts; whereas Latin American countries (and especially Brazil and Mexico), while able to engineer a rapid expansion of exports, were unable to pull the rest of the economy along with it. So, in statistical terms, as GDP growth in Latin American countries is located below their conditional expectations (i.e., given its export growth) consistently enough, the interactive dummy for the region (as in Figure 8.11) ends up being negative and highly significant. The most important issue here to emphasise is that if the dummy is applied to all commodity-exporting countries it becomes non-significant; it is when applied only to Latin American countries that it becomes negative and highly significant—i.e., during this period, the lack of growth-pulling capacities of dynamic exports is a specific Latin American problem!

The underperforming of the Latin American export engine after economic reform is a relatively stable phenomenon throughout the post-1980 period. In Brazil, for example, while between 1950 and 1980 the growth of the previous engine (manufacturing) and overall GDP were very similar (8.8% and 7.3% per year, respectively), since Lula was first elected, the asymmetry between the growth of the new engine (exports) and GDP during this period (2002–2007) could hardly be greater (13.3% and 3.5% respectively; see <http://www.eclac.org>).

Mexico is the country with the largest gap between actual GDP growth and the conditional expectation of this growth (i.e., given its export growth) in the whole sample, making it an extreme example of export-led growth failure. During these two and a half decades, a remarkably dynamic growth of exports (9.2% per year) was associated with an extremely poor growth performance (2.6%).[38] Further, as population grew at a bit over 1.6 percent, per capita GDP growth stood at just under 1 percent per year.[39] Figure 8.13 shows more clearly this phenomenon of booming exports with little GDP-growth tracking.

The Mexican economy's remarkable inability to harness the power generated by its dynamic export expansion seems to be its most important economic failure since the end of the ISI period and the beginning of neo-liberal economic reforms. As Figure 8.13 shows, the long-lasting close relationship between exports and GDP growth, built during ISI, disappeared after the 1982 debt crisis, when the sharp *acceleration* in the rate of growth of exports became associated with a sharp *decline* in rate of growth of GDP—not exactly the Promised Land of the Washington Consensus. In fact, the ratio of GDP growth to that of export collapsed by two-thirds.

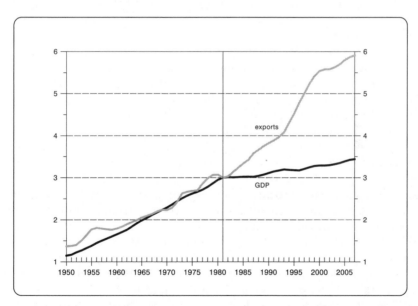

Log scales. Exports do not include oil; 1980 prices. For the convenience of the graph, before transforming the data into logs the original data were first made into a 3-year moving average and then into index-numbers with 1981 as a base year (equal to 20.09; the natural logarithm of this number is 3).

Source: ECLAC's Statistical Database.
Figure 8.13. Mexico: GDP and exports, 1950–2007

As the regression line above has indicated (Figure 8.12), in LA exports are faltering as an engine of growth not because of their lack of own growth, market penetration, or competitiveness, but because of their poor 'GDP-tracking' properties. This is likely to be associated, at least in part, with the lack of 'quality' of its export composition (i.e., in terms of the idiom of Figure 8.10 above, with the region's inability to move from quadrants 2 to 3); and in the case of Mexico, with the lack of 'deepening' of its maquila exports. Orthodox and unimaginative monetary, fiscal, and exchange-rate policies have not helped either. However, as Figure 8.12 indicated, this is also a region-specific phenomenon, likely to be the result of the rigid way in which economic reforms were implemented in the region. For example, if one adds to the above regression a variable for the 'quality' of exports (as in Figure 8.10), other variables to account for factor accumulation (population growth and investment), and others to account for 'production frontier shifters' (such as manufacturing), LA again ends up as the region with the largest negative gap between actual GDP growth and the conditional expectation of that growth.

Ironically, while during the ISI period the main obstacle in LA to the sustainability of growth was an almost obsessive concentration of policy incentives and resources in (non-export) manufacturing, leading to a neglect of exports (hindering growth via a balance of payments constraint), in the post-1980 period the region did exactly the reverse. Though LA certainly succeeded in becoming competitive in world markets for its traditional export products, this effort seems to have had little overall growth-enhancing effect. Lack of growth-enhancing policies, institutions capable of implementing them, adequate structures of property rights, and incentives and macro-stability also matter in this. Product diversification, high levels of investment, and adequate institutions seem to be the conditions that have helped Asian countries successfully take advantage of new 'growth spaces' in a globalized world.

In sum, export-led growth when based on unprocessed primary commodities or 'thin' maquila exports has proved to be a poor engine of growth. The main lesson from post-reform LA is that if middle-income DCs want to insist on this export orientation (or if there is little they can do about it in the short term), policy makers and the capitalist elite of these countries should think about this model only as a 'growth-enabling' export-strategy, not as an export-led growth strategy. That is, a fast rate of growth of (unprocessed) commodity exports or maquila) can at best be expected to provide foreign exchange to *enable* a more dynamic rate of growth in the rest of the economy; that is, to increase the rate of growth of GDP that is sustainable from the point of view of the balance of payments. However, for this growth actually to take place there is still the need for a proper 'engine' to be activated somewhere else in the economy. That is, parallel to commodity or maquila exports there is the need for other sectors or activities to play the role of production frontier shifters, able to set in motion processes of cumulative causation—characterized by their positive feedback loops into the system, capable of generating a momentum of change which is self-perpetuating (as in the Veblen–Myrdal or Young–Kaldor manner).

There's not much evidence from LA since 1980 to indicate that unprocessed primary commodities or maquila exports can play such role—nor that the countries of this region have made much effort in export-upgrading, or in looking elsewhere for an effective engine of growth.

Conclusions

Ultimately, the effectiveness of exports as an engine of growth depends on the capacity of exports to increase both productivity growth and labor absorption not only in the export sector itself but in the overall economy. On the purchasing power of income side there is the additional issue of the terms of trade, as these are the vital link between real GDP growth and real command-GDP growth.

In post-reform LA (with the sole exception of Chile—and only during a specific period that covers about half its post-reform years), the main stylized fact regarding GDP growth is that even in those countries successful in rapidly accelerating the rate of growth of exports, especially Mexico and Brazil, the rate of growth of output has been particularly disappointing. Of course, for those countries that have not even been able to improve export competitiveness, the post-reform economic situation has proved much worse.

For LA and many other DCs the key strategic trade-policy issue is how to invest effectively in product diversification in order to redirect export growth from quadrant 2 to 3 (Figure 8.10). The well-know fact that the design of these policies is sometimes difficult, and that their practical implementation is always so (due to institutional, technological, financial, and other constraints), has become a Latin American (and a South African), but not an Asian, excuse. As discussed above, the movement from 2 to 3 relates not only to the critical supply-side differences between concentrating exports in basic unprocessed primary commodities rather than in products higher up in the value-chain, but also to the rather obvious fact that if for a DC exports are to be an effective engine of growth in an export-led strategy, it is better to be attached to a locomotive (world demand) with effective pulling-power (demand-growth). This could prove, for example, the difference between international trade being a positive- or zero-sum game vis-à-vis competitors.

Export-led growth in post-reform LA has been, at best, a mixed blessing. Although maquila exports have absorbed a significant amount of labour, they have been characterized by little or no productivity growth, and associated with little or no productivity growth in the rest of the economy. In turn, in the few cases of rapid productivity growth in unprocessed commodity exports (e.g. some mining and agricultural products), there is ample evidence that this has been more a 'one-off' type of phenomenon than a process that could be sustained over time. Moreover, this productivity growth has had little 'pulling' effect on productivity growth in the rest of the economy. And from the point of view of command-GDP-growth, except for the short-lived cyclical upswing in commodity terms of trade that started with 9/11, when exports were adjusted by the price of imports, the capacity of export growth to add to the purchasing power of GDP proved equally disappointing.

Using Krugman's terminology, post-reform LA may be a paradigmatic case in which the single-minded emphasis on improved export competitiveness in traditional export products has led policy makers and their economic advisers to forget that what really matter from the point of view of the growth of income in export-led economies are the purchasing power gains arising from specialization. And as Krugman emphasizes, single-minded emphasis on export competitiveness is a very dangerous obsession that tends to skew domestic economic policies.[40]

That is not to say that in open economies 'competitiveness' does not matter; but when the terms of trade are so unstable and downwardly mobile, competitive gains can mean something very different from welfare gains. Therefore, being able to enhance international competitiveness in a given product, even when both the domestic and the international prices are 'right', does not per se justify the continuous concentration of resources in that specific export product in the long run. In fact, one should never forget that when Korea took the decision to 'reinvent' its export sector in the early 1960s, it certainly had no 'competitiveness' problem with its world class silk or its excellent quality seaweed (the country's main export products at the time).

LA's underinvestment in export-product diversification in a world of rapidly changing demand has led the region from being a major player in major products to being a major player in relatively marginal products.[41] In fact, LA has not even sought 'niches' in segmented commodity markets that have emerged from the dissemination of the new technological paradigm (characterized by a 'knowledge society' with flexible production techniques). This underinvestment in part reflects the region's (path-dependent) obsession with traditional products that are often less and less attractive from the point of view of international demand, in which further 'competitive' gains can only be achieved by ever-increasing mass production, more and more optimal routines, greater and greater degrees of standardization, and larger and larger economies of scale.[42] Obviously, LA's underinvestment in productive capacity diversification is the direct result of the fact that every time private investment in the region manages to rise above 15 percent of GDP the capitalist elite begins to experience feelings of vertigo. As a result, LA ends up being like a football team that plays better and better in a league that gets continuously relegated to lower and lower divisions, while EA seems to be a member of a league continually promoted to higher and higher divisions. In fact, in a Ricardian sense, LA's increased export competitiveness has sometimes acted as an 'own-goal' because its standard of living has sometimes actually declined when domestic output growth has been outweighed by deteriorating terms of trade.

The obsession with increased competitiveness in existing export products has led LA to keep shooting at a fixed target, even though world demand became a rapidly moving one. In contrast, East, South-East, and South Asia, aided by their own efforts in institution-building, investment, savings, education, and so on, as well as by Japanese regional leadership, have been increasingly successful in learning how to hit a moving target. Further, as the data have shown, international demand-adaptation and supply-upgrading are closely related phenomena; therefore, predicting the trajectory of this moving target does not seem to be such a difficult task, despite the rapidly changing technological paradigm. Unfortunately, the capacity of the state to 'discipline' the capitalist elite in order to be able effectively to implement an appropriate set of strategic trade and industrial policies is another matter—and one in which LA does not seem to have learnt how to acquire much comparative advantege. In sum, in Foucault's terms what LA requires even to start injecting some dynamism into its growth path is a shift from the current neo-liberal state of affairs—in which 'the state is under the surveillance of the market'—to a more East Asian one where 'it is the market that is under the surveillance of the state' (see Foucault, 2004; for a detailed analysis of this issue, see Palma 2009b).

One of the characteristics of a great deal of the trade literature, even in some of its 'new-trade' brand, is that it has been slow to acknowledge this type of problem. For example, when new-trade theorists criticize traditional neoclassical trade theory, they do so only in relation to issues such as the fact that it has ignored the possibility that a given set of 'right' prices could still generate multiple equilibria due to uncertainties in the economic system (where decisions are taken in a decentralized way); or because it ignores the possibility of the emergence of several types of inefficiency in the social learning process, which in turn could produce inefficient economic outcomes. These could occur, for example, because the information structure is determined by the nature and the extent of these uncertainties, the degree of communication among agents, the pay-off relevance of the decisions to be taken, and the actual range of choices faced by the agents. In other words, in these types of criticism of the neoclassical trade theory, new-trade theory has often tried to identify, and give due relevance to, issues such as the social learning process and the macro-institutional framework of the export sector. It has put emphasis on the actual context in which agents are supposed to learn, and on how this learning is very much determined by the institutional context. Further, it has endogenized the learning process to a (supposedly exogenous) institutional context, and discussed how in this way different export paths could arise. However, the concept of an 'optimal' export path, even though more relative, is still determined by how to maximize an export performance given *present* resource endowments and a set of *contemporary* (more or less) 'right' prices. But it is not

229

at all obvious how the given set of prices will signal medium- and long-term changes in the pattern of international demand and technological change, nor how these prices, or the supposedly 'exogenous' domestic institutional setting, can provide an incentive for diversification of exports towards a flexible pattern compatible with inter-temporal maximization of gains from specialization. In a sense, this new literature returns to the same traditional issue of how to achieve the maximum degree of 'competitiveness' given some existing domestic endowments and current external constraints (now including market failures), but with a much richer way of understanding the dynamics of how this could (or could not) be achieved.

An alternative approach to international trade in DCs should promote the idea that once agents and institutions have learnt how to deal effectively in the 'real' international markets, there is still a need for some vigorous agency (e.g. active trade and industrial policies) steering the economy towards a flexible export productive capacity, which can maximize returns from (often *acquired*) comparative advantages in a world with constantly changing demand patterns and rapid technological change. In this way, a country could attempt to maximize the trade-induced output-growth potentials it gets from an export-led growth strategy as well as welfare gains from international trade. As Stiglitz has repeatedly emphasised, markets do not necessarily lead to these sorts of efficient outcomes by themselves, especially in DCs.[43]

There are obviously many other trade-related issues that cannot be discussed here, such as the crucial one of exhaustible resources (even for resource-rich countries); the optimal taxation policy (especially 'royalties') towards the extraction of non-renewal export-resources; FDI's anti-Latin American bias in the local processing of resources; the upgrading and 'anchoring' of maquila production lines; the perennial lack of innovative Schumpeterian spirit of the Latin American oligarchy; and, in particular, the question of why the region's capitalist elite seem to get altitude sickness every time private investment climbs to about 15 percent of GDP.

In sum, the remarkable asymmetries in terms of gains from specialization between LA and EA (evident, for example, in the negative and significant Latin American dummy in Figures 8.11 and 8.12 above) inevitably lead to a question asked in the spirit of Sugar Kowalczyk (Marilyn Monroe's character in *Some Like It Hot*): why is it that in trade-related issues Latin American countries always seem to end up with the wrong end of the lollipop?

There can be little doubt that at least one important part of the answer is that the Latin American capitalist elite can afford to be so risk-averse in terms of demand-adaptation and supply-upgrading in their trade-related business because they are as effective now (after economic reforms) as they were before in creating structures of property rights and incentives from which lavishly large income streams (rents) can be generated in the domestic economy. After all, according to the World Bank statistics, the median income share of the top

10 percent of income earners in LA is currently above 45 percent (and increasing), while in Malaysia and Thailand it is 35 percent, in India 31 percent, and in Korea only 25 percent![44]

In other words, in post-reform LA the capitalist elite can afford to be so risk-averse in their trade-related business because they have managed to create a political–institutional settlement in which a new distributional coalition has succeeded in imposing a new structure of property rights and incentives that have allowed them, and their populist allies, extravagant forms of predatory capitalism, unproductive rent-seeking, and the economic emasculation of the state.[45] And in terms of their populist allies, one question that begs an answer is why democratic forces in the region were so prepared to believe that such a straitjacketed type of institutionality was the only option open for a return to democracy—for example, the democratic forces in Chile seemed to believe that they could only defeat Pinochet in his 1988-plebiscite if they implicitly agreed that their electoral motto would be 'Liberté, Inégalité, Passivité'.[46] Another, of course, is why almost immediately after the return to democracy did these formerly progressive groups decide to become the new standard-bearers of the neo-liberal orthodoxy?[47]

So, it seems that in their trade-related business the Latin American capitalist elite can perfectively well 'afford' not to make the required investment efforts for demand-adaptation and supply-upgrading, not to be Schumpeterian-innovative, or to take the required risks, because they can count on the fact that their (not very puritanical) share of domestic income will be so plentiful that it will compensate for their (not very Calvinistic) attitude towards trade-related issues. In fact, if one compares the above-mentioned share of national income appropriated by the top 10 percent with the share of private investment in GDP, LA appears even more as an outlier: while in LA the income share of the top decile is approximately *three* times the GDP share of private investment, in India and China this ratio is about 1.7, in Malaysia and Thailand it is only slightly above one, and in Korea these shares of income and investment are actually roughly the same. Perhaps this is what really makes the discreet charm of the Latin American bourgeoisie so unique!

Appendix 1: A demand-adaptability index vis-à-vis (a changing) OECD structure of imports

One set of statistics that can be constructed using the data provided by the Trade-CAN software is a 'demand-adaptability index' of a country to the (changing) structure of imports of the OECD (see Figure 8.4). This index can give an insight into a country's capacity to react to changes in OECD demand for imports.

The 'demand-adaptability index' A_j of a country 'j' to the structure of OECD imports is defined here as $A_j = \sum_{jd} a_{ij}^d / \sum_{jnd} a_{ij}^{nd}$. The numerator $\sum_{jd} a_{ij}^d$ is the country's market share in demand-dynamic sectors ('d'), adjusted by the weight of demand-dynamic sectors in OECD imports; and the denominator $\sum_{jnd} a_{ij}^{nd}$ is the country's market share in non-dynamic sectors ('nd'), also adjusted by the share of these sectors in OECD imports. Therefore, $a_{ij} = \frac{s_{ij}}{S_j}$; where $s_{ij} = \frac{M_{ij}}{M_i}$ is the country 'j' share 's' in OECD imports ('M') of product 'i' (for either 'd' or 'nd' products), and $S_j = M_j = \sum_i s_{ij}$ is the country's total share 'S' in OECD imports ('M')—this, in turn, is the sum of the market shares for different products 'i' of country 'j'. Finally, demand-dynamic products ('d_i') are those import products that increase their shares in OECD imports between two points in time (such that $S_i^d = \dot{S}_i \geq 0$). In turn, non-dynamic products are those that decrease their shares in total imports during this period ($s_i^{nd} = \dot{s}_i < 0$).

Appendix 2: The four quadrants of Figure 8.10

For the export profile of a country to be located in quadrant 1 during a given period of time—i.e. for it to be classified as an 'uncompetitive' country exporting 'non-demand-dynamic' products during this period (e.g. LA in the 1960s)—its export profile should be characterized by both $[M_i/M_{(fy)} < M_i/M_{(by)}]$, and $[M_{ij}/M_{i(fy)} < M_{ij}/M_{i(by)}]$; where 'fy' is final year and 'by' is base year of this period (note that data for all years in the Trade-CAN software are 3-year moving averages). For an export profile to be in quadrant 2—i.e. a 'competitive' country exporting 'non-demand-dynamic' products (e.g. LA in the 1990s)—this profile should be characterized by $[M_i/M_{(fy)} < M_i/M_{(by)}]$ and $[M_{ij}/M_{i\,(fy)} > M_{ij}/M_{i\,(by)}]$. For it to be in quadrant 3—a 'competitive' country exporting 'demand-dynamic' products (e.g. EA in the 1990s)—the conditions $[M_i/M_{(fy)} > M_i/M_{(by)}]$, and $[M_{ij}/M_{i(fy)} > M_{ij}/M_{i(by)}]$ should apply. Finally, to be in quadrant 4—and be an 'uncompetitive' country exporting 'demand-dynamic' products (e.g. Japan and the European Union in the 1990s)—a country's export profile should be characterized by $[M_i/M_{(fy)} > M_i/M_{(by)}]$ and $[M_{ij}/M_{i(fy)} < M_{ij}/M_{i(by)}]$.

Notes

1. If the rates of growth of GDP per capita of the last 5 years in both countries were to continue, China would catch up with Mexico by 2020.
2. See Ffrench-Davis, Muñoz, and Palma (1994) and Palma (2004). For an overview of Latin American economic development throughout the twentieth century, see Ocampo (2004).
3. For example, the combination of the Fed trebling nominal rates and the collapse of commodity prices due to recession in the North led to a *33 percentage-point* increase in the real rate of interest paid by LA for its foreign debt (i.e. when LIBOR is deflated by LA's non-oil export-prices, this rate increased from minus 11.2% to 22.1%; see Palma, 2004). See also Diaz-Alejandro (1984), Marcel and Palma (1988), and Ocampo (2004).

4. The new economic discourse went as far as transforming almost anything previously considered as *virtue* into *vice*, and vice versa. This attitude was best summarized by Gustavo Franco, President of Brazil's Central Bank during the years of economic reform (leading up to the 1999 financial crisis): '[Our real task] is to undo forty years of stupidity ("besteira")' (*Veja* 15–11–1996).

5. Franco again: '[In Brazil today] the alternative is to be neo-liberal or neo-idiotic (neo-burros).' (Ibid.)

6. See, for example, McKay (2002) and Palma (1998).

7. With the exception of post-NAFTA Mexico, this openness was clearly not extended to LA, and especially not to Brazil.

8. This also led to remarkably positive interaction between increases in productivity and wages, particularly in the first-tier NICs (Newly Industrializing Countries).

9. The price of memory chips (per MB of RAM), for example, fell by about four-fifths in 1996 alone, partly resulting from excess supply due to massive expansion of Taiwanese production. Korea was particularly affected.

10. This was reflected in rising debt/equity ratios, which, particularly in Korea, reached vertiginous heights.

11. See Ocampo and Parra (2004), Rodríguez (2006), and Palma (2008).

12. See Blankenburg, Palma, and Tregenna (2008).

13. This long-term trend was temporarily reversed due to 9/11, the Iraq war, frantic speculation in commodities futures, and the rise of China and India (at least in oil and in some minerals and agricultural products) until the 2007 financial crisis. As has so often happened in the past, many policy makers and analysts incorporated a bit too quickly into their analysis the assumption that this post-9/11 cyclical recovery was a permanent state of affairs.

14. See Krugman (1994).

15. To paraphrase Canon's ad, EA's attitude towards exports and comparative advantages could be summarized as 'if anybody can, we can!'

16. See Appendix 1.

17. In 2000, for example, 54% of OECD imports were in sectors that had been 'demand-dynamic' between 1980 and 2000; so an index of 1 for a country in 2000 means that 54% of its exports to OECD markets then were of 'demand dynamic' products.

18. For a critique of the 'resource curse' literature, see DiJohn (2008). For a detailed study of how one particularly successful commodity exporter (Botswana) managed to avoid this supposed 'curse', see Tregenna (2006).

19. On the literature on 'technology-gap' and evolutionary theory, see Cimoli (1994); Dosi et al. (1988) and (1990); Freeman and Soete (1997); Hobday (2003); and Teece (1996).

20. One example of this would be organic agriculture (see Perez, 2008).

21. Sweden had a similar capacity to supply-upgrade its timber exports, as well as the production of inputs for its commodity-extracting industries (see Walker, 2003).

22. Taiwan presents a similar success story of upgrading in the timber-processing industry, but this country had to import the required inputs.

23. On the technological issues involved, see especially Perez (2008).

24. In fact, the first car that Toyota exported to the US (the 'Toyopet') was such a flop that it had to be withdrawn from the market (it was described at the time as just 'four wheels and an ashtray'). As Chang reminds us, 'many [inside and outside Japan]

argued at the time that Toyota should have stuck to its original business of making simple textile machinery...Today, Japanese cars are considered as "natural" as Scottish salmon or French wine' (2007).

25. On the distinction between 'allocative', 'Schumpeterian', and 'growth' efficiencies, see Dosi, Pavitt, and Soete (1990) and the chapter by Cimoli, Dosi, Nelson, and Stiglitz in this volume.

26. See especially Amsden (2001).

27. Sometimes Japan ends up relinquishing its productive capacity in only some inputs of a given product, a process that leads to a regional integration of production lines.

28. In this context, 'the most dynamic sectors' means the sectors in which the US had the highest *increase* in OECD market shares.

29. Not surprisingly, in a series of new trade agreements between the US and Latin American countries, a primary concern of the US has been the opening up of the economies of Latin American countries to its exports of primary commodity (particularly agricultural products).

30. The main limitation of traditional trade statistics (such as those available in the UN Com-trade online database and the Trade-CAN software) is that they refer to *gross* value of exports and not to their value added. As mentioned above, this problem is particularly important in the study of the so-called 'maquila' industry (or purely assembly-type export-operations) of Mexico and some parts of Central America; in fact, the use of these data would distort the comparative regional analysis attempted below. As a result, there is little option but again to exclude Mexico in most of the following comparative analysis, and to analyze Mexico's peculiar export-led growth experience properly separately (see Palma, 2005a).

31. The partial exception is Brazil, which increased its share of exports in 'high-tech' products from 0.3% in 1963 to 3.8% in 1985 and 9.4% in 2000. However, two-thirds of those exports in 2000 consisted of only one (though rather notable) product: aircraft (SITC group 792). In fact, in that year no other 'high-tech' product reached 1% of total exports.

32. For an analysis of the fallacy of composition issue, see Mayer (2003).

33. See especially Kahn (2000).

34. On the issue of the different 'qualities of specializations', see Cimoli and Correa (2005).

35. On this subject, see especially Lagos (2000). On the issue of Chile's and other Latin American countries' 'premature' de-industrialization since economic reform, see Palma (2005b).

36. See especially Moguillansky (1999).

37. Further, the proliferation of the above-mentioned trade agreements between countries of the region and the US (such as those signed by Chile in 2003, and by some Central American countries in 2004), especially due to their asymmetric nature (see, for example, Stiglitz, 2003, and Bhagwati, 2004), would probably make the transition from quadrant 2 to 3 even less likely, unless one considers (against all evidence—see Palma, 2005a) that maquila-type exports are the panacea.

38. One of the most remarkable features of Mexico's poor growth performance is that it took place in a context of both a massive inflow of FDI (well over US$200 billion during this period; see Palma, 2005a) and practically unrestricted market access to the US—the first two items on most DCs' growth agenda...

39. This extremely slow rate of per capita GDP growth contrasts with that achieved by Mexico during its previous politically 'populist', financially 'repressed', and economically 'distorted' four decades (1940–81). During those years, Mexico (with a much faster rate of population growth) achieved a rate of GDP per capita growth of 3.5% per annum. There is little doubt that at the time of its 1982 financial crisis, Mexico needed major political, economic, and institutional re-engineering; however, the chosen path does not seem to have been the most effective. In fact, if before 1980 Mexico doubled its income per capita every 20 years, at the current leisurely pace it would take more than 70 years to do the same...

40. See especially 1997, chs 1 and 2.

41. In 1963, 57% of LA's exports were products included in the OECD list of 20 major import products of the time; by 2000, less than 7% of its exports consisted of products that made the then (new) OECD 'top 20' list. Meanwhile the first- and second-tier NICs and China moved in the opposite direction, with shares increasing from 6% to 64%, 8% to 50%, and 8% to 32%, respectively.

42. In 2000, for example, for all of Chile's remarkable export growth and (horizontal) diversification, two-thirds of its exports still consisted of products that belonged to the 1963 list of 'top-20' OECD imports, while only 2.6% of its exports appeared in the 2000 'top-20' list.

43. See, for example (2002), and the introduction to this volume by Cimoli, Dosi, and Stiglitz.

44. For a comparative regional analysis of income distribution, see Palma (2003).

45. For example, the processes of privatization of public assets in the region compete in their degrees of corruption with those of post-communist Russia. At the same time, the post-reform institutional environment has created a situation in which large corporations in the real and financial sectors can exploit their monopoly power freely, and can count on unlimited bail-outs from governments when things go wrong. In this institutional environment capital can also rent-seek freely from downwardly flexible labor markets, and can be assured that their capital flight will not only be free of regulation but will also be highly exchange-rate-subsidized (for example, foreign asset holdings by Argentinean residents at the time of the 2001 crisis amounted to about $100 billion; this figure was 25% higher than the whole increase in foreign debt since the first election of Menem in 1989).

46. The Latin American economic elite's capacity to transform particularly unequal forms of income distribution achieved during repressive regimes into permanent features of society has become legendary.

47. For an analysis of these issues, see Palma (2009a).

References

Akamatsu, K (1962), 'A Historical Pattern of Economic Growth in Developing Countries'; *The Developing Economies*, 1(2).

Amsden, A (2001), *The Rise of 'the Rest': Challenges to the West from Late-Industrializing Economies*; Oxford University Press.

Bhagwati, J (2004), 'Testimony to the U.S. House of Representatives Committee on Financial Services Subcommittee on Domestic and International Monetary Policy, Trade and Technology', April 1.

Blankenburg, S, J G Palma, and F Tregenna (2008), 'Structuralism', *The New Palgrave Dictionary of Economics*, 2nd Edition, Macmillan.

Capdevielle, M (2005), 'Procesos de producción global: ¿alternativa para el desarrollo mexicano?', *Comercio Exterior*, 55(7).

Chang, H-J (1994), *The Political Economy of Industrial Policy*, Macmillan.

—— (2007), *Bad Samaritans: The Myth of Free Trade and the Secret History of Capitalism*, Random House.

Cimoli, M (1994), 'Lock-In and Specialization (Dis)Advantages in a Structuralist Growth Model', in J Fagerberg, N Von Tunzelmann, and B Verspagen (eds.) *The Dynamics of Technology, Trade and Growth*, Elgar.

—— and N Correa (2005), 'Trade Openness and Technology Gaps in Latin America: a "Low-Growth Trap"?', in J A Ocampo (2005).

Diaz-Alejandro, C (1984), 'Latin American Debt: I Don't Think We Are in Kansas Anymore', *Brookings Papers on Economic Activity*, 2.

DiJohn, J (2008), *From Windfall to Curse? Oil and Industrialisation in Venezuela Since 1920*, Pennsylvanian State University Press.

Dosi, G, C Freeman, R Nelson, and L Soete (1988), *Technological Change and Economic Theory*, Pinter.

—— K Pavitt, and L Soete (1990), *The Economics of Technical Change and International Trade*, Harvest.

Ffrench-Davis, R, O Muñoz, and J G Palma (1994), 'The Latin American Economies, 1950–1990', *Cambridge History of Latin America*, 6, Cambridge University Press.

Freeman, C, and L Soete (1997), *The Economics of Industrial Innovation*, Pinter.

Foucault, M (2004), Naissance de la Biopolitique: Cours au Collège de France, 1978–1979, Gallimard Seuil.

Hobday, M (2003), 'Innovation in Asian Industrialisation: A Gerschenkronian Perspective', *Oxford Development Studies*, 31(3).

Khan, M (2000), 'Rent-Seeking as Process', in M Khan and KS Jomo (eds.), *Rents, Rent-Seeking and Economic Development: Theory and Evidence in Asia*, Cambridge University Press.

Kindleberger, C (1962), *Foreign Trade and the National Economy*, Yale University Press.

Krugman, P (1994), *Peddling Prosperity: Economic Sense and Nonsense in an Age of Diminished Expectations*, Norton.

—— (1997), *Pop Internationalism*, MIT Press.

Lagos, J F (2000), *Chile, de Exportador de Cobre Refinado a Gran Exportador de Concentrados: ¿la segunda fase exportadora?*, mimeo,

McKay, J (2002), Export Structures in a Regional Context and the Flying Geese Paradigm; Ph D Thesis, University of Cambridge.

Marcel, M and J G Palma, (1988), 'Third World debt and its effects on the British economy: a Southern view on economic mismanagement in the North', *Cambridge Journal of Economics*, 12(3).

Mayer, Jorg (2003), 'The fallacy of composition: A review of the literature', *UNCTAD Discussion Papers* 166.

Moguillansky, G (1999), *La Inversión en Chile: ¿el fin de un ciclo en expansión?*; Fondo de Cultura Económica.

Moreno-Brid, J C, J Santamaría, and J C Rivas Valdivia (2005), 'Industrialization and Economic Growth in Mexico after NAFTA: The Road Traveled', *Development and Change*, 13(6).

Ocampo, J A (2004), 'LA in the Long 20th Century', UN, mimeo.

—— (2005), *Beyond Reforms, Structural Dynamics and Macroeconomic Vulnerability*, Stanford University Press.

—— and M A Parra (2004), 'The Commodity Terms of Trade and Their Strategic Implications for Development', ECLAC.

—— —— (2006), 'The Dual Divergence: Growth Successes and Collapses in the Developing World since 1980', DESA.

Palma, J G (1998), 'Does It Make a Difference to Export Micro-Chips rather than Potato-Chips? Comparing Export Structures in East Asia and Latin America', UNCTAD.

—— (2003), 'National Inequality in the Era of Globalisation: What Do Recent Data Tell Us?', in J Michie (ed.), *Handbook of Globalisation*, Elgar.

—— (2004), 'Latin American During the Second Half of the 20th Century: From the "Age of Extremes" to the Age of "End-of-History" Uniformity', in H-J Chang, *Rethinking Development Economics*, Anthem Press.

—— (2005a), 'The Six Main "stylised facts" of the Mexican Economy since Trade Liberalisation and NAFTA', *Journal of Industrial and Corporate Change*, 14(6).

—— (2005b), 'Four Sources of De-Industrialisation and a New Concept of the *Dutch Disease*', in J A Ocampo (2005).

—— (2006), 'Stratégies actives et stratégies passives d'exportation en Amérique Latine et en Asie orientale. La croissance en tant que phénomène spécifique á la composition de produit et spécifique aux institutions', *Revue Tiers Monde*, 186.

—— (2008), 'Raúl Prebisch', *The New Palgrave Dictionary of Economics*, 2nd Edition, Macmillan.

—— (2009a), 'Why Did the Latin American Critical Tradition in the Social Sciences Become Practically Extinct?', in M Blyth (ed.), *The Handbook of International Political Economy*, Routledge.

—— (2009b), 'The Revenge of the Market on the Rentiers.Why neo-liberal reports of the end of history turned out to be premature', Cambridge Journal of Economics 33(4).

Pérez, C. (2002), *Technological Revolutions and Financial Capital*, Elgar.

—— (2008), 'A Vision for Latin America: A Resource-Based Strategy for Technological Dynamism and Social Inclusion', ECLAC.

Pesaran, H, N U Haque, and S Sharma (2000), 'Neglected Heterogeneity and Dynamics in Cross-Country Savings Regressions', in J Krishnakumar and E Ronchetti, (eds.) *Panel Data Econometrics—Future Direction*, Elsevier Science.

Rodríguez, O (2006), *El Estructuralismo Latinoamericano*, Siglo XXI.

Stiglitz, J (2002), *Globalization and its Discontents*, Penguin.

—— (2003), 'Chile perdió soberanía con el TLC con los EEUU', <http://www.argenpress.info>, 18.12.2003.

—— (2004), 'The Free Trade Agreement between Chile and the US', mimeo.

Teece, D (1996), *Strategy, Technology and Public Policy: The Selected Papers of David Teece*, Vol. 2, Elgar.

Trade-CAN (2005), 'Competitive Analyses of Countries', ECLAC–World Bank.

Trần Văn Thọ, Nguyễn Ngọc Đức, Nguyễn Văn Chỉnh, Nguyễn Quán (2000), *The Vietnamese Economy 1955–2000. New Calculations and New Analyses*, Statistical Publishing House: Hanoi.

Tregenna, F (2006), 'Towards a New Understanding of Botswana's Growth Experience', paper presented at the AEA meeting, Boston.

UNCTAD (1996), Trade and Development Report, UN.

Walker, M (2003), 'Resource-Based Industrialisation Strategies: Lessons from the Developed World Experience', mimeo.

WDI (2007), *World Development Indicators*, World Bank.

9

Microeconomic Evolution in High Uncertainty Contexts: The Manufacturing Sector in Argentina

Bernardo Kosacoff and Adrián H. Ramos

Introduction

Various studies have shown that high output volatility: (i) negatively affects long-run economic growth, (ii) imposes high costs in terms of well-being, and (iii) adversely affects the poorest members of society.[1]

The literature shows that these effects are particularly severe in developing countries. In the attempt to explain the negative correlation between volatility and growth, the literature usually focuses on two mechanisms: (i) the fact that greater uncertainty reduces growth as investment falls, and (ii) the consideration that the existence of credit restrictions or imperfect access to capital market adversely affects the impact of short-term volatility on long-term growth by limiting financing options of long-term investment. While those studies tend to stress the aggregate economic effects of real volatility, few scholars attempt to explain the microeconomic aspects of agents' decision-making process and its influence on macroeconomic behavior in the case of countries characterized by high volatility and low institutional quality. The aim of this chapter is to contribute towards filling this gap.

Indeed, this work aims to identify, in an exploratory fashion, some of the effects of real volatility on the structure of the industrial sector and the evolution of the micro-economy of industrial firms, emphasizing that macroeconomic sustainability and the microeconomic structure are two mutually dependent dimensions. The conceptual frames used to advance the understanding of the observed micro-behavior constitute an eclectic collection of fragmented evidence rather than a unified body of theory.[2] First, we present a brief review of industrialization in Argentina since the end of the nineteenth century. In the second section, we analyze the micro-foundations of the decision-making processes in highly volatile contexts, focusing on investment decisions. We will then discuss the accumulation of technological capabilities and skills. The fourth section focuses on the heterogeneity of economic agents. The fifth section concludes.

A brief history of Argentine industrial development

The process of industrialization in Argentina started at the end of the nineteenth century. Initially, the industrial sector was driven by an agro-exporting model based on the production of cereals and meat. This open model persisted until the complete exploitation of the agricultural frontier, which basically coincided with the global turn to wars, economic crises, and protectionism.[3] Similarly to what was happening in other nations, in order to respond to this new scenario, a new economic regime was implemented starting from the thirties onwards. This new regime operated under the form of the so-called 'import substitution industrialization process' (ISI). Thereafter, the industrial sector started to dominate the Argentinean economic structure. Initially, the most prominent economic actors were large state-owned companies in sectors 'of national interest' (like steel, iron, energy, and transport, among others) and small and medium-sized enterprises stimulated by unsatisfied domestic demand and by the high trade tariffs (those firms basically were specialized in the following sectors: clothing, shoes, other consumption durables, simple machinery).

From the fifties onward, the industrial activity was the engine of the economy. Industry absorbed labor and contributed to capital accumulation. In addition, there was a gradual development of remarkable local technological capabilities. At the end of the 1950s, subsidiaries of international companies were already major actors in the local industrial sector.[4] The massive flow of subsidiaries of transnational companies (TNCs) altered the organization of production and shifted the specialization pattern towards more complex and technology-intensive activities, especially in sectors like vehicles, pharmaceutical products, petrochemicals, agricultural equipment, and processed foods.

In the following decade, between 1964 and 1973, industry enjoyed continuous growth, showing constant increases in production. In addition, this period was characterized by a fall in relative prices of industrial goods due to increases in productivity, a rise in industrial exports, an increase in the average size of plants (especially in metal-mechanics, chemicals, and petrochemicals) and by growing employment creation.

In the middle of the 1970s, the Argentinean industrial model faced a set of barriers. These difficulties included aspects related to the general functioning of the economy (balance of trade restrictions and persistent inflation, among others), as well as those derived from the form of industrial organization that was unfolding (plants working at reduced scale, weak subcontracting and specialized supplier networks, low international competitiveness, among others). At the production level, the local answer was an initial attempt to implement reforms calling for opening up the economies and pushing for industrial modernization, in a framework characterized by an abrupt appreciation of the local currency. To sum up, the four decades of ISI laid the foundations for the creation of human skills, engineering capacity, equipment, and a generalized entrepreneurial base. However, when this model came to an end, the prevailing industrial restructuring had a regressive character that did not attempt to rescue the positive aspects of the previous phase.

From 1975 onward, in a context of economic volatility and stagnation, the Argentine industrial sector lost its capacity for productive dynamism, for employment generation, and for leadership in the investment process that had characterized it in the past (Table 9.1). Gradually, the specialization pattern shifted towards the prevalence of natural resource and capital-intensive activities (Bisang et al. 1996; Kosacoff and Ramos, 2001).

The structural pro-market reforms of the nineties (reinforced by the effects of a disproportionate appreciation of the exchange rate) contributed to strengthen this specialization pattern (Table 9.2). Within this context activities based on natural resources and basic inputs, which were already endowed with considerable capabilities, quickly advanced towards the application of the best international practices.[5] Natural resources exports displayed good performance and generated an outstanding mass of foreign currency, although they consisted of products reaching only the first stages of added value (Figure 9.1).[6]

In contrast, there was a remarkable loss of social capital in wide sectors of the economy that could not adapt and the majority of activities resorted to survival strategies, moving from the world of production to the world of

Table 9.1. Employment: sectoral distribution, 1895–2001, percentages

	1895	1914	1947	1960	1970	1991	2001
Primary sector	34.9	26.8	27.2	20.3	16.7	11.5	8.7
Secondary sector	29.8	35.6	29.7	35.4	33.8	25.1	18.3
Manufacturing	*27.1*	*31.3*	*25.0*	*27.8*	*23.9*	*17.5*	*11.4*
Construction	2.6	3.9	4.2	6.4	8.7	6.8	6.1
Electricity, gas & water	0.1	0.4	0.5	1.3	1.2	0.9	0.8
Tertiary (services) sector	35.4	37.6	43.1	44.3	49.5	63.3	73.0
Trade & Finances	13.3	16.2	14.0	13.5	16.7	26.1	1.7
Transport & Communications	3.8	3.4	6.1	7.8	6.8	5.2	6.6
Other Services	18.4	18.0	23.1	23.0	25.9	32.0	64.7

Source: Galiani and Gerchunoff (2003) and authors' calculations based on 2001 Census.

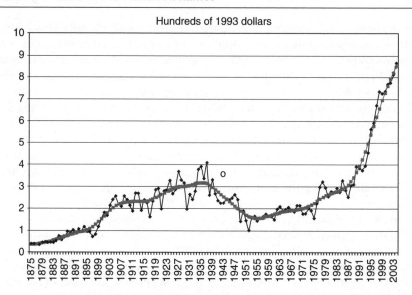

Source: Authors' calculations on the basis of official figures.

Figure 9.1. Export volume per capita and Hodrick–Prescott Trend (1875–2004)

assembly and commercialization of imported inputs and products. The result of these processes was a pattern of specialization in exports that was excessively concentrated in primary products and increases in productivity that occurred concurrently with the expulsion of labor and with negligible promotion of new productive initiatives (Figure 9.1 and Table 9.2).

Both the ISI and the structural pro-market reforms caused imbalances and generated heterogeneous responses. Economic processes are not linear and

Table 9.2. Structure of industrial value added, percentages*

Industrial sectors	1970	1980	1990	1999
Sectors making intensive use of engineering services, except the motor industry (ISIC 381, 382, 383, 385)	13.2	13.4	8.8	10.8
Motor industry (ISIC 384)	10.9	13.1	6.4	9.9
Foodstuffs, beverages, and tobacco (ISIC 311, 313, 314)	33.5	32.5	40.6	38.3
Other sectors making intensive use of natural resources (ISIC 331, 341, 351, 354, 355, 362, 369, 371, 372)	18.3	20.8	24.0	20.2
Sectors making intensive use of labour (ISIC 321, 322, 323, 324, 332, 342, 352, 356, 361, 390)	24.0	20.1	20.2	20.9

* The petroleum refining sector (ISIC 353) has been excluded.

Source: Katz and Stumpo (2001).

therefore it is necessary to avoid falling into oversimplified models of analysis. The stabilization policies of the nineties supposed homogeneous and immediate responses of microeconomic agents. However, the micro-responses to macro-adjustments have been much more complex and diversified from the expected behavior (Kosacoff, 2000). The following pages attempt to analyze this micro-behavior of firms in a context of high macroeconomic volatility focusing on three major aspects: (i) investment decisions and capital accumulation, (ii) technological capabilities and skills, and (iii) heterogeneity between economic agents.

The investment decision and accumulation of capabilities in highly uncertain contexts

Large variations in the price index (above 500%, between 1982 and 1990), hyperinflationary processes, sizable changes in relative prices, and abrupt modifications in policies generated a scenario that threatened investment decisions due to high entrepreneurial risk and high uncertainty regarding future outcomes.

In such a context, firms postpone the decision to incur high sunk costs and delay investments. The economic value of waiting increases and current capital accumulation does not necessarily reflect the net future value of investments. Thus, even in the case of projects with positive net present values, companies may decide to postpone their investments. Within the perspective of real options, the higher the uncertainty, the greater the threshold of profitability that companies will require in order to make their investments (Dixit and Pindyck, 1994).

At the beginning of the nineties, the sudden modification of the competitive environment introduced new uncertainties. The predominant analytical frameworks of the semi-closed economy were useless for evaluating investment decisions in a context of an open economy (Kosacoff, 2000) (Figure 9.2).

The perception of local businessmen of being somewhat unable adequately to respond to the challenge of open economies and high internationalization led many local firms to be absorbed by TNCs or to merge with them (Kosacoff, 2000). Within these circumstances, the strategic position defined by corporate offices of TNCs was crucial in diminishing some of the uncertainties.

In addition, given the change in economic regime of the nineties, it was difficult to discern cycle from trend.[7] As a consequence, some firms and investors made economic decisions based on misleading forecasts. And, at the same time, investment decisions modified economic performance itself and influenced perceptions of other actors, in a circular feedback mechanism. At the end of the nineties, the majority of firms faced difficulties in managing their financial debt, due to rising interest rates, diminishing profits, and

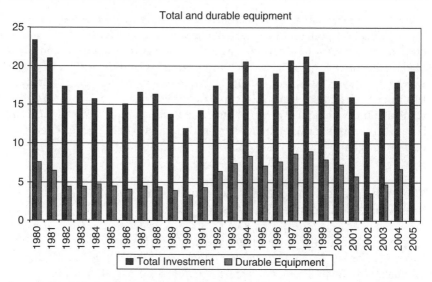

Source: Authors' calculations on the basis of official figures.
Figure 9.2. Gross fixed investment, as percent of GDP (total and durable equipment)

increasing rationing in the financial market. Skyrocketing real interest rates led firms' debt to exceed the value of their assets.

After the devaluation in 2002, the average real exchange rate almost doubled, favoring export growth. Nevertheless, in recent years, most firms— in particular large ones that have reached the limit of their installed capacity and still face excess demand from the domestic market—have chosen to import final goods. In aggregate terms, purchases of foreign goods during the first six months of 2005 were similar to those of 1997 when, with a GDP that was comparable, the exchange rate was considerably lower (Figure 9.3).

There are two major explanations of firms' behavior in this situation. On the one hand, there is the effect of high uncertainty on investment decisions; numerous local companies preferred to import rather than to invest, and to develop complex relationships with suppliers or train human resources. This is so in particular because importing is a short-term action that can be self-financed, while investing implies borrowing today in order to make irreversible commitments involving high uncertainty in the long term.

On the other hand, a version of 'beachhead effect' might apply. In the middle of the eighties many studies focused on the effects of the real exchange rate on the evolution of exports and imports. At that time, the US dollar displayed strong oscillations with respect to the main currencies of the world. Its initial persistent appreciation and the subsequent rise of imports affected the market position of a wide set of local companies of the United

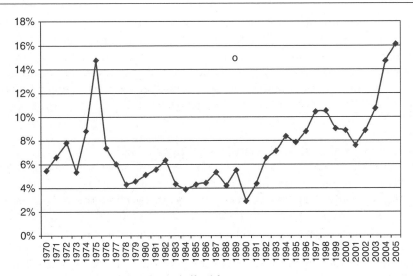

Source: Authors' calculations on the basis of official figures.
Figure 9.3. GDP import coefficient, in current dollars

States and opened up the debate on whether the return to levels considered sustainable would revert the losses in market share.

Several theoretical works emphasized the existence of hysteresis in the interaction between the exchange rate and international trade.[8] The basic assumption behind those models was that a company that does not export must pay a cost of entry in order to access the international market and that this cost is a sunk cost. As a consequence, given the beachhead effect, imports would decrease slower than expected when the currency depreciated, because foreign exporters, once they incurred fixed costs such as the investment in distribution channels, marketing, research, development, reputation, and so on, would only expect to cover operating costs to stay in the market.[9]

A sort of the beachhead effect might explain specific business attitudes in Argentina (Figure 9.3). The persistence of the open economy model stimulated a set of learning processes that were reinforced by a high real exchange rate that later became unsustainable. Actually, the establishment of import channels for local companies during convertibility implied the development of processes of experimentation, routines, and the payment of certain sunk costs that were not compensated once the macroeconomic situation changed.

In general, in contexts of high volatility and low institutional quality, there is great uncertainty about the evolution of the economy; hence, the planning horizon of firms shortens. From a production perspective, microeconomic behavior in most cases translates into defensive strategies that negatively affect the 'animal spirits' and long-term growth. Under these conditions, the predominant attitude is one of reluctance to invest in specific assets and to commit to long-term strategies. Regarding investment in fixed capital, as well as in intangibles, and also in human capital, the maxim seems to be one and only one: *wait and see*. Thus, in Argentina, uncertainty and recurrent macro-economic fluctuations induced microeconomic behavior that resulted in low growth and reinforced tensions at the aggregate level.

Technological capabilities and the supply of skills

In terms of technological capabilities and skills the industrial structure that emerged through the ISI was characterized by a size of plants that did not reach the scale of similar plants in developed countries. In addition, given the immaturity of the productive structure and the absence of local suppliers, the degree of vertical integration was much higher than was predominant in the industrialized world. The layout and organization technologies had a rudimentary character that increased the incidence of dead time (Katz, 1986). The technological challenge for industrial firms was to adapt and assimilate knowledge of foreign origin in a local environment with different prevailing relative prices, less division of labor, and higher transaction costs. However, in order to incorporate knowledge it is necessary to master some additional know-how. Hence, many national and TNCs created internal R&D and engineering departments. However, till the mid-1970s there was no attempt systematically to increase the international competitiveness or export capacity (Katz and Kosacoff, 1998; López, 2002). The ISI strategy allowed the accumulation of knowledge, which, however, did not converge with international standards.

The sudden opening of the economy and the overvaluation of the exchange rate imposed ferocious competition. From a technological perspective, the increasing internationalization of production pushed for a specialization in products that were technically compatible with international standards. In this way, through progressive foreign supply, the process tended towards a reduction of the pre-existing gap in product technology while, at the same time, efforts to develop new products or processes or to adapt foreign technologies were minimized. In addition, this process occurred within a context of continuous weakening of the domestic supply chain.

Thus, the processes of integration in international commercial networks intensified. This tendency resulted in a reduction in the mix of production, which occurred simultaneously with the disintegration of domestic production networks and a stronger reliance on commercial chains (Cimoli, 2005).[10] Innovation activities were particularly concentrated in the acquisition of technology embodied in capital goods.[11] Along the same lines, internal sources of knowledge (R&D),[12] technology transfer, industrial engineering, and management training displayed relatively little importance.

Manufacturing firms scantly invested in innovation activities, and particularly in R&D. Investing few resources in R&D, in absolute as well as relative terms, firms tended increasingly to rely on external sources mainly through the purchase of capital goods and information technology. This combined with the fact that imports became the most dynamic factor of technology supply, particularly when it involved embodied technology but also in the case of the supply of disembodied technology (Yoguel and Rabetino, 2002).

On the other hand, increased international competition forced organizational changes such as: (i) modernization of production processes, which basically introduced flexibility in production management, subcontracting, new quality control systems, and just-in-time techniques, and (ii) consolidation of forms of production that were unusual in the seventies, like clusters and alliances between local and foreign companies; actually large national and international consulting companies were major modernization actors (Fuchs, 1994), and favored the introduction of quality certification procedures (Ramos, 1995).

Another characteristic of the post-reform era is the productive retreat of the technology-intensive sectors. The drop in the output of local pharmaceuticals, capital goods, electronics and telecommunications deprived the local economy of the 'spillover' effects that these sectors normally produce. In general, there is an absence of strategies aiming to conquer new markets in productive sectors with more knowledge content. The economic scheme prevalent after the collapse of convertibility does not yet seem to have induced significant changes in business innovation strategies. A *wait and see* attitude is predominant.

At the same time, however, the expansion of agricultural production during the nineties and the introduction of innovations brought about a radical change in the organization of production in those traditional sectors. The widespread use of technologies originating in the developed world and commercialized in Argentina by TNCs led to the expansion of the agricultural frontier. Some examples are the incorporation of genetically modified soybean, corn, and cotton seeds; a greater use of fertilizers and agrochemicals; the proliferation of direct seeding and double cropping in agriculture; improvements in animal genetics; the development of feedlots in beef production and of new dairy techniques, and the use of new field storage technologies (BID-CEPAL-Ministry of Economics, 2003; Bisang, 2003).

In summary, firms absorbed product and process technologies of foreign origin close to the best international practice that required low adapting efforts. This led to a reduction in product technology asymmetries, but it also implied a significant loss in the generation of domestic capabilities deriving from research and development activities. However, the massive incorporation of imported machinery and equipment was accompanied by organizational changes and greater investment in training. At the same time, the tendency towards de-verticalization of production, which led to the increasing use of imported inputs and components, reduced the probability of creating networks based on local subcontracting and had negative effects on qualifications and skills requirements in the domestic labor market (due to lower direct and indirect labor requirements as well as the losses engendered by the reduction in learning-by-doing processes of human resources).

Heterogeneity and economic agents

One factor that emerges as a distinguishing feature of Argentinean industry is that firms and sectors behave heterogeneously.

On the one hand, a set of companies grew and not only increased their productivity, but they also reached the best international standards in efficiency and practice. Exposure to international markets provided them with the necessary motivation to increase their efforts to achieve higher productivity levels. This group consists of no more than 400 establishments and represents approximately 40 percent of industrial output, particularly in the agro-food sector and the restructured basic input industry created through the public policy efforts of the past. The most representative examples in this sense are the large steel and aluminum plants, oil refineries, petrochemicals, among others. Among them, there are also some firms of the automotive complex, and several enterprises which specialized in the mass-consumption market.

On the other hand, the rest of the production structure has been characterized by a 'defensive' behavior. These firms also increased their productivity; however, they are still far from the international technical frontier and continue to display certain features of the substitution strategy, such as small production scale and limited economies of specialization (Kosacoff, 2000).

In some cases, activities based on natural resources generated downstream effects that also resulted in the attainment of high levels of competitiveness. Such was the case of the candy industry, fine wines, oils, dairy products, lemons, among others. However, these were isolated cases and did not affect the dynamics of the whole production structure.

However, the empirical evidence of the last several years shows that the domestic economy somewhat created capacities to develop more sophisticated production processes based not only on the use of natural resources but also on human capital and technology. Some interesting cases in this respect are EDIVAL and BASSO (engine valves) in the district of Rafaela or TRANSAX (gear boxes) in Cordoba, the production of fine wines in various provinces, ARCOR (candies), the Santa Fe Province dairy complex, and INVAP (nuclear reactors), among others.

EDIVAL is an engine valves producer that reached the international frontier. It created its technological capabilities in the protected market in the 1950s and 1960s and during the 1990s introduced changes in the managerial

strategy to face trade liberalization and the appreciation of the local currency. Within this context, it undertook a risky project: to become a global player in the original equipment supply market. In 2002, once a process of professionalization in company leadership was completed, EDIVAL purchased a plant in Portugal in order to increase its production capacity and get closer to European clients. Today, EDIVAL is the fourth largest valves producer and exporter in the world and has become supplier to automotive producers at their headquarters worldwide, despite the distance that separates them from the city of Rafaela.[13]

INVAP is another example where long-term public intervention played a crucial role. The firm was created by an agreement between the National Commission of Atomic Energy (*Comisión Nacional de Energía Atómica* or CNEA) and the government of the Province of Río Negro. INVAP is well known as an exporter of nuclear plants and equipment for nuclear technology. It has also exported cobalt-therapy machines and automation systems and equipment for industrial projects. INVAP was created from a division of the Applied Research Department. It initiated its activities as a contractor of CNEA in the manufacture of equipment for the supply of combustible elements for a second nuclear plant in an international setting of strong restrictions on the acquisition of nuclear technology. In the eighties, the technological progress made by INVAP allowed it to obtain its first turnkey-plant export contracts. The crisis of the late eighties affected resource availability and the firm incurred drastic employment cut-offs. Some of its former employees created their own companies and became its suppliers. INVAP entered new fields related to space activities and communications and information technology. Finally, the nineties was the decade in which INVAP consolidated its take-off. During this period, it deepened its penetration of foreign markets as a supplier of nuclear technology, which culminated in 2000 with its winning a contract for the construction of a research nuclear reactor for Australia (Lugones and Lugones, 2004).

The perspective provided by evolutionary theory is a central element in the understanding of these long-term processes, with their ups and downs and their co-evolution with macroeconomic dynamics. Despite the striking dearth of company case studies, there are some works that merit mention, such as Gutiérrez (1999), which analyzed the evolution of IMPSA; Kosacoff et al. (2001) which studied the ARCOR group; Ordóñez and Nichols (2003) and the Grobo case; Vispo and Kosacoff (1991) for the analysis of IBM Argentina; Schvarzer (1989) and the experience of Bunge and Born; Artopoulos (2004) and the Teching Group; and Barbero (1995).

During the nineties, along with the privatization of state-owned companies and the reduction in the number of large independent local companies, the presence of foreign companies increased remarkably.[14] Although the presence of foreign capital in manufacturing was not new, it increased substantially.[15] Business structure had already changed considerably at the beginning of the decade, given the active participation of foreign investors in the privatization process. But it is from 1995 onwards that the extraordinary growth in the transfer of private-sector industrial firms takes place.

Notwithstanding the importance of Argentine endowment in natural resources as a location advantage for investments in agro-industrial, mining, and petroleum commodities, FDI concentrated on sectors stimulated by a dynamic demand. Despite the fact that the opening of the economy—within the framework of an exchange rate misalignment—generated an unfavorable bias against domestic production of tradable manufacturing goods, the dynamism displayed by domestic and regional demand in the greater part of the decade became a decisive factor in the investment decisions of TNCs, both for established firms and newcomers.

The imperfections of financial and capital markets and the interest rate differentials between the local and the international market favored the transnationalization process. Furthermore, in certain cases, the technological factor came into play. In sectors that experienced technological progress at an intense pace at the beginning of the 1980s (information technology, telecommunications, machine tools) or in sectors in which access to innovations was difficult (pharmaceuticals), local firms faced adverse effects on their performance, thus favoring the take-over by TNCs.

In the production area, the main concerns regarding new investments were specialization and an increase in the scale of production, which were considered the decisive factors in achieving competitiveness. In the cases of growth by merger or purchase of local companies, the tendency was to vertically dismantle facilities, outsourcing certain sections, and rationalizing activities, downsizing administrative areas and maximizing corporate synergies. It is important to note that in some cases the accumulated equipment imposed technical restrictions on the definition of new projects. In general, only in these cases, and in particular if new investors were involved, transnationalization led to the establishment of new plants or greenfield investment projects.

The transnationalization of the Argentine economy was also reflected in the increasing participation of TNCs in foreign trade (both in imports and exports). The majority of exports were concentrated in a reduced number of sectors based on natural resources, with the exception of the automotive industry. Two other striking facts give the Argentine case a certain singularity: in international terms, the participation of TNCs in trade was comparatively high, and, at the same time, the internal market orientation of their operations was also much greater than in other FDI-receiving countries (Table 9.3).

Only those FDI strategies focused on natural resources generated a positive balance of trade. This occurred as a result of the strong orientation of these activities towards the export market based on natural advantages and their very low import propensity. In contrast, among the firms that engaged in predominantly market-seeking strategies[16]—like the majority of the

Table 9.3. TNCs' strategies in the nineties

Main sectors	Share in FDI flow (%)	Location advantages or attraction factors	Type of investment	Market
Public services	37	Regulation Captive market, monopoly, guaranteed profitability	Market seeking Rent seeking	Internal
Private services (financial and commercial)	11	Regulation Expectations about the internal market	Market seeking	Internal
Food Light chemicals Beverages	6	Expectations about the internal market Market position Natural protection	Market seeking Efficiency seeking	Internal and some Mercosur
Automotive Auto parts	5	Regulation Expectations about the regional market	Efficiency seeking Market seeking	Mercosur
Agro-industrial Commodities Petroleum Mining	28	Natural advantages (frontier expansion) Privatization Regulation	Resource seeking	World Mercosur

Source: Chudnovsky and López, 2001.

manufacturing sector—there was a generalized trade deficit, even in the case of those firms that had a higher export coefficient than the national average and due to their particularly high reliance on final or intermediate imports. Moreover, this group displays a pattern of integration into the foreign market in which exports to Mercosur and imports outside the region are predominant, combined with a strong component of intrafirm trade. As far as the availability of international commercialization channels may be a significant ownership advantage of a TNC, an important expected effect of FDI is its potential contribution to the net generation of foreign currency through exports. However, in the case of Argentina the evidence does not support this argument: the export performance of TNCs seems to be associated with a deployment of strategies of specialization and complementarity among subsidiaries, laid out on the basis of regional commercial preferences.

In fact, despite their preponderant participation in the country's commercial flows and except for the singular case of the development of the automotive complex within the framework of sectoral integration in Mercosur, the strategies displayed by TNCs in the nineties do not appear to have contributed to modify or diversify the traditional pattern of Argentine exports. To the extent that these subsidiaries show a greater import propensity with respect to export—except in the obvious case of sectors based on agricultural resources—their actions are the main source of the trade deficit and, therefore, aggravate external restrictions. In recent years a significant contraction in FDI flows has been experienced. Although it is still difficult to differentiate between temporary and permanent changes, a boom similar to that of the nineties seems unlikely to occur.[17]

An issue generally underexplored by the literature regards the processes of accumulation of idiosyncratic knowledge by managers. Years of high economic volatility, can affect a firm's trajectory and performance. In particular, the latest crisis clearly demonstrated that knowledge accumulated through the years about how to act in the face of changing economic scenarios provided some local companies with a better interpretation of what could happen once the crisis accelerated and became a depression.

Past experiences provide local management with greater flexibility to adapt adroitly, from a financial perspective as well as from a commercial standpoint. In times of crisis, when the decision horizon suddenly shortens, certain business mistakes in short-term decision making related to daily operations can irreversibly lead to a forced company sale or merger, or even permanent closure. These same mistakes, in other contexts, may only translate into a reduction in annual profitability, in economic losses, or into changing the manager of the subsidiary in a country that represents less than one percent of total sales. Therefore, the entrepreneurial capacity for day-to-day crisis management qualifies as an asset, and it represents a structural strength of the firm.

A successful strategy applied by several local companies during the crisis was to protect the company's working capital, which generally meant selling goods and services cash only. Implicitly, this involves the reduction of sales volumes and the loss of a portion of the market to the competition. Lost market share might be difficult to recover in the future. Decisions of this type generate strong internal tension in the attempt to maintain an adequate balance between financial and commercial aspects of the business (Kosacoff et al. 2001).

Conclusion

In Argentina volatility and crisis have been managed purely from a macroeconomic perspective. The government focused on targeting inflation and stabilization policies, disregarding any kind of microeconomic management, likewise any possible interaction between the two was ignored. The predominant view assumed that microeconomic responses of agents to macro shocks were homogeneous and automatic. In this way, there was a sub-estimation of the potential (and averse) feedback effects of macroeconomic policies on micro-behavior, leading to a persistence of adverse conditions. Actually, most of the literature on the Argentinean crisis does not include any kind of microeconomic characteristics as explanatory variables.

Actually, as we have seen in this chapter, the relationship between modes of production, development of technological capabilities, training of human resources, and the dynamics of productivity and competitiveness is affected by output volatility and financial fragility. In turn, those micro-aspects influence macroeconomic management in a circular feedback process. Therefore, consistency between macro- and microeconomic schemes should be taken into account in designing policies for long-term growth. The development of production capacities, besides being country and time specific, is a complex process, which advances in uneven fashion and shows high sectoral-specific features, which are affected and in turn affect macroeconomic patterns. The above observations, based on the Argentine case, aim to contribute to a better understanding of the complex relationship between macro- and micro-behavior.

Notes

1. Cf. Kose, Prasad, and Terrones (2005) and Aizenman and Pinto (2005) survey the economic literature on the topic and Fanelli (2003) studies the Argentine case.
2. Cf. Dal Bó and Kosacoff (1988), and López (2005).
3. Villanueva (1972) and Schvarzer (1996) showed that the strong industrial expansion of the thirties and beginning of the forties did not constitute a rupture with the dominant tendencies since the beginning of the twentieth century.
4. Between 1957 and 1965 approximately 200 subsidiaries of the main international corporations set up their industrial production facilities in Argentina. Cf. Sourrouille et al. (1985).
5. Inherited from sectoral and regional public policies implemented since the beginning of the seventies that originally sought to strengthen the ISI, the production of basic inputs (steel, aluminum, paper, petrochemicals, among others) became the new pattern of industrial specialization as a result of enormous transfers of public resources. Also, after four decades of stagnation, the natural resource sector, with the leadership of agriculture (in particular, of soybean production), expanded again and today is noted for being the most dynamic of sectors, a fact which is reflected in its substantial incorporation of new technology.
6. The performance of these products, along with that of the manufacture of gearboxes, valves, etc., is only comprehensible from an evolutionary perspective that combines routines, learning, and selection. Also, it suggests that the local economy is ready to advance towards more sophisticated productive processes.
7. Cf. Heymann and Sanguinetti (1998).
8. Cf. Baldwin (1988), Baldwin and Krugman (1989). Models were even presented in which those decisions prompted by overvaluation induced a permanent reduction of the equilibrium exchange rate of the economy.
9. Cf. Campa (1993 and 2000), Roberts et al. (1995), Roberts and Tybout (1997).
10. In a study where comparisons were made of scales of production, it was shown that local plants were of smaller size in 78% of the 408 cases analyzed. In the cases where larger or equal scale existed, it was observed that 35% corresponded to the food sector, followed by chemicals–petrochemicals with 30% (Secretaría de Programación Económica-INDEC-CEPAL, 1994).

11. Purchase of capital goods and hardware were more than 70% of expenditures in innovation activities (INDEC–SECYT–CEPAL, 2003). Cf. Anlló and Peirano (2005).

12. The Argentine private sector displays scant participation in R&D (between 20% and 25%) within a domestic outlay (0.4% of GDP in 2003) that is in itself lower than the average in the region and very low when compared to that of other newly industrialized countries (SECYT–Ministry of Education, 2005).

13. Cf. Ascuá (2003).

14. According to official estimates, between 1990 and 2000, 78 billion dollars entered the country in foreign direct investment (FDI); thus, the amount of foreign capital grew at annual rates above 20% and surpassed 80 billion dollars in 2000 (Kulfas, Porta, and Ramos, 2002).

15. While in 1994 there were 69 foreign-owned companies among the largest 200 industrial firms in the country, their participation in this group grew in a sustained fashion, increasing from 87 in 1995 to 129 in 1998. In 1994, sales by foreign companies concentrated 43.4% of total sales by the largest 200 firms, while in 1998 such participation was remarkably higher, reaching 69.2% (CEP, 1999). In 2002, 325 of the largest 500 companies were subsidiaries of TNC and generated more than 80% of the added value of this business elite.

16. Cf. Dunning (1988); Chudnovsky and López (2001).

17. Since the 2001–2002 crisis, the purchase of Argentine companies by Brazilian firms suggests a certain ability by regional firms to take advantage of opportunities that emerge in high instability contexts in which the TNC of the developed world are absent or prefer to be absent.

References

Aizenman J. and B. Pinto (2005), *Managing Economic Volatility and Crises: A Practitioner's Guide*, Cambridge University Press, Cambridge.

Anlló G. and F. Peirano (2005), 'Una mirada a los sistemas nacionales de innovación en el Mercosur: análisis y reflexiones a partir de los casos de Argentina y Uruguay,' *Serie Estudios y Perspectivas 22*, ECLAC, Buenos Aires.

Artopoulos A. (2004), 'Nueva economía en Argentina. El caso de una empresa red: TENARIS,' Presentation for Seminario Interdisciplinario de la Sociedad de la Información, directed by Professor Manuel Castells, Universitat Oberta de Catalunya.

Ascúa R. (2003), *La creación de competencias dinámicas bajo un contexto de inestabilidad macroeconómica: el caso Edival*, ECLAC, Buenos Aires.

Baldwin R. (1988), 'Hysteresis in Import Prices: The Beachhead Effect,' *American Economic Review*, 78(4).

—— and P. Krugman (1989), 'Persistent Trade Effects of Large Exchange Rate Shocks,' *Quarterly Journal of Economics*, 54(4).

Barbero M. (1995), 'Treinta años de estudios sobre la historia de empresas en la Argentina,' *Ciclos*, 5(8).

BID-CEPAL-Ministry of Economics (2003), Componentes Macroeconómicos, Sectoriales y Microeconómicos para una Estrategia Nacional de Desarrollo. Lineamientos para Fortalecer las Fuentes del Crecimiento Económico, Buenos Aires.

Bisang R. (2003), 'Apertura Económica, Innovación y Estructura Productiva: La Aplicación de Biotecnología en la Producción Agrícola Pampeana Argentina,' *Desarrollo Económico*, 43(71).

—— C. Bonvecchi, B. Kosacoff, and A. H. Ramos (1996), 'La transformación industrial en los noventa. Un proceso con final abierto,' *Desarrollo Económico*, Número especial, Vol. 35.

Campa J. (1993), 'Entry by Foreign Firms in the United States under Exchange Rate Uncertainty,' *The Review of Economics and Statistics*, 75(4).

—— (2000), 'Exchange Rates and Trade: How important is Hysteresis in Trade?' IESE Research Paper 427, Universidad de Navarra.

CEP, Centro de Estudios para la Producción (1999), Reporte Industrial 1999. La industria argentina ante los desafíos del próximo siglo. CEP, Secretaría de Industria, Comercio y Minería, Buenos Aires, December.

Chudnovsky D. and A. López (2001), *La transnacionalización de la economía argentina*, Eudeba, Buenos Aires.

Cimoli M. (2005), 'Redes, estructuras de mercado y *shocks* económicos. Cambios estructurales de los sistemas de innovación en América Latina' in M. Casalet, M. Cimoli, and G. Yoguel (eds.) *Redes, jerarquías y dinámicas productivas*. FLACSO-OIT (ILO)-Miño and Dávila.

Dal Bó E. and B. Kosacoff (1998), 'Líneas conceptuales ante evidencias microeconómicas de cambio structural' in B. Kosacoff (ed.), *Estrategias Empresariales en Tiempos de Cambio*. Universidad de Quilmes, Bernal.

Dixit A. and R. Pindyck (1994), *Investment Under Uncertainty*, Princeton University Press, Princeton.

Dunning J. (1988), *Explaining International Production*, Unwin Hyman, London.

Fanelli J. (2003), 'Growth, Instability and the Crisis of Convertibility in Argentina' in FONDAD, *The Crisis That Was Not Prevented: Argentina, the IMF, and Globalisation*, January.

Fuchs, M. (1994), Calificación de los recursos humanos e industrialización El desafío argentino de los años noventa, Working Paper N° 57, ECLAC, Buenos Aires.

Galiani and Gerchunoff (2003) and authors' calculations based on 2001 Census.

Gutiérrez C. (1999), 'Política tecnológica y estrategia empresaria en un caso de transnacionalización: una empresa mendocina de ingeniería,' mimeo.

Heymann D. and P. Sanguinetti (1998), 'Business Cycles from Misperceived Trends,' *Economic Notes*, 2.

INDEC–SECYT–ECLAC (2003), 'Segunda Encuesta Nacional de Innovación y conducta tecnológica de las empresas argentinas. 1998–2001,' *Serie Estudios 38*.

Katz J. (1986), *Desarrollo y crisis de la capacidad tecnológica latinoamericana*, IADB–ECLAC–IDRC–UNDP, Buenos Aires.

—— and B. Kosacoff (1998), 'Aprendizaje tecnológico, desarrollo institucional y la microeconomía de la sustitución de importaciones,' *Desarrollo Económico*, 148.

Kosacoff B. (2000), *Corporate Strategies Under Structural Adjustment in Argentina. Responses by Industrial Firms to a New Set of Uncertainties*, St. Antony's Series, St. Antony's College and Antony Rowe Ltd., Wiltshire.

—— and A. H. Ramos (2001), *Cambios contemporáneos en la estructura industrial argentina (1975–2000)*, Universidad Nacional de Quilmes, Bernal.

Kosacoff B., J. Forteza, M. Barbero, and A. Stengel (2001), *Globalizar desde Latinoamérica. El caso Arcor*, McGraw Hill, Bogotá.

Kose M., E. Prasad, and M. Terrones (2005), 'Growth and Volatility in an Era of Globalization,' *IMF Staff Papers*, 52 (Special Issue).

Kulfas M., F. Porta, and A. Ramos (2002), *La inversión extranjera en la Argentina*, ECLAC/ United Nations, Buenos Aires.

López A. (2002), *Sistema nacional de innovación y desarrollo económico: una interpretación del caso argentino*, PhD Thesis, Facultad de Ciencias Económicas, Universidad de Buenos Aires.

—— (2005), *Empresarios, instituciones y desarrollo económico: el caso argentino*, Working Paper, ECLAC Office Buenos Aires, LC/BUE/L.208.

Lugones G. and M. Lugones (2004), *Bariloche y su grupo de empresas intensivas en conocimiento: realidades y perspectivas*, REDES Centro de Estudios sobre Ciencia, Desarrollo y Educación Superior, Documento de Trabajo 17, Buenos Aires.

Ordóñez H. and J. Nichols (2003), *Agribusiness Turbulent Scenarios, Emerging Economies, Los Grobo Case*, UBA and TEXAS A & M, Enero.

Ramos A. H. (1995), *Hacia la calidad total: la difusión de las normas ISO de la Serie 9000 en la industria argentina*, ECLAC Working Paper 66, Buenos Aires.

Roberts M., T. Sullivan, and J. Tybout (1995), 'Micro Foundations of Export Booms,' Department of Economics Working Paper, Pennsylvania State University.

—— and J. Tybout (1997), 'The Decision to Export in Colombia: An Empirical Model of Entry with Sunk Costs,' *American Economic Review*, 87(4).

Schvarzer J. (1989), *Bunge y Born. Crecimiento y diversificación de un grupo económico*, CISEA/GEL, Buenos Aires.

—— (1996), *La Industria que Supimos Conseguir. Una Historia Político-Social de la Industria Argentina*, Planeta, Buenos Aires.

SECYT–Ministry of Education (2005), *Bases para un Plan Estratégico de Mediano Plazo en Ciencia, Tecnología e Innovación*, Buenos Aires.

Secretaría de Programación Económica-INDEC-CEPAL(1994): *El desempeño de la industria argentina en condiciones de estabilidad económica y apertura externa, período 1991–1992*. Proyecto Competitividad y Estrategias Sectoriales, ARG/93/032, Buenos Aires.

Sourrouille J., B. Kosacoff, and J. Lucangeli (1985), *Transnacionalización y política económica en la Argentina*, CEAL–CET, Buenos Aires.

Villanueva J. (1972), 'El origen de la industrialización argentina,' *Desarrollo Económico*, 47 (12).

Vispo A. and B. Kosacoff (1991), 'Difusion de tecnologías de punta en Argentina. Algunas reflexiones sobre la organización de la producción industrial de IBM,' ECLAC Working Paper 38, Buenos Aires.

Yoguel G. and R. Rabetino (2002), 'La incorporación de tecnología en la industria manufacturera argentina en los noventa: los factores determinantes,' in R. Bisang, G. Lugones, and G. Yoguel (eds.), *Apertura e Innovación en la Argentina. Para Desconcertar a Vernon, Schumpeter y Freeman*. Editorial Miño y Dávila, Buenos Aires.

10

The Impact of Public Policies in Brazil along the Path from Semi-Stagnation to Growth in a Sino-Centric Market

Antonio Barros de Castro

Introduction

This chapter is devoted to the analysis of the interaction between public policies and patterns of growth in Brazil over the last three decades. We begin the analysis when the period of fast industrialization ends and major macroeconomic imbalances emerge. We also discuss the effects of the various macroeconomic cures in terms of patterns of industrial growth. Brazil is possibly the only Latin American country that has emerged from the stabilization cures and liberalization shock with a live and diversified industrial structure. However, at the end of the tunnel of semi-stagnation the international scene has dramatically changed with the emergence of China as a powerful major producer and exporter (including to the markets of other industrializing countries). Hence new challenges, but also new opportunities, have arisen in Brazilian industry. As industrial policies played a crucial role in the early industrialization phase, they are likely to be important—albeit on a different level—in the adjustment to a Sino-centric world.

* The author is grateful to Francisco Eduardo Pires de Souza for his criticism and suggestions.

The long march towards overcoming semi-stagnation

From 1947—when the systematic recording of domestic accounting was initiated—until 1980 the Brazilian economy grew at an average annual rate of 7.5 percent. At that time, the average growth of Asian and Latin American developing countries was 5.7 percent,[1] while the Japanese economy, the unquestioned growth record-holder, achieved an average expansion of 8 percent per annum.

From 1981 until recently, growth has been kept somewhat below 3 percent per annum, except for some short-term expansive peaks. In this 26-year period of modest and unstable growth, two sub-periods can be identified.

In the first long and turbulent phase, running from 1981 to 1999, the immediate reasons why the Brazilian economy proved unable to achieve robust growth were quite clear. A blend of the so-called debt crisis and high inflation from 1980 to 1994 clearly explains the modesty and the instability of growth. In 1994, however, the *Plano Real* defeated inflation, consequently eliminating the most flagrant cause of the Brazilian economy's incapacity to grow on a sustainable basis. Despite that, a period of strong deterioration of the balance of payments began, allowing the current-account deficit to reach 4 percent of the GDP in 1998. Under this framework, aiming to consolidate the victory against inflation, as well as finance and reschedule the foreign debt amid successive international crises, the monetary authorities chose to keep the nominal interest rate at extremely high levels. In this way a phenomenon emerged that is rare in history: exceptionally high interest rates were maintained year after year over a long period. As a consequence, public indebtedness grew rapidly, exports (damaged by an appreciation of the exchange rate) were kept practically stagnant, and credit (both domestic and international) remained severely constrained. In other words, despite the victory over a chronically high level of inflation, powerful factors combined to make steady growth ultimately impossible.

After 1999, however, with the successful transition to a free-floating exchange rate policy and the progressive recovery of the fiscal scene (the primary surplus sprang from −0.88% of GDP in 1997 to 2.92% in 1999), a new panorama came into view. It is true that the quality of the resources used to improve the fiscal situation was very controversial: an increase in tax collecting, which highlighted vices in the tax system,[2] as well as the questionable practice of reducing public investment. Still, the mere quantitative confrontation with the public deficit, combined with improvements such as the Lei de Responsabilidade Fiscal[3] (the Fiscal Responsibility Law), re-established the possibility of solid growth.

On the other hand, it is important to highlight that the end of the 1990s coincided with the end of a cycle of structural reforms. But the connection between these reforms and economic growth—with the exception of commercial liberalization—is something legitimately controversial. Without getting deeply into the topic, which would be a digression from the core of this work, it is worth mentioning that Brazil was one of the Latin American countries which mainly went through structural reforms.[4]

Changes in public policy and advances made on the reforms agenda did not come unaccompanied, however. At this point, it was already possible to note that the thriving and diversified industry inherited from the period of rapid growth had passed the test of the economy's trade liberalization carried out in the 1990s. This does not mean that there were no losses, especially in the industrial fields with high technological density; it means that Brazilian industry, in large measure, preserved the diversity inherited from the period 1950–1980.[5] Moreover, the metal-mechanical industry, already referred to as the *Brazilian industrial fortress*,[6] was invigorated by the liberalization episode. This contrast between the Brazilian economy and the other Latin American economies was accentuated, as the latter had been forced by liberalization to specialize, either in the extraction/processing of raw products or in the labor-intensive steps involved in the conclusion of industrial processes.

The responses to the liberalization challenge were to a considerable degree spontaneously decided by the industrial enterprises. Thus, they freely chose a revision of management procedures, made severe labor cuts, and fostered modernization, together with quality improvement of products, and (some) changes in equipment. The magnitude of this restructuring process (which came at very high cost to employment) can be evaluated by the exceptional pace of growth in labor productivity estimated for the manufacturing industry during the 1990s: something between a minimum of 5 percent, according to the national accounts, and a maximum of 8 percent per annum, according to the Pesquisa Industrial Mensal's (PIM) Monthly Survey of Mining and Manufacturing, issued by the Brazilian Institute of Geography and Statistics (IBGE).[7] It is obvious, however, that this restructuring did not spread all over the industrial apparatus. In fact, firms in the basic inputs sector (steel, etc.), among others, didn't need any technological improvement to be kept near a state-of-the-art level.

If all the improvements observed at the macroeconomic level are considered, as well as the intense modernization of the manufacturing companies, the persistence of low growth from 1999 onward is no longer easily explainable. Furthermore, the expansion initiated months after the substantial devaluation following the January 1999 transition to the floating exchange rate policy seemed to indicate that the economy had recovered its capacity to grow. As a matter of fact, expectations about the performance of the economy remained very optimistic until March 2001 (when the expansion completed a six-quarter period). Immediately afterwards, however, an exceptional conjunction of adversities put a sudden end to the expansive outbreak.

The stop to the expansion at that time combined problems originating in the country itself, such as the suddenly revealed incapacity to satisfy electrical energy demand, with others coming from abroad, such as Argentina's collapse—which showed a contraction of 4.4 percent in 2001 and 10.9 percent in 2002. The mood of the business community turned pessimistic and firms, especially those in the industrial sector, were led to conclude that the domestic market was still subject to harsh contractions—just as it had been in the last two decades of the twentieth century. In fact, the difficulties faced in 2001, followed by new crises in 2002 and 2003, showed that the economy had not yet found its path to expansion. And the overall situation would still suffer the threatening deterioration that occurred towards the end of President Fernando Henrique Cardoso's second term in office, when inflation rose to an annual rate of 29 percent in the last quarter of 2002.

Besides jeopardizing investments, worsening expectations made it very hard at that point to handle the public debt issue. It had been some time since financial resource holders had demanded extremely high interest rates (and very short terms) for refinancing a rapidly increasing volume of debts. In addition, the proportion of dollar denominated public debt reached 50 percent in June 2002 and remained above 50 percent until February 2003. At that point, many questioned the sustainability of the advances recently accomplished at the macroeconomic level, even believing that the situation had reached a point of no return.

However, the new government, which took office in January 2003, faced the incipient inflationary burst with severity and efficacy, managing quickly to resume control over the situation. It is not easy, however, to evaluate the cost of the victory over the so-feared inflationary setback. It is true that trust within the financial establishment was largely regained. The problem, however, was that after two years of extremely modest growth (the economy grew 1.3% in 2001 and 2.7% in 2002), the first year of the new government showed a 1.1 percent growth rate! Moreover, families' consumption was reduced by 0.7 percent in 2003. Similar results unquestionably contributed to reducing the initial enthusiasm for the new government; in particular, weakening strong initial support from non-financial enterprises.

It is important, however, to call attention to other important (and positive) changes that occurred in the difficult period that the economy experienced from 2001 to 2003.

First, let us point out that the renewed frustration with the economy's performance—combined with the substantial increase in the exchange rate—pushed manufacturing firms towards a broad-based reorientation of their strategies. An important result was a much greater focus on foreign markets. Such focus, in turn, was not only about searching for spaces in markets more stable than the domestic one. Data related to foreign sales indicates that, at least since 2003, various segments of Brazilian industry realized that they were able to conquer new markets abroad. There is no doubt that the floating exchange rate, which facilitated the depreciation of the *real*, contributed to the surge of exports. However, it is also important to emphasize that the increase in productivity which took place during the previous decade, as well as certain stimuli provided by public-sector policies, were also behind the outstanding results achieved.

Many accept that trade liberalization decisively contributed to an authentic change in competitive dynamics in the Brazilian market for manufactured goods, forcing firms to close the gaps with foreign competitors in terms of both costs and product quality. Having nearly done that, however, firms discovered that such advances did not suffice. That is to say, the effort made in upgrading products and processes, even if more effective than passive restructuring (limited to cutting waste and personnel), was not sufficient to hold market positions since in several segments new products were quickly being introduced to the market. Hence the necessity to acquire innovative capability in order to compete. To this end, an increasing number of companies initiated an effort to redefine existing products and create new products, markets, and business models.[8]

In that, paradoxically, the legacy of over 20 years of semi-stagnation seems to have fostered the adoption of new and more creative standards of behavior. After all, during the mini growth cycles experienced by companies over the previous two decades new opportunities, in many instances, opened up, but could not be properly exploited: would-be innovations were on hold, waiting for a favorable economic climate in which to be introduced.[9]

With the rapid expansion of exports and an increase in investments (including investments in intangibles), a new framework began to emerge. Specifically, the Brazilian economy, which already had a powerful export agribusiness,[10] proved increasingly able to compete for spaces in several manufacturing markets. In summary, macroeconomic conditions, which had undeniably been improved (and could be made even more buoyant by further growth), were removing the problem of high market instability. At the same time, exports and investments allowed for the development of new growth opportunities.

Figure 10.1 shows the extraordinary performance of Brazilian exports, even when compared with the strong growth in worldwide exports. It must be added that foreign direct investments also seemed to react to the incipient expansion of the Brazilian economy. In fact, in the year Brazil most closely neared new and vigorous growth (2004), foreign direct investments in the country leaped from US$10.1 billion to US$18.2 billion.

The improved conditions for an effective resumption of economic growth depended on other factors, which are worth highlighting.

First, let us point out that in severely fighting inflation and controlling the public debt (which dropped from 52.4% to 44.9% of the GDP between December 2003 and December 2006), the new government revealed that price stability had become (or was becoming) a permanent goal for the country. In other words, price stability had become a sort of 'public good,' changing from the status of a government task out of many to a state duty. This change contributed to the tranquility of the transition from the Cardoso to the Lula administration. After

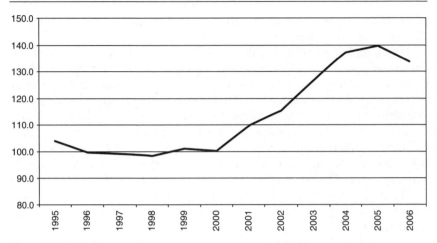

Sources: IMF and Funcex.

Figure 10.1. Brazilian exports/world exports, at constant prices (2000 = 100)

all, the new government brought new players to power, many of whom came from union activism or historically radical leftist groups, as well as a political party that was extremely critical of the country's institutions and policies.[11]

Many detected inconsistency in the new government's preservation of the macroeconomic policy agenda, as well as in the relevance given to the issue of price stability. The administration's deep commitment to social inclusion, however, made it clear that continuity at the macroeconomic level was being combined with the deepening of changes in a direction consistent with the expectations held with respect to Lula's government. We refer in particular to the fact that the reduction in inequality initiated by the end of Cardoso's second term was intensified by the new government. In this respect let us consider two indicators. Inequality, measured by the Gini Index, dropped 4.6 percent from 2001 to 2005 (Figure 10.2), whereas the ratio between the incomes received by the fifth of the population who were richest and the fifth who were poorest declined 21 percent in the same (brief) period of four years.[12] In any case, the massive inclusion of the poor in the consumption of manufactured goods (as demonstrated by several indicators) by widening the market's pyramid base could be preparing the terrain not only for higher growth, but for growth of a different kind (a topic to be discussed below).

Still the semi-stagnation?

The crop of successes harvested in 2004 appeared to many to have put the economy on track for a new expansion cycle. This was not only due to brisker

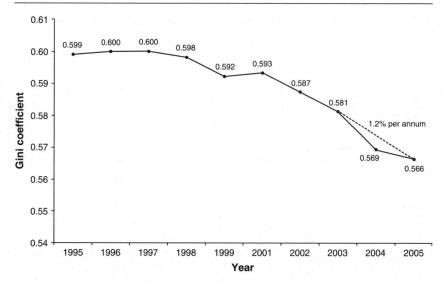

Source: IPEA.

Figure 10.2. Evolution of the inequality in the familial per capita income in Brazil: Gini coefficient 1995–2005

growth. In 2004, when the GDP displayed a respectable increase of 5.7 percent, it also showed traces of a new pattern of expansion. For instance, the volume of exported manufactured articles grew 26.1 percent, while their prices went up by 5.9 percent, indicating that the exporting companies could strongly expand their foreign sales, despite a rise in the average price of their products. Gross capital formation rose 9.1 percent in that year, indicating that the economy was creating additional capacity at a pace much superior to its own (and substantial) rate of growth. In other words, the expansion started to spill over into the future.

Furthermore, simultaneous with the leap in manufactured goods' export rate was a yearly jump in imports of intermediary goods (21% at constant prices), indicating that companies were intensively taking advantage of the openness of the economy to nurture their production and export expansion. A figure illustrating the vigor of the export offensive: in 2004, Brazil was responsible for 48.5 percent of Argentine imports of electrical and electronic goods.[13]

We list in Table 10.1 the segments which most contributed to industrial growth in 2004. The list clearly reveals the leading presence of industrial sectors, which were relatively sophisticated from a technological point of view. It should be underlined that the contribution to growth given by the first three sectors (automotive vehicles, machines and equipment, electronic material and communication equipment) is far superior to their weight in the structure of industry, highlighting their important role as 'engines of growth.' By contrast, the modest contribution to industrial growth by natural resources

Table 10.1. Sectors that contributed to the formation from 75% to 80% of the growth rate of the industry in 2004

Sector	Contribution	Accumulated Contribution	Weight[1]
Automotive vehicles	30.4	30.4	9.2
Machinery and equipment	11.7	42.1	6.5
Electronic material and communication equipment	7.6	49.7	3.9
Food	5.5	55.2	12.0
Other chemical products	5.4	60.6	7.0
Metal products—excluding machines	4.0	64.6	3.6
Office machines and information technology equipment	3.4	68.0	0.9
Rubber and plastic	3.4	71.4	3.9
Textile	3.3	74.7	3.0
Cellulose and Paper	3.2	77.9	3.7
Other	22.1	100.0	
Total	100.0		53.7
Memo:			
Industry Growth Rate		8.3	
Real Effective Exchange Rate (93 = 100)		134.8	

[1] Weight from 1999–2001, updated by using the variation of the production in volume.

processing activities should also be noted. This means that, in flagrant contrast to what was going on in several other emerging economies, manufacturing activities—with growth of 8.5 percent in 2004—were, in more than one sense, heading the expansion.

On the other hand, as agribusiness and mining businesses continued to prove to be highly dynamic, there were plenty of reasons to expect that the country might be able to embark on a steady route of expansion. Seen from this point of view, the economy's good standing could have been considered a preview of what was coming. Within this framework, the unlocking of corporate strategies—particularly in the investment sphere—started to be seen as a major task for public policies. In contrast to the agenda which had prevailed until then and was centered on monetary policy and structural reforms, this meant an enormous change. Ultimately, the main challenge at this point was to adjust the actual expansion pace of the economy to meet the potential of its enterprises.

Despite the substantial widening in the range of policy actions suggested by this change, it is important to call attention to the fact that the new agenda did not consider any discretionary intervention related to the governance of the direction of growth—for example, in terms of sectoral composition of output and investment.

In spite of all that, the growth impulse born in the second half of 2003 faded away in 2005 and 2006: apparently Brazil exchanged a mediocre and brutally unstable growth trajectory for a modest, yet relatively stable one (as shown in Figure 10.3).

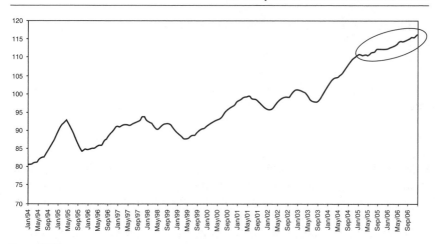

Source: IBGE.

Figure 10.3. Industrial production index with seasonal adjustment (6-month moving averages) (2002 = 100)

And the slowdown occurred in an economy displaying current-account surpluses of around 1.5 percent of GDP per annum and in the process of eliminating the last remaining traces of the turbulence experienced at the transition from Cardoso to Lula.[14]

Moreover, notice that such a disappointing performance occurred against the background of vigorous international growth. If from 1980 to 2000 the average growth of the developing economies was 3.2 percent per annum, from 2000 to 2005 this pace leaped to an average of 5 percent per annum.[15] The bottom line is that notwithstanding the stabilization at the macroeconomic level, resources and human competency accumulated in both the agribusiness and the now internationally exposed industrial fortress. Notwithstanding the sophisticated financial system that the country possesses[16] Brazil appears to be unable to keep the rhythm of growth of the most successful industrializing countries. What are the causes of this? What is hindering the spectacle of growth announced by President Lula?

Limits to growth versus new course of growth

Part of the explanation certainly lies in the macroeconomic management: the monetary policies have yielded aberrant real interest rates and more recently have contributed to currency appreciation. The Central Bank seem to have been guided by what they saw in the rearview mirror and behaved as in the past when the economy several times tottered on the edge of the abyss.

Moreover, a large group of economists were convinced that in the second half of 2004, the economy was bumping up against the ceiling of its productive capacity. Therefore, it was thought, demand had to be restrained. However, such an understanding omits issues of extreme importance.

At that moment the third oil shock had already begun, together with brutal price increases in several commodities. This time, however, the commodity price shock was accompanied—and cooled off—by 'Chinese prices,' as far as manufactured goods are concerned. Among the most immediate results of this important and historically unique episode, one should note the moderate increase in the inflation rate (Table 10.2). This table reveals Brazil's remarkable behavior: its rate of inflation in 2006 is no more than a third of the level reached in 2003! At the same time, with the aim to cool off inflationary pressures, the nominal interest rate was raised from 16 percent to 19.75 percent per annum.

The orientation that prevailed was fundamentally based on the conventional procedures to evaluate the growth potential of economies. But the Brazilian economy was, at that moment, emerging from 25 years of semi-stagnation. Further, the overall rate of investment was rising and manufacturing industry was displaying a truly unpredicted competitive strength.

Once the expansion impetus ceased, the economy faced exchange rate appreciation, which in turn favored a surge of imports boosted by the substitution for intermediary and durable consumption goods domestically produced. At the same time, the rate of growth of manufacturing industry fell substantially more than that of the GDP (Figure 10.4).

It is interesting in particular to compare the leading sectors in 2006 with those of just two years earlier (compare Tables 10.1 and 10.3). First, the number of leading sectors—accounting for around 80% of total growth—shrinks from ten to seven. Second, and more importantly, the extraction and processing of natural resources acquires a much greater weight. Interestingly, office machines and information technology equipment lead in their contribution to growth, reflecting the success of a governmental program named Computador para Todos (*Computers for All*). By contrast, it must be noted that the contributions

Table 10.2. Dynamic of inflation (retail prices), 2000–2006

Year	Developing countries	Brazil
2000	4.0	6.0
2001	4.7	7.7
2002	3.3	12.5
2003	4.2	9.3
2004	4.4	7.6
2005	5.6	5.7
2006	5.5	3.1

Sources: IMF, IBGE, and Brazilian Central Bank.

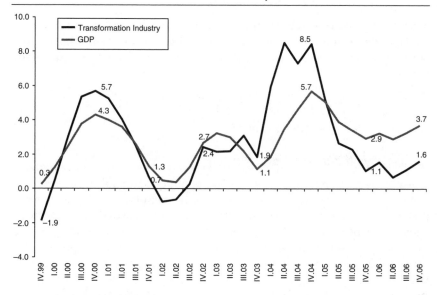

Source: IBGE, Quarterly National.

Figure 10.4. Growth of the GDP and of manufacturing industry (rate [%] accumulated in four quarters)

of automotive vehicles and machines and equipment (the cornerstones of the old Brazilian industrial fortress), which represented 42.1 percent of the country's industrial growth in 2004 (see Table 10.1), were drastically lower in 2006.[17]

In fact, we suggest these changes in the sectoral composition of output are likely to highlight longer-term tendencies whereby the post-stabilization

Table 10.3. Sectors which contributed to the formation from 75% to 80% of the industry growth rate in 2006

Sector	Contribution	Accumulated Contribution	Weight
Office machines and information technology equipment	23.3	23.3	1.4
Extractive industry	16.4	39.7	7.0
Machines, devices, and electric material	10.1	49.8	3.6
Machinery and equipment	8.5	58.3	6.7
Food	6.6	64.9	11.4
Beverages	5.9	70.8	2.6
Basic metallurgy	5.4	76.2	5.9
Other	23.8	100.0	
Total	100.0		38.6
Memo:			
Industry growth rate		2.7	
Real Effective Exchange Rate (93 = 100)		98.3	

[1] Weight from 1999–2001, updated by using the variation of the production in volume.

patterns of growth emerging in the early part of the new century are becoming unviable due mainly to the changing conditions of the international economy, in particular the impact of Chinese booming exports. Let us briefly consider them.

Growth in a Sino-centric market

Tendencies in the Sino-centered economy

A first phenomenon regards the price hike of both oil and metals (Figure 10.5). Chinese growth has a major role in that. For the sake of illustration let us recall that the Chinese economy contributed approximately half of the increase in the demand for copper and aluminum between 2002 and 2005, while being responsible for 29 percent of the global economy's growth over the same period.[18] If Chinese catch-up is not aborted (as the Brazilian catch-up was), the Chinese

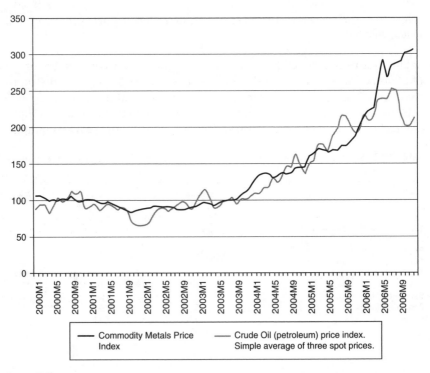

Source: IMF.

Figure 10.5. Oil and metals prices indices, 2003 = 100

demand for raw materials will continue to grow quickly: it is estimated that the consumption of metals, for example, will only decelerate as average income reaches $15,000–20,000. This implies that the pressure over the world's natural resources is likely to continue for many years—a tendency that certainly becomes even more acute if India is included in the picture. Therefore, at least as far as oil and metals are concerned, we are not facing a mere bubble.[19]

Second, concerning manufacturing production, China has emerged as a powerful, highly dynamic, low-cost producer and exporter. Chinese competitiveness is reinforced by a rapid pace of assimilation of new technologies and productivity growth. Moreover, Chinese growth finds a further conducive condition in the undervalued currency—which is apparently there to stay for some years to come.

All of this entails new constraints on the patterns of industrialization and the growth possibilities of other industrializing countries. The peripheral manufacturing industries can no longer rely on the implicit protection that was historically provided by the high wages paid in developed countries. And interestingly, the problem cannot be mitigated by restricting imports: even in a relatively closed economy like the Brazilian one, the prices of several products are dictated more and more by the mere *possibility* of importing them from China.

Third, the two foregoing sets of phenomena had and will continue to have important consequences for resource-rich developing economies.

On the one hand, they drive an improvement on the terms of trade of resource-exporting countries. For an illustration see Table 10.4, where the terms of trade are proxied by the relative prices of exports and imports. Compare, for example, oil-rich Venezuela with resource-poor Central American countries.

The other side of the same coin is the likely possibility that countries well-endowed with natural resources but also with a significant industrial base catch the so-called *Dutch disease*, entailing substantial exchange-rate appreciation

Table 10.4. Latin America and the Caribbean: terms of trade

Countries	2003	2006
Argentina	107.2	111.8
Brazil	97.0	102.4
Chile	102.8	186.9
Colombia	95.2	124.5
Mexico	98.8	107.6
Peru	102.2	150.1
Venezuela	98.7	188.9
Central America	92.6	87.3
Latin America and the Caribbean	98.6	117.5

Source: CEPAL, Balance Preliminar de America y el Caribe, 2006.

(and/or elevation of nominal wages). In turn, this reduces or even turns nega-tive the return from sales of domestic products that do not benefit from the hunger for natural resources, and leads to a substitution of imported goods that is difficult to reverse.[20]

Implications for the Brazilian case

The changes triggered by the trade liberalization of the early 1990s were (finally) being translated into positive results in the first years of this century. In other words, from the industrial point of view, we could say that the Brazilian manufacturing industry not only survived the liberalization shock but was (almost spontaneously) back on a growth track along patterns which appeared to be a sort of open economy version of the old import-substitution newly industrialized country (NIC) model,[21]—itself an acknowledged success from the second half of the 1960s to the first shock of the oil crisis (1973–4).[22]

However, a major emerging challenge—ignored until very recently—was China which, as far as manufacturing is concerned, was taking a course similar to the Brazilian one: (i) organizationally based on a somewhat similar com-bination of subsidiaries of multinational companies and domestic firms and, even more importantly, (ii) based on broadly similar patterns of production largely based on the production of goods originally developed in industrial-ized countries.[23] Moreover, unlike Brazil, the Chinese model displays both a precocious and an aggressive export orientation.

As a consequence, a sizable part of Brazilian industry was and is doomed to face serious problems.

First, Chinese industry still has a substantial advantage in terms of labor costs which persist (even if slowly shrinking) as both wages and manufacturing productivity have been growing in China at double-digit rates.

Second, but relatedly, China has developed growing advantages regarding the scales of production and infrastructures—China invests about 10.5 percent of its GDP in the latter.

Third, China provides the intrinsic attractiveness of offshore investment to multinational corporations (MNCs), and the Chinese government has condi-tioned the implantation of multinational branches in the country upon the acceptance of local partners. Such a policy, combined with the extremely high overall domestic investment rate (supposedly higher than 40% of GDP) has certainly contributed to the rapid dissemination of modern technology in the country.

Fourth, the low wages prevailing in China have apparently contributed to a bias toward cost reduction, as far as the search for innovation is concerned.

Finally, macroeconomic conditions are also important. The renmimbi devaluation (in relation to the dollar) meant that the renmimbi's actual average exchange rate dropped, between 2004 and 2006, 29 percent in relation to the Brazilian currency. Chinese imports became, in principle, 29 percent cheaper in Brazil. (Note that in the case of Brazil an explosion of imports followed at a staggering 47 percent growth rate per year.)

The effective devaluation, combined with proactive policies shaping investment, by the provinces, cities, and other Chinese political entities, has decidedly thickened Chinese industrial value chains well beyond the traditional specialization in the assembly stage.[24]

The overall outcome is that China's points of competitive strength are spreading into new segments and across new sectors. In fact China is presently completing a *sui generis* and comprehensive process of import substitution.

In the Brazilian case, until very recently the domestic market has been subject to the ups and downs of the country's long-lived macroeconomic turbulence. At the same time, in contrast to the earlier import substitution regime of industrialization, some industrial firms began practicing more innovative patterns of behavior, frequently associated with the expansion of the export markets.[25]

There is a sort of paradox here. Given the international circumstances, the Brazilian economy began to pay a price for having developed and somehow consolidated (in the 1990s) a highly diversified industrial system which is increasingly bound to compete with the Chinese one. Conversely, several other Latin American economies were able to adapt to the deep changes brought about by the twenty-first century quite easily. The more natural resources they had, and the more they had previously renounced manufacturing—since commercial liberalization—the easier such an adaptation was. Ultimately, in such cases, there was practically no choice to be made. In other words, those economies that had already accepted the role of raw-material providers prior to the emergence of China had all the more reason to stick to this route as China arose.

In Brazil, however, the issue presents itself quite differently. After successfully restructuring in the 1990s, it is difficult even to imagine that the economy could adapt to a sort of classical international division of labor. From the industrial point of view, Brazil relies today on competencies accumulated and matured through time, often under adverse conditions. At the same time, the country has the world's fifth-largest population, of which 90 percent is considered urban. It is therefore hard to imagine a resource-based pattern of development.

Given this overall framework, it is quite clear that the second liberalization (Figure 10.6) now being experienced by the Brazilian economy poses a number of challenges. It is easy to forecast that a new round of industrial restructuring is necessary. But here we face an important question which has to do with the very nature of economic adjustments spurred by changing relative prices such as those we are now observing, which reward natural resources and punish manufactured products. Do we require, predominantly, a reallocation of factors across different sectors and different products? Or should changes in relative prices be

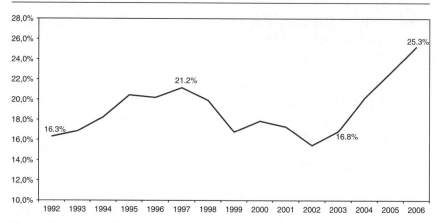

Figure 10.6. Degree of openness of the Brazilian economy: exports + imports/GDP*
*GDP measured at a constant exchange rate, at the average level of 2004–2006.
Sources: Secex/MDIC, IBG, and Branco Central.

confronted primarily through the development of existing capabilities, in many cases in the same sectors and firms? Economists usually favor the former answer which, in turn, relies on a view of readily available solutions and technologies, which can be acquired off the shelf, so to speak. This is a misleading view, however. Rather, capabilities are relatively idiosyncratic resources which are incrementally accumulated, changed, and refined over time.[26]

The Brazilian economy has been accumulating modern skills and capabilities for about five decades. This effort has actually resulted in noticeable outcomes in some areas within the electromechanical field and in energy related sectors. In the aeronautics industry, as well, Brazil is on the international technological frontier. Given that, the new setting could become an exceptional opportunity to build upon old points of strength and develop new ones. In the process, policies are bound to play a very important role.

The National Program for the Acceleration of Growth (PAC) as the preamble for a new agenda of policies and some conclusions

We have already mentioned that a few years after the success of (macro) stabilization policies, attention slowly returned to industrial and technological policies. The policy package announced in March 2004 (Política Industrial, Tecnológica, e de Comércio Exterior), meritorious as it was from some points of view, could not meet the new international challenge. Its basic aim was the strengthening of sectors that generate and disseminate technical progress (semiconductors, software, capital equipment, and pharmaceutical products)—together with non-specified support for innovative initiatives.

And its major implicit assumption was that the leadership in the industrial field was still held by the United States-European-Japanese triad. This, however, was not anymore a hard fact.

Moreover, the modest growth exhibited in 2005 (2.3%, later corrected to 2.9%) contributed to transforming the demand for growth into a public outcry. This led to the launching of a program for the acceleration of growth (the PAC).

The prominence attributed to large infrastructural projects in the new growth program was already present in previously announced—but never implemented—plans. This is somewhat understandable: while the Brazilian economy was under threat of imminent insolvency—and with the government diligently trying to reduce the role of the state—no program requiring a major involvement of the state had much chance of being executed. In addition the infrastructure inherited from the phase of rapid growth was already seriously deteriorated.

Seen by many as a mere repackaging of previously existing projects, PAC may come to be an important step forward beyond a historical phase in which the government's political energy was primarily invested in the effort to promote macroeconomic adjustments and structural reforms. In order to meet its goals, the program intensively turned to the investment capacity of the remaining state-owned companies. This change faced great initial resistance, especially from those who used to see state-owned enterprises as inhabitants of a limbo from which they would only find their way out when privatized.

Further, by making use of the very companies it controls, the government got directly involved in energizing the economy and promoting growth. Consequently, public investment regained attention amongst the government policies. Moreover, by demanding programs and projects from public agencies, as well as by establishing goals and deadlines for their fulfillment, the PAC resurrected the role of technical skills in the public administrations, that had remained idle or were even lost during the long period of semi-stagnation. As a matter of fact, investments in infrastructure constitute the sort of activity that presupposes—and induces—a long-term view.

One of the goals of the PAC is the cooperation and convergence of public and private strategies: out of the total estimated investment included in the PAC (R\$504 billion), nearly 40 percent is supposed to come from the private sector. In short, the PAC—even if it is to experience only a partial implementation—will be contributing to the elimination of merely reactive and predominantly non-cooperative behaviors between the public and private spheres. If so, it will contribute to the building of a new governmental culture, which could well be expanded to similar programs in science and technology, health, and other fields.

But the program is undeniably dominated by the government's concern in recovering investment and consequently 'unblocking' (in the official discourse) growth.[27] Indeed, eliminating the bottlenecks inherited from semi-stagnation, as well as the widely spread reluctance to invest, continues to be a necessary goal. However, the emergence on the international scene of the devastatingly competitive and extraordinarily voracious Chinese economy has added new challenges to and new opportunities for public policies.

The bottom line is that the Brazilian industrial structure can no longer afford a sort of linear (and 'incrementalist') catch-up, since the process is at least partly pre-empted by the fast Chinese catch-up, crowding out other industrializing countries on both the international market and their own domestic markets. Hence, merely raising investment and expanding the infrastructure is a necessary but not sufficient condition to face the challenge. The Brazilian economy needs to redefine its global insertion, taking into account both its revealed advantages and its potential for new developments.

At least in two fields new chances are quite noticeable: ethanol, and oil and gas. Both intensively require hardware—together with a broad range of services. This may be thought of as a very promising new frontier for Brazilian industry. The market itself is providing strong signals in this direction. But long-term targets, governmental coordination, and intense cooperation between state agencies, existing companies, new private investors, technological institutes and universities are necessary to the proper exploration of the new opportunities. In fact singular strategies in each field (ethanol and oil), together with the opportunities born from overall growth might offer the industrial system the necessary new opportunities for both surviving and developing capabilities adjusted to a sustained path of growth in a Sino-centric world market.

Notes

1. This statistic represents the weighted average of the growth rate of 15 Asian and Latin American economies between 1950 and 1980. See Maddison (1992).
2. The Brazilian tax system, conceived in 1967, suffered—with the passing of time and successive crises—such a number of modifications and corrections that it admittedly became an inconsistent collection full of distortions.
3. Other advances would unquestionably be necessary. See Khair, et al. (2006).
4. See Fraga (2004). The article is about the impact of the structural reforms in Latin America, and places Brazil as second in the depth of reforms experienced among the seven strongest regional economies. As for the indicators the author used to examine the reforms, see Lora (2001).
5. See Castro (2001); and Kupfer et al. (2004).
6. The expression was coined by João Furtado in the article 'O comportamento inovador das empresas industriais.' In Velloso and Cavalcanti (2004).
7. See Gonzaga Mibielli (2000).
8. The first broad investigation of the competitive strategies of Brazilian manufacturing industry is found in De Negri and Salerno (2005).
9. See Castro (2005).

10. Agribusiness will not be the focus here, but it is important to point out that this large and diversified sector was a pioneer in growing by incorporating technical progress. See Barros, et al. (2002).
11. A similar combination of discontinuity, at the political level, with continuity in the broader orientations of economic policy seems to have happened in Latin America only in the Chilean transition to democracy.
12. Data was obtained from Paes de Barros R.M. Foguel, and G. Ulyssea (eds.) (2007), *Desigualdade de renda no Brasil: Uma análise da queda recente*, IPEA.
13. Data on imports are from FUNCEX. Data on export shares of electrical and electronic goods are from Sectorial Economic Investigations (IES) (2007), *Valor*.
14. For more about the relation between instability and (low) growth in Latin America, see Zettelmeyer (2006).
15. See World Bank (2006).
16. We refer here to growth potential, that is, not to how much the economy grew in the past (and/or as a function of production), but due to the resources and competences that can be mobilized for growth—including, and highlighting, the knowledge accumulated at the level of enterprises, research institutes, and governmental teams.
17. The changes mentioned here were identified and commented on in Castro and Pires de Souza (2006).
18. See International Monetary Fund (2006), *World Economic Outlook*.
19. See IMF (2004), *World Economic Outlook*, ch. 5: 'The boom in non fuel commodity prices: can it last?'
20. The consequences of the dependence on natural resources (the 'resource curse') are at the origin of CEPAL's advocacy of industrialization. As early as the end of the 1950s, Furtado produced a pessimistic and premonitory report about the Venezuelan case. For many years, mainstream economics tried to deny the specific difficulties that an emerging economy centered in natural resources tends to face. See, for instance, World Bank (2001), *From Natural Resources to the Knowledge Economy*. However, for an assessment of the negative consequences (including at the political level) of the 'resource curse,' see Stiglitz (2006).
21. *The Newly Industrialized Countries: Challenges and Opportunity for OECD Industries*. OECD, 1998.
22. See Batista and dos Santos (2007).
23. For a characterization of the Chinese industrialization trajectory—and some striking differences to the Korean one—see Liu (2005). See also Kroeber (2007).
24. See Cui and Syed (2007).
25. See Arbix, et al. (2005).
26. See Penrose (1995).
27. Primeiro Balanço do PAC, janeiro a abril de 2007 (PAC—First Evaluation, January to April 2007).

References

Arbix G., M. Salerno, and J. De Negri (2005), 'A Nova Competitividade da Industria e o novo Empresariado' in J. Velloso (ed.) *O Desafio da China e da índia: A resposta do Brasil*. José Olympio.

Barros J., J. Rizzieri, and P. Pichetti (2002), 'Effects of Agricultural Research' in M. Barbosa (ed.) *Impacts of the Agricultural Sector Technological Change on the Brazilian Economy*. Empresa Brasileira de Pesquisa Agropecuaria (EMBRAPA).

Batista J. and W. dos Santos (2007), 'A industrialização da pauta de exportação brasileira entre 1964 e 1974: novos dados e índices para o comércio exterior brasileiro do período,' *Revista de Economia Política*, 27(2).

Castro A. (2001), 'A reestruturação industrial do Brasil nos anos 90: Uma Interpretação,' *Revista de Economia Política*, 21(3).

—— (2005), 'A Hipótese do Crescimento Rápido e Sustentável' in J. Velloso and R. Cavalcanti (eds.). *Cinco décadas de questão social e os grandes desafios do crescimento sustentado*. José Olympio, Rio de Janeiro.

—— and F. Pires de Souza (eds.) (2006), 'Especialização e Diversidade na Indústria: O Desafio Contido nos Mais Recentes Dados,' *BNDES: Sinopse do Investmento no. 4*.

Coriat B. and G. Dosi (2002), 'The Nature and Accumulation of Organizational Competences and Capabilities,' *Revista Brasileira de Inovação*, 1(2).

Cui L. and M. Syed (2007), *Is China Changing its Stripes? The Shifting Structure of China's External Trade and its Implications*. International Monetary Fund.

De Negri J. and M. Salerno (eds.) (2005), *Inovações, Padrões Tecnológicos e Desempenhos das Firmas Industriais Brasileiras*, IPEA.

Fraga A. (2004), 'Latin America since the 90s: Raising from the Sickbed?' *Journal of Economic Perspective*, 18(2).

Gonzaga Mibielli P. (2000), 'As Causas do Aumento da Produtividade na Indústria Brasileira nos Anos 90,' PhD Dissertation, Instituto de Economia, UFRJ.

Khair A., J. Afonso, and W. Oliveira (2006), 'Lei de Responsabilidade Fiscal: Os Avanços e Aperfeiçoamentos Necessários' in M. Mendes (ed.) *Gasto Público Eficiente*. Topbooks.

Kroeber A. (2007), 'Inovação: Todo o Errado,' *Carta da China*, Edição Especial. Conselho Empresarial Brasil–China.

Kupfer D., J. Ferraz, and M. Iootty (2004), 'Made in Brazil: Industrial Competitiveness 10 years after Economic Liberalization,' *Cepal Review*, 82.

Liu X. (2005), *China's Development Model: An Alternative for Technological Catch-Up*. Institute of Innovation Research Working Paper, Hiotsubashi University.

Lora E. (2001), *Structural Reforms in Latin America: What Has Been Reformed and How To Measure It*, Inter-American Development Bank, Washington DC.

Maddison A. (1992), *La Economia Mundial en el Siglo XX*, Fondo de Cultura Económica, Mexico.

Penrose E. (1995), *The Theory of the Growth of the Firm*, Revised paperback edition published 1995. Oxford University Press.

Stiglitz J. E. (2006), *Making Globalization Work*, Norton, New York.

Velloso J. and R. Cavalcanti (eds.) (2004), *Cinco décadas de questão social e os grandes desafios do crescimento sustentável*, José Olympio.

World Bank (2006), *Global Economic Prospects: Managing the Next Wave of Globalization*.

Zettelmeyer J. (2006), *Growth and Reforms in Latin America: A Survey of Facts and Arguments*, International Monetary Fund.

11

The Past, Present, and Future of Industrial Policy in India: Adapting to the Changing Domestic and International Environment

*Ajit Singh**

Introduction and overview

In the post-World War II period India was probably the first non-communist developing country to have instituted a full-fledged industrial policy. The purpose of the policy was to coordinate investment decisions both in the public and the private sectors and to seize the 'commanding heights' of the economy by bringing certain strategic industries and firms under public ownership.

This policy program was clearly greatly influenced by close association of the top Indian leaders with Fabian Socialism and UK Labour Party thinkers like Harold Laski. It also drew inspiration from what was then regarded as highly successful Soviet planning for industrial development. Indeed, emulating the Soviet Union, industrial strategy in India was formulated and implemented in the form of five-year plans. This classical Indian state-directed industrialization model held sway for three decades, from 1950 to 1980. The model began to erode in the 1980s. Following a serious external liquidity crisis in 1991 the model appeared to be fundamentally changed, if not abandoned altogether.

* In writing this chapter I have drawn on and updated previous research done either by myself or in collaboration with others. See Singh and Ghosh (1988); Singh (1995, 1998); Dasgupta and Singh (2007).

The pre-1980 Indian industrial policy, as embodied in the five-year plans, has long been the subject of intense criticism from the influential neo-liberal critics of the country's development. As Bradford De Long (2001) puts it:

The conventional narrative of India's post-World War II economic history begins with a disastrous wrong turn by India's first prime minister, Jawaharlal Nehru, toward Fabian socialism, central planning, and an unbelievable quantity of bureaucratic red tape. This 'license raj' strangled the private sector and led to rampant corruption and massive inefficiency. As a result, India stagnated until bold neo-liberal economic reforms triggered by the currency crisis of 1991, and implemented by the government of Prime Minister Narasimha Rao and Finance Minister Manmohan Singh, unleashed its current wave of rapid economic growth—growth at a pace that promises to double average productivity levels and living standards in India every sixteen years.

This echoes *The Economist*'s harsh assessment of the overall Indian record for the first four decades of Indian independence:

The hopes of 1947 have been betrayed. India, despite all its advantages and a generous supply of aid from the capitalist West (whose 'wasteful' societies it deplored), has achieved less than virtually any comparable third-world country. The cost in human terms has been staggering. Why has Indian development gone so tragically wrong? The short answer is this: the state has done far too much and far too little. It has crippled the economy, and burdened itself nearly to breaking point, by taking on jobs it has no business doing. (1991, p 9)

In the mainstream accounts of Indian economic development the move away from India's traditional industrial policy in 1991 towards liberalization, deregulation, and market orientation has been hailed as ushering in a new era of freedom from government controls and one which promises greater prosperity for the Indian people. This unshackling of the economy is credited with achieving the huge increase in India's trend rate of growth of GDP, from the so-called Hindu (Nehru–Mahalanobis) rate of 3 percent to 3.5 percent during 1950–80 to nearly 6 percent to 7 percent per annum over the last two decades. To fulfill its promise, it is suggested that further liberalization is required both in India's domestic economy and in its external economic relations (for example, further privatization, capital account liberalization, increasing foreign direct investment (FDI)). India is regarded as a major beneficiary of globalization by the international financial institutions (IFIs) but is considered to need to go further along this road. However, the present government led by Dr. Manmohan Singh, and including reformers with impeccable credentials in key economic positions (Chidambaram and Ahluwalia), is thought to be hindered in this process by its Communist Party coalition partners.

This chapter takes a rather different view on these matters from that above; specifically, it presents analysis and evidence to support the following theses.

First of all, there has been far greater continuity both in the industrial policy framework over the last five decades and in the economic record than is suggested by the neo-liberal interpretations.

Secondly, the economic growth record of the Nehru–Mahalanobis period (1950–1980), in terms of aggregate statistics, does not adequately reflect the structural achievements of this economic model especially in creating a scientific and technical infrastructure for a modern economy. Furthermore, in the neo-liberal analyses, the enormous internal and external shocks that the economy was subject to for a considerable part of this period (1965–1975) are totally ignored.

Thirdly, the relationship between the post Nehru–Mahalanobis industrial policy and the post-1980 record of faster economic growth is critically examined. Notwithstanding this acceleration in economic growth, students of the current economic regime point to certain observed long-term tendencies which suggest that such growth may not be sustainable. These tendencies include: (i) premature de-industrialization; (ii) slow pace of structural change despite fast growth of the economy; (iii) jobless growth in modern industry and services; (iv) hence, increase in 'informality' of the economy.

Next, the relationship between growth of manufacturing and that of services in an emerging country like India will receive special attention here as it is an issue with enormous general significance for economic development. It will be discussed here within a Kaldorian framework. The main question to be considered is whether due to new technology such as ICT, services could be an additional engine of growth for the Indian economy.

Finally, far from abandoning industrial policy as a relic of the past, it is suggested here that the shortcomings of current economic developments as well as the structural issues outlined above provide fresh challenges, albeit in a different form, for a vigorous industrial policy for the twenty-first century.

The arguments for the above are developed as follows. The second section outlines the Nehru–Mahalanobis model, its rationale, the case of its critics, and its outcomes. The third section considers the important analytical issue of the turning points in Indian economic growth and their implications. The fourth section explores the operation and effectiveness of Indian industrial policy in the post-Nehru–Mahalanobis period by considering the particular but extremely important case of India's IT industry. This case derives its significance in part from the fact that IT is not only modern India's flagship industry, it is also often regarded as being an example of the success of laissez-faire rather than that of industrial policy. The fifth section looks to the future and examines the conceptual issues involved in the analysis of industrial policy for a country like India under a liberalized global international economic regime. The sixth and seventh sections outline a fresh agenda for industrial policy in India for the twenty-first century. The former section considers issues connected with the phenomena of current globalization and the new technological development paradigm, represented by the new information and communication technology. Questions concerning the updating of the old agenda will be taken up in the seventh section. Specifically, the seventh section documents the current issues of jobless growth, slow structural change despite fast economic growth, and hence increasing informality in the economy. It also highlights the seriousness of the distributional issues particularly in light of the anticipated fuller integration of the Indian economy with the world economy. It also provides inter alia an analysis of the role of services and IT services in particular in the future development of the economy. The final section briefly draws lessons for other countries from India's industrial policy experience. For the sake of completeness, and because of the unique institutional position of the Planning Commission in India, an Appendix is provided that summarizes the functions, objectives, and structure of the Commission.

The Nehru–Mahalanobis model: the classical Indian industrial policy framework 1950–1980

In keeping with the ideals of the top leadership, the Indian five-year plans were designed to bring about economic and social development within a 'socialist' framework. The plans pursued multiple objectives of industrialization, raising per capita incomes, and achieving equity in the distribution of gains from economic progress. They also sought to reduce the existing concentration of economic power and to achieve a better regional distribution of industrial development. As far as economic strategy is concerned, several elements were important during the 1950s, 1960s, and most of the 1970s. First, the Indian planners emphasized the role of heavy industry in economic development and sought to build up as rapidly as possible the capital goods sector. Second, the plans envisaged a leading role for the public sector in this structural transformation of the economy. Third, major investments in the private sector were to be carried out, not by the test of private profitability, but according to the requirements of the overall national plan. And lastly, the plans emphasized technological self-reliance, and for much of the period, an extreme inward orientation in the sense that if anything could be produced in the country, regardless of the cost, it should not be imported.[1]

As is well known, the economic rationale for an industrial strategy biased towards capital goods was provided by P.C. Mahalanobis. In the Mahalanobis (1963) model, essentially that of a closed economy, the development of the capital goods industry emerges as the main constraint on economic growth. This model of internal technological and heavy industry development could be rationalized for an open economy of the size of India if one envisages slow rates of growth of the world economy and trade, and, perhaps, falling commodity prices in world markets. Alternatively, it could also be justified in more orthodox terms along the lines that India's dynamic comparative advantage was in industries like steel, for which the country had available the necessary raw materials in close proximity to each other (thus reducing the costs of transportation).

An important drawback of the heavy-industry-biased industrial strategy is that it conflicts with the employment objectives embodied in the five-year plans. The plans sought to square this circle by providing external (against foreign competition) and internal (against domestic competition) protection to a number of small-scale and cottage enterprises for which the capital/labor ratio was very low. Thus, for instance, domestic modern textile factories were limited in how much they could expand their output so that they would not compete with the high-cost products of the cottage industries.

In implementing this industrial strategy, and particularly in making the private sector conform to the requirements of the plans, the government used a wide variety of measures. The most important of these were: (i) industrial licensing: for much of the period, this entailed that any enterprise which wished to manufacture a new article or sought a substantial expansion of its existing capacity had to obtain a license from the relevant government authority; (ii) a strict regime of import controls; (iii) subsidization of exports through special measures; (iv) administered prices; (v) investments by multinationals were generally subject to strict controls; and (vi) Jawaharlal Nehru was an architect of new institutions in all spheres, including notably those for the development of scientific and technical infrastructure, which later blossomed into the information and communications technology industry.

It is also important to observe that the above economic strategy chosen by the Indian leadership was by no means the only feasible one available. In the public debate that took place at the time of the formulation of the early five-year plans, two leading Indian economists, Vakil and Brahmananda (1956) advocated an alternative, more orthodox strategy. After the war, the country had emerged as one of the leading exporters of textiles in the world. Vakil and Brahmananda favored concentration on textile exports, on the development of light industries, and reliance on market forces to achieve industrial development. This kind of alternative strategy was deliberately shunned by the Indian leadership in favor of state-planned industrialization.

This industrial policy framework, as noted earlier, has been subject to intense criticism, particularly by neo-liberal economists, including highly distinguished Indian scholars such as Srinivasan and Bhagwati. Isher Ahluwalia (1991) has best summed up the adverse consequences of this Indian model in the following terms: (i) barriers to entry into individual industries that limited the possibility of domestic competition; (ii) indiscriminate and indefinite protection of domestic industries from foreign competition; (iii) the adverse effects of protecting small-scale industries and regional dispersal of growth on the choice of the optimal scale of production; (iv) barriers to exit by not allowing firms, even when they were non-viable, to close down, and the failure to move the resources to an alternative growing industry; (v) administrative hurdles inherent in a system of physical controls; (vi) increased incentives for rent-seeking activities that resulted in dampening entrepreneurship; and (vii) little or no incentive to upgrade technology.

Other critics (for example, the World Bank) have added to this formidable list: (i) adverse effects of universal credit rationing through the nationalized banking system; and (ii) poor performance of public-sector enterprises.

The first-generation debate between the proponents of the model, for example Chakravarty (1988), and the aforementioned critics were examined in detail in Singh (1991). He concluded that on a long-term view of Indian economic development over the previous four decades as a whole, contrary to what was written in *The Economist*, the record was far from being disastrous. It was clearly not outstanding—it was about average for the developing countries of Asia (the most successful of the three developing continents). Importantly, further analysis suggested that the mediocrity of the outcome was mostly due to the extraordinary and far-reaching economic shocks sustained by the economy during the decade 1965–75. These shocks included the effects of the two wars with Pakistan in 1965 and 1971, suspension of foreign aid for various periods following each of these two wars in 1965 and 1971, the economic effects of the earlier war with China in 1962, drought in the late 1960s, maxi-devaluation of the rupee around the same time, and oil price-rise in 1973–74. In this context, it is a credit to the Indian system that these shocks were contained by prudent macroeconomic policies though these still resulted in slower long-term growth for almost ten years, 1965–75. India ended the 1970s with low inflation and a healthy balance of payments position. Indian economic management of these shocks compares favorably with the experience of Latin American countries during the debt-crisis of the 1980s.

Turning points in India's industrialization and growth record

Economic historians identify two major turning points in Indian GDP growth during the twentieth century. The first and most important one occurred around the early 1950s and a second around 1980. The latter is not quite as important as the former in a hundred-year perspective but is far more so if the shorter and more recent time span of the last half century is considered. These turning points have been the subject of great controversy both in statistical and economic terms. However, there is now fairly wide consensus, as indicated above, on the statistical identification of the two main breaks in long-term economic growth. The early 1950s trend-break relates to the fact that there was a big increase in long-term economic growth in the second half of the twentieth century (independent India) compared to the first half (British-ruled India). The GDP growth rate in the second half was ten times faster than in the first half—nearly 5 percent per annum during 1950–2000, compared with 0.5 percent per annum during 1900–1950.[2]

In relation to the current economic, intellectual, and ideological battles it is the second turning point of the early 1980s that is more significant. What is at issue is whether or not the acceleration in Indian economic growth during the last two decades was a consequence of liberalization of the economy or due to other causes. The essential difficulty here for those who advocate liberalization and globalization as the solution to the problems of the Indian economy, and regard import substitution industrialization under state direction as the main reason for its poor or under-performance, is that the trend growth rate began its rise in the early 1980s rather than in the early 1990s. Serious liberalization, particularly in trade and foreign investment occurred only in the 1990s; it could not therefore be easily regarded as a cause of the trend increase in economic growth which began a full decade before such liberalization.

If the trend increase in long-term economic growth in the early 1980s cannot be attributed to external liberalization which the then finance minister Dr. Manmohan Singh instituted in 1991, how can it be explained? There are at least two plausible explanations, not mutually exclusive, which are particularly promising. One is the suggestion that, although in the 1980s there was very little external liberalization, there was, nevertheless, very considerable deregulation of the domestic investment regime; there were also other important domestic reforms including some liberalization of the financial sector. These reforms, together with changes in the fiscal and monetary policy stance of the government, were sufficient to help raise the long-term growth rate.[3] It must also be emphasized that these internal liberalization measures were adopted in response to the reports of half a dozen high-level government committees, which highlighted the negative outcomes of the investment regime and over-regulation of the economy. In that sense, the reform of industrial policy in the 1980s was endogenous to the Nehru–Mahalanobis model.

The second plausible thesis is that the institutions which had been established in the post-independence period, particularly those in the field of science, technology, and higher education, took longer than anticipated to produce results which would be reflected in GDP growth. It is important to emphasize that India's achievement in science and technology which came to be recognized throughout the world in the last 15 years or so was accomplished by following an educational path dictated by the country's own political economy rather than by implementing policies advocated by the World Bank. Under World Bank policies, India would have been obliged to give primacy to primary and secondary education rather than to tertiary and higher-level education. The country did the contrary, mainly because of the influence of the urban middle classes in policy making and their desire for their offspring to have college education. Although the education standards in these colleges left a lot to be desired, they nevertheless helped produce a huge supply of university graduates in scientific and technical subjects. These colleges, often established by private-sector initiatives, were complemented by the government's establishment of elite institutions, such as the Indian Institutes of Technology (IITs), which are world class. This educational strategy, although in conflict with 'human development,' has clearly not harmed the long-term growth rate of the economy. Indeed, it laid the foundations for later Indian successes in information technology and other areas (Rodrik, 2004).

India's technological success is not limited to the IT industry. Its corporations have been successful in a variety of industries, including in particular, pharmaceuticals and auto components. It is widely recognized that the country also has broad-based technological capability as evidenced by the fact that India is one of the three countries in the world (Japan and the US being the other two) that has built super-computers on its own. It is one of the six countries in the world to launch satellites.

That India's impressive technical and scientific infrastructure was quintessentially established by the government is well acknowledged. How this was done, and is being done, will be illustrated in this chapter by considering the experience of the IT industry, which, as mentioned earlier, is a much disputed case regarding the effectiveness or otherwise of the government's industrial policy.

Industrial policy and IT

The growth of a modern, highly export-oriented IT industry is the arena of one of the main controversies concerning the effectiveness of Indian industrial policy. It is argued in some quarters that the outstanding achievements of the IT industry, to be outlined below, are due to its 'benign neglect' by the government.[4] As the industry was a relatively late-comer on the scene in India, it is thought to have been spared the bureaucratic inefficiencies of heavy government intervention of the Nehru–Mahalanobis period of 1950–1980. Further, it is argued that the industry has been successful precisely because its evolution in the 1990s and 2000s has coincided with the overall liberalization of the Indian economy as a result of reforms ushered in by Dr. Manmohan Singh in 1991.

There is, however, a large body of analysis and evidence that suggests that this characterization of benign neglect by the government is grossly inaccurate and misleading.[5] Before reviewing this literature, it may be useful briefly to indicate some of the achievements of the Indian software industry particularly in relation to exports. Of the 316 Indian software companies that had acquired international quality certification by 2002, 85 were assessed at SEICMM level 5, the highest attainable level. This compares with 42 other companies from the whole of the rest of the world. In addition, software exports from India have been growing at a rate of 30 percent a year in the last three of four years, reaching US$9.2 billion in 2003–2004 and $12.2 billion in 2004–2005. Outsourcing to India by Fortune 500 firms increased from 300 in 2003 to 400 in 2004. Finally, the export intensity of software production in India is more than 70 percent. This compares with an overall export intensity of 10 percent for the whole economy.

India's comparative advantage in software development lies entirely in the availability of low-cost skilled labor. An important issue is how these skills were accumulated. Arora et al. (2001) report that the comparative salaries for software professionals in India were less than a tenth of those of their counterparts in the United States. For example, a programmer's salary in India was 6 percent of that in the US; a software developer's salary in India, although comparatively high, was still 30 percent of that in the US.

This comparative advantage of cheap skilled labor did not arise spontaneously but was helped, in fact established, by the government. The latter took a number of broad as well as specific measures to cultivate this comparative advantage and also helped the industry in other ways.

First, a vast number of engineering colleges were established in both the public and the private sectors, particularly in the South of India where the state governments were highly entrepreneurial. These colleges provided education, including in IT, that was greatly subsidized by the state and central governments. Indeed, the tuition fees were waived in the case of both public and private colleges. This constituted an indirect subsidy to the nascent software industry.

Secondly, the Nehru–Mahalanobis vision, referred to earlier, of creating a broad science and technology base to transform the Indian economy so as to bring about a greater degree of autonomous innovation and development was also fundamental in the development of the IT sector. This policy, as many scholars have pointed out, led to Indian scientists learning by doing in a conscious purposeful manner that had significant public as well as private benefits. Efforts that were argued by many to be tantamount to reinventing the wheel in the event made a major contribution to national development. This occurred not only in relation to IT but also in the case of the growth of the biotechnology and pharmaceutical industries. As the late Sanjaya Lall memorably put it, the Indian scientists and engineers not only mastered the know-how of modern technology, but also excelled in its know-why.

Thirdly, the government's indirect measures significantly helped the industry. Specifically, the government's role in the establishment of Bangalore as a hub attracting the bulk of India's scientific and technological activity was salient to the development of the IT industry. Bangalore first became a centre for cutting-edge defense industries (MIG aircraft production, rocket technology for launching domestically made satellites, giant computers, among other things). The reason Bangalore was favored as a site was because of its distance from India's perceived antagonists, Pakistan and China. Thus, the government's development of a high-technology critical mass of market opportunities and people in and around Bangalore greatly facilitated the emergence of an internationally competitive software sector.

In addition to these extremely important infrastructural factors for the development of the software industry, the government also took suitable specific measures to encourage exports from the sector at each stage of its development. NASSCOM, the highly respected Indian software industry association, fully acknowledges that the government has played a major role in the development of India's IT sector:

The software and services industry has received immense support from the government both at the central and state level. This support, in the form of tax incentives and other benefits has been instrumental in the growth of software and services exports from India. In addition to this, the government has established several task forces that have made far-reaching proposals for the development of this sector. Many of our recommendations for the government are in line with the overall thrust of these task forces.

(NASSCOM, 1999, as cited in Balakrishnan, 2007)

In sum, the IT industry progressed not in the context of benign neglect on the part of the Indian government but through strategic attention by the government to the needs of the industry at each successive developmental stage.

In the general context of the development of science and technology in India, the IT story is instructive. Industrial policy during the last two decades, albeit in a new form, helped the country to develop a highly export-oriented software industry despite liberalization and globalization.

Industrial policy in India's present and future: conceptual issues

Does the internal and external liberalization of the economy since 1980, and particularly the abandonment of the detailed regulation of private-sector investment, mark the end of industrial policy in India? The answer is no. Post-1980 industrial policy changed form and became much more pragmatic. Basically instead of planning inputs and outputs for each firm and each industry, the government adopted indicative planning. However, it did not abandon industrial policy instruments such as very high tariffs by international standards and restrictions on portfolio and foreign direct investment.

It will be argued here that, in the new circumstances, with the opportunity to exploit India's acknowledged lead in the IT industry, as well as other structural challenges facing the economy mentioned in the Introduction, a further change in industrial policy is called for. This does not constitute going back to the Nehru–Mahalanobis model, but, to meet the new challenges and opportunities, it should be a much more vigorous approach than the present one.

It is important to appreciate that industrial policy in India, as in the classic case of post-war Japan, needs to be considered in a broader context of overall development of the national economy. To some extent this is already the position taken by the Planning Commission. Policy has not just been confined to India's upgrading the *industrial* structure and promoting industrial revolution in a broad[6] sense, but has instead provided an overall integrated direction for the development of the whole economy. An important goal of Indian planning has always been, and continues to be, to achieve as high a growth rate as possible, which is compatible with a desired current account balance. Further this ought to be subject to distributional considerations that, as will be argued in the next section, cannot simply be left as an afterthought but must become an integral part of the planning exercise.[7]

India today has an enviable framework for the conduct of comprehensive industrial policy in the broad sense. Many of the necessary institutions required such as the Planning Commission are in place and have broad acceptance among all the political parties and the Indian people. This is one of the reasons why this essay has not concerned itself with the normal starting point of any economic discussion of industrial policy in terms of market failures and externalities. As Dosi et al. have noted in the Introduction to this volume, when considering experience regarding achieving long-run dynamic economic efficiency, market failures and coordination problems are ubiquitous in capitalistic economies, whether developed or developing; these are not minor exceptions as is often implied in orthodox writings. That planning and industrial policy are well embedded in the Indian political economy is a major advantage compared, for example, with Latin American countries who have no such heritage (see Ocampo, 2005 and other chapters in this volume).[8]

A main issue for the future of industry planning in India is what functions, old and new, should the Indian Planning Commission focus on in the years ahead. The Commission must clearly change with the times and continue to be able to provide forward-looking visions of the economy and society. In this context, it is interesting to reflect on the evolution of industrial policy in Japan and in South Korea. In Japan, the Ministry of International Trade and Industry, the traditional government agency which spearheaded the highly successful industrial policy of that country in the 1950s and 1960s, continues to operate but without the coercive powers it had during that period. On the other hand, the Korean government, on its joining the OECD in the early 1990s, ostentatiously abolished its Planning office. Many observers ascribe the Korean crisis of 1997–98 in part to this abandonment of the planning function which meant that the time-inconsistency between foreign exchange inflows and outflows could not be foreseen and resolved in time (Chang, 2003; and Singh, 2002).

In the Indian case, there is a continuing need to guide the country's industrial revolution towards abolishing poverty, providing employment and work to all those who wish to have them, and raising living standards of a billion people while maintaining democracy. The precise role of industrial policy and economic planning in India today and in the future should depend on an analysis of the constraints on the country's industrialization and economic development, which will be outlined below (see also Rodrik, 2004).

The new frontiers for industrial policy in India

There is an important new, as well as an old, agenda for the country's Planning Commission. The new agenda arises in response to globalization and technological change, particularly with respect to information technology. Relevant issues arising from these new phenomena will be examined in this section and those related to the old agenda but requiring updating will be examined in the following section.

I first take up the question of the role of services versus manufacturing in the evolution of the Indian economy in the recent period. There are important analytical questions here which require continuing research as these have salient policy implications for employment, work, and the general well-being of the Indian people. A main issue which has come up during the last decade is the fact that Indian economic growth seems to be led more by services than by manufactures. Contrary to previous historical evidence, for countries at India's level of economic development, the growth of manufacturing has normally been faster than that of services and of GDP growth. The rapid growth of services, as well as the failure of the formal manufacturing sector to create net new jobs despite fast economic growth, has convinced many Indian economists that the high aggregate growth rates of the recent period are fragile. Thus, it is suggested that the recorded growth rate of more than 8 percent per annum for the last three years is in some sense unreal because it is in large part due to the fast growth of services rather than being primarily generated by the contribution of rapid manufacturing growth.

IT, services, and manufacturing

Figures 11.1 to 11.3 provide some of the basic empirical information bearing on these issues. Figure 11.1 indicates that in both the periods 1950–1980 and 1980–1990, the growth rate of industry in India was faster than that of either services or agriculture. However, during 1980–1997, the growth rates of industry and services were more or less equal, with both exceeding agricultural growth. However, Figure 11.1 suggests that services have been growing faster than either industry or agriculture since 1997.

It is normal to indicate the pace of structural change in a developing country by the growth in the share of industry in the country's GDP. Economic history

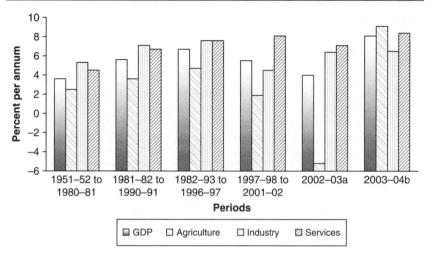

Notes: a: Quick Estimates; b: Advance Estimates for 2003–2004.
Sources: CSO; Economic Survey 2003–04 (Based on Acharya, 2004).
Figure 11.1. Growth of GDP and major sectors in India: 1950–51 to 2003–04

suggests that, when a country begins to industrialize, its share of employment and output in manufacturing rises until a very high level of per capita income is reached, when the share of manufacturing begins to decline. In these terms, Figure 11.2 compares the pace of structural change in the Indian economy with that of other large developing countries in Asia and Latin America. The graph provides information on the share of industry in GDP in a sample of nine Asian and nine Latin American countries. However, so as not to overload the graph the data is displayed only for China and India and the median for

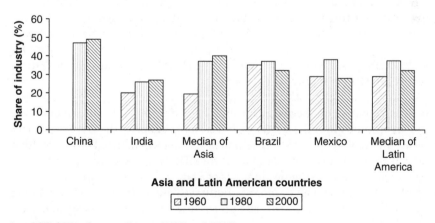

Source: World Development Report, (1982) and (2002).
Figure 11.2. Share of industry in GDP: India, China, Brazil, Mexico, and other countries

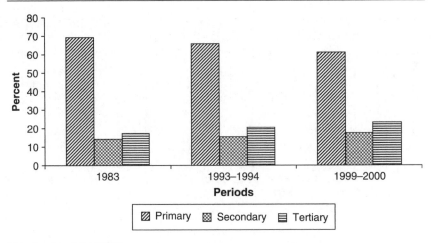

Note: Based on Joshi (2004).
Figure 11.3. Growth of employment by sectors in India: pre-reform and post-reform periods

Asian countries; in the case of Latin America the information is provided for Brazil and Mexico and the median for Latin American countries. The graph suggests that between 1960 and 2000, even though it started at a low level, the share of industry in Indian GDP rose only by 7 percentage points. Most of this increase took place between 1960 and 1980 and there was only a marginal improvement of 1 percentage point between 1980 and 2000. For China, the comparable data is available only for the period 1980–2000. The share of industry is much higher in China than in India but the growth in China's share of industry in GDP during the last two decades is not all that much different from that of India (which to some extent one would expect because of China's starting point being much higher). However, Figure 11.2 also suggests that Brazil and Mexico albeit with higher per capita incomes than that of India have lower proportions of output emanating from the industrial sector in 2000 compared with 1980. There has similarly been an increasing share of services in GDP in most of these countries.

To supplement the data on the growth of value added, Figure 11.3 provides basic information on the expansion and share of employment by sectors in the Indian economy over the last 20 years. The table indicates the share of primary sector in total employment was much greater than in GDP—more than 60 percent compared with 27 percent for GDP (the figure for agriculture). If de-industrialization is defined in terms of a fall in the share of industry in total employment, the Indian economy strictly speaking did not de-industrialize in the 1980s or in the 1990s. The data underlying Figure 11.3 suggests that there was a small increase overall in the share of secondary sector in employment from 13.8 percent in 1983 to 16.8 percent in 1999–2000. This compares favorably with the record of other developing countries including China, as suggested by Figure 11.4. This figure provides evidence of de-industrialization in the above sense in several developing countries. Indeed, Palma (2004) suggests that during the 1990s, de-industrialization has been beginning at an increasingly lower level of per capita income compared with the earlier period.

Figure 11.5 provides information on changes in employment elasticities between the pre-Reform period (1983–84 to 1987–88) and the post-Reform period (1993–94 to 1999–2000) in different sectors of the Indian economy.[9] The figure indicates a sharp fall in the overall employment elasticity of aggregate output in the country from 0.6 to 0.16 between the two periods. Significantly, this suggests that there has been a sizable reduction in employment elasticity in agriculture, manufacturing, and construction. However, Figure 11.5 also indicates that there are a number of service industries including finance, insurance, real estate, and business services which have recorded a trend increase in employment elasticity in the post-Reform period.

Figure 11.6 displays information assembled by Gordon and Gupta (2004) on the growth of services in recent decades in the Indian economy. The figure suggests that it is not only the IT sector in services which has experienced fast growth in the last decade, but so have many other service sub-sectors grown faster than GDP, the fastest growth being recorded in business services, communication, banking services, hotels and restaurants, and community services. However, other services such as public administration, defense, real

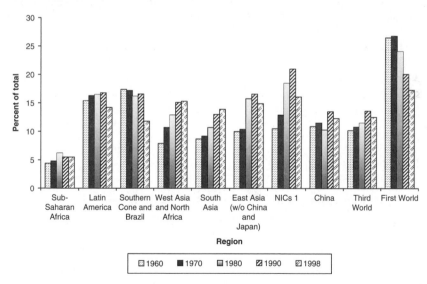

Source: Calculations made using statistics from the ILO Databank. Regional averages are weighted by economically active population (Based on Palma, 2004).

Figure 11.4. Employment in manufacturing: developing regions and China

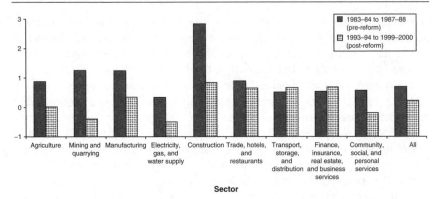

Source: Report of Special Group on Targeting Ten Million Employment Opportunities Per Year over Tenth Five Year Plan, Planning Commission, May, 2002, p. 158 (based on Seema Joshi, 2004).
Figure 11.5. Sectoral employment elasticities in India: pre-reform and post-reform periods

estate, storage, transport, and personal services did not register any acceleration in growth in the 1990s.

With regard to the IT sector itself, although the sector has grown at a much faster rate, its quantitative significance in the overall picture of the economy is rather limited. The sector accounts at present for less than 1 percent of GDP; it employs fewer than one million people in a total labor force of 450 million. The IT sector makes, however, a very important contribution to the balance of payments, accounting for 20 percent of India's exports, and is expected to rise to 30 percent by 2010.

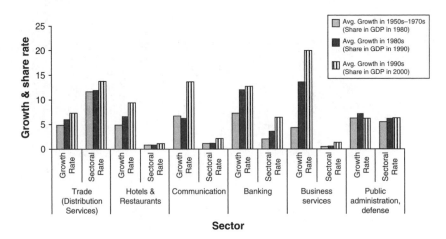

Source: Based on Gordon and Gupta (2004).
Figure 11.6. Growth rates and sectoral shares of services in the Indian economy

It will be appreciated that, despite the IT sector's fast growth and hence its potential for creating jobs, it will be able to *directly* employ only educated people.[10] Joshi (2004) notes that only 5 percent of India's relevant age group receive a college education. The employment needs of the uneducated masses are unlikely to be met directly by the IT industry. To put things in perspective, it may also be noted that in 1999–2000, only 8 percent of the Indian labor force was employed in the organized sector and 92 percent was absorbed by the informal unorganized sector. There is also evidence that a large proportion of informal-sector workers are engaged in tertiary activities especially in large cities.[11]

In detailed analyses Dasgupta and Singh (2005 and 2007) suggest that despite the low direct contribution of the ICT sector to employment, it is as much an engine of growth as manufacturing. These two studies suggest that the growth of both manufacturing and services is closely related to the growth of GDP. In the Kaldor-type structural analysis of economic growth,[12] it is often argued that the high correlation between GDP growth and the growth of services is not due to any independent causal relationships between these two variables but rather due to the fact that the growth of services depends largely on the growth of manufacturing. However, this argument, although it may be applicable to certain services such as retailing and transport, is hardly relevant to services such as those of ICT. The latter may be regarded as causing the expansion of the manufacturing sector rather than the other way round. Dasgupta and Singh's research suggests overall that while manufacturing will continue to be the main engine of economic growth for low-income countries, the ICT services constitute an additional engine of growth. Like manufacturing, ICT services are subject to static and Kaldor's dynamic economies of scale, have positive spillover effects on all sectors of the economy, and help relax at the macroeconomic level the balance of payments constraints.

The main policy implication of these analyses is that India should take advantage of its strength in ICT and use it extensively in all areas of the economy in order to upgrade manufacturing and agriculture as well as services, to compete effectively in the world economy. This would enable the economy to maintain the desired current account balance at a higher growth rate than before. However the introduction of ICT into various areas of the economy would require new institutions and social arrangements, which is one of the major new tasks facing the Indian Planning Commission during the next ten years.

Globalization and income inequality

With regard to the phenomena of globalization, the country faces a host of difficult problems both in the short term and long term. This is in part due to the fact the Indian economy has been one of the most protected economies in the world with some of the highest import duties and non-tariff barriers to trade. Tariffs since 1991, and much more so recently, have been dramatically reduced and other non-tariff trade barriers have also come down as a consequence of India's membership of the WTO. There are, moreover, huge opportunities and challenges for the country in relation to the liberalization of agricultural products currently under negotiation at the WTO. Similar freeing of trade and services is also being negotiated at the WTO. Preparing the country for this gigantic task of integration with the world economy, so as to minimize the losses of integration and maximize the gains, is an important task that will require urgent attention from the Planning Commission as well as other public and private organizations.

However, globalization also has more subtle longer-term implications that need the Commission's attention, namely distribution of the gains and losses from globalization. The main visible gainers from globalization are the vast Indian urban middle class which is numerically very large in absolute terms but proportionately quite small, perhaps 100 million people, which amounts to less than 10 percent of India's population. Whether or not there has been a reduction in poverty in the period since 1991 is still a matter of academic dispute. There is, however, more consensus on the evidence which suggests that income inequality has been increasing rather than falling during the last decade. Cornia (2004) sums up the available evidence on changes in income inequality since liberalization of the economy in 1991: 'In sum, the experience of the 1990s points to a moderate rise in both urban and rural inequality, a larger rise in overall inequality due to a widening of the average urban–rural gap, and a decline in the poverty alleviation elasticity of overall growth' (Ravallion and Datt, 1999).

The effects of globalization on income distribution have been compounded by the information technology revolution. The latter has led to a digital divide, in part because its main beneficiaries are the English-speaking elite. As mentioned earlier only 5 percent of the Indian population is conversant with English, which of course means that in a population of over a billion, there are as many as 50 million English speakers in India. If globalization is to succeed in India with its democratic polity, the question of participation in the digital economy and in the distribution of the gains from the new technology will have to be squarely faced at the national level. The Indian Planning Commission is a body ideally suited to this task as it currently plays a major role in the distribution of resources between states. It is a body that mediates in inter-state conflicts on this issue. This expertise should help the Commission to provide a national forum for discussion and debate and consensus formation on the issue of ensuring that the countryside shares in the wealth created by information and communications technology.

Updating the old agenda

Apart from the above issues arising from ICT and globalization, there are important parts of the old agenda of Indian industrial policy which will need to be addressed urgently and on a continuing basis. First, there is the extremely important question of infrastructure where India is thought to be much behind not only China, but also other countries in the region. Indian infrastructure spending on roads, railways, ports and airports, and so on is about 6 percent of GDP and is considered by the government itself to represent a shortfall of at least another 3 percentage points. The Planning Commission, recognizing the enormity of increasing infrastructure spending to 9 percent of GDP, suggests that it can only be done by creating a partnership with the private sector. This would require the creation of suitable new institutional arrangements if this type of public-private partnership is to succeed.

There are similarly other parts of the old industrial policy agenda that need to be thought afresh. In this context a main issue is that of the efficiency of the public sector. During the last 50 years India has created a vast public sector without much thought being given to its micro economic efficiency. This is not just a question of loss-making public-sector production units (PSUs) but rather the issue of efficient functioning of all non-profit-making public institutions including colleges, schools, and hospitals. A lack of rigor and a sense of mission are lacking in most public institutions. These require public audit committees including NGOs and representatives of other social groups to establish suitable norms of efficiency and to monitor each unit's progress. The government's recent introduction of the Freedom of Information Act should be helpful in this task.

Modern theory of economic development suggests that institutions are arguably the most important deep cause of the long-term increase in standards of living. India, because of its democratic system, rule of law, and protection of property rights, is regarded by many scholars as being well ahead of China in its institutional development. Rodrik and Subramanian (2004) estimate that, given the level of Indian institutional development, the country's per capita income should be three times its present level. This suggests that India's institutional arrangements have become less effective over time and need to be revamped.[13] A good example of this is the Indian civil service which, in many respects, is no longer as efficient as it was in the 1950s and 1960s, due to politicization of the career and promotion prospects of civil service officers. It is therefore hardly surprising that many civil servants have lost self-confidence and are demoralized. They need both to be motivated and, as servants of the people, imbued with a sense of accountability. Indeed, the reform of the civil service is essential for meeting the government's short- and medium-term goals, including delivering health and education to India's villages, but it is also necessary for the long-term development of the country's economy. Hence, an important task for the Planning Commission in the years ahead will be to re-examine India's institutional arrangements in the economic and social sphere.

Conclusion

This chapter has taken a wide view of industrial policy, emphasizing the coordinating role of the government in various spheres. It has examined India's past and present industrial policy and speculated about the role and content of future policy. It has also argued that the Planning Commission constitutes a major institutional advantage for the Indian people. All political parties accept the Commission's important role in formulating industrial policy in a narrow sense and also in guiding India's ongoing industrial revolution in a broad sense. It has been suggested here that industrial policy and planned economic development did not end with deregulation of India's comprehensive and strict investment regime for the private sector. The post-Nehru–Mahalanobis industrial policy has been more pragmatic and less interventionist, focusing more on coordination of economic activity and devising appropriate measures to further develop specific sectors (as illustrated by its role with respect to ICT). This paper argues, in addition, that industrial policy and planning have a potential whole new agenda based on an update of old issues and the need to tackle new issues thrown up by evolving national and international circumstances. A central challenge for the Planning Commission is to exploit India's lead in ICT and its institutional surplus to raise the current 8 percent trend rate of growth to double-digit numbers while promoting equitable distribution of the fruits of economic progress. This would require imaginative applications of ICT and further technological developments in agriculture, industry, and services. The challenge to the Commission would be to help raise productivity growth while also increasing employment. This in turn requires the Commission to shift its emphasis from narrow industrial policy towards questions of distribution and employment, both of which have crucial economic and political dimensions.

What useful lessons can be learned from India's industrial experience over the last five decades? The most striking lesson would appear to be that it is possible for a large country to do exceptionally well in narrow GDP growth terms while following policies not at all approved of by the protagonists of the Washington Consensus. Of course, the IFIs claim that India's success was due to liberalization. Liberalization certainly has occurred in India, but this has been at a deliberately slow pace. During the last five decades India had exceptionally high tariff rates but, even under liberalization, these were maintained at a comparatively high level. Moreover, there were continued restrictions on the entry of multinationals as well as on portfolio investment.

Notwithstanding what, from a neoclassical standpoint, can be considered self-imposed rigidities, the Indian economy achieved very high growth rates in the last two decades. It has done significantly better than the Latin American countries which followed Washington Consensus policies. Looking to the future, it has been suggested here that to meet the challenge of globalization, of new technology, global warming, slow pace of structural change, India will need a much more vigorous industrial policy than it has followed in the last two decades. The Planning Commission will have to give greater weight to creating a national consensus on questions of distribution and the associated problem of employment. In an increasingly globalized and technologically advancing world, promoting industrialization and growth is a multidimensional complex task that requires coordination by the government at various levels. A main lesson to learn from India is the need to establish appropriate institutions to formulate and promote industrial policy and that these need to win wide social acceptance. The optimal industrial policy for other countries can be specified only by examining their past economic history, the kind of economic constraints with which they are faced, and the global economic environment, both current and prospective. Industrial policy is concerned with charting a long-term sustainable path for the economy that is both feasible and ambitious.

Appendix: Composition and functions of the Indian Planning Commission

The Indian Planning Commission was established in 1950 with the following statutory mandate to:

(i) Make an assessment of the material, capital and human resources of the country, including technical personnel, and investigate the possibilities of augmenting such of these resources as are found to be deficient in relation to the nation's requirement;

(ii) Formulate a Plan for the most effective and balanced utilization of country's resources;

(iii) On a determination of priorities, define the stages in which the Plan should be carried out and propose the allocation of resources for the due completion of each stage;

(iv) Indicate the factors which are tending to retard economic development, and determine the conditions which, in view of the current social and political situation, should be established for the successful execution of the Plan;

(v) Determine the nature of the machinery which will be necessary for securing the successful implementation of each stage of the Plan in all its aspects;

(vi) Appraise from time to time the progress achieved in the execution of each stage of the Plan and recommend the adjustments of policy and measures that such appraisal may show to be necessary; and

(vii) Make such interim or ancillary recommendations as appear to it to be appropriate either for facilitating the discharge of the duties assigned to it, or on a consideration of prevailing economic conditions, current policies, measures and development programs or on an examination of such specific problems as may be referred to it for advice by Central or State Governments.

The high status of the Planning Commission within the government is indicated by the fact that the Prime Minister has chaired the Commission since its establishment in 1950. Furthermore, the Deputy Chairman, who is the effective head of the Commission, has always been a member of the Cabinet.

The current membership of the Commission comprises: Dr. Manmohan Singh (Chairman and Prime Minister of India); Shri Montek Singh Ahluwalia (Deputy Chairman); Shri M.V. Rajashekharan; Dr. Kirit Parikh; Prof. Abhijit Sen; Dr. V.L. Chopra; Dr. Bhalchandra Mungekar; Dr. Syeda Hameed; Shri B.N. Yugandhar; Shri Anwar-ul-Hoda.

Over time, the planning function of the Commission has undergone significant transformation. Like the Japanese Ministry of International Trade and Industry, the Indian Planning Commission attempts to build a long-term strategic vision of the future and helps to determine international economic priorities. In parallel, it has shifted from the specification of detailed, mandatory investment plans for the private sector to indicative investment planning, working out sectoral targets and stimulating the economy to grow in the desired direction.

The Planning Commission's functions have devolved in other dimensions. Greater emphasis is now put on achieving efficiency of resource utilization, than on resource augmentation, though the latter is by no means neglected. The Commission also plays a mediatory and facilitating role in the allocation of resources between the central government and the states.

The Commission itself claims that, since the beginning, its approach to policy formation in the critical areas of human and economic development has been holistic. It points to a lack of coordination between ministries with regard to social-sector policies, relating to rural health drinking water, rural energy needs, literacy, and environmental protection. It observes that this has resulted in a multiplicity of agencies. An integrated approach, the Commission argues, can lead to better results at much lower costs.

Notes

1. However, during the late 1970s and in the 1980s, the concept of self-reliance was redefined in less stringent terms. It was interpreted to mean an 'economic base that is sufficiently strong and internationally competitive to generate the export earnings required to pay for needed imports of goods that cannot economically be produced domestically'. See further Byrd (1990).
2. See further Bhalla (2004), Papola (2005).

3. There is a big debate on this issue. See further De Long (2001), Rodrik and Subramanian (2004), Ahluwalia (1988, 2002), Singh (1995, 1998), and Sinha and Tejani (2004). See Kohli (2006) for an interesting political economy explanation of this issue.

4. A leading exponent of this view is a doyen of the Indian IT industry, Mr. Narayana Murthy (2005).

5. See, for example, an incisive analysis of the key issues by Balakrishnan (2006). The latter contribution is a main source of the statistics used in this section unless stated otherwise.

6. Industrial revolution in the broad sense refers to the large trend increase in growth that occurred in England and then in Europe in the nineteenth century as a consequence of industrialization.

7. Some may argue that this is too broad a definition of industrial policy but in the case of a developing economy such as that of India, anything less comprehensive will be inadequate. If we consider the historical experience of Japan and Korea, the exemplar East Asian 'industrial policy' economies, such a policy was considered an integral part of the planning process. Thus, for example, the textile industry remained for long a favored industry in South Korea, not because of its high-technology or skill-formation externalities, but for the reason that the industry made a major contribution to the country's balance of payments. Similarly, in Japan's industrialization in the post-World War II period, domestic interest rates were kept very low to encourage business persons to invest. Therefore industrial policy for economic development must be considered in a wide context. For a discussion of these issues see further Singh (1995), Rodrik (1995), World Bank (1989). It is useful in this context also to note that there is a revisionist literature on industrial policy in Japan and Korea that suggests that these policies were unsuccessful. However, this conclusion is normally arrived at by using a very limited definition of industrial policy which is not compatible either with historical evidence on the actual operation of such policies in exemplar East Asian economies, as well as their perceived logic.

8. A planned economy was supported by Indian businessmen even before the country gained independence. The domestic Indian business groups had formulated the so-called 'Bombay Plan' to guide the development of the economy, see Chakravarty (1988).

9. Employment elasticity of a sector is defined as the percentage increase in the rate of growth of employment in the sector for a given percentage increase in the rate of growth of production in that sector.

10. Unless stated otherwise, the IT sector refers to the design, development, and production of software.

11. The distinction between formal and informal sectors has a rigorous official quantitative basis only with respect to manufacturing. In manufacturing any enterprise employing more than ten people and using electricity is regarded as belonging to the formal sector, otherwise to the informal sector. The distinction between the two sectors is hazier in other areas of the economy. See further Dasgupta and Singh (2007).

12. In modern economics the main theoretical basis for the proposition that 'manufacturing is the engine of growth' in both developed and developing countries is

the work of Kaldor (1966, 1967). See further Dasgupta and Singh (2005 and 2007).

13. For a recent analysis of the degeneration of the Indian civil service, see Appu (2005).

References

Acharya S. (2004), 'India's Growth Prospects Revisited,' *Economic and Political Weekly*, Special Article, October.

Ahluwalia I. (1991), *Productivity and Growth in Indian Manufacturing*, Oxford University Press, Delhi.

Ahluwalia M. (1986), 'Balance of Payments Adjustment in India 1970–71 to 1983–84,' *World Development*, 14(8).

—— (2002), 'Economic Reforms in India since 1991: Has Gradualism Worked?,' *Journal of Economic Perspectives*, 16(3): 67–88.

Appu P.S. (2005), 'The All India Services: Decline Debasement and Destruction,' *Economic and Political Weekly*, 26 February.

Arora A., Arunachalam V.S., Asundi J., and Fernandes R. (2001), 'The Indian Software Services Industry,' *Research Policy*, 30: 1267–87.

Balakrishnan P. (2007), 'Benign Neglect or Strategic Intent? Contested Lineage of Indian Software Industry,' *Economic and Political Weekly*, 9 September.

Bhalla G.S. (2004), 'Is Growth Sans Industrialization Sustainable?' ISID Foundation Day Lecture, Institute for Studies in Industrial Development, New Delhi (May).

Byrd W.A. (1990), 'Planning in India: Lessons from Four Decades of Development Experience,' *Journal of Comparative Economics*, 14(4): 713–35.

Chakravarty S. (1988), *Development Planning: The Indian Experience*, Oxford University Press, Delhi.

Chang H-J. (ed.) (2003), 'Rethinking Development Economics: An Introduction' in *Rethinking Development Economics*, Anthem Press.

Cimoli M., G. Dosi, R. R. Nelson, and J. Stiglitz (2006), 'Institutions and Policies Shaping Industrial Development: An Introductory Note,' LEM Working Paper Series 2006/02.

Cornia G.A. (ed.) (2004), *Inequality, Growth, and Poverty in an Era of Liberalization and Globalization*, Oxford University Press, Oxford.

Dasgupta, S. and A. Singh (2005), 'Will Services Be the New Engine of Economic Growth in India?' Centre for Business Research Working Paper 310, University of Cambridge. Subsequently published in *Development and Change*, November 2005, 36 (6): 1035–58.

—— —— (2007), 'Manufacturing, Services and Premature Deindustrialization in Developing Countries—A Kaldorian Analysis,' in G. Mavrotas and A. Shorrocks (eds.) *Advance Development: Core Themes in Global Economics*, Palgrave Macmillan, Basingstoke, New York.

Datt G. and M. Ravallion (2002), 'Has India's Post-Reform Economic Growth Left the Poor Behind,' *Journal of Economic Perspectives*, 16(3): 89–108.

De Long J. B. (2001), 'India since Independence: An Analytic Growth Narrative,' July, <http://www.j-bradford-delong.net/>.

Economist, The (1991), *A Survey of India*, 4 May.

Gordon J. and P. Gupta (2004), 'Understanding India's Services Revolution,' IMF Working Paper 171, International Monetary Fund, Asia and Pacific Department.

Government of India (2002), *Report of the Special Group on Targeting Ten Million Employment Opportunities per Year*, Planning Commission, New Delhi.

Joshi S. (2004), 'Tertiary Sector-Driven Growth in India–Impact on Employment and Poverty,' *Economic and Political Weekly*, Special Article, 11 September.

Kaldor N. (1966), *Causes of the Slow Rate of Economic Growth of the United Kingdom*, Cambridge University Press, Cambridge.

—— (1967), *Strategic Factors in Economic Development*, New York State School of Industrial and Labour Relations, Cornell University: Ithaca NY.

Kohli A. (2006), 'Politics of Economic Growth in India, 1980–2005 Part I: The 1980s,' *Economic and Political Weekly*, 1 April.

Mahalanobis P.C. (1963), *Approach of Operational Research Planning in India*, Asia Publishing House, London.

Narayana Murthy N.R. (2005), 'The Impact of Economic Reforms on Industry in India: A Case Study of the Software Industry' in K. Basu (ed.) *India's Emerging Economy*, MIT Press, Cambridge, Mass.

Ocampo J.A. (2005), 'Latin America's Growth and Equity Frustrations During Structural Reforms,' *Journal of Economic Perspectives*, 18(2): 67–88.

Palma J.G. (2004), 'Four Sources of De-Industrialisation and a New Concept of the Dutch Disease,' in J.A. Ocampo (ed.) *Beyond Reforms*, Stanford University Press, Palo Alto, Calif.

Papola T.S. (2005), 'Emerging Structure of Indian Economy: Implications of Growing Inter-Sectoral Imbalances,' Presidential Address for the 88th Annual Conference of the Indian Economic Association, Vishakhapatnam (December).

Ravallion M. and G. Datt (1999), 'When Is Growth Pro-Poor? Evidence from the Diverse Experiences of India's States,' World Bank Paper No. 2263.

Rodrik D. (1995), 'Getting Interventions Right: How South Korea and Taiwan Grew Rich,' *Economic Policy*, 20.

—— (2004), 'Industrial Policy for the 21st Century,' CEPR Discussion Paper No. 4767.

—— and A. Subramanian (2004), 'From "Hindu Growth" to Productivity Surge: The Mystery of the Indian Growth Transition,' NBER Working Paper No.10376, <http://www.nber.org/papers/w10376>.

Singh A. (1995), 'The State and Industrialization in India: Successes and Failures and the Lessons for the Future' in H.J. Chang and R. Rowthorn (eds.) *The Role of the State in Economic Change*, Clarendon Press, Oxford.

—— (1998), 'Competitive Markets and Economic Development: A Commentary on World Bank Analyses' in P. Arestis and M. Sawyer (eds.) *The Political Economy of Economic Policies*, Macmillan Press.

—— (2002), 'Asian Capitalism and the Financial Crisis' in J. Grieve-Smith and J. Michie (eds.) *Global Instability and World Economic Governance*, Routledge, London. Also published in *International Capital Market: Systems in Transitions*, J. Eatwell and L. Taylor (eds.), Oxford University Press, 2002.

—— and J. Ghosh (1988), 'Import Liberalisation and the New Industrial Strategy: An Analysis of Their Impact on Output and Employment,' *Economic and Political Weekly*, Special Article, November.

Sinha A.K. and S.Tejani (2004), 'Trends in India's GDP Growth Rate: Some Comments,' *Economic and Political Weekly*, 39(25): 5634–9.

Vakil C.N. and P.R. Brahmananda (1956), *Planning for an Expanding Economy*, Bombay University Press, Bombay.

World Bank (1982), *World Development Report*, Washington, DC.

—— (1989), *World Bank Country Study (1989). India: An Industrializing Economy in Transition*, Washington, DC.

—— (2002), *World Development Report*, Washington, DC.

12

Growth and Development in China and India: The Role of Industrial and Innovation Policy in Rapid Catch-Up

Carl J. Dahlman

Introduction

The objective of this chapter is to review the role of industrial and innovation policy in the development of China and India for insights into rapid catch-up strategies. It will then reflect on the challenges to development policy advice from their experience, as well as from the new more demanding global context.

China and India have used industrial policy extensively. Nevertheless, contrary to the expectations of those who have a negative view of industrial policy, China and India have been growing for the last 25 years at average annual rates of 10.1 percent and 6.3 percent respectively relative to average world growth rate of 3 percent (Table 12.1). However, although they had nearly the same per capita income 25 years ago, their growth performance has differed.

China has been growing at 9–10 percent per year for the last 30 years, while India's increase in growth has been more recent, and has reached 8 percent since 2003. Currently the Chinese economy is almost three times that of India, and its per capita income is more than twice that of India (Table 12.2). They also illustrate contrasting development strategies—China a more traditional labor-intensive export strategy, India a new knowledge-intensive service export strategy.

This chapter will explore the role of industrial policy in their different development strategies and performance. In 1980 India was ahead of China in most economic and social indicators. However, now China is ahead of

Table 12.1. Average annual growth of GDP 1980–2005

	1980–1990	1990–2000	2000–2005
East Asia and Pacific	8.0	8.5	8.4
China	*10.1*	*10.6*	*9.6*
Europe and Central Asia	2.4	−0.7	5.4
Latin America and the Caribbean	1.8	3.3	2.3
Argentina	*−0.7*	*4.3*	*2.2*
Brazil	*2.7*	*2.9*	*2.2*
Mexico	*1.1*	*3.1*	*1.9*
Middle East and North Africa	2.0	3.8	4.1
South Asia	5.7	5.6	6.5
India	*5.8*	*6.0*	*7.0*
Sub-Saharan Africa	1.6	2.5	4.3
All low and middle income	3.3	3.9	5.3
High income	3.1	2.7	2.2
US	*3.0*	*3.5*	*2.6*
World	3.2	2.9	2.8

Source: 1980–1990—WDI 2000; 1990–2000, and 2000–2005—WDI 2007. The region country groupings are those used by the World Bank and top six categories consist of developing countries.

Table 12.2. Current comparison of China and India

Basic indicators	China	India
GNI		
GNI (2005 nominal billion)	2,270	804
GNI as share of Global GDP	5.4	1.9
GNI/capita (2005 nominal)	1,740	730
GNI (2005 PPP)	5,333	2,341
GNI as share of global GDP 2005 (PPP)	9.7	4.3
GNI/capita (2005 PPP)	6600	3486
Exports (2005)		
Merchandise Exports (billion)	762	95
Merchandise Exports % Share of World Total	7.3	0.9
Service Exports (billion)	74	56
Service Exports Share of World Total	3.8	2.9
People		
Population (2005)	1,305	1,095
Population as Share of Global Population	20.2	17.0
Life expectancy at birth	72	64
Poverty		
People living below $1/day (2004–2005)	9.9	34.9
People living below $2/day (2004–2005)	46.7	80.0

Note: In December the International Comparison Program of World Bank released a preliminary report of new PPP price series which adjusted downward by 40% the previous PPP GDP estimate for both China and India. See <http://web.worldbank.org/WBSITE/EXTERNAL/DATASTATISTICS/ICPEXT/0,,menuPK:1973757~pagePK:62002243~piPK:62002387~theSitePK:270065,00.html>

Source: WDI 2007 except for new PPP data.

India in virtually all indicators (except democracy and some elements of the rule of law), in spite of India's recent acceleration of growth rates. In addition, although they are only two countries they are very large. China is 20 percent of world population and 6 percent of world GDP. India is 17 percent of world population and 2 percent of world GDP. In PPP terms China is already 10 percent of world GDP, India is 4 percent.[1] Given current size and growth prospects, they affect the growth prospects for many developing countries, including rather advanced ones such as Brazil, Mexico, and South Africa.[2] Therefore, there are some interesting lessons to learn about the different development experiences of each, as well as to reflect on their implications for development advice.

The development literature has focused a lot on industrial policy.[3] This chapter will argue that industrial policy and infant industry protection have been important in the development of both China and India, and that they would not be the strong global players they are today if they had not had some industrial policy. It will argue that some of the key policy elements that differentiate the performance of the two countries are how they have tapped into global knowledge as well as their education strategies. The chapter will also argue that industrial policy is easier when countries are in the catch-up phase and will focus on three issues that are critical—how were they able to avoid having their industries become permanent infants? what was the role of lax intellectual property protection? and to what extent will they be able to go beyond imitation to technology development?

The chapter will end by summarizing some of the challenges for development policy that arise from the different experience of these two giant countries. Not only are some key elements of the strategies of China and India quite contrary to typical neoclassical development advice. Their strategies are also quite different from each other. In addition, the world has changed. Some of what China and India did is not replicable, in part because of their size, but also because the international system has become more restrictive towards traditional industrial policy. In addition, the global system is now much more demanding and fast paced. Trade is done primarily through global production and distribution networks controlled by multinational companies. It is much more difficult for new entrants to break into these systems because of the higher capabilities and scale required. Thus it is much harder for other developing countries to break in.

Industrial policy

Industrial policy is generally defined as any selective government intervention to promote the development of specific sectors. In both countries the government has been actively involved in industrial policy through virtually all the usual mechanisms: direct state ownership, selective credit allocation, favorable tax treatment to specific industries, tariff and non-tariff barriers to imports, and restrictions on foreign direct investment, local content requirements, special intellectual property rights policies, government procurement, and promotion of large domestic firms.[4] Table 12.3 compares both countries on some of the key elements of industrial policy.

Thus it is clear that both countries have made extensive use of industrial policy. What is interesting is that the countries have had different performance and have pursued different strategies in part as a result of their industrial policies.

One of the main differences in the development strategies of these two giants is the extent, timing, and means through which they have acquired global knowledge. This is also part of the explanation for their different performance and growth paths. As a broad characterization, China has embraced globalization and has been benefiting very much from this. India has been much more autarkic and circumspect. It opened up much later and much more slowly, and is still not as globally integrated as China.

A second major difference has been their education strategy. China invested earlier and more massively in basic education than India. During the Cultural Revolution China actually froze the higher education sector between 1966 and 1976. However, in the 1990s China began to invest massively in higher education and rapidly surpassed India. India on the other hand neglected basic education in its early years, and instead invested in a small number of elite engineering schools and then management schools. While this was controversial at the time, the resulting core of highly educated engineers and managers is part of India's current success story.

A third difference, which is in part the result of the particular type of industrial policies that they followed, is their different industrial structures and differing strengths. China has become a manufacturing hub for the world. India has become a major offshore service center. Hence it is interesting to examine the role of industrial policy in the development of India's competitive information technology services.

Acquiring foreign knowledge

The main means of tapping into global knowledge are trade, foreign direct investment, technology licensing, copying and reverse engineering, foreign education and training, and accessing foreign technical information in print, and now through the Internet. On all these counts, China has been more aggressive and systematic than has India.

Table 12.3. Industrial policy in China and India

	China	India
State ownership	Yes, was extremely high as result of Communist takeover, but thousands of state enterprises have been privatized or shut down as economy has undergone massive restructuring towards market	Yes, strong state control of commanding heights, started with India's first President. Relatively little privatization has occurred, although state ownership was not as pervasive as in China
Subsidized credit	Yes, still significant subsidized credit through state owned banks directed at state enterprises	Yes, still significant directed credit through policy banks and special programs
Tax incentives	Yes, and many have been strongly biased toward foreign investment and high technology	Yes, for targeted sectors and areas
Tariff and non-tariff protection	Yes, but levels have been reduced significantly with WTO entry and are now relatively low	Yes, were extremely high and even though reduced over time, still remain very high by international standards although India is member of WTO
Foreign direct investment targeting	Yes, Initially there was very strong control on FDI. Then strategy changed to opening up to FDI and of getting cutting edge FDI in key areas. One of main means of rapidly modernizing China. Much has come to use China as export platform. Government has been effective at creating strong competition among foreign firms and induced them to bring best technology	*Much less.* There has been much more control of FDI overall and less targeting. India has only recently liberalized FDI regime and begun to target, but still relatively little FDI has been attracted because of high transactions costs and poor infrastructure. Exception has been in software and ICT related services which have not been constrained by regulatory regime or physical investment infrastructure
Average gross FDI/GDP 1995–2004	3.89	0.68
Local content requirements	Yes, important mechanism to develop backward linkages which succeed because of capabilities of domestic firms	Yes, explicit local content requirements in many industrial projects, but not many foreign to participate
Intellectual Property Rights	*Very weak until required to update as part of WTO accession in 2001.* Enforcement is very weak and is likely to become a very controversial issue in future relations with advanced countries	*Weak until completed compliance with WTO requirements in 2005.* Enforcement is weak, though not considered as much of a problem as in China
Government procurement	Yes, important mechanism to develop national firms in many areas. Also effective use of national standards to support competitiveness of indigenous firms	Yes, significant use of government procurement to support domestic industry, including very small firms
Promoting large domestic firms	Yes, multiple instruments used to create world class indigenous (public and private) companies to compete with MNCs domestically and eventually abroad	No. For long time Indian state was against big business and severely restricted growth of large firms. Policy more open now, but still not strongly supportive

Trade

China began opening up to the world much earlier than did India and has become much more integrated into the global economy. The share of imports and exports in China was 71 percent of GDP in 2005 compared with only 37 percent in India (Table 12.4). China's high degree of trade integration was second only to Germany's among the world's large economies in 2005, and it will surpass Germany soon.[5] Purchases of foreign products and services are a key way to gain access to knowledge embodied in those goods and services.

By initially protecting its industries from imports, China developed basic technological capability. Then by opening up to foreign investment in special economic zones with near free trade status it was able to get access to world-class technology and inputs. This worked very well and not only began to modernize China, but also provided needed foreign exchange and employment. The number of these special economic zones was expanded from the initial four to nineteen and then to many more.[6] This program was so successful in generating employment and foreign exchange that by the late 1990s China decided to generalize this free trade status significantly by joining

Table 12.4. Trade

	China	India
Trade as share of GDP		
1990	35.4	16.5
2005	70.7	36.7
Merchandise exports (% of GDP)		
1990	17.5	5.7
2005	34.1	11.8
Manufactured exports (% of merchandise exports)		
1990	72	70
2005	92	70
High tech exports (% of manufactured exports in 2005)	31	5
Commercial service exports (% of GDP)		
1990	1.6	1.5
2005	3.2	7.0
IT services (as % of service exports)		
1990	18.7	42.7
2005	38.6	66.4
Average tariffs (av. simple/av. weighted)		
1990	42.3/40.6*	81.8/83.0
2005	9.2/4.9	17.0/14.5
Royalty and license fee payments ($ mil 2005)	5321	421
Royalty and license fee payments/ million population (2004)	4.08	0.38

* 1992 rather than 1990.
Sources: WDI 2007, and World Bank KAM 2007.

the WTO. This involved committing to a major program of reduction of tariff and non-tariff barriers and opening up to foreign investment not only in the manufacturing, but also in financial and other service areas.

Unlike China, which has significantly removed tariff and non-tariff barriers to trade as part of its joining the WTO, India is still one of the most closed economies in the world. In the 1950s India followed a very autarchic policy of self-reliance, relying initially mostly on massive capital goods imports from the Soviet Union, as was also done by China. Unlike China, India maintained its strongly inward-oriented nationalist policy through the 1980s. It was only after the trade liberalization of the early 1990s that India began to open up more to foreign technology imports. There were also very strong restrictions on direct foreign investment and on the licensing of foreign technology. During this period technology policy focused very much on self-reliance.

Foreign direct investment

The inflows of foreign direct investment into China have been several multiples of those into India (see Table 12.3). This is the result of several factors. First, China opened up its regulatory regime towards foreign direct investment more than ten years earlier and more broadly than did India. Second, China's larger and richer market has been an important pull factor. Third, China has many cost advantages over India, even though its labor costs are now generally higher than India's. Transportation is more efficient, service infrastructure is more developed, and the red tape for trade in physical products is less burdensome. As a result, China has been very attractive not just as a production platform for global markets, but also for production for the Chinese market which soon became the world's fastest growing market. This strong pull on producing in China has also permitted the government to encourage strong competition among foreign multinational firms to bring their very best technology when they locate in China, even though they are very aware of poor intellectual property protection and the risk that their technology will be pirated.

The most important contribution of FDI to China has not been capital since China has had a high savings and investment rate. More important has been access to advanced technology and management through FDI. Equally important is entry into global markets as the foreign investors integrate their Chinese operations into their global supply chains.[7] Moreover the latter does not even require owning production plants in China, but just sourcing from China. An excellent example of this is Wal-Mart which sources over $25 billion from China directly into its retail stores without even using middlemen.

India only began to open to FDI in the 1990s and only slowly and selectively. As a result it got very small inflows. In the last five years India has liberalized

FDI inflows and trade inflows but, as noted, both are still very small compared to those of China. Thus Indian industrial policy has protected domestic industry for too long and also did not take advantage of the technology it could get from abroad, or the economies of scale and scope of pushing its firms to operate globally.

Technology licensing

China has also been much more aggressive in licensing foreign knowledge through formal technology-licensing agreements. Chinese royalty and fee payments are almost 13 times those of India in absolute terms and more than 10 times even in per capita terms.

Diasporas

It should also be noted that both China and India have benefited enormously by drawing on their respective diasporas. However China had done this more systematically and for longer than India. More than one half of the FDI in China has come from Taiwan, Hong Kong, and Singapore. These are market economies which have had great experience operating in the global market. They were already well plugged into global supply chains. They initially moved their more labor-intensive operations into China. As China moved up the technology ladder they have been moving toward more technology-intensive operations. This is particularly true for Taiwanese companies which are now putting some of their most advanced production facilities in China.

In addition, China has set up special high technology parks specifically targeted at attracting back experienced overseas Chinese to set up high tech companies in China. Several of the more than 100 high tech parks in China cater specifically to this diaspora. India has done this much less. Furthermore, China has also made a more sustained effort to attract back Chinese professors and former foreign students to staff the rapid ramp-up of its tertiary education sector. India has had much less success in doing this because it is more constrained by regulations that do not allow its universities to pay professors competitive salaries.

Copying and reverse engineering

While there are no hard data on this, it is quite certain that China has been much abler at copying and reverse engineering than India. Greater access to foreign knowledge through all the formal channels listed above, higher levels of human and technological capital, and a policy (now changing) of ignoring intellectual property rights laws have given China an advantage in copying and reverse engineering foreign technology.

In China, besides the large state-owned firms, thousands of township and village enterprises were developed behind strong trade protection. Some of these, such as Haier, have gone on to become globally competitive companies. In China, the government also negotiated with the large multinationals that wanted access to the Chinese market. Initially they forced companies to go into joint ventures with domestic firms. They also negotiated local content and training requirements.[8] This greatly helped them develop technological and management capability. The government was able to negotiate this because of the attractiveness of the domestic Chinese market to the foreign manufacturers. Once the cost advantage of producing in China became apparent to both the government and to multinational companies, the government relaxed the joint venture requirement in order to encourage the foreign firm to bring its best technology.

Education

Basic education

As a very poor developing country even just 25 years ago, China had very low levels of education. However it has made massive investments in basic education and its literacy rate is 91 percent compared to 61 percent in India. In India there is also a very strong gender bias in literacy. The illiteracy rate is 52 percent among women and 27 percent among men. India's basic education system is still very poor with tens of millions of primary school children out of school.

Secondary education

China invested not only in basic education but also expanded secondary education much more than India, even during the tumultuous period of the Cultural Revolution (1966–1976). By 1980 China had 50 percent higher secondary enrollment rates than India. China increased secondary enrollment rates from 46 percent in 1980 to 73 percent in 2005. India's secondary enrollment rates were only 30 percent in 1980 and it only expanded them to 54 percent by 2005.

Tertiary education

China has undertaken a massive expansion of its tertiary education system starting in the late 1990s to make up for the havoc wreaked on the educational system after the Cultural Revolution. By 2005 its enrollment rate reached 19 percent. Because of China's large population it had more students at the tertiary level than the US and 40 percent were in engineering and sciences. By 2007 China's tertiary enrollment rate reached 21 percent.[9]

In India, Nehru went for a strategy of elite higher education by setting up seven elite Indian Institutes of Technology to develop the technical human manpower necessary to run the commanding heights of the economy and government, and neglected basic education. This decision was controversial until the 1990s as it did not seem to have had a high economic return. However, with the information and communications technology (ICT) and the challenge of the Y2K millennium software bug problem at the end of the 1990s, these early investments paid off. India's English-speaking engineering talent was able to help the global response and is one of the factors in India's strength in knowledge-intensive exports (see below).

Although India has expanded tertiary enrollment rates, it has not done so as fast as China and now is considerably behind. Also, the quality of higher education is poor with the exception of those mentioned above (which produce fewer than 7,000 graduates a year), the Indian Institutes of Science and some of the regional engineering colleges. The low quality of tertiary education and the regulatory constraints on expanding high-quality institutions will be a major bottleneck to India's continued rapid growth in knowledge-intensive services.

Foreign education

China has been sending more tertiary-level students abroad for education and training than India in absolute and relative terms. In 2005, more than 16 percent of the 2.7 million tertiary students studying outside their home country were from China (not counting Hong Kong), and 6 percent were from India (Table 12.5).[10] Foreign education and training are very important means to tap into global knowledge. These students not only learn academic subjects, but a large number of them are researchers at higher education institutions around the world. Many also go on to work in the high technology firms in the United States and Europe. Until a few years ago, many of them stayed on in their host countries. However, in the past five years more of them are returning to China and India, in part because of increasing opportunities and attractive incentive programs designed by their home countries to stem this brain drain. This trend has been stimulated by the more restrictive visa procedures for students following the September 11, 2001 bombing of the World Trade Towers in New York City.

Training

Besides the much lower level of education in India, there is not much training and upgrading of workers skills for those already employed. The exceptions are

Table 12.5. Education

	China	India
Literacy rate, population 15 & above		
1995	80.8	53.3
2004	90.9	61.0
Av. ed. attainment of adult pop. (2000)	6.35	5.06
Basic education	*Universal* but spotty quality	*Incomplete and poor quality*
Secondary education enrollment ratio (%)		
1980	46	30
2005	73	54
Higher education	*Very rapid ramp up*	*Initially high* through Indian Institutes of Technology, relatively little expansion and high variance and much low quality
Enrollment ratio (%)		
1980	2	5
2005	19	12
Students studying abroad (2005)	404,664	139,223
% of World students studying abroad	17	6
Skilled labor	*Well developed* training market inside and outside firms	*Very under developed* Very poorly developed training market

Source: KAM 2007 and WDI 2007, except for students studying abroad, which is from OECD, *Education at a Glance 2007*.

the high technology firms in information services such as Infosys and Wipro (where up to one-third of their workers may be engaged in training at any given time) and a few others. On the other hand, training and retraining is much more prevalent in Chinese manufacturing firms.[11] In addition, in China there are massive training schemes for the millions of rural workers coming into the cities and for the millions of workers being laid off from state-owned enterprises.[12] Thus China is not only providing more formal education to its population, but it is also upgrading the skills of its workforce and keeping them more current with the changing skills needs of the economy.

Development of the ICT service sector in India

One of the hallmarks of the Indian economy is its strong information technology services sector. It also distinguishes it very much from China which is known as an exporter of manufactures rather than an exporter of services. Therefore it is instructive to explore to what extent the development of this sector was the result of far-seeing explicit industrial policies. Paradoxically the dramatic success of this sector was not the result of coherent and explicit industrial policy, but more a case of being well-positioned and the dynamism of the Indian entrepreneurs. Its good positioning came from having developed a core of well-trained engineering talent through the Indian Institutes of Technology and later many Indian engineering colleges. When the world was hit by the Y2K millennium bug scare in 1999, Indian engineers were in high demand to fix the computer and software glitches, although India had already begun to develop software and export software and ICT services. The visible success of Indian engineers in helping to solve the Y2K problems greatly enhanced the reputation of India in the ICT sectors. This led to a strong increase in demand for Indian software services. This was facilitated by the fact that many high-level executives in IT companies in the US and Europe were actually engineers and managers of Indian origin who knew of the capabilities of their compatriots back home and steered business in their direction. Some of them also invested in these Indian firms.[13] Thus the Indian diaspora played an important role here.

Also as the success of Indian software export became known it also led many firms to realize the cost-effectiveness of hiring skilled English-speaking professionals to do ICT-related services to high quality standards at a fraction of skilled labor costs in the US or Europe. This led to an expansion of the demand for IT-enabled highly skilled labor services.

In addition, as the ICT sector was new, it was not subject to the stifling regulations typical in most other sectors of the economy. To the credit of the government, once this sector started to take off it did not try to over regulate it (as happened in Brazil through the Informatics Market Reserve Policy). Rather policy makers supported its rapid development and expansion. They permitted the establishment of efficient broadband and satellite connections for data transfer. They reduced tariffs on the imports of hardware and software tools. They facilitated the creation of software parks with less-onerous labor regulations, and their own electric power suppliers to overcome the problem of the daily power interruptions common in India because of very poor infrastructure services.

Another reason why the ICT service sector took off is that it did not require much infrastructure services other than satellite communications or fiber optic cables. Most sectors that require imports of inputs and components for exports of physical products are not very economically viable because of all the problems with trade and customs clearance, port and transportation costs, and other physical bottlenecks. The magic of ICT services was that they were largely immune from the constraints of the onerous Indian regulatory regime and poor infrastructure and transport services.

Thus, the most successful sector in India was not the result of explicit industrial policy. It was much more the result of the earlier investments in engineering education, the fact that it was in English as a result of the English colonial period, and the luck of having these skills at the turn of the millennium when they suddenly were in very high demand. This is not to minimize the very impressive development of the industry since then including the virtuous cycles driven by Indian entrepreneurial capability, and the stimulus of the Indian diasporas in the ICT industry in the US and Europe. Thus although the government did not lead this sector, at least it has supported it since its emergence.

It should also be noted that, although not as visible because it is not exporting as many IT-enabled services as India because less of its highly skilled labor force is English speaking, China is also becoming a location for knowledge-intensive services. China actually has a larger ICT service industry than India and it is now being actively supported by the government.[14] In addition China is strongly pushing English language training.

Lessons from China's and India's experiences

The entry of China and India on to the world stage is one of the major events of the turn of the century. Both of these countries are benefiting from the rapid generation and dissemination of new knowledge as well as from the greater integration of the global economy. Both countries have become major economies in PPP terms and are having a growing impact on world trade.

China and India have followed different development strategies. China has grown more rapidly and for longer. It has also concentrated its growth more on industry and manufacturing. India's strategy has not pushed industrialization as much. As a result the sector that has been expanding the fastest in India has been services. Since the Y2K bug business at the turn of the millennium its IT-enabled services have become a significant growth engine even though employment in the ICT services still accounts for just 1 percent of its labor force.

The rise of China and India reflect part of a new division of labor. China is positioning itself as the low-cost manufacturing center for the world thanks to the reduction of transportation costs. China has benefited from the unbundling of manufacturing based on logistics of physical trade, aided by ICT and insertion into global production and distribution chains.[15] (However, China is moving to the task of unbundling too as it strengthens its high-level human capital and English-language skills.)

India is positioning itself as the IT-enabled service for the world thanks to the reduction of communications costs and the possibility of trading labor services at a distance. India has benefited from the unbundling of tasks—based largely on possibilities opened up by new ICT infrastructure which has allowed it to overcome constraints of physical infrastructure.

Table 12.6. Differences in economic structure: China and India

	China	India
Development strategy since major regime change in 1947–1949	Starts Communist, moves toward market economy and integrates to world faster	Starts as market economy, goes socialist for 40 years and slowly moves toward market liberalization
Role of government	*Major change* from total state control of centrally planned economy towards a market economy. Share of private sector estimated at over 60% of GDP. Still significant presence of state owned enterprises across economy including banking.	*Some change* from 1950s and 1960s when state acquired control of commanding heights of economy and was anti large private business, toward more business friendly policies since the 1980s, and further liberalization in 1990s and present decade.
Composition of GDP[*] (% distribution by years)	Currently industry sector led	Currently service sector led
Agriculture 1965/1985/2005	39/31/13	47/32/18
Industry 1965/1985/2005	38/46/48	22/29/27
(Manufacturing) 1965/1985/2005	30/34/34	15/19/16
Services 1965/1985/2005	23/23/40	31/39/54
Consumption vs. investment orientation[*]	*Heavily investment oriented.* Investment 36% GDP in 1990, increased to 44% of GDP in 2005, household consumption decreased from 46% in 1990 to 37% in 2005, and government consumption share unchanged. Total consumption only 51% with government consumption 14%.	*Previously heavily consumption oriented.* Household consumption 66% of GDP in 1990, down to 59% in 2005. Government consumption marginally down from 12% to 11%, but investment increased from 24% in 1990 to 33% in 2005 (with surge to 30s only in last 4 years)
Average Gross Investment to GDP 1995–2005[1]	39.2	25.9

[1] WBI KAM 2006.
Source: KAM 2007 and WDI 2007.

The higher growth performance of China over India has been due to in part higher investment rates (Table 12.6). The rate of investment between 1995 and 2005 has averaged 39 percent in China versus 26 percent in India. The higher rate of investment combined with a much greater import of capital goods embodying more advanced technology helps to explain the higher rate of growth in China. As indicated above, China has also made much more extensive use of foreign knowledge through much greater inflows of FDI, greater integration through trade (most of the manufactured imports being capital goods and components), greater formal technology purchases in absolute and relative terms, greater number of students going abroad, greater use of its larger diaspora, and more copying and reverse engineering.

However, if both countries had liberalized from the beginning, it is unlikely that they would be the strong world economic powers that they have become. To a large extent, some of the strengths of both countries are that they developed strong technological capabilities before they liberalized. Because of their high absorptive capabilities and critical mass in education, they have been able to benefit from that liberalization. Therefore it is helpful to review more carefully the nature of the industrial policies and infant industry protection that they followed. Building on what has been presented so far the key to explaining China's greater performance has been its much greater use of FDI as well as greater trade integration.

The justification for the infant industry argument is that a country has to protect the new industries while they learn how to reduce costs and improve quality so that they can compete with established foreign producers. It is expected that over time they will learn by doing and attain scale economies to be able to compete with foreign rivals. From an economic welfare perspective it is argued that the protected industry must become more efficient than the foreign producer to offset the higher costs incurred by domestic consumers during the protection period.

There are typically four types of problems in developing an infant industry.[16] The first is that the acquisition of knowledge for production involves costs and that the knowledge may not be appropriable by the first firm that invests to produce the good or service domestically. The second is that they incur costs in training workers for the new industry and that they may not be able to retain those workers, who may in fact move to other firms. The third is that once the first firm is successful in producing locally, this provides information to other firms who might also invest and drive profits down. The fourth and most common one is that the domestic industries do not grow up to be as efficient as the foreign producers.

The success of the Chinese industrial strategy was to entice foreign firms to locate in export processing zones in China. Since the foreign firms already had the technology and the experience and the links to foreign markets, their costs of learning to produce in the local context were minimal compared to domestic firms that also would have to develop the technology. The government provided infrastructure and fiscal and financial incentives to attract the foreign firms. Once the first firms were successful and discovered that it was in fact more profitable to produce in China than in their other locations, more foreign firms came. Thus the typical technical and market costs associated with infant industries were transferred to the foreign firms. The central and local government absorbed the fiscal and infrastructure costs. But China benefited from massive labor employment and export revenues. China also benefited as workers trained by the foreign firms were lured away and Chinese joint venture partners learned the technology and organization and set up their own firms. In addition, the government initially imposed local content requirements. Unlike the experience in Latin America these local content requirements worked because domestic suppliers quickly developed the skills and the scale economies to supply inputs and components competitively.

In the case of China, it can be argued that since the government was the main force behind the development of the country, and the country has been growing at more than three times the world average, it is one of the most comprehensive examples of successful industrial policy. It could be further argued that the selective liberalization of the economy starting in the late 1970s was part of this industrial policy. A counter argument, of course, is that if China had started these reforms earlier (as was done for example in neighboring Taiwan and Korea), it would have started growing faster earlier.

In the case of India, it could be argued that the slow growth of the Indian economy until the late 1980s was an example of poor industrial policy because of all the constraints the government placed on the growth of the private sector. The subsequent speed-up in the Indian rate of growth can be attributed to the gradual removal of excessive regulatory constraints on the private sector. India's slower rate of growth compared to that of China until recently could also be attributed to its lag in liberalizing the economy.

However, there are three key issues that merit closer attention regarding industrial policy. These are: How were the countries able to avoid having their industries become permanent infants? What was the role of lax intellectual property protection? And to what extent are they going beyond imitation to technology development?

Avoiding permanent infants

Here a distinction needs to be made between China and India. By relying heavily on FDI, China was able to avoid this problem much more than India. By trying to develop technology indigenously India did not develop as broad or as sophisticated an industrial sector as China. Also India's industrial sector is much less competitive than China's as is revealed by its much smaller export sector in relative and absolute terms. One element of why China and India have been able to develop competitive industries behind trade protection is their large market size. That has led to considerable competition within the domestic market even when there was protection from trade.

China's relatively stronger performance has come from greater competition than in India. This has come from three sources. One is the greater openness of the Chinese economy and its greater structural integration through trade into the global economy as has been already discussed in this chapter. A second has been the much stronger emphasis on exports in the case of China.[17,18] As noted, these started with special export processing zones which were multiplied over time. They were complemented with special export incentives including duty drawbacks, subsidized infrastructure, one-stop shops on regulations for setting up enterprises, importing and exporting, and so on. India does not have a very well developed export-promotion system. In addition, as noted earlier, as part of the package of joining the WTO, China has drastically reduced tariff and non-tariff barriers on imports and has a much freer trade regime. This also makes importing and exporting much easier in China. Having to export in competition with the rest of the world also forces exporters to keep up with the new products, designs, and process technologies, quality improvements, and even new business models of competitors. Also, having close exposure to foreign goods and services provides greater opportunity to copy and reverse engineer them.

It should also be emphasized that by being more integrated through trade, China has also developed a much larger industrial sector which is servicing global markets rather than just domestic needs. China's industrial sector is an astounding 48 percent of GDP which is an outlier even by the standards of the former socialist economies.[19] That large export-oriented industrial sector has been instrumental in absorbing millions of workers from the lower productivity agricultural sector and contributed significantly to modernization and the rapid rise of per capital income. India, because it has been more autarkic, as well as because of a much more regulated labor market in the industrial sector, has not had such a dramatic expansion of industry and is still a much more agricultural and agrarian economy.

A third element has been the bias against big business and in favor of small-scale industry in India. The government reserved a good deal of the commanding heights of the economy (power, telecommunications, railways, airlines, chemicals petrochemicals, fertilizers, steel, and heavy capital goods) primarily for state enterprises. It severely controlled the growth of domestic enterprises. In addition some 1500 products were reserved by law for production by small and medium-sized enterprises. As a result much of India's industrial base was not very competitive. The 1980s saw the introduction of pro-business reforms initiated by Indira Gandhi and later carried out by Rajiv Gandhi. These included easing restrictions on capacity expansion by large firms, removal of many price controls, and the reduction of corporate taxes. These were followed in 1991 by a more significant liberalization of the economy as a result of severe balance of payments crisis. These reforms included liberalizing imports, reducing investment licensing, privatizing some state-owned enterprises, allowing automatic approval of direct foreign investment in some sectors, and reducing the number of products reserved for small-scale industry.

China also promoted large state-owned enterprises and for a long time suppressed private business. However, the hybrid township and village enterprises (TVEs) that developed during the 1980s and the 1990s proliferated very rapidly. There was very strong competition among them, and between them and the larger often more inefficient state enterprises. In fact the government strategy eventually turned to growing out of the plan by capping the size of the state sector and allowing growth to come from the expansion of these dynamic TVEs, and eventually the growth of small private firms.[20]

Intellectual property rights

There is no doubt that lax intellectual property rights have been a very important element in the rapid catch-up of these two giant economies. Lax intellectual property rights laws, and when these were upgraded to international standards, weak enforcement, have been key elements of the development strategy of both China and India. The copying and reverse engineering of technology from more advanced countries were critical for the rapid catch-up of the US, Japan, Korea, and Taiwan when they were behind the technological frontier.[21]

Both countries have begun efforts to align their IP rules with international norms, but enforcement is still weak. The complaints about IP violations tend to be stronger regarding China. This is largely because of the greater capability of its firms to reverse engineer or outright copy proprietary foreign technology. Although most multinationals investing in China and India know that their IP is likely to be pirated, they often cannot afford not to be in the Chinese or Indian market. They make their investments with the hope that they can innovate faster than they can be copied, but this is becoming increasingly difficult as the technological capability of these countries continues to improve.[22]

In China, because of the lax enforcement of intellectual property rights, a lot of this technology leaks to domestic producers. Nevertheless the foreign firms continue to bring their best technology because they are competing not just with domestic firms, but with global world-class manufacturers. They try to limit the technology spillover by not having all the elements of their technology package in one facility. However, domestic Chinese firms are catching up quickly. The MNCs cannot resist the advantage of producing in China, even though they realize that their intellectual property is likely to leak out.

In India, strong domestic firms which are now becoming global players, such as Tata, Reliance, Dr. Reddy, and Ranbaxy, developed behind strong trade protection and favorable intellectual property right policies. The development of the strong Indian pharmaceutical industry is particularly relevant. After independence from England the Indian government changed the patent regime they had inherited from the British. They continued to protect pharmaceutical process patents, but not pharmaceutical product patents. Since it is relatively easy to find the molecular composition of drugs and to find alternative manufacturing processes, this allowed Indian pharmaceutical firms to patent alternative ways to produce pharmaceuticals. This asymmetrical type of patent protection led to the development of a strong Indian pharmaceutical industry. When India was finally forced to extend intellectual property protection to pharmaceutical products in 2005, it already had strong Indian pharmaceutical companies. The most successful of these have many new drugs under development, and some of them have even gone on to buy firms in Europe and the US as part of their global expansion.

This whole issue of intellectual property rights is becoming more important for global competitiveness. In the past quarter century the pace of the creation and dissemination of knowledge has accelerated. The nexus of global competitiveness has shifted from natural resources and other static advantages to innovation. The market for knowledge and innovation has become increasingly global. Research is being done in more places, scientific and technical papers are more likely to have co-authors from different countries, and strategic technological alliances are more likely to include firms from more than one country.

Multinational corporations are becoming truly global, conducting R&D as well as production in many countries.[23] This dispersion of high-level activity is generating anxiety about protection of intellectual property (IP). The reigning economic assumption has been that as firms from developing countries gain greater capability and begin to move up the value chain, firms from developed countries can keep ahead by investing more in high-level human resources and in R&D for innovation. That assumption must now be reconsidered in the light of reduced transportation and communication costs, the digitization and outsourcing of knowledge services, and the increasing ability of firms in developing countries to copy and reverse engineer. No longer able simply to outrun the competition from the emerging economies, the United States and other developed countries will have to pay closer attention to IP issues in their relations with China and India.

From imitation to innovation

The final issue is the role of R&D and going from imitation to innovation. Both China's and India's catch-up strategies have benefitted from acquiring knowledge that already exists. Overall, tapping into global knowledge has been much more important in improving the productivity and growth of these economies than has innovation coming from their R&D effort. However, this is beginning to change as they are catching up in many areas and have to make global innovations to get ahead.

Initially, in both countries, R&D was focused on indigenous innovation and on mission-oriented programs in defense[24] and basic industries. Nevertheless, a lot of R&D in public labs and universities as well as in productive enterprises has focused on tracking, assessing, acquiring, and adapting foreign knowledge.

China has followed a five-pronged strategy. One was to import a massive number of turnkey plants, first from the Soviet Union, then turnkey plants and capital goods from the West. A second has been to copy, reverse engineer, and otherwise borrow as much foreign knowledge as possible. As in Japan, and Korea earlier, this has been facilitated by investments in human capital. A third has been to disseminate knowledge internally.

This included the Spark Program to diffuse rural technology and the Torch Program to disseminate high technology. The fourth was to tap foreign knowledge through trade and through direct foreign investment. Now that China is catching up in many sectors and that it is being seen as a major competitor, its fifth prong is to begin to innovate on its own account by increasing investments in R&D. In 1998 R&D spending was 0.85 percent of GDP but it started to ramp up R&D spending in 2003. By 2004 it was spending 1.4 percent (Table 12.7). In 2005 China announced its 15-year Science and Technology Plan with the aim of having R&D expenditures reach 2.0 percent of GDP by 2010 and 2.5 percent (the level of advanced countries) by 2020. Essentially it announced

Table 12.7. R&D inputs and outputs

Indicator	China	India
Researchers in R&D, 2004	926,252	117,528
R&D researchers per million population		
1995	445	157
2004	708	119
Spending on R&D (US$ billions)		
US $ billion nominal 2005	32.7	6.8
US $ billion in PPP 2005*	58.9	18.0
Spending on R&D (percentage of GDP)		
1995	0.85	0.8
2004	1.44	0.85
Scientific and technical journal articles		
1995		
2003	29,186	12,774
Scientific and technical journal articles per million population, 2003		
1995	7.69	10.29
2003	22.7	12.0
Patents granted	448	316
yearly by U.S. Patent		
Office, (average		
2001–2005)		
Patent applications granted by U.S. Patent Office per million population		
1991–1995 average	0.05	0.04
20010–2005 average	0.35	0.30

*Based on the new 2005 PPP series.
Source: Compiled from data in KAM 2007 and World Development Indicators 2007.

that rather than rely mostly on foreign technology it was going to invest more in developing its own technology. At the end of 2006 spending had increased to 1.6 percent of GDP and in PPP terms China surpassed the R&D expenditures of Japan to become the second largest spender (after the US).[25] Although the efficiency of its R&D spending is still low, it is working on improving the administrative and incentive system and getting the productive sector to do more.

China has been increasing its number of scientific and technical publications very rapidly over the past few years. In 2003, it had more than twice as many publications as India, but only 14 percent of the US total. India has also been increasing its scientific and technical publications, but not as fast as China. In addition, citation analysis reveals that China's output is of higher quality than India's.

India has not grown as fast or made as massive an economic transformation as China. India had an inwardly oriented industrial policy for a longer period than China. Like China, it built a lot of technological capability and industrial competence during this period. However, it combined this protectionist trade regime with a protectionist technology regime. It strictly controlled FDI as well as technology imports. However, one of the great successes of this period was the green revolution. The public agricultural research efforts of Indian institutions working with other public research institutions worldwide led to significant improvement in wheat varieties with higher productivity. The dissemination and use of these new improved varieties turned India from a grain importing country with periodic famines to a net agricultural exporter.

The impact of the trade liberalization of the economy in 1991 was significant. Firms which had not had to worry much about efficiency in a protected and over-regulated domestic market suddenly woke up to the need to improve their products and services and to reduce their costs. Some parts of the public research infrastructure responded to the change in the overall incentive regime. The impact of growing competitive pressure was also reflected in an increase in the number of private firms doing R&D, and in the increase in their R&D relative to sales. In addition, in the last five years an increasing number of multinationals (MNCs) are not only producing in India, but are setting up their own R&D centers in India, attracted largely by the lower-cost high-level human capital available locally, as well as the possibility of working round the clock with their other research centers thanks to digital networks.

In India, for 20 years R&D spending as a share of GDP oscillated between 0.8 percent and 0.9 percent, and more than 70 percent of funding came from the government. However, in the past two years there has been increasing spending by the private sector, particularly in information and communications technology, autos, and pharmaceuticals. The bulk of the increase has come from multinational companies that have discovered India as a very cost-effective location for R&D. Recent estimates are that taking into account the recent inflows of R&D by MNCs and the increased R&D by domestic firms, R&D expenditures in India are now 1.1 percent of GDP, and nearly 50 percent now comes from the private sector.[26]

In China there are now more than 750 R&D labs. Part of the reason for the R&D in both countries has been the need for MNCs to do R&D locally to adapt their goods and services to the domestic markets. In addition, MNCs increasingly have begun to set up R&D centers aimed at developing products and services for the global market. The initial motivation was the cost effectiveness of hiring relatively low-wage Chinese or Indian scientists and engineers. However, the rapidly growing demand has revealed that the supply of high-quality researchers was smaller than expected and salaries are rising rapidly. The limited supply of qualified researchers is thus becoming a constraint on MNC-funded R&D, particularly in India.[27]

Thus both countries now have a have critical mass in R&D and are working on increasing as well as improving the efficiency of that R&D. The number of scientists and engineers doing R&D in China is now second only to the United States. The number for India is about an eighth of China's, but there may be some problems in the definitions. China has been ramping up R&D expenditures significantly since 2002. Moreover, unlike as in the typical developing economy, and much more as in a developed economy, the bulk of the spending (65%) was by the productive sector, while in India it was still mostly by public research labs.

Although both countries have made impressive advances in the last five years and have important achievements in international patenting and global innovations, they still have a long way to go to be major global innovators. There are also some indications that as their R&D base gets larger the researchers and public and private labs are becoming more concerned about IPR. The governments of both countries are also making more efforts to enforce IPR legislation. However, from a narrow economic perspective it appears that both countries still stand to gain more from copying and reverse engineering the large and rapidly growing stock of global knowledge than from enforcing strong IPR to stimulate more domestic innovation. Therefore, it is likely that the bulk of their R&D efforts are still going to focus on tapping and adapting global knowledge than in pushing forward the frontiers of science. However, they are already doing more basic research in specific areas and are likely to do even more as they catch up in many areas and need to do fundamental work to deal with some of their unique challenges. More generally they are also facing the difficult problem of how much of their R&D capacity to invest in new fields such as biotechnology and nanotechnology which may be very critical for new techno-economic cycles that may eventually replace the current ICT-led growth paths.[28]

Challenges to development policy

There are three sets of challenges from the Chinese and Indian development experience for development policy advice.

The first challenge is that in many ways these two countries do not conform to many elements of the Washington Consensus, yet have had admirable growth performance: China has been growing at 9–10 percent for more than 30 years, India for the last 4 years—and not directly linked to major policy changes. The main areas in which they have diverged from more neoclassical policy prescriptions have been in having long periods of protection, restrictions on direct foreign investment, and lax intellectual property rights. Neither country would be as strong as it is now if it had not had this type of explicit industrial policy. Trade protection and control of FDI allowed these countries to develop strong domestic capabilities in many sectors before being exposed to global competition. Lax IPR has allowed them to catch up to more technically advanced countries is many areas much faster than they could have through their own effort. They have also invested in education and R&D so they now have a critical mass of engineers and scientists and in R&D-based innovation which they are now beginning to deploy. However, as noted, this industrial policy has been implemented differently with different degrees of success and with different strengths and weaknesses and some differences in industrial structure outcomes.

A second challenge is the novelty that India has managed to achieve very high growth based on high-level human resources and a service-led development strategy. This has a lot to do with the early investments in elite tertiary education and the rise of the ICT sector. The service sector, led by IT-enabled services, has been the backbone of the recent surge in the growth rate of the Indian economy from the 6 percent average of the 1990s to the 8 percent since 2003.[29] IT-enabled services by themselves are still a very small part of the Indian economy. They employ only one million out of the total Indian labor force of about 450 million, and directly contribute only about 1 percent of Indian GDP. However, they have had a multiplier effect on the economy and have also put India on the global map. Multinational corporations have discovered India as a very cost-effective place to do many skill- and knowledge-intensive operations. Many investment banks such as Morgan Stanley are hiring and locating a large part of their investment analysts in India. Thus it is not just arm's length off-shored, IT-enabled services anymore, but FDI in the service sector to supply their global operations. There has also been a rapid increase in the establishment of R&D centers by multinationals in India, attracted by the lower costs and good quality of scientists and engineers. In addition, the reputation India has attracted in IT-enabled and in knowledge-intensive sectors has been leading to increasing investment by foreigner, non-resident Indians, and domestically based Indian capital. The ratio of investment to GDP has increased from 22 percent in 2002 to 30 percent in 2006.

Some observers have made much of the role of the IT-enabled service sector in India's growth arguing that it represents a possible third path of services-led development. However, it should be noted that the service sector growth in India has been much broader based than IT-enabled services. Five of the 15 sub-sectors in the Indian government's classification of services have been responsible for the higher than average rate of growth of the services sector and accounted for 60 percent of the service sector's growth. They are business services, communications, banking services, hotels and restaurants, and community services. In 2003, business services, which include the IT-enabled services accounted for only 1.7 percent of GDP. It needs to be emphasized that the growth of the Indian service sector has been closely tied to the growth of the overall Indian economy and is related to the higher income elasticity of demand for services, outsourcing of services activity from industrial activity (domestically and from abroad), as well as by domestic economic reforms involving liberalization of business activity and international trade. The prospects for continued rapid growth of the service sector in India are good provided that India can reform education (particularly higher education), and improve the overall business and trade environment.

The third major challenge to policy advice to developing countries is that the speed, scope, and impact of China's and India's re-emergence on to world stage are pre-empting some traditional development advice to other developing countries because of first-mover advantage and economies of scale.

China is having four impacts on the global economy. First, the competitiveness of Chinese manufactured exports is reducing the price of labor-intensive manufactured goods to the world as a whole. This benefits consumers in all countries. Second, however, China's competitiveness in manufactured exports is putting a lot of pressure on other exporters of labor-intensive manufactures, which is a negative for many other developing countries that also export labor-intensive manufactures. African countries are feeling the heat of Chinese manufacturing competition. One of the few manufacturing industry exports from African countries was textiles and garments. However, since the removal of the country textile export quotas in 2005 that were part of the multi-fiber textile agreement, many of the exporters and local producers have been put out of business by the more competitive Chinese exporters. Brazilian, Mexican, and many manufactures exporters in other Latin American and Caribbean countries are also facing very strong competition in their home and third markets from growing Chinese competition.

Third, because China is very resource scarce and needs to import natural resources and basic commodities, its rapid growth has increased global demand and raised global prices for commodities. This has provided a windfall for all natural resource and commodity exporters worldwide, from developed and developing countries. While this has stimulated many African and Latin American countries whose growth was stalled or marginal, it is creating a false sense of optimism. Commodity prices are cyclical. Prices will eventually come down. Unless these countries invest these temporary windfalls wisely in strengthening their economic and institutional regime, and investing in education and innovation capability, they are going to be facing much tougher competition in the future. Unfortunately most of these countries are not using these windfalls to strengthen their future competitiveness. Finally, the rapid growth of China offers export and investment opportunities for other countries. However, other than raw materials and commodities, China's imports are components and capital goods. The components are produced mostly by more-advanced East Asian economies such as Korea, Malaysia, Singapore, and Taiwan. The capital goods are supplied mostly by Japan and other more-advanced countries. In addition, many of the companies that were making the components in neighboring countries are moving their operations to China to realize the scale economies.[30]

It is questionable whether the typical advice to developing countries to export labor-intensive manufactures is still valid given the tremendous competitiveness of China in manufactures. China's advantage is not just low labor costs (and it has 250 million more underemployed workers in agriculture that it can shift into manufacturing), but economies of scale and logistics, and the fact that it is already well integrated into global supply and distribution chains through MNCs and its vast Chinese diaspora. In addition, China, and for that matter India, are moving up the technology ladder and exporting more technology-intensive goods.

Likewise it is hard for latecomers from developing countries to break into the IT-enabled service market given India's very strong head start with its advantage of the English language, global reputation, well-established links with foreign buyers of their services, and its own strong global companies such as Infosys, Wipro, and Tata Consulting.

Both countries are also having a major impact on relative wages. Their entry into the global market, added to that of the former Soviet Republics, is doubling the global labor force.[31] This means that the relative returns to labor are falling as these hungry new workforces enter the global market at low wages. Moreover, this is not just through the export of labor-intensive products. Any labor services that can be provided digitally can now be off-shored. As noted, India is becoming a strong off-shoring center for skill- and knowledge-intensive services, scaring the world with the prospect that any jobs that can be done digitally may be off-shored to India and other countries with plentiful educated people who can be accessed through the Internet.[32]

Concern from the new international regime

The importance of industrial policy and lax IPR protection for rapid catch-up strategies having been seen, there are two concerns about the implications of the new international regime for other developing countries.

The first is the concern that comes from the tighter international regulatory regime which to some extent these two countries ignored in their development, but which is becoming more binding. The global trade rules have reduced the degrees of freedom that developing countries have to use some of the industrial policy elements successfully used by China and India, and other economies before them—Korea, Taiwan, Japan, even the US and Germany. This has four components. The first is that there has been a steady pressure from the global system to reduce tariff and non-tariff barriers. Since GATT there has been a trend towards increasing liberalization of trade policy among most countries. In developing countries the average tariff levels have fallen from 34.4 percent in 1980–1983 to 12.6 percent in 2000–2001; in developed countries they have fallen from 8.2 percent in 1989–1992 to 4.0 percent in 2004.[33] The second is that there has also been strong international pressure to adopt stronger protection of intellectual property rights which are more consistent with the regimes of advanced developed countries. The third is that there are also stronger rules about what is permissible in terms not just of tariff and non-tariff barriers, but also subsidies and other indirect support to special industries. The fourth is that there are much stronger teeth in the enforcement mechanisms for both the trade and IPR rules. Countries that do not comply can be hit by countervailing duties. Thus, many of the instruments of industrial policy which were very important for the development of domestic capability in China and India[34] have been outlawed by the evolving international regime. This makes it much more difficult for new players (whether firms, sectors, or whole economies) to enter into existing industries.

The second is the concern that the whole global system has become much more demanding. The market economy is a much more global market because of the reduction of transportation and communication costs, tariff and non-tariff barriers. The share of imports and exports has increased from 38 percent of global GDP in 1990 to 57 percent in 2005. Multinational corporations account for 27 percent of global value added, two-thirds of world trade (half of which is intra-firm),[35] and more than 50 percent of global R&D.[36] They are the main agent of globalization and integration of global markets. Because knowledge is not consumed in use, for the producers of knowledge there is a strong incentive to exploit it over the largest possible market in order to amortize the costs of producing it. There is thus a strong incentive to exploit it on a worldwide scale to get maximum returns. There are large economies of scale in purchasing, branding, advertising, and distribution. Speed to the market and quality are of increased importance to remain competitive. The global trade system is increasingly organized in terms of production and distribution networks controlled by MNCs.[37] To take advantage of this rapid change countries have to have a high elasticity of response—to be able to redeploy resources from less-productive uses to more-productive ones. They need modern and efficient communication systems to be up to date in real time about what is happing in product markets and the international financial system. They also need to coordinate activities and to reduce transactions costs across regions within a country as well as between clusters in the country and abroad. They also need efficient port and transport infrastructure to get products and services to the market.

China and India exemplify some of the characteristics necessary to be successful in the new international regime. These two countries have been able to overcome some of the challenges owing to their large size and the critical mass of skilled people and innovation potential. Most developing countries are being left behind. They do not have the capability to take advantage of the opportunities opened up by this increasingly dynamic and demanding global system. Whole parts of the world are being left out except for the current boom in commodity prices favoring natural-resource exporters. However, commodity prices are very cyclical and they are likely to come down again, which will stifle the recent spurt of growth in many natural-resource exporting countries.

Conclusions

The rise of China and India are somewhat unexpected from the perspective of traditional development policy. They have followed different development paths that challenge the Washington Consensus on infant industry protection, control of FDI, and intellectual property rights. It is unlikely that they would have been able to become such strong global players if they had not first had a period of trade protection and control of FDI, and lax IPR policy to build up domestic capability. Nevertheless, both have benefited greatly from tapping global knowledge and finding appropriate ways to insert themselves into global production and distribution chains.

Their success may also be pre-empting development options for other developing countries. Moreover, their strategies may be hard to replicate. Their protectionist policies, control of FDI, and IPR strategies are much harder to implement now because of the tightening of international rules through the WTO, TRIMS, and TRIPS agreements. Moreover, much of their success stems from their large market size, and their critical mass in high-level human capital and R&D.

While some of the lessons from their development are quite specific to each of these countries (besides their very large size; in China, a strong development-oriented state; in India, having inherited and kept English as an official language which makes it possible to sell services to the rest of the world) other lessons are more general.

One lesson is the importance of opening up to access global knowledge, although they did this at different speeds and with different sequencing. China appears to have benefited from more-effective use of FDI and multi-national companies than India. Some observers argue that Indian firms have more capability than Chinese firms and that therefore India's more indigenous-based strategy may have been better than China's which is too dependent on FDI.[38] However, China has been able to catch up faster as a result both of relying on FDI to show the way, and then taking advantage through supplier and market linkages, as well as exploiting indirect external-ities of informal knowledge flows though copying and imitation. Thus it appears that if the country can capture the externalities of having FDI it may be able to accelerate its growth.

However, there are two caveats to the superior performance of China in the use of FDI. The first is that China was able to bargain effectively with the MNCs because of the tremendous leverage of its large market size. Smaller countries would not have such leverage. The second is that it has been able to capture many spillovers from FDI because it has had a greater capacity to copy and reverse engineer both for products it imports, as well as from FDI in China. The reasons for this greater absorptive capability are the much higher level of average education than in India, and its greater domestic R&D and production capability.

A second lesson is the importance of gradual trade liberalization in order to allow domestic industries to develop the capabilities necessary to compete with foreign firms.[39] However, as noted, there are marked differences between China and India. China has gone much further and benefited much more than India. China also appears to have had an advantage over India in having pursued a more export-oriented strategy starting in the 1980s than India which was much more inward-oriented until the 1990s. Thus it appears that at least in the case of these two countries, export promotion, when combined with effective use of the capabilities of foreign investment, and a competitive domestic environment, has led to more rapid technological learning than would have been achieved by import substitution. More generally, China's superior growth rate is partly explained by its much higher investment rate. Combined with heavy imports of capital goods and heavy reliance on FDI, this has allowed China to adopt more modern technologies much faster than India.

A third is their strong investments in education though different in focus and sequencing. Without its early investments in engineering education, India would not have been well placed to take advantage of the Y2K problem to leverage its growth by expanding its knowledge-intensive exports. Similarly, without its massive investments in basic and secondary education China would not have been able to move so quickly from agriculture into industry, or to become such an export powerhouse in manufactured products. Moreover, the critical mass of highly educated professionals is what is powering both countries' rapid move up the technology ladder to become important global powerhouses.

A fourth lesson is the importance of strong investments in ICT, although again with different emphasis. China has become a major hardware producer and exporter, India in programming, software, and other IT-enabled services. Moreover both countries have invested heavily in the use of ICT. Good ICT infrastructure is allowing them to become major global exporters. The ICT infrastructure connected to logistics and global networks has allowed China to become a major supplier in global production and distribution chains where customer demands in developed countries automatically trigger export production in massive manufacturing centers in China. Likewise, broadband internet connectivity is what has permitted India to export knowledge-intensive services as part of the second unbundling mentioned earlier. A well-developed ICT infrastructure is becoming a critical new infrastructure to compete in the more demanding and rapidly changing international competitive environment.

Fifth, lax IPR legislation, and once the legislation was updated in both countries, lax enforcement, have been important for both countries to play rapid catch-up. Copying and reverse engineering have been very important for domestic Chinese enterprises to catch up very fast. In India, the pharmaceutical sector is an excellent example of the importance of weak IPR to enable catch-up.

Sixth, lax IPR has not meant that R&D effort is not important. Both countries show that it has been important for rapid catch-up as it serves to monitor, assess, acquire, and adapt global knowledge to local conditions. Furthermore, as countries catch up to the global frontier, more fundamental R&D is going to be increasingly important to stay competitive. Both countries are going to face lots of pressures on IPR from developed countries as well as from the growing base of domestic R&D performers, and the balance is likely to turn towards more protection as more global frontier-shifting R&D is done in these countries.

Seventh it also appears that industrial policy is easier during the catch-up phase than for countries that are closer to the frontier as can be anticipated by the problems over IPR. But it is important for leaders also because the market does not always provide correct signals about dynamic as opposed to static efficiencies.[40]

Finally, the differences between China's and India's strategies imply that there is more than one way to development. However, what they have done is difficult to replicate, and their very success is a challenge for the development of other countries. Finding appropriate ways to insert themselves into the global system is very important. China has done this primarily by becoming part of global manufacturing supply chains controlled by MNCs. India has done this primarily by exports of IT-enabled services and skilled human capital, partly through its growing ICT companies, but also as part of off-shored services to MNCs in manufacturing and services. Therefore we need carefully to rethink what is the most appropriate advice to give other developing countries.

Notes

1. These are based on the International Comparison Program's new PPP figures announced in December 2007 which actually reduced the estimates for GDP by 40% for each of them.
2. However both countries still have large poor populations. In India 80% of the population earns less than $2 a day, in China, 47%.
3. See Pack and Saggi (2006) as well as Cimoli, Dosi, Nelson, and Stiglitz in Chapter 2.
4. However, as important as direct industrial policy has been indirect industrial policy which covers the broader macroeconomic and institutional regime issues including: the rate of investment, the cost of capital, the cost of labor, the exchange rate, physical infrastructure, direct and indirect business taxes, and bureaucratic transactions costs. These can be as important as direct elements of industrial policy in affecting competitiveness or growth and will be addressed as necessary.
5. In 2005 the share of merchandise and service trade in GDP was 63.6% and 7.1%, respectively for China, and 62.4% and 12.8% for Germany. Thus China was more integrated in merchandise trade but less in service trade. Because of the faster rate of growth on both types of trade, China will overtake Germany in both the share of trade in GDP and in the absolute volume of trade by 2010.
6. For a good analysis of China's progressive entry into the global system see Barry Naughton (2007), chapter 16: 'International Trade,' and chapter 17: 'Foreign Investment,' pp. 375–424, in *The Chinese Economy: Transitions and Growth*.
7. Gill and Kharas (2007).
8. Motorola, for example, was forced to develop an extensive training program for the management of the 1,000 largest Chinese state-owned enterprises (Dahlman, Zeng, and Wang, 2007).
9. Ibid.
10. OECD (2007c).
11. This is based on firm surveys in China and India done as part of investment climate surveys carried out by the World Bank, see Dutz (2007).
12. See Dahlman, Zeng, and Wang (2007).
13. Pack and Saggi (2006).
14. Gregory, Nollen, and Tenev (2009).

15. See Baldwin (2006) for an explanation of the two unbundlings—of manufacturing due to the reduction of transportation costs, and of tasks that can be digitized and done at a distance through the Internet.

16. See Pack and Saggi (2006).

17. The role of a strong export orientation in helping to avoid permanent infants has been well developed in the literature. See Westphal, Rhee, and Purcell (1981).

18. Another important element of export promotion in the case of China has been the exchange rate. China has pegged the yuan to the dollar for many years. As the US dollar has been depreciating relative to most currencies since 2001 the value of the Chinese yuan has been depreciating too. There was a one-time 2.5% appreciation of the yuan against the US dollar in mid-2005. Through to the end of 2007 the yuan has appreciated by a total of about 12% vs. the US dollar. Many economists argue that the yuan may be still 20% to 25% undervalued relative to the US dollar. It is also argued that China has an explicit policy of undervaluing the yuan in order to support its dramatic export expansion. The real value of the Indian rupee has been maintained more or less constant since the major devaluation of 1991. However, with the recent boom in foreign and domestic investment in India the rupee started to appreciate in 2007.

19. The average GDP-weighted share of industry GDP was 43% in the countries of Europe and Central Asia (the World Bank grouping of the former Soviet Economies) in 1990, which was before the fall of the Soviet Union. Their share of industry in GDP since the reforms has fallen to 32% as many of those countries are de-industrializing. This is particularly true of Russia where the share of manufacturing has been shrinking as Russia has become more specialized in oil and gas and other natural resources.

20. Naughton (2007), see note 6 above.

21. See Chang (2002) for details on the US.

22. Thursby and Thursby (2006).

23. For an excellent exposition on the new conception of the global company from the CEO of IBM, see Palmisano (2006).

24. It should be remembered that both China and India are nuclear powers, and that China is one of only three countries to have put men in space.

25. This was announced by the OECD in 2007 based on the old PPP conversion figures.

26. Dutz (2007).

27. See Dutz (2007).

28. See Perez (2002) for more on techno-economic paradigms.

29. See Gordon and Gupta (2006) and Singh (2007) for good discussions of the important role of the service sector in India's more rapid growth in the 1990s and the most recent period, and for more details about the linkages, opportunities, and constraints to the growth of the Indian service sector.

30. Gill and Kharas (2007).

31. Freeman (2006).

32. See Blinder (2006).

33. UNCTAD (2004).

34. Infant industry protection and the stealing, copying, and reverse engineering of technology were also critical in the development of the US, Japan, Korea, and Taiwan in their catch-up phase. See Chang (2002).

35. UNCTAD (various years).
36. UNCTAD (2005).
37. See Pack and Saggi (2006), Gill and Kharas (2007).
38. Huang and Khanna (2005).
39. More generally an important lesson is that they have moved more gradually rather than trying to develop a globally integrated market economy all at once, as has been the advice often given by textbook economists For example, this was the advice given to the former Soviet Union by key western advisors such as Andreas Schrieffer and Jeffery Sachs; and institutions, such as the World Bank and the IMF.
40. See Pack and Saggi (2006) and Cimoli, Dosi, Nelson, and Stiglitz (Chapter 2) for more on these issues.

References

Baldwin R. (2006), 'Globalization: The Great Unbundling(s),' paper contributed to 'Globalization Challenges to Europe and Finland,' organized by the Secretariat of the Economic Council, Prime Minister's Office (June).

Bergstein C., B. Gill, N. Lardy, and D. Mitchell (2006), *China: The Balance Sheet*, Public Affairs, New York.

Blinder A. (2006), 'Offshoring: The Next Industrial Revolution?' *Foreign Affairs*, 85(2).

Chang H-J. (2002), *Kicking Away the Ladder: Development Strategy in Historical Perspective*, Anthem Press, London.

Cimoli M., G. Dosi, R. Nelson, and J. Stiglitz (2008), 'Institutions and Policies Shaping Industrial Development: An Introductory Note,' this volume.

Dahlman C. (2007), 'China and India as Emerging Technological Powers,' *Issues in Science and Technology*, Spring: 44–53.

—— D. Zeng, and S. Wang (2007), *Enhancing China's Competitiveness Through Life Long Learning*, World Bank, Washington, DC.

Dutz M. (ed.) (2007), *Unleashing India's Innovation: Towards Sustainable and Inclusive Growth*, World Bank, Washington, DC.

Freeman R. (2006), 'Labor Market Imbalances: Shortages, Surpluses, or Fish Stories?' Paper presented at Boston Federal Reserve Economic Conference: 'Global Imbalances—As Giants Evolve,' Chatham, Massachusetts June 14–16.

Friedman E. and B. Gilley (eds.) (2005), *Asia's Giants: Comparing China and India*, Palgrave Macmillan, New York.

Gill I. and H. Kharas (2007), *An East Asian Renaissance: Ideas for Economic Growth*, World Bank, Washington, DC.

Gordon J. and P. Gupta (2006), 'Understanding India's Services Revolution' in W. Tseng and D. Cowen (eds.) *India's and China's Recent Experience with Reform and Growth*, Palgrave, New York.

Gregory N., S. Nollen, and S. Tenev (2009), *New Industries from New Places: The Development of the Hardware and Software Industries in China and India*, World Bank, Washington, D.C. and Stanford University Press.

Huang Y. and T. Khanna (2005), 'China Rethinks India' in E. Friedman and B. Gilley (eds.) *Asia's Giants: Comparing China and India*. Palgrave Macmillan, New York.

OECD (2006), *Science and Technology Scorecard 2006*, Paris.

—— (2007a), *China Innovation Survey*, Paris.

—— (2007b), *Science and Technology Outlook 2007*, Paris.

—— (2007c), *Education at a Glance 2007*, Paris.

Pack H. and K. Saggi (2006), 'Is There a Case for Industrial Policy: A Critical Survey,' *The World Bank Research Observer*.

Palmisano S. (2006), 'The Globally Integrated Enterprise,' *Foreign Affairs*, May–June.

Perez C. (2002), *Technological Revolutions and Financial Capital: The Dynamics of Bubbles and Golden Ages*, Edward Elgar, Cheltenham and Northampton, Mass.

Singh N. (2007), 'Services Led Industrialization in India: Prospects and Challenges' in D. O'Connor (ed.) *Industrial Development for the 21st Century*, United Nations, New York.

Sturgeon T. and R. Lester (2003), 'The New Global Supply-Base: New Challenges for Local Suppliers in East Asia,' MIT Industrial Performance Center Working Paper 03-001.

Thursby, Jerry and Marie Thursby (2006). *Here or There? A Survey of Factors in Multinational R&D Location*, National Academy of Science, Washington, DC.

Tseng W. and D. Cowen (2006), *India's and China's Recent Experience with Reform and Growth*, Palgrave Macmillan, New York.

UNCTAD (various years), *World Investment Report*, UNCTAD, Geneva.

—— (2004), *Development and Globalization: Facts and Figures*, UNCTAD, Geneva.

—— (2005), *World Investment Report: Transnational Corporations and the Internationalization of R&D*, UNCTAD, Geneva.

Westphal L., Y. Rhee, and G. Purcell (1981), 'Korean Industrial Competence: Where Did It Come From?' World Bank Working Paper No 469.

Winters A. and S. Yusuf (2007), *Dancing with Giants: China, India and the Global Economy*, World Bank and the Institute for Policy Studies, Washington, DC.

World Bank (2007 and 2000), *World Development Indicators*, World Bank, Washington, DC.

13

The Political Economy of Industrial Policy in Asia and Latin America

*Mushtaq H. Khan and Stephanie Blankenburg**

Industrial policy—in the definition we adopt here—consists of sector- and industry-specific policies that aim to direct industrialization in line with some definition of the national interest. Whatever the broader national goals of development are, achieving them is more likely if industrialization achieves rapid productivity growth by absorbing and learning to use the best possible technologies. Indeed, sustaining productivity growth in line with international competitors is a fundamental condition for the sustainability of any industrialization strategy. In this chapter, we focus on some very specific problems of achieving and sustaining productivity growth in late developers as *one* of the conditions for a successful industrial policy. We draw a fundamental distinction between sustaining productivity growth in sectors that are *already* market competitive, where the role of industrial policy is limited to regulating the market to ensure sustained compulsions for productivity growth, or maintaining what the World Bank refers to as the 'investment climate,' and achieving rapid productivity growth in sectors or firms that are catching up to become market competitive *in the future,* for which policies target specific firms or sectors. We argue that for late developers, rapid catching-up with more advanced countries is the key. Merely sustaining market competition in the former role of industrial policy creates poor second-best conditions for ensuring rapid productivity growth, as the latter's policies, which accelerate the absorption and learning of advanced technologies, can deliver much more rapid development possibilities. To engage in this debate, we will refer to the non-targeted, investment climate type of industrial policy as 'weak' or 'horizontal' industrial policy and the type of industrial policy that

* The authors would like to thank Jonathan DiJohn for helpful comments on an earlier draft.

aims to accelerate technology acquisition and productivity growth in particular areas as 'strong' or 'targeted' industrial policy.

The case for horizontal or weak industrial policy is that if the state can create general conditions for investments to be secure and profits to be high, this will attract the most profitable technologies to the developing country. However, with current technological capacities, only low-technology and low value-added activities are profitable. Building up technological capacity can yield very high returns in the future but because the 'risk' of failure is uninsurable, private investors are unlikely to play a big role in making investments in learning at early stages of development. Rapid catching-up therefore requires strong industrial policy, described as *some* strategy of targeted technology acquisition that allows the follower country to catch up rapidly with leader countries. While technical progress is possible along the trajectory set by a market-driven strategy, the climb up the technology ladder is likely to be much slower than with an active technology acquisition and learning strategy.

An obstacle for strong industrial policy is that while there is a credible theoretical case for intervention in late developers to assist them to move rapidly up the technology ladder, the institutional and political problems raised are quite different from those faced by earlier developers. If non-market incentives are required for catching-up, the effective implementation of such strategies typically also requires institutional systems of compulsion to supplement the discipline imposed by the market. When states intervene in markets to assist technology acquisition, by definition, they create new incentives and opportunities, and the market on its own may well not suffice as a disciplining mechanism for the resources allocated by the state. The precise nature of the institutional compulsions required depends on the specific mechanisms through which the state attempts to accelerate technology acquisition and investment. The key point that we want to make is that the diversity of the Asian experience tells us that the *compatibility* of the institutional compulsions that industrial policy strategies require to be successful with the organization and structure of political power in that society may or may not allow the effective enforcement of the requisite strategy.

It is not surprising that the institutions required for weak industrial policy should be substantially different from those required for strong industrial policy. Further, the institutions that are appropriate for strong industrial policy can differ substantially between countries depending on the technology acquisition strategy. In principle, we can imagine a number of different strategies that could create both opportunities and compulsions for rapid and effective technology acquisition and learning. But not all strategies are likely to work in every country, and in some countries, the implementation of *any* strategy is likely to require other preconditions.

The strategy that is most likely to be effectively implemented and enforced in a country can depend amongst other things on its internal distribution of organizational power. If the enforcement of critical conditions required for a particular strategy fails, sticking with industrial policy *may* deliver worse outcomes than abandoning it, even though failed attempts at industrial policy may have useful unintended consequences for building up technological capacity that may later be effective in market-based weak industrial policy strategies. This can explain why (i) many *different* strategies have apparently assisted industrial catching-up in East Asia, and (ii) some countries like India have done better by apparently abandoning strong industrial policy regimes. There is some evidence of a similar experience in Latin America, with some countries achieving growth in new sectors that already enjoy international comparative advantage.

This chapter primarily draws on the evidence from Asia, which provides a wide range of industrial sector policy experiences. Success stories such as South Korea and Taiwan are well known, but Asia also provides examples of moderately successful cases such as Malaysia, where foreign multinationals led industrial upgrading. Asia also provides the interesting example of India in recent years, where after a limited liberalization, high-technology sectors that had already achieved the *capacity* to attain international comparative advantage played an important role in driving economic growth, together with the low-technology sectors in which we would expect a country like India to have comparative advantage. There are also cases of moderate growth in Asia, such as Bangladesh where the abandonment of the industrial policy that patently failed in the sixties and seventies has been associated with growth led by low-technology sectors. The conventional interpretation of the Asian experiences by the World Bank and other international agencies has been to identify the successful industrial policy countries as cases of exceptional state capacity, not replicable elsewhere, and to treat the more moderate cases of growth as the norm, proving the efficacy of abandoning industrial policy and following comparative advantage. This interpretation has been a justification for economic reforms in the vast majority of developing countries that have not performed very well.

Our argument is that this interpretation fails to identify the importance of industrial policy in achieving rapid development in the successful Asian countries in a number of important respects. First, although the role of the state in the successful developers is increasingly recognized, the role of industrial policy in the successful developers is underplayed. Secondly, the distinctive feature of successful East Asian developers was *not* that they had exceptional state capacities that are not achievable anywhere else. Rather, the distinctive feature of the success stories was that the particular variant of industrial policy that each tried was *compatible* with internal power balances that allowed the state to create incentives and compulsions in critical areas. Thirdly, the policy conclusion that less successful countries should come away with is *not* how to abandon vestiges of their failed industrial policies at the fastest possible rate, but to identify the type of industrial policy that is implementable in their particular context given critical internal and external political constraints. In many cases, the feasible industrial policy may yield less dramatic results than in the most spectacular of the Asian cases. In others, one must address some of the critical political constraints in order to allow implementation of even limited industrial policies. In both cases, the long-run results are likely to be better than if policy only attempted to create general market conditions for industrial growth using the good governance or good investment climate approaches.

The subsequent argument makes the following points. In the first section, we look at the central argument that makes state assistance so critical in late developers trying to catch up. While there are many reasons why the state has to play a role in the acquisition or development of technology, we only look at the simplest and yet most powerful one to develop our case. This is the problem of organizing learning-by-doing and the uninsurable risks that arise during this process. The second section discusses in similarly simple terms a number of different strategies of coordination and support that states in different Asian countries have used to promote catching-up. The third section looks at our core issue of the compatibility of the institutions of catching-up with the organization of political power and discusses a number of variants in different Asian countries and in Latin America that help to explain the very different experiences of a number of different Asian countries and the difference between them and Latin America. We argue that the coincidence of liberalization with a growth spurt in some Asian countries can be better explained by our alternative analysis that identifies some of the limits of the previous industrial policy regime in these countries. We also extend this analysis to Latin America and argue that the failure of import-substituting industrialization across Latin America, and the consequent liberalization policy shock led to a similar process of shifting to technologies that were already profitable given technical capacities as well as to widespread technological downgrading.

Catching up and the state

Catching up with advanced countries requires rapid and sustained *productivity growth*, which, this volume argues, depends on the creation of new technologies. Markets by themselves may have a role in better resource allocation, but are not sufficient to ensure that productivity growth will be rapid unless appropriate incentives and compulsions exist to induce the creation of new technologies or, in the case of developing countries, learning to use existing technologies effectively. It is possible to analyze these incentives and compulsions in terms of the existence and management of specific rents.

The existence of rents for innovation or to allow learning creates the incentives for particular activities, but we also require institutions that can manage these rents to ensure that they do not last for too long, and that non-performers do not succeed in retaining their rents. If these conditions hold, the appropriate rents and rent-management systems can ensure productivity growth through technological progress or learning (Khan, 2000a).

In late developers, the role of non-market institutions has been critical in explaining success. As mentioned in Cimoli et al. (2009), this volume, the historical evidence suggests that a market economy is necessary but not sufficient for rapid catching-up. If that is so, too much emphasis on developing the conditions for efficient markets can make us lose sight of the other institutional conditions critical for economic success. This is the problem with the focus on good governance and good investment climate conditions in developing countries, which focus primarily on creating conditions for investors exploiting existing comparative advantages. The puzzle for the market-driven view of growth is that England was *not* the area of the world with the most developed markets. Why did rapid productivity growth associated with modern capitalism first take off in England and not in China, India, the Middle East, or other parts of Europe, which at different times were more advanced than England in terms of markets and technology? Marxist historians in the West have put forward two sorts of explanations, and the divide between them is still relevant for understanding contemporary debates on the determinants of and obstacles to the transition to high-productivity economies in developing countries today.

The first explanation argued that capitalism was essentially the *freeing up of market opportunities,* with production growth accepted as an extension of the market economy (Dobb, 1946; Sweezy, 1950; and North, 1990). For instance, feudal obstacles to markets, such as barriers to labor, capital, and the free sale of land, were first overcome in the Western European transition to capitalism because internal and external factors weakened these feudal restrictions and allowed the market to grow. The modern neoclassical economics position, and indeed the US-led international policy consensus generally championing the spread of democracy as a precondition of development have roots here. The policy conclusion that follows is that if political, cultural, and institutional obstacles to competitive markets can be removed, economic growth will accelerate.

In contrast to this position, the argument more closely associated with Marx's own analysis points to the specific institutional conditions of early capitalism that ensured rapid productivity growth in England. The market had existed for thousands of years without leading to rapid productivity growth, so something much more special must have been involved in the relatively rapid growth associated with the development of English capitalism. Rapid productivity growth in England was associated with the emergence of a new system of property rights (a 'mode of production') that required the imposition of a new structure of rights and institutions that *forced productivity growth* in England in a way that did not happen elsewhere.

If this view is correct, it has enormous significance for current debates on the institutional conditions for rapid productivity growth in developing countries. Dynamic economies are unlikely to emerge simply by removing obstacles to the market and trying to make markets more efficient. Rather, we have to ask what rights and institutions are necessary in the context of the contemporary world economy for rapid productivity growth, and we need to examine how these can be introduced. This perspective suggests that development involves a *social transformation* and opens up the possibility that far from market-enhancing strategies being sufficient, the state may have to play a leading role in organizing this social transformation.

Classical capitalism versus late development

Even if we agree that the establishment of capitalism in the early developers required important non-market processes, it is not clear that the property rights and institutions that were appropriate for the early developers are appropriate for late developers. In early developers' 'classical capitalism', the creation of a property-less class of workers and a class of asset owners competing amongst themselves to survive was sufficient to ensure relatively rapid productivity growth. A similar structure of rights in contemporary developing countries may not have the same effect, as developing countries must *catch up* to advanced countries with significantly higher productivity. A catching-up country under free trade would likely be stuck with low-technology production. Though developing countries have much lower wages, they also have much lower productivity in producing high-technology products, due to the absence of appropriate labor and management skills that their schools and universities cannot teach. These skills must be learned on the job, a process described by economists as learning-by-doing (Arrow, 1962; Khan, 2000a). This problem can condemn countries to very slow progress up the technology ladder.

The importance of learning is progressively less the lower the sophistication of the technology involved in production, and the wage advantage of the developing country is more likely to kick in for low-productivity technologies where the unit cost of production in developing countries is likely to be lower than with *potentially* high-productivity technologies. As a result, the developing country appears to have a 'comparative advantage' in producing low-technology products. The developmental state literature (White, 1988 and many others; Aoki, et al. 1997; Woo-Cumings, 1999) and case studies of countries such as South Korea (Amsden, 1989) and Taiwan (Wade, 1990) show that in this context, successful catching-up has required a range of institutions and interventions that are quite different from classical capitalism. The challenge for late capitalism is to address the problem that competitiveness and productivity are both a function of the technology embodied in capital equipment as well as social institutions that impose incentives and compulsions for achieving rapid learning. If these institutions and the associated social compulsions are missing, productivity could be low even with high-technology machinery, and low wages by themselves will not attract investment. However, as we shall see, these incentives and compulsions can vary significantly across countries, even if we look at the limited number of successful Asian developers of the last 50 years (Khan, 2000a).

These considerations mean that the social transformation in late developers is likely to be quite different from that of the early developers. Not only would late developers have to organize a different type of primitive accumulation, to take account of the fact that the scale and capital-intensity of high-productivity production was now much greater, they would also have to organize catching-up strategies to acquire high-productivity technologies that would eventually allow them to compete with advanced countries in high-wage industries. We will see that this imposes new challenges to the state during the social transformation required in late developers.

Strategies of catching up

The conventional explanations of why some countries have been more successful in sustaining high-technology investments have focused on infrastructure and education, but, though important, these aspects of industrial policy do not take us far enough. Investment in infrastructure must simply keep pace with growth: countries such as Taiwan and South Korea in the sixties or China today faced persistent shortages of infrastructure but managed to keep investing at the appropriate pace. So, while infrastructure in general is important, pre-existing levels of infrastructure cannot fully explain why some countries have been much faster in moving up the technology ladder. Similarly, while education and skills can be a constraint in the long run, most developing countries in Asia have a surplus of skilled labor, and many even suffer from the emigration of skilled workers, suggesting that the failure to attract new investment in these countries cannot be explained by shortages in skilled labor.

Infrastructural and educational explanations miss a key factor that determines whether high value-added industries will be successful. That is, *learning* to use high-technology machines, and setting up the internal and external systems that are required to maximize productivity, *takes time*. This means that unless there is some institutional system that can create both the incentives and the compulsions for rapid learning to take place, investment in high-productivity sectors is likely to fail. Since private investors know this, they are unlikely to invest in high-technology industries in a country that lacks the institutions that can induce and compel rapid learning.

The basic problem can be shown using the very simple diagram shown in Figure 13.1. It shows that domestic productivity in the developing country is initially so low, that if it imports the potentially high-productivity foreign technology, it can initially have *higher* domestic marginal costs (line DCE) than the international price PP' set by marginal costs in the advanced country. But this is only because productivity is low because of the absence of learning, not because it is permanently going to be low. Given the lower wages in the developing country, if the advanced technology was used at even a fraction of the productivity achieved in advanced countries, domestic marginal cost could fall to ABQ, allowing the developing country to compete in international markets. How does the developing country overcome this hurdle? The simplest way to acquire the learning is the classical infant industry strategy of providing a conditional subsidy or 'learning rent' for a fixed period, with the condition that the subsidy will be withdrawn at the end of the period, or even earlier if performance is poor. In our diagram, a subsidy of ABCD to the domestic industry allows it to produce OQ_1 of output.

This subsidy need not be a direct financial transfer but could be a combination of hidden benefits that allows the new industry to start 'learning-by-doing'.

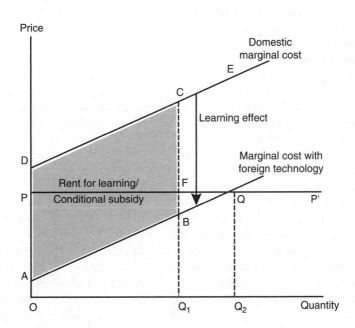

Source: (Khan 2000a: Figure 1.8).
Figure 13.1. Conditional subsidies and rents for learning

If learning can be successfully induced, marginal cost can be reduced to the advanced-country level or even below, given the wage advantage of the developing country. But in the short run, these strategies have a cost, because they allow static inefficiency by allowing a loss-making industry to survive. The short-run cost will only be worthwhile if the subsidy or benefits provided to allow learning actually succeed in generating long-term productivity growth and the country can enjoy higher living standards as a result. In fact, most developing countries that attempted these strategies in the past failed to achieve this productivity growth, and their infant industry strategies ultimately failed. But a few did succeed, and these countries graduated to become the newly industrializing countries especially of East Asia.

The widespread failure of developing countries to catch up with advanced countries is at least partly attributable to the failure of their institutions to compel productivity growth in learning industries, which requires institutions that can manage provided rents and provide credible compulsions and conditions for rapid learning. Thus, the institutions for inducing learning must both provide the incentives for learning and have the credibility to impose costs and sanctions on industries and firms that fail to achieve the required rate of learning. If the state does not have the credibility to withdraw a subsidy when there is underperformance, there will be a short-run cost as well as a permanent cost, because infant industries will never grow up. These conditions are particularly demanding because the optimal period of rent allocation for learning will vary from sector to sector, and across countries depending on the initial capacities of capitalists, managers, and workers.

Figure 13.2 shows that a conceptually optimal period of rent allocation exists for any particular sector and country, but for state institutions to discover this through trial and error requires fairly demanding conditions. Critical conditions for success include a capacity of the state pragmatically to *monitor* and make judgments about performance, and the capacity to *reallocate the subsidies and assets* of non-performers. Inevitably, mistakes are likely to be made, even in the most dynamic countries, but fortunately, all that we require is that state institutions can learn from their mistakes and rapidly correct them. But this in turn requires critical *political capacities*; in particular, the organization of power in society must be compatible with the rent management that state institutions are trying to implement. Otherwise, rent reallocations are likely to be blocked by groups or factions that would lose out from such reallocations, and if this happens frequently enough, the optimal rent-allocation targets are not going to be discovered by any form of trial and error.

However, direct subsidies to infant industries have not always been the route through which late developers have climbed up the technology ladder. Asian countries have used a number of other mechanisms to direct rents to high-technology industries to ensure rapid progress up the technology ladder, and in each case, success has required appropriate institutions to manage these

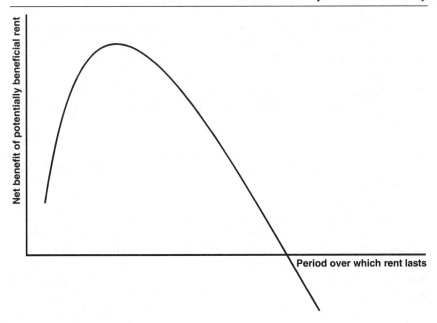

Source: based on (Khan 2000a: Figure 1.7).
Figure 13.2. Rent-management with learning rents

rents, and a corresponding political settlement that allowed this management to be implemented. For example, in the Taiwanese case, state involvement in technology included licensing from abroad, with the state paying for some of the overhead costs of technology acquisition and providing licensed technology to domestic producers at a lower cost. The rent management required in this case was the ability to reallocate licenses and to ensure that the search for technologies driven by the public sector did not get captured by specific interests in manufacturing. A combination of political factors allowed the Taiwanese state to achieve this rent management, as outlined in Wade (1990), and discussed further below. In Malaysia, technology acquisition depended to a significant degree on attracting high-technology multinationals as well as the credibility of the state in providing rents that were implicitly conditional on technology transfer. In this case, rents were available to high-technology foreign investors, but conditional on their ability to bring in superior technologies not otherwise available. The mechanisms through which rents were offered involved prioritization in infrastructure provision, the subsidization of training, and the protection of multinational profits by ensuring that redistributive demands within the country would be satisfied without affecting multinational profits (Jomo and Edwards, 1993; Khan, 2000b).

With the advent of the WTO, organizing direct subsidies to infant industries will be more difficult in the future. Therefore, indirect subsidies, and other benefits for learning industries, and industries bringing in high value-added technologies must be considered. Even industries in advanced countries receive massive implicit subsidies in the form of differential taxation, prioritized infrastructure provision, public subsidies that provide them with an educated and healthy workforce.

States possessing the capacity to manage the rents that are involved in the learning process will inevitably appear different from states whose capacity is limited to maintaining the horizontal competitiveness of markets. In the next section, we will examine some of the diverse ways in which states have managed learning rents during the catching-up period in successful late developers. Here, we present some evidence showing that the crude cross-country data do not support the hypothesis that economic growth in developing countries has been dependent on the achievement of a good investment climate defined by stable property rights, a good rule of law, low corruption, and low expropriation risk. These variables are summarized in Knack and Keefer's consolidated property rights index. Plotting this crudely against the economic growth rates of countries for the 1980s and 1990s (in Figures 13.3 and 13.4) shows that the advocated positive relationship is based on a misreading of the data. While there is a positive relationship when we pool all countries, a closer look at developing countries shows that rapidly growing (converging) and less rapidly growing (diverging) developing countries both

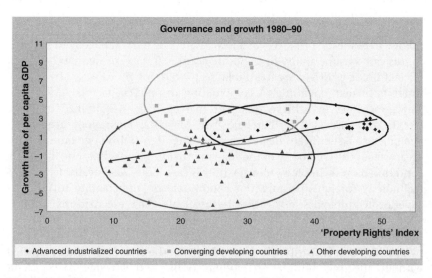

Figure 13.3. The weakness of investment climate explanations of growth 1980–90

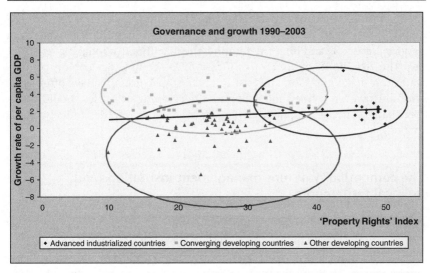

Figure 13.4. The weakness of investment climate explanations of growth 1990–2003

display an almost identical range of variation in terms of their investment climate defined in the conventional way. However, because the number of countries in the converging group was typically smaller, the regression line appears to have a positive slope, even though the goodness of fit is typically very weak (cf. Figure 13.3 and 13.4). The lesson to be learned here is not that investment conditions defined in the conventional sense are unimportant, but rather that rapidly growing countries had institutional capacities for catching up that are not captured in the conventional theoretical models.

Identifying and developing rent-management capacities on a country-by-country basis must be a critical part of any moves towards setting up a developmental state that can organize a strategy for catching up. It follows that assisting developing countries to develop appropriate rent-management capacities can be an important way to help raise living standards more rapidly. While developing countries are often advised to let the market take its course, it is worth noting that rent-management capacities are recognized as extremely important in advanced countries. When the US courts considered whether to allow Microsoft to continue making monopoly profits or to break it up, regulators effectively considered the effects of Microsoft's rents on its rate of innovation and that of its competitors. These are sophisticated state capacities, and while mistakes are occasionally made, advanced countries do not rely on the market alone to ensure rapid innovation and productivity growth. The need for state rent-management capacities is if anything even greater in developing countries. Here the challenge is not the acceleration of innovation but rather the acceleration of learning. However, as in advanced countries, states in developing countries have rent-management systems of varying capacity, and these determine the likelihood of making mistakes and the likelihood of timely rectification. Of course, developing country states can make mistakes, and past interventionist attempts have often gone wrong. However, it does not follow that developing countries should therefore abandon the development of rent-management capacities and rely on the market.

The compatibility of rent-management institutions and political settlements

Our core argument is that managing rents for technology acquisition is not just constrained by state capacities, but also and often primarily by political constraints that prevent specific strategies of rent management from being implemented. The complexity here is that a number of quite different strategies of rent management can be observed in the Asian context, and we argue that this explains why a group of countries with quite different internal political configurations have performed well. Our explanation for this is that while their internal political configurations were different, each of these configurations allowed the effective implementation of different and quite specific strategies of rent management for technology acquisition. At the same time, other Asian countries did far worse when they tried to implement rent-management strategies that were superficially similar to the strategies in one or other of the successful countries, but these strategies were in fact incompatible with their specific internal political configurations. In these cases, which were more numerous, the rents intended to create incentives for technology acquisition became damaging rents that in some cases were much worse in their effect than if they had never been created.

We would like to emphasize an advantage of looking at industrial policy through the lens of rent management: while some rents are critical for enhancing growth prospects in developing countries, others are very damaging (Khan 2000a provides a discussion of different types of rents). From a policy perspective, potentially growth-enhancing rents can become growth reducing if the rent-management capacities of the state are missing. For instance, potentially dynamic infant industry subsidies can become growth reducing for the economy if they are allocated without proper conditions and without the state capacity to monitor and withdraw subsidies in underperforming industries. The configuration of rights and powers that enables emerging capitalism in a developing country to catch up with that in advanced countries is in our view the modern equivalent of the system of compulsion that was created for early capitalism by the distribution of property rights brought about by the primitive accumulation described by Wood (2002). Our argument is that the additional institutional conditions for compulsion, the rent-management strategies discussed earlier and necessary in late developers, can themselves vary significantly given different internal political configurations of power, and their relative success depends on the 'compatibility' of these institutions with these pre-existing distributions of power.

Table 13.1 points out that when we look at the difference between more and less successful examples of learning rents, the critical differences lie in the rent-management capacities of the state. The same is true of redistributive rents, the transfers and subsidies that maintain political stability in all countries. If transfers and subsidies to redistribute incomes are managed well by the state, the result is political stability. If they multiply out of control, the result can be economic stagnation. This too is obvious, but it is often not recognized that effective rent-management capacities are critical for the success of the social transformation that developing countries are experiencing.

Following this framework, we examine actual rent-management strategies in different Asian countries and we look for the institutional and political conditions that allowed the effective implementation of the specific strategy. Conversely, in countries where technological upgrading was relatively much slower, we look at the attempted rent-management strategies and the specific institutional and political capacities that may have prevented the proper implementation of the strategy. This is particularly useful when the rent-management strategies in the successful and less successful countries were superficially quite similar.

Table 13.1. Rents and corresponding rent-management capacities

Type of rent	Rent-management	Economic outcome
Monopoly rent	Created in response to special interest group pressure	Negative
Successful learning rents (infant industry subsidies, prioritization of infrastructure, temporary monopolies)	Benefits conditional on performance, institutional and political capacity for monitoring and rent-withdrawal	Very positive
Failed learning rents	Powerful groups can protect rents, state lacks capacity independently to allocate rents, or monitor or withdraw rents from underperforming enterprises	Very negative
Viable redistributive rents	Extent of redistribution effectively controlled, lobbying for these rents kept separate from management of learning rents	Mildly negative but positive if benefit of political stability included
Damaging redistributive rents	Growing redistribution, unstable coalitions, redistributive coalitions protect inefficient learning rents	Very negative

South and East Asia—diverse industrialization experiences

SOUTH KOREA 1960s TO 1980s

In the South Korean case, technological catching-up was led by large holding companies, the chaebol, who were given various forms of protection and subsidies to allow them to engage in learning and thereby catch up with advanced countries. In a sense, this was the classic infant industry strategy. For this system of rent allocation to work, the state had to operate a rent-management system that involved the setting of export and other performance targets, and making pragmatic judgments about performance based on observed results. The success of the South Korean rent-management system depended critically on a balance of power between the chaebol and the state that prevented inefficient firms from protecting their subsidies if the state decided to withdraw them. The absence of social factions such as the intermediate class factions observed in South Asia or factions led by the landed elites denied the chaebol the opportunity of offering to share rents with powerful social forces in exchange for their support in protecting inefficient rents (Kohli, 1994; Woo-Cumings, 1997; Khan, 1998, 1999). The state on the other hand had no incentive to support inefficient capitalists because it could get bigger economic benefits (and kickbacks) by supporting the dynamic capitalists and weeding out the less dynamic ones (Amsden, 1989; Khan, 2000b). This route of social and economic transformation would be difficult to replicate in many contemporary developing countries where capitalists can easily buy themselves political protection by paying factions within or outside the state to protect their inefficient rents even if other state agencies try to remove them. Moreover, explicit subsidies to large companies like the chaebol would be difficult to organize in the contemporary consensus against explicit subsidies, supported by the WTO and other organizations. Thus, far from being the paradigmatic case of industrial policy, the South Korean success was based on rather unusual conditions. It depended on the compatibility of a specific rent-management strategy with an internal distribution of factional power within the groups that could potentially have offered to make alliances with individual capitalists in exchange for a share of the rents they were getting from the state.

MALAYSIA 1970s TO 1990s

In the Malaysian case, technology acquisition was accelerated by providing incentives for high-technology multinational companies to invest in Malaysia and provide backward linkages to domestic producers. In stark contrast to the experience of many other developing countries, the multinationals that came to Malaysia were mainly high-technology companies. This was not an accident. Malaysia was offering incentives that most developing countries would find very difficult to offer, and even more difficult to manage with credibility without multinationals free-riding on the hidden subsidies and failing to bring in and transfer advanced technologies. The incentives the Malaysians offered took the form of prioritized provision of infrastructure to suit the needs of foreign investors, and the credible protection of foreign investors from internal redistributive demands. The latter was particularly important because Malaysia's internal redistributive needs were entirely met by taxing domestic capitalists. The political arrangements that were arrived at in the early seventies through the National Front government credibly resolved Malaysia's internal redistributive conflicts through internal redistribution. Investors could easily perceive that Malaysia's claim that multinational rents and profits would be protected was a credible promise. Contrast this with the unstable political situation in most developing countries and we can easily see why the typical developing country would not have any bargaining power with multinationals over the type of technology they were offering to bring in. It is not surprising that multinationals in the typical developing country bring in mundane technologies to produce relatively low-quality consumer goods for the domestic market. These technologies offer rapid cost recovery and expose the multinational to the lowest degree of political risk from large sunk costs and lengthy local learning horizons. But equally, for such a strategy to work and for multinationals actually to deliver, the state would also have to have a credible threat of withdrawing privileges from specific companies that failed to meet expectations. The centralized organization of UMNO, the dominant political party in Malaysia, prevented the construction of alliances between particular multinationals and factions within the state whose support could be purchased to protect low-technology investments. These Malaysian conditions were similar to the credible threat that the equally centralized KMT could use in Taiwan in the 1950s to ensure that foreign partners in joint ventures did not free ride on the incentives provided by the state (Wade, 1988). The Malaysian state also ensured that domestic learning would take place by insisting on technology transfer to subcontractors and on local content. But in the end, the Malaysian state could do all this because the platform that Malaysia offered to multinationals was much better than that offered by most of its competitors. Thus, Malaysian success too was based on very specific political conditions that a) allowed multinationals to be offered very attractive incentives; b) credibly protected them from internal redistributive threats; c) prevented them from free-riding. These conditions included the isolation of the predominantly ethnic Chinese capitalists in the domestic society who could be taxed to maintain domestic political stability and who could then be rewarded by ensuring their participation in the backward and forward linkages opened up by multinational investment. At the same time, the centralized organization of the politically dominant intermediate classes ensured that rent allocation to multinationals could be managed without descending into wasteful and unnecessary transfers to foreigners without any technological payback (Jomo and Edwards, 1993; Khan, 2000b). Clearly, it may be difficult for other countries to repeat the Malaysian experience without internal political conditions that allow them to achieve similar things.

TAIWAN 1950s TO 1980s

In the Taiwanese case, an important element of technological progress was the rapid acquisition of advanced technologies by small-scale industries in the private sector. This was driven by a very specific rent-management strategy that deployed the state to acquire high-productivity technologies through state-led technology licensing and subsidizing the provision of this technology to the private sector. At the same time, key intermediate inputs were provided to the private sector through a well-run and efficient public sector. The rent management involved here was in the coordination of acquiring the most appropriate technologies. Once these technologies were made available to the private sector, learning was enforced by ensuring that a relatively large number of firms in the private sector would have access to these technologies, and competition would favor the firms that were better at raising productivity rapidly through learning (Wade, 1990). For this rent-management system to work, the state needed to be able to distance itself institutionally and politically from a competitive private sector, so that rent-seeking by individual firms within this sector did not affect state decisions on technology policy. This too can be difficult to repeat in other countries where the state is not artificially separated from the private sector as it was in Taiwan. Because of historical accidents, the Taiwanese state was led largely by mainland Chinese following their expulsion from mainland China in 1949 and the business sector was composed largely of local Taiwanese. This political distance proved to be very useful in operating this rent-management system because local business interests could not influence state-led technology acquisition to favor particular groups at the expense of national interests, nor could any group use political power to acquire monopoly power in the domestic market. At the same time, the centralized organization of the KMT and the ability of the leadership to override all internal factions (in a context of martial law throughout this period) prevented coalitions from protecting inefficient capitalists or public-sector enterprises.

INDIA 1950s TO 1980

The Nehruvian strategy of catching-up through licensing investments in the private sector, the provision of implicit subsidies to key sectors through protection and subsidized inputs, and technology acquisition driven by significant investments in the public sector had elements of many of the strategies followed in East Asia. Yet the results of the Indian experiment were far less significant in terms of growth of output and productivity, and the attempt was almost entirely abandoned in 1991. But a decade or more before that, the licensing system had effectively collapsed. From 1980 onwards, Indian growth took off led by niche private-sector activities that began to exploit the capacities built up by Indian industrial policy in ways that the industrial policy regime itself could not achieve. If we look at the period prior to 1980, the lackluster results of the Indian strategy can largely be explained in terms of a failure of rent management by the Indian state. Despite the Indian state being aware of its failure at least as early as the mid-sixties (as the Dutt Committee that reported in 1968 outlined in detail), licenses were being used by big business groups to acquire monopoly power and excess capacity, and attempts to reallocate licenses were consistently failing. In addition, in the public sector, subsidies were effectively captured by privileged managers and workers as redistributive rents rather than serving as learning rents that could accelerate catching-up. Ultimately, domestic consumers paid the price by being forced to buy relatively low-quality products in protected domestic markets. A number of political factors in India made these rent-management strategies unworkable. First, business groups in India could rapidly acquire autonomous political power by forming alliances with any of the many numerous political factions that dominated the Indian political process. The availability of a large number of possible protectors of inefficient rents in India in turn reflected the fragmented nature of the intermediate class factions, and their availability for protecting and capturing rents that they saw as redistributive rents. The failure to construct disciplined national organizations that could separate learning rents from redistributive rents is the immediate manifestation of the fragmented clientelism that characterizes Indian politics (Khan, 1998, 2000b). A similar linkup of public-sector employees with broader political factions made restructuring of the public sector just as difficult. Thus while the Nehruvian system was very effective in building up a base of heavy industries and human capital to service these sectors, it failed to generate rapid productivity growth and quality improvements that could have made this industrial policy system viable.

BANGLADESH AND PAKISTAN 1960 TO 1970

Pakistan and Bangladesh provide an example of a somewhat different South Asian rent-management strategy in the sixties that was superficially closer to the South Korean system. But once again, the problem was that this rent-management system was incompatible with the internal power balances that eventually made it impossible to discipline non-performers. In the end, this industrial policy strategy also proved to be unsustainable. The institutional strategy consisted of a combination of import barriers and directed subsidies to a small number of big business groups with an explicit aim of acquiring technology rapidly and turning the Pakistan economy (which included

Bangladesh at that time) into an export-oriented one. Initially, the Pakistan economy was a star performer in the early sixties, with growth rates of output and exports matching those of the East Asian economies. But once the easy import substitution was over and pressure had to be created on the new industrialists to improve productivity and quality, the system ran into trouble. The Pakistani state discovered, like the Indian one, that subsidy recipients in industry had formed alliances with politically powerful factions and realloca-tions of resources were not possible. This was despite the fact that Pakistan was at that time formally a dictatorship (Khan, 1998, 1999, 2000b). Nevertheless, the power of factions led by the intermediate classes could not be overridden, particularly as these factions began to challenge the pro-capitalist strategy of the state by mobilizing broad social groups on ideologies of socialist populism in both East and West Pakistan. Rational capitalists could not but form mutu-ally beneficial alliances with particular factions whereby the capitalist and the faction shared the state-created rent, and the faction protected the capitalist from rent reallocation even though learning and productivity growth was not proceeding according to plan.

INDIA AND BANGLADESH AFTER 1980

While the Indian subcontinent struggled with industrial policies, their imple-mentation and efficacy became increasingly compromised. A series of reforms began in the subcontinental countries that proceeded along different routes towards liberalization. In India, the process formally took off only after the 1991 balance of payments crisis, which was seized on by the reformist Rao government to push through a gradual reduction of the scope of licensing and a gradual reduction of tariff protection. However, India's growth had already taken off around 1980 *before* much of these relatively minor changes had been announced. This, together with the fact that the scope of the liberalization was relatively minor, and could not explain the significant acceleration in growth that had taken place, led economists to suggest that the most import-ant factor was the change in the policy stance of the state. The collapse of industrial policy by the early eighties and the growing number of policy statements in favor of the private sector apparently created new confidence and animal spirits that could explain the acceleration of private investment that triggered the growth spurt (Rodrik and Subramanian, 2004). As Rodrik (2004) later also points out, this is an incomplete explanation because it ignores the capacities that were built up during the industrial policy stage that private entrepreneurs were later to exploit when market opportunities emerged. Thus, India's global comparative advantage in outsourcing, soft-ware, and in some sectors of generic pharmaceuticals did not just emerge overnight once licensing disappeared. Rather, these critical capacities had been built up precisely during the industrial policy period. But, the licensing system, while it failed to provide compulsions for productivity growth across the economy, inadvertently also prevented sectors that had acquired some capacity from taking off under private initiative. Liberalization, or rather the collapse of the licensing system that preceded it, thus worked by allowing niches of capacity to take off even while the overall industrial policy structure had failed.

To a lesser extent, a similar story was unfolding in neighboring Bangladesh. Here the industrial policy regime initiated by Pakistan had collapsed as early as 1971. There followed an interlude of socialist populism that led to a deepening of the crisis as the dominant clientelist factions sought to capture rents by nationalizing the entire manufacturing sector. Liberalization began under military governments, in this case through privatizations and a gradual cutting back of tariff protection as in the Indian case. As in India, the growth spurt that began in Bangladesh in the 1980s was driven by the private sector developing new niche markets. In this case, given the much lower levels of industrial capacity that had been built up during the industrial policy period, the drivers of growth were low-technology sectors like garments, cosmetics, and pharmaceuticals aimed at the domestic market and low-technology primary-sector exports like shrimps. Despite the very vulnerable technological base of the new growth, a decade of rampant primitive accumulation had resulted in the growth of a broad-based emerging small capitalist sector, and these new capitalists have been driving a bottom-up variant of capitalism that has produced growth without rapid technology acquisition.

The preceding analysis has some important implications for the analysis of the liberalization-led growth in India and to a lesser extent in Bangladesh. Rodrik (2004) rightly points out that Indian growth in particular cannot be understood without factoring in the capacities that were built up during the industrial policy phase. However, our analysis suggests that it would be wrong to interpret this as an indication of the success of Indian industrial policy. It is exactly the reverse. The failure of the industrial policy regime to sustain itself meant that capacities were built up that could not be utilized, and it was the collapse of the industrial policy regime that has allowed the exploitation of these capacities in new niche activities. University graduates staffing call centers are the most dramatic indicators of the potential waste that has now become manifest. But more serious is the fact that with the withdrawal of state strategies of subsidizing potential high-productivity sectors, the growth of future capacity is now highly vulnerable. This does not mean that Indian growth is doomed to decline. If growth continues rapidly in such a large economy, multinational-led technology transfer could begin, and could sustain growth in the foreseeable future. But growth could have been even higher and more broadly based if a viable industrial policy could have been implemented. The policy challenge is to identify the sources of industrial policy failure in countries like India and to devise technology acquisition strategies that are compatible with pre-existing political configurations. Alternatively, such an analysis can also open up domestic political debates about how to change political configurations through political activity (as in Malaysia in the late seventies) that may then allow the implementation of other variants of accelerated technology acquisition strategies.

The Asian experience thus provides a range of institutional approaches to industrial policy as well as quite different outcomes. We have tried to make sense of these outcomes by looking at the compatibility of the rent management required under each of these strategies with the evolving political configuration of each country. The relative power of different groups and factions that could intervene in the effective implementation of industrial policy explains for us much of the variance in both industrial policy approaches and their relative success. Some of the important points discussed above are summarized in Table 13.3.

Latin America—a resounding failure?

Unfavorable comparisons of the Latin American industrialization experience with that of East Asia are commonplace (e.g. Chan, 1987; Lin, 1988; Fishlow, 1989; Gereffi, 1989; Gereffi and Wyman, 1990; Harberger, 1988; Jenkins, 1991; Palma, 2004; Ranis and Orrock, 1985; UNCTAD Trade and Development Report 2003). This is not surprising: With the exception of Ecuador and Paraguay that did not begin to industrialize until the late 1960s, Latin America embarked on industrialization many decades before the East Asian NICs. Yet, despite initial successes that saw some of the core countries, such as Brazil and Mexico, forge ahead of the East Asian NICs in the 1960s and into the 1970s, the pace of Latin American industrialization has now fallen far behind the few successful East Asian cases of catching-up. If, between 1945 and 1980, Latin American GDP grew on average at 5.6 percent per annum, and its manufacturing output at 6.8 percent per annum, (Cárdenas, Ocampo, and Thorp, 2000; Haber, 2005), the picture has changed drastically ever since. In the last two decades of the twentieth century, manufacturing value added grew by 9.1 percent in East Asia, 6.5 percent in South Asia, 4.8 percent in the Middle East and North Africa, 1.7 percent in sub-Saharan Africa, and 1.4 percent in Latin America and the Caribbean.

Table 13.2 summarizes basic comparative indicators of growth and productivity performance in the two regions.

Even a cursory glance at the data suggests that Latin America experienced a rupture in its industrialization process in the early 1980s, precisely at a time at which the East Asian NICs managed to transform their initial catching-up efforts into a dynamic and sustainable process of capitalist expansion and development. As Weisbrot notes, '[t]o find a growth performance in Latin America that is even close to the failure of the last 25 years, one has to go

Table 13.2. GDP per capita and per worker relative to the US, gross fixed capital formation in East Asia and Latin America 1960–2004

	Proportion of US GDP per capita (current international $)			Proportion of US output per worker (constant 1996 prices)			Gross fixed capital formation (average growth rates, constant 2000 US $)	
	1960	1980	2000	1960	1980	2000	1965–1980	1981–2004
East Asia								
Hong Kong	0.23	0.58	0.78	0.19	0.46	0.80	6.9	3.8
Singapore	0.17	0.50	0.80	0.21	0.56	0.67[1]	14.2	4.8
Malaysia	0.19	0.24	0.26	0.20	0.28	0.43	11.5	5.1
South Korea	0.12	0.22	0.42	0.15	0.28	0.57	17.9	8.0
Taiwan	0.11	0.27	0.55	0.13	0.32	0.60[2]	n/a	n/a
Thailand	0.09	0.13	0.19	0.07	0.12	0.20	9.6	4.7
China	0.05	0.05	0.11	0.04	0.04	0.09	8.9	12.2
Philippines	0.17	0.15	0.11	0.17	0.20	0.13	7.9	1.3
Latin America								
Argentina	0.60	0.50	0.33	0.62	0.66	0.40	5.1	0.5
Uruguay	0.46	0.36	0.29	0.48	0.46	0.38	8.4	−2.7
Venezuela	0.35	0.39	0.20	0.83	0.55	0.27	4.9	0.7
Mexico	0.33	0.38	0.27	0.44	0.54	0.38	9.4	1.2
Chile	0.31	0.26	0.29	0.38	0.36	0.39	2.4	4.3
Peru	0.26	0.24	0.13	0.33	0.36	0.16	3.6	1.0
Brazil	0.19	0.30	0.22	0.24	0.39	0.30	6.4	0.7
Colombia	0.19	0.20	0.16	0.27	0.31	0.18	[12.9]*)	[4.6]*)
Paraguay	0.15	0.20	0.13	0.24	0.31	0.16	14.2	−1.8
Bolivia	0.17	0.15	0.08	0.22	0.22	0.10	2.1	2.1
.Ecuador	0.17	0.22	0.14	0.20	0.32	0.17	8.4	0.3

[1] Most recent figures from 1996, [2] 1998; *) Figures for Colombia in current US $.

Sources: Calculations from Alan Heston, Robert Summer, and Bettina Aten, Penn World Tables Version 6.1., Centre for International Comparisons at the University of Pennsylvania (CICUP), October 2002 and from World Development Indicators, World Bank, April 2006.

back more than a century, and choose a 25-year period that includes both World War I and the Great Depression' (2006: 2).

This rupture has mostly been attributed to two main factors: first, heterodox and orthodox economists alike criticized the process of heavy (or second-stage) import-substituting industrialization in core Latin American countries, mostly initiated in the 1960s, for having created undesirable and unsustainable macroeconomic imbalances. The mostly heterodox Latin American critics of *cepalismo*—the industrialization strategy advocated by Prebisch and CEPAL (Comisión Económica para America Latina) at the time—scrutinized what they regarded as a distorted and dependant pattern of industrial growth resulting from an incomplete or wrong-headed industrial strategy. *Dependistas* and nationalists alike lamented the bias of industrial development towards the capital-intensive production of consumer durables, underpinning and entrenching inequitable consumption patterns, and the increasing domination of manufacturing by foreign TNCs. The latter were seen not only to siphon off profits freely to their advanced home economies, but also increasingly to expand their activities downstream into the production of wage goods in competition with already hard-pressed domestic producers, rather than to have their technological potential leveraged in favor of the formation of viable national capital good sectors (e.g. Colin, 2004). In addition, both heterodox and (neo-) liberal commentators grew increasingly worried about the monetary and balance of payment crises associated with the second phase of Latin American import-substituting industrialization policies (Cardoso and Fishlow, 1992). Differently from their heterodox colleagues, neo-liberals attributed these latter distortions not to mistakes and imbalances in the chosen industrial strategies, but to the very existence of any such strategy: *cepalismo* had been mistaken in its pessimism about the limited developmental potential of world trade that had grown rapidly after World War II, and Latin America was paying the price for having tampered with free markets through excessive over-regulation and ineffective protectionism, engendering unproductive rent-seeking, corruption, and macroeconomic instability.

Second, external factors are widely regarded to have played a crucial role in the difficulties and decline of the Latin American industrialization experience (e.g. Singh, 1993). Other than much of continental Western Europe after World War II, and East Asia—especially South Korea and Taiwan—in the 1950s and 1960s, Latin America never collected any windfall Cold War funding or soft loans from the US. Quite the contrary—what US-based funding went to Latin America systematically served to undermine the kind of structural changes, such as thorough land reforms, that were essential to successful transformations in East Asia (Kay, 2002). Nor were advanced economies prepared or in a position, in the 1940s, to grant the same market access to light-manufacturing consumer products from Latin America that, two decades later, they provided for very similar export products from what were to become the East Asian NICs.

It is true that had the timing of the Latin American industrialization process been different, and had Latin America occupied a geostrategic frontier position in the Cold War rather than constituting the 'backyard' of the anti-communist US, we might perceivably now be contemplating a success story rather than pondering over the reasons for failure. Similarly, the internal criticisms of the path of forced industrialization in much of Latin America in the post-World War II period certainly pinpointed important problems.

Even so, these observations leave a number of pertinent questions unanswered: Why, for example, have Latin American economies been unable to mobilize their resources under *any policy and political regime* to the same extent as their East Asian counterparts? As is well known, the prolonged and certainly varied Latin American industrialization experience has been characterized by much lower savings rates than in East Asia (Gavin, Hausmann, and Talvi, 1997): the average Latin American savings rate in the period 1960–2005 peaked at 22.5 percent in 1977, compared to performances of 35 percent and above since the early 1980s in the first-tier East Asian NICs, and since the mid 1990s in the second-tier East Asian NICs, such as Malaysia and Thailand.[1] Yet, at one time or another, the majority of Latin American economies adopted very similar industrialization policies to those that played out so favorably in the East Asian NICs: vertical policies to select strategic targets (winners) and concomitant nationalizations, high import tariffs followed by import licensing regimes, a supplementary arsenal of supporting policies including selective and subsidized credit access, tax exemptions, favorable access to foreign exchange, regulations on national content requirements, stimulation of technology transfer and complementary FDI, and export subsidies. If the heterodox critiques of *cepalismo* are correct, and this produced a distorted and dependent pattern of industrial growth, why did the same policies produce such a different outcome in Latin America compared to East Asia? If, on the other hand, liberalization policies were the superior policy choice, as neo-liberal commentators have claimed and many Latin American governments of the 1980s and 1990s have chosen to believe, why did the liberalization shock not yield better results? If South Korea and Taiwan were particularly favored by external factors, such as massive US aid flows, easy market access for manufacturing exports, and political tolerance of radical land reforms, why have second-tier East Asian NICs, such as Thailand and Malaysia that could not count on these factors, recently been more successful than any Latin American economy?

The approach developed in this chapter suggests that the success or failure of rent-management strategies for industrialization is largely determined by the *compatibility* of technological and institutional strategies for late development with political constraints arising from inner-societal power constellations as well as from transnational—external—influences. The East Asian NICs succeeded because their various rent-management strategies to promote industrialization did not lead to political destabilization. In the South Asian subcontinent, a political configuration favorable to highly fragmented clientelist alliances between industrialists and the organizationally powerful middle classes led to the breakdown of more or less classic infant industry strategies.

In Latin America, less fragmented, but no less powerful alliances between strong landed elites and emerging industrialists led to a similar breakdown. Moore (1966), in his seminal work on different routes to industrialization and modern (capitalist) transformation in Western Europe and Asia, characterizes in particular the Japanese and German route to industrialization as an authoritarian/fascist revolution from above. The essential characteristics of this route are the persistence of strong landed elites and the continued use of political rather than market-based mechanisms to ensure an adequate supply of (agricultural) labor and the concomitant failure of emerging industrialists to achieve political emancipation from landed oligarchies on their own.

Instead, the state takes on the task of mediation between landed and industrial interests and, eventually, that of social transformation. In the early stages of industrialization this takes the form of semi-parliamentary 'oligarchic' systems of government. In the later stages of industrialization, the emergence and rapid growth of an urban working class and a growing requirement of state and administrative modernization lead to a 'revolution from above' through inclusive populist-authoritarian regimes, whether of a fascist or a conservative-military nature that 'oversee' capitalist transformation and the eventual decline of landed elites through co-option as well as repression of working-class interests and their middle-class allies. Apart from Germany and Japan, Greece, (to some extent) Italy, Spain, and some Balkan countries are examples of this transition route (Mouzelis, 1986). Latin America shares many of these characteristics, but is different in important aspects: Its colonial history as an exporter of natural resources meant that its landed elites were comparatively much stronger than their European or Japanese counterparts. Importantly, this meant that, other than in many successful late developers, land reforms did not precede industrialization, but were only initiated half-heartedly at late stages of industrialization with the primary goal of creating larger internal markets (Kay, 2002). Furthermore, the timing and external environment of industrialization in Latin America were different: working-class opposition to 'oligarchic' rule and authoritarian transformation emerged later and was weaker than in Europe, not least because of later and dependent industrialization, but was much more premature relative to the formation of an urban middle class. This, in turn, was at least partly a consequence of the minimalist and mercantilist state structure Latin America inherited from colonial domination, which impeded, or at least slowed down, the evolution of a modern and professional state apparatus (Rueschemeyer, Huber Stephens, and Stephens, 1992; Mahoney and vom Hau, 2005).

Together, these and other political factors meant that Latin America, rather than undergoing a successful 'revolution from above', experienced unstable political cycles, alternating between urban populism—of both an authoritarian as well as a more more truly popular kind—and narrowly elitist clientelist regimes. Whereas urban populism refers to attempts by the state to resist the power of landed elites through the mobilization and co-option of working-class and middle-class interest in support of capitalist industrialization, elitist clientelism in the Latin American context refers to alliances that aligned the interests of industrialists, parts of the urban middle classes and landowners against perceived threats from the subaltern classes, including urban and agricultural workers as well as peasants (Mouzelis, 1986). In the South Asian subcontinent, big business groups could form alliances with middle-class factions that, while shifting and fragmented across multiple ethnic, religious, tribal, and political lines of division, ultimately allowed monopolists to build up fairly reliable power bases. While these alliances undermined the state's capacity to impose a national infant industry strategy, they at least rendered possible relatively successful ad hoc private-sector strategies of capital accumulation in niche markets, profiting from previous state-led investments. By contrast, in Latin America, the century-old stalemate between strong landed interests, on the one hand, and gradually consolidating urban and industrial interests, on the other, prevented a *stable* power base for private-sector industrial accumulation from establishing itself. As industrialization proceeded to the more large-scale and capital-intensive second stage of import-substituting industrialization, neither populist states nor clientelist *pactos* could, in the longer term, respond effectively to the growing demands on coordination, planning, and adaptation capacities required for a high-value added large-scale technological strategy. Populist state control as well as clientelist alliances increasingly disintegrated through fractionalization.

BRAZIL 1930s TO 1980s

Following the detrimental impact of the Great Depression on Brazil's coffee-based agrarian export economy, the country embarked on a strategy of state-led industrialization that lasted until the early 1980s. Of the Latin American NICs, the Brazilian industrialization strategy and experience, although much longer drawn out, comes closest to that of South Korea. In both cases an early phase of light import-substituting industrialization, directed mainly at domestic markets, was rapidly followed by a strongly state-controlled 'Big Push' strategy that sought to promote heavy industrialization through the allocation of learning rents to target sectors and industries. In both countries, industrial transformation unfolded under the auspices of exceptionally autonomous states, governed and controlled for most of the relevant periods by authoritarian military regimes. Many of the policy tools employed were similar, including initial high import tariffs, import licensing, directed credit policies, and direct state investment in industry and supportive infrastructure. Initially, at least, results also were comparable: In the period 1900–1987, Brazil was the largest growing economy in the world (Maddison, 1993), with the highest growth performance following a massive build up of productive capacity since the 1950s, in the energy, capital goods, and heavy industry sectors. Between 1950 and 1980, growth rates of up to 10 percent per annum were not exceptional.

There are however important differences with the case of South Korea: Above all, the superficial similarity between the two states in terms of their high degrees of autonomy from society was, in fact, of a very different kind: The South Korean state was not only autonomous, but also very much 'embedded' through close links with the private business sector, ensuring efficient information flows and bargaining mechanisms between these (Evans, 1995; Chang and Cheema, 2001). By contrast, the Brazilian state was autonomous without any such 'embeddedness' in that it represented a centralized, often well-organized, but isolated structure without strong anchors in any section of society. Like the shell of an empty egg, it would crack whenever sufficient pressure came to bear on it. Whereas the South Korean state successfully wedded economic with political exclusion and repression of the 'subaltern' classes whenever industrial transformation caused social tensions, and thus gained a reputation of credible commitment to national and international industrial interests, the Brazilian state was never in a position to wean domestic industrial interests off their fallback alliance with regional oligarchies and their clientelist networks. The reason is, of course, that these networks existed, in the first place, while in South Korea Japanese colonialism had basically eliminated the power of landed elites. In Brazil, private business interests were, at times, co-opted by the state through the appointment of business leaders to cabinet positions; but sustained direct channels of lobbying, bargaining, and interest representation between private business associations and the state remained very fragmented and tied to sectoral rather than national levels (Ross Schneider, 2004). Without such direct 'embeddedness' with the industrial elite, the Brazilian state, autonomous, repressive, and controlling as it became, was left in a technocratic limbo from which to try to promote industrial policies, forever frustrated by stalemates between oligarchic-clientelist networks of landed and industrial elites, on the one hand, and popular demands, that over the long drawn-out process of a relatively early industrialization became increasingly vocal.

COLOMBIA 1930s TO 1980s

Colombia provides a useful contrast to Brazil in the Latin American context. As in Brazil, a very labor-intensive and largely coffee-based agrarian export economy had, by the late nineteenth century, created powerful landed elites operating local and regional clientelist networks that dominated politics and the state. Similarly to most other Latin American economies, Colombia underwent successive stages of easy and heavy import-substituting industrialization, lasting from 1930 to1945 and 1945 to 1967, respectively. Differently from Brazil and many other Latin American experiences, though, the industrialization process remained largely private-led with the state playing a much more indirect role than, in particular, in Brazil, Argentina, and Mexico. The main reason was that following two, even by Latin American standards, very violent periods of civil warfare (The War of the Thousand Days 1899–1902 and La Violencia at the end of the 1940s), the two main clientelist parties, representing a mix of landed and growing industrial interests, took effective control of the state. While tensions between urban industrialists, landed trade and business interests and, to some extent, the military, remained and produced shifting power balances, domestic capitalists, often descended from European immigrants, gradually emerged as the main clientelist 'patrons', running their own networks and influencing state policy-making. Thus, other than in Brazil, private business associations developed relatively strong national channels of direct lobbying and bargaining with the state (Ross Schneider, 2004). This somewhat resembles the Thai process of private capitalist-led industrialization 'from below', that was dominated by a combination of relatively passive industrial policies, a domination of rent-seeking processes by competition between emerging capitalist factions, and a technology acquisition strategy that focused on low-value added, labor-intensive technologies with low adaptation and coordination costs (Khan, 2000b). Industrial policy and state-created rents, in this context, serve the limited purpose of initial support for relatively small-scale private accumulation processes, but are then ideally bid down through private-sector competition.

As in Thailand, an important feature of the Colombian polity post-1950s has been that redistributive factions with effective access to the state were limited to elitist groups, many of which were capitalist-led and -controlled, rather than by organizationally powerful non-capitalist middle- and working-class factions. In both countries, clientelism was thus much less fragmented than, for example, in India, and the redistributive pressure on the state from non-capitalist interest groups less than in more populist and inclusive Latin American states. One indicator of the lower incidence of redistributive claims in the Colombian economy are the, by Latin American standards, relatively low rates of inflation that have also remained fairly stable over the past 50 years (World Bank, 2006). This industrialization 'from below' has, however, been less successful in Colombia compared to Thailand, for a number of reasons: First, competition between capitalist-led factions has been less intensive in Colombia than Thailand. This is, at least in part, explained by the much larger weight of landed elites and interests in the Colombian clientelist settlement. This made entry into high-rent markets more difficult for industrial newcomers who, in contrast to older incumbents, often did not have long-established ties with the landed oligarchy and were thus at a disadvantage in terms of their political bargaining power vis-à-vis the state. Second, the larger role of landed interests in Colombia also meant that the state's capacity to allocate rents to industrialists was more limited by the need to find compromises between industrial and landed interests. Third, key to the relative efficiency of the Thai rent-seeking system was the focus on low value-added labor-intensive technologies that did not require long learning or strong centralized planning efforts. While this was also the case in Colombia during the first phase of import-substituting industrialization in the 1930s and 1940s, the Colombian state did embark, in the 1950s and 1960s, on the promotion of more large-scale capital-intensive industries, such as petrochemicals, basic metals, machinery, transport equipment, and chemical products. This attempt at heavy industrialization was more short-lived in Colombia than in many other Latin American states, and in 1967 was replaced by a mixed strategy of import-substitution, technology acquisition through joint ventures with foreign investors, and export promotion (Ocampo, 1994; Vejarano, 2002). But the earlier attempt at promoting capital-intensive heavy industries was highly unsuitable to the limited rent-allocation and -monitoring capacity of the Colombian state and undermined the relatively low competitiveness of capitalist-led factions even further. In addition, the state's reliance on FDI to promote technology transfer was even less than in Brazil matched by its ability to impose conditionalities conducive to high-productivity technology transfer from TNCs. Despite a moderately successful 'assembly regime', introduced in 1969, that made concessions to foreign 'assemblers' conditional on a rise in domestic components and technical assistance to local suppliers of parts and accessories (mainly in the automobile and electrical appliances industries), the 'Malaysian route' certainly was not open to the Colombian state. Apart from the inability and unwillingness of the clientelist elites to prevent alliances between foreign investors and domestic factions, a fourth and final factor was relevant in this respect: The absence of populism in Colombia and the high degree of exclusion of subaltern and middle classes from the political settlement did not mean that the state was not affected by contestation from outside this settlement. Instead, political contestation by excluded sectors of society took the form of (mostly) rural guerrilla warfare that, while largely confined to remote regions with little government presence, increasingly undermined the political stability of the elitist–clientelist pacts. While elements of such violent contestation 'from outside the political settlement' are also characteristic of Thailand, the extent and longevity of rural warfare in Colombia, as well as the expansion of the drug trade outside the control of the state, have increasingly compromised the state's ability to attract foreign direct investment as an important conduit of technology transfer.

Overall, the Colombian industrialization process was much slower and 'lackluster' compared to that in Brazil: on average, savings rates increased, at best, to only half of those achieved in Brazil between 1950 and 1980, as did the share of manufacturing in GDP. Similarly, average GDP per capita growth rates remained in the 2–3 percent bracket (Maddison, 1992). By contrast, the collapse of state-led industrial policy, when it came, was much less dramatic than in Brazil.

PERU 1950s TO 1980s

A brief mention of Peru serves to highlight a third constellation of power in Latin America that has probably been the most detrimental to the prospects of successful capitalist-led industrial development. Ever since the nineteenth century, this has seen a coalition of heavily foreign-dominated mining and agricultural export interests at loggerheads with a large unionized native workforce. In the case of Peru (as well as Bolivia), the divide between these two sectors is very sharply defined, in racial as well as geographical terms, with a racially mixed middle class playing only a minor role. This constellation of powerful (national and foreign) landed and mineral export interests, on the one hand, and an early mass radicalization *before* the emergence of a viable domestic industrial accumulation process, could not have been less favorable to a state-led catching-up industrialization project. When in 1968, under the combined pressure of popular discontent with foreign ownership, rising costs, limited supplies of some natural resources, and population pressure on land, the military regime of Velasco came to power with a radical agenda of import-substituting industrialization and agrarian in form, it stood little chance of political survival: High import tariff protection, tariff exemptions on imports for manufacturing industries, and general tax exemptions did induce a strong rise in domestic investment and aggregate demand, but they also contributed to a rising public-sector deficit—the fiscal benefits paid out to domestic industrialists between 1971 and 1975 amounted to 92% of total internal financing of industrial investment—and inflationary pressures. Ultimately, the Velasco government lacked allies amongst local industrials whom it distrusted because of their close ties with foreign companies and the landed elite, and it could therefore only opt for nationalization. This not only over-stretched the limited planning and coordination capacities of the Peruvian state (Thorp, 1991)—as late as 1962, taxation in Peru had been contracted out to private firms and until 1969 central bank directors were appointed by private business associations (Cameron and North, 1998)—but it was a doomed strategy given strong US interests in Peru's export sectors. The fate of Allende's Chile did not leave much room for doubt in this respect. While some progress was made with regard to the belated land reform, the powerful opposition of foreign capital and landed elites meant that the only alternative path to late industrialization, given the weakness of domestic capital—a socialist revolution from below—could not succeed. Velasco's regime factionalized and was eventually toppled by a military coup in 1975. No active industrial rent-management regime has been pursued since.

LATIN AMERICA AFTER LIBERALIZATION (1980–2000)

Once state-led catching-up industrialization in Latin America had failed—not necessarily in terms of economic performance during the duration of active industrial policy regimes, but rather in the sense of the compatibility of these regimes with given political settlements outlined above—Latin America underwent a radical liberalization shock. Even though it goes without saying that there were considerable differences in the design, execution, and the impact of these policies between different Latin American countries, the fairly radical shift towards neo-liberalism was sufficiently uniform to allow us to abstract from country particularities and to treat Latin America as a region for the purpose of this brief section.

In these general terms, high levels of external debt and large-scale capital flight—themselves a manifestation of the incompatibility of institutional and technological strategies with political settlements—had made Latin America more vulnerable than most other developing regions to international policy changes, such as the Volcker shock. While the 1980s were dominated by comprehensive free-market reforms, trade liberalization, deregulation, and privatization, the 1990s saw the emergence of passive industrial policies aimed at improving international competitiveness through regional trade integration, mitigating market failure through the provision of public goods, and stimulating productivity growth through the promotion of industries with positive technological externalities (Peres, 1997; Kosacoff et al. 1998; Melo, 2001).

By now, it is clear that the outcome of this policy change has been very disappointing. On the positive side, there were successes in terms of macro-economic stabilization and significant increases in export performances (e.g. Taylor, 2000; Palma, 2005a; Dutrénit and Katz, 2005). More important from a development perspective, however, are the clearly negative effects on productivity growth and domestic technological capabilities (as well as an already highly unequal income distribution), indicating that the increase in exports in many countries has failed to translate into backward linkages to the domestic economy and has, instead, occurred alongside a trend of de-industrialization (see Table 13.2 above; Palma, 2005a and 2005b). In other words, Latin America has returned to its underlying static comparative advantages of natural resources and unskilled labor with detrimental effects on its productivity and growth performance. More specifically, the change in Latin America's productive structure combines specialization in fairly capital-intensive resource-processing industries, mainly in Argentina, Brazil, Chile, and Colombia with a predominance of assembly industries, in particular in Mexico and some Central American countries (Peres, 1997; Dutrénit and Katz, 2005). This has come at the expense of high-technology sectors, such as electronics, semiconductors, and computers (with the possible exception of the medium-technology automobile industries of Argentina, Brazil, and Mexico and the aerospace and computer projects in Brazil) and some more traditional labor-intensive industries (Peres, 1997).

While static efficiency gains did occur, through the weeding out of blatantly inefficient companies (e.g. Ffrench-Davis, 2000 and 2002 for Chile) in the context of greater import competition, and additional resources were freed up through the reduction of some state activity, these additional resources clearly did not translate into productivity increases based on accelerated learning-by-doing. Thus, Cimoli and Katz (2004) show that the major mechanism through which liberalization is argued, by mainstream economists, to entail productivity as opposed to mere (one-off) efficiency gains—the availability of cheap(er) capital goods imports—achieved the direct opposite: In Argentina, Brazil, Chile, Colombia, and Mexico, *all* of five central divisions in the manufacturing sector (metal-working industries, automobiles, food processing, natural-resource processing, and labor-intensive manufacturing industries) actually shrank during the period of liberalization. Ocampo (2004) adds the observation that the process of technological downgrading through the availability of cheaper capital imports was reinforced by a 'disarticulation' (or fragmentation) of the production base into a small group of world-leading, mostly foreign-owned, companies, on the one hand, and a large and increasing number of firms engaged in low-productivity and low-skill activities that by now absorb about 60 percent of the urban workforce. Importantly, there are virtually no technological spillover effects from world-leading to low-skill sectors, or any other macroeconomic linkage effects (Ocampo, 2004; Gwynne 2004 for Brazil; and Palma 2005a for Mexico). Where technological progress is taking place this remains insulated in 'de-linked' or 'disarticulated' MNC-dominated firm clusters that not only fail to engage in significant technology transfer, but partly destroy hitherto productive and viable domestic firms in the supplier chain (e.g. auto-parts industry in Brazil). The case of Mexico's maquila industry is perhaps the prime example, in Latin America, of linkage-less manufacturing (export) growth (Palma, 2005a).

More specifically, Palma (in Chapter 8) provides ample evidence for the fact that the main effect of liberalization, across virtually all of Latin America, has been to reinforce Latin America's commodity bias in the absence of any attempts at 'Schumpeterian' dynamic upgrading into higher-technology, higher-value added *processes* and/or *products*. Put differently, technological improvements have been limited to certain basic commodities, such as copper concentrates in Chile or iron in Brazil, but no attempts have been undertaken to *upgrade* to *different processes* (copper smelting) or product (steel). In fact, in the cited example for Chile, technological downgrading (from smelting back to concentrates) took place. Instead, where high levels of world competitiveness have been achieved within the given production process of commodities, horizontal diversification into other low-value added commodities has taken place. This provides the explanation for export-driven growth (recovery) since the late 1980s/early 1990s, not a 'Schumpeterian' shift to manufacturing exports (especially if one discounts the much-hailed Mexican maquila case as a form of 'fake' upgrading to manufacturing with little or no backward linkages).

The Latin American picture provides a stark confirmation of the argument that catching-up economies, if exposed to international market pressures without any accompanying system of incentives and compulsion to ensure that these market pressures are translated into learning and technology rents, may end up downgrading their technological capabilities. The social costs of this process are also only too well known: the other side of the coin of low inflation and supposed macroeconomic stabilization across all Latin American countries with fiscal deficits below 2 percent of GDP over the past 20 years (with the exception of Brazil and Argentina for particular reasons) has been widespread urban unemployment, increased income inequality, and high and increasing segmentation of labor markets.

Differently from the Asian experience, the Latin American experience thus highlights a situation in which *similar* institutional approaches to industrial policy lead to *differing* outcomes. Not only were the import-substituting industrialization policies of the pre-1980s differently successful, but the recent reactions to the high social and economic costs of the neo-liberal shock therapy applied to virtually all Latin American economies also led to different outcomes: while some countries, such as Chile, Colombia, most Central American economies, and, to some extent, Mexico, remain committed to a neo-liberal policy agenda, at least in purely economic terms, the high social cost of these policies led to regime changes in Venezuela, Bolivia, Ecuador, and, most recently, Paraguay. As with the Asian experience, we argue that these differing outcomes are best explained by analyzing the compatibility of rent-management strategies with underlying political settlements and configurations of power balances. This also means that the new, largely state-led industrial policy regimes in Venezuela and Bolivia, amongst other Latin American countries, may fail, unless they manage to break through the firm grip that constellations of clientelist *pactos* have had on these economies for the best part of two centuries.

Conclusions

In this chapter we have examined the compatibility of the institutions of catching-up with the organization of political power and discussed a number of variants in Asia and Latin America that help to explain their very different experiences. Table 13.3 summarizes these key features of our argument.

We argued that the coincidence of liberalization with a growth spurt in some Asian countries can be better explained by our alternative analysis, which identifies some of the limits of the previous industrial policy regimes in these countries. Extending this analysis to Latin America we argued that the failure of import-substituting industrialization across Latin America, and the consequent liberalization policy shock, led to a similar process of shifting to technologies that were already profitable given technical capacities as well as to widespread technological downgrading.

There are many features which differentiate the Far Eastern and Latin American experiences. First, South Korea and other East Asian NICs proceeded from the first 'easy' stage of import-substituting domestic industrialization to an intermediate phase of 'export-substituting industrialization', replacing their agricultural and resource-based exports by manufactured consumer products, before moving on to the final and heavy stage of industrialization. By contrast, Brazil switched directly from domestic light industrialization to domestic heavy industrialization, skipping the 'export-substituting' phase. This was not for want of trying: subsequent Brazilian governments offered a wide range of export subsidies to domestic and transnational manufacturing producers, and some success was achieved in the 1970s with the share of

Table 13.3. Compatibility of rent management and political configurations

	Industrial policy institutions (rent-management strategy)	Corresponding political configuration	Economic outcome
South Korea 1960s	Targeted learning rents	Limited political power of intermediate class factions to protect inefficient capitalists	Rapid growth and capitalist transformation
Malaysia 1980s 1990s	Public sector and MNC-led technology acquisition	Powerful intermediate classes but centrally organized after 1980 Centralized transfers delink redistributive rents from learning rents	Rapid growth and capitalist transformation
Indian subcontinent 1960s 1970s	Targeted learning rents, public sector technology acquisition	Powerful and fragmented intermediate class factions protect inefficient rents Learning rents regularly become redistributive rents	Many infant industries fail to grow up Moderate growth and slow pace of transformation
Indian subcontinent 1980s 1990s	Liberalization and slow withdrawal of subsidies for learning	Powerful and fragmented intermediate classes remain Growing political fragmentation	Growth led by niche sectors. Higher growth than before but limited to already existing technological capacities
Latin America 1950s to 1980s	Targeted learning rents, public sector and MNC-led technology acquisition	Alternating political cycles of populist regimes and oligarchic clientelism Learning rents rapidly become redistributive rents	Many infant industries fail to grow up Initial rapid growth undermined by foreign debt and balance of payment crises
Latin America 1980s onwards	Rapid liberalization, market-friendly competition policies	'Old' clientelist elites remain powerful, growing political fragmentation Resurgence of populism	Export growth but low productivity growth Technological down-grading and reliance on traditional comparative advantage

manufacturing exports in overall exports reaching levels of 30–50 percent and including some more capital-intensive industries (automobiles, chemicals, aircraft, electrical machinery). But this performance decidedly lags behind that of East Asian NICs and even South Asian economies with shares of 70–80 percent at similar stages of industrialization. Consequently, Brazil lacked an important comparable source of foreign exchange earnings. Second, Brazilian industrialization was not led by large domestic holding companies, as was the case of South Korea. Rather, it came to be led by a combination of state-owned enterprises (SOEs) and TNCs (including joint ventures) (e.g. Gereffi and Wyman, 1990). Despite fairly stringent requirements imposed by the state on joint ventures by TNCs with both SOEs and private capital, the Brazilian state could not successfully impose the Malaysian route: It did not have the overall political credibility nor sufficient effective control of domestic capital to deter TNCs from free-riding through alliances with particular factions. Nor was the Brazilian state in a position to follow the Taiwanese route of state-led technology acquisition in SOEs combined with an efficient technology transfer to a competitive private sector of medium-sized firms, since its relationship with the private sector was certainly characterized by a high degree of structural autonomy, but not therefore also the same degree of *political* autonomy that would have allowed it to impose a competitive structure on industrials without alternative power bases. Put differently, while the Brazilian state employed elements of all successful—South Korean, Taiwanese, and Malaysian—strategies, it could not carry any of these through to their conclusions. Third, the failure, for all these reasons, to mobilize domestic resources to the same extent as the East Asian NICs, by raising the saving rate and earning foreign exchange through manufacturing exports, entailed a growing reliance on foreign borrowing and debt, with a concomitant high vulnerability to the volatility of international, and in particular US, financial capital flows and policy-making.

These differences, we have argued above, have their deeper roots in the underlying political economy.

The three Latin American paths outlined above highlight essential obstacles to late industrial development in Latin America. The institutional approaches to industrial policy were not fundamentally different from those of East Asia. Rather, they consisted of different combinations of successful elements of strategies employed in different East Asian countries (South Korea, Malaysia, and Thailand). As in East Asia, the outcomes were nevertheless different, reflecting different degrees of compatibility of the rent-management strategies adopted and the evolving political configurations in each country. Similar stories to that of Brazil unfolded in Argentina, Uruguay, and Mexico; Chile and Bolivia are closer to the case of Peru; and Venezuela, Colombia, Paraguay, and Ecuador constitute hybrid cases. It goes without saying that the differences in the exact power configurations, and the consequences of their precise incompatibility with institutional approaches to industrial policy are often huge, especially from an inter-Latin American comparative perspective. Thus, for example, in Argentina populism took a less authoritarian turn than in Brazil, mainly because landed elites were less reliant on the supply of cheap agricultural labor, and the urban working classes mobilized earlier than in Brazil. Mexico differed fundamentally from Brazil (and Argentina) in that the traditional oligarchies were overshadowed by an all-inclusive state structure, emanating from an early revolution 'from below', with clientelist networks evolving within this state structure rather than from outside. Similarly, Chile was less dominated by foreign capital than was Peru and a much closer link between landholders and urban entrepreneurs had evolved, mainly in the form of multiple holdings and closer kinship relations. At the same time, radical mobilization was even more virulent than in Peru, not least because of faster urbanization. Finally, Venezuela constitutes a hybrid case between Brazil and Colombia, in that its state became much more inclusive than Colombia's with the consequence that it embarked on more challenging state-led industrialization projects than Colombia and factionalized with a more destructive impact on the effectiveness of industrial policies than in Colombia (DiJohn, 2004). This said, there was, in all its different manifestations, one main obstacle to East Asian style catching-up development in Latin America: the colonial inheritance of strong landed elites and early urbanization. Whether these landed elites allied themselves with emerging industrial interests (as in Brazil and Colombia) or not (as in Peru), or whether early urbanization led to the emergence of radical mass parties with a potential to undermine indigenous capitalist development (as in Peru, and in Colombia until 1949, but not in Brazil), it was ultimately the interplay between these two forces that determined the fate of late industrialization in Latin America. It is worth noting that the only East Asian economy whose performance resembles that of the poorer Latin American countries—the Philippines—shares many of the characteristics that have beset Latin American industrialization, primarily strong landed elites and very belated land reforms.

The hallmark of Latin American liberalization policy—apart from increased income inequality—is a creeping process of technological downgrading, rather than Schumpeterian dynamic upgrading to higher-value added *processes* and/or *products*. In fact, in some countries like Chile, technological downgrading (from smelting back to concentrates) took place. A higher degree of international competitiveness has, instead, been achieved through horizontal diversification into other low-value added commodities. The recent optimistic outlook for exports and overall growth in Latin America (ECLAC, 2004) confirms this trend: it is explained mainly by increased international demand (in particular from China) for low-value commodities, combined with favorable commodity price developments.

From the perspective developed here, this outcome is not surprising: The removal of obstacles to market opportunities does not automatically deliver high(er) productivity growth (other than perhaps in Ricardian commodities) or create dynamic capitalist economies in late developers. Instead, we have argued, what is needed is a system of compulsion that, at least initially, replaces the role played by the market mechanism in early developers to compensate for high private risk and to help overcome structural socio-political obstacles to capital accumulation. To function in this sense, such transitory systems of compulsion must be based on *mutually compatible* technology acquisition strategies and political settlements. Under import-substituting industrialization, formidable obstacles to such compatibility in Latin America meant that (i) the considerable growth in size of industry did not translate into productivity increases to the same extent as it did in some East Asian NICs (e.g. Reynolds 1970 for Mexcio; Díaz Alejandro 1970 for Argentina) mainly because state-created rents deteriorated into redistributive rather than learning rents, and (ii) the political alliances underwriting state-led industrialization factionalized.

Liberalization did nothing to tackle these obstacles in Latin America's various political settlements, described above. Instead, it reinforced existing structural and political obstacles to catching-up industrialization and their main symptoms, namely a weak and risk-averse indigenous industrial class and a domination by foreign capital that operates in its own rather than Latin America's interest. Other than in India, liberalization has thus not even led to a 'niche strategy' based on the exploitation of high-productivity assets created under state-led industrialization by local capital, but has instead resulted in technological downgrading and decline by sending local entrepreneurs scrambling for cover in 'niches' of low-risk, low value-added horizontal diversification of resource-processing industries and leaving the exploitation of high-productivity assets, inherited from import-substituting industrialization to foreign interests. In addition, the failure of liberalization in addressing the underlying socio-political factors that have impeded Latin America's industrialization from the start is confirmed rather starkly by the current stand-off between resurging transformational projects in Latin America: Chavez's populist route in Venezuela, Alan Garcia's and Alvaro Uribe's oligarchic clientelist alternatives in Peru and Colombia, and Evo Morales' renewed attempt at a 'revolution from below' in Bolivia.

Note

1. There have been exceptions to the 'eternal Latin American ceiling' of a 20% savings rate: Brazil in the 1950s–1970s, Argentina in the 1960s and 1970s, Chile in the 1990s all registered savings rates of between 25% and 30%, with oil-exporting Venezuela achieving an average savings rate of over 40% between 1950 and 1975. However, whether or not exceptional circumstances such as the discovery of oil in Venezuela

came into play, even those above-average performances all show a downward trend over time in stark contrast to the sharp upward trend in the East Asian NICs since the 1980s. Nor did they translate into a *sustainable* upward trend of GDP per capita growth rates despite promising performances in Brazil, Mexico, and Colombia in the 1970s (Maddison, 2003).

References

Amsden, A. H. 1989. *Asia's Next Giant: South Korea and Late Industrialization*. Oxford: Oxford University Press.

Aoki, M., H. K. Kim, and M. Okuno-Fujiwara (eds). 1997. *The Role of Government in East Asian Economic Development: Comparative Institutional Analysis*. Oxford: Clarendon Press.

Arrow, K. J. 1962. The Economic Implications of Learning by Doing, *The Review of Economic Studies* 29 (3): 155–73.

Brenner, R. 1976. Agrarian Class Structure and Economic Development in Pre-Industrial Europe, *Past and Present* 70: 30–75.

—— 1985. The Agrarian Roots of European Capitalism, in Aston, T. H. and C. H. E. Philpin (eds), *The Brenner Debate: Agrarian Class Structure and Economic Development in Pre-Industrial Europe*, Cambridge: Cambridge University Press.

Bresser-Pereira, L. C. 1984. *Development and Crisis in Brazil 1930–1983*. Boulder, Colorado, US: Westview.

Cameron, M. A. and L. L. North. 1998. Development Paths at a Crossroad: Peru in the Light of the East Asian Experience, *Latin American Perspectives* 25 (5): 50–66.

Cárdenas, E., J. A. Ocampo, and R. Thorp. 2000. Introduction, in: E. Cárdenas, J. A. Ocampo, and R. Thorp (eds), *An Economic History of Twentieth Century Latin America*, vol. III: Industrialization and the State in Latin America. The Postwar Years, London: Palgrave.

Cardoso, E. and A. Fishlow. 1992. Latin American Development: 1950–1980, *Journal of Latin American Studies*, 24 (Quincentenary Supplement: The Colonial and Post Colonial Experience. Five Centuries of Spanish and Portuguese America): 197–218.

Chan, S. 1987. Comparative Performances of East Asian and Latin American NICs, *Pacific Focus* 2 (1): 35–56.

Chang, H.-J. and A. Cheema. 2001. Conditions for Successful Technology Policy in Developing Countries—Learning Rents, State Structures and Institutions. Maastricht: The United Nations University, INTECH, Discussions Paper Series, 8.

Cimoli, M. and J. Katz. 2004. Reformas Estructurales y Brechas Tecnológicas, in J. A. Ocampo (ed.), *El desarrollo económico en los albores des siglo XXI*. Bogotá: Alfaomega: 242–59.

Colin, M. L. 2004. State and Market in Latin America: The Rise and Decline of Economic Intervention, in Lears J van Scherpenberg (ed.), *Culture of Economy. Economics of Culture*, Universitätsverlag Winter, 32–58.

Connif, M. 1981. *Urban Politics in Brazil: The Rise of Populism 1922–1945*. Pittsburgh: University of Pittsburgh Press.

Díaz Alejandro, C. 1970. *Essays on the Economic History of the Argentine Republic*. New Haven: Yale University Press.

DiJohn, J, 2004. Mineral Resource Rents, Rent-Seeking and State Capacity in a Late Developer: The Political Economy of Industrial Policy in Venezuela 1920–1998. Unpublished Ph.D thesis, Cambridge University.

Dobb, M. 1946. *Studies in the Development of Capitalism*. London: Routledge.

Dutrénit, G. and J. Katz. 2005. Introduction: Innovation, Growth and Development in Latin-America: Stylized Facts and a Policy Agenda, *Innovation: Management, Policy & Practice* 7 (2–3), April–August: 105–30.

ECLAC (Economic Commission for Latin America and the Caribbean). 2004. *Preliminary Overview of the Economies of Latin America and the Caribbean*. Chile: UN Publication, December.

Evans, P. 1995. *Embedded Autonomy. States and Industrial Transformation*. Princeton: Princeton University Press.

Fishlow, A. 1989. Latin American Failure against the Backdrop of Asian Success, *Annals of the American Academy of Political & Social Science* 505: 117–28.

Ffrench-Davis, R. 2000. *Reforming the reforms in Latin America. Macroeconomics, Trade, Finance*. New York: St. Martin's Press.

—— 2002. *Economic Reforms in Chile. From Dictatorship to Democracy*. Ann Arbor: The University of Michigan Press.

Gavin, M., R. Hausmann, and E. Talvi. 1997. Saving Behaviour in Latin America: Overview and Policy Issues, *Inter-American Development Bank*, WP 346, May.

Gereffi, G. 1989. Rethinking Development Theory: Insights from East Asia and Latin America, *Sociological Forum* 4 (4): 505–34.

—— and D. L. Wyman (eds). 1990. *Manufacturing Miracles: Paths of Industrialisation in Latin America and East Asia*. Princeton, NJ: Princeton University Press.

Gwynne, R. 2004. Clusters and Commodity Chains: Firm Responses to Neoliberalism in Latin America, *Latin American Research Review*, 39 (3): 243–55.

Haber, S. 2005. Development Strategy or Endogenous Process? The Industrialization of Latin America, Working Paper, Stanford University, September: <http://www.stanford.edu/~haber/papers/Development_Strategy_or_Endogenous_%20Process-The_Industrialization_of_Latin_America.pdf>.

Hagopian, F. 1994. Traditional Politics against State Transformation in Brazil, in: J. S. Migdal, A. Kohli, and V. Shue (eds), *State Power and Social Forces*, Cambridge: Cambridge University Press.

Harberger, A. 1988. Growth, Industrialization and Economic Structure: Latin America and East Asia Compared, in H. Hughes (ed.), *Achieving Industrialization in East Asia*, Cambridge: Cambridge University Press.

Heston, A., R. Summer, and B. Aten. 2002. *Penn World Tables Version 6.1.*, Centre for International Comparisons at the University of Pennsylvania (CICUP), October.

Jenkins, R.O. 1991. The Political Economy of Industrialisation: A Comparison of Latin America and East Asian Newly Industrialising Economies, *Development and Change* 22 (2): 197–231.

Jomo, K. S. and C. Edwards 1993. Malaysian Industrialization in Historical Perspective, in K. S. Jomo (ed.), *Industrializing Malaysia: Policy, Performance, Prospects*, London: Routledge.

Katz, J. and B. Kosacoff (2000), Technological Learning, Institution Building and the Microeconomics of Import Substitution, in E. Cárdenas, J. A. Ocampo, and R. Thorp (eds), *An Economic History of Twentieth Century Latin America* 3: 154–76.

Kay, C. 2002. Why East Asia Overtook Latin America: Agrarian Reform, Industrialisation and Development, *Third World Quarterly* 23 (6): 1073–102.

Khan, M. H. 1998. Patron–Client Networks and the Economic Effects of Corruption in Asia, *European Journal of Development Research* June 10 (1): 15–39.

—— 1999. *The Political Economy of Industrial Policy in Pakistan 1947–1971*. SOAS Department of Economics Working Paper No. 98, School of Oriental and African Studies, University of London.

—— 2000a. Rents, Efficiency and Growth, in Mushtaq H. Khan and K. S. Jomo (eds), *Rents, Rent-Seeking and Economic Development: Theory and Evidence in Asia*, Cambridge: Cambridge University Press.

—— 2000b. Rent-seeking as Process, in Mushtaq H. Khan, and K. S. Jomo (eds), *Rents, Rent-Seeking and Economic Development: Theory and Evidence in Asia*, Cambridge: Cambridge University Press.

Klarén, P. F. 2000. *Peru: Society and Nationhood in the Andes*. New York: Oxford University Press.

Kohli, A. 1994. Where Do High Growth Political Economies Come From? The Japanese Lineage of Korea's 'Developmental State', *World Development* 22 (9): 1269–93.

Kosacoff, B., C. Bonvecchi, and G. Yoguel. 1998. Argentina: la economía en los años noventa. Contexto macroeconómico, desempeño industrial e inserción externa, in L. J. Garay (ed.), *Argentina, Brasil, México, Venezuela: apertura y reestructuración productiva*. Programa de Estudio. Bogota. Colombia: Study Program 'La Industria de América Latina ante la Globalización Económica'.

Lin, C. 1988. East Asia and Latin America as Contrasting Models, *Economic Development and Cultural Change* 36 (3): S153–S198.

Maddison, A. 1992. *Brazil and Mexico. World Bank Comparative Study: The Political Economy of Poverty, Equity and Growth*. Oxford: Oxford University Press.

—— 2003. *The World Economy. Historical Statistics*. Paris: OECD.

Mahoney, J. and M. vom Hau. 2005. Colonial States and Economic Development in Spanish America, in M. Lange and D. Rueschemeyer (eds), *States and Development. Historical Antecedents of Stagnation and Advance*. New York and Basingstoke: Palgrave Macmillan.

Melo, A. 2001. Industrial Policy in Latin America and the Caribbean at the Turn of the Century. Inter-American Development Bank. Research Department Working Paper Series No. 459.

Moore, B. 1966. *Social Origins of Dictatorship and Democracy*. London: Penguin Group.

Mouzelis, N. P. 1986. *Politics in the Semi-Periphery. Early Parliamentarism and Late Industrialisation in the Balkans and in Latin America*. Basingstoke: Macmillan.

North, D. C. 1990. *Institutions, Institutional Change and Economic Performance*. Cambridge: Cambridge University Press.

Ocampo, J. A. 1994. Trade Policy and Industrialization in Colombia 1967–1991, in G. Helleiner (ed.), *Trade Policy and Industrialization in Turbulent Times*. London: Routledge.

—— 2004. Introducción, in J. A. Ocampo (ed.), *El desarrollo económico en los albores des siglo XXI*. Bogotá: Alfaomega, pp. 13–41.

Paiva Abreu, M de. 2000. Import Substitution and Growth in Brazil, 1890s–1970s, in E. Cárdenas, J. A. Ocampo, and R. Thorp (eds), *An Economic History of Twentieth Century Latin America* 3: 154–76.

Palma, G. 2005a. The Seven Main 'Stylized Facts' of the Mexican Economy since Trade Liberalization and NAFTA. *Industrial and Corporate Change*, November: 1–51.

—— 2005b. Four Sources of 'De-Industrialisation' and a New Concept of the Dutch Disease, in J. A. Ocampo (ed.), *Beyond Reforms: Structural Dynamics and Macroeconomic Vulnerability*. Stanford University Press and World Bank.

Peres, W. 1997. El resurgimiento de las políticas de competitividad industrial, in W. Peres (ed.), *Políticas de competitividad industrial. América Latina y el Caribe en los años noventa*. Mexico, D.F.: Siglo Veintiuno Editores.

Pérez, C. 2004. Cambio Tecnológico y Oportunidades de Desarrollo como Blanco Mobil, in J. A. Ocampo (ed.), *El desarrollo económico en los albores des siglo XXI*. Bogotá: Alfaomega, pp. 205–40.

Ranis, G. and L. Orrock. 1985. Latin America and East Asian NICs: Development Strategies Compared, in E. Durán (ed.), *Latin America and World Recession*, Cambridge: Cambridge University Press.

Reynolds, C. W. 1970. *The Mexican Economy: Twentieth Century Structure and Growth*. New Haven: Yale University Press.

Rodrik, D. 2004. Industrial Policy for the Twenty-First Century. Draft Working Paper Available: <http://ksghome.harvard.edu/~drodrik/UNIDOSep.pdf>.

—— and A. Subramanian. 2004. From 'Hindu Growth' to Productivity Surge: The Mystery of the Indian Growth Transition. Draft working paper Available: <http://ksghome.harvard.edu/~drodrik/IndiapaperdraftMarch2.pdf>

Schneider, R. 2004. *Business Politics and the State in Twentieth-Century Latin America*. Cambridge: Cambridge University Press.

Rueschemeyer, D., E. Huber Stephens, and J. D. Stephens. 1992. *Capitalist Development & Democracy*. Chicago: University of Chicago Press.

Shapiro, H. 2006. Diversity, Growth and Development, *World Economic and Social Survey 2006*, UN DESA Development Policy and Analysis (DPAD).

Singh, A. 1993. Asian Economic Success and Latin American Failure in the 1980s: New Analyses and Future Policy Implications. *International Review of Applied Economics* 7 (3): 267–89.

Sweezy, P. M. 1950. The Transition from Feudalism to Capitalism, *Science and Society* 14 (2): 134–57.

Taylor, L. 2000. External Liberalization, Economic Performance and Distribution in Latin America and Elsewhere. *WIDER UNU Working Papers* No. 215. December.

Thorp, R. 1991. *Economic Management and Economic Development in Peru and Colombia*. Pittsburgh: Pittsburgh University Press.

UNCTAD 2003. *Trade and Development Report*, New York and Geneva: United Nations.

Vejarano, C. P. 2002. Industrialization and Industrial Policy in Colombia: A Tale of Economic Development. Universidad del Rosario, Facultad de Economía. *Serie Documentos*. Borradores de Investigación 31, November.

Wade, Robert 1988. The Role of Government in Overcoming Market Failure: Taiwan, Republic of Korea and Japan, in H. Hughes (ed.), *Achieving Industrialization in East Asia*, Cambridge: Cambridge University Press.

—— 1990. *Governing the Market: Economic Theory and the Role of Government in East Asian Industrialization*. Princeton: Princeton University Press.

Weeks, J. 1985. *Limits to Capitalist Development. The Industrialization of Peru 1950–1980*. Boulder and London: Westview Press.

Weinstein, B. (1994), Not the Republic of their Dreams: Historical Obstacles to Political and Social Democracy in Brazil, *Latin American Research Review* 29 (2): 262–73.

Weisbrot, M. 2006. Latin America: The End of An Era, *International Journal of Health Services* 36 (4), <http://www.cepr.net/columns/weisbrot/2006_06_end_of_era.htm#article>.

White, G. (ed.) 1988. *Developmental States in East Asia*. London: Macmillan.

Woo-Cumings, M. 1997. The Political Economy of Growth in East Asia: A Perspective on the State, Market, and Ideology, in M. Aoki, H. K. Kim, and M. Okuno-Fujiwara (eds), *The Role of Government in East Asian Economic Development: Comparative Institutional Analysis*, Oxford: Clarendon Press.

—— (ed.) 1999. *The Developmental State*. Ithaca: Cornell University Press.

Wood, E. M. 2002. *The Origins of Capitalism: A Longer View*. London: Verso.

World Bank. 2006. *World Bank Development Indicators*, April.

14

The Roles of Research at Universities and Public Labs in Economic Catch-Up

Roberto Mazzoleni and Richard R. Nelson

Introduction

This chapter is concerned with the roles of research in indigenous universities and public laboratories in the processes through which countries behind the technological and economic frontier catch up. Given the purposes of the project of which this chapter is a part, our focus will be on catch-up in industrial technology and practice. However, in much of our analysis, we recognize explicitly that the process of economic development involves building capabilities in a wide range of areas—agriculture, medicine and public health, the ability to manage transportation systems, maintain safe water supply, and many others as well as developing capabilities in industry. We will argue that, for several reasons, the role of indigenous public research in industrial catch-up is more important today than it was in the twentieth century. We also call attention to the fact that building an effective indigenous system of research is no easy task, while offering some guidelines that may be helpful.

However, before getting into these topics, we need to set the stage by considering the process of catch-up more generally, and in historical perspective. It is clear that the process of catch-up involves in an essential way learning about and learning to master ways of doing things that are used by the leading countries of the era. However, the term catch-up seems to connote that the catching-up country simply copies, and this is misleading. While practice in advanced countries does usually serve as a model, what is achieved inevitably differs in certain ways from the template. In part this reflects that exact copying is almost impossible, and attempts to replicate at best get viably close. In part it reflects deliberate and often creative modifications aimed to tailor practice to national conditions.

Most of the writings on catch-up have presumed, explicitly or implicitly, that the key practices that need to be mastered are technologies, in a rather conventional sense of that term, with the know-how involved of the sort that is learned by engineers, and physical and biological scientists, and often embodied in physical things like machines, and specialized materials of various sorts. Certainly a lot of the powerful practice of advanced countries that developing ones are trying to acquire is technology of this sort: product designs, complex production processes, the seeds and pesticides and procedures used in productive agriculture, modern medical practice including the use of pharmaceuticals and sophisticated medical equipment, the technological core of modern air traffic control systems, and the like.

However, a lot of the relevant practice cannot be easily characterized as technology in this narrow sense. Thus complex production processes generally involve large teams of workers, with a division of labor, and a management and control system to generate effective coordination. Modern firms also need to have in place a system for hiring, rewarding, and occasionally releasing labor, and the capability to make the investments needed for effective operation and adjustment to changes in market opportunities and challenges. To operate effectively they must be supported by a system of education and training that gives them access to a labor supply with the needed skills, and a system of banks and other financial institutions that meets their financial needs. As indicated above, later in this essay we will focus on the set of national public institutions that do research and advanced training. All of these involve ways of doing things—practices—but technology in a narrow sense is not at their core.

Nelson and Sampat (2001) have proposed that it may be useful to think of the latter as 'social' technologies, as contrasted with the physical technologies. Rather than being embodied in physical hardware and materials, social technologies are embodied in organizational forms, bodies of law, public policies, codes of good business and administrative practice, customs, norms.

The point of view that we will develop here is that, in this modern age, physical technologies may be much easier to learn and acquire than social technologies, if the capabilities for assimilation are present. However, the phrase 'if the capabilities for assimilation are present' flags several important issues.

First of all, the effective operation of many physical technologies requires the implementation of various social technologies. Thus in the present context it may be far easier to import the machinery and acquire the engineering knowledge to produce modern automobiles or semiconductors than to set up an effective firm organization and management structure to operate the physical technology efficiently, or to set up an effective set of procedures for acquiring inputs, or for marketing.

Second, the broad institutional structure of a nation, and the operation of particular institutions like its education and financial systems, and its system of public research and advanced training, strongly affect both the incentives and the ability to take on board and operate modern industrial, agricultural, or medical practice. Successful economic development generally will require the reform of traditional systems and the setting-up of more modern ones, broadly guided by perceptions of how those systems are structured and work in high-income countries, but tailored to fit in with national conditions and culture. In the past some countries have been able to do this effectively, but success in this endeavor is far from a foregone conclusion.

We proposed above that an effective system of public research has become an increasingly important part of the institutional structure needed for catch-up. We will develop this argument, and some of its implications, shortly. But first we want to lay out some things that seem clear about successful catch-up experience in the past, and some features of the contemporary scene that are different from what they have been.

The catch-up process in historical perspective

The proposition that the economic development process of countries behind the frontier is basically that of catch-up seems so compelling that one might expect that study of the processes involved would be at the center of attention of the contemporary development economics community. But this is not the case.

Understanding differences across countries in their level of economic development and the reasons for economic backwardness was of course a central concern of many of the great classical economists, particularly Adam Smith. But these questions gradually moved to the periphery of the field.

The question came back into focus after World War II. That the development problem was a catch-up problem was put forth explicitly in Alexander Gershenkron's 'Economic Backwardness in Historical Perspective' (1951), which considered the policies and new institutions of the states of continental Europe during the mid- to late nineteenth century as they strove to catch up with the UK and reflected on the relevance of this experience to the post-war world. However, outside the economic historians, few development economists paid attention to the processes of catch-up per se, because most of prevailing economic growth theory saw the principal reason for low productivity and incomes as low levels of physical and human capital, as contrasted with inadequate access to or command over technologies and other practices used in high income countries. Relatedly, imitation of technologies, and practices more generally, in use in advanced countries generally was viewed as relatively easy, if there were no barriers like intellectual property rights, and the needed inputs, particularly physical and human capital, were available. However, learning to do what others already have done often is not easy. Japan was successful at this at the start of the twentieth century, Korea and Taiwan later in that century, and China is proving effective at that task today. But many countries have made hardly any progress.[1]

Moses Abramowitz's propositions about the institutional and political conditions needed for successful catch-up (1986) clearly recognized these difficulties, and generated a small research tradition specifically on the factors conducive to catch-up. Some of this research has been quite illuminating. Scholars like Fagerberg and Godinho (2004), and Bernardes and Albuquerque (2003), have shown that in recent years countries that have caught up rapidly have tended to focus their higher education systems on engineering training, and have developed indigenous research efforts. There are several quite detailed studies of particular countries that have been successful in catching up that delve into the key processes and institutions involved (see for example Kim 1997, and 1999). There are a few studies that have examined how firms in developing countries have caught up in particular industries (e.g. Hobday, 1995). However, these kinds of studies have not been brought together in a systematic way.

Our reading of prior relevant research leads us to propose that, in the past, all successful cases of catch-up have involved the following elements.

First, considerable cross-border flow of people, with a combination of citizens in the then backward country going to learn abroad and then returning, and people from the advanced country coming as advisors or, in some cases, to establish themselves in the developing country. Thus the core of British textile manufacturing methods was brought over to the new United States by British technicians, who stayed. Similarly, there was a significant flow of British technicians to northern Europe in the early nineteenth century, who came with the objective of setting up business on the continent (Landes, 1969; Pollard, 1981; Rosenberg, 1970). The development of Japanese industry in the late nineteenth and early twentieth centuries was helped by technical advisors from abroad, as well as by Japanese returning home after studying Western methods (Odagiri and Goto, 1996). The Korean and Taiwanese electronics industries were developed largely by men who had studied, and often worked, in the United States. While early on the cross-border flows were to a considerable degree the result of individuals' search for economic opportunities abroad, they have increasingly been part of activities carried out by various organizations.

During the twentieth century companies came to play an increasing role in this cross-national learning and teaching process. The new Japanese automobile and electrical equipment companies established close interactions with companies in the United States and Europe that served as their mentors. The development of Singapore was largely driven through the establishment of branch operations by Western multinationals. Hobday (1995) has documented in detail how Korean and Taiwanese companies developed increasing competence working for American and Japanese electronics companies as Original Equipment Manufacturers.

Over the last quarter century an important part of the transnational flow of people in the catch-up process has involved university study abroad in the relevant fields of engineering and applied science. University faculty in the successful developing countries has to a considerable degree been based on nationals who received their training abroad. We believe that this university-mediated transnational conduit of learning will be of particularly great importance during the twenty-first century for countries seeking to catch up. This certainly will be so regarding public health and medical care, as well as regarding manufacturing technology.

A second important element in countries that successfully caught up with the leaders during the nineteenth and twentieth centuries was active government support of the catch-up process, involving various forms of protection and direct and indirect subsidy. The guiding policy argument has been the need of domestic industry in the industries of the day judged critical in the development process for some protection from advanced firms in the leading nations. Alexander Hamilton's argument (1791) for infant industry protection in the new United States was virtually identical to that put forth decades later by Friedrich List (1841) regarding Germany's needs. The policies and new institutions used in Continental Europe to enable catch-up with Britain are documented in Alexander Gershenkron's famous essay. The same story also fits well with the case of Japan, and of Korea and Taiwan somewhat later. In many countries these policies engendered not successful catch-up but a protected inefficient home industry. However, they also were the hallmark during the twentieth century of all the countries that have achieved their goals of catching up.

These policies obviously angered companies in the leading countries, and their governments, particularly if the supported industry not only supplied its home market but began to invade the world market. While the case made after World War II for free trade was mostly concerned with eliminating protection and subsidy among the rich countries, and at that time there was sympathy for the argument that some infant industry protection was often useful in developing countries, the international treaties that have been made increasingly have been used against import protection and subsidy in countries seeking to catch up from far behind.

Our belief is that Hamilton and List were right that successful catch-up in industries where international trade is considerable requires some kind of infant industry protection or other mode of support. The challenge is to find effective means under the new conditions.

Third, during the nineteenth and early twentieth centuries, many developing countries operated with intellectual property rights regimes which did not restrict seriously the ability of their companies in effect to copy technologies used in the advanced countries. There are many examples where licensing agreements were involved, but we believe that for the most part these were vehicles through which technology transfer was effected for a fee or other considerations, rather than instances of aggressive protection of intellectual property by the company in the advanced country.

Like infant industry protection and subsidy, conflicts tended to emerge largely when the catching-up company began to encroach onto world markets, or even to export to the home market of the company with the patent rights. Increasing instances of this clearly were a major factor in inducing the treaty on Trade-Related Aspects of Intellectual Property Rights (TRIPS). But this treaty makes vulnerable to prosecution not just companies in developing countries that are exporting, but also companies that stay in their home markets.

The increased tendency of companies in high-income countries to enforce their intellectual property rights is having consequences regarding agricultural development, and the workings of the public health systems in developing countries, as well as regarding manufacturing development. Patented seed varieties are playing an increasingly important role in modern agriculture. And patented pharmaceuticals are key elements in the attack on a number of diseases that devastate poor countries. The arena of intellectual property is almost sure to become one of considerable international conflict in the immediate future. Developing countries need to learn to be able to cope with this new problem.

Changing conditions: the increased importance of indigenous technological and scientific capabilities

As we have noted, the current and future development environment for countries trying to catch up is different from what it has been, in a number of respects. International treaties, particularly the WTO and TRIPS, have changed the environment for catch-up in important ways. Firms in the advanced countries are likely to press hard for access to markets and in many cases the rights to establish branches abroad. Protection and subsidy of domestic industry is likely to be met by legal and other punitive action on the part of the advanced countries, and hence will have to be more subtle, involving support of sectoral infrastructure, training, and research. Firms in advanced countries also are likely to be far more aggressive and effective in protecting their intellectual property rights, and hence firms and governments in developing countries will have to develop new strategies for access on reasonable terms.

The new legal environment has come into place in a context where both business and finance are operating on a more global frame. Foreign direct investment has played a significant role in the catch-up processes of some successful countries, and is likely to play an even greater role in the future than in the past. So too partnerships between firms in developing countries and companies that possess advanced know-how. At the same time, firms in developing countries can aspire realistically to sell in a world market if their wares are good enough.

Less well noticed, scientific and technical communities in different countries also are now more connected than they used to be.[2] This has come about at the same time that there have been major increases in the power of many fields of applications oriented science, dedicated to achieving understanding of the principles that are operative in an area of practice, so as to provide a base for rigorous training of new professionals who will work in that field, and a scientific basis for efforts to move the technology forward. Included here are such older fields as chemical and electrical engineering, and modern fields such as computer science, biotechnology, and immunology. In recent years these fields of science have become increasingly open to those who have the training and connections to get into the relevant networks.

The implications for catch-up can be profound. On the one hand, in technologies with strong scientific underpinnings, advanced training in the field has become a prerequisite for ability to understand and control; simple working experience no longer will suffice. This fact clearly challenges the capabilities for education and technical training in countries seeking to catch up, even if studying abroad can provide at least a temporary solution to the need for acquiring advanced knowledge in relevant fields. On the other hand, a strong science base significantly reduces the importance of operating apprenticeship abroad, or tutelage by foreign industrial experts. This is not to argue that advanced formal training in a field suffices for mastery. However, in many fields it provides a substantial basis for learning by doing. Moreover, having a domestic base of good scientists provides the basis for breaking into the international networks where new technologies are being hatched.

As a result of these changes, we believe that the development of indigenous capabilities in research and advanced training now are much more important in enabling catch-up than used to be the case, and their importance will grow. As noted at the start of this chapter, our focus here will be on the role of research at universities and public laboratories. However, the roles of such research need to be understood in terms of their operation within a broader National Innovation System.[3] While, the modern conception of a National Innovation System was developed to be useful in thinking about the key institutions involved in technological advance in countries at or close to the frontier (see e.g. Nelson, 1993) recent research has reoriented the concept to provide guidance to countries significantly behind the frontier and striving to catch up (see among others, Kim, 1997, 1999; Albuquerque, 2003; and Viotti, 2002, 2003). We propose that a suitably reoriented concept of a National Innovation System can be a useful tool for considering policies and institutions needed for effective catch-up in the new context.

In the first place, it calls attention to the fact that the process of catch-up involves innovation in an essential way. The innovating that drives the process of course differs from the innovating that has been the central focus of research on technological advance in advanced economies. The new technologies, practices more generally, that are being taken on board, while new to the country catching up, generally are well established in countries at the frontier. And much of the innovation that is required is organizational and institutional. But what is going on in catch-up most certainly is innovation in the sense that there is a break from past familiar practice, considerable uncertainty about how to make the new practice work effectively, a need for sophisticated learning by doing and using, and a high risk of failure, as well as a major potential payoff from success. These aspects of catch-up tend to be denied or repressed in the standard economic development literature.

Second, the Innovation System concept focuses attention on the range of institutions that are involved in the process of innovation. In most industries the roles of business firms is central. However, there has been a tendency of many economists writing about innovation to write as if firms are the full story, neglecting other kinds of institutions that are involved in the processes that support and mold innovation in many modern industries. While in earlier eras such a narrow institutional focus may not have been unwarranted, our argument is that public research institutions are likely to play an important one in the twenty-first century. Perez and Soete (1988), and Bell and Pavitt (1993), argued this point some time ago. But we think it fair to say that standard development economics still is mostly blind to the issues here, and the important functions that public institutions are likely to play.

In the first place, indigenous universities and public laboratories will play an increasingly important role as vehicles through which the technologies and organizational forms of the advanced countries come to be mastered in the developing ones. They will do so partially as an organizing structure for and partially a substitute for international people flows. Indigenous universities will play a key role as the source of students who take advanced training abroad, and as the home of faculty who have been trained abroad. And it is clear that domestic universities must do the bulk of the training of people who will go to industry and other economic activities needing well-trained technical people.

While often overlooked, indigenous research at universities and other public institutions long has been an important element of catch-up in certain important fields for which knowledge originating from abroad was ill suited to national needs. This is especially so in agriculture and medicine. An important part of the reason is that in these areas developing countries often could not simply copy technology and practice in countries at the frontier, but needed to develop technologies suited to their own conditions. Soil and climate conditions tended to be different. The prevalent diseases were different. There is every reason to believe that the importance of having the capability to do effective research and development in these fields will be even greater in the future.

In contrast, while in manufacturing the technologies used in advanced countries may not have been optimal, at least they worked in the new setting with often modest modification, and they generally were available at no great expense. The experience of countries that have successfully caught up in manufacturing over the past half century testifies to the importance of a nation's education system in providing a supply of trained engineers and applied scientists to manufacturing firms catching up. And an important part of the catch-up process has involved firms learning to do R&D on their own. However, while there are exceptions (electronics in Taiwan and Korea and aircraft in Brazil are examples), for the most part research per se in universities and national labs has not in the past played an important role in catch-up in manufacturing, beyond its role in the training function.

But circumstances may have changed. In the new regime of stronger protection of intellectual property, it is going to be increasingly important that countries trying to catch up develop their capabilities to revise and tailor manufacturing technologies relatively early in the game. First of all, this can help companies to develop and employ technologies that avoid both direct infringement of intellectual property that is likely to be enforced aggressively and the need to compete for access to foreign technology through licensing arrangements. Second, over the longer run the development of an intellectual property rights portfolio by firms in developing countries can provide bargaining weight in the complex cross-licensing arrangements that mark many manufacturing industries.

More generally, achieving competence in many areas of manufacturing requires staying up with a moving target. Further, as the frontier is approached, the line between sophisticated imitation and creative design of new products and processes becomes blurry. A strong R&D capability becomes essential. To a considerable extent the R&D needs to go on in firms. However, research in universities and public laboratories can play a strong supporting role.

A look at some selected cases in earlier experiences of catch-up

There has been no systematic study of which we are aware of the roles played by indigenous universities and public labs in earlier experiences of catch-up. What is available is a scattered collection of individual cases, described at different levels of detail. In order to bring some coherence to the present discussion, we will focus here on what is known about the roles of indigenous public research institutions in the successful catch-up experiences of Japan, in the late nineteenth and early twentieth centuries, and Korea and Taiwan later in the last century, supplemented by some instances from the Brazilian experience. Our particular interest is catch-up in industrial technology and practice, and here the studies on which we can draw are very piecemeal. There has been more systematic study of the role of indigenous public research in agricultural development in these countries, and while our focus is not there, we begin this section by summarizing briefly some research on this topic by agricultural economists.

Agricultural development

Very shortly after it came to power in 1868, the new Meiji government, which was committed to the rapid modernization of the Japanese economy, started efforts to improve Japanese agriculture. These efforts included the establishment of both agricultural experimentation stations, and agricultural colleges. At the beginnings of the efforts at agricultural modernization, Japanese experts and politicians had in mind the mechanized agriculture of the United States and (parts of) Great Britain as a model. However, as Hayami and Ruttan note, the very small size of the typical Japanese farm, more generally the very high ratio of farmers and agricultural workers to usable land, made American technology completely inappropriate for most of Japanese agriculture. As attempts at transplant made this fact evident, the orientation of the modernization efforts shifted.

It is interesting that the new orientation was largely toward identifying existing practices of Japanese farmers that were particularly effective. The new agricultural experimentation stations played a major role in this comparative analysis of practice, and in spreading the news regarding best practice to farmers. Teaching at the agricultural colleges became focused on best practice. Under this new regime, a considerable portion of the experimentation that identified better practice was actually conducted by individual Japanese farmers. However, the agricultural experimentation stations also were an important locus of experimentation, and for providing reliable information on the efficacy of different practices to farmers.

Hayami and Ruttan note that much of what was going on at the experimentation stations during this period involved refining, as well as testing, of farmer innovations. During this period, the experimentation station system increasingly established local branches, which was particularly important because the efficacy of practice often was quite vocation specific.

During the 1880s and 1890s, there was increasing recognition in Japanese agricultural circles that, given the low ratio of land to people, improving the productivity of best-practice Japanese agriculture largely meant increasing yields per unit of land, as contrasted with output per worker, as in the United States, and that there was a high premium on the discovery or creation of seeds and methods which effectively could employ high levels of fertilizer. The Japanese agricultural experimentation stations played a major and effective role in moving Japanese agriculture in this direction. Hayami and Ruttan propose that 'the history of seed improvement in Japan is a history of developing varieties that were increasingly more fertilizer-responsive.' The efforts at agricultural experimentation stations involved both systematic selection of existing seed lines, and increasingly the development of new seed lines through hybridization. Again, much of this work necessarily went on at a quite local basis.

Turning to the cases of Taiwan and Korea, it is interesting to note that the agricultural experimentation systems in these countries were begun during the 1920s and 1930s, under Japanese occupation. In both cases, the principal motive of the Japanese was to improve productivity of rice production in these colonies, in the face of rapid increases in the demand for rice in increasingly affluent Japan, and diminishing returns to further applications of fertilizer that were occurring in Japanese agriculture, despite the largely successful research efforts just mentioned. In both Taiwan and Korea, the thrust of the efforts at the new experimentation stations involved crossbreeding of indigenous rice varieties, with a fertilizer-responsive Japanese seed variety. And in both cases the result was significant increases in yields per acre.

In Brazil too, the growth of agricultural production has been since the 1970s shifting from a base in the expansion of cultivated land to one driven by increased yields, and the introduction of new crops and of new varieties of traditional ones. Public research had a strong hand in this transformation. The government created EMBRAPA in 1972 as a public-sector corporation to coordinate the R&D activities in the field of agriculture carried out at a large variety of institutions across the country. The latter include universities, private enterprises, and a number of national, regional, and state-level research institutes. A great deal of the research carried out at regional or state centers focuses on local production systems and aims at adapting to local conditions the result of research conducted at national centers (Dahlman and Frischtak, 1993). It should be noted on the other hand that EMBRAPA is an important node in the linkages between the Brazilian system of agricultural innovation and foreign research centers, with whom it engages in cooperative research activities.

There are several things that we think noteworthy about these quite successful experiences. First, the public research was not particularly 'high science.' Rather, it was pragmatically oriented and highly sensitive to the needs of the users, in this case the farming community. Second, and related, the public research operations had effective mechanisms for two-way communication with the farming community. They most emphatically did not operate as ivory towers. Third, an important part of the effort involved tailoring technologies to local conditions. While this latter requirement is somewhat less important regarding industrial technology, we will argue that the importance of close, two-way interaction with potential users is just as important for making public research concerned with advancing technology as it is for agricultural research.

Industrial development

Universities and public research laboratories also appear to have been important institutional aspects of catch-up in at least a few industrial sectors in these countries. As mentioned above, knowledge of this phenomenon is far from systematic but presently scattered among various case studies. Again we want to sketch an outline of the emerging linkages between these institutions and industrial development in a few countries that have begun to catch up with advanced economies since the late nineteenth century.

Around the time of the Meiji restoration in 1868, absorbing knowledge of Western science and technology had become a crucial component of Japan's industrial development strategy. This goal was pursued through a variety of mechanisms. Crucial among them was the recruitment of foreign professionals to work as consultants and specialized technical personnel for a variety of industrial development projects. Japanese students of Western sciences and technology were likewise sent abroad to visit industrial firms and universities or other educational institutions. But the Japanese government also proceeded to establish educational institutions that could rapidly train indigenous students to serve the industrial development needs of the country. Newly founded universities and specialized schools were organized and staffed at first by large numbers of foreign professors. The early cohorts of students provided the specialist knowledge and skills necessary to staff the emerging bureaucracy overseeing public projects of various kinds, and in particular provided the new generation of professors for indigenous universities and advanced schools. In the early stages of Japan's catch-up experience, there was little emphasis on public research, except in so far as this was part of the training of scientists and engineers.

The task of educating scientists and engineers became the province of public academic institutions.[4] The teaching of natural sciences was promoted at the Tokyo University formed in 1877 by merging together a number of institutions devoted to Western learning. While the faculty of science hosted also a course in engineering, the Japanese government sponsored the development of a specialized institution, the Imperial College of Engineering, which was founded in 1873 with a faculty of eight British professors, offering instruction according to a four-year curriculum modeled after that of ETH in Zurich. The degree program included three years of practical experience that students could acquire at laboratory facilities of the university or later on at an industrial laboratory operated by the Ministry of Industries (Bartholomew, 1989; Odagiri and Goto, 1993). The College merged into the Tokyo University in 1886, where it became part of the Department of Engineering.

The year 1886 marked a reorganization of the Japanese educational system. The government decided to focus its financial efforts on just one national university, renamed the Imperial University of Tokyo, where research activities would be promoted. Until then, Tokyo University was a teaching institution without adequate laboratories and faculty support for the conduct of basic research. In 1885 new facilities were completed as the government strived to turn the Imperial University into a modern research university comparable to its counterparts in Western Europe or the US. The public system of higher education comprised also a large number of specialized training institutions, where instruction was in Japanese language. These were responsible for training a much larger number of students, most of whom found employment at private enterprises. In contrast, most graduates of the Imperial University (about two-thirds in the 1890s) were recruited to public service positions (Amano, 1979).[5]

Historical accounts of Japan's industrial development indicate clearly that many of the pioneers in industries like electrical equipment, chemicals, or iron and steel, received their training in the relevant fields of science and engineering at Japanese universities, often complemented by a period of study and research abroad (Uchida, 1980; Yonekura, 1994). Already at this early stage in the development of Japan's academic system, professors and graduates contributed directly or indirectly to the development of new technologies, and the adaptation of existing ones.[6] In fact, it was a diffuse practice among professors to act as technical consultants for private business enterprises, and to maintain connections with their students as the latter took employment or founded industrial enterprises. During the First World War, when their access to foreign technology was substantially restricted, Japanese companies became increasingly dependent on the technological assistance by university professors. Indeed, while industry need for technological capabilities provided a key rationale for government policies aimed at expanding academic enrollments in fields like applied chemistry, metallurgy, mining engineering, dissenting voices criticized the heavy load of consulting work performed by university professors for its negative effects on the quality of academic research and instruction (Bartholomew, 1989).

The widespread diffusion among academics of consulting for domestic businesses was partly the result of the limited financial support that the government provided for academic research during the period up to the end of the First World War. However, public support for research aimed at industrial development increased during the early twentieth century in response to a variety of factors, including the 1899 reform of the patent law admitting foreign patent applicants and the growth of the government's industrial and military needs. In addition to the formation of testing and R&D programs by private enterprises, the government provided financial support to research and testing laboratories either directly or through public enterprises.

Already in 1900 an Industrial Experiment Laboratory was established to conduct testing and analyses on a contract basis for national firms, consisting of two divisions in industrial chemistry and chemical analysis staffed by 11 members. The Laboratory was expanded in 1906, in the aftermath of the Russo-Japanese war, and then again in 1911. From a staff of 11 at inception, the Laboratory grew to more than 30 members in 1911 when new divisions were created for ceramics, dyeing, and electrochemistry. This institution played an important role in developing techniques and processes that were adopted by chemical firms, including, for example, the synthesis of alizarin (a synthetic dyestuff), and techniques for the production of phosphorus and alkali (Uchida, 1980). In the late 1920s, the Industrial Experiment Laboratory provided Showa Fertilizer Co. with an adaptation of the Haber–Bosch process for the production of synthetic ammonia (Mikami, 1980).

In addition to the Industrial Experiment Laboratory, other specialized public laboratories came into existence after the First World War thanks to public and private funding (Hashimoto, 1999). In addition to providing greater support to public research activities, the Japanese government also supported the creation of private research laboratories, such as the Research Institute for Physics and Chemistry (Riken) established in 1917.[7] The research conducted at these laboratories led oftentimes to the development of new technologies, patented both in Japan and abroad, frequently providing the basis for new products and processes adopted by business enterprises.[8]

The form of government support to the development of technological capabilities reflected of course characteristics of the industrial technologies of interest. Thus, the government promoted the development of iron and steel production primarily by financing and organizing the founding of a large public enterprise, the Yawata Works, that became a center of technological learning for the whole Japanese industry. However, even before this firm established its own formal R&D program in 1916, the government provided its support to organizing the Iron and Steel Institute of Japan in 1915. This institute represented an industrial research center whose membership included representatives of private and public enterprises (both producers and users of iron and steel), as well as of higher education institutions. It diffused technological information among its members through publications, seminars, and the work of its Cooperative Research Divisions launched in 1926 as a mechanism for organizing collaborative research.[9]

A number of features of the Japanese catch-up experience during the late nineteenth and early twentieth centuries can be found in the experience of the two countries whose economic performance during the post World War II years has been most remarkable, Korea and Taiwan. In both countries, the catch-up experience was marked by major investments in higher education, particularly the training of engineers. However, the growth of the educated labor force during the early stages of catch-up in both Korea and Taiwan outstripped the economy's ability to create jobs for graduates of the national universities, so that a phenomenon of unemployment or underemployment began to surface and an outflow of college graduates from the countries. On the other hand, despite significant government support, academic institutions public and private struggled to satisfy the growing demand for higher education with high quality degree programs. As a result, the share of students studying abroad both at the college level and the graduate level increased considerably, contributing further to a general phenomenon of brain drain.

In Korea, early phases of development focused on the acquisition of technological capabilities in mature labor-intensive industries where skill requirements could be met through vocational education or on the job training. Thus, even if the Park government succeeded during the 1960s to increase enrollments in academic science and engineering programs, a matching demand for skilled labor only began to emerge a decade later. Moreover, the educational programs in science and engineering at Korean universities during the 1960s were insufficiently plugged into the realities and needs of industrial development. Rote learning and theoretical knowledge were emphasized in undergraduate and graduate programs that appeared to be geared to preparing students for admission to foreign universities and careers in academia. As a result, an estimated 2,000 Korean science and engineering graduates were living abroad in 1968 (Kim and Leslie, 1998). Similar problems plagued the expansion of the higher education sector in Taiwan. In an effort to meet both growing skill demands in industry and the public's aspiration for higher education, the government created a university level technical program that offered the prospect of an academic degree to students graduating from vocational high schools. But efforts at stemming the outflow of Taiwanese scientists and engineers met at first with limited success.

In hindsight, the repatriation of Koreans and Taiwanese with several years of education and professional research and training outside their home countries has been credited as providing the base of human capital that made it possible for national firms to develop in a short time adequate technological capabilities in a variety of industrial sectors. While the reverse brain drain that occurred over the last quarter century was driven by the growing demand for scientific and technological talent of private-sector firms, early efforts to promote the return home of scientists and engineers were associated with the creation of public research organizations and academic institutions. Already in the late 1960s, awareness of the brain drain problem was an important factor behind the design of public policies whose primary goal was to foster the development of indigenous technological capabilities, and thus to reduce the dependence of national companies on foreign technology.

Consider the origins of the Korea Institute of Science and Technology (KIST). Its establishment in 1966 was the result of several years of negotiations between the Korean and the US governments, during which plans were laid out for creating an organization charged with carrying out contract research for industry and government, along the lines of the Battelle Institute in the US. The contractual basis for the institute's activities was intended to ensure that the scientific objectives of its research be kept close to industrial development needs. Indeed, it was expected that after an initial period of government support, the laboratories would be able to finance their own activities through industry contracts. KIST's initial staff was recruited among the ranks of Korean expatriate scientists and engineers. Thirty-two were appointed and trained in the operations of a contract research outfit at Battelle, which served as KIST's sister institution for the first few years of operation. Surveys and interviews of Korean firms were conducted ahead of the institute's establishment in order to identify the crucial technology areas. KIST was then organized in 31 independently managed laboratories focused on five broad technical areas (food technology, mechanical and chemical engineering, materials science, and electronics). KIST became centrally involved in research projects aimed at various industries, including shipbuilding, steel, chemicals, and industrial machinery (Kim and Leslie, 1998).

While KIST was responsible for the development of several patented technologies and able to generate royalty income from some of them (Lee, et al. 1991), its contributions to the development of indigenous capabilities consisted often of collaborations in technology transfer projects with local and foreign firms, as well as of reverse engineering projects. Together with a rapidly growing array of other public research institutes, KIST played arguably an important role in training personnel for industrial research and in demonstrating the importance of R&D activities to private corporations.

In doing so, KIST, together with other public research institutions and, later on, private enterprises, strengthened the demand for scientific and engineering talent. Around the early 1970s, the graduates of the Korean universities did not adequately meet this demand for the reasons highlighted earlier. Such weakness prompted a US-based Korean scientist, Chung KunMo, to submit a proposal (supported by the Korean Ministry of Science and Technology) to the US Agency for International Development for the creation of a specialized institution offering graduate level education in science and engineering focused on the emerging needs of industrial development. Upon recommendation of a committee headed by Frederick Terman (earlier president of Stanford University), USAID loaned the funds for creating the Korea Advanced Institute of Science (KAIS). The scope of KAIS's educational programs was narrow and focused on the needs of industrial firms like Samsung, Goldstar, and local affiliates of foreign companies, as they had been articulated in a series of interviews conducted by the Terman committee.

The establishment of KAIS created another inducement for Korean scientists and engineers living abroad to return to their home country. It has to be noted though that the research performed by KAIS's faculty was rather applied in nature, and closely related to the research projects undertaken by government research institutes like KIST. Indeed, the similarity in the orientation of training and research projects at these two institutions promoted their merger into the Korea Advanced Institute of Science and Technology (KAIST) in 1982.

An important area of research and instruction was the field of electronics, particularly semiconductor technology. During the 1960s, the growth of the Korean semiconductor industry was largely fueled by foreign direct investment focusing on old technologies and stages of the production process with high labor content. Indigenous research on semiconductors design and fabrication began in 1975 at the Semiconductor Technology Development Center (STDC), whose first project was a collaboration with Goldstar to develop a bipolar IC design through reverse engineering. STDC merged in 1977 with a research department at KIST to create the Korea Institute of Electronics Technology (KIET), which carried out a number of projects aimed at the development of ICs for applications in consumer electronics and telecommunications. All of these projects featured the participation of the leading electronics firms, including Goldstar, Samsung, Daewoo, and Hyundai, whose evolving business interests and technological needs were probably also responsible for the reorganization of public research institutes that led to the creation of the Electronics and Telecommunications Research Institute (ETRI) in 1985.[10]

While the focus of research activities at ETRI might have shifted toward more basic and applied research (Wade, 1990a), the chaebols have continued to collaborate with ETRI and to have a considerable influence on the allocation of public R&D funds to technology areas. These changes in the organization of public research infrastructure and research portfolio ought to be interpreted as an adaptation to the growth in the R&D investment carried out by private-sector firms. Indeed, while the government accounted for more than 80 percent of national R&D funding in 1967 when KIST began operating, the private sector's share of national R&D surpassed 50 percent already in 1977 and exceeded 80 percent in 1988. But while these data suggest that Korea's effective move into high tech industry awaited the development of in-house R&D programs by Korea's large firms (chaebols), it would be misguided to neglect the role played by public research programs in promoting the development of indigenous technological capabilities and in bringing back from abroad a number of very talented researchers, and providing them with research experience.

The Taiwanese catching-up experience during the past 50 years has been also characterized by the rapid growth of enrollments in higher education institutions. Since Taiwan's liberation from Japanese colonial rule, the Taiwanese government committed substantial public resources to education (as a fraction of GNP, education expenditure went from 1.73% of GNP in 1950 to 5.83% in 1985). The growth of the university system in Taiwan was remarkable by any indicator. Between 1950 and 1986, the number of higher education institutions went from 7 to 105, the number of enrolled students from about 6,600 to 440,000, and the number of teaching faculty from 1,000 to almost 22,000 (Hsieh, 1989). Government efforts promoted student enrollment in science and engineering programs, so that these fields accounted for about half of all students in the late 1980s (64% of Master-level students and 48% of doctoral students).

A considerable number of Taiwanese students migrated to foreign higher education institutions. In 1962, about 20 percent of all Taiwanese university-enrolled students were abroad, with the US universities accounting for half of them. The migration of students was particularly strong in the natural sciences: in 1966 one third of the students were pursuing their degrees in US institutions (UNESCO, 1972). Even at the end of the 1970s, the share of non-returning students among those who went abroad to pursue postgraduate studies was greater than 20 percent in the natural sciences and engineering (Hou and Gee, 1993). But, much as we saw in Korea, the large numbers of foreign-trained Taiwanese proved instrumental to the later development of higher education institutions in the country and to staffing the emerging R&D institutes and laboratories in the public and private sectors.[11]

Public research institutions played in Taiwan an even more important role than in Korea. Consider that as late as 1987, the private sector's share of national R&D funding was 80 percent in Korea but only 40 percent in Taiwan. Public investment in science and technology became an important aspect of Taiwan's industrial development policy since the late 1960s and promoted the creation of a number of research institutes during the following decade, including the Institute for the Information Industry (III) and the Industrial Technology Research Institute (ITRI). The latter was formally organized in 1973 with the consolidation of three existing public research laboratories (Union Industrial Research Laboratories, Mining Research & Service Organization, and Metal Industrial Research Institute).

ITRI soon included a new laboratory dedicated to research in electronics and semiconductors technology, the Electronics Industrial Research Center (later renamed Electronics Research and Services Organization, ERSO). ERSO became a key national institution for inward technology transfer, and for the accumulation of indigenous capabilities in industrial research. The typical modus operandi of ERSO's technical projects involved licensing a technology from foreign firms, creating a pilot plant to master the technology and provide training for local personnel. At the conclusion of the project, the technology would be transferred to a spin-off firm. Thus, for example, in 1976 ERSO acquired RCA's metal oxide semiconductor technology and diffused the relevant know-how to a spin-off firm (United Microelectronics Corporation) through a demonstration factory and the transfer of key engineering personnel (Amsden, 2001; Hobday 1995).

Later on, in the 1980s, ERSO promoted the formation of private spin-off companies by contributing venture capital and technological assistance to researchers who intended to exploit technologies developed or acquired through ERSO (Hou and Gee, 1993). Instances of this pattern of technology transfer include specialized companies in various semiconductor-related technologies, such as Taiwan Semiconductor Manufacturing Corp. (a joint venture with Phillips for VLSI chips manufacture), Taiwan Mask Corporation (fabrication masks), and Vanguard International Semiconductor (DRAM manufacturing). But as the local industry developed, established firms became increasingly involved in licensing technologies from ERSO or from foreign firms. Government support to R&D at public research institutes and universities played a rather important role in inducing a qualitative change in the inward transfer of technology taking place as a result of other kinds of activities, including foreign direct investment, joint ventures between local and foreign firms, and subcontracting relations with foreign firms.

An interesting contrast to the cases of Korea and Taiwan is provided by the Brazilian experience. Here too, policy makers have long recognized in words if not in fact the importance of indigenous scientific and technological capabilities toward national economic development. However, the record of accumulation of technological capabilities across the spectrum of industrial sectors in Brazil has been considerably less impressive than those of Korea, Taiwan, or Japan. While the reasons for this fact are too complex to be discussed in this chapter, we would like to draw attention to the fact that higher education and public research institutions did play an important role in the successful development of specific industrial sectors.[12] In particular, the origins of Embraer, currently the world's fourth-largest aircraft vendor, illustrate important aspects of the relationship between education, research, and the development of technological capabilities.

The early phase of development of Brazil's aerospace industry centered in fact on the establishment in 1945 of the Centro Tecnologico da Aeronautica (CTA), a center coordinating the activities of an engineering school and a research institute. Overseas institutions provided both a model for the center and a share of the initial faculty and research personnel at CTA. The engineering school (Instituto Tecnologico da Aeronautica or ITA) was organized in cooperation with MIT, and during the early years of activity many professors came to ITA from MIT and other overseas institutions. Even more important, the cooperation between the two provided an opportunity for ITA students to spend periods of study and research abroad. The successful launch of various undergraduate degree programs and, later on, of a graduate engineering school were undoubtedly related to the creation of a demand for engineers at research institutes located at CTA, and particularly at Embraer, a government-controlled company established in 1969 to develop aircraft based on Brazilian design and engineering.[13]

In turn, access to engineering talent from ITA and to the fruits of R&D activities conducted at the research institutes of CTA was a crucial determinant of Embraer's success, and later of the growth of a cluster of technologically sophisticated enterprises collocated in Sao Jose do Campos. As a result of the public investments in training and research carried out during the 1950s and 1960s, Embraer could quickly accumulate technological capabilities in aircraft design and manufacturing. To be sure, learning at Embraer also proceeded on the basis of joint development projects with and technical cooperation with foreign enterprises. Effectiveness in this learning process enabled Embraer to move quickly on to the conception and direction of aircraft development projects. Existing historical accounts lead us to argue that these developments would have not occurred in the absence of the two-pronged public investment in training and research carried out by the CTA.

Recent studies of how industry draws on university research in the United States

The capabilities of and demands on the university research system in the United States obviously differ from those in developing countries. Nonetheless, we think it useful to discuss briefly the US experience for two reasons. First, it is clear that, for better or for worse, in the minds of many scientists and policy makers in developing countries the current US system is viewed as a model of what a system of university research ought to be. These views often are associated with beliefs about how the current US system is contributing to technological advance in industry that are quite distorted. We want to argue that these beliefs can pull the development of university research systems in developing countries in quite the wrong direction. In contrast, despite the obvious differences in context, we believe that a correct appreciation of the way the US university research system is in fact contributing to industrial development can provide some useful lessons for developing countries.

Second, as successful developing countries move closer to the economic frontier, it is helpful to have an understanding of what an obviously productive, university research system in an advanced industrial nation looks like. As signaled above, our view is that the differences between a system of public research useful in catch-up, and a system useful for economies operating close to the frontiers, is not black and white, and that the latter can grow naturally out of the former.

While our focus in this section will be on the contemporary US system, it is important to put that discussion in historical context. Many authors have argued that, in contrast with the university research systems in the countries of Continental Europe, and the United Kingdom, from its beginnings, research at American universities tended to have a quite practical orientation. Thus the state- and federal government-funded agricultural research system was put in place in response to demands from farmers. In its early years, despite enthusiasm on the part of scientists employed by the system (for the most part chemists) to establish a science-based agriculture, farmers were skeptical, and insisted that the bulk of the efforts on the experimentation stations be directed to identifying best method, and improving it further. Ultimately, the advocates of a science-based agriculture proved the productivity of developing a solid scientific understanding of the chemistry and biology of plant and animal growth, nutrition, insect and other diseases, and so on. But up to the present time, testing of both prevailing and new practice, and reporting results to farmers, continues to be an important activity of public agricultural research. Agricultural research stations tend to be quite responsive to the development of new diseases and other problems facing farmers in their region. Indeed, there are striking similarities between the university based agricultural research system that grew up in the United States, and the one we described earlier that grew up in Japan. And there is good reason to believe that they have been productive for the same reasons.

Similarly, the American engineering schools like RPI, MIT, and the many that affiliated with the land-grant universities, grew up in the nineteenth century largely responding to the demands from American industry (Nelson and Rosenberg, 1994). Originally oriented largely to training young men to work in industry, many of the schools gradually took on a research and consulting role specifically oriented to industry in their region. Thus, Purdue University, located at a major rail hub, developed a strong program of research as well as training in the technologies relevant to railroad equipment. Tulsa University, in the oil country, has had a major research program on the technologies relating to oil exploration and refining. Researchers associated with the University of Minnesota developed a major and successful program to enable taconite iron-ore mining to continue to be profitable in the state, in the face of the mining-out of the richer lodes.

Until after World War II, American university research and advanced training in the fundamental sciences, like physics and organic chemistry, was not particularly strong. A significant fraction of American students seeking to get advanced training in these fields went to the United Kingdom, or Germany, up until the war. The situation regarding government funding of fundamental research, and the strength of American research universities in the basic fields, of course, changed dramatically after World War II. For the past half-century, American universities have been the home of the lion's share of the path-breaking fundamental research going on. Our discussion above, however, calls attention to the fact that American universities have been strong and effective in applications-oriented research for even longer. And the argument we will develop now is that it is a mistake to see the principal contributions of American university research today as largely flowing directly from fundamental research.

Several recent studies have explored which fields of university research are most drawn on by scientists and engineers working in industry (Klevorick et al. 1995; Cohen et al. 2002). The fields tend to be the engineering disciplines, and the applications-oriented sciences, as contrasted with the more basic sciences like physics, and mathematics. In addition to fields like electrical engineering, and pathology, the industry scientists clearly also tended to identify academic chemistry, and academic biology. It is important to note that these basic sciences, like those more specifically aimed to solve practical problems, in fact often involve research that is quite close to applications.

Not surprisingly, the studies of the development of particular technologies that highlight an important university role tend to locate that role in engineering schools, or medical schools.

This is not to play down the importance of the strength of American universities in training and research in the fundamental sciences. Among other things, capabilities and activities here provide an essential support for effective training and research in the applications-oriented sciences. But the latter, not the former, provides the direct links with industrial innovation, even in industries, like those in the United States, generally operating at the frontier.

Another widespread misconception about the ways in which research at American universities has been contributing to industrial innovation is that university research is the principal source of embryonic inventions, which are taken up and commercialized by industry. There certainly are a number of important instances that are like that. Thus, university research gave birth to the modern computer. Some important pharmaceuticals have come directly out of university research, and some important medical devices.

However, responses from industrial scientists and engineers suggest strongly that this is not the principal kind of contribution that university research makes to industrial innovation. One study asked industry respondents to rate the relative importance of three different kinds of inputs of public research to industrial R&D: prototypes, general research findings, instruments and techniques. Virtually all industry respondents said the latter two kinds of research outputs were far more important to them than prototypes. Even in pharmaceuticals, and in electronic devices, where current conventional wisdom has it that the university-created prototypes are highly important, the respondents reported that general research findings, and instruments and techniques created through research, were far more important to them.

Relatedly, the conventional wisdom has it that the principal contribution of university research to industrial innovation is to stimulate, trigger, new industrial R&D efforts aimed to take advantage of those breakthroughs. However, respondents in most industries reported that most of their R&D projects were initiated in response to perceptions of customer needs, or weaknesses in production processes. The principle use of university research results that they reported was in enabling industrial R&D to solve problems effectively in projects so oriented, rather than to trigger new industrial R&D projects.

The respondents' reports on the important channels through which university research results flow to and get used by industry reflect what kind of university research outputs get most used, and how they get used. Respondents in most industries reported that publications, information disseminated at meetings and conferences, informal interactions with university researchers, and consulting, were the most important conduits through which to draw on university research results. Contrary to current conventional wisdom, most industries reported that patents played little role in technology transfer. Even in pharmaceuticals, where university patents were rated an important vehicle of technology transfer, publications, and meetings and conferences were rated as more important vehicles through which industry gained access to the results of university research.

The picture which emerges is that of a university research system helpful to economic development in the United States because important parts of it work at being useful. This is very different from one that proposes that positive effects on economic development flow naturally from the efforts of university researchers concentrating on simply advancing their science. This is not to say the latter is not important. But the US university research system has been as effective as it has been in contributing to economic development because it is not an Ivory Tower.

The challenge of institutional design and development

An influential body of literature argues that government has no business establishing and supporting research programs aimed to help particular economic sectors. First of all, such programs run counter to international treaties regarding the rules of the game under the WTO. Second, in any case governments inevitably make bad judgments when they try to help particular sectors. However, while the ground rules under the WTO inhibit the subsidy of specific commercial products or firms, they do not constrain broad support of R&D and training tailored to meet a sector's needs. And, as the examples we gave showed clearly, such government-supported programs have been very effective in the several successful cases of economic catching-up.

In the preceding two sections we looked briefly at a number of instances and structures of public research contributing effectively to economic progress. We looked at agricultural and industrial development in Japan in the early stages of Japan's successful catch-up experience, at Korea and Taiwan in the last decades of the twentieth century, and at the successful programs in Brazil to support agricultural development and aircraft design and production. We then considered several recent studies of just how university research in the United States has been contributing to technological advance in industry. We think these cases together provide an illuminating picture of the kinds of structures and conditions under which publicly supported research contributes importantly to economic development.

The research programs that effectively contributed to catch-up did not operate within ivory towers. Rather, in every case they were oriented towards an actual or potential user community. They were designed to help solve problems, and advance technology, relevant to a particular economic sector.

As some of the examples suggest strongly, a program of public research can be effective only in a context in which the user community has strong incentives to improve their practices, and the capability to use what is coming out of the research program. They need to be willing and able to try new things, to learn. It is interesting and relevant, we think, that in many of the successful cases, public research was part of a broader structure aimed to improve productivity in a sector which included, as well, education and training programs for people going out to become members of the user community. Thus the agricultural research programs in Japan complemented programs to give Japanese farmers better training. The productivity of the programs of public research in electronics in Korea and Taiwan depended on the major investments that had been made in the training of engineers, who went out into industry, and provided industrial firms with the technical sophistication they needed in order to draw fruitfully from that research. And in turn, a client population, eager for research results that can help them, and capable of recognizing and using those results when they become available, can provide an effective and demanding source of priorities and support for a public research organization.

While there is much to the argument that national governments cannot effectively identify particular firms or narrowly defined commercial products to be supported, the historical evidence indicates that they have much less difficulty in identifying broad economic sectors and technologies where public research can be productive. Programs of support of agricultural research, or research on diseases endemic to a country, simply are not of the kind that can be accused of trying to 'pick winners'. The agricultural research programs we described were focused on the particular problems and opportunities of indigenous agriculture. And for countries significantly behind the technological frontiers, research programs to support the development of indigenous capabilities in manufacturing are able to focus on technologies used in more advanced countries. These are technologies that indigenous firms are going to have to master if they are to be effective operating in the field. Thus, the Korean and Taiwanese programs of public research in electronics, and Brazil's program in aviation technology, were designed to enable domestic capabilities to come closer to capabilities at the frontier.[14]

We note that the fields of research contributing more or less directly to problem-solving and innovation in the user sector were and are largely the applications-oriented sciences and engineering disciplines. This observation is not to denigrate the importance of the development of indigenous capabilities in the basic sciences. Capabilities here are clearly important for training purposes. Engineers, agricultural scientists, medical scientists, need to have solid training in physics, mathematics, chemistry, biology. And problem-solving research in the applied sciences and engineering disciplines often fruitfully draws on relatively recent research results in the more basic sciences. However, all the cases we have considered show the applications-oriented sciences and engineering as the fields of public research where there is direct interaction with problems and opportunities in agriculture, industry, and medicine.

We also note that many of the successful cases and structures that we have considered developed outside the more traditional system of public research in higher education. Earlier we observed that in the contemporary US system, most of the fields of research contributing importantly to innovation in industry usually are housed in engineering and medical schools, rather than in general arts and sciences. Most of the cases we described of successful public-sector R&D in developing countries also were located outside the mainline university structure, in dedicated applications-oriented laboratories. The extent of linkage between institutions supporting engineering, agricultural, and medical research and training, and the broader liberal arts university system, has differed from country to country. But in the cases described earlier, successful systems of publicly supported applications-oriented research and training had their own special structures.

These structures were conducive to two-way interaction between the research institution and the user community. Those involved in the research programs generally were well informed about the nature of prevailing practice in the fields with which they were concerned, and the problems and constraints of practitioners. Crucially, there were a variety of mechanisms through which what was learned and developed in research was effectively disseminated to the user community.

Successful public research programs of other countries can and should serve as broad guides for countries trying to establish their own programs, but as indictors of principles to follow, not as templates. There is first of all the problem that it is very difficult to identify just what features of another country's successful program were key to its success, and which ones were peripheral. Second, what works in one country setting is unlikely to work in the same way in another. Among the several examples our short case studies provide, the highly differing ways that Korea and Taiwan have gone about supporting, successfully, the development of indigenous electronics stands out. Programs of public research need to be free to learn what works and what doesn't, and they need to be designed in such a way as to evolve in response to emerging patterns of development of technological capabilities in the private sector.

While high-level policy can set a frame for the development of a successful program of public research, that frame must have a certain looseness regarding the details. One important reason is the inevitable, and desirable, decentralization of decision-making. Effective research structures can't operate in the setting where what is done is determined by distant, high-level government officials, either directly, or through a highly detailed planning document. The technical expertise resides to a considerable extent with the scientists at the relevant research institute. And it is there that the detailed understanding of the problems and opportunities of the sector being serviced needs to be developed. An effective research program needs to be able to reallocate resources, refocus efforts, as perceptions of problems and opportunities change. Similarly, the problems of information flow, interaction, and mutual influence, between a research institute and the economic sector with which it is concerned, need to be able to develop and change, on the basis of experience which indicates what works, and what doesn't.

But while detailed planning and monitoring by government ministers can hinder the effectiveness of a laboratory, there must be mechanisms in place to prevent a research institution from becoming an ivory tower, focusing on what interests the researchers, or the research director, even if such a program has little to do with the problems and opportunities of the economic sector whose development provides the basic rationale for the research. There needs to be some mechanism by which the user community has a voice in long-run evaluation of a research program.

At the same time, it is important not to have the program captured by prevailing economic interests, First of all, these tend strongly to push the program towards short-run problem solving, and at the expense of research that can have greater payoff over the long run. Second, in many cases potentially the most important research will open up possibilities for new directions and enterprises in the sector in question, which may not be to the interest of existing firms or farmers.

We close by noting that today many countries are beginning to try to use public research as part of their broad strategies for industrial catch-up. There will be accumulating experience in this area, some successful, some not successful, that can help sharpen understanding of what works and what doesn't. An important objective of this chapter is to help catalyze continuing analysis and cross-country discussion of how to use public research programs as an effective support of industrial catch-up.

Notes

1. The different views regarding the importance of learning processes and development of capabilities in economic catch-up are well captured in the contrast between accumulation and assimilation theories of the growth of the Asian Tigers (Kim and Nelson, 2000). The intellectual perils of neglecting the difficulties of learning what others have done, and the associated failures in earlier World Bank development strategies, have been highlighted by Easterly (2001).
2. For example, the share of US science and engineering articles that were the result of international collaborations increased from 10% to 23% over the 1988–2001 period (National Science Board, 2004). Similar trends have been observed in the other countries.
3. Christopher Freeman (1995) has proposed that Friedrich List had something like a National Innovation System in mind when, in the mid-nineteenth century, he was writing about what Germany needed to do to catch up with Great Britain.
4. Private institutions in sciences and technical fields formed early on but owing to the lack of financial support could not maintain scientific and engineering courses on a par with those offered by the public institutions.
5. From all accounts, it appears that the government controlled the growth of the higher education system, including the activities of private institutions. As a result, the otherwise remarkable growth of the Japanese system of higher education did not really result in a trend toward mass higher education, at least until the 1960s. This may help explain why Japan did not experience during the early twentieth century a phenomenon of underemployment of graduates from academic institutions, a problem that surfaced clearly during more recent catch-up experiences.
6. Odagiri (1999) provides a few instances of professors involved in the development of electrical equipment, pharmaceuticals, steel plants, and automobiles.
7. This institute was patterned after the German Physicalische Technische Reichsanstalt established in 1887, and its research mission encompassed both basic research in the fields of chemistry and physics and applied research aimed at industrial technology. This Institute grew considerably in size and range of scientific and technical fields since the mid-1920s when the current director Okochi Masatoshi addressed the financial constraints on the activities of the institute by making a push toward the commercialization of technologies patented by the Institute (Cusumano, 1989).
8. The Research Institute named earlier (Riken) became the core research institute of a new zaibatsu whose subsidiaries operated in a large portfolio of business lines in metals, machinery, photographic equipment, and chemicals (Cusumano, 1989).
9. Yonekura (1994) argues that the activities of the institute, and of its research divisions, consisted mostly of the dissemination of the results of technological research carried out at Yawata Works.

10. The significance of these projects for the chaebols' accumulation of capabilities in semiconductor technology has been evaluated differently by different scholars. Wade (1990a and 1990b) argues that these research collaborations provided the chaebols with technological capabilities that, coupled with other forms of industry support by the government, enabled them to move into the fabrication of semiconductors. On the other hand, Hobday (1995) and Pack (2000) regard the role of KIET as secondary at best, arguing that the relevant sources of technology transfer were foreign firms.

11. Hsieh (1989) reports that in the late 1980s a large majority of the faculty at leading academic institutions in Taiwan (including the Academia Sinica, National Taiwan University, and National Tsing Hua University) held degrees from foreign academic institutions, most notably American ones. Following the establishment of the Hsinchu Science-based Industrial Park in 1980, large numbers of foreign-trained nationals returned home as founders or investors in more than one-half of the new firms based in the Park (National Science Council, 1997).

12. The evolution of the Brazilian system of innovation is analyzed in Dahlman and Frischtak (1993), Schwartzman (1991), and Viotti (2002), among others.

13. On the contrary, the lack of a demand for specialized engineers and metallurgists by either private or public enterprises in the iron and steel sector plagued the development of the Escola de Minas founded in 1875 well into the twentieth century.

14. Reference to the case of Brazilian aviation makes it imperative to observe that in several cases of successful catch-up, governments also played important roles in stimulating or creating a demand for indigenous capabilities in the relevant technologies.

References

Abramowitz M. (1986), 'Catching Up, Forging Ahead, and Falling Behind,' *Journal of Economic History*, June.

Albuquerque E. (2003), 'Immature Systems of Innovation,' Paper prepared for the first conference on Globelics, Rio (November).

Amano I. (1979), 'Continuity and Change in the Structure of Japanese Higher Education,' in W.K. Cummings, I. Amano, and K. Kitamura (eds.) *Changes in the Japanese University: A Comparative Perspective*, Praeger Publishers.

Amsden A. H. (2001), *The Rise of 'The Rest': Challenges to the West from Late-Industrializing Economies*, Oxford University Press, Oxford.

Bartholomew J. (1989), *The Formation of Science in Japan*, Yale University Press.

Bell M. and K. Pavitt (1993), 'Technological Accumulation and Industrial Growth,' *Industrial and Corporate Change*.

Bernardes A. and E. Albuquerque (2003), 'Cross-over, Thresholds, and Interactions Between Science and Technology: Lessons for Less-developed Countries,' *Research Policy*, May.

Cohen W., R. Nelson, and J. Walsh (2002), 'Links and Impacts: The Influence of Public Research on Industrial R&D,' *Management Science*, 48(1): 1–23.

Cusumano M. (1989), 'Scientific Industry: Strategy, Technology, and Entrepreneurship in Prewar Japan,' in W. Wray (ed.) *Managing Industrial Enterprise*, Harvard University Press, Cambridge, Mass.

Dahlman C. and C. Frischtak (1993), 'National Systems Supporting Technical Advance in Industry: The Brazilian Experience,' in R. Nelson (ed.) *National Innovation Systems*, Oxford University Press, Oxford.

Easterly W. (2001), *The Elusive Quest for Growth*, MIT Press, Cambridge, Mass.

Fagerberg J. and M. Godinho (2004), 'Innovation and Catch-up,' in J. Fagerberg, D. Mowery, and R. Nelson (eds.) *Handbook of Innovation*, Oxford University Press, Oxford.

Freeman C. (1995), 'The National System of Innovation in Historical Context,' *Cambridge Journal of Economics*.

Gershenkron A. (1962), 'Economic Backwardness in Historical Perspective' (1951), reprinted in A. Gershenkron (ed.) *Economic Development in Historical Perspective*, Harvard University Press, Cambridge, Mass.

Hamilton A. (1965), 'Report on Manufactures' (1791), reprinted in *The Reports of Alexander Hamilton*, Harper Torch-back, New York.

Hashimoto T. (1999), 'The Hesitant Relationship Reconsidered: University–Industry Cooperation in Postwar Japan,' in L.M. Branscomb, F. Kodama, and R. Florida (eds.) *Industrializing Knowledge*, MIT Press, Cambridge, Mass.

Hayami Y. and V. Ruttan (1985), *Agricultural Development: An International Perspective*, Johns Hopkins University Press.

Hobday M. (1995), *Innovation in East Asia: the Challenge to Japan*, Edward Elgar, Aldershot.

Hou C-M. and S. Gee (1993), 'National System Supporting Technical Advance in Industry: The Case of Taiwan,' in R. Nelson (ed.) *National Innovation Systems: A Comparative Analysis*, Oxford University Press, Oxford.

Hsieh H. (1989), 'University Education and Research in Taiwan,' in P.G. Altbach et al., *Scientific Development and Higher Education: The Case of Newly Industrializing Nations*, Praeger Publishers.

Kim D-W. and S. Leslie (1998), 'Winning Markets or Winning Nobel Prizes? KAIST and the Challenges of Late Industrialization,' *Osiris*, 13(2nd series): 164–85.

Kim L. (1997), *Imitation to Innovation: The Dynamics of Korea's Technological Learning*, Harvard Business School Press, Boston.

—— (1999), *Learning and Innovation in Economic Development*, Edward Elgar, Cheltenham.

—— and R. Nelson (2000), *Technology, Learning, and Innovation*, Cambridge University Press.

Klevorick A. et al. (1995), 'On the Sources and Significance of Interindustry Differences in Technological Opportunities,' *Research Policy*, 24: 185–205.

Landes D. (1969), *The Unbound Prometheus*, Cambridge University Press.

Lee D., Z-T. Bae, and J. Lee (1991), 'Performance and Adaptive Roles of the Government-Supported Research Institute in South Korea,' *World Development*, 19(10): 1421–40.

List F. (1904), *National Systems of Political Economy* (1841), English edition, Longman, London.

Mikami A. (1980), 'Old and New Zaibatsu in the History of Japan's Chemical Industry: With Special Reference to the Sumitomo Chemical Co. and the Showa Denko Co.,' in A. Okochi and H. Uchida (eds.) *Development and Diffusion of Technology: Electrical and Chemical Industries*, 6th International Conference on Business History, University of Tokyo Press.

Mowery D., R. Nelson, B. Sampat, and A. Ziedonis (2004), *Ivory Tower and Industrial Innovation: University–Industry Technology Transfer Before and After the Bayh–Dole Act in the United States*, Stanford University Press, Stanford.

National Science Board (2004), *Science and Engineering Indicators 2004*, National Science Foundation, Arlington, Va.

National Science Council (1997), *White Paper on Science and Technology*, Executive Yuan, Republic of China, Taiwan <http://www.stic.gov.tw/stic/policy/scimeeting/ E-white-paper/index_e.htm>.

Nelson R. (ed.) (1993), *National Innovation Systems*, Oxford University Press, Oxford.

—— and N. Rosenberg (1994), 'American Universities and Technical Advance in Industry.' *Research Policy*, 23: 323–48.

—— and B. Sampat (2001), 'Making Sense of Institutions as a Factor Shaping Economic Performance,' *Journal of Economic Behavior and Organization*.

Odagiri H. (1999), 'University–Industry Collaboration in Japan: Facts and Interpretations,' in L. Branscomb, F. Kodama, and R. Florida (eds.) *Industrializing Knowledge*, MIT Press, Cambridge, Mass.

—— and A. Goto (1993), 'The Japanese System of Innovation: Past, Present, and Future,' in R. Nelson (ed.) *National Innovation Systems: A Comparative Analysis*, Oxford University Press, Oxford.

—— —— (1996), *Technology and Industrial Development in Japan*, Clarendon Press, Oxford.

Pack H. (2000), 'Research and Development in the Industrial Development Process,' in L. Kim and R. Nelson (eds.) *Technology, Learning, & Innovation*. Cambridge University Press.

Perez C. (2002), *Technological Revolutions and Financial Capital*, Edward Elgar, Cheltenham.

—— and L. Soete (1988), 'Catching up in Technology: Entry Barriers and Windows of Opportunity' in G. Dosi, C. Freeman, R. Nelson, et al., *Technical Change and Economic Theory*, Pinter Publishers, London.

Pollard S. (1981), *Peaceful Conquest*, Oxford University Press, Oxford.

Rosenberg N. (1970), 'Economic Development and the Transfer of Technology: Some Historical Perspectives,' *Technology and Culture*, 11(4): 550–75.

—— and R. Nelson (1994), 'American Universities and Technical Advance in Industry,' *Research Policy*.

Schwartzman S. (1991), *A Space for Science*, Pennsylvania University Press.

Uchida H. (1980), 'Western Big Business and the Adoption of New Technology in Japan: The Electrical Equipment and Chemical Industries 1890–1920,' in A. Okochi and H. Uchida (eds.) *Development and Diffusion of Technology: Electrical and Chemical Industries*, 6th International Conference on Business History, University of Tokyo Press.

UNESCO (1972), *Statistics of Students Abroad 1962–1968*.

Viotti E. (2002), 'National Learning Systems: A new approach on technological change in late industrialising economies and evidence from the cases of Brazil and South Korea,' *Technological Forecasting and Social Change*, 69(7): 653–80.

—— (2003), 'Technological Learning Systems, Competition, and Development,' Paper prepared for the first Globelics conference, Rio (November).

Wade R. (1990a), *Governing the Market*, Princeton University Press.

—— (1990b), 'Industrial Policy in East Asia: Does It Lead or Follow the Market?' in G. Gereffi and D. Wyman (eds.) *Manufacturing Miracles: Paths of Industrialization in Latin America and East Asia*, Princeton University Press.

Yonekura S. (1994), *The Japanese Iron and Steel Industry, 1850–1990: Continuity and Discontinuity*, St. Martin's Press, New York.

15

Nationality of Firm Ownership in Developing Countries: Who Should 'Crowd Out' Whom in Imperfect Markets?

Alice H. Amsden

What the entrepreneurial group of Islamic small businessmen most lacks is not capital... or drive... or a sufficient market... It lacks the capacity to form efficient economic institutions; it is a group of entrepreneurs without enterprises.

Clifford Geertz, Peddlers and Princes, Java, 1963

Overview

In theory, the nationality of an enterprise shouldn't matter to economic development. Whether a firm is a foreign-owned subsidiary of a multinational (FOE), or a private nationally owned enterprise in the developing world (POE), development will be the same so long as markets are perfect. In industries in which an infinite number of firms can compete, there need be no crowding out of the momentarily weaker by the stronger. There is plenty of room for all to create new jobs no matter what the nationality of their corporate board or majority shareholders. It follows that government policy should open the doors to one and all.

But this story changes in markets that are monopolistic. Here, arguably, the nationality of ownership does matter. FOEs and POEs make distinct contributions to economic development, but under monopoly, only one species survives—not necessarily because it is better but because it is more experienced. The POE could be as great, if only it had enough time to learn. In fact, many POEs are already entrepreneurial. From ground up, they built most of the new industries of the developing world. FOEs, on the other hand, from subsidiary to headquarters, benefit from a finely tuned, *bureaucratic* management machine. Whether a developing economy is dominated by FOEs or POEs in its mid-tech or mature high-tech sectors thus really matters.

Starting with the 1950s, when the US spurred a managerial revolution that spread to Europe and Japan, multinationals marketed not just capital and technology but also the latest management skills. Through the movement of people, managerial professionalism diffused from FOEs to POEs. All Taiwanese top managers in the electronics industry, for example, had once worked for RCA (Radio Corporation of America)—RCA had located a subsidiary in Asia in search of cheap labor. This was a very important transfer of know-how from North to South.

But the multinational, operating through its subsidiary, is inherently a bureaucratic animal. Strategic decisions must filter from headquarters, then to regional offices, and then to subsidiaries, making three levels of bureaucracy right there. Professional management is one side of the multinational's coin, but bureaucracy and rule-bound decision making is the other.

The POE, by contrast, is likely to contribute Schumpeterian entrepreneurship to development, not bureaucracy. The POE is relatively young, it combines professional management and dynamic family ownership, and it spearheads diversification in countries setting up or restructuring a wide range of promising industries. It, not the FOE, is the agent that opens industries that are new to the developing world. POEs may be adventurous and corrupt (their reputation, with little proof), a little loose with other people's money, but in those developing countries that managed to accumulate modern manufacturing experience, national enterprises are now the incubators of top talent (Morris Chang, the former Vice President of Texas Instruments who presently manages Taiwan Semiconductor Manufacturing Company, spoke of leaving TI because he had reached the 'yellow-glass ceiling'). There are no color bars for national citizens in nationally owned firms.

Entrepreneurship in POEs and bureaucracy in FOEs arise from differences in risk-taking—the FOE is risk averse and the POE is risk loving, given their differences in knowledge, income, and age. The multinational has the knowledge to choose among promising investments around the world, not just in a single country. To decide what actual investments to undertake, it uses bureaucratic processes involving divisions of decision-makers. But however careful, this process may screen out the most profitable and developmental investments due to high estimated risk.

The POE, by contrast, becomes a competitor by reducing the throughput-time of doing business. Its swiftness stems partly from operating within a *business group* that is managed by a single owner that can transfer money and skills to and from organically created affiliates. Groups benefit from the inter-sectoral learning made possible by the absence of operating in a single market (Dosi, 1988). The POE today is typically in its first, second, or third generation of family ownership. It is free from bureaucracy at the top while enjoying professional management at the bottom and middle.

POEs also tend to have more knowledge of the local business environment than FOEs. Charles Kindleberger argued as early as 1970 that proximity creates advantages for the national investor, but he wrote too early to add that the same people who know their own environment also know the leading economies abroad. Knowing both worlds through birth and education, POEs exploit a developing country's high-risk opportunities, because they have no other choice. These lay dormant for so long under the influence of FOEs. POEs pick winners by looking at the earlier behavior or FOEs.

This is the gist of the argument that crowding out of POEs by FOEs in monopolistic industries (mid-tech and mature high-tech) is not development friendly.

FOEs transfer technology, so the argument runs, but clearly they do not do so to their national competitors. Foreign companies transfer knowledge to the developing world but only when they themselves are *located abroad*. Without any ownership strings attached, overseas vendors supply technology to latecomers in the form of capital goods, parts, and components. Sometimes a package with 'supplier's credits' to pay for the capital is included, reducing the need for foreign finance. Foreign capital goods manufacturers, from Sony to Sun Microsoft, are the major sources of technology in industries ranging from steel and petrochemicals to shipbuilding and electronics. No direct foreign investment in these sectors is required for POEs to learn.

Depending on the definition of *foreign direct investment*, the contribution of FOEs to economic development has tended to be exaggerated, especially if an alternative source of capital is available. In order to appear 'open,' countries overstate their foreign investment stock (a firm with only a 10% foreign equity stake may be classified as foreign in one country but not another). In China, around 70 percent of foreign investment is from overseas Chinese, including Chinese from Hong Kong, and the definition of a foreign investment includes the kitchen sink, such as foreign loans, not only foreign equity (Banerjee, 2005).[1] In 2003, under US pressure, 82 countries made a total of 244 regulatory changes regarding foreign direct investment, of which 220 were in its favor (UNCTAD, 2004). The more FDI a developing country has, the warmer a country's political welcome in Washington, so the role of the POE has tended to be understated and misunderstood.

As early as 1982, POEs already showed faint signs of out-performing FOEs. Hyundai Motors, then a baby owned almost exclusively by Hyundai, a Korean business group, out-performed Daewoo Motors, a joint venture between General Motors and Daewoo, another national Korean group (that ultimately went bankrupt from over-expansion) (see Linsu, 1997). The nationally owned firm out-competed the joint venture along every line. If we measure 'commitment' to national development in terms of sunk capital, Hyundai's commitment was larger; as a firm without a leading-edge technology, it had nowhere else to invest than at home. The national company's opportunity costs were higher than the foreign company's. Hyundai's employment was also greater, a key concern of the Korean government at the time. Hyundai's capacity, production, and exports were greater. Although at full capacity, labor and capital productivity were roughly the same in the two companies, given a big gap in capacity utilization, actual labor and capital productivity were far higher in Hyundai.

Mitsubishi Motors sold Hyundai Motors its engine design, which was then perfected to save fuel. Seoul's taxi drivers bought HM's cars, not GM's, out of national pride and fuel efficiency.

The distinction between entrepreneurial and bureaucratic, that makes the POE potentially more valuable than the FOE, takes many forms. A giant multinational, with tacit knowledge, keeps its top managers and engineers at corporate headquarters to oversee non-routine, non-standardized functions, as Raymond Vernon observed in his product cycle theory (Vernon, 1966). This elite, of necessity, is in short supply. Therefore, when a multinational opens a subsidiary overseas, it substitutes top management's insights with bureaucratic rules. It cookie-cuts every foreign operating facility. Within a range, there is no need for innovative managers, so even the transfer of managerial know-how is constrained.

The multinational retains at home its most prized value-added function, R&D. This function never fully migrates even to the biggest markets or labor troves, China or India, despite foreign R&D facilities in these countries (such as General Electric's lab in Bangalore). FOEs' R&D in the developing world barely reaches the level of applied research, let alone basic research (Amsden, Tschang, et al. 2001). The most promising R&D projects are guarded closely by huge corporate labs, huge because they undertake multi-disciplinary tasks, from physics and linguistics to metallurgy and chemistry. GE's Bangalore lab employed maybe 1,000 people and was designed to support all GE's production operations in India, not to launch new products, whereas GE's corporate research laboratory in upstate New York employed at least 5,000 people. Without R&D on the premises, developing countries may not get to produce the hottest-selling models. Daewoo Motors, the GM–Daewoo joint venture, under-performed in Korea because it tried to sell an outdated Opel model from GM-Europe.

A good working hypothesis is that at present, FOEs undertake only beginner-level R&D in most parts of the developing world. As skills rise, headquarters may invite local engineers to participate in a top-level corporate project, but only in a small part of it.

FOEs that are equity investors in the developing world are thus decapitated creatures. They are disfigured because they are missing the top layer of management, including leaders in science and engineering, which are always located at corporate headquarters. If all industry were foreign-owned, a developing country would never develop the top skills and highest-paying jobs (CEO, CFO, Regional Manager, Lead Scientist) that rocket the modern corporation. The developing country would never become advanced enough to earn the entrepreneurial rents that tacit technology and associated brand names earn. The developing world would only experience a brain drain of its best talent, who would migrate to places with high-end jobs. These are some of the opportunity costs of having FOEs crowd out POEs in monopolistic industries.

POEs in developing countries know high risks when they see them, but they don't know investment opportunities elsewhere, and they anticipate ultra-high profits at home; in select under-developed countries, where markets are still young if not virgin and entrepreneurs and government planners know what they are doing, *the expected rate of return is enormous*. Hence, POEs are entrepreneurial. They are the first to create the national enterprises necessary for economic development in conjunction with government support. They assume the lead in overcoming the initial handicaps of lateness. POEs see opportunities first by thoroughly knowing the world around them.

The jury is still out in the FOE–POE rivalry, particularly when joint ventures are taken into account and differences in age and stage of development are controlled for. Imagine if India and China follow in Korea's footsteps and build up their nationally owned automobile industries (which both are trying to do). Then the difficulty of answering the question about future competition between FOEs and POEs becomes clear: who will triumph—Brazil's and Mexico's foreign-dominated automobile industries, with their concern for static efficiency, or Korea's, India's, and China's nationally dominated ones, with their concern for expanding markets? Or will Toyota Motors sweep every board? The answers are not obvious. But if one believes in entrepreneurialism and human capital, versus first-mover advantage and bureaucratic efficiency, then the bet is on Korea, India, and China, all students of Japan.

The national edge

The modern corporation is a microcosm of the modern economy, with all its complex economic, political, and social cross-currents. It is difficult to establish, and only a subset of developing countries have successfully nurtured professionally managed national firms across a wide array of industries. Why has Asia been better than Latin America in building the latest generation of behemoths? Have POEs or FOEs mattered in Asia's rise?

Foreign investors were typically *not* the first to create new industries overseas even before World War II. With the exception of raw material extraction, FOEs were not leaders: 'Throughout the colonial world, while foreign investment undoubtedly speeded up the development of countries (both poor countries and regions of White recent settlement), it is more accurate to think of it as accompanying and reinforcing their growth than as preliminary to it... *the foreign investor usually did not join in until comparatively late in the day, lagging behind rather than running in front'* (Cairncross, 1953, emphasis added). The experience of nineteenth-century America 'strongly supports' this assessment (Kravis, 1970), as does the history of Japan: 'When the Japanese had already demonstrated their general progressive drive and their specific industrial aptitudes, FDI in manufacturing made an appearance' (Reubens, 1955). In India, 'foreigners were responsible for starting the jute industry, a major nineteenth century exporter. The initiative for railroad construction also came from foreigners. But Indians took the lead in creating the cotton textile, power generation, shipping, construction, sugar, iron and steel, engineering, and agricultural implements industries' (Agarwala, 1986). Later, they pioneered in chemicals, electronics, automobiles, and aircraft manufacturing. In all these cases, the POE was first to raise the capital and take the risk in a new industry—new to India. In the Argentine meat packing industry, two local firms were among the original investors, until bought out by foreign meat packers. In China, foreign firms were generally tiny in size, and large enterprises got their start from state-related bureaucrats (Allen and Donnithorne, 1954; Dernberger, 1975; and Feuerwerker, 1958).

Many heavy industries after World War II were developed by state-owned enterprises (SOEs), not FOEs, if only because FOEs were routed out of these industries by government regulations, and POEs didn't have the investment capital. Under colonialism, FOEs got (and mostly retain) secure spots in natural-resource rich industries. In Latin America and Asia, SOEs were instrumental in starting or advancing the petrochemical and steel industries. On average, these two industries accounted for about 80 percent of all state *manufacturing* activity in developing countries. The Crown in Thailand established business groups centered on the manufacture of cement and automobiles. The Indian software industry prides its origins on being private. In fact, the industry started, and started specifically in Bangalore, with the help of a government military R&D installation and a prestigious Indian Electronics Institute, an elite graduate engineering school. The global privatization drive that began under President Reagan sold many SOEs to FOEs. But some of the best SOEs went to national capital, thereby strengthening them (Embraer in the Brazilian aircraft, Sunkyong in the Korean petrochemical industry).

POEs normally remain family owned for at least three generations: a visionary at the top and her close associates rule the roost. Then come professionally trained, salaried managers and engineers. This combination, of professional managers and dynamic owners, is almost as growth-inducing as that of the early Japanese *zaibatsu* (business groups) whose excess demand for capable managers led to outsiders being given a share in ownership; thus, ownership and professional management in Japan were fused early on. In most developing countries there was no fusion, but professional managers went almost to the top of the organizational hierarchy, especially in production engineering. Thus, big business in the advanced developing countries combined raw entrepreneurship in the persona of the ambitious owner and professional expertise in the personae of trained managers. This combination was capable of quick decision-making and project implementation, one that could conceivably challenge the bureaucracy of foreign subsidiaries, regional offices and headquarters. Taiwan's private electronics firms couldn't attract professional managers and engineers unless such professionals were convinced that they were joining a firm that was rationally run. No one wanted to work for a maniac. A new cadre of professional managers disciplined an old cadre of dynamic tycoons.

In Latin America, however, foreign investors got an early start—a conceivable reason behind its lackluster performance compared with Asia's after World War II. As indicated in Table 15.1, Latin America attracted foreign investment far earlier than Asia. Much of the elite in Latin America still considered itself foreign, so foreign investment did not initially meet widespread nationalist opposition, and it found a relatively rich population not under another empire's control. FOEs became part of the woodwork. The subsidiary of an Italian multinational, Pirelli, was established in Argentina as early as 1917 (Barbero, 1990). Afterwards FDI in Latin America rose fairly steadily.[2] Skills and wages in Argentina, Brazil, Chile, and Mexico were high by the standards of Asia, which provided a market for foreign goods. Protective tariffs insured that these goods would be assembled, if not manufactured, locally. When most of the developing world was still under the control of a colonial power, Latin America was nominally free, having thrown off the Spanish yoke in the early nineteenth century. It was easier for FOEs from the US to do business in Latin America than in the colonies of rival powers, so with Washington's support, FOEs became the dominant form of business in Latin American industries.

As World War II approached, foreign investors strengthened their Asian presence. Japan's mobilization for war and invasion of Manchuria in the 1930s provided a lightning rod for regional industrialization. Japan hastily strengthened war-related industries in Korea and Taiwan, thereby planting the seeds for their highly successful postwar industrial promotion systems. Colonial governments in Indonesia and Malaysia responded to Japan's threats with defensive investments, including protectionism against Japanese exports.[3] A bloodless *coup d'état* in Thailand in 1932 ushered in a period of nationalist development initially in collaboration with Japan. While 'economic policy stayed liberal in most (southeast Asian) colonies throughout the late nineteenth and early twentieth centuries,' economic policy was already protectionist when growth resumed in the late 1930s following the Great Depression (Lindblad, 1998).

Table 15.1. Timing of foreign investment in Latin America and Asia, 1977–89 (share of foreign affiliates in local output)

	1977 (%)	1982 (%)	1989 (%)
	Latin America		
United States Foreign Affiliates			
Non-elec mach	22.6	13.5	31.4
Elec mach	31.4	22.6	15.6
Transport eq	64.5	52.2	38.9
All manufacturing	20.0	18.2	15.3
	Developing Asia		
Non-elec mach	3.0	—	—
Elec mach	—	6.2	9.8
Transport eq	—	—	8.5
All manufacturing	3.6	2.2	4.5
Japanese Foreign Affiliates*			
Non-elec mach	—	4.5	6.0
Elec mach	—	8.4	12.9
Transport eq	—	18.7	29.1
All manufacturing	—	5.8	7.8

* Japanese investments in Latin America were negligible and were ignored.

Notes: European OECD investments were negligible and, therefore, were ignored. Data for Japanese foreign affiliates includes affiliates for all those companies in which Japanese ownership is 10% or more. Data for US foreign affiliates include only those companies in which US ownership is at least 50%. Figures from US, Japan and OECD were not aggregated due to missing US observations.

Source: Adapted from Amsden (2001).

The manufacturing experience that a dozen developing countries got from foreign and national enterprise was key to postwar development. *No developing country entered the orbit of modern world industry after World War II, with its own POEs, that didn't have prewar manufacturing experience* (Amsden, 2001). No developing country cultivated a strong cadre of nationally owned firms from scratch.

Manufacturing experience came from one of two basic sources: émigrés and colonial firms (owned by metropolitan-based companies). Foreign immigrants from Europe brought technology to the developing world, especially Latin America, at least since the sixteenth century. First as individuals, then as subsidiaries of foreign companies like Pirelli, their share of the local economy increased. The same is true of Chinese émigrés in Asia. Colonial firms, the second source, didn't transfer technology all that differently, but their investments were more strategic, coordinated, and planned. The critical difference between émigré and colony was that colonialism eventually ended.

After 1945, decolonization, the attainment of independence by a number of former colonies, had a colossal effect on firm ownership. But change was felt only in some parts of the developing world. Because Latin America had achieved political independence in the early nineteenth century, decolonization didn't create any epochal changes. There was no disruption in the ownership of productive assets. FOEs were everlasting, as in the automobile industry. *Given this continuity, any aspiring nationally owned Latin American POE had to confront these dinosaurs in its own backyard.*

Decolonization had a much more cataclysmic effect on colonies that won their political independence after World War II. Decolonization not only meant political independence. It also meant economic independence: *getting rid of unwanted FOEs.* China expropriated foreign capital. Korea and Taiwan retook land, companies, and a modern banking system from Japan. India's independence scared away many British-owned enterprises. Other FOEs were out-competed by Indian POEs. When Indonesia finally got rid of the Dutch in the early 1950s, it inherited some 400 firms and substituted new ownership.

These discontinuities in Asia made it much easier to nurture national enterprises. Decolonization created a *tabula rasa.* POEs became the new entrepreneurs, and growth soared.

The Philippines got its political independence about the same time as its neighbors, but the high income share of American foreign multinationals never changed, despite a fairly well-educated population. African countries were the last to win independence, but their goldmines and plantations remained in foreign hands. The creation of a local African business elite has only begun, as larger numbers of students from the developing world study overseas. In the Middle East, only after 1961 were the Seven Sister oil companies forced to pay higher taxes and royalties, or become nationalized. The catalyst was OPEC, the professionally managed Organization of Petroleum Exporting Countries. OPEC revolutionized ownership in the oil industry. If Africa could reduplicate its expertise (as with AMEC, or African Metallurgy Exporting Countries), it might be able to catch up economically with the richest countries in the Middle East.

Thus, after World War II, the entrepreneurial POE was a major institution in developing the world's most successful countries, mainly in Asia. FOEs, on the other hand, settled in for the long run in the slower-growing regions, Latin America and Africa, with the Middle East's oil industry somewhere in between. Of course, the FOE expects to shed its bureaucracy in the Information Age, although bureaucracy is likely to increase in foreign subsidies. As for the POE, can it move beyond entrepreneurship and become good at managing by the numbers? Does ownership matter when it comes to being good in production management and distribution logistics?

Entrepreneurship and efficiency

Ever since receiving steroids from the state, POEs were disparaged as being inefficient. Inefficiency, however, has often proved to be wishful thinking on the part of POEs' detractors. Virtually every snapshot of a leading POE, in

China or Chile, shows it in a frenzy of minimizing costs, notwithstanding its receipt of government subsidies. Raising productivity and enjoying protection were compatible. POEs (and local FOEs) can raise their domestic price to tariff levels, but still, they can always make more profits if they slash their spending. POEs invested heavily in skills related to production engineering and project execution—stretching existing capacity if they were in slow-growing Latin America, adding new capacity at lightening speed if they were in Asia. As entrepreneurs, POEs were cost minimizers, because it was the rational thing to be.

Initially, technology was always foreign. Rarely was a domestic industry started without technology from abroad. But technology infrequently came from FOEs. *Technology was transferred mainly by foreign capital goods suppliers located overseas.* These vendors were usually happy to transfer information to any customer, and supply them with a road map of where their industry was going. In the case of the developing world's textile equipment in the 1970s, most came from British and Swiss machinery suppliers, who installed textile machinery systems and trained workers to maintain and repair them. If a piece of equipment failed, vendors came to service it at great expense, giving an incentive for local production engineers to be proactive in learning.

Machinery suppliers usually guarantee a buyer a 'rated capacity' below true potential capacity. Therefore, a machinery buyer benefits financially if it can push capacity above the rated level. In the continuous process industries like steel, cement, and pulp and paper, investments to exceed rated capacity were routine.

In mature high-tech industries such as calculators, computers, and cell phones, where global prices were already falling fast and profit margins were thin, POEs had to enter an industry quickly and get a product swiftly out of the door. Taiwan's leading electronics firms did R&D in order to optimize large-scale integration of thousands of components and parts. The better the integration, the shorter throughput times (Amsden and Chu, 2003). POEs were entrepreneurial as well as efficient, the more so if they had both an American and Japanese management background.

Thin air in the stratosphere

At one time, it would have been inconceivable to think that a mega-multinational could do any of its R&D overseas. According to Vernon's product cycle (Vernon, 1966), non-standard projects have to be kept at home in order to be under top management's nose. But, in fact, some R&D has gone overseas, most recently to developing countries with low labor costs. People now regard GE's R&D center in Bangalore, India, with the same awe that they once regarded the Eiffel Tower. But on first observation, the R&D done overseas by multinationals is small in amount and modest in complexity. A study by the OECD of the internationalization of its country-members' R&D suggests this. On average (across countries), OECD countries do only about 12 percent of their R&D in another country. The figure was roughly 10 percent for the US and 2 percent for Japan at the end of the 1990s, although higher for some European countries (OECD, 1998; and Patel and Vega, 1999). In Korea and Taiwan, the proportion of total, country-wide R&D accounted for by FOEs was less than 2 percent, well below their share of output.

Foreign R&D also turns out to be relatively unsophisticated, especially in developing countries. According to two criteria to classify R&D as basic, applied, or another form of research—*the size of R&D operations*, and *the type of mathematics done by researchers, original or algorithmic*—virtually all the R&D undertaken by foreign firms in Singapore and India (Bangalore) is at most applied research (Amsden and Tschang, 2003). An in-depth comparison of R&D in five multinationals and five nationally owned firms in the Korean telecommunications industry concluded that the national firms did more diversified R&D, ranging from some basic to advanced development; the authors warned Korea not to rely on foreign firms for R&D at the frontier.

But R&D is only one among many functions that foreign investors do primarily at home, or possibly in regional offices. Local content tends to be much higher for nationally owned firms than for foreign subsidiaries, the most obvious being foreign assembly operations for export, where most inputs are imported. High importation is partially affected by trade barriers: for most of the period 1950–2000, the US insisted that most of the inputs in products being exported to the US from developing countries be 'Made in America.' The incentives for local content were also different for nationals and multinationals. It often made sense for foreign firms to import components with large scale-economies from a single internal source, outside the country of assembly. It also made sense for nationally owned firms to build their supply chains locally. Daewoo and GM fought constantly over the origin of parts; GM wanted to import them from GM subsidiaries, while Daewoo wanted to make them at home. Hyundai created a local network of parts and components suppliers under the direction of a 'Parts Development Department' that employed 300 engineers. This department was modeled on a Toyota idea. With support from government R&D, nationally owned firms in Taiwan's electronics industry began to import substitute key parts of their computers and cell phones—first CD ROMs and then TFT-LCDs.

Foreign investors do not, and probably cannot be expected to, do their state-of-the-art research outside their corporate labs. If nationally owned companies want to be first with cutting-edge products, earn entrepreneurial rents, and accumulate engineering know-how, then like everyone else they must invest in their own R&D. Like the alchemists—FOEs or POEs—they must slog away, hoping for big results.

Conclusion

Like the Devil, the superiority of the POE over the FOE lies in the details. POEs are not successful in every developing country or every industry. But FOEs and POEs are inherently distinct because of their differing attitudes towards risk. In principle, a joint venture is a substitute for a POE. With a joint venture, the best of the entrepreneurial POE and the best of the bureaucratic FOE can be united in a partnership. In this case, there is no need for local government to treat one type of firm as intrinsically better than another. Joint ventures are often preferred over FOEs by developing countries, from China to India, if no more disaggregated method is possible.

But a joint venture is not necessarily a good substitute for a POE. Entrepreneurs in today's developing countries don't need the expense of a joint-venture partner to buy knowledge about how two worlds work. They already understand how they work because they go to kindergarten at home and university in the US. Many remain in both places as part of a long-term recursive brain drain; entering their home country and then leaving it temporarily for Europe or the US. With greater broadmindedness than the FOE, and with more government support for risk taking, the POE has become a new force in global business.

As POEs have risen, even the nature of foreign investment has changed, giving POEs a larger slice of the pie. At present, a foreign investment in the form of a new, overseas plant is less likely to happen than a foreign investment in the form of outsourcing, where POEs do all the work. RCA made TVs in Taiwan in its own plant. Today, IBM 'makes' computers in someone else's plant in Taiwan.

Given poor infrastructure, the poorest developing countries have secured almost no investment from multinationals except in raw materials. Their resource-intensive industries are typically controlled by foreign firms, many with market power and political clout. The FOE can use diplomacy and a deep pocket to influence public policy making, from a law to a coup. POEs, for their part, have connections to top politicians through childhood ties. Thus, FOEs and POEs divide the terrain for influence-peddling. The difference between them is not in corrupting the rules of law. Instead, the difference lies in investment policies. If profits rise, foreign-owned mining companies tend to reinvest them in the same industry elsewhere, in a different country, with few local jobs or skill formation. POEs, by comparison, are almost always part of a diversified business group (Sumitomo, an old Japanese business group, started in finance). A greater share of their profits is thus likely to be invested in diversifying locally, entering a new industry at home, and possibly a new export market overseas, with many more jobs and skills established.

A country is only credited with those 'foreign investments' that are made by its own POEs, not by its FOEs, who claim their own nationality to identify a new project. A country's outward 'foreign investments' depend on the establishment of homespun POEs, and many potential advantages of globalization only begin with the rise of a cadre of national businesses.

Two questions arise: What is the appropriate government policy towards POEs? This question is difficult to answer because FOEs and POEs usually start off with vastly different endowments, and it is valid to ask whether inequalities in initial endowments should be leveled by governments. Whatever the answer, the time is ripe for rethinking government industrial policy towards POEs because their positive progress has been unexpected and their skill-related benefits have been felt economy-wide.

Second, if POEs in developing countries get the royal treatment from a growth-conscious state, what does the rest of the world get? 'Plenty,' would probably be a fair statement. If POEs from the developing world succeed, as POEs succeeded earlier from Japan, the welfare of the world economy will rise with more competition. A true globalism will appear with multinationals from countries other than just the US, Europe, and Japan. Diversity will prevail, and global income distribution may become less inequitable. As FOEs lose their monopoly power to newcomers, the entrepreneurs who start out behind, they may also face new business opportunities that overtake the joint venture.

Notes

1. 'Without underestimating the capital inflows into China, one has to take note of the fact that the amounts are not strictly comparable with those of India because of the disparities in coverage of data. The coverage of FDI flows in India until 1999–2000 was confined only to equity capital. Apart from equity capital, reinvested earnings and inter-corporate debt transactions, China includes short-term and long-term loans, trade credits, bonds, grants, financial leasing, investment by foreign venture capital funds, earnings of indirectly held enterprises, non-cash equity acquisition, control premium and non-competition fees within FDI. It also includes project imports such as FDI flows, while these are recorded as imports in India' (Banerjee D. (2005), *Globalization, Industrial Restructuring, and Labor Standards*, Sage).

2. The Ford Motor Co. began assembling cars in Argentina in 1917 (Diaz Alejandro C. (1970), *Essays on the Economic History of the Argentine Republic*, Yale University Press, New Haven and London). The *production* of cars by Hyundai in postwar Korea was preceded by the *assembly* of cars by Ford. But it is questionable whether assembly operations should qualify as a second-mover operation. Assemblers transfer *management* skills to locals who then become trailblazers, but by simply assembling, they don't dig their heels into an industry very deep. Usually their parts and components are imported. Their operation, in the form of assembling imported inputs, is more related to foreign trade than foreign investment.

3. In the early 1930s, 'the Netherlands East Indies government had passed the Crisis Import Ordnance designed to impose quotas on a whole range of Japanese goods, and, in the Philippines, Japan was forced by the United States to come to a gentleman's agreement

limiting its cotton exports to that colony. Parallel measures were undertaken in all the insular colonies restricting foreign investment, export of strategic materials, immigration, and land-ownership, all of which were clearly aimed at the Japanese economic advance.' (Peattie M. (1996), 'Nanshin: The "Southward Advance," 1931–1941, as a Prelude to the Japanese Occupation of Southeast Asia' in P. Duus, R. Myers, and M. Peattie (eds.) *The Japanese Wartime Empire, 1931–1945*, Princeton University Press.)

References

Agarwala P. (1986), 'The Development of Managerial Enterprises in India' in K. Kobayashi and H. Morikawa (eds.) *Development of Managerial Enterprise*, University of Tokyo Press, Tokyo.

Allen G. and A. Donnithorne (1954), *Western Enterprise in Far Eastern Economic Development: China and India*, Macmillan, New York.

Amsden A. (2007), *Escape from Empire: The Developing World's Journey Through Heaven and Hell*, MIT Press, Cambridge, Mass.

—— (2001), *The Rise of 'the Rest': Challenges to the West from Late-Industrializing Economies*, Oxford University Press, New York.

—— and Wan Wen Chu (2003), *Beyond Late Development: Taiwan's Economic Restructuring*, MIT Press, Cambridge, Mass.

—— and T. Hikino (1994), 'Project Execution Capability, Organizational Know-how and Conglomerate Corporate Growth in Late Industrialization,' *Industrial and Corporate Change* 3(1): 111–47.

—— and T. Tschang (2003), 'A New Approach to Assessing the Level of R&D,' *Research Policy* 32(4).

—— —— et al. (2001), *Do Foreign Companies Conduct R&D In Developing Countries? A New Approach to Analyzing the Level of R&D with a Study of Singapore*, Asian Development Bank Institute, Tokyo.

Banerjee D. (2005), *Globalization, Industrial Restructuring, and Labor Standards*, Sage.

Barbero M. (1990), 'Grupos Empresarios, Intercambio Comercial e Inversiones Italianas en la Argentina: El Caso de Pirelli (1910–1920),' Estuios Migratorias Latinoamericanos 5(15–16): 311–41.

Cairncross A. (1953), *Home and Foreign Investment, 1870–1913*, Cambridge University Press, New York.

Dernberger R. (1975), 'The Role of the Foreigner in China's Economic Development' in D. H. Perkins (ed.) *The Growth of a Modern Textile Industry and the Competition with Handicrafts*, Stanford University Press: Stanford, Calif.

Diaz Alejandro C. (1970), *Essays on the Economic History of the Argentine Republic*, Yale University Press, New Haven and London.

Dosi G. (1988), 'Sources, Procedures, and Microeconomic Effects of Innovation,' *Journal of Economic Literature*, 26(3): 1120–71.

Feuerwerker A. (1958), *China's Early Industrialization: Sheng Hsuan-Huai (1844–1916) and Mandarin Enterprise*, Harvard University Press, Cambridge, Mass.

Fritsch W. and G. Franco (1991), *Foreign Direct Investment in Brazil: Its Impact on Industrial Restructuring*, Development Centre of the OECD, Paris.

Hymer S. (1976), *The International Operations of National Firms: A Study of Direct Foreign Investment*, MIT Press, Cambridge, Mass.

Kravis I. (1970), 'Trade as a Handmaiden of Growth,' *Economic Journal*, 80(320): 850–72.

Lawrence R. (1993), 'Japan's Low Levels of Inward Investment: The Role of Inhibitions on Acquisitions' in K. Froot (ed.) *Foreign Direct Investment*, University of Chicago for the National Bureau of Economic Research, Chicago.

Lindblad J. (1998), *Foreign Investment in Southeast Asia in the Twentieth Century*, Macmillan in association with the Australian National University, Canberra.

Linsu K. (1997), *Imitation and Innovation: The Dynamics of Korea's Technological Learning*, Harvard Business School Press.

Maddison A. (1995), *Monitoring The World Economy 1820–1992*, OECD, Paris.

Moran T. (1998), *Foreign Direct Investment and Development*, Institute for International Economics, Washington DC.

Mortimore M. (1993), 'Flying Geese or Sitting Ducks? Transnationals and Industry in Developing Countries,' *CEPAL Review* 51: 15–34.

Mouawad J. (2004), 'Irrelevant? OPEC Is Still Sitting Pretty,' *New York Times*, September 3, p. 1, sec. 4.

Organization for Economic Cooperation and Development (1996), *International Direct Investment Statistics Yearbook*, OECD, Paris.

Patel P. and M. Vega (1999), 'Patterns of Internationalisation of Corporate Technology: Location vs. Home Country Advantages,' *Research Policy*, 28: 145–55.

Peattie M. (1996), 'Nanshin: The "Southward Advance," 1931–1941, as a Prelude to the Japanese Occupation of Southeast Asia' in P. Duus, R. H. Myers, and M. R. Peattie (eds.) *The Japanese Wartime Empire, 1931–1945*, Princeton University Press, Princeton.

Reubens E. (1955), 'Foreign Capital and Domestic Development in Japan' in S. Kuznets, W. E. Moore, and J. J. Spengler (eds.) *Economic Growth: Brazil, India, Japan*, Duke University Press, Durham, NC.

US Department of Commerce (various), *U.S. Foreign Affiliates: Direct Investment Abroad*, Washington DC.

United Nations (1963), *The Growth of World Industry, 1938–1961: National Tables*, United Nations, New York.

United Nations Conference on Trade and Development (UNCTAD) (1998), *World Investment Report*, United Nations, Geneva and New York.

—— (2004), *World Investment Report, 2004: The Shift Towards Services*, United Nations, Geneva.

Vernon R. (1966), 'International Investment and International Trade in the Product Life cycle,' *Quarterly Journal of Economics*, 80: 190–207.

16

A Question of Trust: Historical Lessons for Current Development

Colin Mayer

Introduction

What are the financial-sector preconditions for the successful development of financial systems and enterprise sectors? There is accumulating evidence of a relationship between financial development and economic growth. Several studies report a relation between the size of financial systems at the start of a period and subsequent economic growth. If other considerations are controlled for, financial development appears to contribute to growth. A variety of measures of financial development are relevant—the volume of monetary assets, the size of banking systems, and the size of stock markets.[1]

To the extent that it is possible to establish the channel by which financial development contributes to growth, it appears to be through the external financing of firms. Comparing the growth of different industries across countries or different companies suggests that there is an interrelationship between their growth rates, the extent to which they are dependent on external finance, and the development of financial systems in which they are operating (see Rajan and Zingales, 1998). In other words, financial development confers particular advantages on industries and companies that are especially dependent on external finance.

* This chapter was prepared for the Industrial Policies Task Force of the Initiative for Policy Dialogue. I am very grateful to the Task Force and in particular to Giovanni Dosi for very helpful and constructive comments and suggestions. The chapter draws on work that I have done with Marco Becht, Wendy Carlin, Jenny Corbett, Jeremy Edwards, Julian Franks, Zhangkai Huang, Tim Jenkinson, Hideaki Miyajima, Stefano Rossi, Oren Sussman, and Hannes Wagner on contemporaneous and historical aspects of corporate finance, corporate governance, and financial systems in Germany, Japan, the UK, and the US.

These results are consistent with the view that a primary function of financial institutions is to improve allocation of funds within an economy. Institutions that direct financing to activities that are most dependent on external finance assist corporate, industrial, and economic growth. The studies therefore provide empirical confirmation at an aggregate or industry level of the theoretical underpinning of financial institutions.

However, the question that these studies leave unanswered is which institutions are particularly well suited to performing these functions. Do all institutions serve companies equally well or are some institutions particularly well adapted for the financing of, for example, high technology?

The second set of issues concerns the policies that can be used to influence the development of institutions. Over the last few years a literature has emerged emphasizing the important role that legal and regulatory structures play in influencing institutional development. This literature has suggested that protection of investors is a crucial determinant of the development of financial systems. Since, as noted above, the development of financial systems is in turn related to the external financing of firms, this suggests a key role for investor protection in promoting the external financing and growth of firms. The policy message that appears to emerge from these studies is clear: improve investor, in particular minority investor, protection, and financial development, investment, and growth will follow.

This raises the question of what precisely is the relation between legal systems, regulation, and the structure of financial institutions. Is there, as the above literature suggests, a straightforward relation between regulation and the development of institutions? In particular, are certain regulatory rules suited to the financing of high-technology activities?

A third line of investigation has emerged recently that has thrown new light on this topic. This comes from examining the evolution of financial systems and corporate sectors over long periods of time. Long-run evolution studies have now been undertaken for the UK and Germany and are in progress for Japan and the US. They point to the importance of equity finance in the early evolution of capital markets. They also suggest a limited role for formal systems of regulation and instead, informal relations of trust appear to play a critical function.

The second section of the chapter summarizes the literature on comparative financial systems. The third section contrasts ownership and control across countries. The fourth section looks at the influence of law and regulation on these differences. The fifth section discusses politics and finance. The sixth section summarizes the conclusions from the evidence on financial systems, ownership, law, and politics. Three further sections report evidence on the long-run evolution of capital markets in the UK, Germany, and Japan respectively. A final section concludes the chapter.

Market- and bank-oriented financial systems

The most frequent contrast drawn is between the UK and USA on the one hand, and Germany and Japan on the other (see, for example, Edwards and Fischer, 1994; and Aoki and Dosi, 1992). The criteria by which systems are categorized include the size of banking systems and stock markets, the degree of external finance that comes from bank and market sources, and the amount of corporate equity owned by banks. Bank-oriented systems are thought to have large banking systems, high levels of bank finance, and large equity holding by banks. There is thought to be a relation between the structure of financial systems and the balance of economic activities between, for example, innovative and more-traditional industries (see, for example, Carlin and Mayer, 2003).

In fact, the distinction between bank- and market-oriented systems has proven to be fragile (see, for example, Mayer, 1988; Rajan and Zingales, 1995). Japan has a large banking system but also has a well-capitalized equity market. While banks are thought to have been actively involved in corporate activity and, in particular, restructurings in Japan, they have not in Germany. In addition, although early studies of Japan pointed to the advantages of close bank–firm relations, more-recent ones have noted their defects in displaying excessive conservatism in corporate lending and inhibiting restructuring (see, for example, Weinstein and Yafeh, 1998; Kang and Stulz, 2000). Instead, what emerges as a common feature of all developed countries' financial systems is the dominance of internal sources of finance. Retained earnings are by far and away the most important source of finance for companies in developed economies.

Table 16.1 illustrates this in relation to four countries, Germany, Japan, the UK, and the US. It records the proportion of physical investment in the four countries that is financed from internal sources and a variety of different external sources. Over the period 1970 to 1998 the US corporate sector on average raised 96 percent of its financing from internal sources. As Table 16.1 shows, internal sources accounted for more than three-quarters of finance in each of Germany, Japan, and the UK.

Table 16.1 records that a substantial fraction of internal sources is associated with depreciation, that is, the decline in value of the existing assets of the firm. Much of firms' retained earnings are therefore used simply to replace existing rather than to purchase additional new assets. However, even once depreciation is removed, retained earnings are still the most significant source of finance in Japan, the UK, and the US.

If we turn to external finance, there are numerous sources available to firms. Here the most useful distinction is between money raised through financial intermediaries, predominantly banks, in the form of loans and that coming directly from investors via securities markets, in particular through issues of bonds and equities. There is a second fact that applies here with nearly as

Table 16.1. Sources of finance, average 1970–1998

	Germany (1970–1997) (%)	Japan (1970–1997) (%)	UK (%)	US (%)
Internal Sources	79.8	76.1	92.5	96.4
Of which depreciation	71.2	55.2	62.3	76.6
Retained Profits	8.6	20.9	30.2	19.8
Loans	12.4	17.4	13.9	12.6
Bonds	−0.5	4.8	6.5	16.0
New equity issues	0.4	3.8	−6.3	−10.6
Trade Credit	−0.9	−4.9	−0.6	−3.2
Other	9.2	2.7	2.5	−1.3
Statistical adjustment	−0.4	–	−8.5	−9.8
Total	100.0	99.9	100.0	100.0

Notes: This table records the net sources of finance of corporate sectors in Germany, Japan, the UK and the US averaged over the period 1970 to 1997/8. External financing is reported on a net basis, net of the accumulation of equivalent financial assets, e.g. bonds issued by the corporate sector net of purchase of bonds by corporations.

Source: Corbett and Jenkinson (1997) and recent unpublished data from Tim Jenkinson.

much force as the one regarding internal finance and that is that external finance comes predominantly from banks.

Table 16.1 shows that 14 percent of external finance in the UK comes from banks. There are significant variations across countries. Bank finance is, for example, higher in Japan than in the UK and US. However, in Germany, banks account for a slightly smaller proportion of external finance than they do in the market-based systems of the UK and US. The stereotype descriptions of financial systems are not reflected in their corporate finance patterns.

This also holds the other way round. A third feature of corporate financing revealed in Table 16.1 is that securities markets do not in aggregate contribute a great deal to the financing of companies. Bond markets account for less than 10 percent of corporate finance in Germany, Japan, and the UK. In Germany, the negative figure for bonds reveals that companies have actually been net purchasers rather than issuers of bonds. Only in North America have bonds been substantial sources of corporate finance and in the case of the US they are a larger source than banks.

What is even more striking is the small source of funding coming from stock markets. In none of the four countries of Table 16.1 do equity markets provide more than 5 percent of corporate financing. Furthermore, in the two countries with supposedly the largest and most efficient stock markets, the UK and the US, equity financing has in aggregate actually been negative. This reflects a combination of two factors: first, companies have been buying back (i.e. repurchasing) their own shares, in particular in the US, and, secondly, they have been purchasing shares in other companies in the process of acquiring them. Both of these have withdrawn funds from the corporate sector and therefore contributed to a negative net financing figure.

Table 16.1 averages financing proportions over the period 1970 to 1998. Figure 16.1 shows that during this period there were cyclical fluctuations and some trend movements in financing. The most striking cyclical feature, which is observed in all four countries, is the inverse relation between bank finance and internal sources. Bank finance is high when internal sources are low.[2] The most pronounced trend movement is in the US where internal sources increased over much of the period and new equity sources declined. Far from new equity becoming a more significant source of finance in the last part of the century, acquisitions and share repurchases together took an increasing amount of funding out of the US corporate sector via equity markets.

In summary, the above has suggested five stylized facts of corporate finance: (i) Internal funds are the predominant source of finance for companies; (ii) Bank finance is in general the most important source of external finance for companies; (iii) There is an inverse relation between internal sources and bank finance; (iv) Bond markets have in aggregate contributed only a modest amount to the financing of companies in most countries, with the exception of North America; and (v) Stock markets have in aggregate provided little finance for their corporate sectors and there is little association between the size and sophistication of stock markets and the amounts of finance raised on them.

The influence of financial systems on measures of corporate governance is also unclear. Close relations between financial institutions and companies might have been thought to influence incentives and disciplining of management. Systems with close relations have better information flows and thus a firmer basis on which to reward and discipline management. But they lack the powerful incentive and disciplining devices of stock markets. In fact, to the extent that there is evidence on this, it does not point to a clear difference in either incentive arrangements or disciplining across financial systems (see, for example, Kaplan, 1994).

The standard bank–market orientation distinction is neither particularly robust nor insightful. However, there is one important respect in which countries' financial systems do differ. This is the quality of information disclosure. Accounting standards differ appreciably across countries, ranging from the detailed provision of information for investors in some countries, to the most perfunctory disclosure of basic data in others.

There is increasing evidence that, even if other distinctions between market- and bank-oriented systems are not robust, information disclosure is. Rajan and Zingales (2002) describe how industries that are dependent on external finance grow more rapidly in countries with good accounting standards. They provide an interesting explanation for this relationship. They argue that developed financial systems play a particular role in financing activities that possess few tangible assets. The significance of this comes from the fact that tangible assets can be used to offer collateral to banks, and firms that possess tangible assets can, therefore, obtain bank finance. However, firms

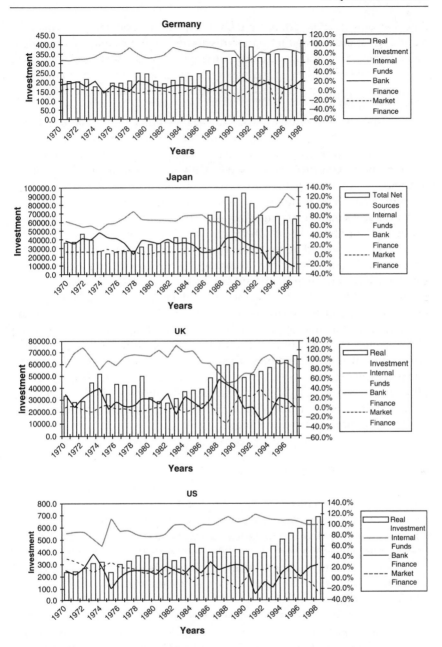

Sources: Corbett and Jenkinson (1997) and recent unpublished date from Tim Jenkinson.
Figure 16.1. Sources of finance in Germany, Japan, UK, and US, 1970–1998

that have few tangible assets are more reliant on market sources, which demand high standards of information disclosure. Activities that are dependent on external equity finance and other intangible inputs, such as skilled labor, should therefore prosper in systems with good accounting standards, and Rajan and Zingales cite evidence, in addition to their own article, in support of this proposition.

In addition to the evidence from aggregate studies there is accumulating information on the way in which individual companies and specific activities are financed. For example, Mayer and Sussman (2005) examine the financing of large investment projects. They record that where firms have substantial financing needs then in the case of large firms these are met from debt, a mixture of bank and bond finance. However, in the case of small firms listed on the UK stock market, external finance comes from stock markets. This again points to the importance of collateral in allowing debt finance to be raised. Large, well-established firms have assets that they can offer as collateral whereas small, particularly high-technology firms do not and are reliant on comparatively expensive equity sources.

This is consistent with the evidence of Singh (see, for example, Singh, 2003) that in contrast to those in developed economies, enterprises in emerging economies raise a large amount of finance externally and a high proportion of this comes from equity markets. In the case of both small high-growing firms and emerging economies, there is a greater dependence on equity sources of finance than in well-established firms and economies. This suggests a life cycle of financing with equity finance being important in the early stages of development of companies and economies and debt finance in more developed and mature firms and economies.

Ownership and control

Having examined financial systems, empirical analysis then turned to international differences in corporate governance and control. Here, pronounced differences, which stood up to close scrutiny, were found, even within developed economies (see La Porta et al. 1999; and Barca and Becht, 2001).

The most striking of these relate to comparisons of concentration of ownership in different countries. There are pronounced variations in ownership concentration in the UK and USA on the one hand, and Continental Europe and the Far East on the other. For example, in France and Germany, in more than 80 percent of the largest 170 listed companies, there is a single shareholder owning more than 25 percent of shares, and in more than 50 percent of these companies, there is a single majority shareholder. In the UK, by contrast, in only 16 percent of the largest 170 listed companies is there a single shareholder owning more than 25 percent of shares, and in only

6 percent is there a single majority shareholder. Concentration of ownership is appreciably higher on the Continent of Europe than in the UK. High levels of ownership concentration have also been reported for the Far East and South America, and ownership is as dispersed in the USA as in the UK.

Not only does the level of ownership differ appreciably between the UK and USA and most of the rest of the world, but so too does the nature of that ownership. In the UK and USA, institutions, such as pension funds, life insurance firms and mutual funds, and individual investors are the main holders of corporate equity. Ownership is dispersed in the sense that no one institution or individual holds a large stake in a single company. This is described as an 'outsider system' (see Franks and Mayer, 1995).

On the Continent and in the Far East, families (or family holding companies) and other firms are the main holders of share blocks. Inter-corporate holdings of large blocks of shares are commonplace, frequently in the form of pyramids of shareholdings, cross-shareholdings, or complex webs. As noted above, in most countries, bank holdings of shares are modest and holdings by the government vary appreciably across countries. This is described as an 'insider system'.

In the insider systems where ownership is concentrated, owners have incentives to be actively involved in the management of firms. In Albert Hirschman's terms, they are more likely to exercise 'voice' rather than 'exit,' which characterizes outsider systems where ownership is dispersed. There is little or no separation between ownership and control, and agency problems should be largely absent.

One implication of this is that ironically in insider systems banks may play a more important role as shareholders than creditors. It is generally observed that banks do not hold a large proportion of corporate equity on their own accounts, except for short periods around the financial distress of their borrowers when they take equity in exchange for impaired loans. However, in the case of Germany, which we describe below, banks hold equity as custodians on behalf of investors. As such they are frequently granted proxy votes that they cast for individual shareholders. This potentially overcomes problems of free-riding in monitoring and control of companies. It also means that banks are able to apply the knowledge that they acquire across industries as well as within particular firms.

But in solving one set of conflicts between owners and managers, insider systems create another, namely between large and small shareholders. Where there are strongly dominant shareholders, minority shareholders are at risk. Insider systems may therefore benefit one class of shareholders at the expense of others. For example, while in principle German banks can use their superior access to information to the benefit of shareholders, there is a potential conflict that arises between their role as custodian and creditor. Franks and Mayer (1998) record that where cases of conflict arise between banks in these two roles then they sometimes behave to the detriment of the shareholders for whom they are acting as custodians.

Why are there such pronounced differences in the ownership and control of companies across countries? One explanation is that the balance of these risks differs across activities and sectors. For some, strong governance is more critical than external financing, while for others the reverse holds. For example, mature industries may be less reliant on external financing than growing industries. Rajan and Zingales (2002) argue that venture capital can be viewed as a transition between different governance and financing arrangements. In their early years, firms have few tangible assets with which to raise external finance and are dependent on the active involvement of a small number of investors. Subsequently, the need for active governance diminishes and requirements for external sources of finance increase. For those firms coming to the stock market, ownership then moves from reliance on a small concentrated group of venture capitalists to dispersed market investors. The implication of this is that real differences in the activities of firms, industries, and economies give rise to differences in the governance and financing needs of firms. There is a complementarity between finance, governance, and real activities, but where causation lies is much harder to establish.

Law and finance

A second explanation for the differences emerged in the next phase of empirical analysis. The observation that the primary conflict in insider systems is not between managers and owners but between majority and minority shareholders led to minority-investor protection as a primary subject of analysis. Regulation can be used to protect minority investors in systems in which ownership is dispersed. In an influential set of articles, La Porta, Lopez-de-Silanes, Shleifer, and Vishny (1997, 1998, 1999, 2000) turned the argument on its head by suggesting that financial structure is a product, not a cause, of legal structure.

The argument ran as follows. Where the law offers little protection, then investors seek direct protection through taking large stakes. Where the law provides strong protection, then minorities can invest with confidence. The structure of financial systems is therefore a product of the legal systems within which they operate.

La Porta et al.'s analysis begins by classifying legal systems into four different 'origins': Anglo-Saxon, French, German, and Scandinavian. By and large, countries of Anglo-Saxon legal origin tend to give external investors the best protection, while countries of French legal origin tend to give investors the worst; countries of German or Scandinavian legal origin are somewhere in between. La Porta et al. go on to demonstrate that financial systems are better developed in countries of Anglo-Saxon legal origin than in those of, in particular, French legal origin. The message that emerges from these articles is clear. Strong minority investor protection is a prerequisite to the successful development of financial systems. Combined with the observation that financial development is associated with subsequent economic growth, the policy prescription is even more powerful. Countries should strengthen minority-investor protection to promote economic growth.

Using several different measures, Beck et al. (2001) report that financial development is further advanced in common-law than in French civil-law systems. Controlling for differences in government and environmental endowments, they find that legal traditions remain an important explanation of cross-country differences in financial development. The difference in financial development between common-law and French civil-law countries is more pronounced than that between common-law and German civil-law countries. This is consistent with the view that it is the adaptability of, rather than the static differences in, legal systems that influences financial development.

Politics and finance

The legal-tradition theories have been subject to criticism from two quarters. The first is that legal origin does not capture relevant features of commercial codes. In certain key respects, differences between common-law systems are sometimes greater than those between civil- and common-law systems. Corporate-insolvency law illustrates the point. Franks and Sussman (2001) examine in detail the evolution of corporate-insolvency law in England and the USA. They report that, despite their common legal origin, corporate-insolvency law in the two countries is quite different. While in England the courts are expected to abide by the terms of debt contracts, in the USA the courts have the power to review the contractual rights of lenders, particularly in regard to liquidation rights of secured creditors.

In the area of corporate governance, Barca and Becht (2001) report higher levels of anti-shareholder devices in the USA than in the UK, with poison-pills, state legislation, and a variety of corporate-board entrenchment devices being widely applied in the USA but not the UK. Corporate governance, as well as bankruptcy, differs significantly between supposedly similar systems.

Conversely, despite their different legal origins, England and Sweden have adopted similar principles of freedom of contracting within the area of corporate insolvency. As a result, in both countries, a secured creditor may exercise his contractual rights and seize the assets of a failed company without any court review. Likewise, in a recent paper, Biais and Recasens (2001) note that deviation from freedom of contracting makes France and the USA, two very different countries according to La Porta et al., quite similar in terms of the powers that they confer on the judiciary to review liquidation decisions.

433

The second line of criticism that has emerged in relation to the law and finance literature is that financial systems are too transient to be explained by immutable legal origins. In an extensive analysis of the evolution of financial systems during the twentieth century, Rajan and Zingales (2003) report that financial systems at the beginning of the century were quite different from those at the end. They argue that these changes appear to have much more to do with the influence of politics than law.

Summary of financial systems, ownership, law, and politics

At the same time as information and incomplete-contract models have provided the basis for the theoretical modeling of a diverse range of institutions, empirical analysis has produced a wealth of information on the operation of these institutions. A number of fundamental insights have emerged.

First, the structure of systems of capitalism is diverse. Very different forms of corporate ownership and control have coexisted in the presence of international trade and financial markets for a long period of time. Whether they will continue to persist with increasing financial integration and trade is much debated and still unclear. It is likely that there will be convergence in financial institutions and instruments before there is convergence in corporate ownership and control.

Second, simple prescriptions about bank- and market-oriented financial systems have not proved valid. Not only is the relevant performance of the two systems uncertain, but it is also unclear whether this is an appropriate basis for classifying financial systems in the first place.

Third, where differences in financial systems do appear robust, in particular in relation to the ownership and control of firms, neither the cause nor the implication of these differences is clear. It is easy to theorize. It is much harder to provide convincing evidence.

Fourth, it is very difficult to find truly exogenous variables in international comparisons of financial systems. Legal origin appeared to provide a way out, but more-detailed analysis of actual legal systems raises questions about the relevance or validity of these variables. Correlations are straightforward, but it is much harder to draw inferences about causality.

Evolution of financial systems: the case of the UK

By some criteria the UK had even more flourishing stock markets at the start of the century than at the end. It certainly had more of them. In the first half of the century from 1900 to 1950, not only was there a flourishing London Stock Exchange but there were also more than 19 provincial exchanges, which specialized in particular industries. For example the Birmingham exchange was important for cycle and rubber tube stocks, Sheffield for iron, coal, and steel, and Bradford for wool. Thomas (1973) describes how 'the number of commercial and industrial companies quoted in the Manchester stock exchange list increased from 70 in 1885 to nearly 220 in 1906. Most of these were small companies with capitals ranging from £50,000 to £200,000' and 'by the mid 1880s Sheffield, along with Oldham, was one of the two most important centres of joint stock in the country, with 44 companies, with a paid up capital of £12 million' (pp. 133 and 124).

One of the features of stock markets around the world today is the modest amount of finance that in aggregate they raise for their corporate sectors, even in countries with large stock markets such as the UK and US. However, stock markets are important sources of finance for two purposes: first for financing small rapidly expanding firms and, secondly, for funding acquisitions by large firms. Equity issues for internal investment are commonplace in recently listed companies and by larger firms taking over others.

To establish the financing patterns of companies early in the twentieth century Franks, Mayer, and Rossi (2005) collected data on all 20 firms that were incorporated in Britain between 1897 and 1903 and are still in existence today. They looked at how much equity they issued and in what form. The answer was that a lot was issued in the form of ordinary equity and some in the form of preference shares that receive dividends ahead of ordinary shareholders. Even at the beginning of the twentieth century there was no evidence of the feature of many countries today, namely the issue of more than one class of ordinary shares (dual class shares). But firms did issue a great deal of ordinary shares.

Strikingly, the main purpose to which equity issues were put at the beginning of the twentieth century is the same as it is today—acquisitions. By far and away the dominant use of equity was to fund acquisitions. Firms grew rapidly through acquiring others and issued equity to do this. So acquisitions have been an important component of the growth of UK firms for more than a century and the existence of a large and vibrant stock market has contributed to this. Again there is no evidence here of a significant change in the structure or functioning of the UK stock market.

What about ownership? When did this become dispersed? Franks, Mayer, and Rossi (2005) took the 20 companies incorporated at the start of the twentieth century and examined the rate at which their ownership became dispersed, in the sense that the minimum number of shareholders required to control a certain percentage (for example, 25%) of their equity increased. They looked at 20 companies that were incorporated around 1900 but died sometime before 2000. They then compared the rate of dispersal of ownership of both the firms that survived and those that died with a third sample of firms that were incorporated around 1960. They used this last sample to provide a post-WWII benchmark against which to compare the rate of dispersion of ownership in the early part of the twentieth century.

What they found was striking. The rate at which ownership of firms at the beginning of the twentieth century became dispersed was very similar to that in the second half of the century. In both cases, ownership was rapidly dispersed. The main reason for ownership rapidly dispersing was not so much that directors and founding families sold their initial shareholdings but that their shares were diluted through takeovers. What happened and continued to happen throughout the twentieth century was that firms issued shares to acquire others and in the process they diluted the shareholding of their directors and founders. For example, if a family initially owned all 1 million shares in a company and issued another 1 million to purchase another firm then the family's shareholding declined from 100 percent to 50 percent.

So the dispersed ownership of firms in the UK is not a recent phenomenon. It set in early in the twentieth century and persisted throughout. It has consistently been associated with rapid growth through acquisitions. Again there is no evidence of the UK stock market having undergone a fundamental shift during the twentieth century.

The stability of the UK financial system during the twentieth century stands in marked contrast to its regulation. At the beginning of the century investor protection in the UK was very weak and UK stock markets were largely unregulated. According to an index of anti-director rights, compiled by La Porta et al. (1998) the UK scored very low, 1 out of a possible 6, about the same score as Germany in 1990.

In contrast to the view that common law is associated with strong investor protection, common law in England contributed directly to the lack of protection of minorities. In a famous case in 1843, *Foss v. Harbottle*, a shareholder sued directors of a company for misuse of company funds. The court found in favor of the directors because their actions had been approved by a majority of shareholders. The basis of the court's reasoning was, that 'if a mere majority of the members of a company . . . is in favour of what has been done then *cadit quaestio*—the matter admits of no further argument.' In the evocative words of a senior English judge, Lord Justice Hoffman (1999), 'Emancipation of minority shareholders is a recent event in company law. For most of the twentieth century minority shareholders were virtually defenceless, kept in cowed submission by a fire-breathing and possibly multiple-headed monster called Foss v. Harbottle. Only in exceptional cases could they claim protection of the court.'

The dominance of the strict majority was enshrined in English law, and those that hoped English common law would rescue Hoffman's oppressed minority were to wait a very long time. Again in Hoffman's words, 'It was not until 1980 that Parliament forged the sword which is now section 459 of the Companies Act 1985 and which enables unfairly treated minority shareholders to slay the dragon.'

Landmark legislation was passed in 1948, when Parliament required substantially increased disclosure from listed companies and empowered 10 percent or more of shareholders to call extraordinary meetings when they were dissatisfied with directors' actions. These provisions marked a step change in La Porta et al's measure of shareholder rights raising it from 1 at the beginning of the century to 3 in 1948. With the passage of legislation in 1980–1985 it rose further to a score of 5, where it remains today.

Thus during the twentieth century there was a substantial increase in investor protection from a virtual absence in the first half to a high degree of protection by the 1980s. But despite this pronounced shift there was no change in the importance of stock markets in terms of their size or usage by the corporate sector. This runs quite counter to the law and finance theories that associate strong investor protection with financial market activity. The UK operated a large and vibrant stock market for the first half of the twentieth century without investor protection. For those who regard regulation as a prerequisite for market development, this is surprising. How could stock markets have flourished in the UK in the absence of investor protection?

One bit of evidence on this puzzle is the orderly way in which some aspects of stock markets operated. The takeover market in the UK is now conducted according to a set of self-regulatory rules known as the Takeover Code. These stipulate how takeovers should be conducted and in particular lay down the basis on which the shareholders of the target firm should be treated. One of these rules states that all shareholders in the target firm should be offered the same price for each of their shares. This is designed to avoid a practice that is common in many countries today by which some, namely large shareholders that own controlling blocks, are offered one price and small minority shareholders are offered another, lower one.

These rules were introduced at the end of the 1960s. Before that the takeover market was essentially unregulated. Directors of acquiring firms therefore could in principle have followed the practice of gaining control of firms by purchasing blocks of shares at one price and offering other shareholders a lower price. This is clearly cheaper than paying everyone the same price. They could have done this but they didn't. Repeatedly they offered all shareholders the same price and also sold their own shares at the same price as was offered to other shareholders. For example, in a letter in *The Times* addressed to the shareholders of John Lysaght the directors made the following recommendation about a proposed takeover by GKN in 1920: 'The offer has been unanimously accepted by the Directors of your company for the whole of their individual shares, and they have no hesitation in recommending its acceptance to the shareholders.' Out of 33 acquisitions that occurred between 1919 and 1939 there was not a single case of price discrimination and in virtually every case almost all of the shares in the acquired company were purchased. In other words a law of one price prevailed without a law of one price being enacted. It occurred by convention rather than regulation.

Why? One clue comes from the observation above on the importance of local stock markets. Writing in 1921 on new shares issues, Lavington notes that 'local knowledge on the part of the investor both of the business reputation of the vendor and the prospects of his undertaking would do a good deal to eliminate dishonest promotion and ensure that securities were sold at fair prices fairly near their investment values.' Concentrating ownership among local investors was recognized as a method of reducing information problems as well as fraud. He cites the views of one broker: 'the securities are rarely sold by means of a prospectus and are not underwritten, they are placed by private negotiation among local people who understand the [cotton] trade' (p. 280).[3] To reduce information problems and fraud, securities were traded in the city in which most investors resided. For example, shareholders in Manchester were anxious that the shares of the Patent Nut and Bolt Co.[4] of Birmingham should be listed in Manchester where most of the shareholders lived (see Thomas, 1973, p. 118).

To quantify this, Franks, Mayer, and Rossi (2005) examined the geographical distribution of the shareholders of one company, GKN, in 1900 and again in 1950. They looked at the addresses of the entire share register of investors in 1900 and measured the distance of their residence from the headquarters of GKN. They found that in 1900, 40 percent of shareholders lived within 5 miles of the centre of Birmingham. By 1950 that had fallen to 5 percent.

The significance of this comes from the fact that at the beginning of the century companies were very dependent on local shareholders to raise finance, in particular for acquisitions. Their reputation amongst local investors was therefore critically important to allow access to external sources of finance. Directors were therefore keen to uphold the interests of their shareholders to allow them to access finance for future expansion. In other words their dependence on local investors for future expansion acted as a commitment device.

As firms expanded through acquisition their activities developed beyond their hometowns. Their shareholder base also expanded and was no longer geographically concentrated. The need for more formal systems of information disclosure through company accounts and listing rules became more acute. The result was the 1949 Companies Act and the London Stock Exchange Listing rules that together substantially strengthened information disclosure.

Regulation not only responded to changing patterns of ownership and financing of firms but in turn influenced subsequent developments. In the first half of the nineteenth century there were a large number of small local banks in Britain that were closely involved in the financing of firms. However, the existence of small banks empowered to engage in note issuance caused serious stability problems. Between 1809 and 1830 there were 311 bankruptcies of local banks. Large banks are less exposed to local market conditions and have more resources available to them than small banks. Encouraged by the

Bank of England, banks withdrew from the illiquid investments in which they were engaged and began to spread their activities geographically, frequently through mergers. A convenient relation emerged by which the clearing banks faced little competition and the Bank of England little financial failure. As a consequence, there is a high level of concentration of corporate lending in Britain and a noticeable absence of local banking.

Similarly, changes in corporate law in Britain in the middle of the twentieth century referred to above prompted a wave of hostile takeovers during the 1950s and 1960s, particularly in response to the greater disclosure of accounting information on the book value of companies. For a brief period of time, the unregulated takeover market encouraged Continental European style ownership patterns with dual classes of shares and pyramid ownership structures. However, these prompted calls for the hostile takeover market to be regulated and in response the Takeover Panel was established and the Takeover Code introduced at the end of the 1960s. This in turn discouraged the persistence of dual-class share ownership and pyramids.

It is therefore important to view regulatory changes as at least in part a response to emerging crises and in turn a determinant of the subsequent patterns of ownership and financing of corporations. Sarbanes–Oxley in the US is the latest example of this: corporate-governance scandals prompted the introduction of significant legislative changes that have in turn affected the structure of ownership and control of US corporations.

Evolution of financial systems: the case of Germany

Ownership of corporations in Germany is today highly concentrated in the hands of families and other companies. Franks, Mayer, and Wagner (2005) provide the first long-run study of ownership and control of German corporations by assembling data on the ownership and financing of firms from samples spanning almost a century from 1860 to 1950. At first sight, German financial markets at the beginning of the twentieth century looked remarkably similar to their UK counterparts. There were a large number of firms listed on German stock markets and firms raised large amounts of equity finance. This runs counter to the conventional view of Germany as a bank oriented financial system. Firms raised little finance from banks and surprisingly large amounts from stock markets.

As in the UK, issuance of equity caused the ownership of founding families and insider directors to be rapidly diluted. Even by the start of the twentieth century, founding family ownership was modest and ownership by members of firms' supervisory boards, which was large at the beginning of the century, declined rapidly thereafter. But there was one important difference between Germany and the UK. In the UK, much of the new equity issuance went to funding acquisitions and mergers. In Germany it did not. To the extent that companies invested in other firms it was in the form of partial share stakes rather than full acquisitions. As a consequence, new equity was frequently purchased by other companies in blocks rather than by dispersed shareholders.

Furthermore, where equity was widely held by individual investors it was generally held on their behalf by custodian banks. Banks were able to cast a large number of votes at shareholder meetings, not only in respect of their own shareholdings which were in general modest, but as proxies for other shareholders. As a result, concentration of ownership did not decline at anything like the rate observed in the UK over the same period. This is the case, even if one assumes that all bank proxies were voted on behalf of dispersed shareholders. Thus, a central conclusion of Franks, Mayer, and Wagner (2005) is that concentration of ownership declined much less than in the UK.

Regulation, or rather existing measures of investor protection, do not explain these differences. Indices of both shareholder anti-director rights and levels of private enforcement are identical and equally low in Germany and the UK in the first three decades of the twentieth century. In this regard, the high level of stock market activity at the beginning of the twentieth century is surprising in both countries. Small investors would not have been expected to subscribe to new equity issues in the absence of either strong anti-director or private-enforcement provisions. Something else must have encouraged them to participate. In the case of the UK, Franks, Mayer, and Rossi (2005) point to the existence of trust relations between investors and firms in local stock markets as the additional ingredient.

Trust mechanisms were different in Germany; Franks, Mayer, and Wagner (2005) argue that they were associated with the role of banks as promoters of new equity issues, custodians of individual shareholdings, and voters of proxies on behalf of individual investors. An English economic historian Lavington (1921) argued that banks provided a more secure basis for the issuance of IPOs in Germany than promoters in the UK whose interests were primarily confined to selling issues rather than ongoing relationships with companies. Regulation at the end of the nineteenth century contributed to this by conferring rights not on minority investors but on the banks, which as the promoters of corporate equity were able to control firms' access to the German stock markets. In the same way as firms in Britain upheld their reputation amongst local investors to gain access to equity markets, so German firms depended on banks as the gatekeepers to securities markets. How the two arrangements compared in protecting the interests of investors is an unresolved issue.

What then was going on? The overall picture that emerges is of firms issuing equity to fund their growth to other companies and individual investors. They were not growing through full acquisitions but through companies taking partial stakes in each other and individuals holding shares via banks. Equity finance was therefore intermediated by companies and banks. In contrast, in Britain, there was little intermediation by financial institutions until the second half of the twentieth century and then it came from pension funds and life assurance companies rather than credit institutions. There has never been significant intermediation by inter-corporate pyramids in Britain.

In essence, Franks, Mayer, and Wagner (2005) document the creation of the 'insider system' of ownership that Franks and Mayer (1995, 2001) describe in modern-day corporate Germany. This is characterized by inter-corporate holdings in the form of pyramids and complex webs of shareholdings, extensive bank proxy voting, and family ownership. What distinguished its emergence from the dispersed ownership of the UK were two things: first, the partial rather than full acquisition of shares by one company in another thereby creating corporate pyramids and inter-corporate holdings and, secondly, the intermediation of equity shareholdings by banks. It is therefore insider not in the sense of ownership by directors but in terms of voting control remaining within the corporate and banking sector rather than being transferred to outside individual shareholders as in the UK and US.

Can regulation explain these developments? At one level, the clear answer to emerge from this chapter is no. Investor protection was equally weak in Germany and the UK in the first three decades of the century when most of the developments documented in this chapter occurred. But that response is probably more a reflection of the inadequacies of existing measures of investor protection than of the irrelevance of law and regulation. By the beginning of the twentieth century Germany had enacted a corporate code that provided more extensive corporate governance than existed in virtually any other country at the time. This may have been critical to the rapid development of the German stock market at the end of the nineteenth and the beginning of the twentieth century. Furthermore, the Exchange Act of 1896 reinforced the control of the banks over German securities markets. Companies became dependent on banks for access to securities markets in the way in which firms in Britain were dependent on local investors for sources of equity. And since banks acted as custodians of minority investor shares, they could also in principle encourage firms to uphold minority shareholder as well as their own interests. Whether they did or whether their dual role as investors and custodians was a source of conflict is a critical issue.

Evolution of ownership: the case of Japan

In many respects the most striking country of the three reviewed here is Japan. As Franks, Mayer, and Miyajima (2006) describe, it is striking because today we regard Japan as the archetypal banking system with companies closely interwoven and largely owned by banks, and stock markets playing little role in the financing and ownership of firms. Whether or not that is true today, it certainly was not earlier in the twentieth century.

On the contrary, in many respects Japan displays the highest dispersion of ownership of the three countries at the beginning of the twentieth century. There were not many firms listed on the Japanese stock markets but ownership of the newly industrialized companies, such as the cotton spinning firms, which were listed at the beginning of the century became dispersed at a remarkably rapid pace. This was so pronounced that measures of concentration are in general lower for Japan than they are even in the stock market economy of the UK at the same time.

A second feature of Japan that is particularly interesting is the rapid change in investor protection that occurred just after the Second World War. The American occupation introduced legislation that transformed weak investor protection in the first half of the century into some of the strongest in the world in the second half of the century. Dispersion of ownership therefore occurred in Japan in the first half of the century in the absence of strong investor protection. The emergence of the insider system of ownership in the second half of the century by which banks and companies had cross-shareholdings in each other occurred against the backdrop of strong investor protection. The move from outsider, dispersed ownership to insider cross-shareholdings therefore coincides with a marked strengthening of investor protection, quite contrary to the predictions of the law and finance literature.

As in Germany and the UK, Japan raises the question of how ownership dispersion occurred in the absence of strong investor protection. Franks, Mayer, and Miyajima (2006) point again to informal arrangements of trust as being critical to the dispersion of ownership. But unlike in the UK these were not attributable to the prevalence of local stock exchanges. Most companies were listed on one of two stock exchanges—Osaka and Tokyo. Nor, unlike in Germany, did banks play an important role in the relations between investors and firms in the first half of the century. Instead, in the first two decades of the twentieth century particular individuals rather than institutions were critical to the ability of companies to be able to access stock markets. These individuals were known as business coordinators and had some of the characteristics of today's private equity investors, particularly business angels. They were prominent members of the business community, sometimes senior figures in the local chambers of commerce, who sat on the boards of several firms. Their reputation acted as a validation of the soundness of the companies with which they were associated.

The role of business coordinators diminished from the 1920s onwards and their place was taken by the family firms, the zaibatsu which were incorporated during and after the First World War and in the 1930s sold their subsidiaries on stock markets. In this case the reputation of the zaibatsu families appears to have been important in facilitating access to stock markets.

In sum, all three of the cases in UK, Germany, and Japan illustrate that it was not investor protection that allowed stock markets to develop at the beginning of the twentieth century. In all three cases, stock markets flourished and owner-ship was dispersed in the absence of strong investor protection. Instead, other institutions and individuals were important in upholding relations of trust between investors and firms. In the case of the UK it was local stock markets, in Germany the banks, and in Japan business coordinators and zaibatsu families.

Conclusion

This chapter has documented the considerable diversity in financial and cor-porate systems that exist across countries. However, that diversity is not primarily associated with the conventional distinction that is drawn between bank- and market-oriented systems. In terms of financing, the similarities across developed countries are more pronounced than the differences with the dominance of retained earnings, the importance of banks to external finance, and the relative insignificance of new equity sources being generally observed in developed economies.

The differences have more to do with ownership and control of companies than financing. Concentrated ownership and control is prevalent in most countries and dispersed ownership and market control restricted to relatively few. Even within these two groups there are considerable variations between family-dominated corporate sectors in some countries and intercorporate holdings in others. These differences may reflect the different needs of corpor-ate sectors and a complementarity between ownership of firms and the types of activities in which they are engaged.

There is a widely held view that strong investor protection is a precondition for the successful development of financial systems and in particular for the emergence of dispersed as against concentrated ownership. For example the World Bank states: 'Protecting investors against self-dealing—the use of cor-porate assets for personal gain—is necessary for equity markets to develop. When small investors see a high risk of expropriation they do not invest—in countries with higher risk of expropriation, investment as a share of GDP is half that in countries with good investor protection. The markets stay under-developed. And fewer firms bother to list' (World Bank, 2005).

This chapter has raised questions as to whether this is indeed the case. Looking at the emergence of early securities markets in developed economies reveals a number of striking features. The first is the importance of equity sources of finance and equity markets. The second is the emergence of these markets in the absence of formal systems of regulation, and the third is the reliance on informal relations of trust. In some countries such as Germany and the US, financial institutions, in particular banks, appear to have played an important role in sustaining relations of trust. In others, such as the UK, trust mechanisms appeared to rely more heavily on close proximity between investors and firms in local stock markets. And in Japan, individuals of high repute, the business coordinators, sustained trust relations at the beginning of the twentieth century.

What has not been explored to date is why trust mechanisms are very different, what is the consequence of those differences, and what factors promoted the emergence of the various forms of trust. Understanding the development of relations of trust is critical to the formulation of policies towards enterprise and financial sectors in emerging and developing economies. It is easier to legislate for investor protection than it is to achieve effective enforcement of investor protection and still harder to promote the conditions for relations of trust. Furthermore, as the cases of Germany, Japan, and the UK illustrate, there comes a point at which trust mechanisms appear to break down and more formal investor protection is required. Is regulation inevitable? Does it undermine the operation of more informal relations or is there a way in which the benefits of trust can be combined with those of formal investor protection. We are just at the start of understanding the processes by which financial markets, institutions, and enterprises develop and until then our policy prescriptions for developing economies will remain tenuous.

Notes

1. See for example the surveys by Levine (1997) and (2005) on this.
2. Mayer (1990) reports correlations between bank finance and internal sources over the period 1970 to 1985 consistently in the range −0.45 and −0.88 in seven countries (Canada, Finland, France, Germany, Italy, UK, and US).
3. Stock exchange introductions (the creation of markets in existing shares) enjoyed complete exemption from prospectus requirements, and lenient 'statements in lieu of prospectus' could accompany private placements (Companies Act 1929, ss. 34, 35, and 355).
4. Patent Nut & Bolt Co. was owned by the Keen family, and merged with Dowlais Iron Company owned by the Guests which in turn developed into Guest and Keen, incorporated in Birmingham in 1900. This is included in our sample.

References

Aoki M. and G. Dosi (1992), 'Corporate Organization, Finance and Innovation' in V. Zamagni (ed.) *Finance and the Enterprise: Facts and Theories*, Academic Press, London.

Barca F. and M. Becht (2001), *The Control of Corporate Europe*, Oxford University Press, Oxford.

Beck T., A. Demirgüç-Kunt, and R. Levine (2001), 'Legal Theories of Financial Development,' *Oxford Review of Economic Policy*, 17: 483–501.

Biais B. and G. Recasens (2001), 'Corrupt Judges, Upwardly Mobile Entrepreneurs and Social Costs of Liquidation: The Political Economy of Bankruptcy Laws,' Université de Toulouse, unpublished manuscript (March).

Carlin W. and C. Mayer (2003), 'Finance, Investment and Growth,' *Journal of Financial Economics*, 69: 191–226.

Corbett J. and T. Jenkinson (1997), 'How is Investment Financed? A Study of Germany, Japan, the United Kingdom and the United States,' *The Manchester School of Economic and Social Studies*, 65: 69–93.

Edwards J. and K. Fischer (1994), *Banks, Finance and Investment in Germany*, Cambridge University Press, Cambridge.

Franks J. and C. Mayer (1995), 'Ownership and Control' in H. Siebert (ed.) *Trends in Business Organization: Do Participation and Cooperation Increase Competitiveness?* Tubingen, Mohr Siebeck. Reprinted in *Journal of Applied Corporate Finance* (1997), 9: 30–45.

—— —— (1998), 'Bank Control, Takeovers and Corporate Governance in Germany,' *Journal of Banking and Finance*, 22: 1385–403.

—— —— (2001), 'Ownership and Control of German Corporations,' *Review of Financial Studies* 14: 943–77.

—— —— and H. Miyajima (2006), 'Evolution of Ownership: The Strange Case of Japan,' mimeo.

—— —— and S. Rossi (2005), 'Ownership: Evolution and Regulation,' European Corporate Governance Institute Working Paper.

—— —— and H. Wagner (2005), 'The Origins of the German Corporation—Finance, Ownership and Control,' *Review of Finance, Springer*, 10(4): 537–85.

—— and O. Sussman (2001), 'Financial Innovations and Corporate Insolvency,' mimeo.

Hoffman L. (1999), Foreword to Hollington R., *Minority Shareholders' Rights*, Sweet and Maxwell, London.

Kang J-K. and R. Stulz (2000), 'Do Banking Shocks Affect Firm Performance? An Analysis of the Japanese Experience,' *Journal of Business*, 73: 1–23.

Kaplan S. (1994), 'Top Executive Rewards and Firm Performance: A Comparison of Japan and the United States,' *Journal of Political Economy*, 102: 510–46.

La Porta R., F. Lopez de Silanes, and A. Shleifer (1999), 'Corporate Ownership Around the World,' *Journal of Finance*, 54(2): 471–517.

—— —— —— and R. Vishny (1997), 'Legal Determinants of External Finance,' *Journal of Finance*, 52: 1131–50.

—— —— —— —— (1998), 'Law and Finance,' *Journal of Political Economy*, 106: 1113–55

—— —— —— —— (1999), 'The Quality of Government,' *Journal of Law, Economics, and Organization*, 15: 222–79.

—— —— —— —— (2000), 'Investor Protection and Corporate Governance,' *Journal of Financial Economics*, 58: 3–29.

Lavington F. (1921), *The English Capital Market*, Methuen, London.

Levine R. (1997), 'Financial Development and Economic Growth: Views and Agenda,' *Journal of Economic Literature*, 35(2): 688–726.

—— (2005), 'Finance and Growth: Theory and Evidence' in P. Aghion and S. Durlauf (eds.) *Handbook of Economic Growth*, Elsevier, The Netherlands.

Mayer C. (1988), 'New Issues in Corporate Finance,' *European Economic Review*, 32: 1167–88.

Mayer C. (1990), 'Financial Systems, Corporate Finance, and Economic Development' in R. Hubbard (ed.) *Asymmetric Information, Corporate Finance and Investment*, Chicago University Press, Chicago.

Mayer C. and O. Sussman (2005), 'Financing Investment: A New Test of Capital Structure,' Saïd Business School, mimeo.

Rajan R. and L. Zingales (1995), 'What Do We Know about Capital Structure? Some Evidence from International Data,' *Journal of Finance*, 50: 1421–60.

—— —— (1998), 'Financial Dependence and Growth,' *American Economic Review*, 88: 559–86.

—— —— (2002), 'Financial Systems, Industrial Structure, and Growth,' *Oxford Review of Economic Policy*, 17: 467–82.

—— —— (2003), 'Great Reversals: The Politics of Financial Development in the 20th Century,' *Journal of Financial Economics*, 69: 5–50.

Singh A. (2003), 'Corporate Governance, Corporate Finance and Stock Markets in Emerging Countries,' Working Paper 258, ESRC Centre for Business Research, University of Cambridge.

Thomas W. (1973), *The Provincial Stock Exchanges*, Frank Cass, London.

Weinstein D. and Y. Yafeh (1998). 'On the Costs of a Bank-centred Financial System: Evidence from the Changing Main Bank Relations in Japan,' *Journal of Finance*, 53: 635–72.

World Bank (2005), 'Doing Business' Website, <http://www.doingbusiness.org/Explore Topics/ProtectingInvestors/>.

17

Competition Policy and Industrial Development

Mario L. Possas and Heloisa Borges

Introduction

Competition policy—especially antitrust—is not usually seen as part of an industrial policy framework. In fact, they are often viewed as conflicting with each other. The present chapter intends to discuss the role that should be ascribed, under an unorthodox framework, to competition policy within, or at least related to, industrial policy.

A general discussion of competition policy will be undertaken in the first section, which will comment briefly on its main objectives and scope. Some basic theoretical issues will be addressed in order to shed some light on what are usually seen as points of conflict between competition and industrial policies. The second section presents the experience of selected developed economies, as well as newly industrialized ones, examining both competition and industrial policies alongside the process of industrial development. It will focus on the unequal emphasis given to each policy through time by different countries and their specific institutional means of enforcing each one. The third section presents some implications stemming from both the general framework and the historical experiences introduced with respect to the design of competition policy in relatively advanced developing economies. A brief conclusion will follow.

Two important points should be kept in mind when reading this chapter. First, when addressing developing economies, our concern is directed towards the newly industrialized ones; economies still in the early stages of industrial development (and even more so economies without significant industrial structure) will not be discussed in detail. Second, this is a qualitative study—that is, limited to identifying and describing patterns of interaction between competition and industrial policies in selected countries. No quantitative attempt is made to measure these policies' impact.

Objectives and scope of competition policy as related to industrial policy

Although other objectives can be added, the main goal of competition policy is to sustain or increase competition within a market environment with a view to preserving or enhancing economic efficiency and social welfare. Both productive and allocative efficiency are expected to increase with the degree of competitiveness of markets, the usual exception being natural monopolies or activities considered to need regulation for some reason (with the possible trade-offs between allocative and dynamic efficiency, discussed in Chapter 2 by Cimoli, Dosi, Nelson, and Stiglitz; see also below).

Note also that competition policy has a much broader scope than antitrust policy, as important as the latter may be (and usually is). While antitrust is mainly defensive, being able to preserve to some extent competitive market structures and conducts—both through prevention and punishment of abuses of market power—competition can be stimulated by many other means, ranging from trade policy (e.g. reducing tariff and non-tariff protection) to some industrial technology policies (e.g. research and development (R&D) and innovation incentives).

Theory and normative issues

Competition policy, in general, and antitrust, in particular, may be viewed as part of a regulatory framework, involving some kind of systematic market intervention. Within that framework, let us distinguish between forms of regulation where intervention measures are continuously active—call them *active regulation*—and other forms, including antitrust, where intervention is not permanent but only triggered by some specific cause, whether structural or behavioral, and whose means are less proactive—call it *reactive regulation*.

For mainstream economists the rationale for both kinds of intervention is market failure. However, from our unorthodox standpoint this is rather misleading.[1] Markets do not fail because they stand far from the ideal of perfect competition, not least because the static model of perfect competition is in no way a theoretical or normative ideal, as Schumpeter showed long ago. The basic reason to support public intervention concerning competition issues through active and reactive regulation is not because markets do not work properly, but because they can and *should*, from a normative standpoint, operate under a permanent pressure to reduce costs and prices and foster innovative efforts. Instead of simply replacing markets with direct state intervention, which does not work in many instances, competition policies ought to be seen as the set of measures providing the incentives as well as the sticks fostering innovative behaviors. In order to reach this target the simple guideline 'the higher the number of competitors, the better,' usually will not do. Indeed, we at least know from Schumpeter that such dynamic competition can be achieved even in oligopolistic industries—indeed *mostly* in such industries.

From this perspective, one can say that laissez-faire economists support free markets for the wrong reasons. They idealize perfect competition for its supposed spontaneous ability to maximize static allocative efficiency, while markets should be seen, as Schumpeter taught us, as powerful mechanisms—under appropriate incentives and regulation—to foster economic progress through innovation. The sort of efficiency that is entailed by this process clearly cannot be reduced to the static allocative one, but instead should be understood, from an evolutionary perspective, as a type of dynamic efficiency where *selection* plays a dominant role.[2]

In turn, such a criterion has two sides, namely, first, the conduciveness of a particular competitive configuration for virtuous corporate behaviors—in terms of technological and organizational innovation and imitation; second, the degrees of *selective* efficiency—in terms of the efficiency and speed by which they weed out far-from-the-frontier technologies and organizational arrangements.

Under such a framework, it becomes easier to acknowledge that competition policy and industrial policy may be brought together on essentially the same normative grounds.

Competition policy as part of an industrial policy

Competition policy may conflict—and often does—with two other typical public policies: trade policy and industrial policy.

Given that trade policy is designed to protect local industries against foreign competition, not to protect local competition or consumers, some degree of conflict is inevitable and the problem is simply how to manage it when it occurs, as long as trade policy is a permanent national policy.

As to industrial policy, conflicts with competition policies, we shall argue, seem to be in some degree overestimated, as competition policy could (and should) be seen as part of, instead of as opposed to, industrial policy, at least in the case of industrialized economies—including newly industrialized countries (NICs).[3] When one takes industrial policies to be 'the aggregate of policies that directly and indirectly affect industrial performance through its impact on microeconomic variables' (Jorde and Teece, 1992, p. 12), they include competition policies. Granted that, however, important trade-offs and complementarity requirements might emerge between competition policies and policies aimed at other objectives—including technological learning and strengthening of the domestic industrial base. Moreover, as we shall argue below, such complementarities and trade-offs are likely to vary according to the degrees of industrialization and the distance from the international frontier of the various countries.

A wider concept of industrial policy is required if one intends to bring into its frame strategic attempts to influence the transformation of an existing industrial structure into a more dynamic and innovative one through learning and capability accumulation, as recorded in most cases of successful industrial and technological catch-up. Competition policy should be seen, at the very least, as a necessary complement to sectoral industrial policies. But it is arguably more than that—it is an integral *part* of it.

In short, competitive pressures on individual firms must be strong enough not only to dissipate monopolistic rents but, more importantly, to induce firms to adopt active competitive strategies instead of just profiting from the incentives provided by industrial and technology policies.

A first angle from which to tackle the possible conflict between competition policies and other industrial policies is in terms of the Schumpeterian trade-offs discussed in Nelson and Winter (1982), that is, the widely accepted fact that 'aspects of the structure that are conducive to innovation' may be detrimental to the achievement of Pareto optimality in the short run' (p. 329). Note that such a trade-off is particularly relevant for industrial development—our main concern here—under at least two aspects.

First, firms in industrializing economies usually face higher constraints (from several sources) that hinder efforts to innovate, to learn, or to keep pace with technical progress, making them more sensitive to all measures curtailing their margins and market shares. Second, and more importantly, the efforts to increase innovative capabilities of local firms usually require protracted learning, which in turn may involve some degrees of protection against competition, especially from potential foreign entrants.

Yet market structures and innovation are related in complex ways, and there is probably no straightforward solution to this trade-off. Not only it is theoretically doubtful whether an optimal trade-off level could ever be devised, but any policy designed substantially to change a given industry structure in a predetermined way is likely to fail, since structure is essentially endogenous to any one regime of Schumpeterian competition (Nelson and Winter, 1982, p. 333).

In this respect, the way antitrust policy is practiced today in many developed countries, though clearly not sufficient in itself to promote competition, steps on relatively safe ground when it limits itself to structural intervention aimed at preventing artificial forms of concentration (e.g. through mergers and acquisitions) from gathering market power and monopoly rents with few or no efficiency gains, as well as repressing anticompetitive behaviors. Moreover, extra profits are accepted and usually not considered illegal when resulting from innovation-driven competition. Curiously, since the old rigid structuralist approach ceased to rule in antitrust (in the late 1980s), not only neoclassical micro theory, but even the Schumpeterian trade-off have been embodied, to some extent, in antitrust laws and practices (although in the latter only implicitly).

As a result, in the last two decades or so, mechanistic measures of industry concentration and market dominance as such have been losing their former prominent place in antitrust policies in favor of a more flexible, analytically oriented view of efficiency-enhancing mergers and acquisitions and a greater concern towards anticompetitive behavior.

Different trade-offs and complementarity requirements characterize different stages of development. As already mentioned, history tells a general story whereby economies in their early stages of industrialization require significant measures of infant industry protection. Indeed, it will be argued below, competition policies tend to appear much later along the development process. Here, our primary concern, however, is the relationship between competition policies and other industrial policies in countries which are still in the process of technological catching-up but already have a significant industrial base, say like Brazil today or Japan half a century ago.[4]

As discussed at length in other chapters of this volume, industrial policies, *in a narrow sense*, refer to that subset of economic policies seeking to provide special advantages or assistance to particular industries or firms (see also McFetridge, 1985). It has also historically been the rule throughout the eighteenth, nineteenth, and twentieth centuries that those which were newly industrialized catching-up economies—including the United States, Germany, and Japan—were driven by the objective of fostering production upgrades and innovative learning by domestic firms. Above some degree of industrialization, however, in order to be effective supply-side policies aimed at increasing capabilities and knowledge accumulation also require some (variable) degree of market selection and regulatory measures curbing rent-seeking behaviors. Let us consider how various countries have dealt with such requirements.

Industrial policy and competition policy: some lessons from international experience

Begin by noticing that it is hard to find a single developed country that has adopted strictly one single policy direction (either pro-competition or discretionary sectoral policies) to the complete exclusion of the other in its development. Industrial development paths, at least from a minimum level of industrialization already achieved, are consistently characterized by some degree of interaction (on different levels) between competition and industrial policies, although this relationship changes over time.

In this study a few countries have been selected with the objective of identifying different patterns of interaction between the two sets of policies, presenting experiences both from developed and developing countries. As expected, differences in competition and industrial policies are observed both across time and across countries, illustrating divergences in policy objectives underlying their application and enforcement.

Moreover, the frameworks in which competition and industrial policies, in the narrow sense, interact in developed and developing countries are rather contrasting and so are the windows of observation of such interactions. At one extreme—in the case of the US—one has the whole period since the Sherman Act to observe the unfolding of competition and industrial policies (albeit often not named in that way). Conversely, most of the countries that industrialized after World War II did not have competition policies until the 1990s.[5] And we know that the lag between introduction of the policies, their implementation, and whatever possible economic effect is quite long. In most developing countries neither the industrialization nor the introduction of competition have been completed, so it is probably too soon to draw conclusions from their preliminary results.[6]

Industrial and competition policies in developed countries (US and Europe): a brief account

The United States is the best-known example of a country approaching the technological frontier at the time when it adopted antitrust legislation as a prominent part of its national economic policy framework. US antitrust laws have been a centerpiece of the country's competition policy for over a century, often taken as a benchmark for assessing policies in other countries.

Since the Sherman Act was passed in 1890, and the current institutional structure was created in 1914, the responsibility for US competition policy has been maintained by two federal antitrust agencies: the Federal Trade Commission (FTC) and the Department of Justice (DOJ) Antitrust Division, each with its own functions: the latter with criminal enforcement power (price fixing and cartel behavior) and an active role in shaping competition policy, and the former more focused on structural issues and their implications for consumers.[7]

We have already mentioned the changes in the general philosophy which antitrust policies underwent. For a good part of the twentieth century the focus was on quantitative structural indicators such as market shares and degrees of concentration taken to suggest the possibility of exercising market power. More recently, starting in the 1980s, such a perspective has shifted toward a much greater emphasis on actual anticompetitive practices and less on structural indicators.

The US convention on competition policy, however, did not prevent the active implementation of industrial policies from time to time—particularly in the process of building new industries during depressions, when economic development was considered more important than competition in some particular markets and placed under the broad heading of 'national security.'[8]

Even nowadays, although the US does not have a coherent, comprehensive industrial policy, the government consistently pursues many specific industrial policies that, together, deeply influence industry evolution and industrial performance. Indeed, the US has a long history of industrial policy, witnessed by the extent to which the state has, in various ways, supported the growth, development, and continuing viability of agriculture and of the aircraft, airline, railroad, automotive, shipping, semiconductors, oil, and banking industries.

Europe has in common with the US the fact that competition policies came much later than the industrialization phase, but national experiences significantly differ. So, for example, in some cases like France the state has a long history of direct intervention in the economy both as a producer and an indicative planner, but competition policies did not play a major role.[9] On the other hand, German competition policies, at least since World War II, look much more like the US ones. The birth of the European Community, and then the European Union, has brought a good part of competition policies— together with the power to legislate and with the enforcing institutions— under the authority of the European Commission, while leaving to national authorities the regulation of national markets.[10] European competition policy was originally built primarily to curb possible distortions in intra-European trade and foster the emergence of a single European market. It has fully taken on board the repression of anticompetitive practices (a famous example is the *EU v. Microsoft* case) and also expanded its reach into industrial policy domains such as state subsidies to firms and the fairness of access to financial resources.

The relationship between such an expansive notion of competition policies and industrial policies in a more traditional sense is a good example of both the possible complementarities and the possible tensions. So, for example, the exercise of competition policies has not interfered with the policies (explicit or implicit) which led to the development of the aeronautical European champion Airbus. On the other hand the expansive interpretation—involving also control over subsidies, etc.—makes discretionary forms of policy measures more difficult to implement.

Industrial and competition policies in Asia

The first Asian case to be examined is Japan. This country offers an interesting basis for analysis both because of its successful industrialization and growth strategy as well as for its policy package. Then, the Korean situation will be briefly examined, along with the infant Chinese and Indian competition policies.

These four Asian examples show distinct patterns of interaction between industrial and competition policies which seem closely associated with the level of development. Since World War II, Japan has been characterized by an emphasis on industrial policy associated with the existence of antitrust rules and a competition policy that comprised non-official exceptions for some industries. Today, however, the country seems to have chosen a set-up based on a more balanced coexistence of industrial and competition policies. Yet during earlier stages of development no competition policies were in place, while industrial policies date back more than a century. Korea seems to be going through a changing process headed towards the Japanese model. China and India, on the other hand, have shown a predominance of industrial policies based on direct state intervention, with some recent competition concerns.

JAPAN

Japan had systematic industrial policies beginning with its early industrializing effort after the Meiji restoration in the late nineteenth century. All the way through most of the post-war years, the chief goal of Japan's economic policy has been development and growth, with competition sometimes seen as inconsistent with that goal.

Indeed, although Japan has had a competition law since 1947 (Act Concerning Prohibition of Private Monopolization of Fair Trade, known as the Anti-Monopoly Act—AMA) throughout the 1960s, 1970s, and 1980s, its competition policy was largely subordinated to policies promoting industrial and trade objectives, and important sectors of the Japanese economy were dominated by officially accepted cartels (see also Evenett, 2005).

At the same time, the systematic manipulation of market and industry structures and the use of 'administrative guidance' with respect to firms and whole industries has always been done with measures which prevented rent-seeking behaviors (more on this in Amsden and Singh, 1994).

Things have changed considerably in the last 15–20 years. Mostly in response to international pressure—particularly in trade disputes with the US—Japan implemented several measures to strengthen its competition law and enforcement capabilities, adopting explicit commitments to increase the resources and the visibility of competition enforcement.[11, 12] The Antimonopoly Law now looks rather similar to the Western model, and the Fair Trade Commission has improved its enforcement record.

Industrial policies also significantly changed, evolving from discretionary promotion of sectors and firms to more 'competition friendly' innovation policies. Even now, however, though there is no general exemption from the competition law, the latter cannot effectively reach most government actions, since competition authorities only deal with voluntary anticompetitive behaviors. So, if a specific statute governs an industry, conduct in accordance with this statute or an order properly issued under it does not violate the law.

KOREA

The Korean case, for both industrial and competition policies, is highly similar to the Japanese one. Korea had a strong, active industrial policy due to government encouragement and provision of direct incentives for the growth of large corporations, the chaebol. Since the national goal was fast economic growth, industrial and trade policies targeted towards maximizing local firms' investment and market share in the global market took priority over other policies. Hence, even though Korea has had for a considerable time an official competition policy, as well as competition laws, as a result of its lax enforcement the country has reached one of the highest levels of industrial concentration in the world.

Only in the early 1980s did competition policies gain relevance. The current antimonopoly law is the 1980 Monopoly Regulation and Fair Trade Act (MRFTA), and the responsibility for its enforcement was given to a new agency, the Korea Fair Trade Commission (KFTC), created within the Economic Planning Board.[13] Even though they were designed to 'mark a significant departure from the tradition of a government-led economy to a market economy based on private initiative and competition,' the continuing price control practices mean that implicit or explicit forms of price collusion remain routine practice.[14, 15]

At the same time, cartels are still tolerated and exceptions to the competition laws and regulations continue to be current practices in Korea (Wise, 2000). In addition, several aspects of Korean competition policy are designed not to promote competition, but to protect the interests of small and medium-sized businesses. Furthermore, while in principle the MRFTA applies to all industries, and exceptions for a few industries were abolished in 1999, some cartels remain protected by particular statutes.[16]

In 2003 the Korean government made a new attempt to enforce competition by laying out a 'Three-Year Market Reform Roadmap' as a proposal for a more transparent market economy. In order to help the implementation of the roadmap, the MRFTA and its Enforcement Decree were revised and entered into force on 1 April 2005, with three main objectives: (i) promotion of market competition, (ii) improvement of regulation on large business conglomerates, and (iii) strengthening of market self-regulation. The results, however, are yet to be seen.

To sum up, recent competition policies in Korea entail broad objectives—ranging from the repression of unfair commercial practices to the protection of consumer rights and the development of small and medium-sized firms, but we are still at an early stage of implementation. The Korean experience is quite similar to the Japanese one, with a gradual introduction of pro-competition measures only beyond a rather high threshold of development.

CHINA

Chinese policies have been characterized by high levels of intervention and the intense use of control mechanisms by the government well past the strict era of communist planning, and central planning mechanisms persist in this century.[17] Industrial policies of various types continue to be formulated at the national level and implemented both at the national and local levels in almost all sectors of the economy.[18]

However, China did not have a competition policy until the early 1980s, and even now the country has no antimonopoly law; provisions controlling monopolies and anticompetitive conducts are distributed among different laws, rules, and regulations.[19] Nevertheless, even a superficial look at the Chinese competition policy (or the absence of it) reveals that what the government calls competition rules are, in fact, an assembly of prohibitions of illegal commercial practices which are only in some cases related to competition. There is no single bureau accountable for competition in China, and there is also no evidence of an active competition policy as defined above.[20]

In sum, there is no interaction between industrial and competition policies, but rather a complete suppression of competition rules under a strongly interventionist industrial policy, replacing the former role of central economic planning.

INDIA

As in China, India's government has traditionally played a significant part in industrialization. Since the end of World War II, the government has tried to guide industrial development through centralized planning and a package of industrial policy measures; and under the 'new policy' regime from the 1990s onward, various industrial policies have continued to be implemented.[21] Competition policies, though, are a much more recent phenomenon.

It is true that India has had a competition law nearly since independence—the Monopolies and Restrictive Trade Practices (MRTP) Act, meant to be implemented by the MRTP commission—but with little or no bite. In fact some commentators suggest that its role has been primarily that of a barrier to import competition.[22] In 2002 a new competition bill was passed, which created the Competition Commission of India (CCI). From an antitrust standpoint, the new law seems rather ambiguous, as it gives the commission powers to take action against restrictive trade practices (such as cartels) but at the same time expressly allows firms that 'contribute to economic development' to cause 'adverse effects on competition.'[23] The same argument is put forward when examining the criteria for determining whether mergers or acquisitions have adverse effects on competition.

When the 2002 Competition Act was introduced, the question of whether or not it was similar to the old law in substance (though not in form) was raised, mostly because it seemed 'not-so-pro-competition.'[24] Since the publishing of the Competition Act was preceded by intense discussions on its form and content, it was determined that there ought to be a transition period during which the implementation of competition policy/law was done gradually.[25, 26]

So far the interaction between competition and industrial policies in India has been very limited. As industrialization and growth have been major policy goals in the country, industrial policies have been predominant over competition policies until recently. In the 1990s this position began to soften, and trade and competition policies became part of the official economic concerns. Presently, the results of the 2002 Competition Act are not clear, but the gradualism in its implementation—combined with the law's exceptions to anticompetitive practices—indicate that competition does not yet seem to be a priority concern for the Indian government.

INDUSTRIAL AND COMPETITION POLICIES IN LATIN AMERICA

Although legal prohibitions of monopolies and anticompetitive conducts can be found in many Latin American countries since the late 1850s, competition policy was not a policy objective in these countries. Competition regulations were regarded only as a means to ban some anti-commercial practices, while state monopolies and price controls were widely used as mechanisms of both industrial and macroeconomic policies. Until recently competition was not part of any structured policy, and had very little enforcement in Latin America.

From the late 1980s throughout the 1990s a transition—not yet concluded—has been taking place in Latin America. As discussed at length in several other chapters of this book, its countries' main industrial policies that have shifted, if at all, from import-substitution industrial policies to horizontal industrial policies compatible with the conditions imposed by the International Monetary Fund and other multilateral organizations. With that shift, competition policies have also gained significance.

In the following we will briefly examine the experiences of Brazil, Argentina, Chile, and Mexico. They show, as to the interaction between competition and industrial policies, a relatively homogeneous pattern. These countries' industrial development was, until the end of the 1970s, based on the predominance of industrial policy over competition policy (nonexistent in most cases), with state direct investment, market protection, and incentives to national companies. Nowadays they again appear synchronized in a regime characterized by greater emphasis on foreign and domestic market competition.

MEXICO

The prohibition of monopolies and monopolistic practices introduced in Mexico in the late 1850s should not be mistaken for an effective competition law. As with virtually all Latin American NICs, Mexico's economic policy was marked by protectionist industrial policies from the end of World War II to the 1980s, and most government industrialization efforts were directed at building an industrial structure by means of import substitution. After the 1982 debt crisis, economic policy changed as the country adopted new economic policies, including trade and financial liberalization, industrial deregulation, and privatization.

Competition policy was introduced in Mexico as a follow up of the 1980s reforms. The starting point was the adoption, in 1993, of the Federal Law of Economic Competition (LFCE) and creation of the Federal Competition Commission (CFC), an agency attached to the Ministry of Economy but with technical and operational autonomy.[27, 28]

In 1995 a National Development Plan was adopted, together with sector 'exceptions' to the trade and competition reforms. In addition, the Industrial Policy and Foreign Trade Program was created, aimed at the coordination of public and private measures onto selected industries.[29] The Secretariat of Economy is the government department now in charge of industrial policy in Mexico, and its declared aim is to enhance industry competitiveness under NAFTA and WTO constraints.[30]

A particular feature of Mexican competition regulations is that the CFC is responsible for determining which economic agents may participate in any privatization procedure. Specific powers were, then, granted to the commission regarding competitive conditions in these markets.[31]

BRAZIL

From the end of World War II until the 1980s Brazil adopted an import substitution industrialization policy that was able to build an almost complete industrial structure. Particularly during the military governments, this strategy led to very high average growth rates. The economy was tightly controlled, through mechanisms including price and wage controls. In addition, major industrial firms either belonged to the state or were private monopolies—or at least very concentrated oligopolies accepted or even induced by the government.

Although there had been a law concerning competition since 1962 (as well as a competition commission—the Administrative Council of Economic Law (CADE)), it mainly dealt with unfair commercial practices. As the law was not applicable either to state-controlled industries or to regulated sectors—the core of the industry, in a sense—competition provisions were not enforced except for a very few cases of abusive pricing.

In the 1980s, however (as discussed in greater detail by Castro in Chapter 10), Brazil went through severe macroeconomic problems. Economic policies then refocused on stabilizing the economy, with a relative neglect of industrial policies. From 1990 onward, industrial policies also switched towards a more liberal approach based mainly on horizontal measures, and a trade reform severely cut import barriers.

Price stabilization was finally achieved in 1994, but by then all attempts to implement a coordinated industrial policy had been virtually abandoned, while economic policy was limited to sustaining economic stability, mostly through restrictive fiscal and monetary policies. In the same period, a new competition law was passed (n. 8.884/94). This law enhanced CADE's powers and made it an independent agency. It also defined the forbidden anticompetitive conducts, imposing far more severe penalties than before. Additionally, two new agencies were created: the Secretariat for Economic Law (SDE) and the Secretariat of Economic Monitoring (SEAE).[32] Not even regulated sectors are exempted from the competition law, and there is no practical case yet of an industrial policy explicitly conflicting with competition rules.[33]

Along with changes in the competition institutional framework, adjustments were made in the whole policy framework. While traditional (sector-specific) industrial policy mechanisms were virtually abandoned, competition enhancement was seen as a tool to promote innovation and competitiveness in industry. In 1995, the Cardoso government issued a policy framework aimed at creating 'the conditions that will enable Brazilian firms to make the transition from the defensive strategies dominant in the initial phase of trade liberalization to more assertive strategies based on increased productivity and technological innovation' (Brazil, 1995).[34]

The outcomes of the policies implemented since the mid-1990s are not yet clear but seem to be of limited reach. As the new regime is recent, and the majority of the policies publicized by the government were not, in fact, implemented, it is risky to try to draw sharp conclusions. Competition, however, has established itself as an important component to be considered in policy decisions regarding industry.

ARGENTINA

Argentina, like its neighbors, adopted import substitution policies that included strong state intervention, protective barriers, and subsidies. The regime lasted until the 1980s, when Argentina too went through a period of high inflation and macroeconomic instability.

There was no competition policy and no competition law until the 1980 Competition Act (n. 22.262) created the CNDC—National Commission for Competition Defense. During the 1980s, though, competition was still not regarded as relevant and the law was not seriously enforced.

In the 1990s a stabilization plan was adopted and, among other reforms, all public companies were privatized and trade and financial barriers were abandoned. In 1999, after the consolidation of the reforms and apparent price stabilization, the competition law was replaced by a new one (n. 25.156) which introduced *ex ante* review and authorization of mergers and acquisitions. This gave CNDC full jurisdiction on competition issues in every sector of the economy and created an autonomous Competition Court to replace the CNDC.

Since 2003 the CNDC reports to the Technical Co-ordination Secretariat of the Ministry of Economy and Production.[35] CNDC is responsible for investigating cases or conducts that might violate the law, and produces reports and recommendations to the Secretariat.[36] The agency also issues non-binding recommendations on competition matters to other governmental agencies.

CHILE

Chile basically followed the same industrialization model as the Latin American countries discussed above. Like Mexico and Brazil, it did have a sort of competition law before the macroeconomic reforms of the 1980s, but the Chilean competition authority, before 1980, took action only in a few cases.[37, 38] At the same time price control mechanisms were in place, and the state controlled many key industries.

During the military dictatorship that took power after 1973, a major free-market reform program was implemented. A Law for the Defense of Free Competition was adopted in December 1973 as part of the military government's program that emphasized trade liberalization, privatization, and deregulation.[39, 40] However, not much effort was devoted to the implementation of competition policies until the end of the 1990s.[41]

By the time the military government was replaced by an elected civilian one, Chile had already privatized electricity, telecommunications, and steel production, and eventually the competition bodies also began playing a more important role in some infrastructural sectors. In 1999, a new law (n. 19.610) changed the competition institutions, replacing the former commissions with a new independent antitrust tribunal. In 2003, law n. 19.911 produced a new competition tribunal.

In 2005 the Ministry of Economics changed and systematized the text of the competition law (decree n. 1/05). The competition tribunal, responsible for the final decision involving competition issues, is now an independent entity with judicial powers. In addition, the competition enforcement agency has extended its powers to investigate and to intervene in every action or agreement that may affect competition.

Conversely, present industrial policy focuses mainly on promoting competitiveness rather than protecting or giving incentives to particular industries. Financial and fiscal incentives are granted for exports and investment in 'horizontal' manners.

Competition policies and development: some conclusions on the historical lessons

The brief overview of the role of competition policies in developed countries and in relatively advanced developing countries highlights a variety of experiences and also a variety of combinations between competition policies and industrial policies of various kinds. Still, some lessons can be drawn.

First, the interaction between competition and industrial policies, and their possible conflict, crucially depends on the levels of development. A historical stylized fact is that a potential conflict between antitrust policy and industrial policy is mainly circumscribed to early stages of industrial development and catch-up. In such contexts, industrial policy usually performs a leading role while antitrust law, if existing at all, tends not to be fully enforced or is partially replaced by surrogate mechanisms of competition. In fact, in all countries competition policies historically came much later than industrial policies aimed at industrialization.

Second, the potential conflict between competition policies and industrial policies tends to fade away in relatively advanced developing-but-industrialized countries.[42] As briefly discussed above, at a relatively advanced stage of indus-trialization there is no significant trade-off between industrial policy—at this point focused on *competitiveness* and *technology catch-up*—and competition pol-icy. There may exist, however, differences between the policies appropriate for frontier countries and those suited for catching-up countries, although we suggest these differences regard mostly *industrial and technological (learning) policies* rather than competition policies (in general) and antitrust (in particular).

Competition policies themselves have significantly changed over the last quarter of a century under the influence of the transition in the US from a rigid structurally oriented static posture to a more pragmatic and, in some ways, more 'Schumpeterian' one. As a result, most antitrust laws and policies now-adays involve (i) *structural* preventive controls, for example, of mergers and acquisitions, and (ii) *conduct* repressive controls of horizontal and vertical anticompetitive strategies and behaviors. Simultaneously, the so-called anti-trust 'efficiency defenses' are increasingly becoming accepted worldwide, as they already are to a good extent in the US. Arguments in court are largely supported by technical tools from economic analysis rather than per se con-siderations and commonplace beliefs. More specifically, the possible *efficiency-enhancing* effects of a merger or of a strategy tend to be carefully analyzed and balanced against the possible welfare and/or competition losses. As Porter (1990) put it, 'when faced with tradeoffs, we should weight progressiveness higher than static efficiency or a snapshot of price-cost margins, because innovativeness is by far the most important source of growth and welfare, greatly outweighing price-cost margins... and even static efficiency' (pp. 662–4). In turn, under the efficiency-enhancing effects—for example in the case of mergers—they not only include the usual static efficiency gains, such as cost-reducing scale effects, but also pro-innovative effects stemming from asset complementarities and R&D risk sharing.

However, some other concerns are found in the literature which appear not to be covered by current antitrust doctrine and practices, and could therefore possibly require specific changes in competition policies for developing economies. One of them is the idea of a trade-off between productivity growth, profitability, and investment, on the one hand, and competition, on the other, which would lead to optimal levels of competition—especially for developing countries in need of fast economic growth—below the maximum, as opposed to the conventional view of as much competition as possibly being an end in itself.[43]

The concept of a higher or lower degree of competition, however, seems to have been caught in the same static trap that we are trying to avoid. Where can a benchmark for maximum competition be found—and would it be perfect competition? And how is its degree to be assessed—would a lower one correspond to higher market concentration, achieved through permissive antitrust rules? If we take a dynamic concept of competition, that is, a Schumpeterian view, as in the first section above, then higher competition should mean higher pressure on several competitive attributes, especially the innovative drive, no matter the degree of market concentration; in this sense there *cannot* be such a thing as too much competition. Moreover, the causal link between profit rates and investment is also very doubtful, on similar grounds. If more competition implies a higher innovative drive, then it also leads *ceteris paribus* to more, not less, productivity growth, through quicker imitation and, most likely, innovation and some related additional investment. High investment rates require many conditions, not only (or necessarily) current profitability: in addition to access to external finance, market growth—which is probably related to *more* competition, not less, as already commented—is paramount. Alternatively, less competition usually implies lower pressure on competitive attributes by firms, whatever the degree of market concentration, and therefore more 'accommodation' to existing market positions and possibly (although this may be difficult to generalize) to lower investment rates, at least in domestic markets.

Another concern is that specific competition policy in late industrializing countries should be devised to cope specifically with local harmful effects of mergers and acquisitions promoted by large multinational corporations, often increasing their market dominance and threatening domestic firms that are building up capabilities to compete in international markets.[44] How frequently these circumstances occur is difficult to assess empirically. In advanced NICs, relatively large local companies facing multinationals and possessing significant market power in domestic markets are far from uncommon, no matter how large their differences in terms of international market shares. Stronger empirical evidence on the real significance of such claims should be provided before major changes in antitrust rules, especially for relatively advanced developing countries, can be justified—such as removing antitrust restrictions to mergers among large local firms.[45]

Conclusion

Once a dynamic view of competition is acknowledged, in which market success and profitability is related more to the innovativeness of firms and their ability to cope with ever-changing environments than to the number of competitors and to static allocative efficiency effects, industrial and competition policies are more easily seen as complementary rather than opposed to each other.

Above a certain industrialization threshold, different national experiences suggest the possibility of several viable combinations of industrial and competition policies, instead of a general and unequivocal trade-off between them. In any case, a stylized fact is that such trade-offs can be very sharp at early stages of industrialization but tend to fade away as catch-up proceeds, turning into a near complementarity. By the same token, such trade-offs tend to be much less common at present in relatively advanced NICs than in their earlier industrialization stages.

It is too early to assess the effects of the current 'quasi Schumpeterian' competition policies, even in frontier countries, and more so in 'advanced NICs' where they have often been introduced—as we saw in the foregoing section—only very recently. What one can say is that a priori such competition policies do not seem to entail systematic trade-offs with technological and industrial policies. Certainly, there are quite a few historical cases when the objective of creating national champions contrasted with any standard competition policy prescription. The development of many Japanese and later Korean industries are good cases in point. However, the success of these experiences was also due to the fact that quasi-monopolistic or oligopolistic domestic firms were forced, quite early on, to compete fiercely on the international markets.

With all the foregoing caveats in mind, the bottom-line message of this essay is that competition policies of various kinds—including antitrust policies—do have an important role to play also in advanced industrializing countries (as opposed to countries at an early stage of industrialization). Of course they cannot come alone: other policies aimed at strengthening the technological capabilities and competitiveness of domestic firms are of paramount importance. But pro-competition provisions should be viewed as a permanent Schumpeterian stick discouraging sheer rent-seeking behaviors and reinforcing the competitive drive of the local economic environment.

Notes

1. See Cimoli et al. in this volume.
2. This could be seen as one of the normative counterparts of Nelson and Winter's (1982) classic evolutionary perspective. Briefly, a *selective* efficiency could be defined as a measure of the extent to which a given market, as a selective environment,

effectively induces an economic *evolution* along an innovative trajectory. Although there is no room here to discuss it in detail, the basic idea is that *selection* is, in principle, what markets can do best, provided some competition policy is not absent.

3. This is clearly not true for those economies—outside the scope of our discussion—still in the early stages of industrial development, which are in need of some kind of significant infant industry protection and where such conflicts might possibly emerge in the case of a competition policy being fully adopted in said early stages. See also below.

4. On the latter cf. Jacquemin (1987) and Johnson (1995), among others.

5. Their introduction has often been part of the International Monetary Fund or World Bank conditionalities, which pushed most developing economies to pass competition statutes over the last 10–15 years. According to Singh (2002), until 1990 only 16 developing countries had formal competition policies. During the 1990s, under pressure and with the technical assistance from international financial institutions and the World Trade Organization, 50 countries have completed their competition legislation, and another 27 are in the process of doing so.

6. According to Scherer (1994), it takes about 10 years for countries to acquire the necessary expertise and experience to implement competition rules effectively. Some experiences shown here have just now completed this period, as others (the Indian one, for instance) have just been implemented. Therefore, there is plenty of information about policy designs and very little information about policy implementation on developing countries.

7. See Foer and Lande (1999).

8. The National Industrial Recovery Act, for instance, was central to the New Deal recovery effort. It was an attempt to promote economic stability by means of an integrated regulatory framework governing production and pricing across sectors. Antitrust was largely eclipsed during this period.

9. See Cohen and Pisani-Ferry (2002).

10. So no attempt is made to interfere with national competition policies as long as they relate only to domestic competition and do not have 'an appreciable impact on actual or potential' trade between EU member states (Lianos, 2002).

11. The perceived laxity of the enforcement of competition law in Japan was a major concern pursued by the US in the Structural Impediments Initiative (SII)—a set of bilateral negotiations initiated in 1989 to address 'outstanding obstacles to trade and investment' between the two countries.

12. As a result, in 1991 the FTC made a formal cartel prosecution for the first time in 17 years.

13. The MRFTA covers all traditional issues of competition policies, like anticompetitive mergers and acquisitions, cartels, resale price maintenance, monopolization, attempts to monopolize, and exclusive transactions. In addition, the law addresses unfair trade practices, as well as undue subsidies, debt guarantees, and equity investment among affiliates of large business groups. Available at the Korea Fair Trade Commission: <http://www.ftc.go.kr/eng/laws/statutes.php>.

14. Available at the Korea Fair Trade Commission: <http://www.ftc.go.kr/eng/>.

15. According to Wise (2000), the government paid special attention to prices in concentrated industries, where market leaders were to report price changes in

advance—pursuant to informal administrative guidance. The Economic Planning Board monitored prices until 1993 and reportedly used the process to stabilize prices.

16. In 1999, the Omnibus Cartel Repeal Act eliminated the statutory authority for 20 cartels that were exempted from the KFTC actions, but although some of these were effective immediately, others will be phased in over a period of several years (Wise, 2000).

17. See Xiao-juan (2002) and Xiaoye (2002).

18. See Lui (2005) and Chapter 12 by Dahlman in this volume.

19. The most important are the 1980 Regulations on Development and Protection of Competition, the 1993 Unfair Competition Law, and the 1998 Price Law (Lin, 2002).

20. According to Xiaoye (2002), the Chinese government has been discussing a Monopoly Act for years now, even though there is no consensus about how to introduce further competition.

21. See Sharma, Jansson, and Saqib (1991), and Singh (Chapter 11) and Dahlman (Chapter 12) in this volume.

22. Bhattacharjea (2003).

23. Chakravarthy (2004).

24. Ibid.

25. Those discussions included the topic of the protections to the domestic industry as well as the relationship between industrial policy, competition policy, and the economic development objectives.

26. The Indian government decided that the Competition Act would be introduced in phases: during its first year (2003), the Competition Commission would carry out only competition advocacy functions (and the old competition law would remain effective); on the second year some provisions would become effective, and that process would continue until all the Competition Act's provisions became effective.

27. It should be noted, however, that although the Competition Law was published in 1992, its rules for implementation were only introduced in 1998.

28. Available at the CFC: <http://www.cfc.gob.mx/>.

29. Available at the Secretariat of Commerce and Industrial Promotion: <http://www.secofi-siem.gob.mx/portalsiem/>.

30. Industrial policy in Mexico has the constraint not to conflict with the competition policy objectives acknowledged in the LFCE, namely, the protection of the competitive process and of free-market access by preventing monopolies, monopolistic practices, etc. Available at: <http://www.cfc.gob.mx/contenedor.asp?P=Results.asp?txtDir=http://xeon2/cfc01/Documentos/>.

31. In regulated infrastructure sectors, for example, a favorable opinion from the commission is necessary for those interested in concessions or licenses issued by regulators. The commission can also determine whether or not the regulators may impose price regulations and access controls (as well as defining if and when, due to market changes, effective competition may be restored and the regulatory controls ended) and address possible competitive effects of proposed changes to federal policies or new laws proposed by the government.

32. The SDE is an agency of the Ministry of Justice responsible for the preliminary investigations and procedures before submitting cases to CADE, which take final decisions in all competition matters, and SEAE is an agency of the Ministry of

Economics that assists SDE's investigations in economic issues. Further information on the Brazilian Competition System can be found in the CADE's website: <http://www.cade.gov.br/>.

33. In cases of anticompetitive conduct in regulated sectors, the respective specific agency contributes technical opinions to the investigations.

34. From the document 'Industrial, Technological and External Trade Policy.' The following government published a similar document entitled 'Guidelines of Industrial, Technological and External Trade Policy' in November 2003. Both documents are available at <http://www.mdic.gov.br>. See also Melo (2001).

35. See the CNCD website: <http://www.mecon.gov.ar/cndc/home.htm>.

36. The Secretariat takes the final decisions in competition matters, but according to the CNDC website, their final decisions regularly follow CNDC's recommendations. On 17 August 2005 the Argentinean Government submitted to the National Congress a draft bill for the amendment of the Competition Law, under which the secretariat of the Ministry of Economy will have a veto right over economic concentrations that require prior approval. Available at: <http://competition.practicallaw.com/jsp/multiJurisUpdates.jsp>.

37. Dating from 1959, Law n. 13.305 ruled on several subjects, not only competition.

38. According to Winslow (2004), from 1963 to 1972 the agency had only seven cases, all minor.

39. Decree Law n. 211 of 1973, modified by Law n. 19.610 from 1999.

40. Competition policy was given little importance during the early stage of the privatization program, but so were the former industrial policies.

41. Winslow (2004).

42. A somewhat similar distinction among developing countries is suggested by Singh and Dhumale (1999) where 'advanced NICs' are clearly distinguished from less-developed economies, although an equally sharp distinction is not made with respect to the appropriate competition policies to follow, as suggested here.

43. Singh (2002), p. 16; also Amsden and Singh (1994).

44. Singh (2002), pp. 12–15; also Singh and Dhumale (1999), p. 5.

45. Singh (2002), p. 20.

References

Amsden A. and A. Singh (1994), 'The Optimal Degree of Competition and Dynamic Efficiency in Japan and Korea,' *European Economic Review*, 28.

Bhattacharjea A. (2003), 'India's Competition Policy: An Assessment,' *Economic and Political Weekly*, 38(34).

—— (2004), 'Trade and Competition Policy,' Working Paper No. 146, Indian Council for Research on International Economic Relations. Available at: <http://www.icrier.org>.

Brazil. President Fernando Henrique Cardoso (1995), *Industrial, Technological and External Trade Policy—Competitive Restructuring and Expansion of the Brazilian Industrial System*, Brasilia: 1995, 19p.

Chakravarthy S. (2004), 'India's New Competition Act 2002—a Work Still in Progress,' *Business Law International*, 5(2): 204–93.

Cohen É. and J. Pisani-Ferry (2002), 'Economic Policy in the US and the EU: Convergence or Divergence?' Prepared for the Harvard Conference on EU–US relations, 11–12 April.

Commission of the European Communities (1994), 'Lignes directrices communautaires pour les aides d'Etat au sauvetage et à la restructuration des entreprises en difficulté,' JOCE, C 368.

—— (2002), 'Industrial Policy in an Enlarged Europe,' Communication 714, European Commission.

Dobbin F. (1997), 'Forging Industrial Policy: The United States, Britain and France in the Railway Age,' Cambridge University Press, Cambridge.

Dormois J.-P. (1999), 'The Idiosyncrasies of Voluntarism' in G. Federico and J. Foreman-Peck (eds.) *European Industrial Policy: An Overview*, Oxford University Press, Oxford.

Evenett S. (2005), 'Would Enforcing Competition Law Compromise Industry Policy Objectives?' Available at: <http://www.evenett.com/chapters/industrialpolicychapter.pdf>.

Federico G. and J. Foreman-Peck (eds.) (1999), 'Industrial Policies in Europe: Introduction' in *European Industrial Policy: The Twentieth-Century Experience*, Oxford University Press, Oxford.

Foer A. and R. Lande (1999), 'The Evolution of United States Antitrust Law: the Past, Present and (Possible) Future.' Available at: <http://www.antitrustinstitute.org>.

Hay D. (1998), 'Industrial Policy in Brazil: A Framework,' Discussion Paper No. 551, IPEA.

Jacquemin A. (1987), *The New Industrial Organization: Market Forces and Strategic Behavior*, MIT Press, Cambridge, Mass.

Johnson C. (1995), *Japan: Who Governs? The Rise of the Developmental State*, Norton, New York.

Jorde T. and D. Teece (eds.) (1992), 'Innovation, Cooperation and Antitrust' in *Antitrust, Innovation and Competitiveness*, Oxford University Press, New York.

Kosacoff B., C. Bonvecchi, and G. Yoguel (1998), 'Argentina: la economía en los años noventa. Contexto macroeconómico, desempeño industrial e inserción externa' in L. Garay (ed.) *Argentina, Brasil, México, Venezuela: apertura y reestructuración productiva*.

Lawless M. and J. Sophister (1999), 'Balancing Industrial and Competition Policies,' Available at: <http://econserv2.bess.tcd.ie/SER/archive/1999/essay13.html>.

Lederman D., W. Maloney, and L. Serven (2003), 'Lessons from NAFTA for Latin America and the Caribbean Countries: A Summary of Research Findings,' World Bank. Available at: <http://www.economia.gob.mx/pics/p/p1763/BM_Lessons_from_NAFTA_full.pdf>.

Lianos I. (2002), 'Report of the Workshop: Competition Policy and Economic Development: The Costs and Benefits of Multilateral Principles on Competition for Developing Economies.' Available at: <http://www.iilj.org/events/details/event-competition-policy_report.html>.

Lin P. (2002), 'Competition Policy in East Asia: The Cases of Japan, People's Republic of China, and Hong Kong.' Prepared for the 28th PAFTAD Conference in Manila, 16–18 September.

Lui L. (2005), 'China's Industrial Policies and Global Business Revolution: The Case of the Domestic Appliance Industry.' *Asian-Pacific Economic Literature* 19(1): 86–106.

McCraw T. (ed.) (1997), *Creating Modern Capitalism: How Entrepreneurs, Companies, and Countries Triumphed in Three Industrial Revolutions*, Harvard University Press, Cambridge, Mass.

McFetridge D. (ed.) (1985), *Industrial Policy in Action*, University of Toronto Press for the Royal Commission on the Economic Union and Development Prospects For Canada.

Marques A. (2002), 'A política industrial face às regras de concorrência na União Européia—a questão da promoção de sectores específicos,' Discussion Paper No. 21, Centro de Estudos da União Européia, Coimbra University.

Matsuura K., M. Pollitt, R. Takada, and S. Tanaka (2003), 'Institutional Restructuring in the Japanese Economy since 1985,' *Journal of Economic Issues*, 37(4).

Melo A. (2001), 'Industrial Policy in Latin America and the Caribbean at the Turn of the Century,' Inter-American Development Bank Research Department, Working Paper 459. Available at: <http://www.iadb.org/res/publications/pubfiles/pubWP-459.pdf>.

METI (2004), 'Key Points—FY 2005 Economic and Industrial Policy,' Available at: <http://www.meti.go.jp/english/policy/FY2005key%20points.pdf>.

Nelson R. and S. Winter (1982), *An Evolutionary Theory of Economic Change*, Harvard University Press, Cambridge, Mass.

Noland M. and H. Pack (2001), 'Industrial Policies and Growth: Lessons from International Experience.' Prepared for the Fifth Annual Conference of the Central Bank of Chile in Santiago, 29–30 November. Available at: <http://www.bcentral.cl/eng/stdpub/studies/workingpaper/pdf/dtbc169.pdf>.

OECD (1999), 'Regulatory Reform in Japan: The Role of Competition Policy in Regulatory Reform,' OECD Reports on the Role of Competition Policy in Regulatory Reform.

—— (2004a), 'Annual Report on Competition Policy Developments in Argentina—2003.' Available at: <http://www.oecd.org>.

—— (2004b), 'Competition Law and Policy in Mexico.' Available at: <http://www.oecd.org>.

Park J. (2002), 'The Two Giants of Asia: Trade and Development in China and India,' *Journal of Developing Societies*, 18(1): 64–81.

Porter M. (1990), 'The Competitive Advantage of Nations,' Free Press, New York.

Rubio L. (1992), 'Política de integración industrial: perspectiva mexicana' in S. Weintraub, L. Rubio, and A. Jones (eds.) *Integración industrial México–Estados Unidos: El reto de libre comercio*. Diana y Centro de Investigación para el Desarrollo: Serie Alternativas para el Futuro, Mexico. Available at: <http://www.cidac.org/vnm/libroscidac/integracion-ind-mex-usa/inte-04.pdf>.

Schatan C. and R. Hernández (2002), 'Políticas de competencia y de regulación en el Istmo Centroamericano,' Serie Estudios y Perspectivas—Sede Subregional de la CEPAL en México, Mexico.

Scherer F. (1994), 'Competition Policies for an Integrated World Economy,' Brookings Institution, Washington, DC.

Sharma D., H. Jansson, and M. Saqib (1991), 'Bureaucracy and Industrial Policy Implementation: The Case of India,' Department of Business Studies Working Paper, Uppsala University. Available at: <http://www.fek.uu.se/forskning/lista.asp?serie=Working%20Papers&year=1991>.

Singh A. (2002), 'Competition and Competition Policy in Emerging Markets: International and Developmental Dimensions,' Discussion Paper Series 18, UNCTAD.

—— and R. Dhumale (1999). 'Competition Policy, Development and Developing Countries,' Working Paper No. 7, Trade-Related Agenda, Development and Equity (T.R.A.D.E.). Available at: <http://www.southcentre.org/publications/workingpapers/wp07.pdf>.

Smith M. (2004), 'Germany's Quest for a New E.U. Industrial Policy: Why it is Failing,' Working Paper No. 11, BMW Center for German and European Studies, Georgetown University. Available at: <http://georgetown.edu/sfs/cges/working_papers.html>.

Stanford, J. (2003), 'Industrial Policy in an Era of Free Trade: What Isn't, and Is, Possible?' Presented to the Analytical Political Economy Conference. Available at: <http://www.caw.ca/whatwedo/research/pdf/stanfordforapecindustrialpolicy.pdf>.

Streeck W. (1992), *Social Institutions and Economic Performance: Studies of Industrial Relations in Advanced Industrialized Countries*, Sage, London.

Vitols S. (1997), 'German Industrial Policy: An Overview,' *Industry and Innovation*, 4(1).

Winslow T. (2004), 'Competition Law and Policy in Chile—A Peer Review.' Available at: <http://www.oecd.org>.

Wise M. (2000), 'Background Report on the Role of Competition Policy in Regulatory Reform.' Available at: <http://www.oecd.org/dataoecd/3/44/2497300.pdf>.

World Bank (1998), 'A Framework for the Design and Implementation of Competition Law and Policy,' Washington, DC.

Xiao-juan J. (2002), 'Promoting Competition and Maintaining Monopoly: Dual Functions of Chinese Industrial Policies during Economic Transition,' *Washington University Global Studies Law Review*, 1(1/2), Presented at the Symposium on APEC Competition Policy. Available at: <http://law.wustl.edu/wugslr/index.asp?id=5866>.

Xiaoye W. (2002), 'The Prospect of Antimonopoly Legislation in China,' *Washington University Global Studies Law Review*, 1(1/2), Presented at the Symposium on APEC Competition Policy. Available at: <http://law.wustl.edu/wugslr/index.asp?id=5866>.

Zysman J. (1983), *Governments, Markets, and Growth: Financial Systems and the Politics of Industrial Change*, Cornell University Press, Ithaca, NY.

18

Latecomer Entrepreneurship: A Policy Perspective

Mike Hobday and Fernando Perini

Introduction

This chapter examines the nature and dynamics of entrepreneurship in developing countries (DCs). It also asks if and how government policies can stimulate, shape, and foster the development of entrepreneurship. In the context of continuing technological progress in the advanced countries, it seems clear that entrepreneurship should play an important role in business growth and the wider processes of keeping up or catching up with the currently developed countries. But what precisely is the role of entrepreneurship in the catch-up context?

The dominant 'Washington Consensus' policy approach to entrepreneurship is to recommend that DCs adopt the policies of the most advanced and successful countries.[1] For example, on the basis of de Soto's work, policy analysts argue that entrepreneurs in DCs suffer from too much bureaucratic 'red tape', poor access to finance, unclear property rights, and excessive informality and illegality. If only these barriers could be removed and firms could be made legal, then innovation and development would follow, so the argument goes.[2] Similarly, because of the perceived role of small and medium-sized enterprises (SMEs) as a source of entrepreneurship and as a carrier of new skills and capabilities in the advanced economies, there are many programs to increase the rate of small firm start-ups in DCs.

To assess these issues, the chapter proceeds as follows. The second section reviews the various definitions and functions of the entrepreneur. It shows that the Schumpeterian model of the entrepreneur as a high-technology risk-taking innovator has been highly influential and argues that this perspective underpins many of the policies towards entrepreneurship in DCs. The third section examines recent research from both developed and DCs concerning the motivation and nature of entrepreneurs, the evolution of entrepreneurial networks, and the role of SMEs. Three following sections provide a critical assessment of current policies towards entrepreneurship, especially those which attempt to counter bureaucracy, reduce informality, and support the fostering of SMEs. The seventh section examines recent evidence on successful firm-level growth within East and South East Asia, touching on the roles of large firms, SMEs, and the subsidiaries of transnational corporations (TNCs). A further section discusses policy directions arising from the above, while the conclusion briefly summarizes the main points.

One important point to note is the lack of data on entry and exit (or 'churn') patterns of entrepreneurial firms in both developed and DCs. The broad statistical evidence presented by Bartelsman et al. (2004) shows that in all countries productivity growth is largely driven by within-firm (i.e. incumbent firm) performance. However, contributions to productivity caused by entry and exit are also highly significant, accounting for between 20 percent and 50 percent of total productivity growth. For all countries, this occurs *via* the reallocation of resources towards more productive uses and the increase in market contestability caused by entry of new firms. Nevertheless, for the DCs, in particular, aggregate data on new entrants probably hides fundamental differences between (a) basic SME entrants (e.g. the self-employed) oriented towards subsistence or survival and (b) SME entrepreneurial entry, focused on innovation, learning, and the development of new skills. Therefore, in the analysis of entrepreneurship it is essential to distinguish between innovation carried out by incumbents versus innovation carried out by new entrants (including SMEs). For policy purposes, it is also necessary to distinguish between survival-based SME entry (e.g. in very poor countries) versus genuine entrepreneurial entry. As we argue, the failure to make these basic distinctions leads to highly questionable entrepreneurial policies in DCs.

Definitions and functions of the entrepreneur

Definitions

The study of entrepreneurship crosses a large number of different disciplines, including economics, development economics, psychology, sociology, business and innovation studies. Clearly, any review of entrepreneurship requires a

Table 18.1. Definitions of entrepreneurs and entrepreneurship

Author	Definition
Richard Cantillon (circa 1730)	Entrepreneurship is defined as self-employment of any sort. Entrepreneurs buy at certain prices in the present and sell at uncertain prices in the future. The entrepreneur is a bearer of uncertainty (Cantillon, 2001).
Jean-Baptiste Say (1816)	The entrepreneur is the agent 'who unites all means of production and who finds in the value of the products... the reestablishment of the entire capital he employs, and the vaiue of the wages, the interest, and rent which he pays, as well as profits belonging to himself' (Say, 1832).
Frank Knight (1921)	Entrepreneurs attempt to predict and act upon change within markets. Knight emphasizes the entrepreneur's role in bearing the uncertainty of market dynamics. Entrepreneurs are required to perform such fundamental managerial functions as direction and control.
Joseph Schumpeter (1934)	The entrepreneur is the innovator who implements change within markets through the carrying out of new combinations. The carrying out of new combinations can take several forms: 1) the introduction of a new good or the same good with improved quality, 2) the introduction of a new method of production, 3) the opening of a new market, 4) the conquest of a new source of supply of new materials or parts, 5) the carrying out of the new organization of any industry. Schumpeter equated entrepreneurship with the concept of innovation applied to a business context. As such, the entrepreneur moves the market away from equilibrium. Schumpeter's definition also emphasized the combination of resources. Yet, the managers of an already established business are not entrepreneurs according to Schumpeter.
Penrose (1963)	Entrepreneurial activity involves identifying opportunities within the economic system. Managerial capacities are different from entrepreneurial capacities.
Harvey Leibenstein (1968)	The entrepreneur fills market deficiencies through input-completing activities. Entrepreneurship involves "activities necessary to create or carry on an enterprise where not all markets are well established or clearly defined and/or in which relevant parts of the production function are not completely known.
Israel Kirzner (1978)	The entrepreneur recognizes and acts upon market opportunities. The entrepreneur is essentially an arbitrageur. In contrast to Schumpeter's viewpoint, the entrepreneur moves the market toward equilibrium.
Rothwell and Zegveld (1982)	Intracorporate entrepreneurship (sometimes called 'intrapreneurship') is related to the creation of a new business inside the large corporation, a phenomenon that increases in importance along with degree of concentration of industry, and particularly of the science intensive industries.

Source: Summarized and amended from <http://www.westaction.org/definitions/def_entrepreneurship_1.html>

definition of both the subject ('the entrepreneur') and the processes undertaken ('entrepreneurship'). Even within disciplines, there is little agreement on a precise definition. Over the past two hundred years or so, observers have adopted their own definitions according to their particular objectives and approach (Table 18.1).

In 1971, Kilby (2003), in his seminal paper 'Hunting the Heffalump' proposed seven theories about entrepreneurship: four theories based on psychological constructs and three based on sociological constructs. He concluded that none of them could be validated or falsified empirically. He reaffirmed this recently (Kilby, 2003, p. 16): 'we still cannot quantify entrepreneurial services, but only infer them from their consequences; investigators improvise proxies drawn from their disciplines, assert that motivating appetite is the maximand of that discipline and then claim to a somewhat skeptical audience that they have captured the determinants of entrepreneurial performance.'

As Cantwell (2001) and many others show, according to Schumpeter (1934) the 'Mark I' (or heroic) individual entrepreneur establishes a temporary monopoly in an output (product) or input (process) market and obtains 'super' profits from innovation, typically associated with higher output prices and lower input costs. In Mark II, recognizing the role of large firms, Schumpeter (1943) emphasized the corporate research and development (R&D) laboratory. Here, innovation occurs in a routine fashion. Cantwell (2001, p. 13) argues that Penrose (1959) offers a neo-Schumpeterian theory of innovation, profits, and growth. Penrose saw the entrepreneurial function as one dispersed within the organization and focused on innovation as a source of profits, achieved through learning to develop new applications based on a firm's specific resources. Penrose also argued that innovative profits should not be understood as returns to temporary positions of monopolistic market power, enjoyed by first movers, but as a return on the capability that enables firms to experiment with new technological combinations and the problem-solving abilities which enable firms to innovate successfully.

Freeman (1994) argues that Schumpeter's early theory over-emphasized the central role of exceptional individuals in technical and organizational innovation and that Schumpeter tended to ignore the changing nature of the entrepreneurial function in subsequent phases of business development which focus on incremental innovation and learning-by-doing in the innovation process.

Contemporary research supports the view that innovation often occurs in an organized manner within large integrated firms. As Pavitt (2004) argues, professional education, the establishment of corporate R&D laboratories, and improvements of techniques of measurement and experimentation have increased the efficiency of discovery, invention, and innovation within large firms allowing increasingly difficult problems to be tackled and solved. Pavitt (2004) contends that at least three forms of corporate specialization have supported innovation: the growth of R&D laboratories specialized in the production of knowledge for commercial exploitation; the growth of many small firms providing the large firms with specialized capital goods; a growing division between private business knowledge and public knowledge developed and disseminated by universities and other publicly funded institutions. Nelson and Winter (1982) and Dosi et al. (2000) also illustrate the importance of the gradual accumulation of capabilities through specific technological paths and learning mechanisms within large firms and in industrial and technological networks. Despite the oft-cited Mark I/Mark II distinction, Mark II activities often proceed hand-in-hand with Mark I processes especially when the latter are undertaken by spin-offs from larger incumbent organizations and managers who leave large firms to 'try their luck' in the marketplace.

In relation to DCs, as we show below, it is important to recognize that the new skills, capabilities, combinations, and industries which entrepreneurs create may well not be new to the world, but only new to the local economy. Indeed, as we argue, entrepreneurs in DCs perform highly specialized 'latecomer' functions different, in many respects, from the conventional Schumpeterian entrepreneur which tends to emphasize the development of new products and technologies. In DCs, entrepreneurs often have to acquire the capabilities for 'behind-the-frontier' catch-up innovation. Also, it is quite probable that the character of latecomer entrepreneurship will vary according to the stage of development and the particular development path of the economy in question. Therefore, this chapter adopts a very broad understanding of entrepreneurship, including technology but not excluding other managerial and social dimensions. For DCs the Schumpeterian vision of the entrepreneur as an innovator whose actions lead to creative destruction needs to be supplemented with an awareness of the latecomer context, for both analytical and policy purposes.

Insights from recent research on entrepreneurship

Recent empirical research challenges mainstream interpretations of entrepreneurship in various ways, pointing to important non-pecuniary motivations of the entrepreneur and showing how entrepreneurship is frequently embedded in social and economic networks which span international boundaries, acting as major forces for national and regional economic development over time. Studies also highlight ethnic and class determinants of entrepreneurial behavior which run contrary to the strictly economic interpretations of the entrepreneur.

Motivations and functions of entrepreneurs

Much of the classic entrepreneurship literature starts from the principle that a considerable supply of entrepreneurs is required to generate capitalist growth. Entrepreneurs are seen as people and/or groups of people willing to take investment risks and capable of organizing others. In a highly influential paper, McClelland and Winter (1969) proposed a direct positive relationship between entrepreneurship achievement and economic growth, based on empirical evidence from the US and North Africa. These types of arguments appeared logical and led to the creation of a large number of centers and educational curricula designed to create an entrepreneurial achievement culture among students in DCs. This line of thought is still prevalent in the DC literature on the psychological traits of the entrepreneurs and in entrepreneurship training and education in DCs (Dana, 2000; Gupta, 1990). However, McClelland and Winter's results were contested from an empirical point of view. Recent studies show (e.g. in India) that entrepreneurship programs have little if any effect on the rate of start-ups. Poojary (1996) shows that entrepreneurs tend to come from traditional trading communities and tend to have little formal training and education. Instead, they are typically indoctrinated in the importance of economic success within their communities. Research in the farm equipment industry in the Punjab in Pakistan reveals that most entrepreneurs lack formal education and instead rely on each other for market and technical information (Romijn, 1999).

Part of the classic interpretation of the entrepreneur is the 'risk taking' function with respect to investment. Entrepreneurs have long been assumed to be more risk-tolerant than the general population and profit, as the reward of risk-taking activities, is often part of the definition of entrepreneurship (e.g. Knight, 1921). However, this view has been challenged by empirical evidence in the US. Xu and Ruef's (2004) statistical analysis of the financial risk-taking propensity of business founders, using a representative dataset of 1261 nascent entrepreneurs and comparison groups in the US consistently shows that nascent entrepreneurs are more *risk-averse* than non-entrepreneurs. They argue that the motivations that individuals have for founding business ventures are often non-pecuniary and that in order to obtain non-pecuniary benefits, they need to be risk-averse in pursing profits, so that they can lower the risk of business closure. Drawing on concepts from organizational sociology and social psychology, they identified two classes of non-pecuniary motivations which often contribute to business formation: (a) autonomy, involving the avoidance of relationships that restrict an individual's actions in professional and personal life; and (b) identity fulfillment, including the need to develop and challenge themselves and establish an enduring personal legacy. In short, companies are often set up to enable personal and financial independence and the freedom of owners to make their own decisions. Instead of assuming that entrepreneurs are profit-maximizing agents, research needs to identify the motivations that entrepreneurs have in founding business ventures. In addition, Xu and Ruef argue that low risk tolerance and non-pecuniary motivation can impact business strategy. For example, firms may restrict the potential growth of the firm in order to achieve the personal goals of the founder. This may explain why many small firms remain small and want to remain small.

Non-profit motivations are also identified in DCs. In Kenya, Nelson and Mwaura (1997) analyzed 30 fast-growing SMEs of between 10 and 100 employees, identifying the strategies of these entrepreneurs through the various stages of growth of their firms. They observed that firms strongly valued personal and financial independence and the ability to make their own decisions without interference from a higher authority. They were also very much concerned with the economic well-being of the family. However, these very motives sometimes prevented the infusion of further resources for expansion and led to managerial problems such as a reluctance to delegate responsibilities to subordinates.

In DCs, the analysis of entrepreneurial profiles varies greatly in terms of background, self-confidence, creativity, independence, and literacy. Relations with economic growth are complex and sometimes contradictory. Kilby (2003) argues that the identification of a unique set of entrepreneurial activities or psychological characteristics, irrespective of time or place, was always misconceived and posed a barrier to improving entrepreneurial practice. For example, the skills and personality attributes required in Schumpeterian (or technology leadership) entrepreneurship is at odds with the adaptive and imitative behavior frequently observed in successful DCs (see the section headed 'Successful firm-level growth in East and South East Asia' below).

The embeddedness of entrepreneurship (in social and economic networks)

Research shows how entrepreneurship is often associated with class and ethnic background and embedded in close social networks. According to Leff (1978), the concentration of economic power in ethnic minorities is a frequently observed characteristic in DCs. Focusing on small-scale entrepreneurship, Sverrisson (1993) attempted to explain why industrial development has proved to be so difficult in sub-Saharan African economies. Sverrisson (1993) analyzed small-scale carpentry enterprise in two African towns, Nakuru (Kenya) and Mutuare (Zimbabwe). He showed that small firms are embedded in rigid production, social, and political networks and alliances which can sometimes retard local innovation and adoption of new and even relatively mature, simple technologies. In line with other studies on Africa, this research shows that within these networks particular social classes take an entrepreneurial lead and, in some cases, arrest the development of other classes by preventing entry. Also, typically, the broad range of customer categories served by each enterprise led to a lack of specialization and division of labor, and a failure to exploit economies of scale and scope. Local firms tended to turn to customers, with whom they had close personal alliances, for production finance, rather than formal financiers or banks so that the majority of the enterprises were not fully integrated into the formal economy and the laws regulating it.

The collective, embedded, informal nature of entrepreneurship is illustrated by research on Pakistan.[3] In a study of the Punjab farm equipment industry Romijn (1999) shows how hundreds of firms progressed from simple fixed structures in the 1960s such as moldboard ploughs and ridges to relatively complex devices such as rotary cultivators with internal power transmission systems. Small-scale farm equipment manufacturers lacked formal technical education and worked closely together to develop and improve on technology. Similarly, Chan (2001) shows how China's entrepreneurial networks share common values and unwritten codes of conduct, firmly embedded in strictly enforced social norms which function to reduce risk and uncertainty. In South India, research shows the importance of social networks of entrepreneurs in the information and communication technology cluster (Taeube, 2004). Membership of these networks can be very useful. According to Schak (2000), Taiwanese SMEs started to operate in networks in response to governmental bias in favor of big business, providing new enterprise with a sense of purpose and direction and formal and informal reward systems.

Evolution of informal networks into formal business activity

Research on both China and India shows that informal entrepreneurial networks can sometimes evolve into highly successful formal centers of regional and national economic growth. An anthropological analysis of the South Indian software cluster indicates that values and casts are closely associated with successful economic behavior. According to Taeube (2004) the software industry is dominated by South Indian Brahmins (traditionally the priestly and knowledgeable cast group), despite the entrepreneurial tradition of the Vaishyas (the merchant or trader cast). This study suggests that a process of social networking among these groups, which started at university and college at home and abroad, was important to the growth of the software cluster.

Recent studies on overseas Chinese networks shows how these informal networks evolved over the centuries to manage and mitigate ever more complex risk-taking activities (Chan, 2001; Chan and Chiang, 1994). Formal overseas Chinese businesses now dominate many branches of the South East Asian economy, controlling more than two-thirds of the region's retail trade and large proportions of the shares of listed equity in South East Asia (Table 18.2). These formal networks coexist with informal practices. So-called *guanxi* (or bamboo networks), for example, continue to link together ethnically homogeneous and disciplined groups of entrepreneurs. These networks are formed on the basis of shared social attributes such as family, kinship, schooling, and friendship. *Guanxi* places considerable emphasis on unwritten codes

Table 18.2. Overseas Chinese holdings in listed companies in South East Asia

	Ethnic Chinese in 1991 (millions)	Percent of population	Share of listed equity (%)
Indonesia	5.81	3.5	73
Malaysia	5.33	29.0	61
Philippines	1.2	2.0	50
Thailand	5.57	10.0	81
Singapore	2.14	77.0	81

Note: Chinese holdings in listed companies not under state or foreign control, as percentage of market value of all shares in such firms.
Source: Sakura Bank, Nomura Research Institute, in *Asiaweek*, October 20, 1993.

of conduct to guard against opportunistic behavior of its members. Chan (2001) argues that *guanxi* functions to minimize risk and reduce uncertainty. However, there is a thin line between *guanxi* as an informal mechanism of exchange and as corrupt practice, given its uncodified and cryptic nature. Many of these networks may well have started out as informal, small-scale endeavors, but, as Table 18.2 confirms, by the early 1990s they represented a large proportion of formal listed equity in the five South East Asian countries mentioned.

As Chan (2001) and others argue, overseas Chinese practices should be viewed as an entrepreneurial approach that has proven economic value under particular, often difficult, circumstances. Overseas Chinese business networks, through large-scale migratory movements, have enabled large numbers of entrepreneurs to engage in investments in increasingly large-scale, high-technology activities upon a basis of trust which is highly valuable in an uncertain and rapidly changing environment.

The role of SMEs and business start-ups

SMEs are often treated as synonymous with entrepreneurs and there are many SME policies to stimulate entrepreneurship in both developed and DCs (see the section headed 'SME policies as entrepreneurship policies' below). However, evidence from both OECD countries and DCs is ambiguous on the role of SMEs in economic growth. SME advocates such as Audretsch and Thurik (2001) strongly associate entrepreneurship with the participation of SMEs, based on research in OECD countries. They argue that an increase in SME activity tends to result in higher subsequent growth rates and a reduction in unemployment. They contend that entrepreneurship generates growth because it serves as a vehicle for innovation and change. The proxies they use for entrepreneurship are the relative share of economic activity accounted for by small firms and the self-employment rate. Economic performance is then measured by economic growth and any reduction in unemployment.

The global entrepreneurship monitor (GEM) (Reynolds et al. 2004), which began as a partnership between the London Business School and Babson College in 1999, purports to provide an authoritative empirical basis for understanding the effects of entrepreneurial activity in the economy. The annual GEM assessment involves surveys of a representative sample of the adult population. In 2003 more than one hundred thousand interviews were completed in 37 developing and developed countries using a standardized methodology. The GEM database provides comparative data on entrepreneurship, which is used to calculate the total entrepreneurship activity (TEA) index which refers to working-age adults in the population who are either involved in the process of starting-up a business or are active as owner-manager of enterprises less than 42 months old.

However, as noted in the introduction, empirical evidence reviewed by Bartelsman et al. (2004) on entry and exit patterns indicates the need to distinguish between (a) small firm, basic entrants including the self-employed (perhaps resulting from structural adjustment programs or recession and mainly oriented towards subsistence or survival) and (b) classical entrepreneurial entry, focused on innovation, learning, and the development of new skills. In the DCs, in particular, the role of new entrants as a carrier of technological advance cannot be captured by aggregate data on entry (or exit) or business start-up participation.

Because of the mistake of conflating start-ups with entrepreneurial activity, the results of the GEM analysis are not credible. Countries such as Taiwan and Hong Kong which have demonstrated their entrepreneurial capabilities find themselves at the low end of the scale. Conversely, countries with poor development records (e.g. Uganda, Mexico, and Venezuela) are right at the successful end. This is because the TEA figures simply report on the numbers of people involved in the creation of new companies as a proportion of the population. They do not reflect on whether these firms are actually engaged in entrepreneurial activity as defined in the 'Definitions' section above. Indeed, far from being an entrepreneurial index, a high TEA may reflect highly undesirable social characteristics, such as rising unemployment, economic decline, and a lack of educational opportunities. As Reynolds et al. (2004) admit, factors which influence a high rate of entrepreneurial activity include low growth in national wealth, a higher prevalence of young adults in the workforce, a larger agricultural sector, reduced social and economic welfare benefits, and less participation in secondary and post-secondary education. This implies that the rate of entrepreneurship is a function of external developmental circumstances rather than vice versa. High rates of entrepreneurship, as measured, can reflect extremely undesirable economic conditions rather than any potential for innovation and growth.

This is a serious issue in many DCs. In Latin America for instance, since the 1980s, the number of microenterprises expanded significantly throughout the region. In Mexico, for example, whereas firms with fewer than 15 employees accounted for 84 percent of all manufacturing firms in 1985, accounted for 93 percent by 1998. Similarly, in Brazil, in just five years, from 1994 to 1999, the percentage of industrial firms with fewer than 10 employees increased from 75 percent to 80 percent. This is hardly a measure of burgeoning entrepreneurship but an indication of economic recession and industrial decline.

The argument that small firms do not necessarily play an important role in entrepreneurial activities is supported by Fehr and Nils-Henrik (1995) in their in-depth analysis of entrepreneurial activity and firm formation in Zambia, based on a survey of 215 firms in manufacturing. They show that small firms, albeit large in number, were relatively unimportant in Zambian manufacturing, both with regard to output and employment and as a source of future growth. The survey concentrated on four manufacturing industries namely food, textiles, wood products, and fabricated metals industries. Enterprises were chosen randomly and covered tiny, informal sector workshops, SMEs, and large, parastatal and foreign-owned companies. The study gathered information on the owner's personal history (including education, experience, and wealth), the start-up of the firm (including financing, investments, and employment) and the firm's development and performance. The study showed that firms which were established at a small scale tend to stay small. Although most surviving firms do grow over time, the smallest entrants very rarely grow to become more than small or moderately sized. The majority of African firms did not grow out of the group of tiny firms; 71 of the 80 firms that were founded by an African entrepreneur started out with less than 10 employees, and of these only 3 (4.2%) eventually employed more than 25 people. Consequently, the small entrants contributed only modestly to manufacturing industrial activity, with regard to employment, capital, and output. Regarding the smallest African firms, while the few that grew made a useful contribution to growth, Fehr and Nils-Henrik argue that from a strictly economic perspective, the small entrants were largely irrelevant, representing only 'noise in the fringe'.[4]

In summary, what recent research indicates for both advanced and DCs is that the capitalist entrepreneur does not have a stable or 'best practice' face represented by the classic individual 'heroic' Schumpeterian entrepreneur. On the contrary, modern entrepreneurship is highly diverse in its nature, embedded in social networks, and stimulated by many diverse factors. Interestingly, some of these networks inhibit while others promote innovation and economic growth. Therefore, one cannot assume that entrepreneurial groups are always positive in relation to economic development. In addition, the tendency to conflate start-ups and SMEs with entrepreneurs fails to distinguish between low productivity non-entrepreneurial firms and genuine innovative entrepreneurial firms. Unfortunately, these confusions sometimes spill over into policy making, an issue to which we now turn.

Policies for entrepreneurship in DCs

This section provides a critical examination of three sets of modern policies towards entrepreneurship: (i) policies to reduce government bureaucracy; (ii) policies to increase the rate of start-ups; and (iii) policies to encourage venture capital. Implicitly, and sometimes explicitly, each of these sets of policies is based on the conventional Schumpeterian view of the entrepreneur. As such, they identify 'best practices' in the now advanced countries and apply them directly to today's DCs.

Policies to reduce and reform government bureaucracy

Some influential policy research is highly critical of the nature and impact of government bureaucracy in DCs. In particular de Soto's writings on poverty, property systems, and capital accumulation highlight government obstructions and impediments to market developments and entrepreneurship in DCs (de Soto, 2000). He identifies explicit obstacles (e.g. excessive state bureaucracy and poor property rights) that increase transaction costs and prevent scale and scope from emerging from basic entrepreneurial activity.[5]

As a typical example, to license a small garment shop (with one worker) in Lima, Peru, de Soto's team attempted to legalize the operation by registering the business according to existing law (de Soto, 2000, p. 28). It took the team of well-educated researchers six hours a day for 289 days. It cost US$1,231 in total (31 times the monthly minimum wage) and required 207 administrative steps, involving 52 government offices. To obtain legal title for the small piece of land took a further 728 steps, a total of 26 months of red tape. De Soto provides many similar examples for the Philippines, Egypt, Haiti, Mexico, and other DCs.

De Soto (2000) argues that most DCs lack a clear and enforceable property system which is one of the important foundation stones of capital accumulation. He concludes that many entrepreneurs and businesses are forced to operate outside the formal capitalist system because of government bureaucracy and inefficiency. Entrepreneurs stand no chance of obtaining loans against their homes, land, or business assets for capital investment. As a result, he contends that a huge amount of 'dead capital' exists in the developing world which is excluded from legal structure of capital accumulation.

De Soto (2000) argues that the total value of real estate held, but not legally owned, by the poor of the Third World and former communist nations is at least US$9.3 trillion. He contends that there would be major benefits from the reform of public bureaucracy and proposes that government should recognize the economic value of assets and make public-sector property officials more accountable. One of de Soto's reform projects was carried out in Peru. According to de Soto, between 1982 and 1996, a relatively small investment (US$17 million by USAID and US$1.2 million from the ILD) managed to incorporate

US$9.4 billion into the formal system between 1991 and 2002. As a result 6.3 million Peruvians below the poverty line legally owned their real estate assets. The value of these formalized real estate assets increased by US$2.2 billion and the income of formalized real estate owners increased by US$3.2 billion; 380,000 business enterprises belonging mainly to the poor were formalized, representing 560,000 additional legal jobs and increased tax revenue by US $300 million a year (source: ILD Website <http://www.ild.org.pe/>). However, other observers question the gains from this and other projects (e.g. Calderon, 2004; Rossini and Thomas, 1990) arguing that household access to formal credit has been disappointing and that the title deeds to property do not necessarily lead to a rise in real credit.

De Soto's arguments and proposals have been highly influential in policy circles such as the World Bank, IMF, UNDP, International Finance Corporation, and International Bank for Reconstruction and Development. For example, they are explicitly referred to in the World Bank's 'Doing Business' database (World Bank, 2004). This aims to provide comparable objective measures of the state of business regulations and their enforcement across 145 economies. The 2005 database (the third edition) argues that poor and DCs impose far more obstacles to entrepreneurship and business development than do more developed economies, involving greater costs, delays, and barriers to owning property, starting-up businesses, declaring bankruptcy, protecting investors, enforcing contracts and legal rights, and in laying off workers.

Djankov and McLiesh (2005), leaders of the Doing Business project, argue that there is a straightforward, positive relationship between the 'ease of doing business' and the human development index, suggesting that reforms could have a positive and widespread impact in developing economies. They contend that more than 2 percentage points could be added to the growth of the 'most difficult countries to do business' if they adopted the regulations that exist in the least difficult ones (Djankov and McLiesh, 2005).

According to Djankov and McLiesh:

It takes 153 days to start a business in Maputo, but two days in Toronto. It costs $2,042 or 126% of the debt value to enforce a contract in Jakarta, but $1,300 or 5.4% of the debt value to do so in Seoul. It takes 21 procedures to register commercial property in Abuja, but 3 procedures in Helsinki. If a debtor becomes insolvent and enters bankruptcy, creditors would get 13 cents on the dollar in Mumbai, but more than 90 cents in Tokyo. Borrowers and lenders are entitled to 10 main types of legal rights in Singapore, but only 2 in Yemen. In Nigeria and Senegal the property registration cost amounts to about 30% of the property value. And even when a formal title is well-established, it will not help to increase access to credit if courts are inefficient, collateral laws are poor and there are no credit information systems, because no one would be willing to lend. Add to this rigid employment regulation, and few people will be hired. Arguably women, young and low-skilled workers are hurt the most: their only choice is to seek jobs in the informal sector.

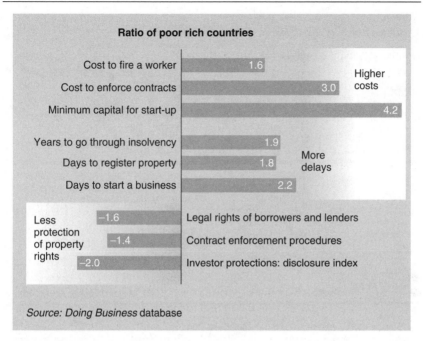

Source: Djankov and McLiesh (2005); <http://rru.worldbank.org/DoingBusiness/>
Figure 18.1. Regulatory obstacles in poor countries

The overall position in terms of regulatory obstacles is presented in Figure 18.1. The benefits of simple regulations in terms of human development (Figures 18.2 and 18.3) according to Djankov and McLiesh (2005) are immense. They also produce figures which suggest a strong positive correlation between the size of the informal sector and regulatory procedures (p. 4). This approach, and the reforms adopted, are best viewed as a subset of the wider range of economic and business reforms contained in the 'Washington Consensus', referred to recently by Rodrik (2004) as the 'augmented Washington consensus' (see Appendix 1 for a detailed discussion).

Although superficially these types of arguments may appear plausible, there are at least four sets of problems with them. First, the policy assumption that there is a linear causal relationship between excessive regulation and low rates of development is questionable. It may be that the economic environment causes low rates of entrepreneurial activity and high rates of bureaucracy, rather than vice versa. Indeed, there is evidence to show that the external environment in terms of innovative demand and opportunity exerts a significant impact on the emergence and development of entrepreneurship (Reynolds et al. 2004; see the section headed 'Insights from recent research on entrepreneurship' above). If this is the case, then regulatory reform alone is

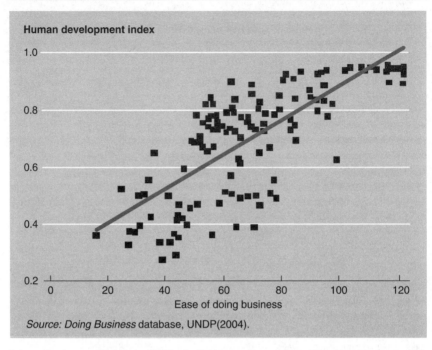

Source: Djankov and McLiesh (2005). Available at: <http://rru.worldbank.org/Documents/DB-2005Overview.pdf>

Figure 18.2. Simple business regulation, more human development

unlikely to produce much entrepreneurial activity. At the very minimum wider economic improvements which lead to more business opportunities would need to precede or accompany regulatory reforms for the latter to be successful. Such economic improvements might require new macroeconomic policies and an entirely different national development strategy.

Second, as Amin (2002) considers, de Soto and similar analyses fail to appreciate the economic functions of the informal sector. Informality is simply treated as a 'problem' to be solved. Amin (2002) argues that informal activities can stimulate growth of the formal market economy by keeping down urbanization costs, contributing to competitiveness, and promoting recycling through buying and selling of waste. In addition, the informal sector constitutes a flexible labor market which absorbs labor from the formal sector in the face of new trade regimes and structural adjustment policies which increase unemployment in the formal sector.[6] As Moore (1997) shows, many thousands of formal sector jobs have disappeared in DCs and the growth of the informal sector is rising rapidly as a result. Amin (2002) illustrates the sheer scale of the informal sector labor force (including self-employed workers, unpaid

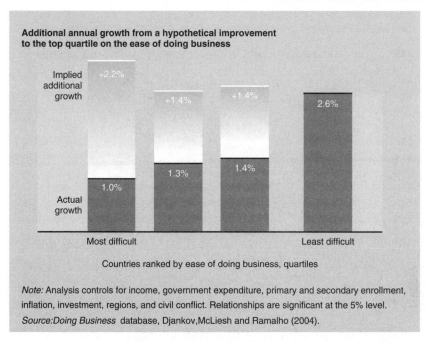

Additional annual growth from a hypothetical improvement to the top quartile on the ease of doing business

Note: Analysis controls for income, government expenditure, primary and secondary enrollment, inflation, investment, regions, and civil conflict. Relationships are significant at the 5% level.
Source:Doing Business database, Djankov,McLiesh and Ramalho (2004).

Source: Djankov and McLiesh (2005); <http://rru.worldbank.org/DoingBusiness/>
Figure 18.3. Ease of doing business is associated with more growth

family labor, and hired labor employed by informal sector enterprises). In many countries this varies between 50 percent and 60 percent of total non-agricultural, urban employment. If extended to include the agricultural sector, the size of the informal sector rises to 90 percent of total employment in India, Bangladesh, and Nepal.

Third, it may well be that informal systems develop and grow and during the development process become increasingly formalized and legal (as has been the case of the overseas Chinese investments which now dominate the listed stock market in South East Asia; see the section headed 'Insights from recent research on entrepreneurship' above). In which case, informality can be a 'stage of development' issue, rather than a problem to be solved. If government attempted to legalize and register informal activity in advance of the formalization stage, this would probably have very little effect on productivity and income growth.

Fourth, de Soto (2000) and Djankov and McLiesh (2005) do not examine cases of success (e.g. in East Asia and South East Asia) where development has widely occurred. So it is not possible to say whether property rights and bureaucracies were any better in these cases than in the cases of failure studied.

In fact, if we look at the position of two of the most successful larger developing nations in the past decade, China and India, we find them very low down on the World Bank's 'Doing Business' 2006 database (India at 115 and China 91 out of 155 countries; World Bank, 2004). This also suggests there is little correlation between the Doing Business rankings and economic success.

Nor is there much explanation of why high levels of bureaucracy exists. It may be that the style, stage, and level of late development has led to high regulation and bureaucracy, as DCs imitate more developed countries and attempt to implement 'good regulatory practices' established by the now developed countries. Or expanding government bureaucracy may be a response to unemployment and low growth. Alternatively, as Krueger (1974) argues, excessive government regulation and intervention (e.g. via the granting of licenses) can function as a means of rent extraction by particular groups in society. The granting of licenses by government officials can lead to competition for very large rents, encouraging bribery and, in the extreme, diverting entrepreneurs into rent-seeking away from innovative activities. If this is a cause, then deep political and institutional changes are needed, which would probably conflict with powerful vested interests. Superficial reform programs merely scratch the surface of the problem and could provide a breathing space for officials to avoid economic restructuring around genuine innovative activity.[7]

The modern policy approaches to bureaucracy are therefore highly dubious and lacking in analytical and historical insight. The policy reforms suggested do not necessarily follow from the problems identified, causation is not established or considered, and the method of calculating benefits (comparing advanced with developing countries) is naïve in the extreme.

SME policies as entrepreneurship policies

Policies to encourage entrepreneurship often take the form of SME promotion and micro-finance programs, arguing that the latter contribute to employment growth and that high-tech SMEs in new economic sectors promote new growth opportunities and enable innovation (e.g. Audretsch and Thurik, 2001). The latter argue that policies for encouraging R&D, venture capital, and new-firm start-ups lead to greater entrepreneurship via SMEs as well as higher economic growth and reduced unemployment. In their words: 'as the evidence shows, just as countries reluctant to shift their industry structures towards smaller entrepreneurial enterprises will be penalized by lower growth rates and higher unemployment, those nations able to harness the forces of technology and globalization by facilitating entrepreneurial activity are rewarded by growth dividends and reduced unemployment' (Audretsch and Thurik, 2001).[8]

However, as we have argued above, there is a major difference between starting a business of whatever form and being an entrepreneur in the sense of being a carrier of new technology, skills, and capabilities. In fact, self-employment, particularly in the informal sector, is often the mark of backwardness and not of dynamism. This point has led to deep misunderstandings concerning the levels and growth of entrepreneurship in DCs.

Overall, the evidence on SMEs calls into question not only the entrepreneurial indices but also policies which aim to increase start-up entrepreneurship in order to generate innovation and development. Indeed, development, historically, has entailed the reduction in the levels of the self-employed (pseudo-entrepreneurial) part of the economy. Furthermore, other evidence questions the role of SME creation in employment and poverty reduction, which is another important argument for SME promotion policies. Using data on SME participation in over 70 developing and developed economies and growth rates during the 1990s, Beck et al. (2003) argue that cross-country comparisons do not indicate that SMEs exert a particularly beneficial impact on the incomes of the poor. Nor is there any significant relationship between SME growth and measures of the depth and breadth of poverty. Beck's statistical evidence does not support pro-SME policies in DCs. Rather, the results show the importance of creating a business environment that fosters competition and commercial transactions for all firms, large, medium, and small.

Nevertheless, SME and microenterprise policies are widely supported by international institutions, donor governments, and nongovernmental organizations. For example, the World Bank Group approved more than US$10 billion in SME support programs over the five-year period ending in 2002 (Beck et al, 2003). Shadlen (2004) argues that there is a danger that further microenterprise promotion will allocate scarce public resources in a way that prioritizes SMEs over industrial integration and dynamism. Shadlen contends, convincingly, that small business policies are best viewed in terms of their contributions toward industrial transformation and economic development in general.

Venture capital policies

As in the case of SME policies, support for venture capital markets is put forward as a means for increasing entrepreneurship in both developed and DCs. These measures are often based on the notable successes of US high-technology firms. However, the data show that even in the case of high-tech start-ups in the developed countries, venture capital is only ever a very minor source of funds for start-up investments, apart from notable cases in the US and Israel (Reynolds et al. 2004). The formal venture capital market is often overestimated in its importance, as a large proportion of investments for start-ups comes from other sources. Instead, informal investments are far more important in start-up and expansion than venture capital.

The availability of venture capital is concentrated in a few developed countries. Overall, fewer that 0.01 percent of nascent entrepreneurs launch their new ventures with formal venture capital or 'business angel' investments. The US accounts for a large proportion of total venture capital (80% of all venture capital worldwide, Reynolds et al. 2004) where it has helped support innovative high growth firms, including Intel, Microsoft, Apple, Dell, Genentech, FedEx, Cisco, Netscape, Google, Ebay, and Amazon.com.

Increasingly though, high-technology start-ups are receiving less support from venture capital even in the US. In the US, speculative capital has shifted away from start-up/early stage investments to acquisition of shares in existing companies (i.e. buy outs), where it now represents more than 80 percent of total funds. Early stage investment accounts for only 4 percent in 2003. The European venture capital market, especially in the UK, was quite significant during the 1990s. However, it reduced dramatically after 2001 (Earley, 2004).

Successful firm-level growth in East and South East Asia

As Amsden (1989), Amdsen and Hikino (1994), and Amsden in Chapter 15 in this volume show, large locally owned firms, often conglomerates, are a frequent element of successful latecomer economic development. In contrast to de Soto (2000) and other studies cited in the 'Definitions' section above, which focus on the failure of entrepreneurship in DCs and barriers to progress, Amsden points to numerous examples of successful firm-level growth in support of national economic development.

While there can be no doubt that in South Korea, India, and other fast-growing economies, large domestic firms play a significant role, there are at least three areas of interest from the perspective of 'latecomer entrepreneurship' (as distinct from 'normal' or advanced-country entrepreneurship) which are important from a policy and analytical perspective.[9] First, what is the nature and path of technological progress of domestically owned, indigenous firms and does this differ from advanced-country enterprise? Second, what is the entrepreneurial role of TNCs, especially in South East Asia, where they dominate exports. As Amsden argues in Chapter 15, TNC investments cannot always be relied upon for development and therefore it is interesting to ask whether there are any lessons from the successful South East Asian cases of TNC-led export development for other developing economies. Third, how important are small firms for entrepreneurial development? Clearly, in the case of Korea and India, small firms appear not to have played a leading role. However, the cases of Taiwan and China suggest there may be a role for SMEs both in support of larger enterprise and as a source from which larger firms emerge. The case of electronics, the largest export sector in East and South East Asia, provides interesting evidence on each of the above questions.

The nature of latecomer technological progress

First, regarding the nature of latecomer technological progress, one very important mechanism for exporting electronics producers over the past 30 years or so, was the original equipment manufacture (OEM) system, where large TNCs based in the developed economies sub-contracted production to local Asian firms. The OEM system evolved and expanded through time, functioning both as an institutional mechanism for acquiring technology and for gaining access to export marketing channels (Table 18.3). The system began experimentally in fairly small ventures in the 1950s and early 1960s, pioneered by US semiconductor assembly producers (e.g. Texas Instruments and IBM). Local firms gained economies of scale and learned basic production operating techniques. Factory workers, technicians, engineers, and managers were trained in what was then modern technology as well as new management techniques, by the large TNCs who wished to gain the advantages of low-cost labor.

In the 1980s, OEM began to be called own design manufacture (ODM) in Taiwan (Johnstone, 1989). Under ODM, the domestic firm carried out most of the detailed product design to an overall design layout from the TNC customer. The TNC continued to carry out the marketing and distribution under its own brand name, thereby continuing to gain most of the value added. However, the local firm was expected to contribute minor product improvements and had to set up the manufacturing processes.

In the 1990s, some of the leading firms began own brand manufacture (OBM), competing directly with international suppliers from Japan, the US,

Table 18.3. Technological development of Korean and Taiwanese firms: from OEM to ODM to OBM

	Technological transition	Market transition
1960s/1970s OEM Original Equipment Manufacture	Local firm learns assembly process for standard, simple goods	Foreign TNC/buyer designs, brands, and distributes/gains non-manufacturing value added
1980s ODM Own Design and Manufacture	Local firm learns process engineering and detailed product design skills	As with OEM, TNC buys, brands, and distributes. TNC gains non-manufacturing value added
1990s OBM Own Brand Manufacture	Local firm conducts manufacturing, product design, and R&D for new products	Local firm has own brand, organizes distribution, and captures all value added

Source: Amended from Hobday (1994).

and Europe. Under OBM, the domestic firm carries out all of the stages of production and innovation, including manufacturing, new product design, and sometimes R&D for new materials and products. At this advanced stage, the local firm would typically have developed its own brand and organized its own distribution abroad, capturing all of the value added associated with production, branding, and distribution. The evidence indicates the progressive move from simple to more complex, technology-intensive tasks. Case studies of firms engaged in OEM show that firms gained technology in a gradual step-by-step incremental manner over periods of 20 or even 30 years and there were often difficulties and setbacks along the way (Cyhn, 2002; Hobday, 1995).

As far as entrepreneurial lessons are concerned, this pattern of development is extremely interesting. What it shows, is that the core technological activity involved was not, in the main, a Schumpeterian, R&D-centered innovation (e.g. for new products or processes) or radical innovation. Instead, successful firms caught up gradually through small, incremental improvements to existing products and processes using engineering and technician skills rather than R&D. The traditional view of entrepreneurship (see the 'Definitions' section above) involving technological innovation and introducing new or improved products to the marketplace or to the world, is replaced by a catch-up model involving behind-the-frontier incremental innovations, including improvements to products and processes, and the introduction of new types of product based on the designs of leading firms.

It should be emphasized that these catch-up processes did not occur in every firm. Nor did they occur without great effort and difficulty. Also, the OEM model applied mainly to low-cost, relatively simple electronics goods, at least until recently. There were also significant differences between exporters. For example, major Korean firms such as Samsung began investing in R&D very early on, and, in some product areas (e.g. microwave ovens) as early as the 1960s, long before they progressed to own brand manufacture. Many firms (e.g. in Taiwan) failed and went bankrupt and some developed financial problems and were taken over by other firms (e.g. Daewoo in Korea).

The role of small firms

The second question relates to the role of small firms in these developments. While in South Korea large firms dominated exports, in Taiwan there was a pluralistic industrial structure which included not only large firms but also SMEs. As Hobday (1995) shows, in contrast with the large industrial groups, such as Tatung, many of Taiwan's start-ups entered in the late-1970s and early-1980s with product innovation/ODM capabilities, often gained by individuals with overseas experience in US firms or universities.

Of these companies ACER is perhaps the best known outside Taiwan. However, many other very fast-growing firms emerged during the 'take-off' phase of growth in the 1980s and early 1990s. First International Computer Inc. became the world's largest producer of circuit boards for PCs in the early-1990s. First International formed joint product development ventures with leading US firms such as Intel, TI, and Motorola to add to its technical abilities. Datatech Enterprises Co. became one of the largest international motherboard producers, with sales of more than US$200 million in 1993. Another entrant, Elitegroup Computer Systems Corporation, claimed a 10 percent world market share in motherboards in 1993. It is impossible to mention all the firms which began small and became large. In computers, around 20 firms produced 54 percent of Taiwan's output in the late-1980s, leaving the other 46 percent to hundreds of SMEs, many of them newly formed, focusing on specialist niches. In 1989 alone at least 30 new firms began laptop production, adding to the rivalry and dynamism of the industry. One of the larger latecomers was Mitac, ACER's arch competitor in computers. Mitac achieved an annual PC turnover of more than 200,000 units in the latter part of the 1980s.

Another latecomer firm Cal-Comp, virtually unknown in the West, became the largest producer of calculators worldwide in 1992 and Taiwan's largest fax machine maker. Under OEM/ODM arrangements, it produced roughly 80 percent of Japanese Casio calculators. Many of Japan's leading fax machine makers established business links with Cal-Comp to benefit from its high-quality, low-cost mass production capabilities. Another barely known was Twinhead, which sold around US$160 million worth of notebook computers in 1992, some under its own brand name.

Not only in Taiwan, but also in Hong Kong (see Berger and Lester, 1997; Hobday, 1995) and increasingly in China, new start-ups play an important role in each economy's dynamism, both as a source of larger firms and as subcontractors to large local and foreign firms. Later entrants, such as ACER, were able to enter at a level closer to the technology frontier set by leading TNCs, avoiding the 1970s phase of consumer electronics. These small firms were carriers of capabilities new to the economy, and complemented the entrepreneurial role of large firms in the region.

Entrepreneurship within TNC subsidiaries

Regarding the role of TNCs, while Amdsen (Chapter 15) is correct to question the developmental role of TNC subsidiaries with their HQ and R&D functions typically located in advanced countries, under some circumstances TNC subsidiaries can play an important part in entrepreneurial development and economic development more generally. For example, South East Asia has depended heavily on TNC subsidiaries for exports of electronics, the largest industrial and export sector in Singapore, Malaysia, Thailand and a rapid growth export industry in Indonesia, the Philippines, and Vietnam. This also

Table 18.4. Technological progress in South East Asia

	Singapore	Malaysia	Thailand	Indonesia	Vietnam
1960s	Assembly				
1970s	Process eng*	Assembly	Assembly		
1980s	Product dev**	Process eng	Assembly	Assembly	Assembly
1990s	R&D	Product dev	Process eng	Process eng	Assembly

Notes: *Process engineering; **Product development.
Source: based on empirical research (see text for references).

applies to recent Chinese exports. Gaulier et al. (2004) show that FDI conducted by foreign affiliates is responsible for a large and growing share of export growth. In 2003 FDI accounted for more that 55 percent of total exports compared with only 20 percent in 1992. Within processing zone activities (e.g. electronics), FDI accounted for around 80 percent in 2003.

Table 18.4 presents a simple stages model of the processes of technological advance in electronics based on research in the region (see below). TNC subsidiaries in Singapore, the first developer, gradually learned assembly technology in the 1960s, progressing to process engineering in the 1970s and minor product improvements in the 1980s (Hobday, 1995), rather similar to the path of development of the locally owned East Asian firms. Recent research shows R&D increasing during the 1990s as wages rose and skills improved in Singapore (Wong, 1992, 1998).

TNC subsidiaries in Malaysia began assembly production in the 1970s. Technology transfer from parents enabled the rapid start-up of new export factories, the expansion of existing investments, and a progressive upgrading of the type of products being exported. While there was nothing especially new in TNC investments in these countries, in the past TNC investments had been carried out mainly to serve domestic markets or to engage in tariff hopping, rather than technology transfer to enable exports.

Technological learning continued and successively higher levels of technology were attained in Malaysia and the other South East Asian economies. However, these remained somewhat behind Singapore through the 1980s and 1990s, lacking in R&D and new product development capabilities (Ariffin and Bell, 1998; Bell et al. 1996; Rasiah, 1994). Nevertheless, assembly personnel, technicians, engineers, and managers within the TNC subsidiaries in Malaysia and Thailand, as in Singapore before them, acquired useful manufacturing process skills and some limited product design capabilities and, in some cases, R&D skills.[10] A similar pattern also appears to be beginning in Indonesia and Vietnam but the TNCs have yet to achieve the levels of capability development of earlier entrants.[11]

From an entrepreneurship perspective, the role of staff members, particularly managers, within the subsidiaries was not directly to risk their investment capital or to develop technology new to the world or the market. Instead, it was to increase the skills, capabilities, and efficiency of local plants so that managers could bargain with the parent HQs for further investments. This latecomer 'intrapreneurial' role involved ingenuity and, some would say, creativity in developing new 'behind-the-frontier' improvements to existing manufacturing processes.

As in the case of locally owned firms in Korea and Taiwan, the main focus of TNC subsidiaries was technical and engineering skills aimed at assimilating and improving on existing technology, rather than R&D-based or radical innovation. Some studies (e.g. in Malaysia) show that the subsidiaries had to struggle for many years to overcome obstacles and acquire technology from their parents.[12] There is also abundant case study research in Singapore, Malaysia, and Thailand which shows that some subsidiaries have learned to innovate over time and play significant roles within the TNC (e.g. in semiconductors and hard disk drives in Malaysia). Research also shows that there are different propensities to innovate according to TNC corporate strategy, company culture, and ownership (Guyton, 1994; Hobday and Rush, 2005).

Although there is little direct research on intrapreneurship within the subsidiaries of TNCs, it can be inferred from case research that TNC subsidiaries have contributed not only to the export-led growth of Singapore, Malaysia, Thailand, the Philippines, Vietnam, Hong Kong, and China but also to the growing levels of skills and capabilities in the electronics sector. An interesting question is whether or not the presence of intrapreneurship is a necessary condition for the rapid firm-level growth witnessed. Or, alternatively, is it possible to have such growth with a 'passive' TNC subsidiary? The evidence suggests that the former is correct and that many of the subsidiaries have upgraded technologically through time by investments, technological efforts, and growing managerial capability (Ngoh, 1994; Lim, 1991; Arrifin and Bell, 1998; Intarakumnerd and Virasa, 2002; Hobday and Rush, 2005). Often this process is driven by competition with the subsidiaries of rival TNCs in the same country. In addition, it is driven by competition for investment by subsidiaries of the same TNC in other countries, particularly lower-cost countries such as China.

The fact that many TNC subsidiaries take initiatives and learn to innovate should not come as a surprise. Research on TNCs in advanced countries shows how subsidiaries manage to distribute and integrate their global activities relying on their networks of subsidiaries to produce and, in some cases, to innovate (Bartlett and Ghoshal, 1987, 1987a, 1989; Ghoshal and Nohria, 1989).[13] Over time, some subsidiaries mature to become world product design centers and/or centers of excellence for particular technological activities (Kogut, 2002; Fratocchi and Holm, 1998) indicating that innovative capabilities have been acquired by the subsidiary. Technological improvements by subsidiaries can be an effective way to promote the overall competitiveness of the TNC (Egelhoff et al. 1998).[14]

Some research on subsidiary initiatives (e.g. Birkinshaw, 1997) goes further, arguing that subsidiary initiatives are, in fact, the normal manifestation of dispersed corporate entrepreneurship. The initiative process typically involves the identification of an opportunity at the subsidiary level, subsequent nego-tiations with the HQ, and, finally, the commitment of resources to a new initiative by the HQ.

However, in the DCs, TNC learning and intrapreneurship does not neces-sarily occur, despite high-profile and costly policies of encouragement, as in the case of TNC subsidiaries within the Brazilian telecommunications sector where results have been disappointing despite large subsidies from govern-ment to conduct R&D locally (Lacerda, 2003; Galina and Plonski, 2002; Galina, 2003; Perini, 2004a, 2004b). In addition, even within the successful South East Asian cases, there are different propensities to innovate among TNC subsidiaries, with some failing to move to higher stages of technology over many years (Hobday and Rush, 2005). Therefore, one cannot assume that all TNC subsidiaries will automatically evolve to higher stages of technological capability.

Policy directions

There can be no simple 'blanket solutions' to the problems of entrepreneur-ship and development. As Gerschenkron (1962) showed, latecomer economies face very different external circumstances to now developed countries and have very different resources and institutional capabilities, precisely because they are latecomers. Therefore, each case must be considered on its own merits and one cannot simply transpose lessons from earlier to new developers, as occurs in the anti-bureaucracy and Doing Business 'best practice' recom-mendations. As Rodrik (2004) points out, DCs differ considerably in terms of causes of arrested development. In some cases, bureaucracy may be a factor, in others it may not. Even in cases where it is a factor, other problems (e.g. macroeconomic instability) may also be preventing development. Therefore, any program of DC reform must be tailored to the specific needs, problems, and capabilities of the individual DC, taking into account the precise causes of arrested development.

Most mainstream, conventional, policy approaches towards entrepreneur-ship (implicitly if not explicitly) are based on a developed country 'Schumpe-terian' notion of the entrepreneur and modeled on business and policy practices now carried out in highly advanced countries, and not oriented towards the needs of developing economies. Modern policies also exhibit a great deal of confusion, with new small start-ups being treated as synonymous with entrepreneurship when, in fact, an upsurge in numbers of small firms and self-employed in DCs is often a sign of development failure, rather than entrepreneurship.

Entrepreneurship policies which seek to increase the numbers of SMEs and self-employed are deeply flawed. These policies are unlikely to stimulate entrepreneurship and the development of new skills and capabilities unless the wider macroeconomic context provides the demand conditions and business opportunities necessary for entrepreneurship to thrive.[15] These demand conditions have to be created through policies which stimulate industrialization, including trade, macroeconomic, industrial, technological, and competition policies (see Chapters 8, 10, and 11 by Palma, Castro, and Singh respectively). In other words, integrated and effective overall development strategies need to be in place, as occurred in the successful export-led growth experiences of the East and South East Asian economies.

Regarding the removal of bureaucracy and other measures to improve the business environment, the conventional approach of applying policy measures based on best practices from the now advanced countries is inappropriate for DCs. As Gerschenkron (1962) showed, individual latecomer economies have limited resources and weak institutional capabilities compared with advanced countries. Therefore, they cannot (and should not) merely imitate the now-developed economies. Instead, they need to develop their own paths, based on their particular stage of development and institutional capacity. Excessive bureaucracy, for example, may be a symptom of much deeper political economic problems. If bureaucracy reflects corruption in firm–state relations, as some argue, superficial reforms might simply delay or obviate the need for the deep political changes required to address these difficulties. Alternatively, bureaucracy may be an employment creation mechanism in very poor countries, functioning as a social safety net, in which case policies would be needed to address this specific problem. Simply recommending the adoption of the best practices of the most advanced economies is highly unlikely to address or change the conditions which lead to bureaucracy.

Many of the problems underlying questionable SME policies arise from a misconception of the function of the entrepreneur in DCs. While the classical view of the individual heroic entrepreneur as the commercial exploiter of new technology has its place in the developing world, evidence from the successful Asian cases shows that the primary role of the entrepreneur is to enable technology transfer, catch-up, learning, and 'behind-the-frontier' incremental innovation, rather than new product development or radical technological advance. 'Schumpeterian' technological development occurs mainly in the industrially advanced countries and this creates a flow of opportunities for the accumulation of technological capabilities in DCs. In Asia, entrepreneurs were the human agents responsible for acquiring this technology from abroad and creating learning mechanisms for technology transfer and business development. Entrepreneurs were responsible for integrating local production into international value chains and for continually upgrading domestic business and technology in order to keep up and, in some cases, catch up with the advancing technological frontier.

In Asia, this 'latecomer entrepreneurship' was embedded within existing firms and business networks which crossed international boundaries. Therefore, in formulating policy, it is important first to ask what precisely are the latecomer entrepreneurial functions required to support development in particular DCs, rather than assuming the Schumpeterian entrepreneur, as classically understood, should be promoted.

In non-Asian latecomer economies, business development is also likely to require highly specialized catch up entrepreneurial functions, capable of absorbing foreign technology and creating capabilities and industries new to the local economy, rather than the world. This latecomer function may be embedded in new start-ups, but it is more likely to be a latent potential, embedded in large local firms (see Amsden in Chapter 15) and in large numbers of existing SMEs and, as in the case of South East Asia, the subsidiaries of foreign TNCs. By contrast, the Schumpeterian small-firm entrant engaged in developing novel technology for new markets is likely to play a far less important role in DCs. While catch-up may include some leadership entrepreneurial activities (e.g. new opportunity search and limited R&D) much of it will be typically concerned with improvements to existing processes, products, organizational structures, and ways of conducting business.

Finally, in cases where entrepreneurial failure (i.e. an insufficient supply of capable firms and managers) is a major barrier to development, the evidence from East and South East Asia suggests an important (often overlooked) if implicit role for policy. For example, in the case of South Korea, the government supported a 'big business' Japanese style zaibatsu model by financing and supporting the chaebol and, in doing so, created a class of latecomer entrepreneurs and managers capable of absorbing and improving on foreign technology. In the case of Singapore, the then government, rightly or wrongly, believed that the entrepreneurial potential was inherently too weak to lead industrialization. It therefore sponsored and subsidized the entry of foreign TNC subsidiaries, and allowed them a degree of operational freedom which was highly unusual (and unpopular) at that time in the developing world. Malaysia and Thailand also enacted policies to attract exporting TNCs to lead industrialization from the 1960s onwards. In each of these cases, policies towards entrepreneurship were (usually implicit) parts of wider strategies towards industrialization, involving export-led growth, fierce internal competition, macroeconomic stabilization, basic education (to achieve high levels of numeracy and literacy), and technical education relevant to the stage of industrialization.

Conclusion

This chapter shows that the Schumpeterian notion of the entrepreneur as a high-technology risk-taking innovator has been highly influential in the formation of modern day policies toward entrepreneurship in DCs. This has led to dysfunctional policies towards entrepreneurship, particularly those which attempt to counter bureaucracy by adopting the practices of the highly developed economies. Polices of promoting SMEs and supporting venture capital are also unlikely to have much impact on the progress of entrepreneurship and productivity in DCs. Indeed, 'blanket policies' aimed at the indiscriminate support for new entrants will do little to cope with informality but could well maintain and expand the low-productivity sector.

There can be no simple policy solutions or standard measures to address entrepreneurial problems or wider developmental failures. There can be many causes of arrested development and each strategy must address the primary causes of failure, taking into account the particular circumstances, resources, and opportunities of the DC in question. Policies also need to be informed about the specific nature and role of latecomer entrepreneurship as distinct from 'leadership' or Schumpeterian entrepreneurship. Latecomer entrepreneurship is required to create local industries, generate new skills and capabilities, enable local technological learning, and acquire and improve upon technology from abroad. All entrepreneurial policies should be carried out within, and as part of, a coherent national development strategy to stand any chance of success.

The East and South East Asian evidence of successful firm-level growth shows that large firms, SMEs, and the subsidiaries of foreign TNCs all have a part to play in latecomer entrepreneurial progress. While governments may not wish to rely unduly on any particular industrial grouping, wherever possible, policies should stress the accumulation of technical and managerial skills in firms and industries linked into international value chains with high growth potential, in order to break free of low-productivity activities and generate new opportunities for catch-up growth.

Appendix 1: The Washington Consensus

Rodrik (2004) is highly critical of the Washington Consensus approach to DC reform put forward by the World Bank and other institutions. The 'Doing Business' reforms described in the sections above can be viewed as a subset of the wider package of reforms which the current policy consensus regularly recommends to DCs. The Washington Consensus approach has now been augmented to include new 'rules of good behavior for promoting economic growth' as shown in Table 18.5. The 'Doing Business' reforms described above are included in items 8 to 13 in the list shown in the table.

Table 18.5. Rules of good behavior for promoting economic growth

Original Washington Consensus	"Augmented" Washington Consensus: ... the previous 10 items, plus
1. Fiscal discipline	11. Corporate governance
2. Reorientation of public expenditures	12. Anti-corruption
3. Tax reform	13. Flexible labor markets
4. Interest rate liberalization	14. Adherence to WTO disciplines
5. Unified and competitive exchange rates	15. Adherence to international financial codes and standards
6. Trade liberalization	
7. Openness to DFI	16. "Prudent" capital-account opening
8. Privatization	17. Non-intermediate exchange rate regimes
9. Deregulation	18. Independent central banks/inflation targeting
10. Secure Property Rights	19. Social safety nets
	20. Targeted poverty reduction

Source: Rodrik (2004).

Rodrik's main argument against any 'laundry list' of reforms is that the recommended reforms are 'based on what a rich country *already* looks like' which may have taken decades or even centuries to achieve. In addition, the agenda comes without any way of determining priorities, and the amount of administrative capacity, human resources, and political capital needed to complete the vast agenda of institutional reforms simply does not exist in most DCs (Rodrik, 2004).

Rodrik's arguments are reminiscent of those made by Gershenkron (1962, 1963) in his debate with Rostow (1960) over the validity of deriving lessons from the stages of development of the now developed countries for DCs, which Gershenkron argued was intellectually flawed in the extreme. The modern Washington Consensus approach is actually even less valid than Rostow's approach, because at least Rostow recognized that DCs needed to progress incrementally through phases of development, whereas the Washington Consensus reforms ignore this, recommending the current policies of now developed countries and claiming that rapid growth will follow.

In his critique of Rostow (1960), Gerschenkron argued that the study of industrial development of the past could not provide a model for today's policy makers wishing to promote economic development. He showed that the idea of identifying the preconditions which were 'missing' in a particular DC (e.g. in terms of investment, institutions, and technology or today's 'rules of good behavior') and then installing them was not a logical strategy for achieving a take-off to sustained growth, but was an example of historical determinism. Instead, he argued that each country needed to develop its own development agenda based on the institutional capacities, stage of development, problems and opportunities facing the particular country. Of course, some things could be learned from earlier industrializers but no direct model could apply (Gerschenkron, 1962).

Regarding the Washington Consensus reforms as Rodrik (2004) puts it:

Yet the agenda comes without a way of determining priorities. Too often, the result is that policy effort is spread too thinly over too many different areas: governments are overwhelmed with the range of things that need to be done, copies of Western legislation or 'best-practice' codes are adopted without much consideration of their suitability and adaptability, and too little effort is made to render the reforms politically popular and ultimately sustainable ... The implicit, and sometimes explicit, approach seems to be to say: 'well, we know that all of these things cannot be done at once, but more is better than less, and the more countries can do the better.' So they and the governments they advise proceed opportunistically, and try to complete the enlarged agenda as best as they can, as completely as they can, and as quickly as they can ... After much effort, governments may find that economic performance has hardly improved ... Finally, there is something intellectually worrisome about the Augmented Washington Consensus, in that it is entirely unfalsifiable. Such is the nature of the agenda that if a country adopts it and fails to grow, it is always possible to find something wrong with what the government did. So in the end it is the policymakers who end up being chastised for the 'incompleteness' of their reforms. And if enough countries find themselves in this predicament, then it must be time to augment the list further by adding yet other needed reforms.

Rodrik and colleagues' own historical study of spurts of growth during the last 50 years shows that the vast majority of growth take-offs are not produced by significant economic reforms, and the vast majority of significant economic reforms do not produce growth take-offs (Hausmann et al. 2004). Like Gerschenkron (1962), Rodrik argues for a country specific 'diagnostic' approach to growth strategies which identify and address the 'binding constraint' or most significant bottleneck to growth. Rodrik cites as examples of such constraints a lack of investment funds, high costs of capital, and the inability of firms to appropriate returns on investment. Other barriers to development might include macroeconomic instability, political instability (including war and conflict), corruption, and a lack of obvious investment opportunities for achieving dynamic comparative advantage through specialization.

Notes

1. For a discussion of the Washington Consensus, see Appendix 1.
2. See de Soto (2000) for a highly influential book on bureaucracy and development.
3. For a general discussion of embeddedness see Granovetter (1985).
4. By contrast, small firms have played an important role in some parts of Asia (e.g. Taiwan and China, see above under 'Successful firm-level growth in East and South East Asia') indicating that the context in which small firms operate is all important.
5. Hernando de Soto is President of the Institute for Liberal Democracy (ILD).
6. Under these conditions informality can be seen as a rational and socially responsible response to harsh economic reality and falling opportunities in the formal sector.
7. Krueger (1974) argues that, in extreme cases, the perception that businesses become successful by exerting influence or bribing officials 'to do what they ought in any event to do' (p. 302) undermines the link between pecuniary reward and business efficiency as well as trust in the motives and actions of government. Favoritism towards certain groups can lead to the perception that government policy is a mechanism for rewarding the already rich and influential. In such cases, policies can divert the attention of entrepreneurs away from innovative activities towards

capturing rents; the natural tendency is further expansion of bureaucracy and red tape, rather than a reduction. Unless the 'fundamentals' (i.e. the structures, incentives, and interest groups which perpetuate the system) are understood and somehow addressed, reform is unlikely to work because bureaucracy is merely a symptom of deeper problems. Whether these extreme cases are widespread or important problems is not clear from the evidence and is an important area for further research.

8. In fact, for European countries, Acs and Varga (2004) analyze the GEM database but find no significant support for the hypothesis that entrepreneurship facilitates a knowledge spillover mechanism leading to economic growth.

9. For an explanation of the concept of the latecomer firm, see Hobday (1995).

10. For stages in general in Thai industry, see Intarakumnerd and Virasa (2002); for firm-level development stages see Chairatana (1997); for electronics in Thailand see Poapongsakorn and Tonguthai (1998).

11. See Ca and Anh (1998) for Vietnam, and Thee and Pangestu (1998) for Indonesia.

12. See Ngoh (1994) for the case of Motorola, and Lim (1991) for the case of Intel.

13. The use of foreign TNCs to lead industrial development occurs widely in the developed countries. For example, Scotland, Ireland, and parts of England have benefited from large-scale investments in electronics, semiconductor components, and automobiles.

14. These findings were developed mainly within Canada (Birkinshaw, 1997) and then expanded to other developed countries where subsidiaries have proved effective in promoting growth (Holm and Pederson, 2000; Delany, 1998; Egelhoff et al. 1998).

15. Policies which encourage the start-up of SMEs and self-employment may have a beneficial effect on poverty, although even this is contested by some (e.g. Beck et al, 2003).

References

Acs Z. and A. Varga (2004), *Entrepreneurship, Agglomeration and Technological Change*, Max Planck Institute for Research into Economic Systems, Germany.

Amin A. (2002), *The Informal Sector in Asia from the Decent Work Perspective*, International Labour Organization (ILO).

Amsden A. (1989), *Asia's Next Giant: South Korea and Late Industrialization*, Oxford University Press, New York.

—— and T. Hikino (1994), 'Project Execution Capability, Organizational Know-How and Conglomerate Corporate Growth in Late Industrialization,' *Industrial and Corporate Change*, 3(1): 111–47.

Ariffin N. and M. Bell (1998), 'Firms, Politics and Political Economy: Patterns of Subsidiary–Parent Linkages and Technological Capability-Building in Electronics TNC Subsidiaries in Malaysia' in K.S. Jomo, G. Felker, and R. Rasiah (eds.) *Industrial Technology Development in Malaysia*, Routledge, London.

Audretsch D. and R. Thurik (2001), *Linking Entrepreneurship to Growth*, STI Working Paper 2001/2, France.

Bartelsman E., J. Haltiwanger, and I. Scarpetta (2004), *Microeconomic Evidence of Creative Destruction in Industrial and Developing Countries*, draft report, World Bank, Washington, DC.

Bartlett C. and S. Ghoshal (1989), *Managing Across Borders: the Transnational Solution*, Harvard Business School Press, Boston.

—— —— (1987), 'Managing Across Borders: New Strategic Requirements,' *Sloan Management Review*, 28(4): 7–17.

—— —— (1987a), 'Managing Across Borders: New Organisational Requirements,' *Sloan Management Review*, 29(1): 43–53.

Beck T., A. Dermirgüç-kunt, and R. Levine (2003), *Small and Medium Enterprises, Growth, and Poverty: Cross-Country Evidence*, World Bank Policy Research Working Paper 3178.

Bell M., M. Hobday, S. Abdullah, N. Ariffin, and J. Malik (1996), *Aiming for 2020: A Demand-driven Perspective on Industrial Technology Policy in Malaysia*, Final Report to Ministry of Science, Technology, and Environment (Malaysia), World Bank/UNDP.

Berger S. and R. Lester (eds.) (1997), *Made by Hong Kong*, Oxford University Press, Hong Kong.

Birkinshaw J. (1997), 'Entrepreneurship in Multinational Corporations: The Characteristics of Subsidiary Initiatives,' *Strategic Management Journal*, 18: 207–29.

Ca T. and L. Anh (1998), 'Technological Dynamism and R&D in the Export of Manufactures from Vietnam' in D. Ernst, T. Ganiatsos, and L. Mytelka (eds.) *Technological Capabilities and Export Success in Asia*, Routledge, London.

Calderon J. (2004), 'The Formalisation of Property in Peru 2001–2002: The Case of Lima,' *Habitat International*, 28(2): 289–300.

Cantillon R. (2001), *Essays on the Nature of Commerce in General*, Transaction Publishers, Somerset, N.J.

Cantwell J. (2001), 'Innovation, Profits and Growth: Schumpeter and Penrose,' Working Paper No. 427 (Vol. XIII), University of Reading.

Chairatana P. (1997), 'Latecomer Catch-up Strategies in the Semiconductor Business: the Case of Alphatec Group of Thailand and Anam Group of Korea,' MSc Thesis, SPRU, University of Sussex, England.

Chan K. (2001), *Chinese Business Networks*, Prentice Hall, Singapore.

—— and C. Chiang (1994), *Stepping Out: The Making of Chinese Entrepreneurs*, Centre for Advanced Studies, National University of Singapore and Prentice Hall, New York.

Cyhn J. (2002), *Technology Transfer and International Production: The Development of the Electronics Industry in Korea*, Edward Elgar, Cheltenham.

Dana L. (2000), 'Creating Entrepreneurs in India,' *Journal of Small Business Management*, 38: 86.

Delany E. (1998), 'Strategic Development of Multinational Subsidiaries in Ireland' in J. Birkinshaw and N. Hood (eds.) *Multinational Corporate Evolution and Subsidiary Development*, Macmillan, London.

de Soto H. (2000), *The Mystery of Capital: Why Capitalism Triumphs in the West and Fails Everywhere Else*, Basic Books, New York.

Djankov S. and C. McLiesh (2005), *Doing Business in 2005: Removing Obstacles to Growth*, a co-publication of the World Bank, the International Finance Corporation, and Oxford University Press.

Dosi G., R.R. Nelson, and S. Winter (2000), *The Nature and Dynamics of Organizational Capabilities*, Oxford University Press, New York.

Earley R. (2004), *Global Private Equity: Trends in Investment and Fund Raising*. 5th International Venture Capital Forum.

Egelhoff W., L. Gorman, and S. McCormick (1998), 'Using Technology as a Path to Subsidiary Development' in J. Birkinshaw and N. Hood (eds.) *Multinational Corporate Evolution and Subsidiary Development*, Macmillan, London.

Fehr M. and Nils-Henrik (1995), 'The African Entrepreneur: Evidence of Entrepreneurial Activity and Firm Formation in Zambia,' Working Paper, World Bank, Washington, DC.

Fratocchi L. and U. Holm (1998), 'Centres of Excellence in the International Firm' in J. Birkinshaw and N. Hood (eds.) *Multinational Corporate Evolution and Subsidiary Development*, Macmillan, London.

Freeman C. (1994), 'The Economics of Technical Change,' *Cambridge Journal of Economics*, 18: 463–514.

Galina S. (2003), *Desenvolvimento Global de Produtos: o papel das subsidiárias brasileiras de fornecedores de equipamentos do setor de telecomunicações*, Escola Politécnica, São Paulo.

—— and G. Plonski (2002), 'Global Product Development in the Telecommunication Industry: An Analysis of the Brazilian Subsidiaries Involvement' in S. Antipolis (ed.) *9th International Product Development Management Conference*, France.

Gaulier G., F. Lemoine, and D. Unal-Kesenci (2004), *China's Integration in Asian Production Networks and Its Implications*, Paper Prepared for Conference 'Resolving New Global and Regional Imbalances in an Era of Asian Integration,' Tokyo (June 17–18), CEPII (Centre D'Etudes Prospectives Et D'Informations Internationales, Paris, France).

Gerschenkron A. (1962), *Economic Backwardness in Historical Perspective: A Book of Essays*, Belknap Press, Harvard University, Cambridge, Mass.

—— (1963), 'The Early Phases of Industrialisation in Russia' in W.W. Rostow (ed.) *The Economics of Take-off into Sustained Growth*, Macmillan, London.

Ghoshal S. and N. Nohria (1989), 'Internal Differentiation within Multinational Corporations,' *Strategic Management Journal*, 10: 323–37.

Granovetter M. (1985), 'Economic Action and Social Structure: The Problem of Embeddedness,' *American Journal of Sociology*, 91(3): 481–510.

Gupta S. (1990), 'Entrepreneurship Development Training Programmes in India,' *Small Enterprise Development: An Internal Journal*, 1: 15–26.

Guyton L. (1994), *Japanese FDI and the Transfer of Japanese Consumer Electronics Production to Malaysia*, Report Prepared for UNDP, K.L., Malaysia.

Hausmann R., D. Rodrik, and A. Velasco (2004), 'Growth Diagnostics,' Harvard University, unpublished manuscript. Available at <http://ksghome.harvard.edu/~drodrik/papers.html>.

Hobday M. (1994), 'Export-Led Technology Development in the Four Dragons: The Case of Electronics', *Development and Change*, 25(2): 333–61.

—— (1995), *Innovation in East Asia: The Challenge to Japan*, Edward Elgar, London.

—— and H. Rush (2005), *Technological Upgrading of Foreign Transnational Subsidiaries in Developing Countries: The Case of Electronics in Thailand*, SPRU/CENTRIM, Brighton, UK, Mimeo.

Holm U. and T. Pedersen (2000), *The Emergence and Impact of MNC Centres of Excellence: A Subsidiary Perspective*, St. Martin's Press, New York.

Intarakumnerd P.* and T. Virasa** (2002), 'Taxonomy of Government Policies and Measures in Supporting Technological Capability Development of Latecomer Firms,' *Science, Technology and Innovation Policy Research Department, National Science and Technology Development Agency (NSTDA), Thailand and **College of Management, Mahidol University, Thailand, NSTDA Working Paper.

Johnstone B. (1989), 'Taiwan Holds Its Lead. Local Makers Move into New Systems,' *Far Eastern Economic Review*, August 31, pp. 50–1.

Kilby P. (2003), 'The Heffalump Revisited,' *Journal of International Entrepreneurship*, 1: 13–29.

Kirzner I. (1978), *Competition and Entrepreneurship*, University of Chicago Press, Chicago.

Knight F. (1921), *Risk, Uncertainty and Profit*, Houghton Mifflin, Boston.

Kogut B. (2002), 'International Management and Strategy' in A. Pettigrew, H. Thomas, and R. Whittington (eds.) *Handbook of Strategy and Management*, Thousand Oaks, London and Sage Publications, New Delhi.

Krueger A. (1974), 'The Political Economy of Rent-Seeking Society,' *The American Economic Review*, 64(3): 291–303.

Lacerda A. (2003), Globalização e Inserção Externa da Economia Brasileira: Política Econômica, Investimentos Diretos Estrangeiros e Comércio Exterior, na Década de 1990, *Departamento de Economia*, Campina, UNICAMP.

Leff N. (1978), 'Industrial Organization and Entrepreneurship in Developing Countries: The Economic Groups,' *Economic Development and Cultural Change*, 4: 661–75.

Leibenstein H. (1968), 'Entrepreneurship and Development,' *American Economic Review*, 58(2): 72–83. Papers and Proceedings of the Eightieth Annual Meeting of the American Economic Association (May).

Lim P. (1991), *Steel: From Ashes Rebuilt to Manufacturing Excellence*, Pelanduk Publications, Pataling Jaya, Malaysia.

McClelland D. and D. Winter (1969), *Motivating Economic Achievement*, Free Press, New York.

Moore M. (1997), 'Societies, Polities and Capitalists in Developing Countries: A Literature Survey,' *The Journal of Development Studies*, 33: 287–363.

Nelson R.E. and M. Mwaura (1997), 'Growth Strategy of Medium-Sized Firms in Kenya,' *The Journal of Entrepreneurship*, 6: 53–74.

Nelson R.R. and S. Winter (1982), *An Evolutionary Theory of Economic Change*, Belknap Press, Harvard University, Cambridge, Mass.

Ngoh C. (1994), *Motorola Globalisation: The Penang Journey*, Lee and Sons, K.L. Malaysia.

Pavitt K. (2004), 'The Process of Innovation' in J. Fagerberg, D. Mowery, and R. Nelson (eds.) *Handbook of Innovation*, Oxford University Press, Oxford.

Penrose E. (1959), *The Theory of the Growth of the Firm*, Oxford University Press, Oxford.

Perini F. (2004a), 'Managing Innovation between Global and Local Innovation Systems: Coordination Mechanisms in Brazilian ICT Private Research Institutes,' DRUID Summer Conference 2004: Industrial Dynamics, Innovation and Development, Maastricht, Netherlands.

Perini F. (2004b), 'Micro-Dynamics of Subsidiary Development; Subsidiary Initiatives, Coordination Mechanisms and Technological Capability Accumulation in the Brazilian ICT Sector,' Presented at the PRIME Doctoral Conference, SPRU, University of Sussex, Brighton, UK.

Poapongsakorn, N. and Tonguthai, P. (1998). 'Technological Capability Building and the Sustainability of Export Success in Thailand's Textile and Electronics Industries' in D. Ernst, T. Ganiatsos, and L. Mytelka (eds.) *Technological Capabilities and Export Success in Asia*, Routledge, London.

Poojary C. (1996), 'What Creates an Entrepreneur? Some Observations from Micro Study,' *The Journal of Entrepreneurship*, 5: 253–60.

Rasiah R. (1994), 'Flexible Production Systems and Local Machine Tool Sub-Contracting: Electronics Components Transnationals in Malaysia,' *Cambridge Journal of Economics*, 18(3) 279–98.

Reynolds P., W. Bygrave, E. Autio, and A. Others (2004), *Global Entrepreneurship Monitor: 2003 Executive Report*, Babson College, Babson Park, Mass.; London Business School, London.

Rodrik D. (2004), 'Rethinking Growth Policies in the Developing World,' *Locu d'Agliano Lecture in Development Economics*, Torino, Italy.

Romijn H. (1999), *Acquisition of Technological Capability in Small Firms in Developing Countries*, Macmillan, London.

Rossini R. and J. Thomas (1990), 'The Size of the Informal Sector in Peru: A Critical Comment on Hernando de Soto's El Otro Sendero,' *World Development,* 18(1): 125–35.

Rostow W. (1960), *The Stages of Economic Growth: A Non-Communist Manifesto*, Cambridge University Press, Cambridge.

Rothwell R. and W. Zegveld (1982), 'New Ventures and Large Firms: The Search for Internal Entrepreneurship' in *Innovation and the Small and Medium Sized Firm: Their Role in Employment and in Economic Change*, Frances Pinter, London.

Say J. (1832), *A Treatise on Political Economy; Or the Production, Distribution, and Consumption of Wealth*, Grigg & Elliot, Philadelphia. (Translated from 4th edn.)

Schak D. (2000), 'Networks and their Uses in Taiwanese Society' in Chan Kwok Bun, ed., *Chinese Business Networks: State, Economy and Culture*, Prentice-Hall, Singapore.

Schumpeter J. (1934), *The Theory of Economic Development*, Harvard University Press, Cambridge, Mass.

—— (1943), *Capitalism, Socialism and Democracy*, Allen and Unwin, London.

Shadlen K. (2004), *Democratization Without Representation: The Politics of Small Industry in Mexico*, Pennsylvania State University Press, University Park, Pennsylvania.

Sverrisson A. (1993), *Evolutionary Technical Change and Flexible Mechanization: Entrepreneurship and Industrialization in Kenya and Zimbabwe*, Lund Dissertations in Sociology 3, Lund University Press.

Taeube F. (2004), 'Culture, Innovation and Economic Development: The Case of the South Indian ICT Clusters' in S. Mani and H. Romijn (eds.) *Innovation, Learning and Technological Dynamism of Developing Countries*, United Nations University, Hong Kong.

Thee K. and M. Pangestu (1998), 'Technological Capabilities and Indonesia's Manufactured Exports' in D. Ernst, T. Ganiatsos, and L. Mytelka (eds.) *Technological Capabilities and Export Success in Asia*, Routledge, London.

Wong P. (1992), 'Technological Development through Sub-Contracting Linkages: Evidence from Singapore,' *Scandinavian International Business Review*, 1(3): 28–40.

—— (1998), 'Patterns of Technology Acquisition by Manufacturing Firms in Singapore,' *Singapore Management Review*, 20(1): 43–64.

World Bank (2004), *Doing Business in 2005,* a co-publication of the World Bank, the International Finance Corporation, and Oxford University Press.

Xu H. and M. Ruef (2004), 'The Myth of the Risk-Tolerant Entrepreneur,' *Strategic Organization*, 2: 331–55.

19

Intellectual Property and Industrial Development: A Critical Assessment

Mario Cimoli, Benjamin Coriat, and Annalisa Primi

Introduction

Intellectual property rights (IPRs) are a set of legal regimes of a broad scope that range from patents that protect inventions, to copyrights, which relate to original forms of expression such as literary and artistic work, and, among others, trademarks that protect words and symbols that identify goods and services. IPRs confer an exclusive (and in the case of patents and copyright, temporary) right to the exploitation and commercialization of intangible assets.[1] Therefore, the IP regime establishes an institutional framework to manage access, exploitation, and transfer of knowledge, technology, and information. In the last decade, the emergence of new technological paradigms—mainly Information and Communication Technology (ICTs), biotech and nanotech, the reshaping of world IP systems, and the explosion in patenting—led much of contemporary attention of scholars, policy makers, and civil society to focus on the relationship between intellectual property and development.

A complete analysis of the changes in IP regimes and their impact on the rate and direction of inventive activity goes beyond the scope of this chapter; here we would like to stress the connection between IP regimes and industrial development. Evidence shows that IP regimes usually convolve with production transformations, as pulled by the production side. Frontier countries, particularly the US, strategically use IP regimes as mechanisms to protect certain accumulated capabilities of national production and research agents. Business methods and genetic engineering are research fields of growing importance in the US, and are sectors in which national research centers and enterprises already possess a considerable relative advantage. There is nothing accidental in the public authorities' decision to preserve national dominance in those fields by means of patent protection. This is a de facto industrial policy, aiming at preserving comparative advantages in given technological trajectories for certain economic agents. IP laws are mechanisms to preserve dominant positions in given fields, not mechanisms to create them.

Our thesis is that asymmetries in technological capacities (between firms and countries) are likely to persist over rather long periods of time, beyond the legal mechanisms defining the appropriability and transferability conditions of technologies. As regards the behavioral foundations of innovative and imitative activities, we are quite skeptical about their reduction to linear and deliberate profit maximizing choices. 'Getting the IPRs right' is not an optimal solution for fostering industrial development and catching up. Legal appropriability mechanisms, that is, prevailing intellectual property norms, classify as second-order effect factors, with respect to production and technological capabilities in shaping innovative and imitative conducts. The analysis of TRIPS' flexibilities shows that any use of existing policy space is subject to decisions that go beyond the pure IP domain and that concern trade, industrial, and technology policy issues. No flexibility will be used simply because it is legally feasible—national policies and priorities shape market and non-market incentives and transform legal feasibility into action. Frontier countries have been using and use IP as a de facto industrial policy measure to sustain the competitiveness of their industries and to protect dynamic advantages in certain technological trajectories. Developing countries should learn from them and strategically fine-tune IP regimes according to their industrial development needs.

This chapter, far from being an exhaustive analysis, serves as a road map for analyzing the relationship between intellectual property and industrial development, in the light of public policy perspective.

In the first section we analyze the changes introduced in the US IP system beginning in the 1980s and the consequent reconfiguration of international IP regimes. In this respect, we present a taxonomy of TRIPS' flexibilities and a synthetic analysis of TRIPS 'extra' and 'plus' provisions included in recent bilateral trade agreements, analyzing the relationship between industrial development strategies and IP management. Next, we examine the dynamics of patenting, stressing the relationship between IP and production structure specialization. On that basis, we present an analysis of current markets for knowledge, exploring potential participation in and exclusion from those markets for developed and developing countries. An overview of current IP dilemmas and the analysis of the relationship between production structure and IP management are necessary steps in defining a strategic approach to industrial development. The chapter concludes by stressing the importance of including IP issues in the renewed debate on policies and institutions shaping industrial development, avoiding incurring oversimplified IP for development agendas.

The reshaping of intellectual property regimes

Intellectual property regimes are, as all economic and legal institutions, context and time specific, and they are subject to change. In terms of evolution of intellectual property rights, if a lesson can be derived from history, it is that systems evolved as pulled by the production side. When, in a given country, the introduction of IP protection could bring about a pecuniary gain in a given sector or area, the system was adapted, or a negotiation initiated to grant the right of appropriation of the relative rent. In contrast, sectors, lobbies (and countries) attempted to block the introduction of IP protection in cases in which they were net importers of the product or service in question.[2]

The transformation of intellectual property regimes has gone hand in hand with the different phases of development of modern economies.[3] Intellectual property systems have evolved from regulations of national scope, which prevailed during the 'inward' stage of development of early industrializers, towards regimes of supranational scope. This transformation has taken place as foreign trade and interaction among countries have become more necessary and more frequent; as different technological paradigms emerged, increasing articulation and diversification of production processes, thus augmenting the relevance of know-how, technical information, knowledge and the consequent value of their appropriability.

However, since the 1980s, there has been a radical reshaping in the management and the structure of IP regimes at the global level. Such changes are occurring in a context of growing trade integration and in a system of open economies, where trade liberalization has been coupled with pressures to strengthen intellectual property rights on an international scale.

In this regard, the changes in intellectual property regimes concern two different, although related, domains: (i) the modification of prevailing norms and the generation of a new set of incentives deriving from jurisprudential rulings within the US system, and (ii) the increasing relevance of intellectual property in multilateral and bilateral trade negotiations and in international disputes between countries. In this respect, the adoption of the TRIPS agreement in 1994 marked a milestone in the big push towards the homogenization of IP minimum standards of protection.

A new set of incentives in the US IP laws and the 'American preference'

Beginning in the 1980s, intellectual property protection has been (deliberately) intensified, in the United States through various channels: extension of patentable subject matter, extended time protection, and increased target of subjects who can exert intellectual property rights. Subsequent to these changes, there has been an upsurge in patenting activity. A deep analysis of these issues goes beyond the scope of this chapter;[4] it suffices here to recall two major changes: (i) the extension of patent subject matter and (ii) the Bayh–Dole Act, and to highlight their use as (informal or de facto industrial policy) mechanisms to support technological development in national research centers and firms.

THE EXTENSION OF PATENTABLE SUBJECT MATTER

According to US law, 'Whoever invents or discovers any new and useful process, machine, manufacture or composition of matter, or any new and useful improvement thereof, may obtain a patent...'.[5] Nowadays in the US, the most probable answer to the question, 'Can I patent that?' is likely to be yes, as Hunt (2001) argues in his critical paper on the introduction of patents for business methods in the US economy. The above-mentioned relaxation of patentability criteria, due to some Supreme Court rulings, led to an extension of the patentable subject matter. In fact, US firms increasingly use patents to protect physical inventions as well as more abstract ones, such as computer programs or business models and methods.[6]

According to US jurisprudential tradition, laws of nature, and hence mathematical formulas, could not be the subjects of a patent (cf. *Gottschalk v. Benson*, 1972). However, in 1981 the *Diamond v. Diehr* Supreme Court decision paved the way for computer software and business methods' patentability by asserting that 'a claim drawn to subject matter otherwise statutory does not become non-statutory simply because it uses a mathematical formula, computer program or digital computer'.

The Court of Appeals for the Federal Circuit (CAFC), instituted in 1982, also played a decisive role in the extension of patentable subject matter through several jurisprudential rulings that reversed the prevailing doctrine. The *State Street Bank and Trust v. Signature Financial Group* (1998) CAFC decision allowed the patentability of business methods when the claimed invention satisfies the requirements of novelty, utility, and non-obviousness. This decision also made the utility requirement more lenient.

Through a reinterpretation of patentable subject matter and of previous rulings, the *State Street v. Signature* decision reversed the prevailing doctrine and allowed patenting of algorithms as long as they are applied in a useful way, that is, as long as they produce 'a useful, concrete and tangible result'. According to this decision, registrants seeking patent protection for business methods or algorithms are not required to disclose their computer methods.[7] Contrary to the previous Supreme Court decision, a mathematical formula and a programmed digital computer are currently patentable subject matter under chapter 35, p. 101 of the US Code.[8] This tendency favors the engendering of what has been called the *patent thicket*, considered to have negative potential effects on future rates of innovations in the context of incremental innovations: for example in the software industry, in which each application might be built upon a series of hundreds of patented algorithms (Shapiro, 2001).

The extension of the patentable domain also involved living entities. The 1980 *Diamond v. Chakrabarty* Supreme Court decision stated that 'a live, human made micro-organism is patentable subject matter',[9] paving the way for a series of rulings which led to the patentability of partial genes sequences (ESTs[10]), including genes crucial to treating illnesses (Orsi, 2002). Another decision worth mentioning is *re Brana* 1995. This ruling established the presumption of utility and reversed the jurisprudence that supported the circumspect practice of the USPTO in granting patents in this field. *Re Brana* recognizes the validity on patent claims on discoveries not yet made or not yet materialized.

In the US patent law, *utility* is an essential criterion for patentability. *Utility* refers to the industrial and commercial advances, 'useful arts', enabled by the invention. Relaxing the meaning of *utility* transforms non-patentable subject matters into patentable ones. Again, the *re Brana* Court decision is remarkable. Partial sequences of ESTs were classified as useful due to their potential contribution to future advances in knowledge, and this sufficed for these entities' patentability, despite their value as research tools.[11] Disavowing a previous Supreme Court ruling that explicitly warned against inhibiting future research by restricting access to knowledge, *re Brana* allowed patent applicants the right to make extensive claims with reference to 'virtual' inventions, that is, inventions that have not yet been made and that cannot be predicted. Patents were transformed from a reward granted to the inventor in exchange for the disclosure of the invention into a veritable hunting tool.[12] Patents might result in a *monopolistic right of exploration* granted to the patent holder even before any invention has been made and a fortiori disclosed.

Subsequent rulings and Supreme Court decisions engendered a new patent regime that creates conditions for transforming research advantages into competitive advantages, guaranteeing an upstream protection of the research product, which results in the right to exclude rival firms from benefiting from basic discoveries (Coriat and Orsi, 2002). The resulting fear is that the system is moving toward the dissipation of the traditional 'open science' paradigm (Dasgupta and David, 1994). The new regime covers areas for software and living entities, key inputs, research tools, and raw materials for other areas of innovation (Arrow, 1962; Shapiro, 2001). In a context in which innovation is increasingly cumulative in nature, the progressive enclosure[13] of technical knowledge, which is at the basis for subsequent advancements in science and innovation, may induce a sort of 'lock-out' of potential innovators that are not yet in a dominant position, or, on the contrary, may give excessive bargaining power to small, technology-intensive firms with no physical processing or distribution capacity.

A complete analysis of the changes in US IP law and their impact on the rate and direction of inventive activity is beyond the scope of this chapter, however, we would like to stress the connection between the reshaping of IP regimes and the dynamics of research and industrial development in the US. Business methods and genetic engineering are research fields of growing importance in the US, and are sectors in which national research centers and enterprises already possess a considerable relative advantage. There is nothing accidental in the public authorities' decision to restrict access to a discovery in order to preserve it by means of patent protection in those fields. This is clearly a de facto industrial policy, intended to preserve comparative advantages in given technological trajectories for certain economic agents.

THE BAYH–DOLE ACT

The inclusion of provisions that allow granting patents through *exclusive licenses* only to US manufacturing firms, as it is stated in section 204 of the Bayh–Dole Act, which sets the conditions for 'American industry preference', responds to the same de facto industrial policy strategy. In 1980, the US Congress adopted the Bayh–Dole Act, which is embedded in title 35, chapter 18, of the US Code under the label of 'patent rights in inventions made with federal assistance'. This Act sets the principles for patenting inventions realized by institutions receiving federal funds for R&D, and introduced two basic changes in the US IP regime: (i) it established a new principle that gives to institutions (universities and public research laboratories) receiving public funding the right to patent their discoveries; and (ii) it affirmed the right to license the exploitation of those patents as *exclusive rights* to private firms, and/ or to engage in 'joint ventures' with them. The literature has already extensively analyzed the impact of this Act on the rate and direction of innovative activities. Scholars have stressed the fact that the enactment of the Bayh-Dole Act established a new IP regime that threatens the previously dominant open science principle.[14] The possibility of granting exclusive licenses on research findings obtained by the main centers of scientific knowledge, such as universities and public laboratories, creates a basis for appropriating basic knowledge, which should, by definition, constitute the knowledge base available to all national innovation system agents. Dasgupta and David (1994) emphasize the fact that this appropriation of knowledge is achieved through a series of 'bilateral monopolies' that universities and public laboratories share with private for-profit organizations, thus contributing to the commoditization of research outcomes (Eisenberg, 2000; Orsi, 2002).

The literature stressed the fact that this Act introduced a fundamental shift in the way in which patenting is justified. In terms of incentive theory, the inventor's reward justification fades since, as Mazzoleni and Nelson (1998) noted, the invention is made with federal financial assistance, hence inventors receive an a priori reward. The rewarding function of the patent weakens when the inventor is the beneficiary of financial assistance. In contrast, shifts in the US patent system introduced a different (and new) type of incentive: the inducement to transfer from public research to marketable products, favoring the appropriation of research results to firms that have not been engaged in fundamental research. Firms are induced, through the benefit of exclusive licenses, to commercialize outcomes of publicly funded research even before those outcomes are obtained. In this respect Mazzoleni and Nelson (1998) discuss an 'induced commercialization theory'. Patents no longer reward the inventor *ex post*—instead, the *ex-ante* reward transmogrifies the patent's status from an exploitation right to an exploration right.

The extension of patents' domain and the 1980 Bayh–Dole Act modified the academy–enterprise links in knowledge generation and diffusion. From 1991 to 2000 patents applications from universities grew about 240 percent. In reality, the public nature of basic knowledge is shifting towards the private and club goods domain, where access is ruled by market mechanisms. The Bayh–Dole Act, especially paragraph 204, reversed the previous system under which free access to basic research outcomes was granted equally to all firms that profited differently from the available knowledge pool depending on their specific assets and capabilities.

However, beyond the debate on access and commercialization of knowledge, there is an additional provision, scantly addressed by the literature, which we believe deserves consideration: the 'preference for the United States industry' stated in section 204 of the Bayh–Dole Act. According to section 204, the right to patent and sell discoveries as exclusive licenses does not apply 'unless ... any product embodying the subject invention or product through the use of the subject invention will be manufactured substantially in the United States'.[15] In this way, intellectual property management has entered clearly the domain of strategic industrial and trade policy.[16] Exclusive licenses of outcomes of inventions made with federal assistance are, with no surprise, strategically reserved to US industries. Moreover, this preference is granted as early as the exploration phase, helping to create entry barriers to foreign firms. The US administration seems deliberately to provide domestic firms with an opportunity to develop a whole set of legally guaranteed rents, even before the investment in R&D has taken place, thus reverting the traditional patent logic of rewarding a prior effort *ex post*. A virtual *rent market* at bargain basement prices is being set up for American companies.[17]

Internationalization of IP protection and management

The use of IP mechanisms as strategic tools for promoting industrial and technological development also characterizes international IP management. Historically, the territorial scope of intellectual property protection extended through time from national borders to the international arena as international trade increased and economies became interdependent.[18] The 1883 Paris Convention on protection of industrial property and the 1886 Berne Convention, which regulates the protection of original forms of expression such as artistic and literary works, represented the first stages of the internationalization of intellectual property protection.[19] Those agreements responded to the lack of effective protection felt by foreign IP rights holders from countries in the technological frontier to countries with less strict IP regimes. In this way, IP laws were used as mechanisms to preserve dominant positions in given fields (not as mechanisms to create them).

The 1994 adoption of the Trade-Related Aspects of Intellectual Property Rights (TRIPS) agreement and the various chapters on IP included in the bilateral trade and investment agreements are the major factors reshaping IP regimes at the international level in recent decades. The US stance towards IP protection is strictly related to trade balance concerns, production structure specialization, and the lobby of certain industries and corporations (usually knowledge-intensive sectors such as pharmaceuticals, software, microelectronics, entertainment, and biotechnology and chemicals; Cottier, 1991). The increasing connection between trade and IP issues led to a shift in the international arena in matters related to industrial development (i.e. those de facto industrial policy issues related to IP and innovation incentives). Increasingly, intellectual property issues enter into the multilateral and bilateral controversies;[20] countries should recognize the implicit component of industrial policy in IP decisions in order to push for resolutions that support their national development interest.

International harmonization of IPRs is meant to prevent free-riding by competitors and to level the playing-field, two issues that both favor the technological leaders, so it is by no means unintentional that developed countries advocate international harmonization and rising standards of protection. However, much is yet to be understood regarding the position of developing and emerging economies in this sphere. On the one hand, IP negotiations suffer from strong imbalances in negotiating capacities and preparedness between developed and developing economies. Likewise, no one can deny the asymmetric bargaining power of the US, for example, with respect to small developing economies. On the other hand, developing countries share some responsibilities in the current international management of IPRs. Although it is undeniable that developed economies' interests are shaping the international management of IP, there are cases in which developing countries, and especially countries with certain industrial capabilities, are not creating opportunities or profiting from flexibilities which actually exist or might be exploited. Countries that recognize the relationship between industrial capabilities and IP issues can strategically use and tailor the IP systems to their needs—in terms of political economy, having a national strategy for industrial and technological development lays the foundations for using IP for development. In this light, there are two aspects worth noting: (i) TRIPS as a baseline agreement setting minimum standards and the flexibilities included in it; and (ii) the TRIPS plus and extra provisions in bilateral agreements.

A TAXONOMY OF TRIPS' FLEXIBILITIES

TRIPS establishes homogeneous minimum standards of protection among WTO members, introducing two basic principles in IP management: the national treatment and the most favored nation treatment (TRIPS, Articles 3 and 4). According to these principles, each WTO member is required to treat nationals of other member states at least as well as its own nationals, and to treat all other member states on an equivalent basis in relation to the protection of intellectual property. TRIPS resulted in the expansion and the strengthening of IPRs, thus pushing for foreign countries' establishing a system that reflects the priorities of the US regime.

The adoption of TRIPS raised concerns regarding its implications for developing countries including the risks of homogenizing IP systems among countries with asymmetric technological capabilities and at different development stages.[21] For the purposes of this chapter, it suffices to recall some basic features of this agreement and to highlight the relationship between its provisions and industrial development. Though the interest today has shifted from the multilateral to the bilateral level, it is worth identifying some (although scant) flexibilities that exist in the TRIPS agreement and to identify the effective policy spaces which might allow countries to use IP management strategically according to their industrial development priorities. In fact, TRIPS includes some special and differential treatment provisions and flexibilities that might be used to pursue industrial development objectives (Table 19.1).

First, special and differential treatment provisions (SDT) confer specific rights to developing and least developed countries (LDC) in the framework of TRIPS, recognizing their status as developing economies. However, SDT do not eliminate the one-size-fits-all nature of the agreement; SDT simply grant a time lag for implementing the homogeneous minimum standards established by TRIPS. SDT do not confer the right to implement an IP regime in accordance with the stage of development of the economy, but simply recognize the right to benefit from transitional periods for the implementation of the agreement (transitional periods, Art. 65 and 66). The provisions related to technical and financial cooperation and technology transfer open a window of opportunity, but they are not legally binding, hence their effectiveness, in practice, is scant unless countries decide to exert it.

Second, Article 31 establishes the conditions under which the governments of member states are allowed to issue a compulsory license. A government may authorize a party other than the patent holder of an invention to use that invention, even without the consent of the patent holder, when that party has unsuccessfully tried to obtain such a license on 'reasonable commercial terms within a reasonable period of time'. The conditions under which it is possible to issue a compulsory license restrict the potential use of this flexibility, being difficult to fulfill and subject to subjective interpretation of 'reasonable'.

Table 19.1. SDT, flexibilities, and self-determination provisions. A taxonomy of TRIPS' (effective) policy degrees of freedom

Provision	Article of reference	(Effective) policy degrees of freedom
Special and Differential Treatment (SDT)		
Transitional periods	**TRIPS, Art. 65, par. 2–5** Developing countries are entitled to delay for a given period the date of application of (given) provisions of the agreement **TRIPS, Art. 66.1** Least developed countries (LDCs) are entitled to delay for a period of 10 years the application of TRIPS provisions, other than Articles 3,4 and 5. Upon motivated request by a LDC the Council for TRIPS may accord extensions of this period	The Dhoa Declaration on TRIPS Agreement and Public Health extended the window for LDC's even beyond the original TRIPS allowance
Technical and financial cooperation	**TRIPS, Art. 67** On request and on mutually agreed terms and conditions, developed countries shall provide technical and financial cooperation to developing and LDCs	Non-legally binding provision
Technology transfer	**TRIPS, Art. 66.2** Developed countries should provide incentives to enterprises and institutions in their territory to promote and encourage technology transfer to LDCs **Doha Declaration, Art. 7** It reaffirms the commitment of developed countries to provide incentives to promote and encourage technology transfer	Non-legally binding provision
Flexibilities		
Compulsory licensing (CL)	**TRIPS, Art. 31** Governments are allowed to authorize a party other than the holder of a patent on an invention to use that invention without the consent of the patent holder, on the condition that efforts have been made to obtain the authorization from the right holder on reasonable commercial terms within a reasonable period of time. In case of national emergency, other circumstances of extreme urgency and public non-commercial use the requirement of prior efforts does not apply	Only countries with certain production and technological capacities may make use of this provision. If the country is credible (in terms of industrial capacities, market structure, and public policy) this instrument can be used as a negotiation threat. Strong political will and commitment is necessary. TRIPS does not stipuiate the grounds upon which a compulsory license should be granted. Thus member countries can make provisions for CL on any ground. TRIPS only mandates certain procedural prerequisites such as voluntary negotiation prior to the grant of a license etc. In the case of national emergencies, or if the CL is being granted to remedy an anticompetitive practice, then these

(cont.)

515

Table 19.1. (*Continued*)

Provision Special and Differential Treatment (SDT)	Article of reference	(Effective) policy degrees of freedom
		prerequisites need not be met. If the country in question lacks the necessary manufacturing and technological capacities, the Doha declaration and its 2003 implementation provide for a CL that would enable export from countries that have such manufacturing capabilities
Exhaustion (national, regional and international exhaustion) (Parallel imports)	**TRIPS, Art. 6** For the purposes of dispute settlement under this Agreement, subject to the provisions of Art.3 and 4, nothing in this Agreement shall be used to address the issue of the exhaustion of IPRs. This article addresses the exhaustion of IPRs that is crucial in international trade because it addresses the point at which the IPR ceases. This provision implicitly addresses the issue of parallel imports (i.e. products placed on the market in one country and subsequently imported into a second country without the permission of the owner of the intellectual property right in the second country)	The only obligations under the TRIPS Agreement that can be used by one country to challenge another country's position on parallel imports are those relating to national treatment (Article 3) and most-favored-nation treatment (Article 4). The exhaustion regime of IPRs depends on national laws
Exceptions to rights conferred	**TRIPS, Art. 30** Members may provide limited exceptions to exclusive rights conferred by a patent, provided that such exceptions do not unreasonably conflict with a normal exploitation of the patent and do not unreasonably prejudice the legitimate interests of the patent owner, taking account of the legitimate interests of third parties	National law can introduce exceptions according to Art. 30
Bolar exception	The Bolar exception was first introduced in the US Drug Price Competition and Patent Term Restoration Act in 1984 following the court ruling Roche vs Bolar Pharmaceuticals. The US law enables testing to establish bio-equivalency of generic drugs before patent, expiration. This mechanisms allows generic producers to place their products on the market when the original patent expires	According to a WTO dispute settlement in April 2000 Canadian law conforms to TRIPS in allowing manufacturers to exploit this exception. (WTO case "Canada: Patent Protection for Pharmaceutical Products"). This exception has been explicitly adopted by Canada, Australia, Israel, Argentina, and Thailand. In the EU it has been used in case by case to solve disputes. In the Canadian case, the WTO upheld the "Bolar" provision but struck down the "stockpiling" provision, stating that this contravened Article 30

Source: Authors' elaboration.

However, the quite restrictive a priori effort requirement does not apply in the cases of national emergencies, extreme urgency, and public non-commercial use.

Developing countries make scant use of compulsory licensing, because of its restrictive requirements, but also due to serious industrial limitations. In the case of pharmaceuticals, most developing countries lack the know-how and the production and technological capabilities to carry out the reverse engineering. Also, in many cases, a lack of market incentives precludes use of this flexibility in absence of a more long-term industrial policy supporting their engagement in such productive effort.[22] In fact, until 2005, no use was made of these flexibilities. However, if a compulsory license is granted to remedy an anticompetitive practice, then the prerequisites established by Art. 31 need not be met. If the country in question does not have the manufacturing and technological capabilities, then the Doha declaration and its 2003 implementation provide for a compulsory license that would enable export from countries that have such manufacturing capabilities (Basheer, 2005). Canada and Rwanda recently exploited this space for Triavir, an HIV drug. Further, Thailand, soon followed by Brazil, recently issued compulsory licenses to produce some key drugs for the treatment of the HIV pandemic.

Third, parallel imports, which refer to the different exhaustive regimes of patent protection (national, regional, or international), are products purchased in one market and subsequently sold in a second market without the authorization of the right holder. Thus, prior to a patent's expiration, countries can take advantage of products manufactured under license in other countries or for other markets and profit from international price differentials. Developing countries make scant use of this mechanism, in part due to the lack of qualified technical personnel and institutional apparatus needed to carry out this practice. Further, this policy space is at risk as banning parallel imports is often a prerequisite for entering into a bilateral trade negotiation with the US.

Finally, Article 30 of TRIPS established the 'exceptions to rights conferred'. Member countries 'may provide limited exceptions to the exclusive rights conferred by a patent, provided that such exceptions do not unreasonably conflict with a normal exploitation of the patent and do not unreasonably prejudice the legitimate interests of the patent owner, taking account of the legitimate interests of third parties'. In the cautious language of TRIPS, this article recognizes the right to provide limited exceptions to the rights conferred by a patent, including the Bolar exception, also known as *early working*, which allows generic producers to import, manufacture, and carry out experiments on patented products before the patent expires. In other words, the Bolar exception allows firms to carry out experimental R&D to produce generic products without violating the patent. Certain thresholds of technological and production capacities, as well as public and private incentives to engage in such research efforts, are needed to engender a demand for using this flexibility, and most developing countries lack the first, that is, the production capacities, or the second, that is, the incentives and the appropriate sets of policies.

Ultimately, any use of existing policy space is subject to decisions that go beyond the pure IP domain and concern industrial development issues. No flexibility will be used simply because it is legally feasible; national policies and priorities shape market- and non-market incentives and transform legal feasibility into action.

TOWARDS A TRIPS PLUS WORLD

Nowadays TRIPS' flexibilities are threatened by the elevation of minimum standards caused by IP provisions in bilateral trade agreements. All bilateral agreements (FTAs and BITs) signed between the US and developing economies after the ratification of TRIPS engendered higher IP standards of protection than those included in TRIPS. (Fink and Reichenmiller, 2005).[23]

Section 301 of the 1974 Trade Act allows the US 'to impose trade sanctions against foreign countries that maintain acts, policies and practices that violate, or deny US rights or benefits under trade agreements, or are unjustifiable, unreasonable or discriminatory and burden or restrict US commerce'. Section 301, as amended by the Trade and Tariff Act of 1984, includes a set of specific provisions, the Special 301,[24] that were intended to promote and ensure international compliance with intellectual property rights. The 1988 Omnibus Trade and Competitiveness Act reinforced this provision, especially strengthening unilateral trade retaliation instruments, in particular Section 301.[25] The Special 301 requires the United States Trade Representative (USTR) to identify foreign countries denying adequate and effective protection of IPRs or fair and equitable market access for US nationals that rely on IP protection. Thus, the US benefits from the unilateral right of reprisal against countries that are deemed as denying adequate and effective protection to US firms' IPRs, even when these countries are complying with international agreements in this area. In particular, the right of the USTR to undertake unilateral action ensues when an 'unjustifiable, unreasonable or discriminatory' behavior is detected in trading partners. Paradoxically it can happen that, according to Bayard and Eliott, an action is deemed 'unreasonable' when it appears to be 'inequitable and unfair in some way or another, even if it does not necessarily violate the United States' international rights, or even if it isn't incompatible with them' (Bayard and Eliott, 1994).

In 2005, the USTR declared that the US was 'committed to a policy of promoting increased intellectual property protection' and that it will use 'all statutory tools to improve intellectual property protection in countries where it is inadequate' in order to protect its industries. Even though the policy language has softened in the last three years, the US still makes no mystery of its strategy for securing fair and equitable market access for US products. 'This Administration is committed to using all available methods to resolve IPR related issues and ensure that market access is fair and equitable for U.S. products..., requiring authorized use of legal software by government ministries, proper implementation of the TRIPS Agreement by developed and developing country WTO members, and full implementation of TRIPS Agreement standards by new WTO members at the time of their accession' (USTR, 2007).[26] IP issues are shaped to protect national interest (i.e. national firms).

A shift in US trade diplomacy (Fink and Reichenmiller, 2005) focuses now on bilateral trade and investment agreements, which reduce many of the flexibilities that were available in TRIPS,[27] especially including TRIPS extra and plus provisions.[28] The strategic protection of US industry through different channels has been at the hub of the US approach towards development and competitiveness. For example, free trade agreements (FTAs) extend patent terms beyond the 20 years established by TRIPS by introducing extensions for delays caused by the regulatory approval process or delays in the patent granting process itself. This is particularly relevant in the case of pharmaceuticals because, as the process for approval of marketing a new drug can last years, patent protection can be extended far beyond the standard 20-year term.[29] In certain cases, the requirement of novelty is relaxed, and patenting of new uses for existing products is allowed. FTAs also restrict TRIPS' flexibilities, often used as a means to ban parallel imports (Maskus and Chen, 2002). Usually, FTAs include provisions which create obstacles to compulsory licensing, such as the requirement to obtain the consent of the patent holder to market a generic drug before patent expiration and the data test exclusivity.

In bilateral agreements, 'intangibles' seem to be the counterweight for 'tangibles'. Developing countries engage in these negotiations seeking privileged market access for their products (especially agricultural and textiles) and concede on the US request on IP. This is a risky business for a number of reasons. First, bilateral FTA IP provisions raise welfare concerns because they affect key issues such as public health, as many relate to the pharmaceutical industry and generic production of patented drugs. Further, the advantages of the privileged market access will tend to decrease as more countries enjoy that privilege. Finally, restrictive IP regimes reinforce the technological dominance of frontier economies, hampering the structural change required to develop new products and processes for which enjoying preferential market access could really make the difference.

The US monitoring activity and negotiating strategy are empowered by the threat of reprisals and the counterweight concessions in other areas of international trade.[30] Though the various activities are formally labeled as trade policy intended to foster competition and free trade, it is evident that these instruments are tailored to maintain the competitiveness of national firms in given priority sectors. Hence again, IP issues enter into the de facto industrial policy space. This might be legitimate from the point of view of the US, but from that of developing countries? The US strategically manages all policy spaces in order to defend its national interest and 'prefers' its industries. Developing countries, in turn, often appear to prioritize blaming the aggressive US attitude over designing and implementing industrial policies to strengthen the economic and academic actors, or in pursuing myopic negotiating strategies privileging static comparative advantages, rather than dynamic ones, adversely affecting long-term industrial development.

Identifying the changes in IP management within the US system and at the international level is only the first step in proposing a pragmatic development agenda capable of going beyond good intentions and declarations. Clarifying the relationship between patenting and production structure specialization and recognizing that the rationale for patenting is moving away from the traditional interpretation of markets for technologies are the necessary next steps.

The relationship between production structure specialization and patenting

Patenting has intensified in the last decades. Year after year, patent offices receive a growing number of applications, and they are granting more patents. In the United States Patent and Trademark Office (USPTO), the number of granted patents exponentially increased since the 1960s, showing a remarkable jump in 1998; in 2006 the USPTO granted 173,771 utility patents.[31]

The increase in patenting activity is registered globally. Though the leading economies in terms of technological and industrial capabilities still are major players, activity has also intensified in emerging economies and developing countries, paving the way for a reconfiguration of the traditional knowledge club. Nevertheless, the three major patent offices remain in North America, Japan, and Europe, which collectively have the highest share of patents at the global level.[32]

According to USPTO data the United States, Japan, and Germany accounted for almost 80 percent of total granted patents in the USPTO since the 1970s. Nevertheless, when considering the total number of patents granted in the United States to non-residents, we note that whereas in the 1960s the three main countries were Germany, England, and France, which had 58.8 percent of the total patents issued to non-residents, in 2003 the three main stakeholders were Japan, Germany, and Taiwan, which accounted for 67.3 percent of total patents granted to non-residents. If we consider the five major patenting economies, excluding the US, we note that, from the 1970s, Taiwan and Korea replaced France and Canada.

This *sorpasso* is not surprising given the structural changes experienced by those countries. In the last few decades those economies have radically transformed their production structures by intensifying their specialization in knowledge-intensive sectors (Amsden, 1989; Wade, 1990; Jomo, 1997; Cimoli et al. 2005). The combination of selective industrial, technological, and trade policies in support of domestic industries and the gradual opening-up to foreign trade as production sectors achieved international competitiveness had generated the technological capacities that lie at the root of the intensification of patenting activity. In fact, once a production system has been transformed into a knowledge generator and disseminator, patents become necessary in order to appropriate the rents stemming from innovative efforts.

Despite the patenting dynamism of emerging countries, the knowledge club persists. The North–South asymmetry in the dynamics of patenting activities corresponds to the North–South asymmetry in technological intensity of production structures and specialization patterns. That is, countries' participation in world patenting depends on the dynamics of their production structures and their processes of structural change.

Developing countries spend few financial resources on R&D,[33] as they are in general specialized in low-knowledge intensive activities, especially natural resources and labor-intensive industries, and their domestic innovation efforts are basically adaptive in nature and rarely encompass inventions and scientific discoveries. Consequently their patenting activity is scarce. In contrast, industrialized countries are more specialized in knowledge- and technology-intensive sectors and they invest more resources in R&D; it therefore comes as no surprise that they are also leaders in the number of patents applied for and granted (Aboites and Cimoli, 2002; Cimoli et al. 2005; Montobbio, 2006).[34]

R&D efforts do not depend exclusively on the specialization pattern, but a minimum efficient scale of industries specializing in key sectors is a precondition for generating a system that is willing to invest in R&D. The specialization pattern and R&D efforts are, in turn, related to patenting activity. It seems to be a self-reinforcing circle: those who specialize in more technology-intensive sectors display more patent-intensive activity and, of course, host the more relevant patenting offices.

Contrary to the argument championed by the TRIPS' advocates, stronger and homogeneous patent regimes have not accelerated the pace of innovation in developing countries. Asymmetry between developed and developing countries in patenting activity, reflecting diverging specialization structures, also emerges when considering *who* patents in given sectors. In the USPTO, patents in the electronics-related sectors show the highest dynamism during the 1990s, correlated to the information technology revolution. The leading patentees in those sectors are the US and the South East Asian countries. On the other hand, European countries' patent pattern persists in its traditional field of expertise, chemistry, while Latin America continues to file applications in mechanical technologies. In fact, developing countries concentrate their occasional patenting in traditional sectors, while developed and emerging economies concentrate their patenting patterns in new technological paradigms. This, of course, is not independent of the fact that the developed and emerging countries have been shifting their specialization patterns towards these dynamic areas.

Ranking countries according to their technological production capacities and to their innovative performance helps to clarify our point. In Figure 19.1 we order countries along the horizontal axis according to the intensity of their technological specialization with respect to the frontier (which in this case is proxied by the US). At the same time, we measure their patenting activity: for each country or group of countries, we plot on the vertical axis the cumulative share of all patents applied for at the three major world-patenting offices (Europe, Japan, and North America). The figure portrays what we call a *knowledge curve*, showing the comparative technological intensity of production structures of countries and their relative patenting behavior.

First, we observe a clear differentiation between industrialized and industrializing countries. The US, Japan, Canada, Emerging Asia, and the European countries all show similar production structures as regards the share of technology-intensive sectors within total manufacturing value added. The share of those sectors varies between 45 percent for the average of European countries considered and 65 percent in the US. Asian countries were successful in

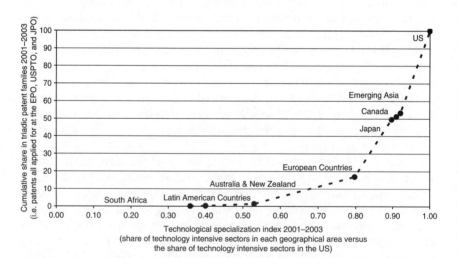

Technological specialization index 2001–2003
(share of technology intensive sectors in each geographical area versus
the share of technology intensive sectors in the US)

Note: Emerging Asia includes: India, The Republic of South Korea, and Singapore. Latin American countries include: Argentina, Brazil, Chile, and Mexico. European countries include: Finland, France, Ireland, Israel, Norway, Sweden, and the UK. The specialization index for each group of countries is calculated as the simple average of the index value for each member country.

Source: Own elaboration, OECD Patent Database 2006, ECLAC-Padi and OECD-Stan.

Figure 19.1. The knowledge curve: production structure specialization and patenting

fostering the development of technology-intensive industries by combining selective import substitution policies with an aggressive export-oriented strategy (Amsden, 1989; Wade, 1990; Jomo, 1997). On the contrary, in Latin America and in most African countries, the opening-up process of the 1990s and the increasing exposure to external competition pushed developing countries to specialize further according to their static comparative advantages. In addition, trade negotiations frequently led developing countries to cede on intellectual property as a counterweight to market access for their produce—textiles and agriculture. Consequently, in developing countries the share of technology-intensive sectors does not exceed 30 percent on average, the rest of production being concentrated in labor- and natural resource-intensive sectors.

Second, from the vertical axis, the figure shows the asymmetry in innovativeness—as measured by patent applications—which corresponds to and derives from the specialization pattern. Patenting results from innovation and defensive strategies which are not homogenous across sectors. Behavioral microfoundations of innovation activities, patenting, and rent appropriation through patents are strictly industry specific. Corresponding to the relative intensity of production specialization, the US, Japan, and the European countries show the highest shares in the triadic patent family, respectively accounting for 46.7 percent, 32.5 percent, and 15.56 percent of total patent applications.[35] Emerging Asia accounts for 2 percent of that total, while South Africa, Latin America, and Australia and New Zealand, in accordance with their low-tech specialization pattern, account for residual international patent activity. The timing effect is interesting: South East Asian countries first reoriented their production structures towards technology-intensive sectors, and then their patenting activity skyrocketed, although they are still residual actors in the global patent game. When and if those emerging economies will erode the position of major IP players is still an open question.

Participation and exclusion in the (new) markets for knowledge[36]

When *The Economist* entitled its special issue 'A Market for Ideas' on 20 October 2005, it was clear that firms (and countries) were facing a reconfiguration of traditional markets for technologies, and that patents were moving away from their usual domain of 'temporary monopolies' granted to inventions with industrial applicability.

According to the literature, when the right to produce some artifact, or the knowledge and the know-how required to produce it are clearly separated from the product or the service they are destined to produce, a line emerges between the market for tangibles and the market for the technologies necessary to produce them (Eaton and Kortum, 1996; Arora, Fosfuri, and Gambardella, 2001).

The idea of *markets for technologies* implies that there are firms that are specialized in providing technologies and enterprises able—and willing—to use these technologies to produce and sell artifacts to consumers. In this view, patents allow for specialization and division of labor between technology providers and users, fostering efficiency in markets for technology. The primary function of this market is to favor the diffusion and the transferability of innovation through licensing. The value of patents mainly derives from usability in tangible production, and it is strictly related to the subjacent technology.

A number of studies show the growing importance of patents and the increase in the use of technology licenses in transfers, acquisitions, and cross-licensing among companies (Grindley and Teece, 1997; Thurow, 1997; Grandstrand, 1999; Guellec, Martínez, and Sheenan, 2004).[37] At the same time, global cross-border transactions in intangibles are increasing (Figures 19.2a and 19.2b). Payments and receipts for royalties and licensing fees can be interpreted as good proxies, respectively, for global demand and supply of knowledge. The share of global payments for royalties and licenses fees in world imports of goods and services tripled from the mid-1980s to 2006 (WB, 2007). The concentration of the market for intangibles, in demand and

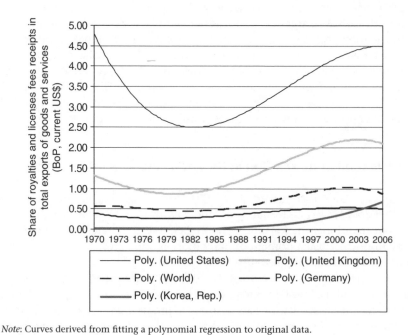

Note: Curves derived from fitting a polynomial regression to original data.
Figure 19.2a. Markets for technologies: trends in intangible world exports of selected economies

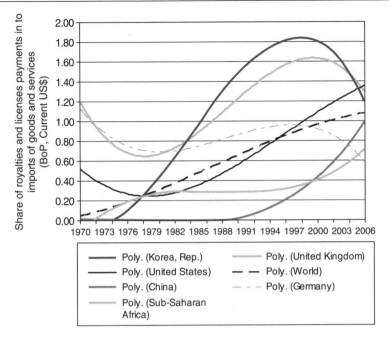

Note: Curves derived from fitting a polynomial regression to original data.

Source: Own elaboration of the basis of WDI database. Curves show the tendency of the share of royalties and licenses fees receipts (payments) as percentage of total exports (imports) of goods and services.

Figure 19.2b. Markets for technologies: trends in intangible world imports of selected economies

supply, showed a decreasing pattern by the end of the 1970s, reflecting the repositioning of countries in international specialization and the virtuous structural changes of some emerging and dynamic economies.

In the early 1970s, the US accounted for 80 percent of world receipts for royalties and licenses fees, followed by the UK with 12 percent. In 2005, 46 percent of world receipts for royalties and licenses fees accrue to the US, followed by Japan with 14 percent and the UK with 12 percent. Knowledge supply is more concentrated than knowledge demand, meaning that there are more countries that increasingly demand knowledge than countries that supply it, but this is not extraordinary: as a matter of fact, knowledge production is sticky. As economies develop they are likely to extend their knowledge demand more rapidly than their capacity to produce it. In 2005, we must include 12 countries in order to reach the 80 percent of global demand for knowledge.[38] However, the importance of technology markets and the increase in worldwide transactions of intangible goods explain only some of the dynamics related to the recent explosion in patenting and the new trends in firms' and universities' patenting strategies. The answers to the questions 'why do firms patent?' and 'what do firms do with patents?' go beyond the logic provided by the market for technology approach. Patents today are peculiar kinds of strategic assets, whose value is increasingly disentangled from the subjacent technology, and increasingly dependent on non-rational expectations regarding possible future technological conditions.

The emergence of new technological paradigms entails a redefinition of *innovation*, how it is generated, and through what means it can be diffused and appropriated. In new technological paradigms, primarily ICT, biotech, and nanotech, innovation is increasingly incremental and cumulative in character, intensive in interrelations between firms (countries and institutions), and entails an increasing relevance of science. The concepts of replicability, usability, and copying are constantly redefined, the potential technological interrelations are multiple, and uncertainty regarding future possible outcomes is even higher than under past technological paradigms. In this scenario, the traditional vision of markets for technologies is reconfigured into what we might call *new markets for knowledge*.

On one hand, the redefinition of boundaries between science and business engendered by new technological paradigms and the expansion of patent subject matter modified the traditional open science conception engendering the generation of a *market for science* where R&D labs and universities patent (and commercialize) their inventions. The adoption of the Bayh–Dole Act in 1981 represents a critical turning point in this area (Jaffe, 2000; Mowery et al. 2004). The increase in patenting activity of universities challenges the traditional open science paradigm according to which publicly funded research was supposed to increase the pool of available knowledge, since the filter to use and exploit this knowledge rested on technological and production capacities of agents, routines, and tacit knowledge beyond any legal effort to protect it (Rai, 2001; Dasgupta and David, 1994; Mowery et al. 2004). This market results in an *anterior* market, to which firms have to revert when results of universities' research are subject to proprietary regimes. The rationale for the market derives from the latent and diffused demand for science induced by new technological paradigms (which increasingly rely on pure science for their inventions) and by the changing behaviors that seem to have pushed forward the frontier of private knowledge.

At the same time, increasing cumulativeness and uncertainty in the nature of technical change and the reshaping of legal frameworks that rule the knowledge domain towards more extensive IP protection induce firms to play with patents in additional arenas. These dynamics lead to the generation of what we call *secondary markets for science and technology*. Firms might benefit from patents beyond the monetary (or non-monetary) rents deriving form technology licensing. Firms might patent to block the entrance of competitors, to secure their dominant position in given technological trajectories, to increase their bargaining power in cross licensing or, among other reasons, to protect themselves in case of infringement trials. The rationale behind the patenting behavior is primarily strategic, defensive, or blocking. In this case, the value of patents is, to a major extent, a function of uncertain expectations regarding future non-deterministically foreseeable technological scenarios.

This market is liquid in the sense that patents are easily tradable without requiring firms to have the necessary technological and production capacities to translate the invention into practice (at the time of transaction). Patents monetize because they loose the weight and the density of the technological component and they easily circulate without having to be necessarily entangled in any final artifact. At the same time, a given share of patents is not evenly traded and it remains 'sleeping'. Just as in derivative financial markets the value of the transaction is disentangled from the present value of the share object of transaction, in this case patents are valued according to their potential future value. The decision to patent goes beyond the expectation of incorporating the patented invention into (direct or indirect) production. Firms patent to create barriers to competitors, and to create the possibility to participate in oligopoly rents that will be generated in the future by potential additional discoveries or incremental innovations based on their patents (Levin at al. 1987; Cohen at al. 2000).

Patents enter into firms' portfolios as a signal of (technological) reputation. Patents acquire a value per se, independently from that of the subjacent technology, and they might be kept dormant in firms' portfolios.[39] The utility of patents goes beyond the appropriability function. The willingness to patent can be assimilated to the decision to buy a lottery ticket. Even though the probability of winning is extremely low, the winning prize or the value assigned by each individual to the eventual win is high enough to encourage the patenting behavior (Scherer, 2001; Lemely and Shapiro, 2005). The difference in the current scenario is that uncertainty concerns not only the possibility to win, but also the prize itself. When a firm patents an invention with the idea of engaging in the secondary market, there is no guarantee that the invention, that is, the patent, will reach a certain value in the future.

Moreover, the value of a patent can directly depend upon the value of other patents to which it can be linked through patent-pools, for example. This might contribute to explain why firms carry out extensive patenting strategies even though it is widely acknowledge that patents have a highly skewed value distribution, (i.e. in every technological field there is a limited number of valuable patents and an enormous number of patents with much less value). Given high entry barriers determined by risk propensity and high enforcement and legal capacities, the secondary market is a highly concentrated one where the value of patents is increasingly disentangled from the subjacent technology and increasingly related to their potential (future) value.

527

Production structure specialization, technological capabilities, institutions and legal infrastructure shape participation and exclusion in these new markets for knowledge.

First, in the case of the markets for technologies, developing countries lack production and technological capabilities that would enable them to participate in those markets. It is difficult for them to play the role of specialized technology providers. At the same time, they face serious constraints as demanders of technology, due to production specialization and to scant technological capabilities necessary to decode and use patent information productively. Socio-institutional factors, infrastructure, and current scientific and technological capabilities strictly shape the arena of production possibilities. Even in an extreme scenario in which all patent information is freely available to developing countries it is unlikely that this would generate increased activity by local manufacturing firms. Typically, industrial and technology policies would be necessary in order to create the incentives for entrepreneurial efforts.

Second, the same discourse applies to the case of the markets for science. Developing countries in general lack scientific and technological capabilities. Beyond legal frameworks, those countries suffer from a chronic deficiency in researchers and quality of infrastructure and systemic environment for science and scientific research. Obviously the current debate regarding proprietary versus open science is of concern for developing countries, but they should avoid blaming patents as the only barrier to their scientific catching-up. Public support for research and development, the recognition of the profession of researchers, capacity building in scientific research and development, and investment in top quality infrastructure for research are more relevant factors than patent protection for developing countries to play a role in scientific research.

Finally, considering the emerging dynamics of what we have called secondary markets for knowledge and the kind of speculative patenting behavior that is taking place, it is clear that this arena is for the leading innovative actors who recognize and value innovation as a strategic asset for future competitiveness. In these markets the value of patents is increasingly disentangled from the subjacent technology. Hence, production and technological capacities are not seen as major entry barriers, but this means that main barriers here are the capacity and the capability to carry out a strategic management of intellectual property, which stems from and exceeds production and technical capacities. Without those capacities it is difficult to participate in these markets; agents might not even recognize the rationale for them. The explosion of patenting activity deriving from competitive behaviors of agents coping with uncertain future outcomes and extensive patenting may induce a slowdown in the rate of technical change which is already alarming actors on the frontier— consider the self-evident negative consequences of patent thickets in the context of incremental innovations. These issues will be of concern in developing countries as well.

Secondary markets for knowledge in which firms bet on future uncertain outcomes shape firms' patenting behavior. In this context, costs and barriers to entry for new actors (firms and countries) are high, litigation and enforcement costs may be prohibitive, and different forces press towards concentration. Barriers to entry in the secondary market go beyond production and technological capabilities; they derive from firms' risk-propensity and size, as well as the existence of needed complementary markets and institutions to make this secondary market work. Although there are spaces for the entrance of new actors into certain technological trajectories, in developing countries this would not easily happen through market forces alone.

Concluding reflections on policies and strategic IP management

Recently, in the US many voices have raised concerns regarding the 'perverse' dimensions of the new IP system on US innovation performance. Likewise, some rulings have contributed to a slight moderation of the original aims of the pro-patent movement. The relaxing of the patentability criteria has led to a proliferation of patent grants that piqued skeptics who see the counter-innovative incentive potentiality of the patent thicket (Shapiro, 2001) and has brought the patent debate into a hypersensitive field, dealing with basic research issues such as health concerns (Rai, 2001). Preeminent scholars, as well as influential public and private institutions, have tried to introduce some limits to the patenting fury. Among them Nelson (2003) stresses the importance of keeping the scientific commons outside any form of IP protection in order to maintain strong and creative innovative activities. On the institutional side, a report written by the National Research Council (Merril et al. 2004) leveled a series of serious critiques of the new US IPR regime and called for a general reform of the US patent system focused on the restoration of more seriously grounded standards of patentability.

In the countries on the technological frontier, especially the United States, the discussion on intellectual property follows a dual track. On one hand, foreign policy defends the strengthening of intellectual property standards of protection abroad. Weak protection and the asymmetry between the systems of the developed countries and those of the developing countries resemble a systemic fault which prevents the potential transfer of knowledge and technical progress derived from trade liberalization. Investing and marketing in a context of scarce protection of intellectual property is a risk that few are prepared to take. On the other hand, the debate surrounding domestic concerns is polarized between the powerful groups, (i.e. big corporations in sectors such as pharmaceuticals and chemicals, as well as the courts), which advocate growing standards of protection, and the academics and civil society, who are concerned about the proliferation of patenting activities and its effect on the long-term innovating capacity of the economic system. At the same time, voices of concern are arising even from the business side, when big firms envisage the possibility of small firms controlling up- and downstream patents, thus increasing their bargaining power.

In developing countries, particularly in Latin America, the inclusion of protection of intellectual property in trade negotiations has brought the topic into political debates. However, the discussion is primarily characterized by the paradox of adopting favorable positions on trade liberalization in tangible sectors and, at the same time, accepting the adoption of protection measures in the area of intellectual property and intangible goods. The Latin American stances are varied but, in general, a lack of strategic perspective on the role that the protection mechanisms for intellectual property in general, and patents in particular, can play in the generation of endogenous technological capacities prevails. Most discussions conclude by prioritizing the technology transfer potential of IP, without considering the structural capacities of transferring *what* to *whom*. However, some developing countries, such as Brazil and India, are beginning to manage IP issues strategically, in accordance with the transformation of their production structures and their national industrial development strategies.

In general, the capacity to innovate, though partially the result of a random process concerning something new and unexpected, entails a degree of stickiness shaped by scientific, technological, and production capabilities. However, technological dominance is not a permanent feature. History demonstrates that with the right combination of (formal and informal) policies and innovation potential among other assets, a firm or sector can take off. Lack of strategic vision and short-term demands jeopardize learning processes and the development of scientific and technological capabilities, which are localized and gradually built up in a continuous process of trial, error, and feedback (Atkinson and Stiglitz, 1969).

Ultimately, countries differ in production structures, technological capabilities, development stages, and in the structure of their national systems of innovation (Cimoli and Dosi, 1995). However, the center–periphery relationship between countries with a first-class membership in the knowledge club and those who are at the margins also exists within countries. Structural heterogeneity is, unfortunately, a persistent feature of developing and industrializing countries, where islands of excellence (of foreign or national firms) coexist with the rest of the economy which usually shows extremely low productivity and organizational levels and which is primarily oriented inward. Dual economies require dual policy models in order to orient their industrial development. This also holds true in the intellectual property domain, where developing countries face the challenge of strategically managing IP systems in order to use them as complementary tools in their industrial development strategy.

'Getting the IPRs right' is far from being the solution; there is too much variation in the meaning of *right* in intellectual property regimes across countries with profound differences in technological and production capacities. Our suggestion is that first, countries should have a clear vision for their industrial development, and second, countries should balance IP regimes in order to cope with the needs of the different segments and stages of their production and scientific structures. Awareness and political will in these fields are the keys for moving forward.

We do not presume in this chapter to propose a solution for the IP and industrial development debate. It would suffice for us to call the attention of those concerned with the innovation for development discourse to the need to avoid converting the patent debate into a *much ado about nothing* discourse.

The existence of unexploited technological opportunities, together with the relevant knowledge base and a set of appropriability conditions, combine to define the boundaries of the set of potential innovations: those which are actually explored might critically depend on socio-economic traits of production and organizational systems and on a set of formal and informal policy interventions in support of the generation of certain scientific, technological, and production capacities. Considering that technology is highly specific and embedded in routines and procedures, that knowledge has a strong tacit component, and that learning is a trial and error process which entails non-substitutable experiences, those enmeshed in the patent controversy who often blame or bless patents for their effects on innovative conducts are losing their relevance. We hope that our reasoning contributes to an inclusion of intellectual property management in the current renewed discourse on policies and institutions shaping industrial development. Seeking more balanced and tailored IP systems is necessary, and emphasis should be placed both on industrial policies for creating technological and production capabilities and on strategic IP management to uphold the industrial development effort.

Notes

1. The origins of the protection for intellectual property trace back to medieval times, when *guildes* used to grant exclusive property rights. 'Patent' literally means open letter, emphasizing the disclosure function of the special privilege, but the British monarchy used patents as a reward mechanism which conferred an exclusive right to commerce in specific commodities—a means for creating artificial monopolies. The first patent law is said to be the Venetian one of 1474. While the English Statute of Monopolies of 1623 allowed only the monopolies made by 'true and first inventor' and regarding 'method of manufacture'.
2. One well-known example may suffice. The US was a net importer of literary and artistic work in the nineteenth century, and its copyright statute of 1790 only granted protection to US residents. The US managed to delay the extension of

copyright protection to foreign residents until 1891; at that time, when the US amended its copyright act, it was registering a surplus in the trade balance for literary works (see Scherer, 2005, whose work has clearly insisted on this point).

3. On this topic see Machlup and Penrose, 1950; David, 1993; and Moncayo, 2006, among others.
4. There is a conspicuous body of literature analyzing the changes in IP laws and court rulings, and the boom in patenting activity. See Kortum and Lerner, 1999; Hunt, 2001; Gallini, 2002, among others.
5. US Code, title 35, part II, chapter 10, paragraph 101.
6. Amazon's 'one click' patent granted in 1999 by the USPTO is a clear example.
7. Smets-Solanes (2000) presents evidence on several cases of patented business models that do not disclose the computer processes and algorithms involved.
8. Regarding software patentability, see Liotard (2002), Samuelson (1998), and Mergès (2001). See the Besen and Raskind (1991) survey on IP, as well.
9. In Europe, in spite of the 1998 EU Directive, this process of extension of the new right regarding living entities met serious opposition.
10. Expressed Sequence Tags or 'partial sequences' of genes. The utilization of this process constitutes an advance in the methods that can be used to identify complete sequences of genes.
11. It is worth noting that this evolution of the American law would have been impossible per se under the Continental European law, according to which a key distinction separates 'discoveries' (pertaining to knowledge) and 'inventions' (pertaining to applied arts), the latter being the only patentable subject matter. We should, however, further specify that even under American law, the observed changes were neither grounded in objective fact nor even foreseeable. On this point, see the discussion in Orsi (2002).
12. This is despite the fact that the Supreme Court had specifically warned that '*a patent is not a hunting license*' in its *Brenner v. Manson* ruling. (cf. on this point, Orsi, 2002, and Eisenberg, 1995).
13. The idea that the new IP regime can be analyzed as a new 'enclosure' movement is at the heart of a series of works and studies first introduced by Boyle. For a restatement of the issues at stake, see Boyle (2003).
14. See Mowery at al. 2004; Mazzoleni and Nelson, 1998; Mowery et al. 1999; and Dasgupta and David, 1994 for interesting analyses regarding the effects of the introduction of the Bayh–Dole Act in the US IP regime.
15. A dispensation is given in case 'unsuccessful efforts have been made to grant licenses to potential licensees that would be substantially likely to manufacture in the USA, or where under the circumstances domestic manufacture is not commercially feasible' (section 204 of the Bayh–Dole Act).
16. For an unmitigated argument in favor of such a strategic industrial policy thesis, see the collection of articles published by Tyson (1996), former Head of the Council of Economic Advisers under President Clinton.
17. Entry costs are reduced since the discovery has already been funded publicly.
18. In the nineteenth century, as industrialization proceeded and costs and time of replicating literary works declined, net producers of such, primarily England, pushed for international recognition of intellectual property protection. In 1883

there were 69 international agreements on IP, mainly related to trademark protection (Ladas, 1975).

19. These two conventions were followed by the 1891 Madrid agreement on industrial trademarks and the 1925 The Hague agreement on industrial design, and other similar international agreements. In 1893 the Office for the Protection of Intellectual Property (BIRPI) was created; it was an antecedent of the World Intellectual Property Office, established in 1967, under whose current administration are various international treaties for the protection of intellectual property.

20. The Glivec case is emblematic: in 2006 Novartis, the Swiss multinational company, challenged the contentious Section 3d introduced via the 2005 Amendments to India's Patent Act, claiming it was in breach of India's obligation under the TRIPS agreement. According to Section 3d, the mere discovery of a new form of a known substance which does not result in the enhancement of the known efficacy of that substance is not patentable. The Chennai high court dismissed the contention, saying that the issue should be settled by the WTO's dispute settlement board.

21. See Aboites and Cimoli, 2002; IPRC, 2002; Drahos, 2002. For an analysis of TRIPS and development see UNCTAD–ICTSD, 2005.

22. See Coriat, Orsi, d'Almeida, 2006 for a detailed presentation of the international controversies concerning TRIPS and Health.

23. FTAs and BITs are country specific, but common elements are present, especially with reference to IP protection strengthening.

24. The Special 301 Report is an annual review of the global state of intellectual property rights (IPR) protection and enforcement, conducted by the Office of the USTR pursuant to Special 301 provisions of the Trade Act of 1974 (Trade Act).

25. A more detailed analysis is offered in Coriat (2000). On this topic, see also Zhang (1994).

26. According to the 2007 Special 301 Report main priorities are counterfeiting and piracy and other critically important issues, including 'internet piracy, counterfeit pharmaceuticals, transshipment of pirated and counterfeit goods'.

27. Agreements concluded in recent years include 'the Republic of Korea FTA (KORUS FTA), Panama Trade Promotion Agreement, Bahrain FTA, Oman FTA, Morocco FTA, the Peru Trade Promotion Agreement, the Colombia Trade Promotion Agreement, and the Central America–Dominican Republic Free Trade Agreement (CAFTA–DR) which covers Costa Rica, El Salvador, Guatemala, Honduras, Nicaragua, and the Dominican Republic. In regions such as the Middle East and Asia, the United States has used an increasing number of trade and investment framework agreement (TIFA) negotiations to enhance intellectual property protection and enforcement' (USTR, 2007).

28. Fink and Reichenmiller (2005) provide a clear and extensive revision of IPRs provisions included in US FTAs.

29. Some FTAs also extend the term for copyright protection up to 70 years after the death of the author, in contrast with the 50-year term of the TRIPS agreement.

30. The first USTR action under the Section 301 dates back to 1985, carried out against Brazil, with respect to the Brazilian Computer Law. The second action regarded Korea in 1986. The same unilateral approach can be found in the trade treaty, signed in 1983 with the Caribbean countries, entitled the Caribbean Basin Economic

Recovery Act, which allowed to the President of the US the right to assess whether the signatory Caribbean countries were complying with the treaty's requirements and implementing satisfactory IPRs policy, being these the mandatory preconditions for enjoying the tariff preferences (Bayard and Eliot, 1994). Finally, NAFTA required Canada and Mexico to base their legislation on the US law as a precondition to benefit from free trade preferences.

31. These are USPTO data; the pattern is the same if we consider the case of triadic patent families; from 1985 to 2005 triadic patent applications grew from 22,879 to 52,864, showing a cumulative increase of 230% in 20 years (OCED Patent Database). Several studies analyze this increase in patenting activities. See Kortum and Lerner, 1999; Hall, 2004; Guellec, Martínez, and Sheehan, 2004, among others.

32. The relationship between patents granted to residents and to non-residents usually shows asymmetric patterns in developed and in developing economies. In the former, patents granted to residents usually outweigh those granted to non-residents, whilst in the latter, the ratio is the other way round. This is obviously related to the asymmetry in technological capabilities and specialization patterns between developed and developing economies.

33. The US and Canada account for 41.9% of world R&D expenditure, Europe 28.2%, and Asia for 27.3%, while Latin America and the Caribbean (accounts for 1.3% of world expenditure), Oceania (1.1%), and Africa (0.2%) evidently play a more residual role (RICYT, 2004). Data refers to 2003 OECD, UNESCO, and RICYT estimates, based on current US dollars.

34. There is consensus on the fact that R&D expenditures are positively correlated with patenting activity, though the relationship between patenting activity and innovation is not deterministic. For an interesting evaluation of the effectiveness of patents as innovation indicators, see Grilliches, 1990.

35. This affirmation can appear tautological given that we are considering patents all applied for in the US, Europe, and Japan; however, the home country bias effect is not relevant for our analysis, as we are interested in comparing the intensity of patent application across world countries in a general way. Calculating the share of triadic patent families for all countries excluding the US, Europe, and Japan would not alter the order: South Africa still accounts for the lowest share and emerging Asia the highest.

36. This section is mainly drawn from Cimoli, M. and Primi, A. (2008), 'Technology and intellectual property: a taxonomy of contemporary markets for knowledge and their implications for development,' LEM Working Paper Series, 2008/06.

37. Grindley and Teece (1997), for example, analyze the growing use of technology licenses by large corporations such as IBM, Hewlett-Packard, and AT&T during the 1990s.

38. In order of decreasing contribution to total demand, these countries are: United States, Ireland, Japan, United Kingdom, Singapore, Germany, Canada, China, Korea, Netherlands, France, Spain.

39. Following a survey of the EU regarding the value and the use of invention patents in Germany, France, Italy UK, Holland, and Spain, sleeping and blocking patents account for 18% in the case of SMEs and 40% of big firms and universities (Cesaroni and Giuri, 2005).

References

Aboites, J. and M. Cimoli (2002), 'Intellectual Property Rights and National Innovation Systems: Some Lesson from the Mexican Experience', *Revue d' Economie Industrielle*, 99, pp. 215–33.

Amsden, A. (1989), *Asia's Next Giant: South Korea and the Last Industrialization*, New York, Oxford University Press.

Arora, A., A. Fosfuri, and A. Gambardella (2001), 'Markets for Technology: Why Do We See Them, Why We Don't See More of Them and Why Should We Care', in Arora, A., A. Fosfuri, and A. Gambardella, *Markets for Technology: The Economics of Innovation and Corporate Strategy*, Cambridge, MIT Press.

Arrow, K. (1962), 'Economic Welfare and Allocation of Resources for Inventions', in, R.R. Nelson, ed., *The Rate and Direction of Inventive Activity*, Princeton, NJ, Princeton University Press.

Atkinson A. B. and J. E. Stiglitz (1969), 'A New View of Technological Change,' *The Economic Journal*, 79(315), pp. 573–57.

Basheer, S. (2005), *Limiting the Patentability of Pharmaceuticals and Micro-Organisms: A TRIPS Compatibility Review*, UK, Oxford Intellectual Property Research Center.

Bayard, T. and K. Eliott (1994), *Reciprocity and Retaliation in US Trade Policy*, Washington DC, Institute for International Economics.

Besen, M. and Raskind (1991), 'An Introduction to the Law and Economics of Intellectual Property', *Journal of Economic Perspectives*, 5(1), Winter, pp. 3–27.

Boyle J. (ed.) (2003), 'The Public Domain', in *Law and Contemporary Problems*, Special Issue Volume 66 Winter/Spring 2003 Numbers 1 & 2.

Cesaroni, F. and P. Giuri (2005), 'Intellectual Property Rights and Market Dynamics', LEM Working Paper Series, 2005/10.

Cimoli, M. and G. Dosi (1995), 'Technological Paradigms, Patterns of Learning and Development: An Introductory Roadmap', *Journal of Evolutionary Economics*, 5(3), pp. 243–68.

—— —— R. R. Nelson, and J. E. Stiglitz (2008), Institutions and Policies Shaping Industrial Development: An Introductory Note, in this volume.

—— G. Porcile, A. Primi, and S. Vergara (2005), 'Cambio estructural, heterogeneidad productiva y tecnología en América Latina', in Cimoli, M., ed., *Heterogeneidad estructural, asimetrías tecnológicas y crecimiento en América Latina*, CEPAL–BID.

—— and A. Primi (2008), 'Technology and intellectual property a taxonomy of contemporary markets for knowledge and their implications for development' LEM Working Paper Series, 2008/06.

Cohen, W. M., R. R. Nelson, and J. P. Walsh (2000), 'Protecting their Intellectual Assets: Appropriability Conditions and Why US Manufacturing Firms Patent (or not)', NBER, Working Paper, 7552.

Coriat B. (2000), 'Entre Politique de la Concurrence et Politique Commerciale: quelle place pour la politique industrielle de l'Union Européenne' in Lorenzi, Cohen (eds.) *Les politiques Industrielles Européennes*, Cahiers du Conseil d'Analyse Economique, 1ier Ministre, La Documentation Française, Paris.

—— and F. Orsi (2002), 'Establishing a New Regime of Intellectual Property Rights in the United States. Origins, Content, Problems', *Research Policy*, Vol. 31, (8–9), pp. 1491–507.

Coriat B. and C. d'Almeida (2006), 'TRIPS and the International Public Health Controversies. Issues and Challenges' *Industrial and Corporate Change*, Vol. 15, issue 6, pp. 1033–62.

Cottier T. (1991), 'The Prospects for Intellectual Property in GATT', *Common Market Law Review*, 28, pp. 383–414.

Dasgupta, P. and P. David (1994). 'Toward a New Economics of Science.' *Research Policy*, 23(5), pp. 487–521.

David, P. A. (1993), 'Intellectual Property Institutions and the Panda's Thumb: Patents, Copyrights and Trade Secrets in Economic Theory and History', in Wallerstein, M. B., Mogee, M. E., and Schoen, R. A., eds., *Global Dimensions of Intellectual Property Rights in Science and Technology*, Washington DC, National Academy Press.

Drahos, P. (2002), 'Developing Countries and International Intellectual Property Standard Setting', Commission Background Paper 8, <http://www.iprcommission.org>.

Eaton, J. and S. Kortum (1996), 'Trade in Ideas: Patenting and Productivity in the OECD', *Journal of International Economics*, 40, pp. 251–78.

Einsenberg, R. (1995). 'Corporate Strategies and Human Genome' in *Intellectual Property in the Realm of Living Forms and Materials.*, Acte du Colloque Académie des Sciences, Octobre, eds. Technique et Documentation, pp. 85–90.

—— (2000), 'Analyse this: A Law and Economics Agenda for the Patent System', *Vanderbilt Law Review*, 53(6).

Fink, C. and P. Reichenmiller (2005), 'Tightening TRIPS: The Intellectual Property Provisions of Recent US Free Trade Agreements', World Bank Trade Note, no. 20, February 2005.

Gallini, N. (2002), 'The Economics of Patents: Lessons from the Recent US Patent Reform', *Journal of Economic Perspectives*, 16, pp. 131–54.

Granstrand, O. (1999), *The Economics and Management of Intellectual Property*, Cheltenham, Edward Elgar.

Grilliches, Z. (1990), 'Patent Statistics as Economic Indicators: A Survey', *Journal of Economic Literature*, 28, pp. 1661–707.

Grindley, P. C. and D. J. Teece (1997), 'Managing Intellectual Capital: Licensing and Cross-Licensing in Semiconductors and Electronics', *California Management Review*, 29, pp. 8–41.

Guellec, D., C. Martínez, and J. Sheehan, (2004), 'Understanding Business Patenting and Licensing: Results of the Survey', Chapter 4 in Patents, Innovation and Economic Performance. OECD, Conference Proceedings, OECD, Paris.

Hall, B. H. (2004), 'Exploring the Patent Explosion', NBER Working Paper No. 10605.

Hunt, R. M. (2001), 'You Can Patent That? Are Patents on Computer Programs and Business Methods Good for the New Economy?', *Business Review*, Q1, 2001, Federal Reserve Bank of Philadelphia.

IPRC, Intellectual Property Rights Commission, (2002), 'Integrating Intellectual Property Rights and Development Policy', London, UK.

Jaffe B. J. (2000), 'The US Patent System in Transition: Policy Innovation and the Innovation Process', *Research Policy*, 29, pp. 531–57.

Jomo, K. S. (1997), *South East Asia's Misunderstood Miracle: Industrial Policy and Economic Development in Thailand, Malaysia and Indonesia*, Westview Press.

Kortum, S. and J. Lerner (1999), 'What Is behind the Recent Surge in Patenting', *Research Policy*, 28, vol. 1, pp. 1–22.

Ladas, S. (1975), *Patents, Trademarks and Related Rights: National and International Protection, vol.1*, Cambridge, Harvard University Press.

Lemely, M. A. and C. Shapiro (2005), 'Probabilistic Patents', *Journal of Economic Perspectives*, 19(2), pp. 75–98.

Levin, R. C., A. K. Klevorick, R. R. Nelson, and S. G. Winter (1987), 'Appropriating the Returns from Industrial Research and Development', *Brookings Papers on Economic Activity* 3, pp. 242–79.

Liotard, I. (2002), 'La Brevetabilité des logiciels: les étapes clés de l'évolution jurisprudentielle aux Etas Unis', *Revue d'Economie Industrielle*, n. 99, pp. 133–57, Paris, France.

Machlup, F. and E. Penrose (1950), 'The Patent Controversy in the Nineteenth Century', *Journal of Economic History*, X(1), in Towse R. and Holzhaner, R. (eds.), 2002, *The Economics of Intellectual Property, vol. II*, Elgar Reference Collection.

Maskus, K. and Y. Chen (2002), 'Parallel Imports in a Model of Vertical Integration: Theory Evidence and Policy', *Pacific Economic Review*, 7, pp. 319–34.

Mazzoleni, R. and Nelson, R. R. (1998), 'The Benefits and Costs of Strong Patent Protection: A Contribution to the Current Debate', *Research Policy*, 1998, vol. 27, issue 3, pp. 273–84.

Mergès R. (2001), 'As Many as Six Impossible Patents before Breakfast: Property Rights for Business Concepts and Patent System Reform', *Berkeley Technology Law Journal*, Vol. 14, pp. 577–615.

Merril S.A, R. Levin, and M. B. Myers (2004), *A Patent System for the 21st Century*, National Resaerch Academy, The National Academies Press, Washington DC, <http://www.nap.du>.

Moncayo, A. (2006), 'Bilateralismo y multilateralismo en materia de patentes de invención: una interacción compleja', background paper, *Sistemas de Propiedad Intelectual y Gestión Tecnológica en Economías Abiertas: Una Visión Estratégica para América Latina y el Caribe*, Estudio OMPI–CEPAL.

Montobbio, F. (2006), 'Patenting Activity in Latin American and Caribbean Countries', background paper, *Sistemas de Propiedad Intelectual y Gestión Tecnológica en Economías Abiertas: Una Visión Estratégica para América Latina y el Caribe*, Estudio OMPI–CEPAL.

Mowery, D. C., R. R. Nelson, B. N. Sampat, and A. A. Ziedonies (1999), 'The Effects of the Bayh–Dole Act on US University Research and Technology Transfer' in Branscomb L., Kodama F., and Florida R., (eds.), *Industrializing Knowledge: University–Industry Linkages in Japan and the United States*, MIT University Press, Cambridge, Massachusetts, ch. 11, pp. 269–306.

—— —— —— —— (2004), *The Ivory Tower and Industrial Innovation: University Industry Technology Transfer before and after the Bayh Dole Act*, California, Stanford University Press.

Nelson, R. R. (2003), 'The Market Economy and the Scientific Commons', LEM Working Paper Series, 2003/24.

Orsi, F. (2002), 'La constitution d'un nouveau droit de la propriété intellectuelle sur le vivant aux Etats Unis : Origine et signification d'un dépassement de frontières', *Revue d'Economie Industrielle*, n. 99, 2° trimestre, pp. 65–86.

Rai, A. K. (2001), 'Fostering Cumulative Innovation in Biopharmaceutical Industry: The Role of Patents and Antitrust', *Berkeley Technology Law Journal*, 16(2).

RICYT (2004), 'El Estado de la Ciencia, RICYT-Red de Indicadores de Ciencia y Tecnología: principales indicadores de ciencia y tecnología', Buenos Aires, Argentina.

Samuelson, P. (1998), 'Economic and Constitutional Influences on Copyright Law in the United States', <http/www.berkeley.edu>.

Scherer, F. M. (2001), 'The Innovation Lottery', in Rochelle Dreyfuss et al. eds., *Expanding the Boundaries of Intellectual Property*, Oxford University Press.

—— (2005), *Patents: Economics, Policy and Measurement*, Edward Elgar.

Shapiro, C. (2001), 'Navigating the Patent Thicket: Cross Licenses, Patent Pools, and Standard-Setting', in Jaffe, A. B., Lerner, J., and Stern, S. (eds.), *Innovation Policy and the Economy* (Vol. I), NBER Innovation Policy and the Economy Series, the MIT Press, Cambridge, Massachusetts, pp. 119–50.

Smets-Solanes, J. P. (2000), *Stimuler la concurrence et l'innovation dans la société de l'information*, Document de Travail, Version 1.0, beta 5, polycopié.

Thurow, L. C. (1997), 'Needed: A System of Intellectual Property Rights', *Harvard Business Review*, pp. 95–103.

Tyson, L. (1996), *Who's Bashing Whom? Trade Conflicts in High Technologies Industries*, Washington DC, Institute for International Economics.

UNCTAD–ICTSD (2005), *Resource Book on TRIPS and Development*, Cambridge University Press.

USTR (2005), *2005 Special 301 Report*.

USTR (2007), *2007 Special 301 Report*.

Wade, R. (1990), *Governing the Market: Economic Theory and the Role of Government in East Asian Industrialization*, Princeton, NJ, Princeton University Press.

WB (World Bank) (2007), World Development Indicators (WDI), 2007, The World Bank Group.

Zhang, S. (1994), *De l'OMPI au GATT. La protection internationale des droits de propriété intellectuelle*, ed IITEC, Paris.

Part IV

Conclusion

20

The Future of Industrial Policies in the New Millennium: Toward a Knowledge-Centered Development Agenda

Mario Cimoli, Giovanni Dosi, and Joseph E. Stiglitz

A major thread running through this book has concerned the conditions hindering or fostering the process of knowledge accumulation and its effective economic exploitation, and the role in all that of policies and institution-building along the *great transformation* toward an industrial economy.

Some chapters have taken a centennial comparative perspective, others have investigated the experience of specific countries or the impact of specific policies. All add to the understanding of the mosaic of ingredients and processes which drive industrial catch-up.

Indeed, many lessons can be usefully drawn from the ways by which 'the West grew rich' (paraphrasing Rosenberg and Birdzell, 1986), including of course the package of policy instruments which allowed Western Europe, North America, Japan, and—more recently—a few developing countries to get out of the poverty trap and join the club of increasingly wealthy exploiters of new technologies.

The lessons from the past, however, are useful in so far as they apply also to the future. Hence, the normative conclusions of this book have to start with some words on the possible discontinuities that 'globalization' (with the meanings that one has tried to clarify in the chapter by Castaldi et al.) has implied vis-à-vis previous development patterns. In particular, what about the millenarist notion according to which discretionary industrial, technology, and trade policies *might have been necessary* in a world of nation states which constrained the full display of 'market forces', but are redundant or harmful nowadays? In fact, the evidence we review in more detail in Castaldi et al. above, and in Stiglitz (2006), suggests that the secular divergences in technological capabilities, growth rates, levels of per capita income (across and within countries) have continued, if not increased, under the last decades of globalization. Countries differ—possibly even more so than in the past—in their capabilities of absorption of production technologies and product design capabilities developed in 'frontier' countries. If anything has changed, it is that under multiple forms of localized increasing returns, greater degrees of international integration fostered by globalization—when left to themselves—may well lead to phenomena of increasing national and international differentiation with self-reinforcement and lock-in onto particular production activities, specialization patterns, and technological capabilities (or lack of them). Globalization is by itself no recipe for some sort of natural catch-up in technological capabilities and for easy convergence in incomes. On the contrary, more interdependent economies are likely to require *more* and *more sophisticated* measures of policy intervention by the weaker countries. It was already so when Hamilton was trying to design an industrialization strategy for the new-born United States in a world of British-dominated 'globalization', and it continues to be so nowadays.

Moreover, yet other aspects of unbridled 'globalization', which cannot be discussed at length here, add to the demands for policy governance. So, as we comment in Stiglitz (2006), in the new millennium, and in the last part of the previous one, income distribution has dramatically changed against wages and in favour of profits, with 59 percent of the world population living in countries with increasing inequality, while only 5 percent live in countries with increasing equality (ILO, 2004; Cornia et al. 2005). Further, 'globalization' has favoured the transformation of employment in both developed and developing countries working against organized labour and against employment guarantees. It has made acute the conflict between the requirements of 'international competitiveness' and social norms (e.g. on work safety, working hours, environmental protection, child labour, etc.). It has brought pressure on national governments to dismantle social welfare systems in countries which have them and to prevent their establishment in countries which do not have them yet. Finally, it has made it harder to impose fiscal levies on 'mobile factors'—i.e. capital—as compared to 'immobile' ones—i.e. labour (on all these points, more in Stiglitz, 2002 and 2006; and Rodrik, 1997).

Of course, the urgency to govern these consequences of the contemporary regime of international economic and political relations complement the more specifically 'developmental' reasons motivating industrialization policies. Concerning the latter, while the basic historical lessons, to repeat, continue to hold, the political and ideological context has indeed changed, entailing also the actual *or perceived* disempowerment of national or even supranational institutions (such as the European Union) of many of the policy instruments which historically allowed the governance of the political economy of industrial development. Needless to say, also the mechanisms and degrees of disempowerment are different across the world: in some cases, as mentioned in other chapters, it is an item of packages imposed at gunpoint from the outside, in other (even less justifiable!) cases, it is a self-inflicted hardship peddled by 'market talibans'. Indeed, there is nothing new in the fact that countries that have been successful in reaching the technological and income frontier next tend to 'kick away the ladder' (Chang, 2002; and Reinert, 2007) which allowed them to get there in the first place, and rebuild a free-market virginity. What is specific of this globalization wave is the formation of an increasingly 'globalized' ruling class, often with a degree in economics obtained in Anglo-Saxon countries (generally the USA) who take home policy medicines which frequently the country of origin itself finds too unpalatable to swallow.

However, such disruptive sides of the current globalization mode luckily are short of the point of no return. Fortunately, policy making continues to have a lot of unexploited degrees of freedom, and in different ways this applies from Brasilia to Brussels to Washington. As the orgy of market fanaticism is wearing out, finally hit by the evidence of its failure, this book comes at a high time of renewed reflection and tries to offer a fresh look at the policies and institutions fostering technological and organizational learning and industrialization across and within countries.

In fact, most of the chapters discuss extensive, empirical evidence on development as a process that links micro learning dynamics, economy-wide accumulation of technological capabilities, and industrial development. Different learning patterns and different national 'political economies' yield of course different patterns of industrialization. However, it happens that all the countries which are nowadays developed undertook indeed relatively high degrees of intervention to support the accumulation of technological capabilities and the transformation of their organization of production especially in the early period of industrialization.

We have emphasized from the start of this book the futility of the search of any 'magic bullet' driving industrialization. The process of accumulation of technological and organizational capabilities does play a crucial role—as highlighted by many contributions to this volume—but such process has to be matched, first, by a congruent 'political economy' offering incentive structures conducive to 'learning-based' rent-seeking while curbing rent-seeking *tout court*, and, second, by a congruent macroeconomic management. By the same token, it is futile to search for any 'magic policy recipe' automatically yielding industrialization and catching-up.

However, as one is able to identify some regularities in the ingredients and processes driving industrialization, so one can trace some basic ingredients and principles that *successful* policy arrangements historically had and have in common. Let us spell out some of them.

Emulation and, sometimes, leapfrogging as a general principle inspiring policies

Emulation—we borrow the term from Reinert, above—is the purposeful effort of imitation of 'frontier' technologies and production activities irrespectively of the incumbent profile of 'comparative advantages'. It often involves explicit public policies aimed at 'doing what rich countries are doing' in terms of production profile of the economy and it always involves microeconomic efforts—on the part of individuals and, more so, firms—to learn how to do things others in frontier countries are already able to do. It is a familiar story over the last three centuries. It dates back at least to the case of England vis-à-vis the Low Countries in the period preceding the Industrial Revolution, and it applies all the way to the contemporary Chinese industrialization.

Emulation concerns primarily—as it ought to—products and processes based on new technological paradigms. In one epoch it meant mechanized textile production and the construction of the related machines. Later it was steel production, electricity-based products and machinery, and internal combustion engines. Nowadays it has to do first of all with information and telecommunication technologies.

In fact, it sometimes happened that catching-up countries not only emulated the leading ones, but 'leapfrogged' in some of the newest most promising technologies. It happened in the nineteenth-century United States and Germany which forged ahead of England in electromechanical engineering, consumer durables, synthetic chemistry.

But why should everyone emulate frontier technologies in the first place, rather than being guided by one's own 'comparative advantages'? Or, as the skeptics often put it, isn't it absurd to suggest that everybody should specialize in ICT production?

This very question, in our view, reveals a dangerous albeit widespread confusion between absolute and comparative advantages (more in Dosi, Pavitt, and Soete, 1990). Typically, relatively backward economies display an *absolute disadvantage in everything*, that is, they are less efficient in the production of every commodity, and in fact the disadvantage in many commodities is likely to be infinite in the sense that they are not able to produce them at all. Catching-up entails closing the gap in production knowledge and learning how to produce novel goods (which at the beginning are generally novel only for the catching-up country, even if 'old' for the world). This is particularly important with respect to new technological paradigms because such technologies are most often *general purpose*: they influence directly or indirectly most production activities. For example, it was so in the past (and it continues to be so nowadays) in the case of mechanical engineering and electricity as it is today the case of ICT technologies.

Moreover, goods and pieces of equipment based on the new technological paradigms generally entail higher elasticity of demand and richer opportunities for further technological advance (cf. Dosi, Pavitt, and Soete, 1990; and the chapters by Castaldi et al. and Cimoli et al.). Hence emulation of frontier countries in these activities implies, other things being equal, higher growth possibilities and a greater potential for productivity growth and, eventually, domestic product innovation.

The issue of *comparative* advantage is a quite distinct one. The point is made also in Reinert's chapter. It is trivially true that any economy has comparative advantages in something or other. So, when comparing an advanced ICT economy and a Stone Age one, it is straightforward that the latter is likely to have a 'comparative advantage' in stone-intensive products! However, the distribution of the overall ('world') income between the two depends in the first place on the magnitude of absolute advantages (i.e. seen the other way round on the *technological gaps*) between the two economies. Learning and catching-up affect precisely the profile of such advantages/gaps. In the process, changing comparative advantages are only the byproduct of the different rates at which learning occurs in different activities.

The complementarity between technological learning and the development of production capacity

We have already emphasized above (cf. the chapter by Cimoli et al.) the difference between technological knowledge and sheer information, bearing important implications in terms of 'stickiness' and difficulty in the transmission of the former—embodied as it generally is in specific people, organizations, and local networks. A consequence is also that learning rarely occurs so to speak, 'off line', especially in the initial phases of industrialization. Rather it goes together with the acquisition of production equipment, and with the efforts of learning how to use it and how to adapt it to local conditions (more in Bell and Pavitt, 1993). In turn, this goes hand in hand with the training of workers and engineers and the formation of managers capable of efficiently running complex organizations. These are also the reasons why it is dangerous to see industrialization—even in its early stages—simply as a matter of diffusion: the adoption and use of equipment, both when acquired 'turnkey' from abroad, and more so when the technologies are in the form of 'blueprints' or licenses, require a lot of local painstaking learning efforts.

Of course, no policy maker is in the position to fine tune the details of the production activities together with the patterns of learning which the economy has to exploit. Such details of the actual dynamics depend a good deal on the details of corporate strategies and, indeed, on chance. So, just to give an example, there was no way that the Korean policy makers could know that opportunities would arise, or even less 'plan', say, a learning push in semiconductor memories rather than microprocessors. However, policy makers ought to be acutely aware of the fact that future capabilities build upon, refine, and modify incumbent ones: hence the policy goal of building *good path-dependencies* (the point resonates with similar advice by Hausmann and Rodrik, 2006, when addressing the patterns of product diversification along the development process).

Moreover two fundamental caveats must be kept in mind.

First, a useful distinction can be made between *production capacity*—covering the knowledge and organizational routines needed to run, repair, and incrementally improve existing equipment and products—and *technological capabilities*—involving the skills, knowledge, and organizational routines needed to manage and generate technical change (Bell and Pavitt, 1993, p. 163). It happens that the kinds of activities which foster the accumulation of technological capabilities increasingly involve specialized R&D laboratories, design offices, production engineering departments, and so on. Second, 'while various forms of "doing" are central to technological accumulation, learning should not be seen simply as a doing-based process that yields additional knowledge simply as the by-product of activities undertaken with other objectives. Learning may need to be undertaken as a costly, explicit activity in its own right through various forms of technological training and deliberately managed experience accumulation' (*ibid.* p. 179). Interestingly, the transition from the production capacity phase to the technological capabilities phase has been managed superbly well by countries like Korea and Taiwan and it is where, on the contrary, most Latin American countries got stuck.

The necessity of nurturing infant industries

Consider again the caricature of a Stone Age economy and an ICT economy, and allow them to interact. Two properties are quite straightforward. First, the patterns of economic signals will be quite biased in favor of stone-intensive product in one country, and ICT-intensive in the other (i.e. precisely their current 'comparative advantages'). Hence if the former country wants to enter the ICT age it has purposefully to *distort market signals* as they come from international exchanges (on the assumption that there are some: it could well be that the ICT economy is unwilling to absorb any stone product!). Second, it is quite unlikely that the stone producers even under the 'right' kind of signal, will be able instantly to acquire the knowledge to produce competitive ICT products.

Certainly, all individuals take a long time to learn new skills. Turning violinists into football players and vice versa is rather hard, if at all possible. And, even more so, this applies to organizations and organization-building.

Even when the transformations are possible, they require time, nurturing, and care. If a newly converted violinist, ex-football player, is made to compete with professional violinists, he will make a fool of himself. If a catching-up company is suddenly made to compete with the world leaders it will most likely disappear. Often, it is even a daunting task to learn how to make—no matter how inefficiently—a product which might indeed be rather standard in technologically more sophisticated economies: additionally demanding competitive efficiency is like asking the violinist to run the 100 meters in around ten seconds after some quick training rounds.

Safeguarding the possibility of learning is indeed the first basic pillar of the *infant industry logic*.

On the incentive side, to repeat, market signals left to themselves are often not enough and indeed frequently *discourage* the accumulation of technological capabilities in so far as they ought to occur in activities currently displaying significant comparative *disadvantages* and thus also unfavourable current profitabilities. Incidentally note, also, that financial markets are meagre instruments, if instruments at all, for translating a future and uncertain potential for learning into current investment decisions (more in Stiglitz, 1994). Thus, there are also sound learning-related reasons why the historical evidence shows that, just prior to industrial catching-up, average industrial import tariffs are relatively low; they rise rapidly in the catching-up phase, and they fall after a mature industrialization. Indeed, it is during the catching-up phase that the requirement for distorting (international) market signals is more acute, precisely because there are young and still relatively fragile learning infants. Before, there are no infants to speak of. After, there are adults able to swim into the wild international ocean by themselves.

Some decades ago, there was the old adage 'what is good for General Motors is good for the United States'. Turning it upside down, the developmental policy heuristics is 'let us make "good" (that is, viable, and in the future, profitable) for, Toyota, Sony, etc., and later Samsung, Lenovo, etc. what is good for Japan, Korea, China, etc.'. Doing that, however, does not involve only 'signal distortion'. As many of the Latin American experiences have shown, this is far from enough. Partly it has to do with the fact that many forms of protection entail the *possibility* of learning but not, in the language of Khan and Blankenburg (above), the 'compulsion' to innovate as distinct from the sheer incentive just to exploit a monopoly rent, no matter how inefficient and lazy is the potential 'learner' (more on this below). Partly, it has to do with the *conditions of capabilities accumulation and the characteristics of the actors involved*.

After all, even under the best intentions and incentives, our violinist not only will take time to learn but will be able to develop his/her football skills only in a team. In turn, most often, the team will not be the making of sheer self-organization, especially when production entails relatively complex

547

products, as it usually does. At the same time, violin players might not be the best candidates for football playing, irrespectively of the incentive structure. Out of metaphor, and contrary to the 'De Soto conjecture', industrialization might have rather little to do with the sheer award of property rights and with the establishment of firms as legal entities (cf. Hobday and Perini, above). Of course, the legal context does matter and is likely to be a conducive condition (even if cases like China show the possibility of a fast take-off even under a regime of poor property right protection and a blurred rule of law). However, this is far from sufficient. In fact, it is quite misleading to think that all over the world there are plenty of sources of technological knowledge just waiting to be exploited—the lag being due mainly to institutional and incentive-related forces. On the contrary, irrespective of the opportunities for the entrepreneurial exploitation of technological knowledge which the 'international knowledge frontier' *notionally* offers, the fundamental gap regards precisely the *lack of capabilities* in exploring and exploiting them. This is a crucial bottleneck for development: such gaps apply to rather simple capabilities which even casual visitors to developing countries notice (whenever walking out of IMF-paid hotels . . .), regarding—at early stages of development—even rather basic activities such as accessing the Internet or processing a credit card and apply, much more so, to firm-level capabilities such as drilling an oil well (or, at early stages, even keeping an existing well working). As discussed in the chapters by Cimoli et al. and by Mazzoleni and Nelson, above, 'horizontal' policies of education and training, together with the activities of technical support to firms by public institutions, can go a long way in the capability-enhancing direction. But even that is not likely to be enough. In fact policies are often bound to get their hands *explicitly* dirty with respect to the *nature, internal structure, and strategies of a few corporate agents* themselves.

Fostering the emergence of, and on a few occasions explicitly building, technologically and organizationally competent firms are indeed fundamental *infant nurturing tasks*.

Needless to say the absence/existence of mature technological capabilities and 'dynamic capabilities' for changing them (cf. Teece, Pisano, and Schuen, 1997) in any one country is not a binary variable. However, the distribution is highly uneven. So, one could list several dozen countries which can hardly show any. Other countries do display some technologically progressive organizations in a bigger sea of less dynamic firms. In fact, even the most developed countries present only a fraction of technologically dynamic organizations within a much greater population of firms. (Note that all this applies to both 'high-tech' and 'low-tech' sectors as conventionally defined.) In a sense, industrialization has to do with the properties of changing distributions between 'progressive' and 'backward' firms.

How do policies affect such a dynamic? The chapter by Dahlman, above, is quite revealing. He reports on China and India, but the historical lesson goes well beyond these two country cases. Policies happened to involve

(i) state ownership; (ii) selective credit allocation; (iii) favourable tax treatment to selective industries; (iv) restrictions on foreign investment; (v) local context requirements; (vi) special IPR regimes; (vii) government procurement; (viii) promotion of large domestic firms. In a nutshell, this is the full list of the capital sins which the market faithful are supposed to avoid!

There is here again a widespread misunderstanding to be dispelled, which goes under the heading of 'picking-the-winner' or 'national champion' fallacies. Why should governments foster national oligopolists or monopolists in the first place? And how could governments be more 'competent' than markets in selecting who is technologically better or worse?

There certainly are unintentional or even counter-intentional outcomes of discretionary industrial policies. Of course, untainted pro-market advocates typically quote among OECD countries the failures of the computer support programmes and the Concorde project in Europe as archetypes of such 'government failures' to be put down on the table against 'market failures'. Economists more sympathetic to the positive role of the public visible hand, including us, would find it easy to offer the cases of Airbus or ST Microelectronics again in Europe, Petrobras and Embraer in Brazil, and so on, among many others, as good counterexamples. However, our point goes well beyond this. The 'picking-the-winner' idea basically builds on the unwarranted myth that there are many 'competitors out there' in the market, and the government has the arrogance of 'knowing better' than the market in their selection. This is often far away from reality in developed countries and, even more so, in catching-up ones. When the US government sponsors Boeing, cutting every possible 'fair trade' corner, and the European Union matches-up with EADS/Airbus, there is little resembling governments messing around with the 'invisible hand of markets', selecting politically appointed winners out of a multitude of candidates instead of letting 'competition work its way'. Rather we observe the 'public hand' shaking, twisting, helping a quite *visible* corporate hand, often represented by one or very few members of international oligopolies with their own capabilities and strategic orientations which might or might not match the long-term interests of the countries where they are located. This applies, *much more so,* to developing countries where often governments face the task of helping the birth and growth of *one or very few* candidates eventually to join the same quite exclusive clubs.

And in fact it happens that the major vehicles of learning and catching-up in all episodes of successful industrialization, with the possible exception of little Singapore, have been *domestic* firms—sometimes alone, sometimes in joint-venture with foreign MNCs—but rarely MNCs themselves. This holds from German and American industrialization all the way to current China—possibly the case nearest to a two-pronged strategy, both fostering the development of domestic firms and trying to squeeze out of foreign MNCs as much technological knowledge as possible.

An ensemble of 'infant nurturing' measures, we have suggested, has been a major ingredient of development policies throughout the history of industrialization, and it continues to be so today. Historically, the 'infant learners' had to be shielded or helped in the domestic and international markets essentially in their interactions with the more efficient and more innovative firms from 'frontier' countries. This happens to a large extent also today. However, the unique feature of the current 'Sino-centric' world—as Castro, above, puts it—is that many catching-up countries are, so to speak, caught between two fires: the developed world is still ahead of them, but at the same time China quickly reduces its absolute disadvantages across the board, in both more traditional productions and in activities based on the newest technological paradigms. And it does so at rates higher than its catching-up in wages (notwithstanding the fast growth of the latter). The outcome is an absolute *cost* advantage in an expanding set of goods including those which were/are central to industrial production of many low- and middle-income countries. In that respect the magnitude and the speed of Chinese industrialization risk exerting a sort of crowding out effect vis-à-vis the industrializing potential of many other countries. So, for example, Brazil—a country indeed on the upper tail of the distribution of industrializers in terms of technological capabilities—turns out to be a very 'high-wage' country as compared to China, but so are also other less-developed Latin America countries, and even African countries are losing cost-based international (and domestic) competitiveness vis-à-vis China. A reason to give up the 'infant nurturing' philosophy? In our view it is not: on the contrary, it adds to the reasons to practice various combinations of the 'capital policy sins' mentioned above. And it ought to push toward a more explicit use of the domestic or regional markets as venues for emerging national industries even when the latter tend to be squeezed on the international arena between 'advanced productions' and Chinese exports.

Infant industries under the new international trade regime

There is another big novelty in the current organization of international economic relations, namely the regulatory regime stemming from the World Trade Organization (WTO) and the TRIPS agreements (more on them below). This historically unprecedented regime indeed implies a significant reduction in the degrees of freedom developing countries can enjoy in their trade policies, while notably all catching-up countries in the preceding waves of industrialization could exploit a large menu of quotas, tariffs, and other forms of non-tariff barriers. Just as an illustration, note that in developing countries the average industrial tariffs have fallen from nearly 35 percent in the early 1980s to 12 percent at the turn of the millennium (conversely, in developed countries they have halved from around 8% to 4%: *for industrial goods*; agriculture is quite a different matter...). Together, there are also stronger constraints on what is admissible in terms of subsidies and other discretionary forms of support to firms and industries. Member countries of the WTO which do not comply may be hit by countervailing duties and other retaliatory measures. As a consequence, quite a few of the instruments for industrial policy which have been a common practice at least from the times of the US declaration of independence all the way to the development of domestic technological capabilities in China and India have been outlawed in the new international trade regime. In turn this state of affairs makes it more difficult for new players—new firms and new emerging economies—to enter existing industries.

What can be done?

Quite a few things can be done also within the existing agreements, full as they are of loopholes and of provisions for exceptions, generally put there by the negotiators of developed countries with an eye on their special interests— ranging from dubiously defined 'anti-dumping measures' to national safety and security considerations. Developed countries (in fact, frequently, *the very representatives of special industrial interests* in person, mostly from the US, EU, and Japan), have been quick in exploiting these provisions. Developing countries have rarely done so, overwhelmed by the power of the money, the political clout, the lawyers' sophistication, the power of blackmail by stronger states. At least equally common has been so far the unawareness of these opportunities for pragmatic management, certainly thickened—we caricature on purpose—by Chicago-trained ministers of the economy truly believing that all problems come from the fact that trade liberalization has not gone far enough, and directors-general of the ministry of trade who had been taught that the Heckscher–Ohlin–Samuelson theorem on gains-from-trade is the last word on the subject. In this respect, we believe that if catching-up countries could display the same amount of pragmatism (someone would say *cynicism*) currently practiced by, for example, US representatives at the WTO, many degrees of freedom could be regained *even under current rules*. In that, BRIC countries (Brazil, Russia, India, China) and South Africa could play a very important role. Notwithstanding the deep differences amongst these economies and political systems, they have the skills to negotiate, together with the sheer economic size, and the technological capabilities to imitate (or even to forge ahead in new technological paradigms, as in the case of Russia). When (unfortunately too rarely) a BRIC country has put its cards on the table, it has been remarkably successful. Recall the example of the Brazilian negotiations with Big Pharma on the conditions of production and distribution of retroviral drugs. Indeed, this is a case to be studied, improved upon, and repeated more often.

There are other things that must be avoided at all costs: among them, *shy away from 'bilateral' agreements.*

In brief, 'bilateral' agreements are WTO-plus, and, in terms of Intellectual Property Rights, 'TRIPS-plus' agreements, whose bottom line is to close the loopholes/exceptions/safeguard clauses of the original WTO and TRIPS agreements, freezing them in favour of companies and industries from the developed world. So, a bilateral agreement, most often with the US, offers 'preferred country clauses', typically concerning textile exports and the like, which we know do not matter much, if at all, since Chinese exports are more competitive even if one takes away all tariffs on the developing country's export. On the other more subtle side, the provisions of the bilateral agreement often involve the unconditional acceptance of the IPR regime imposed by the developed partner (we shall come back to that) and curbs on imports from third-world countries of commodities produced under the various waivers still contemplated under the WTO. So for example, if the Brazilian government is able to have internationally recognized its possibility to produce and sell, say, a certain pharmaceutical drug, the bilateral agreement is generally preventing the signee from buying it, forcing the country to accept all the conditions (and prices!) of Pfizer, Glaxo, and the like. In the short term, the neglect of the issue by any minister of finance and trade of, say, Colombia, Morocco, or Jordan—the names are from the list of countries which signed bilateral trade treaties with the US—appears to be quite reasonable. No firm in these countries would be able in the near future to produce, say, any retroviral drug, but at the same time such deals increase the obstacles to catching-up for the whole group of industrializing countries. Come as they may, bilateral agreements give very little to the country signing them, because in any case China tends to be better and cheaper in the productions concerning the 'upside' of the agreement, and put in place many obstacles to the possibilities of technological learning by the developing country—with added constraints on those countries already trying to catch up.

While there are significant and still largely unexploited degrees of freedom unintentionally provided by the current international trade institutions and rules, the straightjacket is likely to remain too tight. As Dahlman, above, remarks, if China and India 'had liberalized from the beginning it is unlikely that they would be the strong economic powers that they have become. To a large extent, some of the strengths of both countries are that they developed strong capabilities before they liberalized'. The point applies of course also to the countries which are beginning now their process of capability accumulation. But then the conclusion is that some trade renegotiation is going to be necessary.

It is reasonable for example, as discussed in Akyüz's chapter, to switch to a regime whereby the object of multilateral agreements are *average* industrial tariffs as distinct from tariffs that are line-by-line or apply to specific products and sectors (in which case the special corporate interests from developed countries are generally able to exert much greater firepower).

The system is simpler than the current structure of tariff commitments and would also reconcile multilateral discipline with policy flexibility since countries would be subject to an overall average ceiling while maintaining degrees of freedom for discretionary sectoral strategies. In practice it would have the effect of balancing tariff increases and reductions, since a country would need to lower its practiced tariffs on some products in order to be able to raise them on others. This would encourage governments to view tariffs as temporary instruments and focus their efforts to ensure that the tariffs effectively serve the purpose they are designed for, that is to provide a breathing space for infant industries before they mature and catch up with their counterparts in more advanced countries.

Moreover, within such a logic, the average ceiling itself ought to depend on the levels of technological and economic development, rising as the catch-up process is put in motion and falling as industrialization becomes ripe.

A management of the distribution of rents favourable to learning and industrialization

The other side of 'infant nurturing' policies discussed above regards the rent distribution profile that they entail. We have already emphasized that offering an opportunity of learning via, say, a temporary trade barrier, does not imply per se the incentive to do so by rather simply exploiting the rents stemming from the protection. As outlined above by Khan and Blankenburg, successful industrialization policies have all come with rent-management strategies providing for *compulsions* for learning and accumulation of both technological capabilities and production capacity. There are three sides to such strategies.

First, on the 'carrot' side, policies must be able to transfer resources to the 'progressive actors': fiscal policies, subsidies, preferential credits, grants are among the possible means. In fact, fiscal policies are particularly important in the transfer of resources from those activities which benefit from (cyclical or, even more so, trend) improvements in the terms of trade of natural resources—in the form of export levies, royalties indexed on the final price of the commodities, fines and taxes discouraging environmental damage. Moreover, the construction of industrialization-friendly financial institutions is of paramount importance. In some historical cases, it has meant steering in a pro-development fashion the financing strategies of large private conglomerates, like the Korean chaebols. In other historical examples it involves state-owned development banks like BNDES in Brazil. Conversely, the absence of 'industry-friendly' intermediation of finance is a major bottleneck for both learning and investment—as witnessed by most Latin American countries over the most recent decades.

Second, on the 'stick' side, governments must have the credibility to commit to developmental rents for periods that are sufficiently long but not too long (of course how long will depend on the sectors, the nature of the technologies, the distance from the international frontier, the initial capabilities of managers, technicians, workers, etc.). In that, of course, the critical requirement is the credible commitment to stop all rent-yielding measures after some time and, in any case, to withdraw them and impose sanctions on firms and industries failing to achieve technological, investment or export targets. A good case in point has been the 'stick-and-carrot' allocation of scarce foreign currency to firms in Korea in the first industrialization phase as a function of export targets.

Third, the nurturing of domestic oligopolists has to be matched by measures fostering competition. There is a general lesson coming from the experiences of Korea, and some decades before, Japan, whereby quasi-monopolistic or oligopolistic domestic firms were forced, quite early on, to compete fiercely on the international markets. And, together, above some threshold of industrial development, antitrust policies are an important deterrent against the lazy exploitation of 'infant protection'.

Indeed, the management of rent distribution in its relation with industrial learning is one of the most difficult and most crucial tasks of any industrialization strategy, as it concerns the overall distribution of income, wealth, and political power across economic and social groups. So for example, well beyond the pitfalls of single policy measures, one of the deeper underlying weaknesses of the industrialization process in most Latin American countries has been the absence of 'pro-developmental' social coalitions with the strength to channel resources toward industry (that is, both industrial firms and urban workers). In this respect, the recent episodes of resistance to export levies by land owners in Argentina is just another symptom of a quite diffused anti-industrial political economy, often linking together agricultural, financial, and mining interests.

Tight intellectual property rights regimes never help industrialization and sometimes harm it

It has already been discussed in this book that all past episodes of successful industrialization have occurred under conditions of *weak* IPR protection. All catching-up countries—including, to repeat, at one time also the United States and Germany—have done so through a lot of imitation, reverse engineering, and straightforward copying. But these activities are precisely what strong property right protection is meant to prevent. How effective IPR are in achieving this objective depends a lot on the technologies and the sectors (more in the chapter by Cimoli, Coriat, and Primi; and in Dosi, Marengo, and Pasquali,

2006), but certainly when they are effective they are likely to represent an obstacle to domestic technological learning. Conversely, if IPR protection *may* represent an incentive to innovate in *frontier* countries—a claim indeed quite controversial, not supported by particularly robust evidence (cf. again Dosi et al. 2006, for a discussion)—there is no evidence that they have any positive effect in spurring innovative activities in catching-up countries. Certainly, successful industrializers at some point start innovating and also patenting, but typically—a century ago as well as today—they file their patent claims in frontier countries where their strongest competitors are likely to be based. At the same time, the domestic IPR regime has been characteristically weak. The situation, however, has recently changed with TRIPS agreements which have basically extended the tightest IPR rules of developed countries to all the signing countries, including developing ones, and has been made even worse by the already mentioned bilateral agreements. Further, TRIPS has taken away the possibility of differentiating the regime of protection across products and technologies. For example, as already mentioned above, even countries like Italy and Switzerland were not granting IPR protection to pharmaceuticals (indeed an area where patents are very effective appropriability devices) until the 1980s. This is not possible any longer under the new TRIPS rules. Finally, one is witnessing an unprecedented aggressiveness in IPR enforcement by developed world MNCs, even when the stakes are low and the moral outrage is rampant, as in the case of retroviral drugs to be used by third-world patients.

What can catching-up countries do?

In principle, the first and easiest thing to do is to *be aware* and never buy the story that 'IPR are good for development because they are good for innovation.' On the contrary, in many technological areas they are largely irrelevant for both innovation and technological catching-up. In other areas like, as a prime example, *drugs*, they are definitely harmful for imitation and capability building in catching-up countries (while they have indeed a dubious effect on the rates of innovation in frontier countries). A consequence of such an awareness is also the need for greater efforts to build institutional capabilities and a clear 'technology acquisition strategy' to orient negotiations and dispute settlements.

Second, and relatedly, TRIPS agreements contain a series of loopholes, safeguard clauses, and exceptional provisions—for example, concerning compulsory licensing—which catching-up countries have still to learn how to exploit.

Third, the most advanced among catching-up countries ought to strive to offer relatively less-developed ones appealing regional agreements which could be viable alternatives to the bilateral agreements with the US (and the EU) generally containing IPR provisions even stricter than TRIPS.

Last but not least, also in this case, as in the trade of goods—already discussed—a new wave of multilateral negotiations are likely to be needed aimed at (i) reducing the breadth and width of IPR coverage; (ii) expanding the domain of *unpatentability*—from scientific knowledge to algorithms to data; and, (iii) conditioning the degrees of IPR protection on the relative level of economic and technological development of each country.

After all, the current international IPR regime is largely the response to the special appropriability interests of a small *subset* of developed countries' firms—to simplify to the extreme, Big Pharma and biotech, Microsoft and Hollywood. A reform in the directions just indicated would benefit catching-up countries, but also first-world consumers, without doing any harm to the overall rate of innovation.

Avoid the natural resource curse

The availability of natural resources—from minerals to hydrocarbons to agricultural land and forestry—at a first look appears as a blessing, an easy shortcut to development, especially in times of rising terms of trade like the recent ones. In fact, it may turn out in the long-run to be a curse. Exports of natural resources may induce the 'Dutch disease': as was noticed around forty years ago in the gas-exporting Netherlands, exchange rate appreciation was 'crowding out' industry by making it internationally less competitive. In turn, in so far as manufacturing and other increasing return activities such as knowledge-intensive services are at the core of technological learning, the 'Dutch Disease' also reduces the future learning potential. Production activities in natural resources are typically capital-intensive with a reduced demand for skilled labour. They favour polarization in income distribution. The big stakes involved in exploration and mining rights are easily conducive to corruption among bureaucrats and politicians. And the problem has been recently compounded by privatization generally occurring under rapacious terms in favour of foreign mining companies and to the almost exclusive domestic benefit of a few corrupt officials and middlemen. Of course in modern history resource abundance has sometimes been conducive to growth, the most noticeable case being the nineteenth-century United States. However, this has occurred precisely through a capital-intensive and resource-intensive *industrialization* process (Rosenberg, 1963; David and Wright, 1997). Without that, resource abundance can sustain growth for some time especially when terms of trade improve and sectoral productivity is rising, but in the long term the small size in terms of overall employment of the resource-exploiting sector, the failure to tackle income inequality, and the scarce overall learning efforts tend to erode the economic benefits derived from natural resource exports. In fact, in order to avoid the resource curse, rents have to be purposefully distributed *against* comparative advantages, fostering diversification of production in knowledge-intensive activities.

The necessary consistency between macroeconomic and industrial policies

As abundantly shown by all the chapters above addressing the Latin American experience over the last two decades, there are macroeconomic policies which kill most learning efforts together with most firms carrying the related learning capabilities. The sudden and indiscriminate dismantling of trade barriers can easily do that, especially if it comes together with reckless (non) management of exchange rates, characterized by vicious cycles of appreciation followed by sudden devaluations. And the cycles have been only amplified by the stubborn refusal to utilize controls over capital movements, especially short-term movements. Blind trust in the 'magic of the market place' and the associated lack of fiscal policies and demand management increase output volatility. In turn, the latter, together with the endemic financial fragility of many developing countries' firms means induced waves of corporate mortality and with that also the disappearance of the capabilities of technological accumulation which the disappearing firms embodied. And even among surviving firms, behaviours tend to become more short-termish and the economy tends to respond more to financial signals than to long-term learning opportunities (more on the consequences of 'Washington Consensus' macro policies in Ocampo and Taylor, 1998; and Stiglitz et al. 2006). The comparative tales of Latin American countries as compared to, for example, Korea or Malaysia, tell the importance of the vicious feedbacks between macro policy shocks prescribed by orthodox recipes and micro dynamics (in Latin America) versus the virtuous feedbacks between more interventionist and 'Keynesian' macro policies and continuing industrial expansion even under severe financial crises (e.g. in Korea).

A new development pact: the courage of imagining a novel international 'consensus'

We began this book with the inevitable reference to the 'Washington Consensus' and the damage done by the almost religious implementation of such an extremist version of economic orthodoxy. The times of the 'Consensus' are over, buried by the weight of its economic failures, in addition to its massive social disruptions. This book, rather than proposing amendments to the failed consensus, has tried to build on a different diagnosis of the obstacles to and drivers of development, centred on the conditions for the accumulation of technological and organizational knowledge and on the political economy sustaining or hindering it.

Far too much reliance has been put in the current analyses of development on a highly simplified and indeed misleading economic model whereby 'technology' is just information in principle freely available to every country and every economic agent all over the world. On the contrary, even a slightly more

557

sophisticated understanding of the nature of productive knowledge has crucial economic ramifications which put in the forefront the enormous asymmetries in the international distribution of such knowledge, the difficulties in its accumulation, and the interactions between what economic agents know how to produce and search for, the incentives they have to do so, and the role of public policies in shaping both.

The foregoing analyses, from different angles, offer a rich alternative menu of industrial policies—in their broadest definition. Many of such policies, as we have discussed in these conclusions, may be implemented, albeit with daunting difficulties, even under the current regime of international economic relations, largely built under the political atmosphere of the Washington Consensus. Developmental pragmatism is much better than nothing, and certainly better than anti-developmental fanaticism! However, we would like to conclude this book with a more comprehensive and daring policy vision. This alternative view—we are tempted to call it the 'Rio Consensus', acknowledging the venue where we began discussing this book—contains also a plea for an alternative view of governance of international economic relations. Indeed, a *new pact*, involving four major elements.

First, we have discussed it repeatedly above, on the 'take side' for developing countries there ought to be much greater provision for 'managed trade'—a word used for too long to protect vested interests of *first*-world lame ducks—in order to allow, on the contrary, *infant nurturing*, albeit with time limits and under transparent conditions. The higher the distance from the international technological frontier, the higher also the degrees of 'nurturing' that should be allowed. Together, the new WTO pact should prescribe much more stringent conditions under which 'anti-dumping' measures can be called for. (Notice that under current practices the punitive measures may be implemented first, while still waiting for the definitive ruling, with the likely consequence that the developing country's firm dies before having its rights recognized.)

Second, one need not be a development-friendly economist to acknowledge the profound anti-developmental bias of agricultural trade policies in all developed countries. There is a curious paradox here. Agriculture is the sector which most resembles textbook economics, made of many relatively small price-taking producers, with little possibility of exploiting monopolistic rents. This sector is indeed the one where all developed countries massively 'distort market signals', and with no gains in terms of learning opportunities of any kind: just a pure rent-extraction, with a huge loss by a multitude of developing countries' farmers and developed countries' consumers alike. Any new trade deal is bound to involve the dismantling of arrangements which are massively damaging to the cotton producer of West Africa, the Brazilian soya producer, as well as the Detroit or London consumer, without any 'dynamic' benefit for any economy.

Third, we have already emphasized the need for a reform of Intellectual Property Right regimes at the international level, and domestically within developed countries, toward a *reduction* of IPR protection in terms of domains of patentability and patent scope. Add to that some proportionality between degrees of development and degrees of IPR protection that multilateral agreements should require. Again, it is a 'win–win' reform that finds an increasing number of advocates also in frontier countries and even among a part of *frontier firms*, worried that the current system might simply lead to 'patent arms races', stockpiling otherwise useless patent thickets, just waiting to be used for threat or retaliation. And in fact the rates of innovation stagnate, while the cost of litigations soar: in the US litigation costs are estimated to be around one third of the total R&D expenditure of American industry!

Fourth, untamed globalization of production activities has been a powerful vehicle for a huge income transfer from labor to *first-world* capital. The delocalization of production, say within NAFTA, from the US to Mexico, or from all of the OECD countries to China, has meant and means of course much lower wage costs. In the change, very little goes to the wage of the Mexican or Chinese worker, little becomes a price gain, say, for the US shopper at Wal-Mart, most goes to the companies which relocate the production of intermediate and/or final products. The relocation also has indirect effects since it makes it harder and harder for the first-world workers to negotiate on wages, working conditions, pensions, or even to defend the status quo. Symmetrically, in most developing countries the nearly 'unlimited supply of labor' maintains the bargaining power of local workers at nearly zero. One of the overall outcomes has been wages that in the US have stagnated for at least 15 years, despite steady productivity growth; and the widening gap between productivity and wages has certainly not gone to the workers of Tijuana or Shanghai. The new pact should correct for all that and allow for the possibility of developed countries to require for their imports the fulfilment of standards concerning child labor, work conditions and working hours, the right to unionize, and environmental respect. Unconditional free-traders would certainly accuse these measures of being protectionism in disguise. On the contrary, in our view, they are going to be beneficial also to catching-up countries, to their workers and to the environment.

In fact they would make a major contribution to redress a worldwide tendency toward ever-growing income inequalities, within a larger pro-development international deal fostering knowledge accumulation and industrialization in catching-up countries.

References

Bell, M., and Pavitt, K. (1993). 'Technological Accumulation and Industrial Growth: Contrasts Between Developed and Developing Countries', *Industrial and Corporate Change*, 2: 157–210.

Chang, H.J. (2002). *Kicking away the Ladder: Development Strategy in Historical Perspective*. London: Anthem Press.

Cornia, G.A., Addison, T., and Kiiski, S. (2005). 'Income Distribution Changes and Their Impact in the Post-World War II Period', in G.A. Cornia (ed.), *Inequality, Growth, and Poverty in an Era of Liberalization and Globalization*. New York/Oxford: Oxford University Press.

David, P.A., and Wright G. (1997), 'Increasing Returns and the Genesis of American Resource Abundance', *Industrial and Corporate Change, 6*.

Dosi, G., Marengo, L., and Pasquali, C. (2006). 'How Much Should Society Fuel the Greed of Innovators? On the Relations Between Appropriability, Opportunities and Rates of Innovation', *Research Policy*, 35(8): 1110–21.

—— Pavitt, K., and Soete, L. (1990). *The Economics of Technological Change and International Trade*, Brighton:Wheatsheaf, and New York: New York University Press.

Greenwald, B., and Stiglitz, J.E. (2006). 'Helping Infant Economies Grow: Foundations of Trade Policies for Developing Countries', *The American Economic Review*, 96(2): 141–6.

Hausmann, R., and Rodrik, D. (2006). 'Doomed to Choose: Industrial Policy as Predicament', CID Working Paper. Center for International Development at Harvard University.

Hirschman, A.O. (1958). *The Strategy of Economic Development*, New Haven/London: Yale University Press.

—— (1971). *A Bias for Hope*, New Haven: Yale University Press.

Humphreys, M., Sachs, J.D., and Stiglitz, J.E. (eds.) (2008). *Escaping the Resource Curse*, New York, Columbia University Press.

ILO (2004). *A Fair Globalization: Creating Opportunities for All*, Geneva: International Labor Office.

Kim, L., and Nelson, R.R. (2000). *Technology Learning and Innovation: Experiences of Newly Industrializing Economies*, Cambridge: Cambridge University Press.

Ocampo, J.A., and Taylor, L. (1998). 'Trade Liberalization in Developing Economies: Modest Benefits but Problems with Productivity Growth, Macro Prices, and Income Distribution', *The Economic Journal*, 108, 1523–46.

Reinert, E.S. (2007). *How Rich Countries Got Rich . . . and Why Poor Countries Stay Poor*, London: Constable.

Rodrik, D. (1997). *Has Globalization Gone Too Far?*, Washington, DC: Institute for International Economics.

—— (2008). 'Goodbye Washington Consensus, Hello Washington Confusion?', *Journal of Economic Literature*, forthcoming.

Rosenberg, N. (1963). 'Capital Goods, Technology and Economic Growth', *Oxford Economic Papers*, 15: 217–27.

—— and Birdzell, L.E. (1986). *How the West Grew Rich: The Economic Transformation of the Industrial World*. New York: Basic Books.

Stiglitz, J.E. (1994). *Whither Socialism?* Cambridge, MA: MIT Press.

—— (2002). *Globalization and its Discontents*, New York/London: W.W. Norton & Company.

—— (2006). *Making Globalization Work*, New York/London: W.W. Norton & Company.

—— Ocampo, J.A., Spiegel S., Ffrench-Davis, R., and Nayyar, D. (2006). *Stability with Growth: Macroeconomics, Liberalization, and Development*. New York/Oxford: Oxford University Press.

Teece, D., Pisano, G., and Shuen, A. (1997). 'Dynamic Capabilities and Strategic Management', *Strategic Management Journal*, 18(7): 509–33.

INDEX

Index